W9-AGJ-711

INTRODUCTION TO PERSONALITY

THE WILEY BICENTENNIAL–KNOWLEDGE FOR GENERATIONS

Each generation has its unique needs and aspirations. When Charles Wiley first opened his small printing shop in lower Manhattan in 1807, it was a generation of boundless potential searching for an identity. And we were there, helping to define a new American literary tradition. Over half a century later, in the midst of the Second Industrial Revolution, it was a generation focused on building the future. Once again, we were there, supplying the critical scientific, technical, and engineering knowledge that helped frame the world. Throughout the 20th Century, and into the new millennium, nations began to reach out beyond their own borders and a new international community was born. Wiley was there, expanding its operations around the world to enable a global exchange of ideas, opinions, and know-how.

For 200 years, Wiley has been an integral part of each generation's journey, enabling the flow of information and understanding necessary to meet their needs and fulfill their aspirations. Today, bold new technologies are changing the way we live and learn. Wiley will be there, providing you the must-have knowledge you need to imagine new worlds, new possibilities, and new opportunities.

Generations come and go, but you can always count on Wiley to provide you the knowledge you need, when and where you need it!

WILLIAM J. PESCE
PRESIDENT AND CHIEF EXECUTIVE OFFICER

PETER BOOTH WILEY
CHAIRMAN OF THE BOARD

INTRODUCTION TO PERSONALITY

Toward an Integrative Science of the Person | 8th Edition

WALTER MISCHEL
Columbia University

YUICHI SHODA
University of Washington

OZLEM AYDUK
University of California, Berkeley

JOHN WILEY & SONS, INC.

Publisher *Jay O'Callaghan*
Acquistions Editor *Christopher Johnson*
Assistant Editor *Maureen Clendenny*
Marketing Manager *Emily Streutker/Jeffrey Rucker*
Production Manager *Dorothy Sinclair*
Senior Production Editor *Sandra Dumas*
Designer *Hope Miller*
Photo Editor *Jennifer MacMillan*
Photo Researcher *Elyse Rieder*
Production Management Services *Pine Tree Composition, Inc.*
Cover image: *Ocean Park #70 by Richard Diebenkorn (1922–1993.) Courtesy of the Estate of Richard Diebenkorn.*
Wiley Bicentennial Logo Design *Richard J. Pacifico*

This book was set in Times by Laserwords Private Limited, Chennai, India and printed and bound by R.R. Donnelley/Crawfordsville. The cover was printed by R.R. Donnelley/Crawfordsville.

The book is printed on acid-free paper. ♾

ISBN 978-0470-08765-7

Printed in the United States of America

10 9 8 7 6 5 4 3 2 1

PREFACE AND TEXT ORGANIZATION

Personality psychology was established as the area within psychology devoted to studying the person as a coherent and unique whole (Allport, 1937). The hope was for personality psychology to become the hub where all the levels of analysis devoted to understanding the organization and functioning of the person, and the nature of important individual differences, would become integrated to give a "big picture" view.

In spite of that integrative goal, for many years the field of personality—and particularly its texts, including earlier editions of this one, which was first published in 1971, became divided into alternative competing approaches and theories. The implication was that if a given approach at a particular level proved to be "right" and useful, the other approaches and levels were bound to be somehow "wrong" or less important. The questions usually asked were: "Which one is best? Which one is right?" Some texts even invite the student to take from the course whatever perspective felt most right to them. While this type of approach may be understandable early in a field's history or pre-science stages, it risks becoming embarrassing in a maturing science, and can leave students more confused than illuminated. One would be surprised by a textbook offering, for example, "alternative views of organic chemistry."

Over the years it has become increasingly clear that the different theoretical approaches to personality ask different questions and address different phenomena at different levels of analysis. Consequently they usually deal only with selected aspects of personality versus the construct in its entirety. Historically, this was understandable, given the limits to what any one researcher or theorist can know and study, especially as the knowledge base in the area grew at an accelerating pace. But this approach also undermined the original ambitious mission of personality psychology to become the hub and locus of integration. And it made it difficult if not impossible for the student to emerge with a "big picture" view of how the diverse concepts and findings from a century of work added up, undermining the take-home message from the course, and leaving the student without a sense of how the pieces fit together. Now, however, an exciting change is taking place, moving personality psychology into a new stage (e.g., Carver, 1996; Cervone & Mischel, 2002; Duke, 1986; Mischel, 2004, 2005; Morf, 2003). One gets a sense of this movement toward integration just from some of the titles of the articles, for example; "Rethinking and Reclaiming the Interdisciplinary Role of Personality Psychology: The Science of Human Nature Should Be the Center of the Social Sciences and Humanities" (Baumeister & Tice, 1996). Fortunately, the explosion of research findings at different levels of analysis, and in closely related areas of the larger science, continues to be so great that the pieces of the puzzle are coming together, at least in outline. The insights from different levels complement each other increasingly well and help to build a more integrated and cumulative view of the person as a whole.

This eighth edition of ***Introduction to Personality*** reflects these new developments, and gives the student a picture of the field as a cumulative, integrative science that builds on its rich past and now allows a much more coherent view of the whole functioning individual in the social world. Building on the large changes in this direction begun in the last edition, this revision, subtitled *Toward an Integrative Science of the Person,* is committed to making that integration, and its practical applications and personal relevance to everyday life, even more clear and compelling for our students.

At the same time, the text continues to provide coverage of the essential features and contributions from the field's rich heritage. To do so, this edition first covers in a balanced manner the key ideas and pioneering work that shaped the field for many decades in the last century. But the focus is on distilling how findings at each level of analysis still speak to and inform each other, and how they add to the current state of the science and its continuing growth.

We use a variety of features to help the student to see the interplay among the insights obtained at the six major levels of analysis, namely the Trait-Dispositional, Biological, Psychodynamic-Motivational, Behavioral-Conditioning, Phenomenological-Humanistic, and Social Cognitive Levels. Throughout the book, we show how the discoveries made at each level enrich the understanding of the whole. We also show how each level has practical applications for benefiting personal adjustment, self-understanding, and effective coping. As in the last edition, we highlight the "personal side of the science" by inviting students to ask specific questions about how each level applies to them. Consistent with the theme of integration, *part preludes* orient the reader to each major section of the text that follows by placing it in a broader conceptual framework. Review sections conclude each part with a segue into the next part to enhance the integration.

After providing a solid background in the six levels of analysis, and pointing out their interconnections, the final part of this text—*Integration of Levels: The Person as a Whole*—continues to be the most notable innovation, found in no other current personality text. In this edition it has been extensively revised and consists of three fresh, integrative chapters that focus on the contemporary scene. These chapters demonstrate the complementary relations among all the levels for gaining a rich sense of the personality system and the person as a whole. They illustrate the type of integrative system that draws on findings at the vanguard of personality science, as well as on the enduring contributions from work at each level of analysis reviewed throughout the text. In these chapters we examine the person engaged in goal pursuit and self-regulation, functioning and adapting proactively within his or her context and culture.

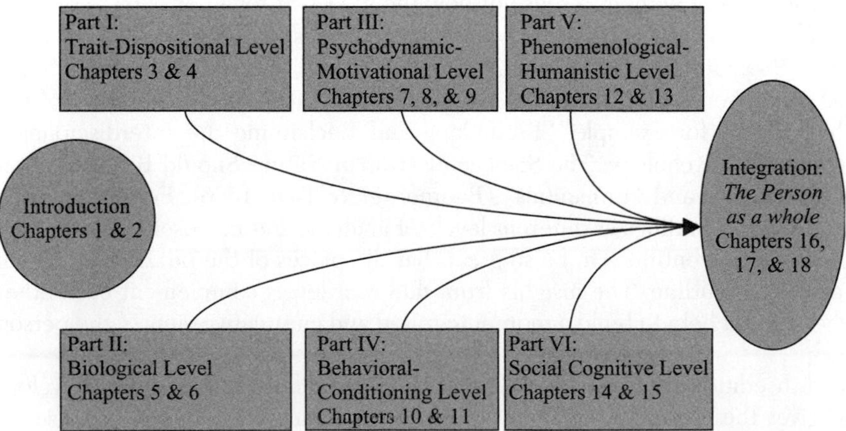

Organization of the text.

The organization of the entire text is depicted in the graphic at the bottom of page iv, showing the six levels and their flow into the integration presented in the last three chapters that illustrate how each contributes to the total picture of the person.

Much of the text was rewritten for this edition, retaining only its best, time-tested features. The extensive rewriting reflects the continuing growth and transformation of personality psychology in recent years. But it is also driven by our goal to make the book even more readily accessible to today's students, and to make mastery of the material personally involving and enjoyable as well as informative and stimulating.

Based on previous teaching experience—cumulatively the authors have spent more than 50 years teaching the undergraduate course in personality—new features facilitate mastery of the material. One important pedagogical feature, continued and expanded from the last edition, consists of *focus questions*, which occur in the margin of the book adjacent to important concepts and facts. The focus questions are designed to facilitate active processing of content by the reader and to function as study guides and retrieval cues. Their inclusion was based on educational research in controlled studies that showed that questions like ours significantly enhanced retention of facts and concepts. With our own students, this approach has proven so successful (increasing test scores appreciably in groups of randomly selected students who used such questions compared with others who were not provided with them) that we have made it an integral learning tool in this text. To highlight important points effectively, detailed, comprehensive bullet point summaries end each chapter, and overview-summary sections occur within chapters as needed.

Updated and greatly expanded instructor and student materials also have been developed, including the sections described below.

INSTRUCTOR MATERIALS

- Comprehensive sets of test questions for each chapter.
- Two sets of powerpoint slides. One set corresponds directly to each text chapter; the other was used by the authors in teaching Introduction to Personality.
- A case study viewing an individual from multiple levels of analysis ("Case of Lourdes").
- Video of the basic Mischel delay of gratification measure showing young children's diverse reactions. This video has attracted extensive media and professional attention, and is vivid and of great interest to students. It compellingly illustrates classic personality research and provides a memorable supplement to Chapter 17 lectures.
- A bibliography of recommended readings listed by chapter to supplement references throughout the text.
- Sample syllabi for semester and quarter systems; tables of contents for each chapter; selected tables and figures from the text for overheads or handouts.

STUDENT MATERIALS

- Practice questions, recommended readings, key terms with definitions organized by chapter.
- Sample personality questionnaires which can be used to self-test various aspects of personality learned in the course.
- Links to websites with additional measures and information to compliment themes in the text and to facilitate further exploration of personality psychology.

Preparation of each edition feels like a wonderful adventure in which we learn much about our own field. We hope that both instructors and students will share our excitement about the current state and future of personality psychology, and our appreciation for the richness of its heritage. Your comments on earlier editions continue to help shape and reshape each edition of this text, and we trust that we have heard and been responsive to your suggestions. One of these changes is seen in the new arrangement of part and chapter sequences. As shown in the Contents, the part and chapter sequence now reflects feedback from instructors' recent experience with this text, as well as our own teaching. Specifically, the Biological Level now follows right after the Trait-Dispositional Level, allowing a clearer sense of the close connections between them. Likewise, the Phenomenological-Humanistic Level comes directly before the Social Cognitive Level, making it clear how the latter built on the former, particularly on George Kelly's contributions.

This extensive revision by a new team of authors (Ozlem Ayduk replaces Ron Smith) contains more than 25% fresh material. The book has been updated and reorganized to reflect the continuing rapid growth and transformation of personality psychology while also remaining true to, and respectful of, the field's rich history of theories and methods for understanding personality. We present personality as a vibrant, expanding field that speaks directly to how students live their lives and how they think about themselves.

Walter Mischel
Yuichi Shoda
Ozlem Ayduk

ACKNOWLEDGMENTS

The authors owe a great debt to more people than can be acknowledged here. Walter Mischel had the extraordinary benefit of studying and working directly with historical pioneers who helped build the field, and who influenced him profoundly. These notably included his mentors George Kelly and Jules Rotter at Ohio State University, and Gordon Allport, Henry Murray, and David C. McClelland, who were his senior colleagues at Harvard University, and he remains grateful to them all. The same is true for his many close colleagues during more than 20 years at Stanford University, and an even longer span that continues at Columbia University. He is especially grateful to his many wonderful students, truly too many to even name here, who made life in psychology exciting for him for what is now more than half a century.

Yuichi Shoda owes his beginning in psychology to the confluence of idealistic subculture at UC Santa Cruz in the early 1980s, with Elliot Aronson, Tom Pettigrew, Brewster Smith, and in particular, David Harrington. Through the years at Stanford and Columbia as a graduate student, he was fortunate to absorb by osmosis the philosophies and approaches to science of such mentors and colleagues as Lawrence Aber, Ozlem Ayduk, Albert Bandura, Geraldine Downey, Carol Dweck, E. Tory Higgins, David Krantz, Robert M. Krauss, Rodolfo Mendoza-Denton, Philip K. Peake, Ewart Thomas, Jack Wright, and, above all, Daniel Cervone, whose infectious love of good ideas and dedication to our field drew Yuichi to it and sustained him throughout. The University of Washington is now his intellectual home, and he is grateful for the inspiration and support provided by his colleagues Ron Smith, Tony Greenwald, and Brian Raffety, and his many students, most recently Vivian Zayas. Most important of all, however, he has had the privilege of pursuing a shared vision of personality as a dynamic, multifaceted, yet coherent whole, with his mentor and friend, Walter Mischel, for over two decades. This textbook is an expression of this vision.

Ozlem Ayduk is indebted to the social-personality faculty at Columbia University (including Walter Mischel, Geraldine Downey, Yuichi Shoda, E. Tory Higgins, and Carol Dweck) who trained her and other fellow graduate students fortunate enough to be at Columbia in how to be social-personality psychologists, rather than social and/or personality psychologists. The idea that the effect of situations cannot be well understood without taking into account individual differences in people's responses to those situations, while at the same time, that the situation needs to be incorporated into our very conceptualization of personality still guides and inspires her current research.

In the preparation of this edition, Rodolfo Mendoza-Denton and Ethan Kross played significant roles, commenting on drafts and contributing to them. Diane Leader and Vivian Zayas went far beyond the usual expectations for reviewer feedback and devoted enormous care to detailed comments that substantially enhanced earlier drafts of this edition, and we are grateful to them.

A special large debt is owed to Amy Blum Cole and Deniz Cebenoyan who generously helped to prepare endless drafts of the manuscript, commenting and working diligently and constructively on it from its earliest versions into its final production. They also have worked closely and long with the first author to develop a greatly expanded set of innovative instructional supplements as well as a new carefully designed and pretested set of materials for the Instructor's Manual.

The editorial and production staff, and particularly Maureen Clendenny, Patty Donovan, and Chris Johnson, worked hard and intensively to make the project go well, and were a pleasure to deal with from start to finish. We thank them sincerely. We also are grateful to the exceptionally helpful reviews and support from the reviewers listed below, and apologize to those who contributed but remain anonymous.

Donna Goetz, Elmhurst College
Dianne Leader, Georgia Institute of Technology
Mindy Mechanic, California State University at Fullerton
Herbert Mirels, Ohio State University
Karen Prager, University of Texas at Dallas
Robert Weiskopf, Indiana University
Vivian Zayas, Cornell University

Tables 1 and 2 present a suggested list of chapter assignments for a quarter system, or a semester system.

TABLE 1 Suggested Schedule for a Quarter System

Week 1	**INTRODUCTION** CHAPTER 1 *Orientation to Personality* CHAPTER 2 *Data, Methods, and Tools*
Week 2	**PART I: THE TRAIT-DISPOSITIONAL LEVEL** CHAPTER 3 *Types and Traits* CHAPTER 4 *The Expressions of Dispositions*
Week 3	**PART II: THE BIOLOGICAL LEVEL** CHAPTER 5 *Heredity and Personality* CHAPTER 6 *Brain, Evolution, and Personality*
Week 4	Exam 1 **PART III: THE PSYCHODYNAMIC-MOTIVATIONAL LEVEL** CHAPTER 7 *Psychodynamic Theories: Freud's Conceptions*
Week 5	CHAPTER 8 *Psychodynamic Applications and Processes* CHAPTER 9 *Post-Freudian Psychodynamics*
Week 6	**PART IV: THE BEHAVIORAL-CONDITIONING LEVEL** CHAPTER 10 *Behavioral Conceptions* CHAPTER 11 *Analyzing and Modifying Behavior*
Week 7	**PART V: THE PHENOMENOLOGICAL-HUMANISTIC LEVEL** CHAPTER 12 *Phenomenological-Humanistic Conceptions* CHAPTER 13 *The Internal View*
Week 8	Exam 2 **PART VI: THE SOCIAL COGNITIVE LEVEL** CHAPTER 14 *Social Cognitive Conceptions*
Week 9	CHAPTER 15 *Social Cognitive Processes* **PART VII: INTEGRATION OF LEVELS: THE PERSON AS A WHOLE** CHAPTER 16 *The Personality System: Integrating the Levels*

TABLE 1 *(Continued)*

Week 10	CHAPTER 17 *Self-Regulation: From Goal Pursuit to Goal Attainment* CHAPTER 18 *Personality in Its Social Context and Culture*
Week 11	Final Exam

TABLE 2 Suggested Schedule for a Semester Course

Week 1	**INTRODUCTION** CHAPTER 1 *Orientation to Personality*
Week 2	CHAPTER 2 *Data, Methods, and Tools* **PART I: THE TRAIT-DISPOSITIONAL LEVEL** CHAPTER 3 *Types and Traits*
Week 3	CHAPTER 4 *The Expressions of Dispositions* **PART II: THE BIOLOGICAL LEVEL** CHAPTER 5 *Heredity and Personality*
Week 4	CHAPTER 6 *Brain, Evolution, and Personality*
Week 5	Review and integration of Parts I and II Exam 1
Week 6	**PART III: THE PSYCHODYNAMIC-MOTIVATIONAL LEVEL** CHAPTER 7 *Psychodynamic Theories: Freud's Conceptions* CHAPTER 8 *Psychodynamic Applications and Processes* CHAPTER 9 *Post-Freudian Psychodynamics*
Week 7	**PART IV: THE BEHAVIORAL-CONDITIONING LEVEL** CHAPTER 10 *Behavioral Conceptions* CHAPTER 11 *Analyzing and Modifying Behavior*
Week 8	Review and integration of Parts III and IV Exam 2
Week 9	**PART V: THE PHENOMENOLOGICAL-HUMANISTIC LEVEL** CHAPTER 12 *Phenomenological-Humanistic Conceptions* CHAPTER 13 *The Internal View*
Week 10	**PART VI: THE SOCIAL-COGNITIVE LEVEL** CHAPTER 14 *Social Cognitive Conceptions* CHAPTER 15 *Social Cognitive Processes*
Week 11	Review and integration of Parts V and VI Exam 3
Week 12	**PART VII: INTEGRATION OF LEVELS: THE PERSON AS A WHOLE** CHAPTER 16 *The Personality System: Integrating the Levels* CHAPTER 17 *Self-Regulation: From Goal Pursuit to Goal Attainment*
Week 13	CHAPTER 18 *Personality in Its Social Context and Culture* Review and integration, Parts I to VII
Week 14	Final Exam

BRIEF CONTENTS

CONTENTS

PART IV
THE BEHAVIORAL-CONDITIONING LEVEL

▶CHAPTER 10
BEHAVIORAL CONCEPTIONS **245**

▶CHAPTER 11
ANALYZING AND MODIFYING BEHAVIOR **270**

PART V
THE PHENOMENOLOGICAL-HUMANISTIC LEVEL

PART VI
THE SOCIAL COGNITIVE LEVEL

▶CHAPTER 18

PERSONALITY IN ITS SOCIAL CONTEXT AND CULTURE **466**

CHAPTER 1

ORIENTATION TO PERSONALITY

WHAT IS PERSONALITY PSYCHOLOGY?

What *is* personality? The term "personality" has many definitions, but no single meaning is accepted universally. In popular usage, personality is often equated with social skill and effectiveness. For example, we may speak of someone as having "a lot of personality" or a "popular personality," and advertisements for self-help courses promise to give those who enroll "more personality."

Less superficially, personality may be taken to be an individual's most striking or dominant characteristic. In this sense, a person may be said to have a "shy personality" or a "neurotic personality," for example, meaning that his or her dominant attribute appears to be shyness or neurotic behavior, respectively.

In personality psychology, the concept goes much beyond these meanings. It has many aspects, reflecting the richness and complexity of the phenomena to which the term refers. Here is an example of one aspect of the concept.

Stable, Coherent Individual Differences

Charles and Jane both are first-year college students taking an introductory course in economics. Their instructor returns the midterm examination in class, and both receive a D. Right after class, Charles goes up to the instructor and seems distressed and upset: He sweats as he talks, his hands tremble slightly, he speaks slowly and softly, almost whispering. His face is flushed and he appears to be on the verge of tears. He apologizes

Different people respond differently to similar events.

(*Source*: Photo Alto/Getty Images)

for his "poor performance," accusing himself bitterly: "I really have no good excuse—it was so stupid of me—I just don't know how I could have done such a sloppy job." He spends most of the rest of the day alone in his dormitory, cuts his classes, and writes a long entry in his diary.

Jane, on the other hand, rushes out of the lecture room at the end of class and quickly starts to joke loudly with her friend about the economics course. She makes fun of the course, comments acidly about the instructor's lecture, and seems to pay little attention to her grade as she strides briskly to her next class. In that class, Jane participates more actively than usual and, surprising her teacher, makes a few excellent comments.

This example illustrates a well-known fact: Different people respond differently to similar events. One goal of personality psychology is to find and describe those individual differences between people that are psychologically meaningful and stable.

1.1 Which two aspects of individuality give rise to the concept of personality?

Though the concept of personality has to do with how an individual differs from others, it implies more. Personality refers to qualities of individuals that are relatively stable. If a person's behavior changes from time to time, then it may not be indicative of personality. But sometimes the *change* in the person's behavior can also be meaningful and tell you something more about the individual. Suppose on the second day, the course in which Jane was more upset than Charles was English Composition in which their essays were read aloud to the class. Not only was the subject matter different from economics, they also learned that their classmates thought poorly of the essays they wrote. Now, does this additional information help make sense of their behaviors? If you answered yes, think about why.

One possibility is that with the new information about what happened on the second day, one can begin to see why their behaviors changed from the first day to the second day. One can begin to form a mental picture of the kind of person who doesn't seem upset by a bad grade in Economics but is devastated by a poor grade in English and/or her peers' unenthusiastic response to her essay. Similarly, one may form an impression of a person who is very upset by a poor grade in Economics but is unaffected by a bad grade in English Composition or his peers' reactions. The information about the circumstances may make the change from day 1 to day 2 a source of insight. The change is potentially meaningful, because even though on the surface Charles and Jane's behaviors changed, there may be coherence in the way they changed; that is, coherence in the pattern of change in an individual's behavior may be another key component of personality.

1.2 How do situational factors (circumstances) contribute to perceived personality coherence?

Predicting and Understanding

The term "personality" usually implies continuity or consistency in the individual. Personality psychologists therefore ask questions like: How consistent are the observed differences between people? How would Charles and Jane respond to a D in physical education? How would each respond if they were fired from their part-time jobs? What do the differences in the reactions of the two students to their grade suggest about their other characteristics? For example, how do they also differ in their academic goals and in their past achievements and failures?

1.3 Describe two goals of personality psychologists.

The observed differences may be meaningful indicators of individual differences in the personality of these two students. Identifying consistent, stable individual differences is an important goal for personality psychologists—and for everyday life—because it makes it possible both to describe people and to try to predict their future behavior, and so to get to know what we can expect from them.

In addition to mapping out the differences between people in terms of their characteristic ways of behaving—that is, thinking, feeling, and acting—personality psychologists try to understand what it is that underlies these differences. They ask: Why did Jane and Charles react so differently to the same event? What within each person leads to his or her distinctive ways of behaving? What must we know about each person to understand—and perhaps sometimes even predict—what he or she will think and feel and do under particular conditions? Personality psychologists ask questions of this sort as they pursue the goal of trying to explain and understand the observed psychological differences between people.

Defining Personality

The definition begins with the assumption that there are stable individual differences. It is further assumed that these differences reflect an underlying organization or structure. In one classic and still influential working definition, the idea of organization is central to the definition. Personality psychology is "... the dynamic organization within the individual of those psychophysical systems that determine his characteristic behavior and thought" (Allport, 1961, p. 28).

As the science matures, there is a growing consensus about the findings and concepts that have stood the test of time. Consequently, a unifying conception of personality and, more modestly, at least a broadly acceptable definition, is becoming possible. A good candidate for such a definition was offered by Pervin (1996, p. 414):

> *Personality is the complex organization of cognitions, affects, and behaviors that gives direction and pattern (coherence) to the person's life. Like the body, personality consists of both structures and processes and reflects both nature (genes) and nurture (experience). In addition, personality includes the effects of the past, including memories of the past, as well as constructions of the present and future.*

Consistent with that definition, David Funder (2001, p. 198) defines the mission of personality psychology as needing to "account for the individual's characteristic patterns of thoughts, emotion, and behavior together with the psychological mechanisms—hidden or not—behind those patterns."

As discussed above, individual differences are always a core part of the definition of this field, but they are not all of it. Thus the term personality psychology does not need to be limited to the study of differences between individuals in their consistent attributes. Rather, "personality psychology must also . . . study how people's [thoughts and actions] . . . interact with—and shape reciprocally—the conditions of their lives" (Mischel, 1981b, p. 17).

This expanded view recognizes that human tendencies are a crucial part of personality. But it also recognizes the need to study the basic processes of adaptation through which people interact with and change the conditions of their lives, and how those conditions, in turn, influence them and their behavior. Personality thus includes the person's unique patterns of coping with, and transforming, the psychological environment. This view of personality focuses not only on behavioral tendencies but also on psychological processes (such as learning, motivation, and thinking) that interact with biological-genetic processes to influence the individual's distinctive patterns of adaptation throughout the life span.

1.4 Cite five aspects of the construct of personality as currently conceived.

In summary, to capture the richness of human behavior, the personality construct has to encompass the following aspects:

- Personality shows continuity, stability, and coherence.
- Personality is expressed in many ways—from overt behavior through thoughts and feelings.
- Personality is organized. In fact, when it is fragmented or disorganized it is a sign of disturbance.
- Personality is a determinant that influences how the individual relates to the social world.
- Personality is a psychological concept, but it also is assumed to link with the physical, biological characteristics of the person.

THEORY AND LEVELS OF ANALYSIS IN PERSONALITY PSYCHOLOGY

Early "Big Picture" Theory

Personality psychology is a relatively young science, but it has been practiced from the time that people began asking questions about human nature: Why am I anxious for no apparent reason? Who can I trust? Who do I select for a mate? Who am I?

In Western societies, since the time of the ancient Greeks, philosophers have long pondered questions about human nature and attempted classification schemes for making sense of the varieties of individual differences in important attributes and their causes. As early as 400 B.C., Hippocrates philosophized about the basic human temperaments (e.g., choleric, depressive), and their associated traits, guided by the biology of his time. For example, he thought physical qualities like yellow bile, or too much blood, might underlie the differences in temperament. He began a tradition—trait and type psychology—whose modern versions date to the start of the last century. It is a tradition that is still very much alive and well, although completely transformed in current scientific practice, drawing extensively both on modern measurement methods and on the biology of today.

Aristotle postulated the brain to be the seat of the rational mind, or the "conscious and intellectual soul that is peculiar to man" (Singer, 1941, p. 43). This view has become a foundation of the Western view of human mind. For example, in his dualistic view of the human being as consisting of mind and body, Descartes viewed the mind as what gives us the capacities for thought and consciousness, which sets us apart from the physical world of matter. The mind "decides" and the body carries out the decision.

In the early 1900s, Sigmund Freud, living and working in Vienna as a physician, upset the rational view of human nature that characterized his time with a powerful and comprehensive theory of personality. Freud's theory made reason secondary and instead made primary the unconscious and its often unacceptable, irrational motives and desires, thereby forever changing the view of human nature. The tradition he began also continues to influence contemporary personality psychology, but again in ways that are greatly changed from Freud's original ideas, both by the work of his many followers and by developments in other areas of the science that made it possible to reinterpret much of his work and to revise it as needed.

From Grand Theories to Levels of Analysis

In the first half of the 20th century, personality psychology was inspired by grand theories of personality that were being developed by several "big picture" innovators: Each proposed distinctive conceptions of the nature of personality, and tried to present a comprehensive view of all of personality in all of its diverse aspects. Like Freud, many of these theorists were working in western Europe as therapists treating psychologically disturbed and distressed individuals. As practicing therapists, they used the cases of their patients as the basis for broader generalizations on the nature of personality. Consequently their ideas helped to shape clinical psychology and psychiatry as well as personality psychology. One hazard here was that because their work was based on their experience with emotionally disturbed patients, they may have focused more on the disturbed aspects of personality than on its healthier versions in less troubled people.

Broad theories like Freud's provide an orientation and perspective that stimulates different types of research within the field and different types of real-life applications, such as clinical practice with people experiencing psychological problems. Most notably, they lead to different lines of research and to different forms of therapy or intervention designed to modify or enhance personality constructively. They also lead to different approaches to assess personality and to think about persons, including oneself, and thus matter a great deal to the image one develops of personality and individuality, and indeed of oneself as a person. As such they are valuable.

1.5 What are the scientific shortcomings of broad theories of personality?

Many such grand theories sprang up in the first half of the last century, not just in the tradition of Freud, who was widely rejected in many American psychology departments, but in different directions, as discussed throughout this text. In spite of the growth of personality psychology as a field of scientific research, however, most of the grand theories of personality did not lend themselves to precise scientific testing that allowed them to be either supported or disconfirmed clearly on the basis of empirical studies (Meehl, 1990, 1997). Reasons for this range from the difficulty of specifying the theoretical premises in testable terms, to various types of experimental and statistical limitations in conducting and evaluating the test results.

But even beyond these limitations, grand theories often function more like general guidelines or orientations for studying personality and interpreting the results from a particular perspective or framework. Thus it is difficult to firmly reject or support a given theory on the basis of empirical studies. As one pundit put it, many big theories in all areas of science generally are never really disconfirmed: They just die of loneliness as they gradually are replaced by approaches that seem more fruitful and lead to more informative new research that raises new questions and suggests new—always tentative—answers.

In the second half of the last century, after World War II, American personality psychology grew into a substantial field in its own right. It was influenced by European psychology but also developed in its own directions within the larger science of psychology. The influences in the United States came from traditions that sprang up in university psychology departments that were devoted to turning psychology away from philosophy and into science. Researchers working both with normal and disturbed populations developed and applied increasingly sophisticated scientific methods to address many central issues in personality psychology. In time, it became possible to examine important questions about personality with research evidence that accumulated at a rapid rate and pointed to exciting new directions as the science evolved.

From the 1960s to about the 1980s, the field of personality psychology was full of seemingly insoluble controversies among apparently irreconcilable broad theoretical approaches. The result was much debate and new research that helped to clarify important questions but that also created much divisiveness among alternative viewpoints.

In contrast, in the current scene there are numerous encouraging signs of integration and constructive syntheses of the insights coming from theorists and researchers that are working at different **levels of analysis**, addressing different aspects of personality. It is increasingly seen that each level has its legitimacy and usefulness, and each requires distinctive methods and concepts. But the findings from different levels do not necessarily conflict. On the contrary, they usually add to a fuller understanding and clarification of the whole. Each level of analysis yields many solid answers—as well as raising new questions—and each contributes to building a cumulative and coherent view of personality and human nature.

▶ LEVELS OF ANALYSIS: ORGANIZATION OF THIS BOOK

1.6 Personality is studied at which six levels? What questions about ourselves does each level suggest?

In this book you will learn some of the major theoretical approaches to personality that have guided thinking and research, and see how research and theory-building is done at each level of analysis. We survey some of the main concepts developed to describe and understand the important psychological differences among people, and we consider the concepts and findings that are central to diverse views of human nature.

To capture the essentials, this text is organized into the six major levels of personality study from a century of work in psychology as a science and profession. Each part of the text presents the main concepts, methods, and findings associated with that level of analysis, and each focuses attention on distinctive aspects of personality. Each level adds to the appreciation of the richness and complexity of personality. Each level also led to discoveries that have important practical and personal applications that we will examine. In combination, the six levels provide an overview of the many complex and diverse aspects of human personality. The final part of the text shows how the levels interconnect and become integrated to give a more coherent view of the person as a whole. The organization of the text highlights how each level adds to the whole, and suggests their evolving integration. You can see this organization at a glance in Figure 1.1.

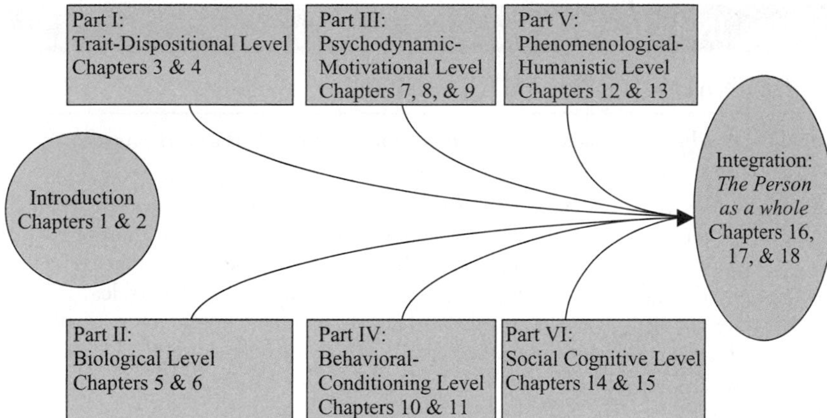

Figure 1.1 Organization of the text.

After an Introduction section that gives an overview of the data, methods, and tools of the science, Part I presents contributions from the Trait-Dispositional Level; Part II focuses on those coming from the Biological Level; followed by Part III, the Psychodynamic-Motivational Level; Part IV, the Behavioral-Conditioning Level; Part V, the Phenomenological-Humanistic Level; and Part VI, the Social Cognitive Level. Below we look at an overview of each of the levels. As Figure 1.1 suggests, the contributions from each level are cumulative and come together in the final Part VII, Integration of Levels: The Person as a Whole, which explicitly shows their interconnections. Each level asks distinctive questions, although both the questions and the levels overlap.

Almost everyone becomes interested in the science of personality because they want to understand people, and particularly themselves and those they care about, as fully as possible. In this sense, the science of personality also has a distinctly personal side: the questions that researchers ask at each level in formal scientific terms also have personal relevance. Often they are asked more informally by most people. Therefore, to make those connections explicit, the key questions pursued at each level of analysis are summarized in *In Focus 1.1*, and phrased in personal ways that invite you to ask them about yourself.

The Trait-Dispositional Level

The Trait-Dispositional Level seeks to identify the types of stable psychological qualities and behavioral dispositions that characterize different individuals and types consistently. In everyday life, people may ask themselves questions like those listed for this level in *In Focus 1.1*: "What am I like as a person? How am I different from other people 'on the whole'? In what general ways are people different from each other?" Using the natural language of trait terms, people often ask and answer such questions easily, not just about themselves but about other people: He or she seems friendly, assertive, aggressive, submissive, conscientious, and so on. Examples of such traits used in current research include broad characteristics such as agreeableness, conscientiousness, and open mindedness. Studies at this level also examine the stability and consistency of traits and types over the course of time throughout the life span.

1.7 Describe the focus of the Trait-Dispositional Level of analysis.

IN FOCUS 1.1

THE PERSONAL SIDE OF THE SCIENCE

Some key questions at different levels of analysis phrased as questions that can be asked about oneself:

- ***Trait-Dispositional Level:*** What am I like as a person? How am I different from other people "on the whole"? In what general ways are people different from each other? Does what I usually do and think and feel depend mostly on myself or on the situation in which I find myself? When and how is my behavior influenced by the situation? How does my personality influence the situations I choose to be in? How does my personality influence the effects that different kinds of situations have on me?
- ***Biological Level:*** What in my personality comes from the genes I inherited? How is my personality a reflection of my life experiences? How does my personality reflect my basic biological predispositions? Can my experiences change my biology? For instance, does my brain change when I'm depressed? How do the same experiences affect people with different genetic predispositions? Why is my personality so different (or similar) to my siblings? How does my biology influence my pursuit of life goals? How does evolutionary theory help me understand dating and social behavior today?
- ***Psychodynamic-Motivational Level:*** Does what I do sometimes puzzle me? How and why? What are the real motives that drive or underlie my behavior? How can I explain irrational fears and anxieties? How do I try to protect myself psychologically against getting hurt? How much of what I do is unconscious or done without awareness? What might be some unconscious influences on my behavior? Do I have motives that make me uncomfortable? If yes, what do I try to do about that?
- ***Behavioral-Conditioning Level:*** How is what a person *does* linked to what happens to him or her when he or she does it? How are important behavior patterns, including emotions and fears, learned? How does what I do and feel depend on my earlier experiences? How can my behavior and feelings be modified by new learning experiences? Do aspects of my personality depend on the contexts in which I am? How am I different when with a good friend at school and when with my family at home for the holidays? Why?
- ***Phenomenological-Humanistic Level:*** Who am "I" really? Who do I want to become? How do I see myself? How do I see my parents? What do I feel about myself when I don't meet my parents' expectations? How is my real self different from the self I would ideally like to be? What is my ideal self? How am I different from my mother but similar to my father?
- ***Social Cognitive Level:*** What is the role in personality of what people know, think, and feel? How does what I know, think, and feel about myself and the social world influence what I do and can become? What can I do to change how I think and feel? Will that change my personality and behavior? How much of who and what I am and do is "automatic"? How much is open to "willpower" and self-regulation? How do willpower and self-regulation work? How can I enhance my control over my life?

This level of analysis has become one of the most vigorous and widely researched in recent years. This progress has been supported by the development of some straightforward, well-established self-report methods that are being used by researchers throughout the world. Consequently, the usefulness of trait-level analyses is being extensively investigated and has led to findings on the stability of personality over time. Work at this level is also yielding a broad taxonomy for classifying individuals with regard to major traits, providing a map on which people, groups, and even cultures can be compared. Especially in recent years, researchers at this level also have been getting answers to questions such as: Does what we do and think and feel characteristically depend mostly on the individual or on the situation? How do the two—the person and the situation—interact?

The Biological Level

An important goal of personality study at the biological level is to try to specify the role of genetic determinants and of the social environment in shaping who and what we become. The focus in much of this work in the past has been to answer the age-old question: How much of personality reflects nature, and how much nurture—and above all, how do these two sources of influence interact in shaping our characteristics? When you learn what is now known at this level of analysis, you will be able to answer questions like: "To what extent does my personality come from my parents and the genes I inherited from them? To what extent is my personality a reflection of my life experiences? To what extent does my personality reflect my basic biological predispositions?"

1.8 What kinds of biological factors are known to underlie individual differences in personality?

This level of analysis also addresses the fact that humans are biological beings who evolved in adaptive ways that endowed the species with biological characteristics, constraints, and possibilities. These influence human nature and the way we fight, mate, socialize, and create. The goal at this level of analysis is to examine how aspects of personality may have evolved in response to the evolutionary pressures and history that shaped our species over time. Here is an example of the kinds of problems it studies and the questions this level asks:

Consider two identical twin baby girls who were separated at birth and grew up in very different worlds. Jane was raised on a rural Iowa farm, an only child, with hard-working but unloving parents. Nahid's life unfolded in the capital of Iran, nurtured by loving parents in a large, middle-class family. The identical twins started life with the same DNA and therefore with virtually identical brains. Suppose the twins were reunited at age 30 and tested extensively. How similar will their personalities turn out to be?

The Psychodynamic-Motivational Level

The Psychodynamic-Motivational Level probes the motivations, conflicts, and defenses, often without one's awareness, that can help explain complex consistencies and inconsistencies in personality. Questions you might ask yourself when thinking about this level of analysis (*In Focus 1.1*) include: "Does what I do sometimes puzzle me? How and why? What are the real motives that drive or underlie my behavior? How can I explain irrational fears and anxieties? How do I try to protect myself against getting hurt psychologically?"

1.9 Which aspects of personality are addressed at the Psychodynamic-Motivational Level of analysis?

Work at this level is relevant for understanding many puzzles of personality, for example, when people turn out to be more complex and unpredictable than expected and seem to change as one knows them better. Here is an example:

Roberto was confusing his girlfriend. Before they moved in together, she thought she knew him—warm, friendly, fun, and easy to be with. Later she began to see the sadness, the inside rage, the fears, and the unpredictability. She felt she was getting more smoke than light—the longer she knew Roberto, the less she felt she really understood him, and she was beginning to lose her trust. One day, he stayed in bed most of the day. When asked what's going on he'd say, "I'm fine," denying any anxiety or depression, and he seemed to mean it. Roberto was reassuring, yet she remained quite unconvinced.

Roberto's girlfriend intuitively understood that what Roberto said and seemed to honestly believe was not necessarily the whole story and that there were other reasons that he could not acknowledge even to himself. The kind of insight needed to understand Roberto's behavioral and emotional inconsistencies is at the heart of the psychodynamic motivational level of analysis.

Much of the work at this level has been done in psychological therapy situations, beginning with Sigmund Freud a century ago. He worked, for example, on the case of Hans, a 4-year-old child who had developed an irrational fear of going outdoors because horses might be there and he had become terrified of them even though he had never been hurt by one. Freud created a theory that used the concept of the unconscious and the child's unacceptable sexual and aggressive wishes to explain how a fear like that could have developed.

An important key here was the discovery that certain impulses, such as a young child's aggressive impulses toward his father, are treated by society as taboo and punished, making the child anxious. If the impulses still persist but create painful anxieties, the child may unconsciously redirect them at other objects, for example, by becoming afraid of horses, which remind him of his father who might punish him.

The Behavioral-Conditioning Level

1.10 What questions about personality are addressed at the Behavioral-Conditioning Level?

As *In Focus 1.1* indicates, work at this level of analysis has asked questions like: "How are important behavior patterns, including emotions and fears, learned? How does what I do and feel depend on my earlier experiences? How can my behavior and feelings be modified by new learning experiences?"

Consider this dilemma:

Jake was upset because he could not accept the management job he had been so eager to get when he learned that it was on the 80th floor: just the thought of riding up in the elevator terrified him—but he had never been afraid of elevators in the past.

Work at the Behavioral-Conditioning Level also tries to provide accounts of irrational behaviors that perplex the people who are tortured by them, similar to many of the same basic personality phenomena that Freud discovered at the Psychodynamic-Motivational Level. But they get there through a different route and reach different conclusions that lead to important revisions in some of the earlier ideas for dealing with such problems.

The Behavioral-Conditioning Level analyzes specific patterns of behavior that characterize individuals and the situations or conditions that seem to regulate their occurrence and strength. It studies the determinants of learning and applies learning principles to modify problematic patterns of behavior, including emotional reactions like fears. Behavioral analyses focus on a specific, problematic or otherwise important behavior—such as the stutter of a person suffering from public speaking anxieties, or one's inability to stay concentrated on studying before exams. Then they analyze the situations or conditions that seem to control that behavior, that is, the conditions in which the stutter or the studying becomes worse or improves. Finding the conditions under which the problem improves becomes the basis for designing treatments to modify the behavior to help reduce or eliminate the problem. Behavioral analyses have helped us understand the conditions through which behaviors relevant to personality—from stutters through poor self-concepts, to troublesome behavior in interpersonal relationships—are learned and can be modified.

The results have been applied to help people overcome a variety of serious personal difficulties, ranging from common but debilitating fears, to weight problems, to learning deficits and handicaps, to increasing personal assertiveness and self-esteem. Originally this level of analysis dealt mostly with learning and conditioning based on animal work because studies of the brain were invasive and dangerous, making experiments with humans unethical. In new directions, behavioral levels of analysis have a second life because advances in brain imaging, for example, and in the modern study of mental processes make it possible to analyze mental functions previously considered too mysterious for behavioral study with the objective methods of science.

The Phenomenological-Humanistic Level

Each person sees the world subjectively in his or her own personal ways. To understand this privately experienced side of personality, we must examine the nature of subjective experience; we have to try to see how people perceive their world. Workers at this level of analysis are genuinely interested in hearing and exploring fully the answers people give to questions (from *In Focus 1.1*) like these: "Who am I really? Who do I want to become? How do I see myself? How do I see my parents? What do I feel about myself when I don't meet my parents' expectations?"

1.11 What is the major focus of the Phenomenological-Humanistic Level of analysis?

Here is a sample of self-reported personal feelings taken from a self-description by a college student about to take a final examination:

> *When I think about the exam, I really feel sick . . . so much depends on it. I know I'm not prepared, at least not as much as I should be, but I keep hoping that I can sort of snow my way through it. . . . I keep trying to remember some of the things he said in class, but my mind keeps wandering. God, my folks—What will they think if I don't pass and can't graduate? Will they have a fit! Boy! I can see their faces. Worse yet, I can hear their voices: "And with all the money we spent on your education." Mom's going to be hurt. She'll let me know I let her down. She'll be a martyr . . . Oh hell! What about Anne [girlfriend]? She's counting on my graduating. We had plans. What will she think? . . . I've got to pass. I've just got to. . . . What's going to happen to me? . . . The whole damn world is coming apart. (extracted from Fischer, 1970, pp. 121–122)*

Work at this level begins by listening closely and trying to understand the individual's experience as he or she perceives it. The focus is on subjective experience, feelings, the personal view of the world and the self. The focus also is on people's positive strivings and their tendencies toward growth and self-actualization.

These concerns require studying the internal or mental processes through which individuals interpret experience. A distinguished psychologist, Ulric Neisser, for example, put it this way (1967, p. 3): "Whether beautiful or ugly or just conveniently at hand, the world of experience is produced by [the person] who experiences it." That statement, of course, does not imply that there is no "real" world out there, but just that it is the *experienced world* that is basic for understanding phenomena like personality and the important differences between people. Ideally, researchers at this level would like to look at the world through the eyes of the persons they are studying, to stand in that person's shoes, to know emotionally as well as intellectually what it might be like to *be* that person.

For many years this level of analysis was treated with suspicion by the rest of the field, but beginning in the 1980s there has been an explosion of solid research on the self, close relationships, and identity. This work is restoring the self as an important concept in current personality psychology. It is addressing the processes through which each person develops a sense of self and identity—a conception of who one is and wants to be. This research is telling us much about how people create a life story or inner narrative that can provide life with a sense of purpose and direction (e.g., McAdams, 1995, 2005). Much work at this level also explores links between the self and personality adjustment, mental health, and positive functioning (e.g., Diener & Lucas, 2000; Duckworth, Steen, & Seligman, 2005).

The Social Cognitive Level

1.12 How does the Social Cognitive Level of analysis differ from the behavioral-conditioning approach?

The focus of personality research at this level includes the person's social knowledge of the world, and how people make sense of other people and themselves and cope as they negotiate their interpersonal lives. Questions that you might ask about yourself at this level of analysis (*In Focus 1.1*) are: "How does what I know, think, and feel about myself and the social world influence what I do and can become? What can I do to change how I think and feel?"

This level examines individual differences in how social knowledge is used in dealing with the world, in the construction of the self, in self-regulation, and in self-control. The specific focus is on the individual's characteristic ways of thinking and processing information, both cognitively and emotionally, as determinants of his or her distinctive and meaningful patterns of experience and social behavior. For example:

> *Yolanda and Virginia, now college students, both lost their young mothers last year from breast cancer. Both women know that their total family histories put them at high risk for having a genetic predisposition for this type of cancer early in life. At the college health service the specialist they see points out the risks of their situation in great detail. He urges that they adhere strictly to monthly breast self-examination as an important part of their health-maintenance program.*
>
> *When Yolanda tries self-examination, she remembers the risks the doctor described and she imagines them vividly. Her thoughts flow from anticipating finding the lump, to thinking "I'm going to die," to a flood of panic feelings. She thinks "what will be will be" and stops trying to self-examine. When Virginia begins, she also remembers the physician's words but she imagines that if there is a lump she will find it early, it can be removed, and she can be successfully treated. She thinks: Above all I will have at least some control over my fate.*

An important challenge at this level is to understand such internal mental and emotional processes and their links to the characteristic behavior patterns that may enduringly distinguish different individuals and types of people. The goal is not only to "get inside the head" but to understand the stable mental-emotional processes and structures that generate the diverse individual differences that are observed. Most attention in recent years is given to studying the basic psychological processes through which individuals construct, interpret, and understand their social-personal world. Questions here include: How do individuals come to deal with their worlds in the stable cognitive, emotional, and behavior patterns that characterize them? What is the "self" and how do self-concepts and perceptions about the self influence what the person thinks, feels, and becomes?

Levels of Analysis Applied to Understand Unexpected Aggression: The Texas Tower Killer

The different levels of analysis discussed throughout this text can complement each other constructively. Taken together, they increase the total understanding of personality as a whole. To illustrate, we next look at the types of questions that each level asks when confronted by the real-life puzzles of personality. In this example, you can see that the phenomena addressed by all levels interact concurrently within a personality.

The example here is the case of Charles Whitman, a University of Texas college student. Late one hot summer night, Charles Whitman killed his wife and mother. The next morning he went to a tower on the University of Texas campus and opened fire on the crowded campus below with a high-powered hunting rifle. In 90 horrifying minutes,

Charles Whitman: The Texas Tower Killer

(*Source*: © AP/Wide World Photos)

he killed 14 people, wounded another 24, and even managed to hit an airplane before he was killed by police. After the Whitman incident, the first question asked was a familiar one: What caused this mild-mannered young man to explode into violence?

The night before the killing, Whitman wrote the following letter, reflecting his internal subjective experiences at the time:

> *I don't really understand myself these days. I am supposed to be an average, reasonable, and intelligent young man. However, lately (I can't recall when it started) I have been the victim of many unusual and irrational thoughts. These thoughts constantly recur, and it requires a tremendous mental effort to concentrate on useful and progressive tasks. In March when my parents made a physical break I noticed a great deal of stress. I consulted a Dr. Cochrum at the University Health Center and asked him to recommend someone that I could consult with about some psychiatric disorders I felt I had. I talked with a doctor once for about two hours and tried to convey to him my fears that I felt overcome by overwhelming violent impulses. After one session I never saw the doctor again, and since then I have been fighting my mental turmoil alone, and seemingly to no avail. After my death I wish that an autopsy would be performed on me to see if there is any visible physical disorder. I have had some tremendous headaches in the past and have consumed two large bottles of Excedrin in the past three months.*

The **Phenomenological-Humanistic Level** would focus directly on these words by Whitman and try to illuminate Whitman's own views of what he did and why, and of what he believed was happening to him, beginning with the letter he wrote, and extending in various other directions. The concern would be to understand how his perceptions and interpretations of what was happening to him misguided him to the actions that then erupted explosively. In the effort to unscramble his confusions and misperceptions, attention would be focused on his disturbed sense of self and his panic in trying to deal with the internal conflicts, loss of control, and feelings of fragmentation, despair, and helplessness that he was experiencing. In these efforts, work at this level and work at the psychodynamic level would become complementary, with researchers at both levels converging on some of the same questions, albeit with somewhat different concepts and methods.

Applied to the Whitman case, at the **Trait-Dispositional Level** of analysis, the main questions will be: Would Whitman be likely to have a distinctive trait profile on personality tests (to be described in the next chapter) that show, for example, high levels of angry hostility, impulsiveness, and neuroticism, with poor impulse control and little ability to handle stress? If he was not characterized by such a profile before the incident, did Whitman undergo personality change, at least as defined at the trait level? Or were there any subtle indications in his behavioral tendencies that might have allowed one to predict his actions? The profile resulting from personality tests would provide a rich description of his characteristics. Many of these might not have been evident from his previous behaviors, but might now help one to make sense of his violent outburst and the character traits with which it was consistent.

At the **Biological Level**, to understand Whitman, one would begin by considering the possible links between the brain and aggression that might underlie his ferocious outburst. To understand the Whitman case at this level, a postmortem examination was conducted to follow up on his reference to intense headaches. It revealed a highly malignant tumor in an area of the brain hypothesized to be involved in aggressive behavior. Some experts therefore suggested that Whitman's damaged brain might have predisposed him to violent behavior. On the other hand, although many efforts have been made to locate and study areas of the brain involved in aggressive behavior, even with modern methods these relations are still poorly understood, and emerging evidence suggests that the relationship between brain areas and behavior is not simple. Certain areas of the brain may have coordinating functions in aggression, and we also know that these regions are closely regulated by other areas of the brain that process information coming in from the environment. Certain kinds of brain damage or disorders can produce violent and unpredictable behavior in humans, too. In the majority of individuals who behave aggressively, however, there is no evidence of brain damage, although the aggression is being triggered by a variety of brain mechanisms.

Nevertheless, biological and genetic factors do appear to play a more general role in aggressive behavior (Baron & Richardson, 1994; Loehlin, 1992). Identical twins, who are genetic copies of each other, are more similar in their aggressive and dominant behavior patterns than are fraternal twins, who differ genetically from one another (Plomin & Rende, 1991). This is the case even if the identical twins are raised in different homes with presumably different social environments (Bouchard, Lykken, McGue, Segal, & Tellegen, 1990). But, behavior geneticists also remind us that genetic factors never operate in isolation; they always interact with environmental factors. In recent years, new discoveries about the brain, and new methods of studying its activities, have encouraged great interest and much research at this level. If Whitman were tested today, biological-level measures (such as brain scans) would allow much fuller analyses of the links between his thoughts, actions, and brain processes. Most important, as you will see later in this text (Chapter 17), recent advances in the study of brain mechanisms are giving us an increasingly clear picture of the neural mechanisms in the brain that can go wrong when people have violent outbursts of aggression (Davidson, Putnam, &

Larson, 2000). Recent work at this level, discussed in the final part of the text, also makes it clear that the biological and the psychological aspects of personality are in a continuous reciprocal influence process, each affecting the other. Consequently, contributions from the different levels of analysis again continuously enrich each other.

At the **Psychodynamic-Motivational Level**, to understand Whitman's violence one might first focus on the "unusual and irrational thoughts" to which he referred and to his "overwhelming violent impulses." Using the methods of psychodynamic theory (Chapters 7, 8, and 9), one seeks to understand the unconscious conflicts and struggles that underlie them. According to psychoanalytic theory, for example, human aggression is an outgrowth of the continuous conflict between strong and often unconscious impulses and the defenses developed by the ego to keep them in check. Might Whitman's defenses against his own anger and hostility have become so rigid and extreme that he could not express his aggressive impulses even in indirect or disguised forms? A question asked at the psychodynamic level then is: Have the unreleased pressures built up to an explosion point? Work at this level assumes that the provocation that triggers unexpected destructive outburst is usually trivial. Instead, it searches to try to infer underlying conflicts and unconscious dynamics that might account for the unexpected and seemingly inexplicable change in his typical behavior.

At the **Behavioral-Conditioning Level**, the focus is on the ways in which the person's behavior reflects and is shaped by his or her learning history and present life conditions. Applied to Charles Whitman, at this level, one would seek the answer in Whitman's previous learning experiences and the culture in which he grew up. A question at this level would be whether there was a history of fascination and rewarding experiences with guns, as well as exposure to role models that displayed violent behaviors. One may also ask whether there was an influence by the culture or subculture and the rewards it offered for aggression in diverse forms. Perhaps the environment in which he developed had primed him to solve his problems in a violent manner, particularly when he was overwhelmed by the recent life stresses that he described in his letter.

At the **Social Cognitive Level**, how people perceive and interpret events, and the internal states and mental-emotional processes that these perceptions activate, determine how they behave. To understand what Whitman did requires understanding these mental and emotional processes that were activated in him at the time of his outburst, the specific situations he was exposed to, and his characteristic cognitive and affective dynamics that generated his extraordinary aggression. Perhaps his aggression was prompted by perceptions that he had been terribly wronged in ways that allowed him to justify his actions at least to himself. By blaming a person or group for real or imagined wrongs, people can create an image of a hated enemy fully deserving of whatever aggression is directed toward them. But why did Whitman do something so extreme that most people would not do under similar circumstances, and with equally good reasons? What was going on in Whitman's mind that was so different and that could plausibly account for the extremeness of his aggression? What kinds of skills, self-regulatory controls, and values did he lack that could allow such behavior? What were the beliefs and expectations that led him to his actions? These are the kinds of questions that drive work at this level of analysis. While there is no way to answer such questions in hindsight, the challenge is to be able to do so—at least sometimes—in advance. In pursuing the answers, work at this level and at several of the other levels converges and each again complements the others.

1.13 How do the six levels of analysis address different potential causes of Charles Whitman's killing spree?

Sometimes stable individuals exhibit extreme and unconventional behavior, as displayed in astronaut Lisa Marie Novak's case

(*Source*: JSC/NASA Media Services)

The Whitman case is an extreme example, but by no means unique. Forty years later, NASA astronaut Lisa Marie Novak, infatuated with a fellow astronaut who was involved with another woman, drove 900 miles to confront her romantic rival, an Air Force Captain. Before leaving, she packed her car with large trash bags and various weapons, including a knife and a BB Gun, and in her eagerness even wore a diaper to avoid stopping on the 10-hour drive from Houston to Orlando. She was a respected, intelligent individual in her field of expertise, and the extreme behavior in her personal life, which ultimately led to an attempted murder charge, was a shock to those who thought they knew her well. We see these complexities of personality dramatized by the media, but they also surprise us often in everyday life.

Integration of Levels: The Person as a Whole

In sum, the different levels all add their distinctive insights to understanding the total person "as a whole" and they inform each other and interact. In this text we focus first on each level separately so that each can be studied in depth, and then consider their interconnections and integration in the final part's three chapters. When taken together, the work done at these different levels addresses every conceivable cause for any behavior or mental event central for personality. At times, to be sure, work at the different levels can also produce critical findings that contradict each other and generate real conflicts. That has happened often in the field's history, and will continue in the future as it does in every science. But those are some of the most exciting moments in science and often set the stage for dramatic progress. In fact, in recent years, personality psychologists working at different levels seem to be crossing more freely over what used to be rigid boundaries. As one reviewer of ongoing work within diverse research orientations put it:

> *Their research programs frequently inform one another. The complementary findings are beginning to portray a coherent (albeit incomplete) picture of personality structure and functioning. Personality psychologists have found common ground. (Cervone, 1991, p. 371)*

A more comprehensive view of the person has been emerging that seeks to incorporate many of the insights and findings from each of the diverse levels within one broader, unifying framework (e.g., Baumeister & Tice, 1996; Carver, 1996; Cervone & Mischel, 2002; Mischel & Shoda, 1998). If this trend continues, it promises to be an exciting time for the field. It indicates that personality psychology is becoming a more cumulative science in which knowledge and insights add to each other, allowing each generation of researchers to revise earlier conclusions and to build progressively on each other's work. If so, major contributions provided by each stream of work will ultimately become more integrated, retaining those elements that stand the test of time and research as the science matures.

1.14 What kinds of theoretical integrations are occurring as personality psychologists seek a unified understanding of the person?

Boundaries are also being crossed productively between personality psychology and related fields, both at more molar, social-cultural levels of analysis (e.g., Nisbett, 1997) and at more molecular levels, particularly in cognitive neuroscience and in behavioral genetics (Lieberman, 2007; Ochsner & Lieberman, 2001; Plomin, DeFries, McClearn, & Rutter, 1997; Rothbart, Posner, & Gerardi, 1997; Wager, Jonides, Smith, & Nichols, 2005). It has long been the hope of personality psychology that it could some day provide an integrated view of the person (e.g., Allport, 1937) that at least begins to capture the complexity and depth of its subject matter: optimists in the field are beginning to think that day might not be too far off (Cervone & Mischel, 2002, Chap. 1).

Practical Applications: Coping and Personal Adaptation

To speak to why most people really want to study personality, we also look at how the discoveries made already can allow a better understanding of oneself as a person and as at least a partial architect of one's own future. Personality theories are often *applied* to help improve the psychological qualities of one's life. Even people whose problems are not severe enough to seek help from professionals still search for ways to live their lives more fully and satisfyingly. But what constitutes a fuller, more satisfying life? Given the diversity and complexity of human strengths and problems, it seems evident that simple notions of psychological adequacy in terms of "good adjustment" or "sound personality" are naive. More adequate definitions of "adaptation" and "abnormality," of "mental health" and "deviance," hinge on the personality theory that is used as a guide. The work discussed through the text offers distinctive notions about the nature of psychological adequacy and deviance. On closer examination, it will be seen that even these conceptions from different levels of analysis in fact have clear, common themes. But each also adds to the strategies that can be chosen to try to change troublesome behaviors and to encourage better alternatives.

1.15 In what sense is personality an applied science?

Many personality psychologists are searching for useful techniques to deal with the implications of personality for human problems, such as depression, anxiety, and poor health, and to foster more advantageous patterns of coping and growth. In addition to having enormous practical and social importance, attempts to understand and change behaviors provide one of the sharpest testing grounds for ideas about personality.

These efforts include different forms of psychotherapy, drugs, and physical treatments, various special learning programs, and changes in the psychological environment to permit people to develop to their full potential. Research on these topics informs us about the usefulness and implications of different ideas about personality change in normal, well-functioning people as well as in those who are distressed. The concepts, methods, and findings relevant to personality assessment, change, and growth are discussed at many points as they apply to each of the major approaches and the levels of analysis that they guide.

SUMMARY

WHAT IS PERSONALITY?

- The term "personality" implies stable and coherent individual differences that can be described or predicted.
- In personality psychology, "personality" refers to the person's unique patterns of coping with and transforming the psychological environment.
- Personality psychologists study how personality dispositions and psychological and biological-genetic processes influence people's distinctive patterns of behavior.

THEORY AND LEVELS OF ANALYSIS

- In the first half of the last century, grand theories of personality (e.g., those of Freud) developed, introducing many lines of research and therapeutic practices.
- Work in personality psychology can now be grouped into six different major levels of analysis.
- These six levels provide an overview of the many complex and diverse aspects of human personality.
- The Trait-Dispositional Level tries to identify consistencies in the basic expressions of personality, conceptualized as stable personality characteristics.
- The Biological Level explores the biological bases of personality, including the role of heredity, the brain, and evolution.
- The Psychodynamic-Motivational Level probes the motivations, conflicts, and defenses—often unconscious—that may underlie diverse aspects of personality.
- The Behavioral-Conditioning Level analyzes specific patterns of behavior that characterize individuals and identifies the conditions that regulate their occurrence.
- The Phenomenological-Humanistic Level focuses on the inner experiences of the person and his or her way of seeing and interpreting the world.
- The Social Cognitive Level shares the focuses with the Psychodynamic, Behavioral, and Phenomenological Levels, but places a greater emphasis on scientifically rigorous analysis of the patterns of thoughts and feelings and the role of situational contexts on them.
- The example of Charles Whitman shows how each level of analysis contributes to a fuller understanding of individual personality and behavior.

TOWARD AN INTEGRATIVE SCIENCE

- Work at each level provides basic concepts and strategies for seeking information about people and for constructively changing maladaptive behavior patterns.
- An increasingly comprehensive view of the person seems to be emerging that incorporates many of the insights and findings from each level of analysis.
- Boundaries are also being crossed between personality psychology and other related fields.

PRACTICAL APPLICATIONS

- The findings of personality psychologists address diverse human problems, such as depression, anxiety, impulse control, and poor health.

KEY TERMS

CHAPTER 2

DATA, METHODS, AND TOOLS

WHY A SCIENCE OF PERSONALITY?: BEYOND HINDSIGHT UNDERSTANDING

2.1 Describe and compare two basic approaches to understanding behavior and its causes. What are the advantages of a scientific approach to understanding?

Much of our lives are spent trying to understand, after the fact, our own and others' behavior. In the words of the Danish philosopher Sören Kierkegaard, "Life is lived forwards, but understood backwards." And, as the saying goes, hindsight is 20/20. Past events can be explained in many ways, and there is no sure way to determine which, if any, of the alternative explanations is the right one.

Furthermore, we see only through our own eyes, and are convinced we see the truth, without realizing how different other accounts of the same event can be when seen through different eyes. This is vividly illustrated in Akira Kurosawa's classic film *Rashomon*, which tells the tale of the rape of a woman and the murder of a man, seen entirely in flashbacks from the perspectives of four narrators. Each story makes perfect sense when taken by itself, but together, they do not add up and the contradictions become evident. The characters are the same in all four versions of the story, as are many of the details. But much is different, as well. The film never tells what really happened, leaving the viewer with a feeling of ambiguity and an appreciation of how what we see depends on who we are. In real life, we don't have the moviegoer's advantage of viewing the same event through different people's eyes. Rather, like the characters in the film, we only see our own version, through our own glasses that give us our 20/20 vision.

It is not that after-the-fact understanding is useless. Often, there may be no alternative and hindsight can help one at least try to make sense of events that otherwise cannot be understood. But that is very different from the essence of scientific inquiry. A science begins by creating a language to describe phenomena in a way that allows a single common understanding to emerge, in order to avoid multiple alternative accounts that vary with each observer. The goal is not just to find a common understanding, but to be able to use it to make accurate predictions and to test if they really are accurate, remaining ready to disconfirm and modify them if they are unsupported. Therefore, researchers try to arrange conditions under which they can test hypotheses about the various causal factors that might influence the occurrence of the behavior or event of interest. If one understands the causes of a given behavior, then it may be possible to predict when it will occur again, and when it will not, with reasonable accuracy. In time, this knowledge also makes it possible to build a theory to understand what is the process or mechanism that underlies the behavior being studied. That is why, at least in the

IN FOCUS 2.1

GARY W., THE TEXT'S CASE—GARY'S SELF-DESCRIPTION

I'm 25 years old, and a college graduate. I'm in business school working toward an MBA.

. . .I'm an introspective sort of person—not very outgoing. Not particularly good in social situations. Though I'm not a good leader and I wouldn't be a good politician, I'm shrewd enough that I'll be a good businessman. Right now I'm being considered for an important job that means a lot to me and I'm sweating it. I know the powers at the office have their doubts about me but I'm sure I could make it—I'm positive. I can think ahead and no one will take advantage of me. I know how to work toward a goal and stick with whatever I start to the end—bitter or not.

The only thing that really gets me is speaking in a large group, talking in front of a lot of people. I don't know what it is, but sometimes I get so nervous and confused I literally can't talk! I feel my heart is going to thump itself to death. I guess I'm afraid that they're all criticizing me. Like they're almost hoping I'll get caught with my pants down. Maybe I shouldn't care so much what other people think of me—but it does get to me, and it hurts—and I wind up sweating buckets and with my foot in my mouth.

I'm pretty good with women, but I've never found one that I want to spend the rest of my life with. Meanwhile I'm enjoying life. I hope someday to find a woman who is both attractive and level headed. Someone who is warm and good but not dominating and who'll be faithful but still lead a life of her own. Not depend on me for every little thing.

My childhood was fairly typical, middle class, uptight. I have an older brother. We used to fight with each other a lot, you know, the way kids do. Now we're not so competitive. We've grown up and made peace with each other—maybe it's just a ceasefire but I think it may be a real peace—if peace ever really exists. I guess it was his accident that was the turning point. He got pretty smashed up in a car crash and I guess I thought, "There but for the grace of God."

Dad wasn't around much when we were growing up. He was having business troubles and worried a lot. He and Mother seemed to get along in a low-key sort of way. But I guess there must have been some friction because they're splitting now—getting divorced. I guess it doesn't matter now—I mean my brother and I have been on our own for some time. Still, I feel sorry for my Dad—his life looks like a waste and he is a wreck.

My strengths are my persistence and my stamina and guts—you need them in this world. Shrewdness. My weaknesses are my feeling that when it comes to the crunch you can't really trust anybody or anything. You never know who's going to put you down or what accident of fate lies around the corner. You try and try—and in the end it's probably all in the cards. Well, I guess that's about it. I mean, is there anything else you want to know?

view of most personality researchers, we need a science of personality. And that in turn requires attention to the methods and tools needed to pursue that goal.

Personality psychologists are committed to studying persons by means of scientific methods. But they are equally eager to avoid oversimplifying their subject matter and reducing the complexities of personality into a stereotypically "scientific" collection of formulae and variables. They recognize that "the most distinguishing feature of persons is that they construct meaning by reflecting on themselves, their past, and the future" (Cervone & Mischel, 2002, p. 5).

In that spirit, it makes sense to begin the study of persons by asking individuals how they see and understand themselves, and what they are like in their own eyes—while also recognizing that this personal "internal" vantage point will necessarily be limited and incomplete. So, that is what we will do, as we begin this text by considering a case study of Gary W. As you proceed through the text, you will learn about Gary's personality and the information made available about him, which is based on his clinical files but was modified sufficiently in order to protect confidentiality and to illustrate points in the text.

In Focus 2.1 presents some of what Gary said when "asked to describe yourself as a person"—an exercise that you the reader may also want to try on yourself. He was asked to describe himself on his first visit to the university campus clinic in the psychology department of a large university.

The impressions Gary gives us about himself, while interesting, are of uncertain value: We know neither their accuracy nor their meaning. Then how can we find out more? To convert personality speculations about people into ideas that can be studied scientifically, researchers must be able to put them into *testable* terms using good measures. There is a wide range of these available, as considered next.

▶ THE RANGE OF PERSONALITY-RELEVANT MEASURES

Imagine going to a hospital for a comprehensive checkup. You may see a radiologist who would take X-rays and perform CAT scans. You may see an endocrinologist who analyzes the levels of various hormones in your blood. You may see a neurologist who performs a variety of diagnostic tests to study the functioning of your nervous system and taps your reflexes. You may see an immunologist who examines your immune system, and you may see a cardiologist who specializes in determining how well your heart is working. All these experts will offer a snapshot of a given aspect of your body. Yet they all reflect one thing, your body, which is a *system* of many, many interdependent components. The different levels of analyses of personality psychology work in a similar way. Each will provide data about one aspect of your total functioning personality, and an ultimate challenge is putting them all together for an understanding of how the personality as a system operates.

2.2 How do levels of analysis contribute to the diversity of personality measures available to personality psychologists?

Psychologists approaching personality at different levels of analysis obtain information about people from many sources and through a wide range of strategies. The result is a collection of diverse observations about many aspects of persons. A central goal of personality psychology is to figure out how these diverse aspects about an individual relate to each other and help us to understand what is going on in the individual as a whole. But before we get there (which we will, in Chapter 16), we need to first see just what kinds of data are available; and the range is huge. This chapter is an introduction to the sources and types of data that are made available from each level, and to the concepts and tools used to make sense of those data.

Interviews

2.3 Describe some strengths and weaknesses of interviews.

A valuable source of information is the **interview**—a verbal exchange between the participant and the examiner, favored particularly by workers at the Psychodynamic-Motivational Level and those at the Phenomenological level. Some interviews are tightly structured and formal: the examiner follows a fixed, prescribed format. For example, in research to survey people's sexual activities, the interviewer might follow a standard series of questions, starting with questions about the person's earliest experiences and going on to potential problems in current relationships.

The interview is the oldest method for studying personality, and it remains the most favored for psychodynamic research and assessment (Watkins, Campbell, Nieberding, & Hallmark, 1995). Its usefulness as an assessment tool depends on many considerations, including how the interview is guided and structured, and how the interviewee's responses are recorded, coded, and interpreted. Each of these steps requires attention to the same issues that apply to other methods that rely on the clinician's judgment. In recent years, unobtrusive video and sound recording has made the interview a method that is more open to manageable scoring, coding, and data analysis. These procedures often can be made even more flexible by computerized programs. The interview therefore is being used with renewed interest in efforts to systematically improve psychodynamic assessment (Horowitz, Rosenberg, Ureno, Kolehzan, & O'Halloran, 1989; Perry & Cooper, 1989).

Interviews, while popular, tend to be expensive and time consuming to conduct, as well as to code or score, because it is not easy to have all interviews with different people conducted the same standard way so that they can be compared easily. Therefore many researchers use various standardized tests, often in the form of ratings and self-reports. Ratings and self-reports were used particularly early in the field's development, as discussed in *In Focus 2.2*.

IN FOCUS 2.2

EARLY PERSONALITY MEASUREMENT

Interest in self-description or self-report as a method of personality assessment was stimulated by an inventory devised during World War I (Watson, 1959). This was Woodworth's *Personal Data Sheet*, later known as the *Psychoneurotic Inventory*. It was aimed at detecting soldiers likely to break down under wartime stress. Because it was impractical to give individual psychiatric interviews to recruits, Woodworth listed the kinds of symptoms psychiatrists would probably ask about in interviews. He then condensed them into a paper-and-pencil questionnaire of more than 100 items. Examples are: "Do you wet your bed at night?" and "Do you daydream frequently?" The respondent must answer "yes" or "no" to each question. Soldiers who gave many affirmative responses were followed up with individual interviews. This method was valuable as a simplified and economic alternative to interviewing everyone individually. Often questionnaires are still employed as substitutes for interviews.

The Woodworth questionnaire was not used widely, but it was a forerunner of the many other self-report devices that flourished in the 1920s and 1930s, and new versions of similar measures are still used. These self-reports compared people usually with respect to a single summary score. This total score served as an index, for example, of their "overall level of adjustment," just as single scores were developed to describe the level of "general intelligence." In addition to efforts to assess adjustment, attempts to measure individuals on various personality dimensions soon became extremely popular.

Tests and Self-Reports

A **test** is any standardized measure of behavior, including verbal behavior.

Many tests are in the form of **self-reports**—a term that refers to any statements people make about themselves. Respondents are asked to react to sets of questions or items with one of a limited number of prescribed choices (e.g., "yes," "no," "strongly agree," "frequently," "don't know"), not unlike multiple choices on tests in academic courses. Examples are shown in Figures 2.1 and 2.2.

Self-reports offer quick ways of getting information the person is willing and able to reveal. For example, Table 2.1 shows a self-report measure of anxiety with multiple items. The responses are scored and added to estimate the person's overall self-reported level of anxiety.

Some tests involve **performance measures**. For example, researchers interested in seeing how personality measures in childhood predict academic performance in later life might use measures like the SAT as an outcome assessment. Likewise, those interested in anxiety might use a measure in which the ability to repeat long strings of numbers under difficult, stressful conditions is measured. On this measure, the examiner verbalizes long lists of numbers and the respondent has to repeat them backward, knowing that a poor score will be taken as an index of low intelligence.

2.4 Differentiate between performance and self-report tests.

Projective Measures

Projective tests were developed more than 60 years ago and continue to be popular in clinical use. With these methods, assessors present the person with ambiguous

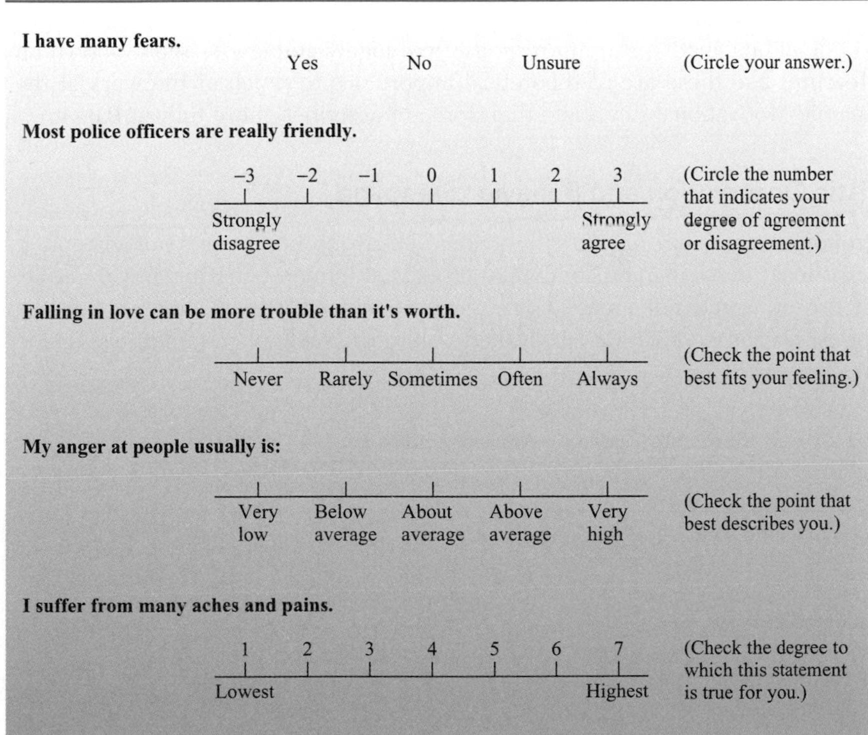

Figure 2.1 Examples of different types of structured test items.

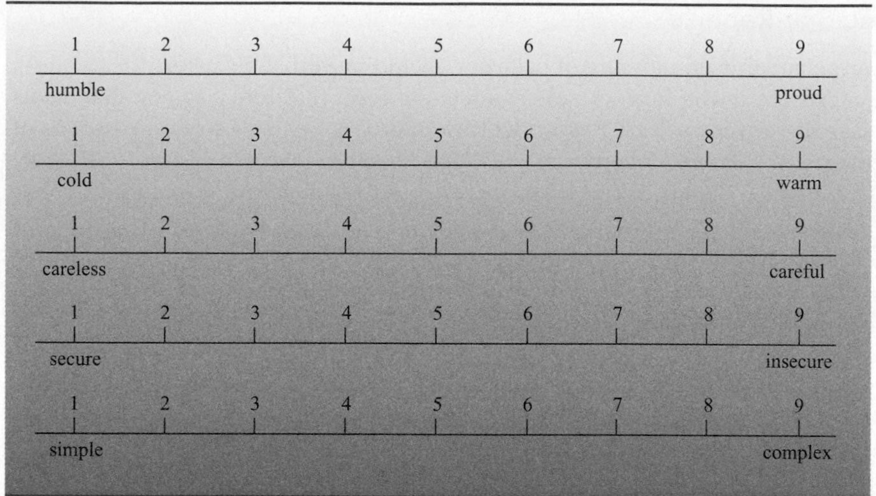

Figure 2.2 Examples of adjective scales. Rate yourself for the degree to which these terms describe you. (Check the point that describes you best on each scale.)

Source: Adapted as illustrations, selected from 40 adjective items used by McCrae and Costa (1985) to identify personality dimensions from ratings and questionnaires. McCrae, R. R., & Costa, P. T., Jr. Updating Norman's "adequacy taxonomy": Intelligence and personality in dimensions in natural language and in questionnaires. *Journal of Personality and Social Psychology, 49*, 710–721. © 1985 by the American Psychological Association. Reprinted with permission.

2.5 What are projective tests? With what level of analysis are they most often associated?

stimuli and ask them ambiguous questions that have no right or wrong answers. For example, they ask "What could this remind you of?" [while showing an inkblot], or ask you to tell an imaginative story in response to a highly ambiguous scene shown on a card. Measures like these are of theoretical importance to much of the work at the Psychodynamic-Motivational Level and therefore are described more fully in Part I.

Naturalistic Observation and Behavior Sampling

Just as astronomers cannot manipulate the actions of heavenly bodies, psychologists often cannot—or should not—manipulate certain aspects of human behavior. For example, one could not or would not create home environments in which children become delinquent or marital conflicts are provoked. Although such phenomena cannot be

TABLE 2.1 Items Similar to Those on Anxiety Scales

Item	Responses indicative of anxiety
I cannot keep my mind focused on anything.	True
I am a worrier.	True
I am often afraid.	True
I feel safe most of the time.	False
I don't fret a lot.	False
I sleep well before exams.	False
Often I think I am nervous.	True

Note: The participant must respond "true" or "false."

manipulated, often they can be observed closely and systematically. Ethical considerations often prevent psychologists from trying to create powerful, lifelike experimental treatments in the laboratories (see Consent Form, Figure 2.5).

Even when some variables can be manipulated in experiments, the investigator often prefers to observe behavior as it naturally occurs, without any scientific interference. Some of the most informative work using this method, called *naturalistic observation*, comes from students of animal behavior, who unobtrusively observe the moment-by-moment lives of such animals as chimpanzees in their natural environment. Such methods have been adapted to study families interacting in their own homes (Patterson, 1990).

Gerald Patterson and coworkers at the Oregon Social Learning Center developed a behavioral coding system having 29 categories with very specific definitions. Both parents' and children's behavior could be coded, including specific types of aversive behaviors (e.g., yelling, negativism, hitting, whining, refusing to comply). In one large project, trained observers came to the families' homes at dinnertime, when problem interactions most often occur. Every interaction of the child with another family member was coded, so that it was possible to study the entire sequence of interactions. The data indicated that in distressed families, the problem children's aversive behaviors continued in "chains" over longer periods of time, with an escalating pattern of hostile interchanges with family members. When the parents in the problem families reacted with punishment, it tended to prolong the escalation of aggression as the child reacted with defiance or resumed aversive behaviors shortly afterward. These behaviors translated into poor social skills, noncompliance at school, poor school achievement, rejection by peers, and, in many cases, antisocial behavior as an adolescent (Patterson & Fisher, 2002).

In clinical applications, observation may give both client and assessor an opportunity to assess life problems and to select treatment objectives. Direct observation of behavior samples also may be used to assess the relative efficacy of various treatment procedures.

Observers may study children from behind a one-way mirror so that they are not seen by the individuals being observed (Mischel, Shoda, & Rodriguez, 1989). Observation is a commonplace method in everyday life; through observation we form impressions and

Concealed video cameras and one-way mirrors allow unobtrusive observation by researchers who remain unseen by participants.

(*Source*: Marcia Weinstein)

learn about events and people. However, observation as a scientific tool is distinctive in that it is conducted as precisely, objectively, and systematically as possible. When observers are not visible by the individual observed (e.g., when observing through a one-way mirror, or by video camera), the effect of the observers' own behaviors is minimized.

Remote Behavior Sampling: Daily Life Experiences

2.6 Describe and compare naturalistic observation and remote behavior sampling methods.

It is not practical or possible for behavioral assessors to follow people around from situation to situation on a daily basis. In addition, assessors are frequently interested in unobservable events, such as emotional reactions and thinking patterns, that may shed considerable light on personality functioning. Through remote behavior sampling, researchers and clinicians can collect samples of behavior from respondents as they live their daily lives. A tiny computerized device carried by respondents pages them at randomly determined times of the day. When the "beeper" sounds, respondents record their current thoughts, feelings, or behaviors, depending on what the researcher or therapist is assessing (Barrett & Barrett, 2001; Conner, Barrett, Bliss-Moreau, Lebo, & Kashub, 2003; Csikszentmihalyi, 1990; Singer, 1988; Stone, Shiffman, & DeVries, 1999). Respondents may also report on the kind of situation they are in so that situation–behavior interactions can be examined. The data can either be stored in the computer or transmitted directly to the assessor.

Remote sampling procedures can be used over weeks or even months to collect a large behavior sample across many situations. This approach to personality assessment has great promise, allowing researchers and clinicians to detect patterns of personal functioning that might not be revealed by other methods (Stone et al., 1999).

Many personality researchers have moved outside the lab to study people's daily experiences by obtaining the person's self-reported reactions to daily experiences that cannot be observed directly (Bolger & Romero-Canyas, in press; Tennen, Suls, & Affleck, 1991). For example, researchers use daily mood measures on which participants indicate the degree to which they experienced various emotions (such as enjoyment/fun, pleased; depressed/blue) in each reporting period (Larsen & Kasimatis, 1991). Such reports can be linked to other aspects of experience, such as minor illnesses and psychological well-being (e.g., Emmons, 1991). Likewise, daily reports of everyday reactions to various stressors and hassles, such as interpersonal conflicts at home, can be related to other measures of personality (Bolger & Schilling, 1991; David, Green, Martin, & Suls, 1997).

2.7 Describe methods that are used in remote behavior sampling research.

Experience samples also are used to study reactions to common life problems such as adjusting to college life in terms of such personal tasks as getting good grades and making friends (e.g., Cantor et al., 1991). Examples of different behavior sampling methods are shown in Table 2.2.

Physiological Functioning and Brain Imaging

Personality researchers have long searched for practical methods to assess emotional reactions. One of the classic measures of physiological functioning is the **polygraph**, an apparatus that records the activities of the autonomic nervous system. Measures of bodily changes in response to stimulation also provide important information, especially when the stimuli are stressful or arousing. The polygraph apparatus contains a series of devices that translate indices of body changes into a visual record by deflecting a pen across a moving paper chart. A popular component of polygraphic measurement is the **electrocardiogram (EKG)**. As the heart beats, its muscular contractions produce patterns of electrical activity that may be detected by electrodes placed near the heart

TABLE 2.2 Illustrative Methods for Sampling Daily Life Experiences

Methods	Examples	Source
Preprogrammed time samples	Digital watch alarm signals time for respondents to record their tasks, behavior, and perceptions at the moment	Cantor et al. (1991)
Systematic diaries	Self-reports of reactions to daily stressors (e.g., overload at work, family demands, arguments)	Bolger & Schilling (1991)
Sampling emotions, symptoms, and other internal states	Self-ratings of emotional states (e.g., pessimistic–optimistic, full–hungry), occurrence and duration of symptoms (e.g., backache, headache), reported personal strivings and well-being	Larsen & Kasimatis (1991); Emmons (1991); Diener et al. (1995); David et al. (1997)

on the body surface. Another component is the changes in blood volume that may be recorded by means of a **plethysmograph**. Other useful measures include changes in the electrical activity of the skin due to sweating (recorded by a galvanometer and called the **galvanic skin response** or **GSR**), changes in blood pressure, and changes in muscular activity (Cacioppo, Berntson, & Crites, 1996; Geen, 1997).

2.8 What types of physiological measures are used to measure biological aspects of personality?

Intense emotional arousal is generally accompanied by high levels of "activation" in the brain (Birbaumer & Ohman, 1993; Malmo, 1959). The degree of activation in the cerebral cortex may be inferred from "brain waves" recorded by the **electroencephalograph (EEG)**, as illustrated in the records shown in Figure 2.3. As

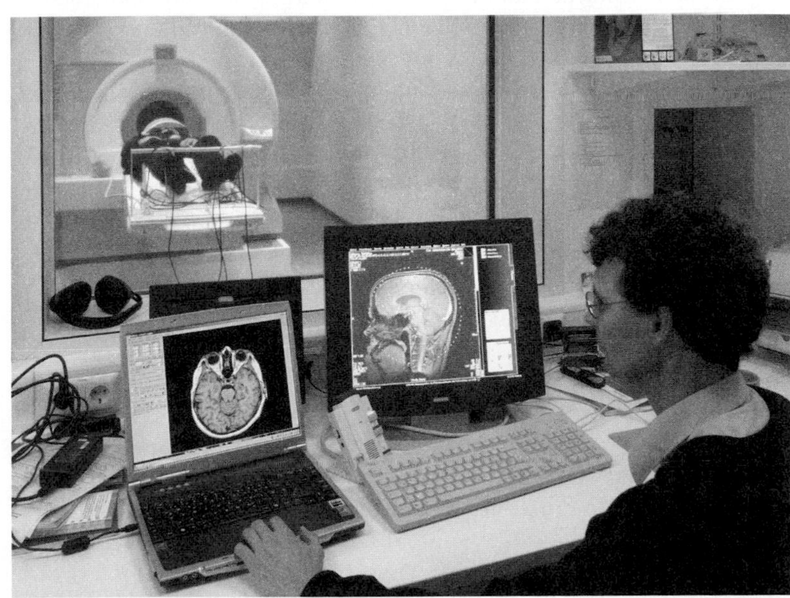

Advances in brain imaging offer a new way to study mental activity.

(*Source*: Landov LLC)

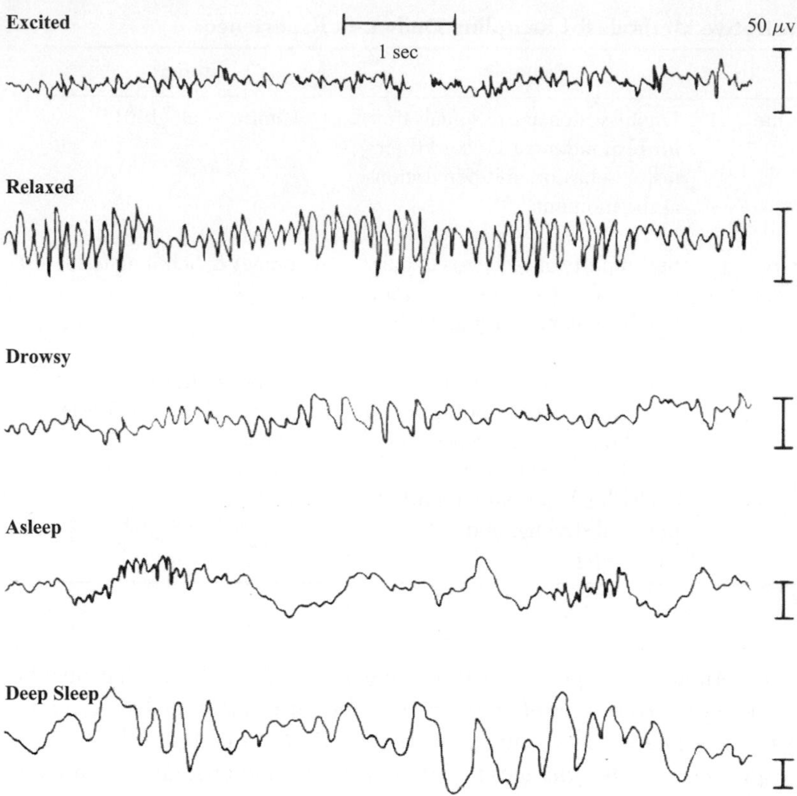

Figure 2.3 Various human EEG patterns under several arousal states.

Source: Jasper, H. (1941). In Penfield & Erickson (Eds.), *Epilepsy and cerebral localization*. Courtesy of Charles C. Thomas, Publisher, Springfield, IL, and of Wilder Penfield Archive.

the EEG patterns in this figure indicate, the frequency, amplitude, and other characteristics of brain waves vary according to the participant's arousal state, from deep sleep to great excitement.

The biological level of analysis has achieved increasing influence in the study of personality, thanks to technical advances in the measurement of physiological reactions, genetic functions, and brain processes, as you will see in later chapters. For example, new brain imaging procedures make it possible to examine relations between neural functions and behaviors. **Positron emission tomography (PET) scans** measure the amount of glucose (the brain's main fuel) being used in various parts of the brain and provide an index of activity as the brain performs a particular function.

Functional magnetic resonance imaging, or **fMRI**, measures the magnetic fields created by the functioning nerve cells in the brain and with the aid of computers depicts these activities as images. These pictures virtually "light up" the amount of activity in different areas as the person performs mental tasks and experiences different kinds of perceptions, images, thoughts, and emotions. They thus allow a much more precise and detailed analysis of the links between activity in the brain and the mental states we experience while responding to different types of stimuli and generating different thoughts and emotions. These can range, for example, from thoughts and images about what we fear and dread to those directed at that we crave the most. The result is a virtual revolution for work that uses the biological level of neural activity to address questions of core interest for personality psychology.

Laboratory Methods of Social Cognition

In current personality and social psychological research, some investigators are trying to understand individual differences in emotional and cognitive reactions to different kinds of social stimuli that occur often outside the individual's awareness and control. To illustrate, one method is called the **sequential priming-pronunciation task** (e.g., Bargh, Raymond, Pryor, & Strack, 1995).

This method was used to test the hypothesis that certain types of people are more prone to become hostile when they feel rejected (Ayduk, Downey, Testa, Yen, & Shoda, 1999). On a computer screen, participants were shown **target** words related to hostility such as "anger," "rage," and "revenge." These words appeared one by one, and the participants were asked to read them aloud as soon as they appeared. A microphone connected to the computer detected the onset of their vocalization, and measured the elapsed time between the presentation of a target word on the screen and the onset of vocalization. On average, participants were able to start saying the word about 3/4 of a second (750 milliseconds) after the word appeared on the screen.

If this had been all there was to the experiment, it would just have been a trivial study of how quickly people can say a word after they see it. How did the researchers use this task to assess people's tendency to have hostile thoughts when they feel rejected? They did so by "priming." **Priming** refers to presenting a stimulus just prior to another stimulus. The stimulus presented first is called the prime, and the stimulus presented shortly after the prime is called the target. Participants are asked to ignore the prime, but perform a task with the target, such as reading it aloud. Researchers have found that the time it takes for people to start the task, called the **reaction time**, is affected by the nature of the prime. In the experiment Ozlem Ayduk and her colleagues (1999) conducted, some prime words, such as "abandon," "exclude," and "ignore," were related to rejection. Other prime words, such as "disgust," "itch," and "vomit," were also negative but not directly related to rejection. After measuring the reaction times for saying the hostility-related target words (i.e., the lengths of time it takes to start reading a hostility-related target word after it appeared), the researchers asked: Does it matter which kind of prime word was presented right before the target word they read aloud? Do participants start reading the hostility-related target word more quickly when it was preceded by a rejection-related prime word, compared to non-rejection-related prime words? It turned out that the answer depends on the participants' level of sensitivity to personal rejection.

At the beginning of the study, prior to the computer task, participants took a test to measure their level of rejection sensitivity. People who score high on this test tend to believe it's a matter of time before other people reject them, and they are highly anxious about the possibility of being rejected. During the computer task, rejection-sensitive subjects started saying the hostility-related target words more quickly after they saw the rejection-related prime words, compared to when the prime words were not related to rejection. The opposite happened if a subject was low in rejection sensitivity: It took them longer to start saying a hostility-related target word when it was preceded by a rejection-related prime word, compared to when the target word was preceded by other prime words.

A great deal of research in cognitive psychology has shown that people can process stimuli (e.g., reading a target word aloud) faster when they are already having thoughts and feelings related to the stimuli (e.g., Bargh et al., 1995). In the case of this experiment, therefore, the researchers concluded that among women who are especially sensitive to rejection, hostility was closely linked to the feeling of rejection and therefore once they saw words related to rejection, they automatically started having hostility-related thoughts, which facilitated saying the hostility-related target words aloud. Among people low in rejection sensitivity, feeling rejected did not lead to hostility.

In sum, assessment of the effect of different kinds of primes allows researchers a glimpse into their automatic reactions – the thoughts and feelings they automatically have when in response to what they see, and what they think and feel. These reactions are automatic because people have such reactions without intending to, and without being able to control them even if they tried to do so. Most importantly, research has shown that people differ reliably and meaningfully in such automatic reactions. Priming is one of the central methods to assess them.

To gain insight into how information may be organized in people's minds, **memory tasks** are used to examine the types of mistakes people make in remembering. For example, in a study by Cantor and Mischel (1977), participants read a story about a person who was either described as extraverted or introverted, depending on the condition the participants were in. Then, after a short delay, they were given a memory test in which they were asked to decide which words on a list were actually in the earlier stories to describe the person. Some of these words were never used to describe the person in the story. The results showed that participants who read about a person described as an extravert later erroneously remembered the person as having extraverted traits (e.g., outgoing, sociable) that had not been presented in the story. Similarly, those who read about a person described as an introvert later erroneously remembered the person having introverted traits (e.g., quiet, shy), even though these words were not originally used to describe the person in the story. Such a false-alarm effect shows that people routinely extract the "gist" of information about a person they encounter. Similar memory tests in turn can be used to assess what people see in other people. For example, in a study by Sedlins and Shoda (2007), subjects read the names of movie stars such as Natalie Portman and Katie Holmes. More women than men later erroneously thought they saw Meryl Streep, suggesting that in their minds Natalie Portman and Katie Holmes represented "women movie stars." In contrast, other subjects confused these young actresses with Ben Affleck, suggesting that in their minds, Natalie Portman and Katie Holmes represented "young movie stars." Thus memory tasks can be used to assess how an individual organizes his or her knowledge about the world, and people may differ importantly in the organizational schema they use to do so.

▶ CONCEPTUAL AND METHODOLOGICAL TOOLS

Constructs and Operational Definitions

To conduct scientific research (or even to carry on intelligent discourse), it is necessary to clearly identify and specify the phenomena that one wants to understand. The vocabulary of psychology is filled with terms like aggression, extraversion, intelligence, stress, learning, and motivation. All of these are simply words or concepts—scientists prefer the term **constructs**—that refer to classes of behaviors, thoughts, emotions, and situations. Every personality term that we discuss in this book is a construct (including the term *personality*). These words represent nonmaterial ideas—concepts and not things—and they may have different meanings for different people. For example, the term *dependency* refers to a particular class of behaviors, but the specific types of behavior that are labeled "dependent" may differ from one person to another. Unless two people have a common definition of what dependent means, they can't be sure they're communicating effectively when they talk about "dependent" people. "What do you mean by that?" is a question psychologists must answer very precisely if they are to study a psychological phenomenon.

2.9 What are psychological constructs? Why do they require operationalization?

Operationalization translates these constructs into something observable and measurable. It refers to the specific procedures used to produce or measure it in a particular study. Sometimes, a construct is operationalized in terms of a condition to which someone is exposed. For example, the construct hunger could be operationally defined as "the number of hours that a person is deprived of food." At other times, a construct is operationalized in terms of some behavior of the participant. Thus, we could also define hunger in terms of people's ratings of how hungry they feel or in terms of how much effort they will make to obtain food. Regardless of the method used to operationalize a construct, it cannot be studied scientifically unless it can be tied to something observable.

An Example: Defining the Construct of Aggression

To illustrate these points, let us consider the construct of aggression. If we ask the question, "What is aggression?" we are trying to specify the meaning of the construct itself. That's no easy matter, for the term is used in many different ways in our daily discourse, and with different connotations. Thus, an athlete may be praised for being an "aggressive competitor," whereas an "aggressive schoolyard bully" may evoke disapproval.

Researchers have offered various construct definitions of aggression. An early one was "the delivery of noxious stimuli to another organism" (Buss, 1961). Other psychologists found the definition too broad. For example, if a person accidentally bumps into you, it may be aversive, but is it aggression? If a doctor gives a child a painful vaccination, she's hurting her—but is it an act of aggression? Over time, these concerns were addressed with more elaborate definitions. Today, a definition adopted by most psychologists who study aggression is the following: **aggression** is "any form of behavior directed toward the goal of harming or injuring another living being who is motivated to avoid such treatment" (Baron & Richardson, 1994, p. 7). Notice that this definition has a number of facets:

2.10 How have psychologists defined aggression at a conceptual level?

1. Aggression is behavior, not an emotion. The behaviors may take many forms, including physical and verbal acts. It may even involve not doing something, as when a person deprives another of something needed and thus harms that individual.
2. Aggression is motivated behavior, with the intent being to hurt another. Thus, unintentional acts that harm another would not be considered aggression.
3. The target of the behavior is a living being, not an inanimate object. However, if the purposeful destruction of an inanimate object, such as a prized vase, harms another person, the act would be considered aggression.
4. The recipient must be motivated to avoid the treatment. Thus, an assisted suicide would not be classified as an aggressive act if the deceased person wanted to die, even though it may legally be classified as manslaughter.

Given a working definition of the construct, we must find a way to operationally define it in terms of observable events if we are to study it scientifically. A variety of operational definitions, some quite ingenious, have been used to measure individual differences in aggression. Here are a few of the ways that aggression has been operationally defined and measured in various studies:

2.11 What kinds of measures have been used to provide operational definitions of aggression?

- Archival records, such as school suspensions, rates of violent behavior, or arrests for such acts.

- Verbal reports of aggressive behavior, obtained in interviews and on questionnaires.
- Scores on personality measures designed to measure aggressiveness.
- Ratings and reports from others on a person's aggressive behavior.
- Observations of aggressive behavior in natural and laboratory settings.
- Unnecessary honking of one's automobile horn at other motorists.
- Administration of electric shock or aversive noise to another person in a laboratory setting.
- Written or spoken insults during laboratory interactions with another person.
- Negative evaluations of another person who has provoked study participants.

ESTABLISHING RELATIONSHIPS AMONG OBSERVATIONS

Once observations are made, the next step is to determine the relationships among them. First, how objective is the measure: Do the measured results fluctuate across different occasions? Do multiple observers agree with each other? Are self-reports and observers' ratings consistent with direct observations of relevant behaviors? Second, how does the measure relate to measures of other constructs: Is social anxiety related to loneliness? Do extraverts have happier lives than introverts? What personality factors distinguish happily married couples from those headed for divorce? Do firstborn versus later-born children differ in personality? Is the amount of television violence a child is exposed to related to antisocial aggression later in life? These and countless other psychological questions ask about *associations* between naturally occurring events or variables.

Correlation: What Goes with What?

Data that psychologists who study personality collect, regardless of their source, are conceptualized as variables. A **variable** is an attribute, quality, or characteristic that can be given two or more values (hence "variable"). For example, a person's height is a variable, and a psychological characteristic such as attitude toward premarital sex can be quantified using a 7-point scale in which 0 is neutral, +3 is extremely positive, and −3 is extremely negative (Figure 2.1). Often, two or more variables seem to be associated—seem to "go together"—in such a way that when we know something about one variable, we can usually make a good guess about the other variables. For example, people who are taller generally tend to weigh more; when we know how tall someone is, we can roughly predict the person's weight. This "going together," "co-relationship," or joint relationship between variables is what psychologists mean by the term **correlation**.

2.12 What is meant by correlation?

The degree of relationship or correlation may be expressed quantitatively by a number called a **correlation coefficient**. Correlation coefficients can range from −1.00 through .00 to +1.00. A coefficient of +1.00 means that there is a perfect positive relation between X and Y—that is, the person having the highest score on X also has the highest score on Y, the person having the second highest score on X has the second highest score on Y, and so on. A correlation of −1.00 signifies a perfect negative relation so that the higher a person's score is on X, the lower the score on Y. A correlation of .00 means that there is no relation at all between X and Y. The correlation coefficient thus indicates both the direction (positive or negative) and the strength of the statistical relation between the two measures.

2.13 What is a correlation coefficient? In what two ways do correlation coefficients differ?

Suppose we want to know how scores on a psychological test of anxiety are related to students' performance. We can obtain a score on each of the two measures for each student in our sample and graph these data in a scatter plot like those shown in Figure 2.4. Each point in the scatter plot represents the intersection of an individual participant's scores on the two variables of interest, which we'll call variable X (anxiety) and variable Y (average performance level).

The scatter plots in Figure 2.4 illustrate three kinds of correlational results: positive, in which high scores on anxiety are related to high performance averages; negative, in which high scores on anxiety are related to low performance averages; and a zero correlation, in which there is no relation between the two variables and the data points are scattered about in a random pattern. Correlations can be any value between +1.00 and −1.00. As mentioned above, a correlation of 0 (i.e., no relationship whatsoever) indicates the weakest relationship. The closer to +1.00 or −1.00 the correlation, the more strongly the two variables are related. Thus, a correlation of −.59 indicates a stronger association between X and Y than does a correlation of +.37. In case you're wondering about the previous examples, moderate negative correlations (typically around −.30) exist between anxiety and student performance. As a basis for comparison, a correlation of about +.50 exists between height and weight in the general population.

Interpreting Correlations

2.14 If we square a correlation coefficient, what does the product tell us?

One useful feature of the correlation coefficient is that by squaring the coefficient, we arrive at an estimate of what percentage of the variation in one of the variables is accounted for by differences in the other. For example, squaring the correlation of −.30 between anxiety and grade point average tells us that 9% of the total group variation in grades can be accounted for (linked to) differences in anxiety ($-.30 \times -.30 = .09$). This means that there can be 10 other variables, each accounting for 9% of the total variance in grades, that are totally unrelated to anxiety and with each other (i.e., each can have a +.30 or −.30 correlation with grades, while the correlations among them and with anxiety are 0.0). Together, these 11 variables would account for 99% of the variance.

Correlations that are even close to perfect are very rare in psychology, showing that although many psychological variables are, indeed, associated with each other, the association usually is not very strong. Correlations of about .30 to .50, either positive or negative, are fairly common in psychology. Such correlations may allow predictions that significantly exceed chance guesses, but they are still far from perfect. Statistical computations are used to evaluate the **statistical significance** of particular correlation coefficients reflecting how unlikely a given association would be if it were generated just by chance.

Correlations are useful, but they do not indicate cause and effect. If variable X and Y are correlated with each other, there are actually three possibilities:

2.15 A statistically significant correlation coefficient allows what causal interpretations?

1. Variable *X* causes Variable *Y*.
2. Variable *Y* actually causes Variable *X*.
3. A third factor (Variable Z) causes both *X* and *Y*, so that there's no direct causal relation between *X* and *Y*.

Consider the positive correlation between people's shoe sizes and height. Does it mean larger shoes cause people to grow taller (the first possibility above), or does it mean that greater height causes larger shoes (the second possibility), or does it mean that a third factor was responsible for both (e.g., genes and nutrition that influence physical

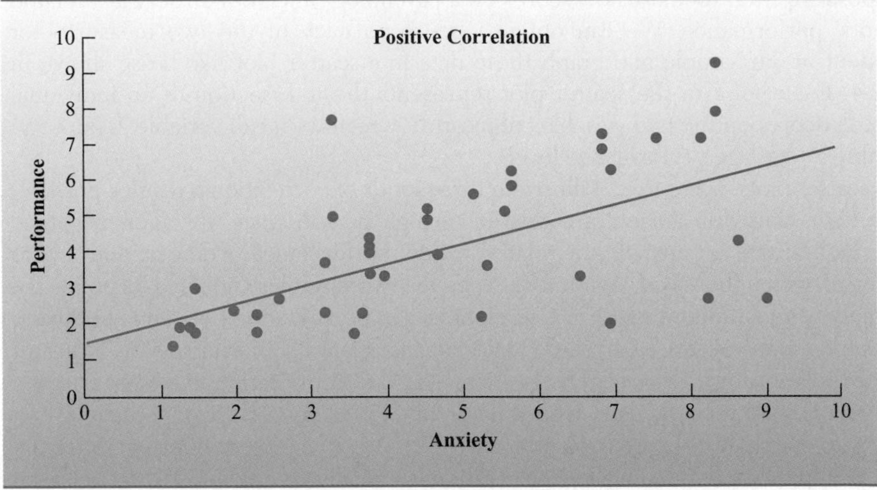

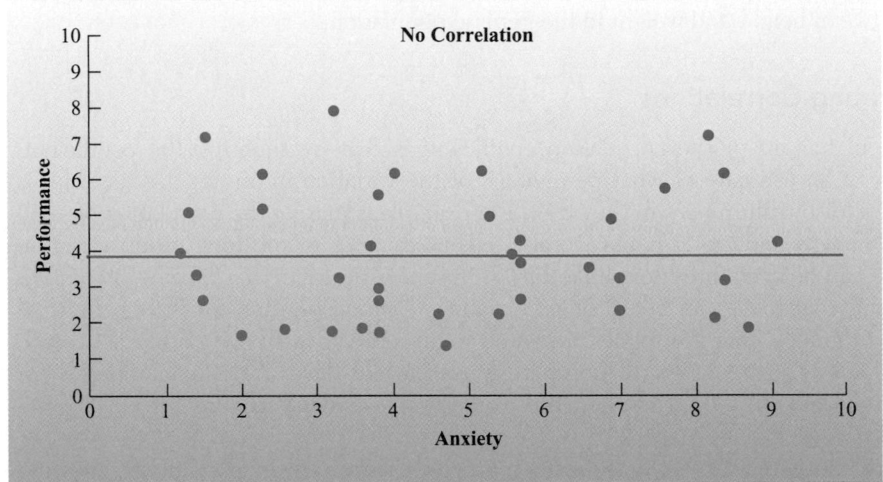

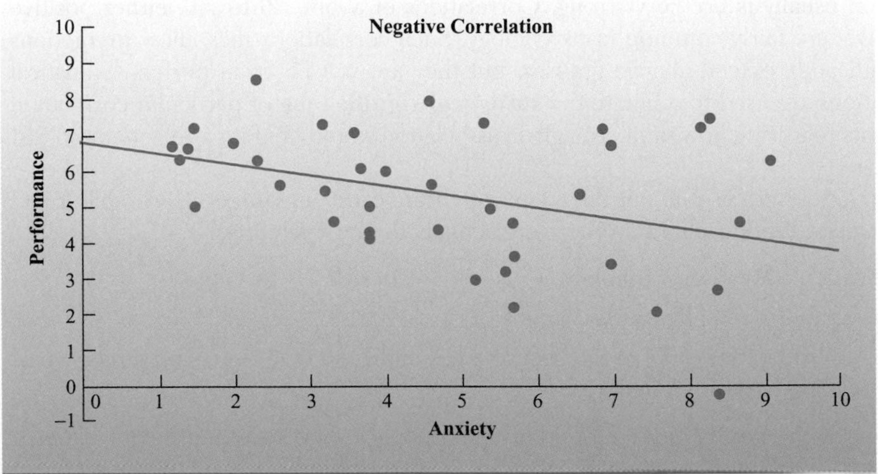

Figure 2.4 Examples of positive correlation, no correlation, and negative correlation between anxiety levels and performance levels.

growth determined height and foot size, the latter of which is in turn reflected in shoe size)? The correlation would only alert you to the many things that might make the two tend to occur together.

Although correlations among measures do not allow us to establish causality, they are useful in prediction. If two measures are highly related, either positively or negatively, knowledge of the score on one measure allows us to predict (with some uncertainty) the score on the other. Admissions officers use college entrance examination scores to predict probable college grades and success because these measures are positively correlated. Insurance premiums are likewise established on the basis of correlations among certain risk factors and medical/accident outcomes. In a sense, your insurance company is betting that you will not demolish your car, become seriously ill, or die before you are statistically "supposed to" based on the information about you, such as your driving record and whether or not you smoke. Because insurers' predictions are based on sound correlational data, the odds are in their favor.

RELIABILITY AND VALIDITY OF OBSERVATIONS AND MEASURES

In order to be scientifically useful, the observations and measures we use to operationally define the constructs we wish to study must have certain characteristics. First, they must be consistent, or reliable, in a number of ways. Second, they must be valid indicators of the constructs we are interested in. Much scientific activity is devoted to developing reliable and valid measures, because without good measurement tools, scientific activity cannot proceed.

Reliability: Are the Measurements Consistent?

2.16 What is meant by reliability of measurement?

A number of techniques are available for estimating the consistency or "reliability" of personality measures. When the same test is given to the same group of people on two occasions, a retest correlation or "coefficient of stability" is obtained. This measure provides an index of **temporal reliability**. Generally, for measures of constructs that are expected to remain stable, temporal reliability of a measure should be high.

Other reliability estimates are more concerned with the consistency with which different parts or alternate forms of a test measure behavior. The correlation between parts of a single form is called **internal consistency**. A special type of internal consistency is measured by the correlation between scores on alternate forms of a test administered to the same set of people. For example, a test of anxiety may be given before an intervening procedure, such as psychotherapy, and an "alternate form" of the same measure, using items that are not identical to the form used earlier, is given after the intervention. By using two different forms, researchers can avoid the contaminating effects of administering the same form twice. But it is important that the alternate forms produce results that are consistent with each other. Otherwise, they may be measuring different constructs, rather than being alternate forms of the same construct.

If subjective judgment enters into scoring decisions, a special kind of reliability check is needed. This check is called **interscorer agreement** or consistency. It is the degree to which different scorers or judges arrive at the same statements about the same test data. For example, if three judges try to infer personality traits from a person's interview behavior and dream reports, it would be necessary to establish the degree to which the three assessors reach the same conclusions. As noted before, interscorer agreement is easiest to achieve when scoring is objective, as on highly structured tests (e.g., when all answers are given as either "yes" or "no").

Validity: What Is Being Measured?

2.17 What is meant by validity of measurement? Distinguish between content and criterion validity.

If a woman's family and friends independently rate her as very friendly, does it mean she is really friendly? The agreement among the raters shows that they are reliably reflecting something. But is that something what we are intending to measure? One needs validity research to establish the meaning and implications of the test scores.

Content Validity

Content validity is the demonstration that the items on a test adequately represent a defined broader *class* of behavior. For example, judges would have to agree that the different items on a "friendliness" questionnaire all in fact seem to deal with the class or topic of friendliness. In practice, content validity often is assumed rather than demonstrated. Even if the content validity of the items is shown acceptably, it cannot be assumed that the answers provide an index of the individual's "true" trait position. We do not know whether or not the person who says she is friendly, for example, is really friendly. A self-description is a self-description, and a description by another person is another person's description, and the relationships between such data and other events or measures have to be determined.

Criterion Validity

To go beyond description of the sampled behavior, one has to determine the relationship between it and the score on other measures that serve as referents or standards, thus providing **criterion validity**. For example, psychiatrists' ratings about progress in therapy, teachers' ratings of school performance, the person's behavior on another test, or self-reported progress on another occasion may be selected as criteria. Criterion validity may be established by a correlation among concurrently available data (such as current test score and present psychiatric diagnosis). This is called **concurrent validity**. Criterion validity also can be predictive if it comes from correlations between a measure and data collected at a later time, for example, pretherapy diagnosis and adjustment ratings after a year of psychotherapy. The term for that is **predictive validity**. Correlations may be looked for between data that seem to have a strong surface similarity in content, such as a child's arithmetic performance on an IQ test and his future success in an arithmetic course. Or they may be sought between measures whose contents appear quite dissimilar, such as a patient's drawings and a psychiatric diagnosis.

Tests based on criterion validity may be used for various practical purposes, depending on their specific validation procedures. Obviously a test may have criterion validity with regard to criteria measured roughly at the same time and still be unable to predict future behavior. Likewise, a test may have predictive validity without concurrent validity if, for example, it can predict suicide 5 years before a patient kills himself but relates to no other measure at the time of administration.

2.18 What is construct validity? How is it established?

Construct Validity: Validity of the Construct Itself

The concept of "**construct validity**" was introduced in response to a frank acknowledgment that there often is: "... no existing measure as a definitive criterion of the quality with which he is concerned. Here the traits or qualities underlying test performance are of central importance" (American Psychological Association, 1966, pp. 13–14).

Traditionally, construct validity involves the following steps. The investigator begins with a hunch about a dimension on which individuals can be compared, for example, "submissiveness." The researchers might regard submissiveness as a "tendency to yield to the will and suggestions of others" (Sarason, 1966, p. 127). To study this tendency, they devise a measure of submissiveness. They have no one definite criterion, however,

IN FOCUS 2.3

SOMETIMES DIRECT SELF-REPORT MEASURES WORK BEST

At the height of the Cold War, and the start of the Kennedy administration in Washington in the early 1960s, the Peace Corps was established. Its first mission for personality psychologists was to develop and evaluate assessment procedures to identify people who would do well in their foreign assignments (e.g., in Nigeria, in Colombia). Most important, it was to screen out those likely to produce internationally embarrassing gaffes that would hit the front pages of newspapers. That happened when a Peace Corps worker dropped a postcard on which she had described her disgust and disdain at the culture and social conventions she encountered in Africa. A first goal was to predict the probable success of Peace Corps teachers in Nigeria. Ratings and judgments of the trainees were made during their 2-month training period at Harvard University, by the faculty, by the assessment board for the project, and by interviewers. The expert judgments were strongly intercorrelated, showing that the assessors shared similar impressions of the candidates' personalities in training. Independently, field performance of the Peace Corps volunteers when they were on their assignments as teachers in Nigeria was assessed about a year after their arrival. The simple direct self-reports and self-ratings of anxiety and attitudes to authority taken during training modestly but statistically significantly predicted field performance. They did much better than the far more costly and time-consuming evaluations by expert judges, which failed completely to predict how the candidates performed when in Nigeria (Mischel, 1965). As this early example shows, sometimes simple ratings can be more useful than much more expensive procedures that require lots of judgments and clinical inferences—a fact that by now has often been found in the research literature (e.g., Spitzer, Kroenke, & Williams, 1999).

but instead the validity of the measure is indicated by the degree to which it predicts behaviors hypothesized to reflect the construct it measures (e.g., submissiveness). If the prediction turns out to be accurate, our confidence in the construct validity of the measure is increased. But what if the predicted behavior was not observed? Perhaps the measure does not reflect the construct. Or, perhaps the hypothesis is wrong. To resolve this dilemma, construct validity research will turn to test other hypotheses about behaviors believed to reflect submissiveness. If many of these behaviors are successfully predicted by the measure of submissiveness, our confidence in the measure is increased, and our confidence is decreased in the first hypothesis that failed to receive support. Construct validity therefore follows an ever-evolving spiral of increased precision in both the measures and the hypotheses about the construct (West & Finch, 1997).

▶ THE EXPERIMENTAL APPROACH

So far, we have looked at examples of research strategies that examine the relationships between naturally existing differences among people in various personal qualities as well as behavior. Now suppose, for example, that researchers have shown that people high in their overall rated levels of frustration tend to behave more aggressively. Next they may want to examine the hypothesis that frustration is in fact what causes or increases aggression. To test such a hypothesis they could use an experimental method in which the experimenter varies one or more factors and then measures how another variable has been affected. The logic behind this approach is that if two or more groups of equivalent or well-matched participants are treated identically in all respects but the variable that is intentionally varied, and if the behavior of the groups differs, then that difference in behavior is likely to have been caused by the factor that was varied.

2.19 What is the advantage of experimental research over correlational research?

Independent and Dependent Variables

In psychological experiments, the researcher is interested in relations between conditions that are manipulated and behaviors that are measured. The condition that is controlled or manipulated by the experimenter is called the **independent variable**; the resulting behavior that is measured is called the **dependent variable**. To look at it another way, the independent variable is the cause, or the stimulus, and the dependent variable is the effect, or the response. Both the independent and dependent variables reflect underlying constructs that have to be operationally defined.

Experimental and Control Groups

Suppose that we want to test the hypothesis that frustration increases aggression. Frustration and aggression are both constructs that can be applied to a variety of circumstances and behaviors. To test the hypothesis experimentally, we need to operationally define both frustration and aggression. To operationally define frustration, we do the following: Participants are given a set of 15 items with strings of 7 random letters and told that the letters can be rearranged into words. Any person who can unscramble them within 10 minutes will win a monetary prize. However, half of the participants are given letter sets that are impossible to solve, which we assume will be frustrating to the participants. This group is called the **experimental group**. To be sure that the frustration has an effect on subsequent aggression, a second group is given a set of easily solvable scrambled words. This group that is not subjected to the frustration is the **control group**.

2.20 Differentiate experimental and control groups.

After the participants are exposed to the frustrating or nonfrustrating condition, they participate in a second, supposedly unrelated, experiment where they are asked to assist the experimenter in a study of the effects of punishment on learning. They are seated before a box with 10 buttons that deliver increasingly intense levels of electric shock. Whenever the learner (seated in an adjoining room) makes a mistake, the participant selects the shock level and presses the button. In reality, the learner is not being shocked, but the participant does not know that. The average intensity of shocks administered by each participant is the operational definition of that person's aggression.

To make the experimental and control groups as similar as possible in all respects other than exposure to the frustration, we assign participants to the experimental and control groups on a random basis. To guarantee random assignment, we can assign each person a number and then either draw numbers out of a hat or use a table of randomly ordered numbers devised by statisticians for this purpose. Random assignment is intended to minimize group differences on other factors (such as intelligence or social class) that might affect the dependent variable.

Double-Blind Designs

2.21 Why do experimenters employ (a) random assignment to conditions and (b) double-blind designs?

Many studies have shown that if experimenters expect to obtain certain results, they are more likely to get them (Rosenthal & Rubin, 1978). In some of these studies, experimenters showed participants a standard set of facial photographs and obtained ratings of how successful the persons in the photos had been. Some of the experimenters were told that the people in the photos had been very successful and that most past participants had rated them as being successful. Other experimenters were told just the opposite. Actually, the people in the photos had been rated by earlier participants as being neither successful nor unsuccessful. Experimenters who expected "successful" ratings tended to get more of them, and those who expected low success ratings tended to receive such ratings, even though they apparently did nothing intentional to influence their participants.

Because of potential problems involving experimenter expectancy effects, experiments are usually set up so that an experimenter collecting data from participants is unaware of the experimental condition to which the participants have been assigned. When both the participant and the experimenter are blind to the independent variable manipulation, the design is referred to as a **double-blind experiment**.

Some types of behavior can be studied only in their natural settings where little or no control is possible; others can be studied under highly controlled laboratory conditions. The decision to study behavior in a natural setting as opposed to a laboratory involves some important trade-offs. On the one hand, identifying the true causes of behavior in a real-world setting poses problems because there is no way to rule out other possible causes by controlling them. On the other hand, when people are observed in their native habitat, the researcher can be more confident that the results can be applied to other, similar real-life settings. In case studies and in observational research carried out in natural settings, it is also possible to observe the full complexity of person–environment relations. This very complexity, however, can make it difficult to identify the causal factors with complete confidence.

Because of the advantages and disadvantages of the various personality research methods, many personality psychologists stress the desirability of using all of the methods, moving from the real world to the laboratory and back again. When consistent results are found in both settings, we can have increased confidence in our observations. In many instances in personality research, the movement is from observations made in natural settings to the laboratory, where greater control of variables is possible.

ETHICS IN PERSONALITY RESEARCH

2.22 What measures are taken by personality researchers to protect the privacy and well-being of participants in their studies?

Some of the studies we have reviewed above involved exposing participants to frustrating conditions or using deception. Although the large majority of personality research does not involve such manipulations, some studies do. Sometimes, in order to study important problems, personality researchers walk an ethical tightrope, balancing the importance of the knowledge to be gained and the benefits that may result from its application against the use of deception or the exposure of participants to stressful conditions. When personality data are collected from people who can potentially be identified, invasion of privacy issues also arise.

The desire to protect the privacy and welfare of human participants has resulted in a set of explicit ethical guidelines. For example, according to the research guidelines of the American Psychological Association (APA), participants cannot be placed in either physical or psychological jeopardy without their informed consent. A typical consent form is shown in Figure 2.5. As the form indicates, participants must be told about the procedures to be followed and warned about any risks that might be involved. If deception is necessary in order to carry out the research, then participants must be completely debriefed after the experiment and the entire procedure must be explained to them. Special measures must be taken to protect the confidentiality of data, and participants must be told that they are free to withdraw from a study at any time without penalty.

When children, seriously disturbed mental patients, or others who are not able to give true consent are involved, consent must be obtained from their parents or guardians. Strict guidelines also apply to research in prisons. Inmates cannot be forced to participate in research, nor can they be penalized for refusing to do so. In research dealing with rehabilitation programs, inmates must be permitted to share in decisions concerning

CONSENT FORM

FOR PARTICIPATION IN AN EXPERIMENT IN ____________________

PSYCHOLOGY IN THE LABORATORY OF ____________________

1. In this experiment, you will be asked to
2. The benefit we hope to achieve from this work
3. The risks involved (if any)

CONSENT AGREEMENT

I have read the above statement and am consenting to participate in the experiment of my own volition. I understand that I am free to discontinue my participation at any time without suffering disadvantage. I understand that if I am dissatisfied with any aspect of this program at any time, I may report grievances anonymously to ____________________

Signed: ____________________

Date: ____________________

Figure 2.5 A typical consent form for participation in a psychological study. Ethical standards require that participation in research comes only after volunteers understand the task and freely consent.

program goals. Researchers who violate the code of research ethics face serious legal and professional consequences.

The ethical and moral issues in psychology are not simple ones. They are quite similar to those that confront medical researchers. In some instances, the only way to discover important knowledge about behavior or to develop new techniques to enhance human welfare is to deceive participants or to expose them to potentially stressful situations. To help researchers balance the potential benefits against the risks involved and to ensure that the welfare of participants is protected, academic and research institutions have created scientific panels that review every research proposal. If a proposed study is considered ethically questionable, or if the rights, welfare, and personal privacy of participants are not sufficiently protected, the methods must be modified or the research cannot be conducted.

SUMMARY

STUDYING PERSONS: SOURCES OF INFORMATION

- Psychologists want to understand personality to predict future behavior and understand present and past behavior.
- Case studies are a method used to evaluate the individual intensively. They can be conducted at each level of analysis and over many occasions. The case of "Gary W." will be used as a case example throughout the text.
- Psychologists utilize various types of personality tests or structured interviews to assess personality in a quantifiable way.
- Naturalistic observation is especially useful when aspects of behavior cannot—or should not—be manipulated.
- Direct behavior measurement samples behavior in diverse situations. It includes both verbal and nonverbal behavior, as well as physiological measurements of emotional reactions.
- Through remote behavior sampling and daily diary studies, researchers can collect samples of behavior from respondents as they live their daily lives.
- To measure changes in the autonomic nervous system, researchers often utilize data from the EKG, plethysmograph, galvanic skin responses (GSR), and EEG.
- PET scans and fMRI help to examine neural activity in the brain.
- Researchers utilize a variety of methods in laboratory settings, such as priming and memory tasks, to better understand underlying cognitive processes.

CONCEPTUAL AND METHODOLOGICAL TOOLS

- Constructs are concepts that refer to classes of behaviors and situations.
- Operationalization refers to the specific procedures used to produce or measure constructs in a particular study.

ESTABLISHING AND QUANTIFYING THE RELATIONSHIPS AMONG OBSERVATIONS

- The correlational approach utilizes statistical analysis to measure whether two phenomena or *variables* are related to one another.
- The degree to which two variables are related is mathematically represented by the correlation coefficient.

RELIABILITY AND VALIDITY

- Reliability is found when the results of a measure can be repeated both within the confines of the study and with different investigators.
- Validity refers to how well an assessment device actually measures what it claims to measure. It includes content validity, construct validity, and criterion validity, both concurrent and predictive.

THE EXPERIMENTAL APPROACH

- The experimental approach tries to demonstrate causal relations by manipulating one variable—the independent variable—and measuring the effects on a second variable—the dependent variable.
- In order to minimize experimenter expectancy effects, experiments may be set up to be double-blind.

ETHICS IN PERSONALITY RESEARCH

- To help researchers take into account the privacy and welfare of their participants, the American Psychological Association (APA) has set up guidelines to ensure that participants cannot be placed in either physical or psychological jeopardy without their informed consent.

KEY TERMS

aggression 31
concurrent validity 36
constructs 30
construct validity 36
content validity 36
control group 38
correlation 32
correlation coefficient 32
criterion validity 36
dependent variable 38
double-blind experiment 39
electrocardiogram (EKG) 26
electroencephalograph (EEG) 27
experimental group 38
functional magnetic resonance imaging (fMRI) 28
galvanic skin response (GSR) 27
independent variable 38
internal consistency 35
interscorer agreement 35
interview 22
memory tasks 30
operationalization 31
performance measures 23
plethysmograph 27
polygraph 26
Positron emission tomography (PET) scans 28
predictive validity 36
priming 29
reaction time 29
self-reports 23
sequential priming-pronunciation task 29
statistical significance 33
target 29
temporal reliability 35
test 23
variable 32

PART 

THE TRAIT-DISPOSITIONAL LEVEL

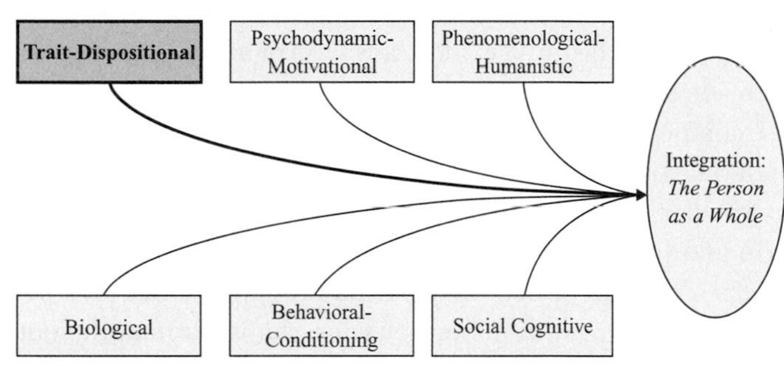

PRELUDE TO PART I: THE TRAIT-DISPOSITIONAL LEVEL

"My roommate is a really closed-in person who just doesn't like to relate. Regardless of how nice I try to be to her the most I get is courtesy—and she seems like that with everybody—a loner. She's a total contrast from the fun-lover I was so lucky to have last year."

Individuals differ consistently from each other in their personality characteristics. These differences are readily perceived and with much agreement among observers, including in the self-perceptions of the people who are being characterized. Researchers at this level of analysis search for these differences, and attempt to find those that are most important, consistent, and perhaps even universal.

Two questions drive work at the Trait-Dispositional Level:

- What are the basic psychological qualities that characterize people?
- How can the consistent differences between people in these qualities be best captured and described?

Theory and research at this level to answer these questions provides one of the most productive and enduring traditions for the study of personality. The answers have contributed greatly to the measurement, description, classification, and analysis of personality since the start of the field. Most work at this level of analysis has been driven by the assumption that the important qualities that characterize a person consist of a finite number of broad traits. Traits are conceptualized as individual differences in tendencies to show consistent behavior across many different situations and with much stability over time (e.g., McCrae, Costa, Del Pilar, Rolland, & Parker, 1998).

Researchers at the Trait-Dispositional Level also assumed that traits are quantifiable—some people are more sociable than others, and some are more modest than others, for example. Guided by these assumptions, one goal has been to develop methods to quantify people's social–personal traits. The methods then have been used to create taxonomies for classifying and capturing the fundamental traits of personality so that people can be compared on the amounts of the different traits that they possess.

From the start of the field, work at this level has provided both concepts and methods for describing and comparing human individual differences on a vast array of attributes and qualities, and many of the highlights are discussed in Chapter 3. It gives an overview of major work in the early phases of this tradition. The chapter then turns to the current developments and advances that now provide measures for comparing people on the main traits that have emerged from a century of active research. In the last few decades of the 20th century, work at this level of analysis has experienced a great resurgence and made significant advances.

Chapter 4 examines how traits are expressed in behavior. It shows that people are characterized not only by broad traits. People also display patterns of behaviors that are connected to particular types of situations in distinctive ways. For example, the phrase "Monica is warm and friendly when starting a relationship but she begins to withdraw when people get really close to her" may accurately capture that this person shows a distinctive "*if* . . . *then* . . ." pattern in her behavior: she is warm at the outset but cools as a relationship becomes close. Such patterns can also provide clues to characteristic underlying motivations and goals that may enrich the understanding of the individual's personality. This part of the text examines the various types of consistency that characterize personality, the attempts to measure them, and the theories that have been developed to try to account for them, at the trait-dispositional level of analysis.

THE PERSONAL SIDE OF THE SCIENCE

Some questions at the Trait-Dispositional Level you might ask about yourself:

- What am I like as a person?
- How am I different from other people "on the whole"? In what general ways are people different from each other?
- Does what I usually do and think and feel depend mostly on myself or on the situation in which I find myself?
- When and how is my behavior influenced by the situation?
- How does my personality influence the situations I choose to be in?
- How does my personality influence the effects that different kinds of situations have on me?

CHAPTER 3

TYPES AND TRAITS

"My father is a really great guy. He's absolutely dependable; I can always count on him."

"Nancy's very quiet and withdrawn. She never says hello to anybody."

Descriptions like those above are examples of everyday trait psychology. We see analyses at the trait level whenever people describe and group the differences among themselves into slots or categories. We all tend to classify each other readily on many dimensions: sex, race, religion, occupation, friendliness, and competitiveness are a few examples. Good–bad, strong–weak, friend–enemy, winner–loser—the ways of sorting and classifying human characteristics and attributes seem virtually infinite.

Most sciences classify and name things in their early efforts to find order. You see this, for example, in the classification system of biology, in which all life is sorted into genera and species. This effort to categorize also occurs in psychology, where, as the oldest and most enduring approach to individuality, it is known as the **trait approach**. Many psychologists working at this level of analysis try to label, measure, and classify people, often but not always using the trait terms of everyday language (e.g., friendly, aggressive, honest) in order to describe and compare their psychological attributes and to make sense of them (John, 1990).

3.1 What are the general goals of the trait-dispositional approach to personality?

▶ TYPES AND TRAITS

Traditionally, analyses at this level have been guided by the assumption that behavior is primarily determined by stable generalized **traits**—basic qualities of the person that express themselves in many contexts. Many investigators have searched vigorously for these traits, trying to find the person's position on one or more trait dimensions (e.g., intelligence, introversion, anxiety) by comparing the individual with others under similar uniform conditions. Guided by the belief that positions on these dimensions tend to be stable across situations and over time, the focus in the study of individuality at this level becomes the search to identify the person's basic stable and consistent traits or characteristics.

3.2 Differentiate between traits and types.

Types

Some categorizations sort individuals into discrete categories or *types* (Eysenck, 1991; Matthews, 1984). As noted in the text's introduction chapter, in the ancient theory of temperaments the Greek physician Hippocrates assigned persons to one of four types: *choleric* (irritable), *melancholic* (depressed), *sanguine* (optimistic), and *phlegmatic* (calm, listless). In accord with the biology of his time (about 400 B.C.), Hippocrates attributed each temperament to a predominance of one of the bodily humors: yellow bile, black bile, blood, and phlegm. A choleric temperament was caused by an excess of yellow bile; a depressive temperament reflected the predominance of black bile; the sanguine person had too much blood; and phlegmatic people suffered from an excess of phlegm.

Other typologies have searched for constitutional types, seeking associations between physique and indices of temperament. Such groupings in terms of body build have considerable popular appeal, as seen in the many stereotypes linking the body to the psyche: Fat people are "jolly" and "lazy," thin people are "morose" and "sensitive," and so on.

One of the important typologies used repeatedly by personality theorists has grouped all people into **introverts** or **extraverts**. According to this typology, the introvert withdraws into herself, especially when encountering stressful emotional conflict; prefers to be alone; tends to avoid others; and is shy. The extravert, in contrast, reacts to stress by trying to lose himself among people and social activity. He is drawn to an occupation that allows him to deal directly with many people, such as sales, and is apt to be conventional, sociable, and outgoing.

The very simplicity and breadth that makes such typologies appealing also reduces their value. Because each person's behaviors and psychological qualities are complex and variable, it is difficult to assign an individual to a single slot. Nevertheless, important typologies continue to be explored and are useful for many purposes. For example, the Type A pattern is particularly interesting because some of its ingredients, particularly chronic levels of hostility and anger, seem to have value in predicting a variety of dangerous health outcomes, most notably a proneness to premature coronary disease (see *In Focus 3.1*).

Traits: Individual Differences on Dimensions

Traits Defined

While typologies assume discontinuous categories (like male or female), most traits are measured on continuous dimensions like "friendliness" (see Figure 3.1). On such dimensions, differences among individuals may be arranged quantitatively in terms of the degree of the quality the person has (like degrees of "conscientiousness"). Psychological

IN FOCUS 3.1

AN EXAMPLE: TYPE A PERSONALITY

In collaborative research, psychologists and physicians have looked at the psychological variables in men at higher risk of coronary heart disease early in life. A coronary-prone behavior pattern was identified (Friedman & Roseman, 1974; Glass, 1977) and designated as *Type A*. This behavior pattern is characterized by:

1. ***Competitive Achievement Striving.*** Type As are likely to be involved in multiple activities, have numerous community and social commitments, and participate in competitive athletics. In laboratory studies, they are persistent and behave as though they believe that with sufficient effort they can overcome a variety of obstacles or frustrations.
2. ***Exaggerated Sense of Time Urgency.*** Type As show great impatience and irritation at delay (e.g., in a traffic jam, on a waiting line, when someone is late for a meeting).
3. ***Aggressiveness and Hostility.*** Type As may not be generally more aggressive than other people, but they become more aggressive under circumstances that threaten their sense of task mastery, for example, when under criticism or high time pressure.

Individuals who manifest these behaviors to a great degree are called Type As. Those who show the opposite patterns of relaxation, serenity, and lack of time urgency are designated as Type B. The two types differ in many ways, including in their family environments (Woodall & Matthews, 1989).

A number of studies have suggested that Type A people may have at least twice the likelihood of coronary heart disease as Type B people. They also smoke more and have higher levels of cholesterol in their blood. Type A people also tend to describe themselves as more impulsive, self-confident, and higher in achievement and aggression. Both Type A men and women fail to report physical symptoms and fatigue (Carver, Coleman, & Glass, 1976; Weidner & Matthews, 1978). This tendency to ignore symptoms may result in a Type A individual failing to rest or to seek medical care in the early phases of heart disease and may be one reason why these people push themselves into greater risk of premature death from coronary heart disease. Identifying individuals at high risk for heart disease and teaching them to pay more attention to physical symptoms may be an important part of programs aimed at reducing the toll of heart disease.

But the relationship between the total pattern of Type A behavior and coronary disease may be weaker than was suggested initially, especially among high-risk people (Matthews, 1984). Rather than looking at the relationship between the Type A pattern as a whole and coronary disease, it may be more useful to isolate such specific components of the pattern as anger and hostility. These components were found to be related to coronary disease even in the more recent studies (Miller, Smith, Turner, Guijarro, & Hallett, 1996). In sum, it now seems that specific behaviors, rather than the more global typology, are linked to a higher risk of coronary disease.

measurements usually suggest a continuous dimension of individual differences in the degree of the measured quality: most people show intermediate amounts, and only a few are at each extreme, as Figure 3.1 shows. For example, on the introversion–extraversion typology, individuals differ in the extent to which they show either quality but usually do not belong totally to one category or the other. It is therefore better to think of a psychological continuum of individual differences for most qualities or traits.

3.3 Describe the characteristics of the Type A personality and its significance for physical health.

Traits are assumed to be quantifiable and scalable:

> *By [scalability] we mean that a trait is a certain quality or attribute, and different individuals have different degrees of it.... If individuals differ in a trait by having higher or lower degrees of it, we can represent the trait by means of a single straight line.... Individual trait positions may be represented by points on the line.* (Guilford, 1959, pp. 64–65)

In its simplest meaning, the term "trait" refers to consistent differences between the behavior or characteristics of two or more people. Thus, a trait may be simply defined

3.4 What is meant by the scalability of a trait?

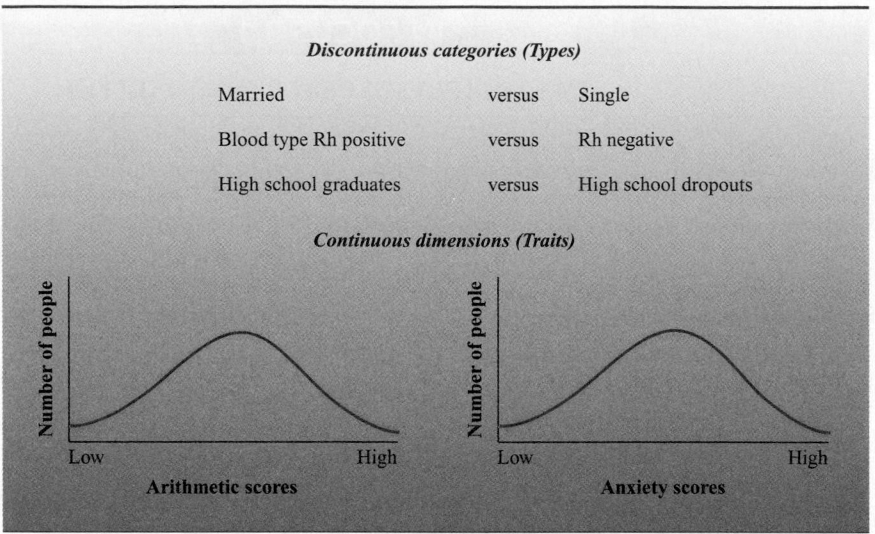

Figure 3.1 Examples of discontinuous categories (types) and continuous dimensions (traits).

as ". . . any distinguishable, relatively enduring way in which one individual varies from another" (Guilford, 1959, p. 6).

The search for traits begins with the commonsense observation that individuals often differ greatly and consistently in their responses to the same psychological situation or stimulus. That is, when different people are confronted with the same event—the same social encounter, the same test question, the same frightening experience—each individual tends to react in a somewhat different way. The basic idea that no two people react identically to the same stimulus is shown schematically in Figure 3.2. Moreover, in everyday life most of us are impressed with the distinctive *consistency* of one individual's responses over a wide variety of stimulus situations: We expect an "aggressive" person to differ consistently from others in his or her responses to many stimuli.

3.5 What everyday observations stimulate the search for traits?

Describing and Explaining

In addition to using trait labels to describe individual differences, some theorists also see traits as explanations: In their view, the trait is the property within the person that accounts for his or her unique but relatively stable reactions to stimuli. Thus, the trait becomes a construct to explain behavior—a hypothesized reason for enduring individual

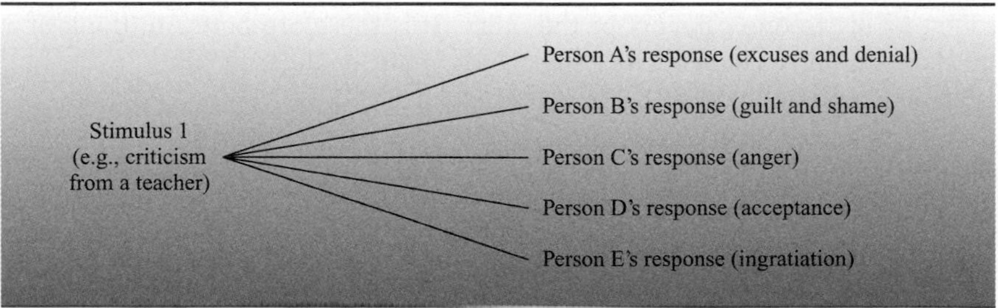

Figure 3.2 Individual differences in response to the same stimulus. The trait approach emphasizes consistent differences among people in their response to the same stimulus.

differences. Before looking at formal trait theories, however, we should consider how traits are used informally by people in daily life. Indeed, we are all trait theorists in the sense that we generate ideas about our own dispositions and the characteristics of other people.

Trait Attributions

When people describe each other in daily life, they spontaneously use trait terms. We all characterize each other (and ourselves) with such terms as aggressive, dependent, fearful, introverted, anxious, submissive—the list is almost endless. We see a person behaving in a particular way—for example, sitting at a desk for an hour yawning, and we attribute a trait, "unmotivated" or "lazy" or "bored" or "dull."

3.6 Describe and contrast the descriptive and explanatory uses of traits.

These simple trait attributions are often adequate to "explain" events for many everyday purposes in commonsense psychology (Heider, 1958; Kelley, 1973; Ross & Nisbett, 1991). In these commonsense explanations, traits are invoked not just as descriptions of what people do but also as the causes of their behavior. Thus in everyday practice, traits may be used first simply as adjectives describing behavior ("He behaves in a lazy way"), but the description is soon generalized from the behavior to the person ("He *is* lazy") and then abstracted to "He has a lazy disposition" or "He is unmotivated." These descriptions pose no problems as long as their basis is recalled—he is seen as behaving in a lazy way and no more. A hazard in trait attribution is that we easily forget that nothing is explained if the state *we* have attributed to the person from his behavior ("He has a trait of laziness") is now invoked as the *cause* of the behavior from which it was inferred. We then quickly emerge with the tautology, "He behaves in a lazy way because he has a lazy disposition," or because he is "unmotivated." The utility of trait terms therefore depends on their ability to make predictions about people's behaviors in a new situation based on their behaviors observed in the past in a different situation.

The trait approach to formal personality study begins with the commonsense conviction that personality can be described with trait terms. But it extends and refines those descriptions by arriving at them quantitatively and systematically. Efforts to explain individual differences by formal trait theories face some of the same problems that arise when traits are offered as causes by the layman. However, using scientific methods, numerous safeguards have been developed to try to control some of these difficulties, as discussed in later sections.

▶ TRAIT THEORISTS

There have been many different trait theorists, and three of the most influential were Gordon Allport, Raymond B. Cattell, and Hans J. Eysenck.

Gordon Allport

Gordon Allport's 1937 book *Personality: A Psychological Interpretation* launched the psychology of personality as a field and discipline. In this book and many later contributions, he made a convincing case that a distinctive field was needed, devoted to understanding the person as a coherent, consistent whole individual. His view of personality was broad and integrative, and he was sensitive and attentive to all its diverse aspects. Reacting against the tendency of researchers to study isolated part processes, such as learning and memory, in ways that failed to take account of individual differences,

Gordon Allport (1897–1967)
(*Source*: Courtesy Harvard University News Office)

he wanted the field to pursue two goals. One was to understand the differences between people in personality; the other was to see how the different characteristics and processes (like learning, memory, and biological processes) that exist within an individual interact and function together in an integrated way. His vision underlies much of what is still the definition and main mission of personality psychology today, as discussed in the introduction of this text. In particular, Allport's conception of traits continues to guide much of the work at the trait-dispositional level of analysis. In Allport's theory, traits have a very real existence: They are the ultimate realities of psychological organization. Allport favored a biophysical conception that

3.7 In Allport's theory, what are the characteristics of traits? How are traits linked to basic psychological processes?

> *does not hold that every trait-name necessarily implies a trait; but rather that behind all confusion of terms, behind the disagreement of judges, and apart from errors and failures of empirical observation, there are none the less bona fide mental structures in each personality that account for the consistency of its behavior. (1937, p. 289)*

According to Allport, traits are determining tendencies or predispositions to respond. In other words, a trait is

> *a generalized and focalized neuropsychic system (peculiar to the individual) with the capacity to render many stimuli functionally equivalent, and to initiate and guide consistent (equivalent) forms of adaptive and expressive behavior. (1937, p. 295)*

Thus, Allport believed that traits are relatively general and enduring, and that they were able to make, as quoted above, "many stimuli functionally equivalent." By that

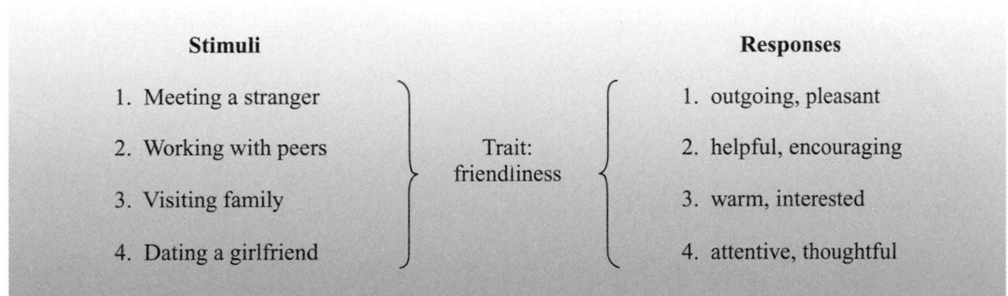

Figure 3.3 An example of a trait as the unifier of stimuli and responses.

he meant that they unite many responses to diverse stimuli, producing fairly broad consistencies in behavior. This relationship is seen in Figure 3.3.

Allport was convinced that some people have dispositions that influence most aspects of their behavior. He called these highly generalized dispositions **cardinal traits**. For example, if a person's whole life seems to be organized around goal achievement and the attainment of excellence, then achievement might be his or her cardinal trait. Less pervasive but still quite generalized dispositions are **central traits**, and Allport thought that many people are broadly influenced by central traits. Finally, more specific, narrow traits are called **secondary dispositions** or "attitudes."

3.8 Differentiate between Allport's notions of cardinal and central traits. What is their relation to secondary dispositions?

Allport believed that one's pattern of dispositions or "personality structure" determines one's behavior. This emphasis on structure rather than environment or stimulus conditions is seen in his colorful phrase, "The same fire that melts the butter hardens the egg" (1937, p. 102). Allport was a pioneering spokesman for the importance of individual differences: No two people are completely alike, and hence no two people respond identically to the same event. Each person's behavior is determined by a particular **trait structure**.

Allport thought that traits never occur in any two people in exactly the same way: They operate in *unique* ways in each person. This conviction was consistent with his emphasis on the individuality and uniqueness of each personality. To the extent that any trait is unique within a person rather than common among many people, it cannot be studied by making comparisons among people. Consequently, Allport urged the thorough study of individuals through intensive and long-term case studies, and did pioneering work at the Phenomenological-Humanistic Level of analysis, as discussed in later chapters. He also believed, however, that because of shared experiences and common cultural influences, most persons tend to develop some *roughly* common kinds of traits, and they can be compared on these common dispositions. It is this part of his many contributions that makes his ideas still central for work at the Trait-Dispositional Level.

Raymond B. Cattell

Raymond B. Cattell (1950, 1965) is another important trait theorist. For Cattell, the trait is also the basic unit of study; it is a "mental structure," inferred from behavior, and a fundamental construct that accounts for behavioral regularity or consistency. Like Allport, Cattell distinguished between **common traits**, which are possessed by many people in different degrees and **unique traits**, which occur only in a particular person and cannot be found in another in exactly the same form.

Raymond B. Cattell (1905–1998)

(*Source*: Times Newspapers Ltd., London)

Cattell also distinguished **surface traits** from **source traits** (see Table 3.1 for selected examples). Surface traits are clusters of overt or manifest trait elements (responses) that seem to go together. Source traits are the underlying variables that are the causal entities determining the surface manifestations. For Cattell, source traits can be found only by means of the mathematical technique of factor analysis (discussed later in this chapter). Using this technique, the investigator tries to estimate the factors or dimensions that appear to underlie surface variations in behavior. According to Cattell, the basic aim in research and assessment should be identification of source traits. In this view, these traits are divided between those that reflect environmental conditions (**environmental-mold traits**) and those that reflect constitutional factors (**constitutional traits**). Moreover, source traits may either be *general* (those affecting behavior in many different situations) or *specific*. Specific source traits are particularized sources of personality reaction that operate in one situation only, and Cattell pays little attention to them.

3.9 Describe Cattell's approach to identifying the structure of personality traits. What three types of data were used to discover source traits?

Cattell used three kinds of data to discover general source traits: (1) *life records*, in which everyday behavior situations are observed and rated; (2) *self-ratings;* and (3) *objective tests*, in which the person is observed in situations that are specifically

TABLE 3.1 Surface Traits and Source Traits Studied by Cattell

Examples of Surface Traits (Cattell, 1950)	Integrity, altruism—dishonesty, undependability Disciplined thoughtfulness—foolishness Thrift, tidiness, obstinacy—lability, curiosity, intuition
Examples of Source Traits (Cattell, 1965)	Ego strength—emotionality and neuroticism Dominance—submissiveness

Note: These are selected and abbreviated examples from much longer lists.

designed to elicit responses from which behavior in other situations can be predicted. The data from all three sources are subjected to factor analysis. In his own work, Cattell shows a preference for factor analysis of life-record data based on many behavior ratings for large samples of persons. Some 14 or 15 source traits have been reported from such investigations, but only six have been found repeatedly (Vernon, 1964).

In Cattell's system, traits may also be grouped into classes on the basis of how they are expressed. Those that are relevant to the individual's being "set into action" with respect to some goal are called **dynamic traits**. Those concerned with effectiveness in gaining the goal are **ability traits**. Traits concerned with energy or emotional reactivity are named **temperament traits**. Cattell has speculated extensively about the relationships between various traits and the development of personality (1965).

Hans J. Eysenck

The extensive research of Hans Eysenck in England complemented the work of the American trait theorists in many important ways. Eysenck (1961, 1991) extended the search for personality dimensions to the area of abnormal behavior, studying such traits as neuroticism–emotional stability. He also has investigated introversion–extraversion as a dimensional trait (although Carl Jung originally proposed "introvert" and "extravert" as personality types). Eysenck and his associates have pursued an elaborate and sophisticated statistical methodology in their investigations of these personality dimensions. In addition to providing a set of descriptive dimensions, Eysenck and his colleagues have studied the associations between people's positions on these dimensions and their scores on a variety of other personality and intellectual measures, and developed an influential model of personality designed to account for the roots of these traits in ways that connect to the Biological Level of analysis, and will be considered in those sections of the text.

3.10 According to Eysenck, which two trait dimensions can be used to describe individual differences in personality?

Hans J. Eysenck (1916–1997)

(*Source*: Courtesy Hans J. Eysenck)

Eysenck emphasized that his dimension of introversion–extraversion is based entirely on research and "must stand and fall by empirical confirmation" (Eysenck & Rachman, 1965, p. 19). In his words:

> *The typical extravert is sociable, likes parties, has many friends, needs to have people to talk to, and does not like reading or studying by himself. He craves excitement, takes chances, often sticks his neck out, acts on the spur of the moment, and is generally an impulsive individual. He is fond of practical jokes, always has a ready answer, and generally likes change; he is carefree, easygoing, optimistic, and "likes to laugh and be merry." He prefers to keep moving and doing things, tends to be aggressive and loses his temper quickly; altogether his feelings are not kept under tight control, and he is not always a reliable person.*
>
> *The typical introvert is a quiet, retiring sort of person, introspective, fond of books rather than people; he is reserved and distant except to intimate friends. He tends to plan ahead, "looks before he leaps," and mistrusts the impulse of the moment. He does not like excitement, takes matters of everyday life with proper seriousness, and likes a well-ordered mode of life. He keeps his feelings under close control, seldom behaves in an aggressive manner, and does not lose his temper easily. He is reliable, somewhat pessimistic and places great value on ethical standards.*

Eysenck and his colleagues recognized that these descriptions may sound almost like caricatures because they portray "perfect" extraverts and introverts, while in fact most

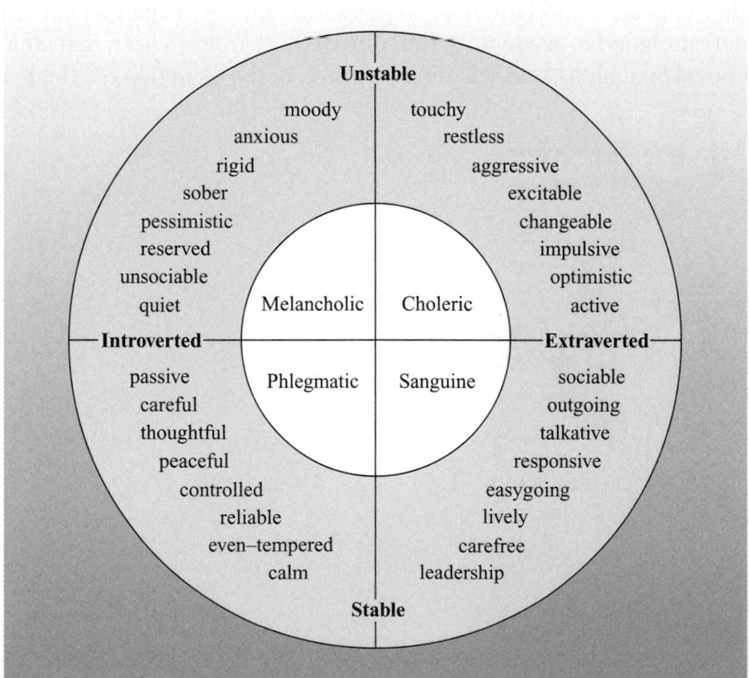

Figure 3.4 Dimensions of personality. The inner ring shows the "four temperaments" of Hippocrates; the outer ring shows the results of modern factor analytic studies of the intercorrelations between traits by Eysenck and others (Eysenck & Rachman, 1965).

TABLE 3.2 Sexual Activities Reported by Introverted (I) and Extraverted (E) Students[a]

		Males		Females	
Activity		I	E	I	E
Masturbation at present		86	72	47	39
Petting at 17		16	40	15	24
at 19		3	56	30	47
at present		57	78	62	76
Coitus (intercourse) at 17		5	21	4	8
at 19		15	45	12	29
at present		47	77	42	71
Median frequency of coitus per month (sexually active students only)		3.0	5.5	3.1	7.5
Coitus partners in the last 12 months	one	75	46	72	60
(unmarried students only)	two or more	18	30	25	23
	four or more	7	25	4	17

[a]The numbers are the frequencies of endorsements by each group.

Source: Based on data from Giese, H., & Schmidt, S. (1968). *Studenten sexualitat*. Hamburg: Rowohlt; cited in Eysenck, H. J. (1973). Personality and the law of effect. In D. E. Berlyne & K. B. Madsen (Eds.), *Pleasure, reward, preference*. New York: Academic Press.

people are mixtures who fall in the middle rather than at the extremes of the dimensions (see Figure 3.4). As Figure 3.4 shows, Eysenck suggested that the second major dimension of personality is **emotional stability** (or "neuroticism"). This dimension describes at one end people who tend to be moody, touchy, anxious, restless, and so on. At the other extreme are people who are characterized by such terms as stable, calm, carefree, even-tempered, and reliable. As Eysenck stressed, the ultimate value of these dimensions will depend on the research support they receive.

To clarify the meaning of both dimensions, Eysenck and his associates have studied the relations between people's positions on them and their scores on many other measures. An example of the results found is summarized in Table 3.2, which shows self-reported differences in the sexual activities of extraverts and introverts (reported in Eysenck, 1973). As expected, the extraverts generally reported earlier, more frequent, and more varied sexual experiences. While the groups differed on the average, there was still considerable overlap, making it difficult to predict any particular individual's behavior from her introversion–extraversion score alone. But the results of many studies of this type provide an increasingly comprehensive picture of Eysenck's dimensions. In addition, Eysenck's ideas are notable in stimulating a search for the biological foundations of dispositions, and are discussed in that context.

COMMON FEATURES OF TRAIT THEORIES

Now consider the principal common characteristics of trait approaches.

Generality and Stability of Traits

Trait theorists often have disagreed about the specific content and structure of the basic traits needed to describe personality, but their general conceptions have much similarity and they remain popular (Funder, 1991). They all use the trait to account for consistencies in an individual's behavior and explain why persons respond in different ways to the same stimulus. Most view traits as dispositions that determine such behaviors. Each differentiates between relatively superficial traits (e.g., Cattell's surface traits) and more basic, underlying traits (e.g., Cattell's source traits). Each recognizes that traits vary in breadth or generality. Allport puts the strongest emphasis on the relative generality of common traits across many situations. Most theorists also recognize some fluctuations, or changes in a person's position with respect to a disposition. At the same time, each is committed to a search for relatively broad, stable traits.

3.11 What is the importance of behavioral consistency in trait theories?

Traits and States Distinguished

It is one thing to be irascible, quite another thing to be angry, just as an anxious temper is different from feeling anxiety. Not all men who are sometimes anxious are of an anxious temperament, nor are those who have an anxious temperament always feeling anxious. In the same way there is a difference between intoxication and habitual drunkenness ...

Cicero (45 B.C.)

This ancient wisdom (quoted in Chaplin, John, & Goldberg, 1988) is used by modern trait theorists to illustrate a distinction that is often made, both intuitively and by trait psychologists, between *traits* and *states* (Chaplin et al., 1988; Eysenck, 1983). Both traits and states are terms that refer to the perceived attributes of people. Both refer to categories that have fuzzy boundaries, and both are based on prototypes or ideal exemplars (e.g., Cantor & Mischel, 1979). The difference between them is that prototypic traits are seen as enduring, stable qualities of the person over long time periods and internally (e.g., biologically) caused. In contrast, prototypic states refer to qualities that are only brief in duration and attributable to external causes, such as the momentary situation (Chaplin et al., 1988). Examples of terms that people tend to classify as traits are gentle, domineering, and timid, while terms like infatuated, uninterested, and displeased tend to be seen as states.

3.12 How does an anger state differ from an anger trait?

Search for Basic Traits

Guided by the assumption that stable dispositions exist, trait psychologists try to identify the individual's position on one or more dimensions (such as neuroticism, extraversion). They do this by comparing people tested under standardized conditions. They believe that positions on these dimensions are relatively stable across testing situations and over long time periods. They paid less attention to the effects of environmental conditions on traits and behavior. The search for traits, and for useful ways to measure them, in modern personality psychology has a long history, and it began in response to urgent practical considerations at the time of World War I, as was discussed in Chapter 2.

Quantification

A main feature of the trait approach has been its methodology, and you saw many examples in Chapter 2 of self-report questionnaires and ratings by self and others. This methodology is "psychometric" in the sense that it attempts to measure individual differences and to quantify them. Psychometricians study persons and groups on trait dimensions by comparing their scores on tests. To do this, they sample many people, compare large groups under uniform testing conditions, and devise statistical techniques to infer basic traits. Their methods over the years have become increasingly sophisticated and effective for meeting a wide range of measurement goals (e.g., Jackson & Paunonen, 1980; John, 1990).

Aggregating across Situations to Increase Reliability

Although they acknowledge that the situation is important, many psychologists working at the trait level are convinced that past research has underestimated the personal constancies in behavior. They point out that if we want to test how well a disposition (trait) can be used to predict behavior, we have to sample adequately not only the disposition but also the behavior that we want to predict (Ajzen & Fishbein, 1977; Block, 1977; Epstein, 1979, 1983). Yet in the past, researchers often attempted to predict single acts (e.g., physical aggression when insulted) from a dispositional measure (e.g., self-rated aggression on a personality scale). Generally, such attempts did not succeed. But while measures of traits may not be able to predict such single acts, they may do much better if one uses a **multiple-act criterion**: a pooled combination of many behaviors that are relevant to the trait, and a pooled combination of many raters (e.g., McCrae & Costa, 1985, 1987).

The methods and results of this line of research are illustrated in a study in which undergraduate women were given the "dominance scale" from two personality inventories (Jaccard, 1974). The women also were asked whether or not they had performed a set of 40 dominance-related behaviors. For example, did they initiate a discussion in class, argue with a teacher, ask a male out on a date. The dominance scales from the personality inventories did not predict the individual behaviors well. But the researcher found that when the 40 behavioral items were summed into one pooled measure, they related substantially to the personality scores. Namely, women high on the dominance scales also tended to report performing more dominant behaviors, and the reverse was also true. Thus a longer, aggregated, and therefore more reliable behavioral measure revealed associations to other measures (the self-reports on the personality tests) that would not otherwise have been seen. Similar results were found when the behaviors were measured directly by observation (e.g., Weigel & Newman, 1976).

3.13 How did the Jaccard and Epstein studies illustrate the value of aggregating behaviors?

In the same direction, it has been shown that reliability will increase when the number of items in a test sample is increased and combined. Making this point, Epstein (1979) demonstrated that temporal stability (of, for example, self-reported emotions and experiences recorded daily, and observer judgments) becomes much larger when it is based on averages over many days than when it is based on only single items on single days. His demonstrations also indicate that even when one cannot predict what an individual will do in a specific situation, it is often possible to predict the person's overall standing relative to other people when the behaviors are aggregated (combined) across many situations (Epstein, 1983).

▶ TAXONOMY OF HUMAN ATTRIBUTES

A widely shared goal is to find a universal taxonomy or classification system for sorting the vast array of human attributes into a relatively small set of fundamental dimensions or categories on which most individual differences can be described. From this perspective, psychologists attempt to identify "the most important individual differences in mankind" (Goldberg, 1973, p. 1).

Psycholexical Approach

Researchers in this approach assume that the most significant individual differences—those that are most important in daily human relationships—enter into the natural language of the culture as single-word trait terms. They use a variety of methods to identify basic trait terms in the language and to categorize them into smaller groupings. This is an enormous classification task, given that English includes thousands of trait terms (over 18,000 in one count of the dictionary). The hope is that an extensive, well-organized vocabulary for describing human attributes in trait terms will lead to better theories of personality and better methods of personality assessment.

3.14 Describe the assumptions underlying the psycholexical approach to identifying the major traits that underlie personality.

This research strategy is called the **psycholexical approach**. Its basic data are the words in the natural language that describe human qualities. In these studies, many people are asked to rate how well each of many trait terms describes or fits a particular person they know well. In some studies, this is a peer; in some studies, participants rate how well the words describe themselves. In each study, the results are then analyzed to see which sets of trait terms tend to cluster or "go together" when individuals are described. Using statistical procedures, the researchers try to specify a small number of factors or dimensions that seem to capture the common element among adjectives that are closely associated (e.g., Goldberg, 1990).

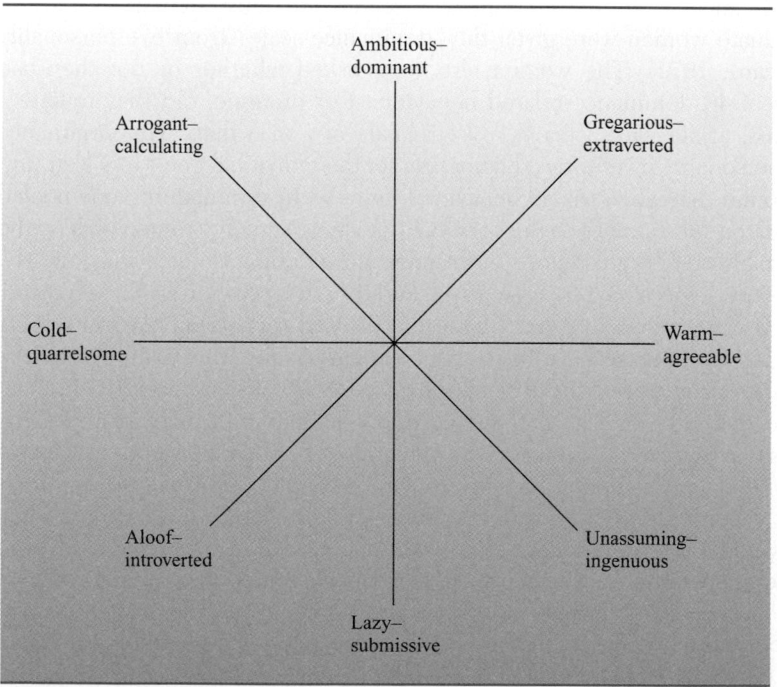

Figure 3.5 Wiggins's (1980) taxonomy of the interpersonal domain.

Source: Wiggins, J. S. A psychological taxonomy of trait-descriptive terms: The interpersonal domain. *Journal of Personality and Social Psychology*, 37, 399, fig. 2. © 1979 by the American Psychological Association. Reprinted with permission.

This approach was illustrated in an early attempt to find a comprehensive taxonomy of the **domain of interpersonal behavior** (Wiggins, 1979, 1980) that yielded the dimensions shown in Figure 3.5. Note that each dimension is bipolar, that is, has two opposite ends or poles. The dimensions are structured in a circular pattern like a pie. Each pole is made up of a set of adjectives so that *Ambitious (Dominant)*, for example, is defined with such terms as persevering, persistent, industrious. The opposite pole, *Lazy (Submissive)*, includes such terms as unproductive, unthorough, unindustrious. Wiggins reports that these dimensions fit well the results of earlier descriptions of the interpersonal domain (Leary, 1957). They seem to be reasonably robust and useful when different samples of people are rated on them and continue to be revised and refined (Wiggins, Phillips, & Trapnell, 1989).

The "Big Five" Trait Dimensions

For many years in the long search for a universal taxonomy of traits, researchers disagreed as to which personality dimensions they should use to describe personality. Some proposed as many as 16; others, as few as two or three (Vernon, 1964). More recently, however, some consensus has grown among many researchers to focus on five dimensions of personality (Goldberg, 1992; John, 1990; McCrae & Costa, 1985, 1987, 1999) that emerge from ratings using English-language trait adjectives.

Trait terms number in the thousands, as a look at the dictionary makes clear. But they have to be simplified and organized to become manageable units for describing people systematically. Consider, for example, the mass of data yielded by responses to a self-report measure with 550 items answered by 100 persons. To extract order from such a stack of facts, investigators searching for underlying traits try to group responses into more basic clusters. For this purpose, many trait psychologists turn to **factor analysis**. This is a mathematical procedure that helps to sort test responses into relatively homogeneous clusters of items that are highly correlated. Using this method, and working in the psycholexical approach, a number of researchers have reached reasonable agreement about the five types of dimensions or factors on which English trait terms may be clustered, often called the "Big Five Structure" (e.g., Goldberg, 1992; John, 1990).

Factor Analysis to Find Trait Dimensions: The NEO-PI-R and Big Five

Factor analysis is a very useful tool for reducing a large set of correlated measures to fewer unrelated or independent dimensions. As such, it can be a powerful aid to psychological research by clarifying which response patterns go together. Suppose, for example, that 50 students have answered 10 personality questionnaires, each of which contains 100 questions. A factor analysis of this mass of information can show which parts of the test performances go together. It essentially finds and connects the items that tend to "go together" (covary) with each of the other items in the total set. The analogy would be a procedure that allows you to go to a stack of several hundred unsorted books in the library and that finds and groups together those that are alike on certain dimensions (e.g., size, color, length, language, content areas) but different in other respects.

A series of pioneering studies (Norman, 1961, 1963; Tupes & Christal, 1958, 1961) investigated the factors obtained for diverse samples of people rated by their peers on rating scales. The scales themselves came from a condensed version of the thousands of trait names originally identified by Allport and Odbert's search many years earlier for trait names in the dictionary. After much research, 20 scales were selected and many judges were asked to rate other people on them. The results were carefully factor analyzed.

TABLE 3.3 The Big Five Factors and Illustrative Components

Factor (Trait Dimension)	Adjective Items[a]
I. **Neuroticism (N)** (negative emotions—e.g., anxiety, depression)	Calm–worrying Unemotional–emotional Secure–insecure Not envious–jealous
II. **Extraversion (E)** (versus closed-minded)	Quiet–talkative Aloof–friendly Inhibited–spontaneous Timid–bold
III. **Openness to Experience (O)** (versus closed-minded)	Conventional–original Unadventurous–daring Conforming–independent Unartistic–artistic
IV. **Agreeableness (A)** (versus antagonism)	Irritable–good natured Uncooperative–helpful Suspicious–trusting Critical–lenient
V. **Conscientiousness (C)**	Careless–careful Helpless–self-reliant Lax–scrupulous Weak-willed–Goal-directed

[a] Illustrative adjectives describing the two ends of the scales that comprise the dimension.

Source: Adapted from McCrae, R. R., & Costa, P. T., Jr. (1987). Validation of the five-factor model of personality across instruments and observers. *Journal of Personality and Social Psychology, 52*, 81–90. Essentially similar results were found in John, O. P. (1990). The big-five factor taxonomy: Dimensions of personality in the natural language and questionnaires. In L. A. Pervin (Ed.), *Handbook of personality: Theory and research* (pp. 66–100). New York: Guilford Press; and in Normak, W. T. (1963). Toward an adequate taxonomy of personality attributes: Replicated factor structure in peer nomination personality ratings. *Journal of Abnormal and Social Psychology, 66*, 574–583.

3.15 How was factor analysis used to identify the Big Five traits that are thought by some theorists to describe personality? Describe the five factors using the acronym OCEAN to capture their first letters.

The same set of five relatively independent factors appeared consistently across several studies and continues to form the basis of what has become the **Big Five Structure** (e.g., Goldberg, 1992; John, 1990). It consists of five factors measured with a personality inventory now called the **NEO-PI-R** (Costa & McCrae, 1997), as shown in Table 3.3.

The Big Five factors include: **Neuroticism (N)**, for example, worrying and insecurity; **Extraversion (E)** or surgency (positive emotionality), as reflected by terms like friendly, talkative; **Openness to experience (O)**; **Agreeableness (A)**; and **Conscientiousness (C)**. See Table 3.3 for descriptions of each factor. In the NEO-PI-R, each factor is also more finely described in terms of a number of different facets through which it may be expressed, illustrated in Table 3.4.

The Big Five resemble the dimensions initially proposed by Norman (1963) and found repeatedly in research, although sometimes given slightly different names. Each dimension includes a collection of bipolar rating scales, such as "calm–worrying" and "timid–bold," that refer to types of feelings or behaviors. For each dimension, Table 3.3 gives examples of the adjectives describing the two ends of some of the rating scales used.

To illustrate the type of research that underlies the development of the Big Five, in one study, 187 college students rated how well each of 1,710 trait terms described him or her (Goldberg, 1991). Statistical analysis showed that these terms clustered into five major factors or dimensions much like the Big Five (McCrae & Costa, 1987). Thus, when people are described with trait terms like those shown in Table 3.3, a reliable clustering

TABLE 3.4 Illustrative Facet Scales for the Big Five Factor

Neuroticism: anxiety, angry hostility, depression, impulsiveness, vulnerability
Extraversion: warmth, gregariousness, assertiveness, activity, excitement-seeking positive emotions
Openness to Experience: fantasy, aesthetics, feelings, actions, ideas, values
Agreeableness: trust, straightforwardness, altruism, compliance, modesty, tender-mindedness
Conscientiousness: competence, order, dutifulness, achievement, striving, self-discipline, deliberation

Source: Reproduced by special permission of the Publisher, Psychological Assessment Resources, Inc., 16204 North Florida Avenue, Lutz, Florida 33549, from *The NEO Personality Inventory—Revised*, by Paul Costa and Robert McCrae, Copyright 1978, 1985, 1989, 1992 by PAR, Inc. Further reproduction is prohibited without permission of PAR, Inc.

occurs consisting of five large descriptive categories or factors, called **super traits**. This Big Five Structure seems to characterize major dimensions of personality in natural English-language words. A number of personality trait questionnaires and personality ratings using these types of trait terms provide descriptions of persons that seem to fit the Big Five reasonably (Costa & McCrae, 1992a; Costa, McCrae, & Dye, 1991).

Considerable stability over time has been demonstrated on trait ratings and questionnaires related to the Big Five (e.g., McCrae & Costa, 1990) even for long time spans. Stability tends to be particularly high during the adult years (Costa & McCrae, 1997; McCrae & Costa, 1999). It is notable that in spite of the many changes that often occur in life structures during adulthood over long time periods—including the changes produced by marriage, children, divorce, residential and occupational moves, and health issues—the status of most individuals on the Big Five dimensions tends to show high stability (see Table 3.5).

3.16 How stable are the Big Five dimensions over time?

TABLE 3.5 Stability of NEO-PI Scales (Ages 25–56)

NEO-PI Scale	Men	Women
N (Neuroticism)	.78	.85
E (Extraversion)	.84	.75
O (Open minded)	.87	.84
A (Agreeable)	.64	.60
C (Conscientiousness)	.83	.84

Note: Retest interval is 6 years for N, E, and O scales, 3 years for short forms of A and C scales.

Source: Adapted from *Personality in Adulthood* (p. 88), by R. R. McCrae and P. T. Costa Jr., 1990, New York: Guilford Press.

EVIDENCE AND ISSUES

Overview of Usefulness of the Big Five

An explosion of research has documented the robustness of the Five Factor Model, or Big Five. The kinds of evidence that has accumulated is impressive (e.g., McCrae & Costa, 1997, 1999; McCrae et al., 1998), and too large to summarize beyond the general conclusions to which it leads:

- The Big Five Factor Structure has often been replicated in research by diverse investigators using a variety of English-speaking samples.

- Especially the N, E, and A factors listed in Table 3.3 have been found to replicate well even when the languages, cultures, and item formats used differ. Replicability has been reported for diverse languages and language families that span Sino-Tibetan, Uraic, Hamito-Semitic, and Malayon-Polynesian.

3.17 Cite four lines of evidence for the generality of the Five Factor Model.

- Overall, the results are impressive and broadly generalizable across diverse cultures throughout the world (e.g., McCrae et al., 1998), although unsurprisingly some of the factors may take different forms in extremely different samples and cultures.
- The factor structure of individuals as described by this model tends to be relatively stable in adults over long periods of time.
- The Big Five has some predictive validity for important life outcomes and diverse other links to personality measures.

In short, the total evidence is impressive for the broad robustness and potential of this taxonomy as a comprehensive descriptive system for describing people in trait terms at a broad, highly abstract, or super trait level. The value of having such a robust and comprehensive trait map for describing and comparing people is considerable and widely recognized (e,g., MacDonald, 1998).

The Big Five dimensions offer a useful replicable taxonomy of trait terms, potentially not only in the English language but across diverse languages (Costa & McCrae, 1997; DeRaad, Perugini, Hrebickova, & Szarota, 1998; McCrae et al., 1998). Its focus on language as the route for identifying what humans care about with regard to personality makes good sense. It is based on the idea that the languages people develop contain clusters of trait terms that go together and that reflect what they care about when they describe and evaluate other people and themselves (Saucier & Goldberg, 1996). Factor analysis has been used effectively to identify these clusters, and they provide a robust view of personality qualities that matter to people in everyday life. Given that trait judgments are widely used and can have important consequences, it also becomes interesting to ask how such judgments of what someone (or something) "is like" are made, and that question is addressed in *In Focus 3.2*.

Stability of Traits over Time

Are a person's qualities stable? Do early characteristics predict later qualities? When parents say "Fred was always so friendly, even as a little baby," are their comments justified? Can we predict the 6-year-old's behavior from responses in the first year of life? Is there much continuity in the qualities and behaviors of the child throughout childhood? Research has made it clear that although behavior depends on context, and the same person may be quite different in very different contexts, there also is significant trait stability over time, particularly after the first few years of life.

3.18 At what point does temporal stability begin to emerge, and which behaviors show stability?

Many important connections have been found over time in the life course. For example, lower sensitivity to touch on the skin in the newborn predicted more mature communications and coping at age $2\frac{1}{2}$ and at age $7\frac{1}{2}$. High touch sensitivity and high respiration rates at birth were related to low interest, low participation, lower assertiveness, and less communicativeness in later years (Bell, Weller, & Waldrop, 1971; Halverson, 1971a, 1971b). But these links between newborn and later behaviors were exceptions, and the associations that were found generally were not strong. So there are some connections between a newborn's qualities and characteristics later in life, but in the individual case, one could not predict confidently from responses at birth to later characteristics:

IN FOCUS 3.2

PROTOTYPES: "TYPICAL" PEOPLE

Psychologists concerned with the classification of human attributes also try to identify how we judge the **prototypicality** or "typicality" of different members of a category, whether it is a trait category, such as one of the Big Five, or an everyday, "natural" category, such as the category "birds." To demonstrate the idea of typicality to yourself, think of the most typical, representative, or "birdlike" bird. You probably will think of a bird that is something like a robin or a sparrow—not a chicken or an ostrich. The point is simply that some members of a category (in this case, birds) are better or more typical examples of a category: Some reds are "redder" than others, some chairs are more chair-like than others. This point has been elegantly documented for everyday categories of natural objects like furniture (Rosch, Mervis, Gray, Johnson, & Boyce-Braem, 1976). Thus natural categories may be organized around *prototypical* examples (the best examples of the concept), with less prototypical or less good members forming a continuum away from the central one (Rosch, 1975; Tversky, 1977).

The important point here is that trait categories, like other categories, often are not well-defined, distinct, nonoverlapping categories in which each member of a category has all its defining features. (While many birds sing, not all do, and some nonbirds surely do.) Well-defined, nonoverlapping categories are built into artificial, logical systems, but they are rare in the real world. If we turn from the abstract world of logic and formal, artificial systems to common, everyday categories—to furniture, birds, and clothing—the categories become "fuzzy." As the philosopher Wittgenstein (1953) first pointed out, the members of common, everyday categories do not all share a set of single, essential features critical for category membership. If you closely examine a set of natural objects all labeled by one general term (like "birds") you will not find a single set of features that all members of the category share; rather, a *pattern* of overlapping similarities—a *family resemblance* structure—seems to emerge.

"Typicality" and "family resemblance" and "fuzziness" also may characterize everyday judgments about categories of people (Cantor & Mischel, 1979; Cantor, Mischel, & Schwartz, 1982; Chaplin et al., 1988; John, 1990). When making these judgments while forming our everyday impressions of people, we seem able to agree about who is a more or less typical or even "ideal" kind of personality, just as we agree that a robin is a more birdlike bird than a chicken. For instance, such qualities as "sociable" and "outgoing" are the characteristics of a "typical extravert."

The study of prototypicality rules and family resemblance principles in judgments of people helps in understanding how consistency and coherence are perceived in spite of variations in behavior (Kunda, 1999; Mischel, 1984). To illustrate, someone who really knows Rembrandt's work, who has seen dozens of his paintings, can easily identify whether a previously unseen painting is a real Rembrandt, an imitation, or a fake. The art expert seems able to extract a central distinctive gist from a wide range of variations. The same processes that permit such judgments must underlie how we identify personality coherence in the face of behavioral variability, and agree that someone is or is not a "real" introvert, or an anxious neurotic, or a sincere, friendly person. One attractive feature of this prototypicality approach to traits is that it seems highly compatible with attempts to quantify interpersonal behavior into dimensions of the sort discussed throughout this chapter (John, Hampson, & Goldberg, 1991).

> *To use an analogy, newborn behavior is more like a preface to a book than a table of its contents yet to be unfolded. Further, the preface is itself merely a rough draft undergoing rapid revision. There are some clues to the nature of the book in the preface, but these are in code form and taking them as literally prophetic is likely to lead to disappointment. (Bell et al., 1971, p. 132)*

As one progresses beyond the "preface of the book" to the first few chapters (to the early years of life), continuities in development become increasingly evident (Block & Block, 1980; McCrae & Costa, 1996; Mischel et al., 1989). Children who are seen as more active, assertive, aggressive, competitive, outgoing, and so on at age 3 years are also more likely to be described as having more of those qualities later in development, for example. In sum, the specific links between qualities of the child, say in the 4th year and in the 8th year, may be complex and indirect. But a thorough analysis of the patterns suggests that some significant threads of continuity emerge over time (Caspi, 1987, 1998; Caspi, Roberts, & Shiner, 2005). Thus childhood characteristics may be connected coherently to later behavior and attributes to some degree (Arend, Gove, & Sroufe, 1979; Block, 1971; Mischel et al., 1989). Experiences in the early pages of the book affect what happens in the later pages, although these early experiences do not prevent the possibility of genuine changes later.

The amount of stability or change over time varies for different types of characteristics and different types of experiences at different points in development (Caspi, 1998; Caspi & Bem, 1990; Caspi et al., 2005; Srivastava, John, Gosling, & Potter, 2003). For example, consider a large study (799 people) of Big Five trait stability spanning the 40 years between elementary school and midlife (Hampson & Goldberg, 2006). Stability across the 40-year interval was highest for Extraversion (e.g., .29 correlation), and Conscientiousness (e.g., .25), less for Openness (e.g., l6), even less for Agreeableness (e.g., .08), and zero for Neuroticism. Unsurprisingly, in adulthood when smaller time intervals were examined (1–3 years), correlations were much higher (e.g., .70–.79). Overall, the findings point to some continuity in some characteristics, especially in adulthood over short time spans, and, as the authors noted, importantly depend on the specific ways in which the stability data are obtained and analyzed.

A set of interesting studies of lives over many years indicate that "ill-tempered boys become ill-tempered men" (Caspi & Bem, 1990, p. 568). These continuities in development reflect the fact that stable qualities of the individual, whether adaptive (such as the ability and willingness to delay gratification), or aversive and maladaptive (such as inappropriate displays of temper), can have profound "chain effects" that quickly accelerate. Beginning early in life, they can trigger long sequences of interconnected events that impact on the person's subsequent opportunities and options, often greatly limiting them. As Caspi and Bem (1990) note, a child's ill temper rapidly produces trouble in school, making school a negative experience for the child him- or herself. At the same time it also provokes the school authorities, ultimately leading to expulsion from school—an outcome that permanently limits occupational opportunities and constrains the future. The unhappy network of consequences is illustrated in Figure 3.6.

The network of outcomes associated with early ill-temperedness is broader than just school and career. For example, Caspi and Bem (1990) reported that almost half of the men (46%) with a history of ill-tempered behavior as children were divorced by age 40 while only 22% of the other men studied were divorced at that age.

Taken collectively, studies of individual differences on trait dimensions after early childhood have produced many networks of meaningful correlations. These associations tend to be larger and more enduring when people rate themselves or others with broad trait terms (e.g., Block, 1971; Caspi & Bem, 1990; Costa & McCrae, 1988; E. L. Kelly, 1955). Such ratings suggest significant continuity and stability in how people are perceived over the years as well as in how they perceive themselves. For example, long-term stability was shown using rating methods in some early landmark studies that closely followed children into adulthood (Block, 1971), as summarized in Table 3.6. It is also high on many personality trait inventories, and ranges on average from median correlations of .34 to .77 (Costa & McCrae, 1997).

3.19 What is the temporal stability of results derived from self-descriptions and ratings?

When one looks closely at how people actually behave in specific situations, sampling it objectively by different, independent measures, however, the association generally tends to be much more modest. Thus while people often show consistency in what they say they are like on questionnaires and ratings, these characterizations often do

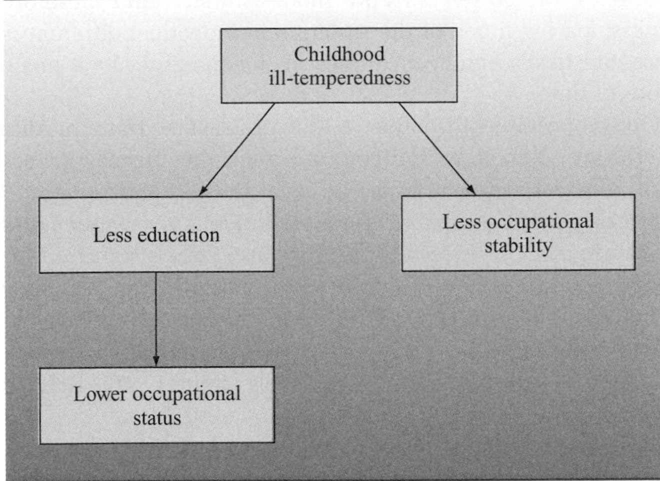

Figure 3.6 Some long-term outcomes associated with childhood ill-temperedness. Statistically significant correlations are shown. Data are for 45 men from middle-class origins.

Source: Figure and data adapted from "Moving against the world: Life-course patterns of explosive children," by A. Caspi, G. H. Elder, Jr. and D. J. Bem (1987). *Developmental Psychology, 23*, 308–313.

not accurately predict what they do, as noted even by advocates of trait-level analysis (Funder, 2001), and discussed in the next chapter. Therefore, one has to be cautious about generalizing from a person's personality test behavior, including the robust and well-established measures of the Big Five, to his or her behavior outside the test.

Big Five Differences Predicting Life Outcomes

An important issue is whether individual differences in traits dimensions are also meaningfully related to important life outcomes. Data suggest that they indeed do, as

TABLE 3.6 Examples of Significant Stability over Time in Ratings of Personality

	Correlations From		
	Junior to Senior H. S.	Senior H. S. to Adulthood	Item Rated
Males	.57	.59	Tends toward undercontrol of needs and impulses; unable to delay gratification
	.58	.53	Is genuinely dependable and responsible person
	.50	.42	Is self-defeating
Females	.50	.46	Basically submissive
	.48	.49	Tends to be rebellious, nonconforming
	.39	.43	Emphasizing being with others, gregarious

Source: Based on Block, J. (1971). *Lives through time*. Berkeley, CA: Bancroft.

illustrated below. In these studies, the correlations are modest in size, and therefore of limited predictive usefulness, leaving much of the variation in individual differences unexplained. But they also are statistically significant, indicating meaningful, albeit small, relationships over long periods of time.

Juvenile delinquency. One important life outcome that personality traits predict is juvenile delinquency. Youths are defined as "delinquent" when they display antisocial tendencies and unlawful behavior, often resulting in legal problems, arrests, and confinement, making it unsurprising that compared to nondelinquent youths they also tend to be lower in Agreeableness on Big Five self-descriptions. They also are lower in Conscientiousness, which is related to difficulties in impulse control. Similarly they are lower in Open-mindedness (O) reflecting rigidity as well as lower intelligence. Finally, delinquent youth tend to be higher in Extraversion as they probably are high in excitement seeking and in personal tempo and activity levels (John, Caspi, Robins, Moffitt, Stouthamer-Loeber, 1994).

Academic achievement. There is a small but significant relationship between Conscientiousness and academic achievement. People who are high in C tend to work harder, and know how to stay task focused, which translates into greater academic success (Chamorro-Premuzic & Furnham, 2003; Luciano, Wainwright, Wright, & Martin, 2006). Open-mindedness and academic achievement also are correlated (Hair & Graziano, 2003), perhaps because high O people may be internally driven to learn and more engaged with behaviors that promote learning (Komarraju & Karau, 2005).

Longevity. High Conscientiousness (C) in childhood is related to longevity and the effect size is as big as male–female differences (Friedman et al., 1995). A plausible reason for this correlation is that conscientious people adhere more closely to health-protective and health-care regimes, as well as taking fewer risks that can jeopardize health and survival. Interestingly, children who are cheerful and optimistic in childhood tend to die earlier in adulthood. Research indicates that cheerful children grow up to be more impulsive adults engaging in risky behavior and hence they are at greater risk for mortality (Martin et al., 2002).

Interracial attitudes. As another example of these links, and as noted earlier in this chapter, more Open-mindedness (O) by White participants also has been shown to relate to their more open-minded interracial attitudes, both in self-reports and in less negatively racially stereotyped judgments of Black individuals viewed in computer-presented informal interviews (Flynn, 2005).

In sum, consistent with these examples, a comprehensive review of studies using a variety of personality trait measures to predict important life outcomes concluded that although the effects tend to be small, they do as well as the correlations obtained from measures like socio-economic status or cognitive abilities. As they authors emphasized, they therefore have value for many goals psychologists care about, and encourage more investigations of how traits develop, and the mechanisms through which they might influence all sorts of life outcomes (Roberts, Kuncel, Shiner, Caspi, & Goldberg, in press).

Limitations, Concerns, Contributions

At the same time that studies of broad traits, and particularly the widely used Big Five, created much enthusiasm, critiques showing the limitations of the model and the approach itself continued (e.g., Block, 1995; Borsboom, Mellenbergh, & Van Heerden, 2004; McAdams, 1992; Pervin, 1994).

Limitations of Factor Analysis

First, as was recognized long ago (e.g., Overall, 1964), factor analysis cannot establish which characteristics of persons or things being measured are "real," "basic," or "primary." The factors obtained are simply names that the researcher *gives* to the correlations found among the particular measures. In other words, factor analysis yields a greatly simplified patterning of the data put into it. The results of factor analyses depend on what is put into the procedures, such as the test items and the people selected by the researcher, and on the details of his or her procedures and decisions (see, e.g., Mischel, 1968). However, it cannot go beyond the limitations of the original tests or measures. And what comes out of the analysis depends on many decisions by the investigator (e.g., in the type of factor analysis he or she conducts). Consequently, while the factor analytic search for hypothesized underlying traits may yield mathematically pure factors, their psychological meaningfulness and relevance for the person's actual behavior has to be demonstrated. Factor analysis does not reveal the basic traits of persons any more than it reveals the nature of the knowledge in the books in the library sample when the librarian is sorting them into different categories (e.g., psychology, chemistry, dictionaries).

Are Traits Causal Explanations or Descriptive Summaries?

The most enduring and difficult question at the trait level of analysis concerns the causal status of traits. The question is, do traits, when defined and studied in the ways described in this chapter, really serve to explain individual differences or do they simply provide useful ways to measure and describe those observed differences on the dimensions selected by the researchers? In other words, the same problems may arise that were discussed earlier in this chapter under "trait attributions" when trait terms are used to explain the causes of the very behavior that is being described in everyday common speech: Ronnie's roommate is behaving in a lazy way, never doing the chores expected, and to explain it to her friend, Ronnie says "it's because she's lazy."

Sensitive to this potential circularity when traits are used as causal explanations, not all theorists working at this level of analysis view traits as causes. Buss and Craik (1983) are a notable case in point. They moved away from the traditional trait view of dispositions as underlying internal causes (or explanations) of cross-situational consistencies in behavior. Instead, they see dispositions like the Big Five as summary statements of **act trends** or behavioral trends, not explanations. In this view, dispositions are natural categories made up of various acts. The acts within a category differ in the degree to which they are prototypical or ideal members. Most importantly, this view of dispositions emphasizes that dispositions do not provide explanations of behavior; instead, they are summary statements of behavioral trends that must themselves be explained (Buss & Craik, 1983; Wiggins, 1980).

3.20 What did Buss and Craik suggest about a causal interpretation of personality traits?

This revised view of dispositions reflects attempts to take account of the explanatory limitations of classical global trait theories like Allport's (1937), which have been widely criticized for several decades (Mischel, 1968; Ross & Nisbett, 1991; Wiggins, 1980). It is a revision, however, that is by no means completely shared: some voices still call for a return to the earlier approach to traits as global entities that provide adequate explanations (Funder, 1991). And it is common for theorists and researchers (e.g., McCrae & Costa, 1999) within the modern trait approach to view traits like those in the Five Factor Model as causal entities and explanations of behavior as Epstein (1994), Mischel and Shoda (1994), Pervin (1994), and many others noted in a special journal issue devoted to these concerns (e.g., Pervin, 1994).

Reacting against this trend to act as if trait descriptions provide causal explanations of underlying mechanisms, Block (1995), while himself a major contributor to the trait-dispositional level of personality, provided a detailed analysis of the confusion this usage creates. He showed both logically and technically why labeling a person's position (e.g., low on "Conscientiousness") with regard to the Big Five, or on any other descriptive taxonomy, is unjustified and does not provide any understanding of the personality processes that underlie and account for the labeled phenomena that need to be clarified.

Links between Perceiver and Perceived: Valid Ratings

Finally, one of the important concerns about the usefulness of trait ratings, like those used to find the Big Five, for many years was that they may reflect the social stereotypes and concepts of the judges rather than the trait organization of the rated persons. Mulaik (1964), for example, conducted three separate factor analytic studies, using many trait-rating scales, to determine the degree to which the method reveals the subject's personality factors as opposed to the rater's conceptual factors. The judges in one study rated real persons on the scales, including family members, close acquaintances, and themselves. In a second study, they rated stereotypes like "suburban housewife," "mental patient," and "Air Force general." The raters in the third study rated the "meaning" of 20 trait words. There was much similarity between the factors found for ratings of real persons and those found for ratings of stereotypes and words. Results like these led many investigators to conclude that personality factors that emerge from ratings may reflect the raters' conceptual categories rather than the traits of the subjects being judged (Mischel, 1968; Peterson, 1968).

3.21 What evidence exists that trait ratings may be influenced by stereotypes and preconceptions? Cite research evidence that trait ratings can nonetheless predict independent behavior ratings reflecting the same traits.

It is quite possible that raters' stereotypes and preconceptions enter into these ratings, and it is also the case that different investigators may arrive at somewhat different views of trait organization. Nevertheless, a few basic trait dimensions have been found over and over again, as the evidence for the Big Five makes clear. And, most importantly, the characterizations of people on these dimensions, based on ratings by peers, reasonably agree with the self-ratings of the rated individuals themselves (e.g., McCrae & Costa, 1987). Thus, even if stereotypes and oversimplifications enter into these judgments, as they probably do, they are made reliably, shared widely, and seem significantly linked to qualities of the rated persons (Funder & Colvin, 1997).

Consequently there are many applications of the Big Five. The Big Five measures have been especially popular in the corporate domain, especially to try to predict a candidate's job performance. Several reviews concluded that Big Five factors are related to job performance (Hogan, 1991; Schmidt, Ones, & Hunter, 1992), with implications for personnel selection. Barrick and Mount (1991), for example, concluded that a high level of Conscientiousness was a valid predictor of success for all jobs. Tett and colleagues (1991) showed that the ability of Agreeableness to predict job success depended on the particular job requirements. Interestingly, some personality measures do better at predicting job performance over other, more cognitive ability measures (McHenry et al., 1990). This suggests that a person with lower intellectual abilities may outperform another person with higher abilities due to the nature of his or her personality characteristics (see Goldberg, Grenier, Guion, Sechrest, & Wing, 1991). People whose personality is compatible with job requirements are likely to perform better than people whose personality is incompatible.

Summary

In sum, there has been extensive debate about the limitations and usefulness of trait ratings and the meaning of the trait factors found with them (e.g., Block, 1995; Block, Weiss, & Thorne, 1979; Pervin, 1994; Romer & Revelle, 1984; Shweder,

1975). Nevertheless, it is clear that the descriptions of people obtained from different raters in different contexts often agree with each other. This basic conclusion was reached more than four decades ago and still stands. To illustrate, in one classic study, agreement was found between peer judgments on dimensions of aggressive and dependent behavior and separate behavior ratings of actual aggressive and dependent behavior (Winder & Wiggins, 1964). Participants were first classified into high, intermediate, and low groups on aggression and dependency on the basis of their peer reputations. Separate behavior ratings made later indicated that the three groups differed from each other significantly in the amount of aggression and dependency they displayed in an experimental situation. Similarly, college students were preselected as extremely high or low in aggressiveness (on the basis of ratings by their peers). They tended to be rated in similar ways by independent judges who observed their interaction (Gormly & Edelberg, 1974). Thus, there are linkages between a rater's trait constructs and the behavior of people he or she rates (e.g., Funder & Colvin, 1997; Jackson & Paunonen, 1980; McCrae & Costa, 1987; Mischel, 1984).

For many years, most researchers studied either the judgments of the perceiver or the behavior of the perceived; they rarely considered the fit between the two. One study tried to relate observers' overall judgments of children's aggressiveness (and other traits) to the children's independently coded actual behavior (Mischel, 1984; Wright & Mischel, 1987). Specifically, their trait-related acts were recorded during repeated observation periods on 15 separate occasions distributed across three camp situations during a summer. Examples of behaviors coded as aggressive are: "I'm gonna punch your face" or "Let's go beat up . . ." or lifting a dog by his collar and choking him.

The first question was: Do raters' judgments of the child's overall aggression relate to the actual frequency of the child's aggressive acts as coded by other independent observers? The results clearly answered the question: Yes. Thus, children who are rated by independent observers as more aggressive, actually tend to be aggressive more frequently. For instance, they yelled and provoked more. Most interesting, however, was that these differences were seen only in certain situations, namely in those stressful situations that greatly taxed or strained the competencies of the children.

One needs to recognize the constraints and limitations of work at the broad super trait level of analysis, but also to appreciate its important contributions. In thinking about the meaning and uses of traits, keep in mind that even if traits like the Big Five don't explain why people behave as they do, they are valuable for many goals. Such terms are used by people in daily life to characterize and evaluate themselves and other persons. These personality judgments have links to the judged person's actual behavior, although that behavior may be visible only in certain types of situations in which the relevant individual differences emerge. They are providing a common map for comparing individuals, groups, and even cultures on meaningful dimensions or factors of trait terms. And they raise fascinating questions about the possible bases of these traits, their functions, and the ways they are expressed in behavior in the life course.

Interaction of Traits and Situations

It has become increasingly recognized that a comprehensive approach to the study of traits must deal seriously with how the qualities of the person and the situation influence each other—that is, their "interaction" (Higgins, 1990; Magnusson, 1990; Mischel & Shoda, 1998). The behavioral expressions of a person's traits depend on his or her psychological situation at the moment. For example, rather than exhibit aggression widely,

3.22 How can the study of interactions between traits and situations contribute to an understanding of personal individuality?

an individual may be highly aggressive but only under some set of relatively narrow circumstances, such as when psychological demands are very high (Shoda, Mischel, & Wright, 1994; Wright & Mischel, 1987). Moreover, this aggressiveness may be expressed in some ways (e.g., verbally) but not in others (e.g., physically). The implications of these specific interactions for contemporary personality theory will become evident when we consider the topic of interaction and the nature of consistency in the next chapter.

▶ SUMMARY

TYPES AND TRAITS

- Personality types refer to discrete categories of people that have similar features of characteristics (physically, psychologically, or behaviorally).
- Carl Jung divided people into two types: introverts (withdrawn, shy) and extroverts (sociable, outgoing).
- Traits are basic, stable qualities of the person. Unlike types, traits are continuous dimensions on which individual differences may be arranged.
- Trait theorists conceptualize traits as underlying properties, qualities, or processes that exist in persons.
- Trait constructs have been used to account for observed behavioral consistencies within persons and for the behavioral differences among them.

TRAIT THEORISTS

- In Gordon Allport's theory, traits are the general and enduring mental structures that account for consistency in behavior.
- According to Allport, traits range from highly generalized cardinal traits to secondary traits or more specific "attitudes."
- For Allport, "personality structure" is the individual's stable pattern of unique dispositions or traits, and he urged the intensive study of the individual.
- R. B. Cattell distinguished between surface and source traits, environmental-mold and constitutional traits, and general and specific traits.
- Through factor analysis, Cattell tried to estimate the basic dimensions or factors underlying surface variations in behavior.
- According to Hans J. Eysenck, individual differences can be measured on two, continuous trait dimensions: introversion–extroversion and emotional stability–neuroticism.

COMMON FEATURES OF TRAIT-LEVEL ANALYSES

- Trait theorists assume traits to be general, underlying dispositions that account for consistencies in behavior.
- Some view traits as causes and explanations for behaviors; others interpret them as summaries of behavioral tendencies.
- Some traits are considered to be relatively superficial and specific; others are more basic and widely generalized.
- Traits are seen as enduring, stable qualities of the person over long time periods, while states refer to qualities that are brief in duration and attributable to external causes.
- This level of analysis tries to identify and measure the individual's position on one or more dispositional dimensions.
- Psychometric strategy is used to sample, quantify, and compare the responses of large groups of people to discover basic traits.
- To test the stability of a given trait, psychologists sample the individual's behavior over the course of multiple situations.

TAXONOMY OF HUMAN ATTRIBUTES

- The psycholexical approach to personality categorizes natural-language trait terms in order to describe and understand basic human qualities.
- The "Big Five" identified five primary dimensions of personality through factor analysis: Neuroticism, Extraversion, Openness to new experience, Agreeableness, and Conscientiousness.
- Each of the five dimensions (or factors) includes specific personality characteristics represented as adjectives on a bipolar scale (e.g., quiet–talkative, suspicious–trusting).
- The NEO-PI-R is a widely used personality inventory designed to rate individuals on these Big Five factors.
- Certain life outcomes such as juvenile delinquency, academic achievement, longevity, and interracial attitudes can be predicted by Big Five trait measures.
- Trait research focuses on correlations among trait ratings obtained from self-reports, paper-and-pencil inventories, and questionnaires. The results often show significant stability in traits over time and between independent raters.
- There is increasing recognition that the qualities of the person interact with those of the situation(s) in which he or she functions.

► KEY TERMS

ability traits 53
act trends 67
Agreeableness (A) 60
Big Five Structure 60
cardinal traits 51
central traits 51
common traits 51
Conscientiousness (C) 60
constitutional traits 52
domain of interpersonal behavior 59
dynamic traits 53
emotional stability 55
environmental-mold traits 52
Extraversion (E) 60
extraverts 46
factor analysis 59
introverts 46
multiple-act criterion 57
NEO-PI-R 60
Neuroticism (N) 60
Openness to experience (O) 60
prototypicality 63
psycholexical approach 58
secondary dispositions 51
source traits 52
super traits 61
surface traits 52
temperament traits 53
traits 46
trait approach 45
trait structure 51
unique traits 51

CHAPTER 4

THE EXPRESSIONS OF DISPOSITIONS

Carmen and Dolores are both moderately high on measures of extraversion and their total scores on that scale are similar. But those who know the two well also see a distinctive difference between their patterns of typical behavior. Carmen is more outgoing in big groups and you count on her to be the center of attention and the life of the party at campus events. When with just a few people having dinner, however, she tends to be more on the quiet side. She also seems to have many casual acquaintances but few intimate friends that she really relates to. Dolores, in contrast, is at her warmest in one-on-one relations—she is the close friend you are sure to have fun with when in a small group or just going out together for the evening.

Do differences like these tell us something about the nature of traits and dispositions? This chapter examines that question, and the answers have yielded some surprises. In Chapter 3 we saw that people differ on many personality dimensions. Some people may be perceived as distinctly more benevolent, benign, congenial, cordial, generous, good-humored, gracious, likable, sociable, and welcoming than others. Observers tend to agree with each other about peoples' personal qualities. And these qualities are stable over time, sometimes over many decades. Is there also a distinctive *pattern* in the behaviors individuals engage in, and the thoughts and feelings they express characteristically? What are these patterns and what do they mean? In what ways are one person's behavior patterns distinct from those of other people? This chapter explores the question of the regularities and distinctiveness that exist in the observable patterns of thoughts, feelings, and behaviors that characterize different individuals and types.

▶ TRAITS, SITUATIONS, AND THE PERSONALITY PARADOX

Individual Differences in Behavior Tendencies

Some people may be more likely to behave in a friendly manner, some tend to behave more aggressively than others, some often show disagreeable behavior—the list of individual differences in behavior tendencies is long. And for every type of behavior, one also can think of a corresponding personal quality that makes a person display that behavior more often, or more strongly, than other people. Think of adjectives that describe a type of behavior: helpful, kind, agreeable, conscientious, or aggressive. For every adjective like that there is a noun that refers to a personal quality: helpfulness, kindness, agreeableness, conscientiousness, and aggressiveness. In fact, for any given type of behavior, one can hypothesize a corresponding personal quality that leads people to enact it. The grammatical convention in English makes it easy to name these qualities: just attach *-ness* at the end of the adjective.

The Intuitive Assumption of Consistency

As you saw in Chapter 3, people differ in their personality characteristics, and many if not all of such characteristics do take the form of xxx-ness, where xxx refers to a type of behavior. It seems obvious that people differ reliably in their tendency to display any given type of behavior. So, if you meet a person who behaves in a very friendly manner, you might think she has a friendly personality, and expect that next time you see her, she will behave in a friendly way also. That is, to the extent that people differ reliably in their tendency to display a behavior, we expect them to behave in a similar way in a variety of situations. Of course our behaviors do vary from one situation to another; everyone is more somber when her softball team has suffered a season-ending loss in a close game, compared to winning a championship. But the person who is particularly excited after her team's success may be the one who manages to find something to laugh about in a crushing loss. In short, if in one situation a person displays more of behavior X than other people, then we expect her, in other situations as well, to display more of that behavior than other people.

4.1 What was the surprising result of research on the consistency of behavior across situations? What did behavioral specificity suggest about personality dispositions?

So many trait theorists were surprised and distressed by the results when in the 1960s and 1970s researchers studied not just peoples' self-reports about what "they are like," but rather looked at what they actually did specifically in different situations. These studies examined the **cross-situational consistency** in behavior, that is, the individual's consistency across different types of situations (e.g., from home to school to work). This literature, beginning in the 1920s (e.g., Hartshorne & May, 1928; Newcomb, 1929), and many times later (e.g., Mischel, 1968; Mischel & Peake, 1982; Pervin, 1994; Peterson, 1968; Shoda, 1990; Vernon, 1964), showed cross-situational consistency was much less than expected. This was found for such traits as rigidity, social conformity, dependency, and aggression; for attitudes to authority; and for virtually any other personality dimension (Mischel, 1968; Pervin, 1994; Peterson, 1968; Vernon, 1964). The gist of these findings was that the aggressive child at home may be less aggressive than most when in school; the man exceptionally hostile when rejected in love may be unusually tolerant about criticism of his work; the one who melts with anxiety in the doctor's office may be a calm mountain climber; the high risk-taking entrepreneur may take few social risks.

Thus although intuitively we assume that individuals do differ consistently in the kinds of behavioral tendencies that they exhibit in many different situations, on close observation it turns out that this is often not the case. When this discrepancy between intuition and data was recognized it became a challenge to the field that deeply influenced its future course (Mischel, 1968, 1973, 2004).

The 1968 Challenge

The reaction was most intense when Mischel (1968) challenged the field by concluding that although overall cross-situational consistency in behavior was not zero, it was much less than had been assumed traditionally at the trait level of analysis. Most disturbing to the field at the time was that Mischel (1968, 1973) suggested these findings reflected not just limitations in the methods that have been used but also in the core assumptions about the nature of consistency and coherence in personality. The question then became: Where is the consistency of personality that intuitively seems to characterize individuals?

The Paradox Defined

4.2 How did the personality paradox create conflict in the field of personality while promoting the position of situationism?

The Mischel (1968) book *Personality and Assessment* created a challenge that upset the field of personality for many years and generated what Bem and Allen (1974) called the **personality paradox**: Namely, the data from extensive research indicated low cross-situational consistency of behavior. Nevertheless, human intuition, and a long tradition of Western thought dating to the ancient Greeks, led to the conviction that the opposite was true. Which one was right, the research or the intuition? A long **person versus situation debate** resulted and persisted for many years.

The Person versus Situation Debate

This debate consisted of a prolonged and heated controversy about personality traits, consistency, and the role of the situation that consumed much of the agenda of personality psychology in the 1970s and early 1980s.

Situationism

At the height of the debate, many social psychologists amassed evidence for the power of the situation as the main determinant of behavior. Some also argued that often the situation is so powerful that individual differences and personality don't make much difference. The emphasis on the power of situational variables, and the belief that personality was less important than the situation, was named **situationism**. This view also proposed that laypeople tend to make erroneous explanations of the causes of other people's behavior. The error is that they systematically neglect the role of the situation and instead invoke personality dispositions as favorite—but incorrect—explanations of social behavior (e.g., Nisbett & Ross, 1980). Called the **fundamental attribution error**, the tendency to focus on dispositions in causal explanations soon was seen as a mistake committed by laypersons in everyday life, as well as by the psychologists who study them (Ross, 1977).

4.3 What is the fundamental attribution error? How was it used to promote situationism?

Evidence of systematic judgmental errors in personality assessment and inferences, of course, had been noted often in the past. Before, however, the limitations of judgments about personality had been dismissed as merely due to unreliable, imperfect methods, open to correction by improving the quality of measurement. Now, instead, they were read as reflecting human nature (e.g., Nisbett & Ross, 1980). In its most extreme form, some critics argued that personality was mostly a fictitious construction in the mind of the perceiver (e.g., Shweder, 1975).

Revival of the Traditional Paradigm

At the opposite pole, many personality psychologists renewed even more intensely their efforts to retain the traditional paradigm for the study of traits. In the early 1980s, a resurgence of the factor analytic approach occurred in the study of traits, as was described in Chapter 3. It was founded on an agreement among many researchers to reach a consensus concerning the set of major traits or basic dispositions needed for a comprehensive taxonomy of personality using factor analyses based on trait ratings, in the form of the "Big Five" (e.g., McCrae & Costa, 1999). Many similar factor analytic studies and taxonomies had been done in earlier years, and their strengths and limitations had been duly noted (e.g., Fiske, 1994; Mischel, 1968; Peterson, 1968). The difference now was that they agreed about what those factors were and proposed that the Big Five at least approximated the basic structure of personality. It turned out that this consensus actually was a useful way to revitalize enthusiasm for the study of traits, by showing the usefulness of the broad trait level of analysis for many goals, as you saw in the last chapter.

The Role of the Situation

To understand this debate and the passions it stirred requires a quick look at the history of personality psychology. Since the inception of the field a century ago, the trait level of analysis was mostly devoted to studying the person apart from the situation. In contrast, the field of social psychology was devoted to understanding the general effects and power of situations regardless of individual differences. In that framing, in social psychology the person became the **error variance**—the noise—that had to be removed. In contrast, in personality psychology it was believed that one had to remove the effects of situations—and treat them as noise or error—in order to glimpse the true situation-free personality that remained consistent.

Given the way that the mission of personality and social psychology as disciplines was defined then, many personality psychologists heard a strong argument for the importance of the situation as trying to undermine personality as a field and as a construct. In contrast, many social psychologists hailed evidence for the power of the situation and interpreted it as pointing to the relative insignificance of individual differences in personality. The mistaken belief that to the degree that the person was important, the situation was not, and vice versa, led to the unfortunate person versus situation debate. Its resolution is discussed throughout the remainder of this chapter.

▶ INCORPORATING SITUATIONS INTO TRAITS

If we accept that people's behaviors vary widely across situations, how do we reconcile that with our intuitive conviction that each individual is characterized by stable and distinctive qualities? What remains consistent through the changing stream of thoughts, feelings, and behaviors? How might one capture what is constant? The finding of large variations in a person's behaviors across situations challenged the ultimate goal of personality psychology, which is to identify the coherence and stability that underlie individuals' thoughts, feelings, and behaviors.

Within the patterns of variation shown by an individual, however, there may be a distinctive temporal order, a stable pattern over time that is unique to each person. On the surface, the thoughts, feelings, and behaviors of an individual may vary considerably, and this may appear to go against the assumption that personality is relatively invariant or consistent over time and across situations. But when we look beneath the surface, and focus on just how the variation occurs, and on what external and internal situations it depends, there may be a regular pattern that is distinctive for each individual (e.g., Brown & Moskowitz, 1998; Fleeson, 2001; Larsen & Kasimatis, 1990).

When Gordon Allport founded the field of personality in 1937, he wanted to make the search for such patterns in the stream of behavior central. He urged, "... the constant return to the observable stream of behavior, the only basic datum with which the psychology of personality has to work...." And further: "Unless full recognition is given to this continuous, variable and convergent character of behavior, the theory of traits will become a purely fanciful doctrine of "little men within the breast ..." (Allport, 1937, p. 313). At first, Allport's hopes and warnings seemed to fall on deaf ears. Perhaps they were expressed too early in the field's development to be realized, and that may still have been true when a similar challenge and questions were raised 30 years later (Mischel, 1968; Peterson, 1968). Qualitative case studies and life histories and narrative accounts, or direct observations of one person tracked across diverse situations, of course were possible. They were informative, and done in clinical case studies and life histories, particularly in work at the psychodynamic and the phenomenological levels of analysis (see also McAdams, 2006; Runyan, 2005, in press), as later chapters discuss. But quantitative studies of the behavior of many individuals systematically observed across a set of situations over multiple occasions in the natural stream of behavior were rare, and for a good reason. Because they demanded extremely extensive observation of social behavior as it unfolds naturally, sampled repeatedly, such work could not be done until video cameras and adequate computers became available. With these tools in hand in the early 1980s, such studies became possible (e.g., Mischel & Peake, 1982; Mischel & Shoda, 1995; Shoda, Mischel, & Wright, 1993, 1994).

If ... Then ... Situation–Behavior Signatures

The situations in which particular behaviors do and don't occur can be informative, as illustrated in a simple analogy with the diagnosis of problems in an automobile (see *In Focus 4.1*). In both people and machines, when the situation changes, so do the behaviors, but the relationship between the situations and behaviors may be stable, and informative. In the case of people, it can tell us a lot about the underlying personality system. For instance, suppose two professors on the whole display the same average amount of sociability. However, the first one is extremely sociable and warm with students but unfriendly and cold with colleagues. In contrast, the second professor shows the opposite pattern, and is unfriendly and disinterested with students but very sociable with colleagues. Research indicates that many people are reliably characterized by such patterns. Such profiles seem to constitute a sort of **signature of personality** that does reflect some of the essence of personality coherence and promises to provide a route to glimpse the underlying system that generates them (Mischel & Shoda, 1995; Shoda, Mischel, & Wright, 1994).

4.4 What are behavioral signatures? How does this "*if ... then ...*" concept preserve the coherence and consistency of personality?

IN FOCUS 4.1

LOOKING UNDER THE HOOD

Like people, automobiles also can easily be described on many trait-like dimensions (Epstein, 1994). Are they gas guzzlers or economical? Are they clunky or speedy? Silent or noisy? Generalizations like that can be very useful in orienting buyers toward a particular kind, but only provide remote, indirect cues about the *mechanisms* that produce these differences—about what is going on under the hood (Cervone, 2005).

Every car owner knows this, and realizes that when experts want to understand anything about the characteristics of a car—for example, its "noisiness"—they try to diagnose the *conditions* under which the particular noises occur: *When* does the car emit that particular screeching sound? Only when it's accelerating (loose fan belt)? Or only when trying to shift gears (transmission issue)? Information about how the car behaves in relation to different driving situations provides diagnostic information about the car itself.

Likewise, a focus on the conditions under which an individual behaves in a particular way can be basic for understanding personal dispositions and give insights about what is underlying the behavior. As described in the text, even if two individuals display the same overall average level of behavior, depending on the pattern of *where* it is displayed, one may reach drastically different inferences about the individual (Kammrath, Mendoza-Denton, & Mischel, 2005; Mendoza-Denton, 1999; Plaks, Shafer, & Shoda, 2003; Shoda & Mischel, 1993). Consider, for example, the dimension of "dependability." Suppose Joan is dependable when it comes to work, consistently putting it above all else, but her friends and family know they cannot count on her for social or family obligations. Jane, on the other hand, is extremely dependable when it comes to interpersonal obligations, but is late and sloppy when it comes to her work. Even though, on average, both might be seen or rated as equally dependable, their distinct patterns—if observed repeatedly and across multiple samples of situations—may be highly informative about differences in their motivations, goals, and values (Hong & Mallorie, 2004; Mendoza-Denton, Ayduk, Shoda, & Mischel, 1997).

To give another example, in situation A, people rarely initiate personal interactions, while in situation B, they commonly do so. Suppose also that Mark tends to become irritated when he thinks he is being ignored (likely to happen in situation A), whereas April is happier when she is left alone and even becomes irritated when people tell her personal stories about themselves (which happens often in situation B). Then Mark will become irritated in situation A, but not in situation B, and April will show the opposite ***if . . . then . . .* pattern**, annoyed if B, but not if A. These feelings further activate other thoughts and feelings in each situation in a characteristic pattern for each individual. If so, then even if both people have similar overall levels of irritability, they will generate distinctive, predictable *if . . . then . . .* patterns.

The point is that an individual's personality may be seen not only in the overall average frequency of particular types of behavior shown but also in when and where that behavior occurs. The *if . . . then . . .* patterns of situation–behavior relationships that unfold—if they are stable—can then provide a key to the personality. Thus, an expression of personality coherence is eliminated when the situation is removed by aggregating the behavior across different situations or by ignoring the situation altogether.

Evidence for Signatures Indicative of Personality Types

Researchers have tested this proposition and found clear support for it (Shoda, Mischel, & Wright, 1989, 1993a, 1993b, 1994). In these studies, children were systematically observed for more than 150 hours per child in a residential summer camp setting over the course of 6 weeks (e.g., Shoda et al., 1993b, 1994).

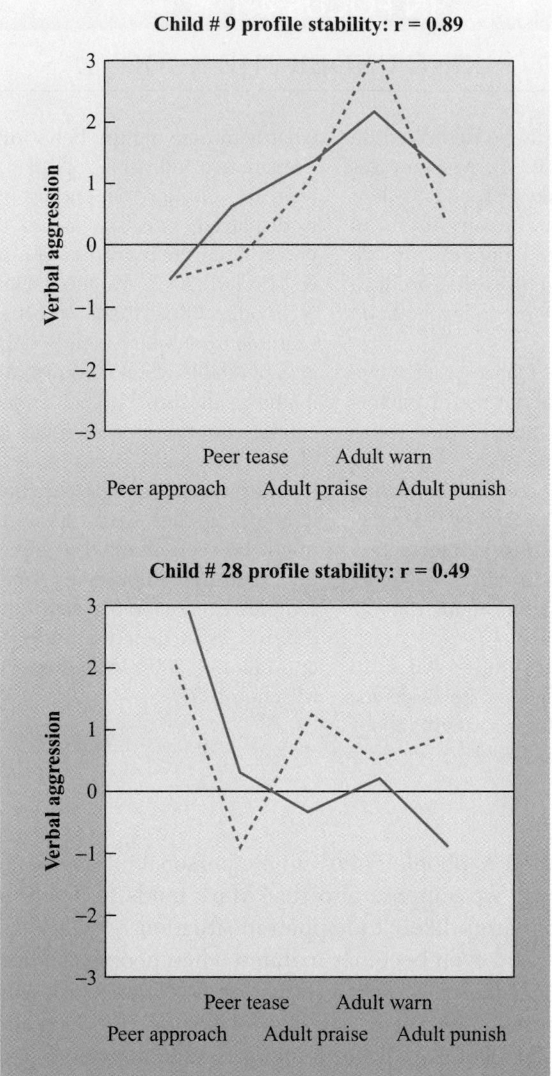

Figure 4.1 Individual *if . . . then . . .* situation–behavior signatures for two children. Their aggressive behavior was observed in five different situations many times. Half of the observations are shown as dotted lines, half as solid lines. Profile stability is the correlation between the two sets of observations.

Source: Shoda, Y., Mischel, W., & Wright, J. C. Intra-individual stability in the organization and patterning of behavior: Incorporating psychological situations into the idiographic analysis of personality. *Journal of Personality and Social Psychology,* 67, 674–687, fig. 1. © 1994 by the American Psychological Association. Adapted with permission.

As predicted, children tended to display stable, distinctive patterns of *if . . . then . . .* relationships. To illustrate (Figure 4.1), some children were consistently more verbally aggressive than others when warned by an adult, but were much less aggressive than most when their peers approached them positively. In contrast, another group of children with a similar overall average level of aggression was distinguished by a striking and opposite *if* . . . *then* . . . pattern: they were more aggressive than any other children when peers approached them positively, but were exceptionally unaggressive when warned by an adult (Shoda et al., 1994). A child who regularly becomes aggressive when peers try to play with him is quite different from one who expresses aggression mostly to adults who try to control him, even if both are equal in their overall aggressive behavior. In short, stable *if* . . . *then* . . . personality signatures, not just stable levels of average overall behavior, were found to characterize individuals, and their patterns seem to be meaningful reflections of the personality system. Evidence for such behavioral signatures has now been obtained even when using very different methods in adult participants in a major German observational study of twins (Borkenau, Reimann, Spinath, & Angleitner, 2006), and in diverse other samples (e.g., Fournier, Moskowitz, & Zuroff, in press).

To summarize, individuals differ stably in their distinctive *if* . . . *then* . . . strategies and behavior patterns. Consequently, they will behave in their characteristic ways within a given type of situation, but they will *vary* their behavior predictably when the "if" changes, thus producing behavioral variability across situations. Then, by aggregating behavior across situations in their search for broad behavioral dispositions, researchers risk eliminating the distinctive individuality and stability that they are trying to find! Like their handwritten counterpart, behavioral signatures can be seen as an expression of individuality that identifies the person. To illustrate this more concretely, Gary W.'s behavioral signatures are summarized next.

Gary W.'s Behavioral Signatures

Gary's behavior depends on the situation as well as on the type of behavior involved. For example, while he may respond pessimistically and with defensive withdrawal in many interpersonal situations, when tasks call for quantitative skills he is self-confident and optimistic. And while on average Gary is not a "generally aggressive person," he does have disruptive outbursts of anger, especially when he feels ignored or rejected. It is notable that, *if* Gary feels provoked or threatened in an intimate relationship with a woman, *then* he becomes vulnerable to outbursts of rage. On the other hand, *if* he feels secure, *then* he can be extremely caring. Such *if* . . . *then* . . . relationships provide a window for seeing Gary's unique but stable patterns, the "signature" of his personality. In short, this perspective emphasizes that both the person and the situation need to be considered when trying to predict and understand individuals and the important, consistent ways they differ from each other.

Consider the differences between Gary W. (dotted line) and Charles W. his older brother (solid line). Figure 4.2 illustrates their self-reported (in daily diaries) emotional states (from extremely stressed, upset, and negative affect at the top of the scale to extremely pleased and positive at the bottom). As the figure shows, Gary and Charles are similar in becoming very upset in situation 1. This is when they feel "provoked or threatened" in close personal relations with women. They differ, however, in the other events that upset them most. In situation 2, public speaking (e.g., in seminar presentations), Gary becomes distressed; Charles enjoys those occasions and looks forward to them. Likewise, while Gary becomes extremely unhappy and "mad" when he gets negative feedback about his work (situation 4), Charles readily dismisses complaints from unhappy patients or colleagues as "part of the grumbling you have to expect. . . . There are always people you can't please." Interestingly, the pattern reverses when the brothers must deal with quantitative work problems (situation 3), for example, when writing research reports in their technical specialties. Gary finds those tasks a "real high—a challenge"; Charles experiences them as anxiety-provoking, fearing that his

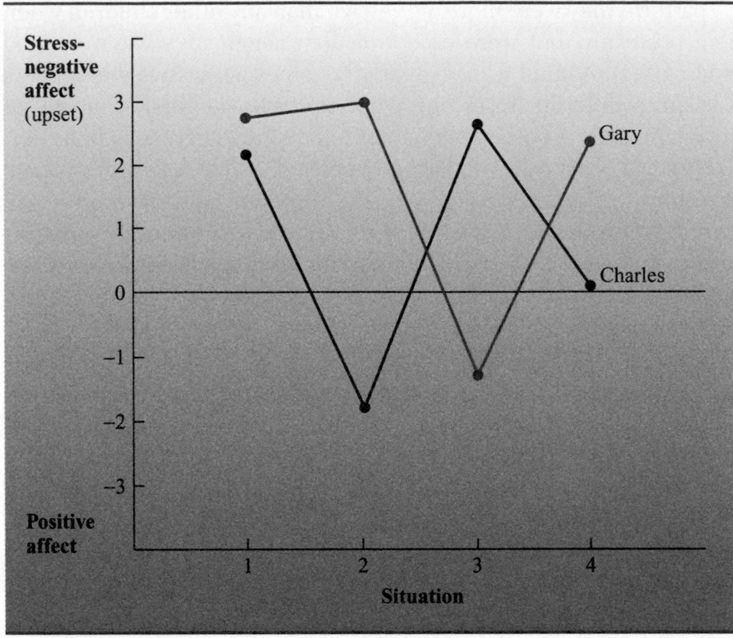

Figure 4.2 Illustrative *if . . . then . . .* signatures. Self-reported stress and emotion, for Gary and Charles, in four situations (sampled repeatedly in daily diaries for 3 months).

inadequate grasp of the quantitative method he uses in his medical research will be revealed.

Two Types of Consistency

In sum, consistency can be found in personality and in behavior in relation to situations, and it has been found, but not where many researchers had long been looking for it. The consistency in personality they were looking for is found in two different forms or types, and both need to be considered together to see the coherence and stability that characterizes individuals. Each gives an incomplete picture when considered alone. Each type has its distinctive uses, advantages, and limitations. When both types are taken into account the personality paradox noted at the start of this chapter dissolves.

4.5 Differentiate between Type 1 and Type 2 consistency.

- ***Type 1: Average overall levels of behavior tendencies.*** The first or "classic" form of consistency is seen in the overall average differences in the levels of typical behavior of different kinds (such as aggressiveness, sociability) that characterize the individual. The trait level of analysis captures these by aggregating indices of what the individual is like and does across many different types of situations, as when people are described with regard to their status on broad factors, as discussed in Chapter 3.
- ***Type 2: If . . . then . . . (situation–behavior) signatures.*** These consistencies are seen in patterns of stable links between types of situations and types of characteristic behavior, as illustrated in the signatures of the aggressive behavior characterizing different individuals in the camp study (Shoda et al., 1993b, 1994), and related research (e.g., Borkenau et al., 2006; Fournier et al., in press; Moskowitz, 1982, 1988, 1994).

Uses of the Two Types of Consistency

Is it more useful to try to infer broad traits or situation-specific signatures? The answer always depends on the particular purpose. Inferences about global traits may have limited value for the practical prediction of a person's specific future behavior in specific situations, or for the design of specific psychological treatment programs to help facilitate constructive change. But broad traits have many other uses. Indeed, they have value for everyday inferences about what other people seem like on the whole, as when you get first impressions about a stranger, or form a quick opinion about a new acquaintance (e.g., McAdams, 1999). With people we know well and who are important to us, however, we also want to know "what makes them tick." Therefore, we try to understand their goals, motivations, and feelings in order to make sense of the *if . . . then . . .* patterns—the personality signatures that characterize them as we get to know them better (Chen-Idson & Mischel, 2001).

4.6 What are the practical advantages of the two methods of studying consistency? What is required in order to obtain Type 1 consistency?

The first type of consistency—average overall behavior tendencies on broad dimensions—can be enhanced by the method of aggregation introduced in the last chapter. In this method, behavior on a dimension is simply averaged across many different situations to estimate the person's overall true level of the characteristic. Bolstered by this method, the case can be made that global dispositions as traditionally conceptualized are "alive and well" if one routinely aggregated multiple observations and measures across different situations. That serves to eliminate the role of the situation by averaging it out. This strategy now acknowledges that specific behaviors across different types of situations could not be predicted by such a model (e.g., Epstein, 1979), and continues to treat the situation as a source of noise by removing it as before. On the positive side, by aggregating the individual's behavior across many different kinds of situations, it is in fact possible to increase greatly the strength of the overall average differences that will be found between individuals "on the whole" for diverse traits (e.g., Epstein, 1983).

Inferences about broad traits also have practical value for gross initial screening decisions (as in personnel selection), studying average differences between groups of individuals in personality research (Block & Block, 1980), or the layman's everyday perception of persons (e.g., Funder & Colvin, 1997; Schneider, 1973; Wright & Mischel, 1988). And as was seen in the last chapter, when measures are combined or aggregated over a variety of situations, one can demonstrate stable differences among individuals in their relative overall standing on many dimensions of social behavior, and these differences have been shown to be related to important life outcomes (e.g., delinquency, longevity).

In sum, overall average differences between individuals can be obtained easily, particularly with rating measures, and used to differentiate among people in "what they are like" on the whole (Funder & Colvin, 1997; Kenrick & Funder, 1988). For other goals, however, more specific levels of analysis that consider *if . . . then . . .* situation–behavior signatures and that take the situation into account may be more useful. The impact of any situation or stimulus depends on the person who experiences it, and different people differ greatly in how they cope with most stimulus conditions. It is a truism that one person's favorite "stimulus" may be the stuff of another's nightmares and that in the same "stimulus situation" one individual may react with aggression, another with love, a third with indifference. Different people may consistently act differently in particular classes of situations, but the particular classes of conditions tend to be narrower than traditional trait theories have assumed (e.g., Cantor, 1990; Cantor & Kihlstrom, 1987; Mischel, 1990). For purposes of important individual decision making, one may need highly individualized assessments of what the specific situations mean to the person.

4.7 In what situations are behavior signatures a more useful way to approach personality consistency? When is it difficult to predict behavior using Type 2 consistency?

The significant consistency that exists is at least in part reflected in stable patterns of behavior *within* similar types of psychological situations (Mischel & Peake, 1982;

Mischel & Shoda, 1995). As the similarity between situations decreases, so does the cross-situational consistency of the person's behavior (Krahe, 1990; Shoda, 1990; Shoda et al., 1994). Then it becomes difficult to predict from what individuals did in one type of situation to what they will do in a very different type of situation. On the other hand, within particular types of situations, individuals do show characteristic stable patterns. These patterns are expressed as stable *if* ... *then* ... relationships, such that when the situation (the "if") remains stable (e.g., if "teased by peers about his glasses and appearance"), then so does the behavior (e.g., he becomes physically aggressive). So for the people we know well, we have a sense not only of what they are like in general (in trait terms) but also of what they are likely to do in particular types of situations (e.g., at the holiday dinner, in an argument about money, on a date).

To illustrate these abstract points more concretely, think again about Gary. It is certainly possible to form some generalizations about his seemingly major qualities, strengths, and problems. Such generalizations help us to differentiate Gary from other people, and to compare him with them. Suppose that we learned, for example, from trait tests that Gary tended to be low on Extraversion, relatively high on Neuroticism and Anxiety, high on Conscientiousness, and intermediate on both Sociability and Open-mindedness scales. Such characterizations may help one to gain a quick overall impression of Gary. But in order to predict what Gary will do in specific situations, or to make decisions about him (as in therapy or vocational counseling), it would be necessary to conduct a much more individually oriented study that considers the specific qualities of Gary as they relate to the specific situations of interest in his life.

Just when does Gary become more—or less—neurotic and anxious? Under what conditions does he *not* avoid close relations with people? When is he likely to be more and less sociable in ways that are distinctive and predictable? The analysis and prediction of specific behavior requires that we ask questions like these to link behavior to conditions, and to capture their distinctive pattern and meaning, in addition to painting personality portraits with more general characterizations that also have their many valuable uses. You also have to ask questions like these if you want to look under the descriptions of behavior in search of the mechanisms and psychological processes that underlie them, as was discussed in *In Focus 4.1*.

▶ INTERACTIONISM IN PERSONALITY PSYCHOLOGY

Interactionism in personality is the idea that the individual's experience and action cannot be understood as the result of separate personal and situational factors. Rather, it is a product of dynamic interactions between aspects of personality and situations (Magnusson, 1999; Magnusson & Endler, 1977; Mischel, 1973). Interactionism focuses on how the expressions of the stable personality system are visible in the person's unique *patterns* of *if* ... *then* ... situation–behavior relationships.

The Meaning of Person–Situation Interaction

In the interactionist view, knowledge of individual differences often tells us more if it is combined with information about the conditions and situational variables that influence the behavior of interest. Conversely, the effects of conditions depend on the individuals in them. Thus, the interaction of individual differences and particular conditions, and not just the individual or the context separately, is important (Bem & Funder, 1978;

Magnusson, 1990; Shoda et al., 1994; Wright & Mischel, 1987). *If . . . then . . .* behavioral signatures of individuals, and those of groups of individuals such as "narcissists," illustrate the basic principles of interactionism.

4.8 What is meant by a person–situation interaction? What does it add to a knowledge of a person's traits?

An Example: Uncertainty Orientation

An example of **person–situation interaction** involving an individual difference dimension comes from research on **uncertainty orientation**. This personality dimension is defined at one end by individuals who are relatively comfortable dealing with uncertainty and strive to resolve it, and on the other end by those who are more uncomfortable with uncertainty and likely to avoid situations that increase their subjective sense of uncertainty (Sorrentino & Roney, 1986, 2000). Now consider this question: Would experiencing a situation in which one didn't have control over the outcome make people approach, rather than avoid, new information? Would students do better on a test if they are told that the test is diagnostic of an important ability? The answers to these questions depend on an individual's uncertainty orientation. For those who are high in uncertainty orientation (i.e., those who are comfortable with uncertainty and seek to master it), the answer is yes to both questions. But for those who are uncomfortable with uncertainty, the answer is very different (Huber, Sorrentino, Davidson, & Epplier, 1992). For example, they do better on a test if they are told it is not diagnostic of important abilities (Sorrentino & Roney, 1986). Further, when individuals low in uncertainty orientation experience uncontrollability, they avoid new information, especially if they are also mildly depressed (Walker & Sorrentino, 2000). So it all depends on the interaction between the type of person with the type of situation: the situation that suits one person may distress another.

4.9 How does research on uncertainty orientation illustrate the value of an interactionist approach?

Note that differences in personality are expressed here not in the overall average behavior tendencies but rather in the different effects of situations, be it the experience of uncontrollability or the perceived meaning of a test. A similar insight was captured in an example Gordon Allport (1937) used (mentioned in Chapter 3). He asked: What is the difference between butter and raw eggs? They differ in the *effect* of cooking heat: as heat increases one softens and melts, but the other one hardens. The question of which is harder *in general* is meaningless unless one specifies the temperature. It results in one answer if the food is in the refrigerator, but another if the food is in the frying pan. Depending on the situations in which participants in a study find themselves, one would make opposite predictions for their behavior. And that, put most simply, is the basic **principle of interactionism**.

Definition of Triple Typology

In a thoughtful analysis of the importance of interactions for personality psychology and for understanding personality dispositions, Daryl Bem (1983) summarized a mission of personality psychology, or any science for that matter, with great simplicity. Whether or not one is studying molecules, plants, or people, there are millions of specific instances of them. A goal of science is to produce a way to categorize them into a manageably small number of *meaningful* categories. Because objects can be categorized in many arbitrary ways, "meaningful" of course is the key concept. In what sense should it be meaningful?

4.10 What is the basic question posed in Daryl Bem's triple typology?

Bem's answer to that question was that a meaningful way to categorize people, behaviors, and situations was one that allows accurate statements in the form "*this type of person will do these types of behaviors in these types of situations.*" This is a **triple typology** in the sense that it classifies together three categories: types of people, types of behavior, and types of situations. A meaningful system of categorizing people, behaviors, and situations is one that allows the personality psychologist to spell out precise *if* . . . *then* . . . regularities in describing types of people. For example, "narcissists" is a meaningful way of categorizing people (e.g., Morf & Rhodewalt, 2001b) that allows one to say, "*if* they encounter situations that can be seen as an opportunity to bolster their grandiose self-concept, *then* they will seek to demonstrate their superiority." Note that the *if* . . . *then* . . . statement describing narcissists already contains references to types of behaviors and types of situations. That is, "seeking to demonstrate their superiority" is a type of behavior, and "situations that can be seen as an opportunity to bolster their grandiose self-concept" is a type of situation. There are meaningful categories of behaviors and situations precisely because they allow a simple description of narcissists in one *if* . . . *then* . . . statement. The practical challenge of course is to find meaningful categories of people, behaviors, and situations.

4.11 Describe the approach taken to produce a triple typology of hostility. What psychological processes underlie the tendency to keep anger in or let it out?

In one promising direction, modern computer technology is beginning to provide hope that a triple typology is in fact attainable. For example, Van Mechelen and his colleagues have devised a computer algorithm that simultaneously tries out many different ways to categorize people, behaviors, and situations. It searches for the best system of typologies that allow the fewest number of *if* . . . *then* . . . statements to describe the data with the least amount of errors (Claes, Van Mechelen, & Vertommen, 2004; Van Mechelen & Kiers, 1999; Vansteelandt & Van Mechelen, 1998). To see how this works, read *In Focus 4.2*.

Interaction as a Rule in Science

Although the concept of interactionism has been controversial in personality psychology, the fact that organisms and environment interact to determine behavior and development is a general conclusion in most sciences dealing with living organisms. In biology, evidence of organism–environment interaction is commonplace. As Lewontin (2000) points out, genetic and environmental influences are intertwined, making development "contingent on the sequence of environments in which it occurs" (p. 20). In the example of plant growth, Lewontin notes that cloned samples of seven different individuals of a given plant species that were grown at different elevations showed little cross-environment consistency in the rank-ordering of their size of mature plants, because a particular plant that flourishes at one altitude may readily have below-average growth in another context. Consequently, one has to represent plant growth not in terms of the average growth tendencies of an individual organism but in graphs that take into account the environment in which the organism develops. To understand plant growth and predict the size of a given plant relative to others, one has to take into account the particular environmental conditions that are present—in other words, one has to identify and understand the *if* . . . *then* . . . contingencies.

4.12 How general is interactionism throughout the sciences? Give some examples.

Other examples abound in the biological sciences, including an analysis of the "plasticity" (modifiability) of neural systems (Edelman, 1992; Kolb & Whishaw, 1998) and the ways in which cultural and biological factors interact in human evolution (Durham, 1991). Ehrlich (2000), focusing on the interplay of genetic endowment and environmental experience, obtained similar findings for the importance of interaction. He concluded that the psychologist's typical strategy of partitioning the determinants of behavioral characteristics into separate genetic versus environmental causes was no more sensible than asking which areas of a rectangle are mostly due to length and which mostly due to width. Yet curiously the implications of interactionism for understanding the multiple cognitive, behavioral, and physiological mechanisms through which personality functions have been extremely difficult to accept in traditional trait-level analyses of personality (as discussed in Cervone & Mischel, 2002, Chap. 1).

IN FOCUS 4.2

A TRIPLE TYPOLOGY FOR HOSTILITY

To test their methodology, the researchers asked study participants to describe what specific responses they would exhibit when faced with a specific type of situation. They chose these situations carefully to get a wide spectrum of potentially frustrating situations in order to obtain a variety of response patterns. Some of the situations they used were: you are in a restaurant and have been waiting a long time to be served (low frustration); you are trying to study and there is incessant noise (moderate frustration); your instructor unfairly accuses you of cheating on an examination (high frustration). The responses provided were also intended to reflect a wide variety of potential hostile responses, such as turning away; wanting to strike something or someone; hands tremble; heart beats faster; cursing; becoming tense; feeling irritated; or becoming enraged (taken from S-R Inventory of Hostility; Endler & Hunt, 1968).

When the data were analyzed by a computer program designed by Van Mechelen and colleagues, the result was a grouping of people, behaviors, and situations. In this classification, Van Mechelen and colleagues found several groups of people, with each group characterized by a set of *if . . . then . . .* statements describing how its members tend to display specific types of behaviors in specific types of situations. For example, one group or "type" was likely to respond to a situation that is highly frustrating by becoming tense, having their heart beat faster, sweating, and having their hands tremble. People of another type would respond to the same type of situations by wanting to strike something, cursing, and becoming tense or irritated. In a situation that is not very frustrating, such as when you accidentally bang your shins against a park bench, neither type of people would respond in a hostile manner. Because these person types directly reflect *if . . . then . . .* behavioral signatures, this sort of typology can be used to predict the probability of a certain type of individual producing certain types of behaviors when faced with a certain type of situation.

After Van Mechelen and his colleagues formulated these typologies, they were able to examine some of the psychological processes that linked the type of person to the type of situation–response patterns they produced. They designed a questionnaire that asked about the participant's interpretation of situations, expectations about the consequences of different types of behavior, and whether they kept their anger in or let it out. These questions were designed to engage thoughts and feelings that were related to hostile and aggressive behavior. For example, participants were asked to agree or disagree with the following statements: "When other people get me in trouble, I rapidly think that they do it on purpose" (interpretation); "I think that, in general, the expression of anger is not appreciated by others" (expectation); "I easily suppress feelings of frustration" (anger-in); "When I feel frustrated, I show it easily" (anger-out) (Vansteelandt & Van Mechelen, 1998). They also asked the participants to fill out a questionnaire designed to measure the participant's ability to tolerate frustration (Van Der Ploeg, Defares, & Spielberger, 1982). The researchers then looked at how the person types related to the presence or absence of each of the types of thoughts and feelings measured.

Their findings showed the feasibility of forming meaningful categories of people, behaviors, and situations simultaneously. They also indicated that the resultant typology provided glimpses into the internal psychological processes that underlie the observed *if . . . then . . .* behavior signatures characteristic of various types. The different types were clearly different in the patterns they used for responding to different types of frustrating situations from very mild to the highly frustrating.

Resolution of the Personality Paradox

If stable *if . . . then . . .* situation–behavior patterns are meaningful reflections of one's personality, they also should be linked to the person's self-perceptions about his or her own consistency. The relationship between the stability of the person–situation profile that characterizes an individual in a particular domain of behavior and the self-perception of consistency has been closely examined. The results directly speak to Bem's classic "personality paradox," which, as you saw earlier, has motivated much of the research agenda in studies at the trait level. As Bem pointed out in the 1970s, while our intuitions convince us that people have broad behavioral dispositions that we believe are seen in extensive consistency in their behaviors across situations, the research results on cross-situational consistency in behavior persistently contradict our intuitions (Bem & Allen, 1974). To try to resolve this dilemma, and prove our intuitions are better than our research, Bem and Allen noted that traditional methodologies assume that all traits belong to all persons. But if a given trait is in fact irrelevant for some people, their inconsistency with regard to it will obscure the consistency of the subset of people for whom the trait is relevant. Therefore, Bem and Allen (1974) reasoned that a solution to the consistency problem requires first selecting only those persons who perceive themselves as consistent in the given disposition. We then should expect to find high cross-situational consistency in their behavior in that domain, but not in the behavior of those who see themselves as inconsistent with regard to it, or to whom it is irrelevant.

4.13 Are self-perceptions of behavioral consistency related to actual consistency? Consistency of what?

Initially, Bem and Allen (1974) obtained some encouraging support for this prediction. A few years later, in a more comprehensive test in a large field study at a midwestern college, researchers observed behavior relevant to "college conscientiousness" and friendliness as it occurred over multiple situations and occasions (Mischel & Peake, 1982). Each of the 63 participating college students were observed repeatedly in various situations on campus relevant to their conscientiousness in the college setting. The specific behaviors and contexts selected as relevant were supplied by undergraduates themselves in pretesting at the college. Conscientious behaviors were sampled (observed) in various situations such as in the classroom, in the dormitory, and in the library, and the assessments occurred over repeated occasions in the course of the semester.

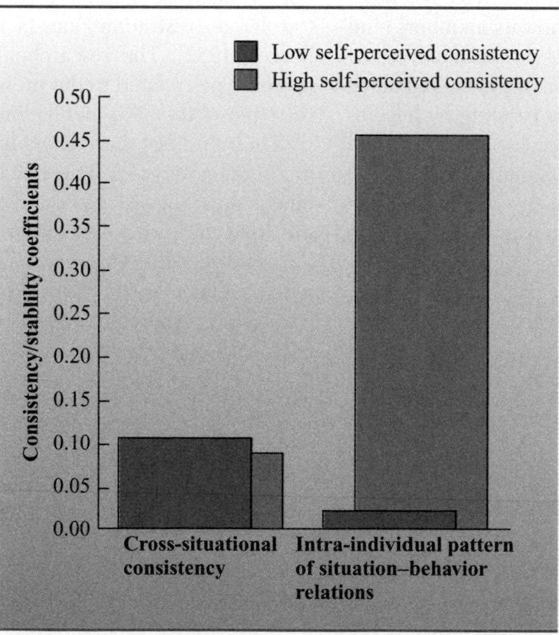

Figure 4.3 Cross-situational consistency and the stability of *if* . . . *then* . . . signatures for people high versus low in self-perceived consistency in conscientiousness. Self-perceived consistency is predicted by stability of the *if* . . . *then* signatures.

Source: Based on data from Mischel, W., & Shoda, Y. (1995). A cognitive-affective system theory of personality: Reconceptualizing situations, dispositions, dynamics, and invariance in personality structure. *Psychological Review, 102*, 246–268.

These data were used to examine the links between the students' self-perceptions of consistency and their actual behavior (Mischel & Shoda, 1995). As the first set of two columns of Figure 4.3 shows, those who perceived themselves as consistent (the first light column) did not show greater overall cross-situational consistency than those who did not. In contrast, the second set of columns clearly supports the hypothesis of coherence in terms of pattern stability: For individuals who perceived themselves as consistent, the average *if* . . . *then* . . . situation–behavior signature stability correlation was near .5, whereas it was trivial for those who saw themselves as inconsistent.

In short, the self-perception of consistency seems to be predictable from the stability in the situation–behavior signatures. That, in turn, indicates that the intuition of personality consistency is not an illusion. But it is based on the stability of the person's specific prototypic behaviors over time, not, as had so long been assumed, on the broad consistency of behavior across many different kinds of situations.

Summary: Expressions of Consistency in Traits–Dispositions

This chapter started with the basic personality paradox as the problem to untangle. To recapitulate, the construct of personality rests on the assumption that individuals are characterized by distinctive qualities that are relatively invariant across situations and over a span of time. This assumption seems also intuitively true. The paradox was that in a century of personality research, evidence showed that individual differences in social behaviors tend to be surprisingly variable across different situations. Research that sought regularities in the patterns of variability has begun to provide a resolution of this paradox. Namely, the variability across situations seen as the person's behavior unfolds across different situations is not simply random fluctuations. Rather, it in part is a stable and meaningful characteristic of an individual that may provide a window into the underlying system that produced them. This type of behavioral signature of personality is lost if one treats the situation as error or noise and eliminates it by simply averaging behavior over diverse situations.

4.14 How does the concept of behavioral signatures help resolve the personality paradox? What does this resolution suggest about how we might view the coherence of personality?

The intuition of consistency in the behavior of the people we know and in ourselves, then, is neither paradoxical nor illusory. It just turns out to be based on a different type of behavioral consistency than the one for which psychologists searched for so many years. Such variability seems to be an essential expression of the enduring underlying personality system itself and its organization. The person–situation debate is resolved not just by recognizing that the person and the situation both are important—a fact that has long been acknowledged. Rather, it dissolves if one thinks of personality in ways that make the predictable variability of behavior across situations an essential aspect of its behavioral expression in the form of meaningful and stable interactions between types of persons and types of situations. Furthermore, as was shown mathematically by Shoda (1990), to the degree that people are characterized by stable and distinctive patterns of variations in their behavior across situations, their level of cross-situational consistency cannot be very high, and we should not expect it to be. Likewise, the "situation" is not necessarily a source of error to be removed in the search for personality. Rather, it is a locus in which personality is expressed and within which it can be more fully understood. The challenging question then becomes: what is the nature of that underlying system and organization that accounts for the two types of behavioral consistency that have been found to characterize people stably? That is the question we continue to pursue in the rest of this text.

SUMMARY

TRAITS, SITUATIONS, AND THE PERSONALITY PARADOX

- Despite intuition and a long tradition of Western thought, researchers found it difficult to show that individuals display highly consistent types of behavior across a variety of different situations.
- In the person–situation debate, it seemed that psychologists had two choices: Either they could view situation information as "noise" that obscures the true, consistent personality, or they could recognize the power of situations, and treat the person as error variance.

INCORPORATING SITUATIONS INTO TRAITS

- Alternatively, psychologists could take into account situational features when interpreting individual behavior patterns.
- Personality may be seen both in the overall average frequency of behaviors and in the link between the type of behavior and the type of situation in which it occurs.
- The *if ... then ...* situation–behavior signatures that have been studied show significant stability. Two types of personality consistency emerge, (1) the average of overall behavioral tendencies and (2) distinctive *if ... then ...* situation–behavior signatures.
- Measures of traits are often not able to predict single acts, but they may predict a pooled combination of behaviors across different situations.
- Knowing what a person does in specific types of situations can help us understand more about the person's underlying personality system.

INTERACTIONISM IN PERSONALITY

- *Interactionism* is the idea that the individual's behaviors are the product of dynamic interactions between personality and the psychological environment.
- Some personality psychologists try to categorize people, situations, and behaviors into triple typologies.
- Biological sciences treat the dynamic interaction between organisms and their environments as a given.
- The intuition of consistency is neither paradoxical nor illusory: Personality coherence is seen in the individual's meaningful, stable situation–behavior signatures.

KEY TERMS

cross-situational consistency 73
error variance 75
fundamental attribution error 74
if ... then ... pattern 77
Interactionism 82
person versus situation debate 74
person–situation interaction 83
personality paradox 74
principle of interactionism 83
signature of personality 76
situationism 74
triple typology 83
uncertainty orientation 83

TAKING STOCK

PART I

THE TRAIT-DISPOSITIONAL LEVEL

▶ OVERVIEW: FOCUS, CONCEPTS, METHODS

As we conclude Part I and the presentation of work at the trait-dispositional level of analysis, we pause to put it in perspective and consider the essence of its contributions. So much has been done within trait-dispositional approaches that it becomes easy to lose the essential characteristics, which are summarized in Table A. The summary reminds you that the main aim of the trait approach was to provide methods to infer and quantify people's social–personal traits. In classic trait theories of personality, these traits were assumed to be stable and broadly consistent dispositions that underlie a wide range of behaviors across a number of related situations. As summarized in Table A, traits are inferred from questionnaires, ratings, and other reports about the subject's dispositions. Usually, the person's self-reports are taken as direct signs of the relevant dispositions. For example, the more often you rate yourself as aggressive, the more you are assumed to have an aggressive disposition. The focus of research is on measurement to develop quantitative ways of finding and describing important stable individual differences. Traditionally, the trait approach has recognized that behavior varies with changes in the situation, but it has focused on individual differences in the overall response tendency averaged across many situations. Individual differences on any given dimension are more visible in some situations than in others, and not all dimensions are relevant for all individuals. Some psychologists within this perspective now view traits as "act trends"—summaries of behavior—rather than as explanations or determinants of behavior.

Increasingly, some theorists and researchers also try to take systematic account of the situation as it interacts with the individual's qualities and are incorporating the

TABLE A Dispositions Expressed as Overall Behavioral Tendencies

Basic units	Inferred trait dispositions
Causes of behavior	Generalized (consistent, stable) dispositions
Behavioral manifestations of personality	Direct indicators of traits
Favored data	Test responses (e.g., on questionnaires); trait ratings including self-ratings
Observed responses used as	Direct signs (indicators) of dispositions
Research focus	Measurement (test construction), description of individual differences and their patterning; taxonomy of traits
Approach to personality change	Not much concerned with change: Search for consistent, stable characteristics
Role of situation	Acknowledged but of secondary interest

TABLE B Dispositions Expressed as *If . . . Then . . .* Behavioral Signatures

Basic units	*If . . . then . . .* behavioral signatures of personality
Causes of behavior	Underlying personality processes/dynamics
Behavioral manifestations of personality	Patterns of behavioral signatures; inconsistencies across different kinds of situations
Favored data	Behavior sampling, situation-specific diaries, field studies of behavior in context as it unfolds naturally, *if . . . then . . .* self-reports, person × situation interactions
Observed responses used as	Indicators of underlying personality processes (e.g., motives, goals)
Research focus	Identifying stable personality signatures and understanding their meaning
Approach to personality change	By understanding the meaning of the personality signatures and modifying them if desired (discussed in Part VII)
Role of situation	Essential; needs to be incorporated into the conception and measurement of dispositions and personality

situation into the conception and assessment of personality dispositions. This alternative approach, summarized in Table B, includes the overall level of a given type of behavior in the study of individual differences. It focuses, however, on the situation-specific expression of traits in the form of stable *if . . . then . . .* situation–behavior signatures of personality. These signatures are seen as a second type of behavioral consistency that needs to be captured in a comprehensive assessment of dispositions. They provide clues to the motives, goals, and other aspects of the personality system that may underlie them. As Table B indicates, that requires sampling behavior in relation to the situations in which it occurs, and leads to alternative methods for measuring and thinking about personality and its expressions.

▶ ENDURING CONTRIBUTIONS OF THE TRAIT-DISPOSITIONAL LEVEL

Research and theory at this level of analysis represents one of the longest and richest research traditions in the study of personality. For a century, it has made essential contributions to the quantification and objective measurement of personality, for evaluating test results and for measuring treatment effects. From the start of the field, it has provided both concepts and methods for describing and comparing human individual differences with regard to a vast array of attributes. Its yield has been great, identifying and quantifying the consistencies that characterize different individuals and types of people on trait dimensions. It now provides reliable taxonomies for describing people, identifying their stable positions on a map of trait factors. The Big Five provides such a map, which is currently state-of-the-art, and there is considerable, although by no means complete, consensus that it usefully captures much or most of the trait domain. It is useful for many goals, enabling descriptions of the broad trait differences that characterize individuals and groups, and it has greatly stimulated research in the area.

It helps psychologists to capture the general gist of what individuals or groups and even cultures "are like on the whole" and to obtain a broad impression that compresses much information.

Nevertheless, work at this level has limitations that even its advocates recognize. Basically, it is not that the work is wrong or technically flawed. The limitation, rather, is that it is only one piece—an extremely important piece—needed for putting together a conception of the whole of personality and all its diverse aspects, and therefore it is incomplete. It offers a first part or stage for an account of personality. Oliver John (1990), a major leader in research on the Big Five, also has been one of its most perceptive critics. He sees that the categories are at such a broad level of abstraction that "they are to personality what the categories 'plant' and 'animal' are to the world of biological objects—extremely useful for some initial rough distinctions, but of less value for predicting specific behaviors of a particular object" (p. 93). An ideal taxonomy, in John's view, needs to be built on causal and dynamic psychological principles and needs to be cast at different levels of abstraction from the broad to the more specific. The rest of this text discusses each of those other levels, and as noted in the Introduction, illustrates their integration in the final part.

The challenge for the trait level will be to connect its work to that coming from the other levels (e.g., John, 2001; Mischel, 2004; Mischel & Shoda, 1998). That also will make it possible to link the individual's position on trait maps to the underlying psychological processes needed to help us understand more about the "why" of personality, that is, to what the mechanisms are that underlie and generate their observed consistencies. Even when we know that someone generally "is a sociable person," for example, the psychologist still needs to explain and understand *why* the person is that way and why and how the psychological and behavioral expressions of his or her sociability take the particular forms that they do.

Work at this level of analysis also has shown that the consistency that characterizes people is seen in their stable *if* . . . *then* . . . patterns, as well as in their overall average levels of different types of behaviors. Thus, within particular types of situations, individuals do show characteristic stable patterns, and these are reflections and expressions of their underlying personalities. Capturing these signatures, clarifying the underlying processes that generate them, and linking them to work at other levels of analysis will be an important piece of the agenda for the future. These signatures, as well as the overall average levels of behavior that characterize the person at the super trait level, will together provide useful windows for studying the underlying organization and nature of personality.

PART 

THE BIOLOGICAL LEVEL

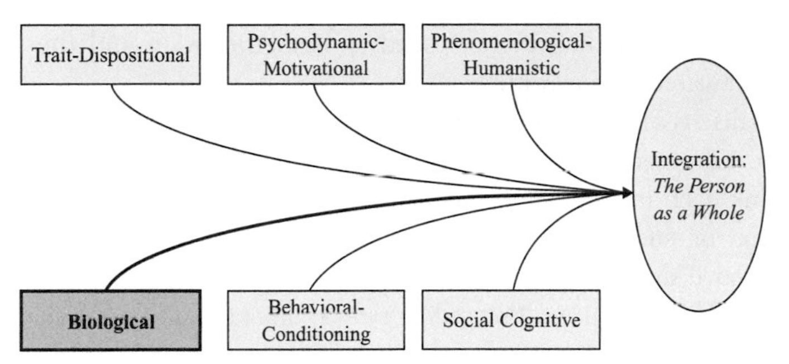

PRELUDE TO PART II: THE BIOLOGICAL LEVEL

Two identical twin girls were separated at birth, adopted and raised apart in different families from birth on. Nahid's life was spent in the capital of Iran while Jane grew up in the middle of the United States on a farm in rural Iowa. As identical twins, the two shared the same genetic heritage equally at the outset and consequently started their development with essentially identical brains and physical-biological structures. Nevertheless, the two girls grew up and experienced their lives in very different families, social worlds, and cultures. One was reared by loving parents in a family that adored her, surrounded by six siblings, four older than she and two much younger. The other twin grew up as the only child with a neglectful, depressed mother and an alcoholic, abusive stepfather. If the twins are reunited at age 30 and tested extensively, how similar will their personalities turn out to be?

At the Biological Level of Analysis researchers want to answer the age-old question: how much of personality reflects nature, and how much nurture—and how do these two sources of influence interact in shaping human characteristics?

A second question also comes from the recognition that we humans are biological beings. It asks: what are the consequences of having evolved as creatures within the animal kingdom? Evolution endowed us with a host of biological characteristics, constraints, and possibilities that influence who and what we are and do and can become—from eating, drinking, and breathing, to fighting, mating, socializing, and creating. Work at this level shows that people are not simply a blank slate; we are born with a wide range of mechanisms that make it possible to perform an impressive array of complex feats of information processing that facilitated the evolutionary fitness of our species. Like other species, we are the products of the evolutionary processes that shaped us. Consequently, a major goal at this level of analysis is to examine the ways in which personality may have evolved in response to the evolutionary pressures and history that shaped our species over the span of time.

Work at the biological level for many years had little to say about the specific ways in which biology influences individuals' experiences and behaviors that interested personality psychologists. In just a few years that picture has changed dramatically: new ways have been found for examining the links between activity in the human brain and the thoughts, feelings, and behavioral tendencies of the person as they occur. The most dramatic advances are in brain imaging technology. These methods now allow studies of the relations between what happens at the brain level and all the psychological levels. These relations are beginning to be traced as both the brain and the psychological processes are activated concurrently.

Chapter 5 discusses genes, heredity, and the interplay of genetic and social influences on personality. Chapter 6 considers the specific biological processes and brain mechanisms that link each individual's genetic background to central aspects of personality and social behavior, such as emotion and motivation. Then we turn to the evolutionary processes that have shaped the genes over the course of the species' development, and examine the implications for understanding personality at that level of analysis.

THE PERSONAL SIDE OF THE SCIENCE

Some questions at the Biological Level you might ask about yourself:

- ▶ What in my personality comes from the genes I inherited?
- ▶ How is my personality a reflection of my life experiences?
- ▶ How does my personality reflect my biological predispositions?
- ▶ Can my experiences change my biology; for instance, does my brain change when I'm depressed?
- ▶ How do the same experiences affect people with different genetic predispositions?
- ▶ Why is my personality so different from (or similar to) that of my siblings?
- ▶ How does my genetic inheritance influence my pursuit of life goals?

CHAPTER 

HEREDITY AND PERSONALITY

Talk to most people about personality characteristic and one of the first questions raised is: How much of this is inherited? Our genes dictate whether we will be male or female, blue eyed or brown eyed, curly haired or straight haired. But do the genes also underlie aspects of personality? If the answer is that they do, the next question is, How much? Do they affect sexual preferences and choice of partners? Are they reflected in tendencies to develop severe mood disorders and mental illness? Do they even influence attitudes and political views?

The rapidly growing field of **behavior genetics** studies the role of genes in social behavior and personality. Current work on these topics is vigorous and moving in many new directions. It is propelled by better methods for studying the inheritance of personality characteristics and by rapid advances in genetics research. In this chapter, we examine the genetic and biochemical roots of personality, including temperament, attitudes, beliefs, and behavior. We then consider the interplay between genetic determinants and social factors, such as the family and culture in which the child develops, as influences on personality.

Let's begin with a concrete example. Consider these two statements about race:

> *When capable black college students fail to perform as well as their white counterparts, the explanation often has less to do with preparation or ability than with the threat of stereotypes about their capacity to succeed.* (C. Steele, 1999, p. 44)

> *The mechanism by which racial preferences engineer "inclusion" is a tolerance of mediocrity in minorities—allowing mediocrity to win for them what only excellence wins for others.* (S. Steele, 2000)

The first author, Claude Steele, is a social psychologist and a member of the National Academy of Sciences. The second author, Shelby Steele, is a writer who received the National Book Critic's Circle Award in 1990 for his book *The Content of Our Character: A New Vision of Race in America*. He is a member of the National Association of Scholars, and was awarded the National Humanities Medal in 2004. Claude Steele is a professor in the Psychology Department at Stanford University. Shelby Steele is a research fellow at the Hoover Institution, also at Stanford University. Both have written extensively about the academic performance of African Americans. But they strongly disagree with each other. Shelby Steele's account is embraced by those with conservative political beliefs, and Claude Steele's by those with liberal beliefs. Although their ideas are sometimes diametrically opposed to each other, they also share much in their background. They were born on the same day, in the same city, in the same family. In fact, they are identical twins.

▶ GENETIC BASES OF PERSONALITY

The Human Genome: The Genetic Heritage

As we near the second decade of the 21st century, staggeringly large advances have been made in our knowledge of the genetic bases of life. With every new insight gained, for example from the Human Genome Project, controversies sprout about the implications and the hazards of each new discovery. The arguments become especially heated about the implications for understanding the heritability of personality characteristics and behavioral tendencies—from thrill-seeking, alcoholism, and criminal tendencies to sexual attitudes and political conservatism. The conclusions reached influence how we judge other peoples' behavior and our own. If genes underlie antisocial and violent behavior, can one hold criminals responsible for their crimes? Can reform and change be possible? Is biology destiny? How you see the role of heredity in personality affects not just your view of human nature. It also can change your personal sense of your own possibilities and limitations in trying to build a life.

Inside DNA: The Basic Information

The genetic heritage of each human being is contained in a large molecule called DNA (deoxyribonucleotides), arranged in 23 pairs of chromosomes. A DNA is a long string of small units called nucleotides, of which there are only four types: A, T, G, and C. These are strung together in the form of a long string (e.g., AATATAACTTCCGGTGCAACGTATT...), just as words in English are a string of letters. Imagine a book with about a billion words, organized in 23 chapters, and a virtually identical "version B" of the same book. That is what the **human genome** basically is, except the "alphabet" of DNA only has four letters, rather than the English

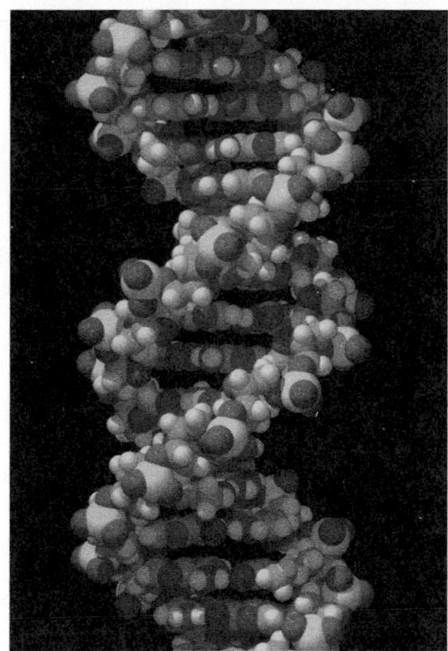

The genetic heritage of each human being is contained in the DNA molecule.

(*Source*: Kenneth Eward/Biografx/Photo Researchers, Inc.)

language's 26. Each of about a trillion cells in the human body houses within its nucleus a complete and identical sequence of DNA. Each contains about 1.5 gigabytes of genetic information, an amount that would fill roughly two CD-ROMs. Discoveries about just how this information underlies the form and function of living organisms are quickly changing the understanding of nature–nurture and person–environment relations.

5.1 What is the human genome? How does it contribute to human similarities and differences?

Not Really a Blueprint

Although DNA is popularly described as a "blueprint," that analogy is far from accurate. Just think about this: Considering that each and every cell (with very few exceptions) in our body contains completely identical DNA, why do some of these cells become nerve cells, while others become skin cells, and others form highly specialized cells in different organs performing highly specialized functions?

While this question is the target of intensive research and a full understanding of it may still be decades away, a key to solving this puzzle lies in the fact that most of the DNA, in any cell, does nothing. As an analogy, think about all the words in this text. You and all other students in this class have a copy of this book. But do these words do anything while the book is in your backpack, or on the bookshelf of your dorm room? The words do not do anything unless they are read. The part of the book that you read depends on what is going on in your mind, and around you. If you are particularly interested in biology, you may start the book by reading this chapter. But if tomorrow's midterm exam is on trait approaches, then that in turn may make you more interested in reading Chapter 3 instead.

DNA–Environment Interactions

In the case of DNA, "reading" the DNA results in making the particular type of protein specified by the part of the DNA that was read. And what gets read in turn is determined by what's going on in the cell (e.g., what other proteins and other molecules are floating around in the cell), which in turn is influenced by what's going on outside the cell, the molecules (e.g., hormones) that are floating around, as well as the nature of the neighboring cells. Ultimately, all these are influenced by the environment outside the person—the person's physical and social environment.

A **gene** is a region of DNA that influences a particular characteristic in an organism, and is a unit of heredity. Genes typically contain a stretch (or stretches) of DNA that specify the structure of a protein to be made, as well as a stretch called the regulatory sequences, which control whether or not, and how much of, the protein is made. Sometimes different proteins can be made based on the same gene, determined by the interaction between the cellular environment (what's going on inside the cell) and the regulatory sequence.

Individual Differences in DNA

Although any unrelated people share about 99.9% of their DNA sequence, people's DNA are not identical (i.e., unless they are identical twins—more on this later). These occasional differences could in turn have significant consequences. For example, what do you think of a friend who says she asked her rabbi for guidance? And how about another friend who says she asked her rabbit for guidance? The presence or absence of the letter *t* in an otherwise identical sentence can lead to quite different impressions. Similarly, sometimes a minor difference in a DNA sequence can lead to profound differences in the nature of the proteins made based on the sequence. So it would not be surprising if the relatively minute variations in the DNA sequences among people can lead to some significant differences in their physical and behavioral characteristics.

5.2 How much DNA do strangers from different races share?

Even an extremely brief description (and one mostly relying on analogy) of the DNA such as the above makes it clear that variations among people in their DNA sequence could have important variations in how they look, think, feel, and behave. At the same time, it should also be clear the nature and magnitude of the variations would depend on the environment, most immediately the intracellular environment but ultimately the physical and social environment to which a person is exposed.

Biological Switches

What a cell becomes is determined by biological switches outside the cell that turn the specific genes in the cell on or off. As Marcus (2004) notes, although it is the genome that provides the options, it is the environment that determines the options that become activated. The discovery of the fundamentally interactive nature of gene–environment interconnections applies not just to understanding how our bodies develop, but equally to how the mind functions, and how personality is organized and expressed (Gazzaniga & Heatherton, 2006). A surprising example comes from a much simpler species (see *In Focus 5.1*).

5.3 Does the environment change DNA?

In the past, the search for the biological bases of personality has focused on the kinds of genes that different types of people might possess, and hunted for specific genes that might underlie different personality types and characteristics. The new look, and it is still very new, changes the focus from just looking to see who has what kinds of genes. Instead, the goal now is to understand just how the genes are turned on and off by the physical and social-psychological environment and expressed, and the specific ways in which this process influences how we think, feel, and behave. As Gazzaniga and Heatherton (2006, p. 75) say: "Although there is evidence that people might possess specific genes that have specific effects, it is the expression of those genes ('turning on and off') as much as mere possession that makes us who we are."

IN FOCUS 5.1

EVEN THE BEES DO IT: GENE–ENVIRONMENT INTERACTIONS IN SOCIAL BEHAVIOR

The *foraging* gene affects naturally occurring variation in insect behavior. There are two different variants of this gene commonly present in populations of *Drosophila melanogaster* (fruit flies). One variant is associated with collecting food over a larger area than the other variant. This therefore is an example of how different variants of a gene can result in significant differences in behavior.

But there is also evidence that environment affects the expression of these genes, resulting in different behaviors. Specifically, studying honey bees, a group of researchers showed that this gene is also involved in developmental changes in behavior induced in part by the social context. Adult worker bees perform tasks in the hive such as brood care ("nursing") when they are young, and then shift to foraging for nectar and pollen outside the hive. But the age of onset for foraging is not rigidly determined; it depends on the needs of the colony, mediated in part by social interactions with older individuals and chemical signals from the brood and queen bee.

To investigate the role of the *foraging* gene in such a contextually induced shift in behavior, the researchers manipulated colony social structure to obtain precocious foragers. They established "single-cohort colonies" initially composed only of 1-day-old bees and found the absence of older bees resulted in some colony members initiating foraging as much as 2 weeks earlier than usual. Molecular assays showed that the foraging gene was expressed two to four times more in these bees than in their same-age counterparts in other colonies.

It is important to note that the DNA of these bees itself remains unchanged as the bees assume different roles in their colony. Division of labor (e.g., foraging vs. nursing) in honey bees reflect not differences in the DNA, but their expression, reflecting the effects of age, social interactions, colony needs, and resource availability. Other examples include changes in brain expression of a gene as the bees make the transition from pollen versus nectar foraging.

Source: Based on Ben-Shahar, Y., Robichon, A., Sokolowski, M. B., & Robinson, G. E. (2002). Influence of gene action across different time scales on behavior. *Science*, *296*, 741–744.

5.4 How does the example of the bees show the effects of environment on DNA expression?

The vast majority of human genes are the same for every human being, resulting in the enormous similarities that people share—10 toes, 10 fingers, 32 teeth, two arms, two legs, two eyes, two ears, one heart, and so on. But a relatively small minority of genes are different for different persons and these make each individual genetically distinctive. They are the ones that influence the diverse variations among people in such characteristics as eye color and height—and perhaps in aspects of personality and social behavior not anticipated until recently. The question to which we turn here is the role of these genetic differences between individuals as influences on personality.

Most of what is known about the genetic roots of personality comes from studies that compare the similarity in personality shown by individuals who vary in the degree to which they share the same genes and/or the same environments. Therefore, the "genetic" and "environmental" influences on personality discussed next do not refer to the effects of specific genes and specific environments. Rather, they refer to the overall effects of these two types of determinants on individual differences on average. To anticipate what you will see in this chapter, genetic research on personality is producing a huge and complex literature, but it has a clear message: Genes play a role in personality, and it appears to be a larger one than earlier research had suspected (e.g., Eaves, Eysenck, & Martin, 1989; Loehlin, 1992; Loehlin & Nichols, 1976; Plomin et al., 1997). For example, it is now widely believed that such dispositions as extraversion–introversion (Chapter 3) have a biological-genetic basis (Bouchard et al., 1990; Eysenck, 1973; Plomin & Caspi, 1999; Tellegen et al., 1988). How these dispositions are expressed in behavior, however, depends importantly on the interactions with the environment throughout the course of development. Now let us look at some of the evidence that leads to that conclusion.

▶ TWIN STUDIES

The Twin Method

5.5 How do twin studies shed light on genetic factors in personality?

Most often, heredity studies use the **twin method** to assess genetic influence. This method simply compares the degree of similarity on measures of personality obtained for genetically identical twins—those who are from the same egg or **monozygotic (MZ)**—as opposed to twins who are fraternal or **dizygotic (DZ)**, that is, with each from a different fertilized egg (Plomin et al., 1997). Identical twins are as close to genetically identical as people get, but fraternal twins—like other siblings—are only 50% similar genetically. To the degree that genetic factors affect personality, it follows that identical twins must be more similar than fraternal twins with regard to that characteristic.

Results of Twin Studies

5.6 What do twin studies find regarding the degree of resemblance in personality as compared with other characteristics?

A pioneering study with nearly 800 pairs of adolescent twins and measuring dozens of personality traits reached a conclusion that has stood the test of time (Loehlin & Nichols, 1976): Identical twin pairs are much more alike than fraternal twin pairs. The resemblance within identical twin pairs tends to be strongest for general ability. The resemblance is somewhat lower for personality inventory scales and lowest for interests, goals, and self-concepts (see Table 5.1). For personality, twin correlations are about .50 for identical twins and .25 for fraternal twins. This same study also found that nearly all personality traits measured by self-report questionnaire show moderate genetic influence.

The Big Five

Genetic research on personality has focused on five broad dimensions of personality—the Big Five (Goldberg, 1990), discussed in Chapters 3 and 4. Extraversion and Neuroticism

Studies comparing identical twins and fraternal twins help specify the role of genes in personality.

(*Source*: (left) Photodisc/Getty Images, Inc; (right) Todd Warnock/Taxi/Getty Images)

TABLE 5.1 Resemblance of Identical and Fraternal Twin Pairs: Typical Correlations within Pairs

Trait Area	Identical Twins	Fraternal Twins
General ability	.86	.62
Special abilities	.74	.52
Personality scales	.50	.28
Ideals, goals, interests	.37	.20

Source: Adapted from *Heredity, Environment, and Personality: A Study of 850 Sets of Twins*, by John C. Loehlin and Robert C. Nichols, Copyright © 1976. By permission of the University of Texas Press.

have been studied the most. Extraversion includes sociability, impulsiveness, and liveliness. Neuroticism (emotional instability) includes moodiness, anxiousness, and irritability. Table 5.2 summarizes results for Extraversion and Neuroticism (Loehlin, 1992). Results from five twin studies in five different countries, using a total of 24,000 pairs of twins, consistently indicate moderate genetic influence. Correlations are about .50 for identical twins and about .20 for fraternal twins.

The role of heritability in extraversion and neuroticism has been studied extensively, but much less genetic research has been done for the other three Big Five traits, namely, Agreeableness (likeability, friendliness), Conscientiousness (conformity, will to achieve), and Culture (openness to experience). These qualities have been investigated with diverse measures (rather than one standardized test) that also make it more difficult to compare results across different studies. Nevertheless, results of twin and adoption studies with measures related to these three traits also suggest genetic influence for agreeableness, conscientiousness, and culture at least to a moderate degree (Loehlin, 1992).

TABLE 5.2 Resemblance of 24,000 Pairs of Reared-Together Twins in Five Countries and Identical Twins Reared Apart

	Correlations within Twin Pairs		
	Identical Twins Reared Together	Fraternal Twins Reared Together	Identical Twins Reared Apart
Extraversion	.51	.18	.38
Neuroticism	.46	.20	.38

Source: Adapted from Loehlin, J. C. *Genes and environment in personality development.* © 1992, reprinted by permission of Sage Publications, Inc.

Temperaments

The term **temperaments** refers to traits that are visible in early childhood (Buss & Plomin, 1984), and seem especially relevant to the individual's emotional life (Allport, 1961; Clark & Watson, 1999). Dispositions usually considered temperaments include the general level of emotionality, sociability, and activity. These temperaments are usually assessed through parental reports about their children on temperament rating scales (Rothbart, Derryberry, & Posner, 1994). In adults, they typically are assessed by self-report measures (e.g., Buss & Plomin, 1984), with items like those shown in Table 5.3.

TABLE 5.3 Self-Report Items to Assess Temperament in Adults

EMOTIONALITY (easily aroused physiologically to experience negative emotions)
Many things annoy me.
I get emotionally upset easily.
SOCIABILITY (seeks social interaction)
I prefer working with others rather than alone.
I like to be with other people.
ACTIVITY (overall energy level, tempo/speed, intensity or vigor)
My life is fast-paced.
I usually seem to be in a hurry.

Note: Participants rate on five-point scales the degree to which items like these apply to them, from "not typical" of me to "very typical" of me. Based on Buss, A. H., & R. Plomin. (1984). *Temperament: Early developing personality traits* (Table 7.3). Hillsdale, NJ: Erlbaum. Copyright, 1984, reprinted by permission.

Emotionality, also called **emotional reactivity**, is often defined as the tendency to become aroused easily physiologically (by ready activation of the autonomic nervous system) and especially to experience frequent and intense negative emotions such as anger, fear, and distress (Buss & Plomin, 1984). Not all researchers agree with this definition, however. They find that the intensity with which an individual experiences emotions is independent of how often he or she has such feelings (Larsen, Diener, & Emmons, 1986). That suggests that these two components of emotionality need to be considered separately, and that both need to be taken into account. For example, if Jane rarely experiences fear but becomes unbearably fearful in some situations, her emotional life would be quite different from someone who is often moderately fearful but never intensely afraid. Further, positive and negative emotions can function independently and they need to be measured separately. For example, people who often experience positive emotions may or may not also experience negative emotions often.

In spite of these variations, there is agreement that emotionality is an important aspect of temperament. There also is some evidence that emotional reactivity at high levels may be a long-term risk factor for emotional disorders, and for some somatic diseases. Studies by Strelau and Zawadzki (2005), for example, suggest that this temperament trait may increase the individual's risk to react to life stressors by depression, and may in turn lead to increased likelihood of physical disorders.

Sociability refers to the degree to which the person seeks to interact with others and to be with people. (As such, it overlaps with the concept of extraversion versus introversion, introduced in Chapter 3.)

Activity may be defined with regard both to the vigor or intensity of responses and their tempo or speed. It refers to stable individual differences on a dimension that ranges from hyperactivity to extreme inactivity (e.g., Thomas & Chess, 1977).

In these dispositions genetic endowment seems to have a significant part and the evidence is increasingly strong (e.g., Clark & Watson, 1999; Plomin, 1990; Rowe, 1997). Figure 5.1 illustrates these types of results more concretely. It shows that on the dimension of emotionality, identical twins are rated as much more similar by their mothers than are fraternal twins.

Although the results are impressive, they are not easy to interpret. Some of the greater similarity found may reflect that the mothers themselves may treat the identical

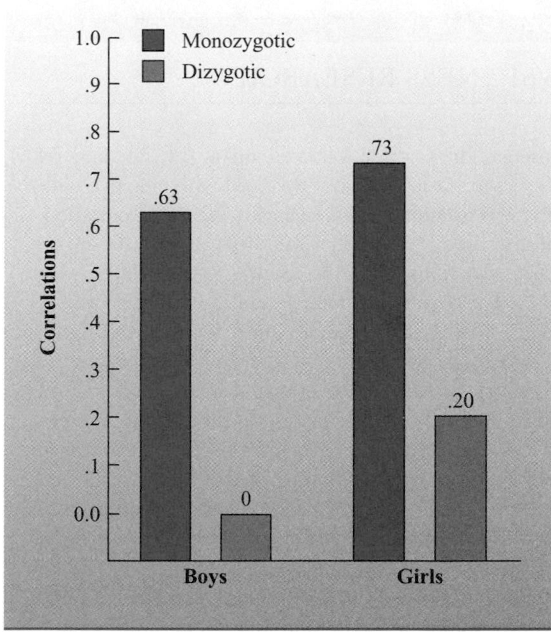

Figure 5.1 Similarity of emotionality: mother's ratings of monozygotic and dizygotic twin pairs.

Source: Correlation coefficients for degree of similarity from data in Buss, Plomin, and Willerman (1973).

twins more similarly, as might other people in the environment. The mothers also may have been influenced in their ratings not only by the twins' behavior but by their own expectations and preconceptions for identical versus fraternal twins. Nevertheless, results like these tend to be obtained so consistently that they suggest a significant genetic role in personality with regard to the temperaments of emotionality, activity, and sociability (Buss & Plomin, 1984; Plomin et al., 1997). A comprehensive review of this research concluded that ". . . one-third to one-half of individual differences in temperamental traits can be attributed to genetic variation among children" (Rowe, 1997, p. 378).

5.7 In twin studies, how strongly do genetic factors seem to influence temperament? Why are these results difficult to interpret?

Genetic researchers investigating differences between children in temperament could not use self-report questionnaires with their young participants and therefore used other measures, such as direct ratings of the children's behavior by observers (e.g., Cherney et al., 1994; Goldsmith & Campos, 1986; Saudino & Plomin, 1996). With few exceptions (confined to the first few days of life), observational studies of young twins show genetic influence for diverse characteristics. These characteristics include the degree to which the child's behavior is inhibited—an aspect of fearfulness (e.g., Robinson, Kagan, Reznick, & Corley, 1992); shyness both when observed at home and in the laboratory (Cherney et al., 1994); activity level (Saudino & Eaton, 1991); and empathy (Zahn-Waxler, Robinson, & Emde, 1992). Findings from these studies are especially valuable because they go beyond those that rely on self-reports—which are by far the most common—to closely observe what the child is doing. A notable example of research on temperaments that goes much beyond self-reports comes from Jerome Kagan's long-term research on inhibition and shyness (*In Focus* 5.2).

IN FOCUS 5.2

INHIBITED CHILDREN: KAGAN'S SHYNESS RESEARCH

Jerome Kagan (2006) argues that **inhibition** is one of the major dimensions of temperament, and finds early individual differences exist on this dimension and endure in the course of development. The inhibition construct is similar to the neuroticism component of the Big Five. It refers to the extent to which infants are wary of novelty and unfamiliarity. Inhibited or "shy" children react to unfamiliar people or situations with fear. They try to avoid those situations, and take much longer to relax when they are in them. They tend to have phobias when they grow up.

Kagan's research program, spanning over four decades, examined how early these individual differences emerge, how stable they are over time, and whether or not they are biologically based. In one study, he observed identical and fraternal twins when they were 4 months old. The twins were videotaped in response to novel stimuli such as a stranger or a balloon popping. They were also exposed to familiar stimuli such as a mother's face or her voice. To measure how fearfully reactive children are to unfamiliarity, the videotapes were coded for such behaviors as the arching of the back, unhappy facial expressions, and crying. Kagan and colleagues found that in their sample 20% of children were inhibited, 40% were low reactive or uninhibited, and 40% were mixed.

These children were followed up at 14, 24, and 54 months of age. At later follow-up, the highly reactive children showed greater fearful behavior, heart acceleration, and higher blood pressure when they were put in an unfamiliar situation. At age 54 months, the inhibited children talked less with unfamiliar adults who were trying to interact with them in the lab and tried to avoid them. Furthermore, a moderate heritability influence was found (using the heritability index discussed in *In Focus 5.3*) at 14 months and at 24 months of age. In short, temperamental differences in inhibition emerged as early as 4 months of age, were stable across the first 4 years of life, and showed moderate heritability, suggesting a biological-genetic component in its development (Robinson, Kagan, Reznick, & Corley, 1992).

Although this research has demonstrated considerable stability in inhibition, the inhibited child under some conditions can change over time. For example, inhibited infants grew up to be less inhibited preschoolers if they had mothers who were not overly protective and placed reasonable demands on them (Fox, Henderson, Rubin, Calkins, & Schmidt, 2001). Still, complete and consistent crossover transformations from one extreme to the other were unlikely.

5.8 How did Kagan use a twin study to evaluate the heritability of inhibition?

Attitudes and Beliefs

Genetic influences also seem to play a role in individual differences in attitudes and beliefs. Results come from a number of twin studies (Eaves et al., 1989), including one of twins who were adopted and reared apart (Tellegen et al., 1988). To illustrate, a substantial genetic influence was found on *traditionalism*, a general orientation that taps conservative (as opposed to liberal) attitudes on diverse topics and many other attitudes also seem to show genetic influence (Eaves et al., 1989; see Plomin et al., 1997).

5.9 How strongly are attitudes influenced by genetic factors? Which attitudes seem most strongly influenced?

Attitudes that are more heritable may differ from those that are less heritable systematically, and examining such differences sheds some light on the nature of genetic influences. For example, in one study the researcher separated many specific attitudes into two sets (Tesser, 1993). One set contained those that twin studies had found were more heritable (such as attitudes about the death penalty and about jazz). The other set consisted of those that were less heritable (such as attitudes about coeducation, straightjackets, and the truth of the Bible). Then the researcher set up experimental situations designed to change these attitudes in college students. He found that the more heritable attitudes were harder to influence and also more important in determining the person's judgments of interpersonal attraction.

Aggressive and Altruistic Tendencies

Research with adult twins also points to the influence of genes on other aspects of social behavior. For example, self-reports on aggressiveness questionnaires were obtained from a large number of twin pairs in England (Rushton, Fulker, Neale, Nias, & Eysenck, 1986). The twins answered such questions as: "I try not to give people a hard time" and "Some people think I have a violent temper." The altruism questionnaire asked for the frequency of such behaviors as "I have donated blood" and "I have given directions to a stranger." Within the identical (monozygotic) twin pairs, the answers were more similar than would be expected by chance whereas between fraternal twins, the correlation was merely at a chance level. These results occurred both for the males and for the females. Using sophisticated statistical techniques, the researchers estimated that genetics accounted for approximately 50% of the individual differences in test answers.

Romantic Love and Marriage

Although genes seem to directly or indirectly influence individual differences on most measures of personality, as well as on social attitudes, including peoples' self-esteem (e.g., McGuire, Neiderheiser, Reiss, Hetherington, & Plomin, 1994), one area that seems to be beyond DNA is romantic love. A behavior genetic twin family study focused on the genetic versus environmental influences on individual differences in adult romantic love styles. The participants were drawn from 890 adult twins and 172 spouses from the California Twin Registry married for an average of a dozen years (Waller & Shaver, 1994). Six different love styles were measured, ranging from one that values passion, excitement, intimacy, self-disclosure, and "being in love from the start," to one that values a relationship that is affectionate and reliable and has companionship and friendship (with items like "It is hard for me to say exactly when our friendship turned into love").

The findings showed that how people love is almost completely due to the environment and essentially unaffected by genetic influences. In fact, this is one domain in

How people love is mostly influenced by their environment, not their genetics.

(*Source*: LWA/Dan Tardd/Getty Images, Inc)

which it is the family environment that turned out to be particularly important (Waller & Shaver, 1994). As the researchers noted ". . . love styles may be learned during early familial or shared extra-familial interactions and subsequently played out in romantic relationships" (pp. 272–273).

But while love styles at least so far seem not heritable, the propensity to get married is. Johnson and colleagues (2004) studied over 7,000 women and men, including many complete twin pairs. According to their findings, the tendency to get married is itself genetically influenced.

Twins Reared Apart

5.10 What is the special value of comparing twins raised together and apart?

To try to separate the role of genetics and environment, it is especially informative to assess identical twins who have been reared apart in different families. Reports have come from two large-scale studies of twins reared apart in Minnesota (Bouchard et al., 1990; Tellegen et al., 1988) and in Sweden (Pedersen, Plomin, McClearn, & Friberg, 1988; Plomin et al., 1988). The results surprised even many of the researchers who have long been convinced that genes affect personality.

In this research, for more than a decade, Bouchard, Tellegen, and their associates studied a sample of identical (monozygotic) twin pairs reared apart who were separated early in life (on average before the end of the second month). They grew up in different families, but mostly in English-speaking countries. As adults, their responses were assessed on many medical and psychological measures, including personality questionnaire scales and intelligence tests (as seen in Table 5.4). Most had not seen each other for an average of about 30 years, although some had contact over the years. Comparisons were made with a larger sample of twin pairs who had been reared together and grew up in Minnesota.

There were instances of dramatic psychological similarities within the twin pairs, even for twins who grew up in radically different environments for 30 years or more in many cases. These twins seemed to share some quite distinctive mannerisms, postures, attitudes, and interests. For example, in some cases they posed alike for photos. Some turned out to have virtually the same height, the same weight, the same number of marriages and children, the same drinking and smoking habits, the same mannerisms, the same clothes, food, and jewelry preferences, similar physical symptoms—and similar

TABLE 5.4 Names of Personality Scales in Studies of Twins Reared Apart and Together

Well-being	Control
Social Potency	Harm Avoidance
Achievement	Traditionalism
Social Closeness	Absorption
Stress Reaction	Positive Emotionality
Alienation	Negative Emotionality
Aggression	Constraint

Note: On most scales, identical twins reared apart were as similar to each other as those reared together. The main exception was "social closeness" (on which those raised together were more similar).

Source: Tellegen, A., Lykken, D., Bouchard, T., Wilcox, K., Segal, N., & Rich, S. (1988). Personality similarity in twins reared apart. *Journal of Personality and Social Psychology, 54*, 1035 (Table 3).

scores on personality tests (e.g., Segal, 1999). Many also quickly felt a close emotional connection with each other even though they had spent their entire lives apart.

There also were strong similarities in many of the test results of the identical twins. Especially interesting, the similarity was almost as high for the monozygotic twins who grew up in different homes as it was for those raised within the same family (as was seen in Table 5.2). Bouchard and colleagues (1990) attributed approximately 70% of the individual differences found in intelligence to heredity. They interpreted the effects of heredity on personality (as assessed on their questionnaires) to be approximately 50% and the effects of family environment to be trivial (Tellegen et al., 1988). Likewise, twin studies of the Big Five factors suggest "The shared genes, not the shared experiences, mainly determine the family resemblance of 'blood relatives'" (Rowe, 1997, p. 380).

Beyond Self-Report Measures

One of the most surprising findings from genetic research on self-report personality questionnaires is that of the many traits that have been studied, virtually all show genetic influence. That may be because all these traits in fact reflect genetic predispositions. But at least some of the similarity may lie in the eyes of the beholder. For example, identical twins who have a higher level of frustration tolerance may *think* and honestly say that they experience less negative emotions than others, worry less, and rarely feel anxious, not because they experience these feelings less than others, but because they are less bothered by them. It is therefore particularly important to use measures of personality other than self-report questionnaires to investigate whether or not this result is somehow due to biases in the self-report measures themselves.

5.11 Describe the difficulties that attend the use of self-report measures to assess heritability.

To address this, researchers gave a measure of the Big Five personality factors to almost a thousand pairs of twins (Riemann, Angleitner, & Strelau, 1997) in Germany and Poland. They also obtained ratings of each twin's personality by two different peers (who agreed reasonably with each other in their ratings about each twin's personality).

On average, ratings by the peers correlated .55 with the twins' self-report ratings, providing moderate validity for those ratings. Table 5.5 shows twin correlations for the "Big Five" personality traits, which are similar to those summarized in Table 5.2, with average correlations of .52 for identical twins and .23 for fraternal twins. The fact that

TABLE 5.5 Twin Study Using Self-Report and Peer Ratings of "Big Five" Personality Traits

	Correlations within Pairs			
	Self-Report Ratings		Peer Ratings	
	Identical Twins	Fraternal Twins	Identical Twins	Fraternal Twins
Extraversion	.56	.28	.40	.17
Neuroticism	.53	.13	.43	-.03
Agreeableness	.42	.19	.32	.18
Conscientiousness	.54	.18	.43	.18
Culture	.54	.35	.48	.31

Source: Riemann, R., Angleitner, A., & Strelau, J. (1997). Genetic and environmental influences on personality: A study of twins reared together using the self- and peer report NEO-FFI scales. *Journal of Personality, 65*, 449–476. With permission from Blackwell Publishing.

the peer ratings also indicated genetic influence helps support the conclusions reached earlier based on self-report questionnaires.

The German Observational Study of Adult Twins (Borkenau, Rieman, Spinath, & Angleitner, 2006) also examined genetic and environmental influences on person × situation interactions, measured as *if . . . then . . .* behavioral signatures of personality like those described in Chapter 4 (Mischel & Shoda, 1995). The researchers used videotaped performances of the behavior of 168 monozygotic and 132 dizygotic twin pairs in 15 situations. These tapes were observed by 120 judges who had never met the twins. Four independent judges observed one twin of each pair in one situation. The researchers analyzed twin similarities in the *if . . . then . . .* behavioral signatures using a variety of standard methods. They then partitioned genetic and environmental contributions to trait levels and to *if. . . then . . .* personality signatures. Borkenau and colleagues concluded that genes accounted for about 25% of these signatures. Thus, unsurprisingly, identical twins are more similar in these signatures and in their stable person × situation interactions compared to fraternal twins.

5.12 How are heritability coefficients computed? What do they tell us?

So far in this chapter we have reviewed some of the main findings that show significant effects of one's genetic heritage on the personality that develops. Most of these studies use the heritability index to estimate the size of these effects. Because the method and the conclusions it allows are easy to misunderstand, they need to be examined carefully. *In Focus 5.3* discusses these misunderstandings and clarifies the meaning of this index.

IN FOCUS 5.3

UNDERSTANDING HERITABILITY AND THE HERITABILITY INDEX

There are many misconceptions about the implications of heritability for personality. Let's address some of the most common.

The Heritability Index. Correlations like those shown in Table 5.5 are used by behavioral geneticists to estimate the percent of the variation in scores measuring individual differences that is attributable to genetic factors. The computation of this index is straightforward, but its interpretation is not. To compute it, pairs of same-sex fraternal and identical twins are compared on particular variables. For each type of twin, the researchers compute a correlation among pairs of identical twins to index their similarity, as well as a correlation among pairs of fraternal twins. Subtracting the latter from the former, and then multiplying the result by two, results in the heritability index. It is an estimate of the role of heritability in accounting for individual differences on the variable studied. Results using these estimates to date suggest that heritability plays an important role in many aspects of personality.

The Meaning of High Heritability. Twin studies are a valuable first step toward answering whether genetic factors contribute to individual differences in personality. But the heritability indexes they compute have to be interpreted cautiously for several reasons (e.g., Dickens & Flynn, 2001):

- First, **heritability estimates** always are limited to the specific population that was studied in the research reported and for which they were computed. This is a crucial caution that behavioral geneticists generally emphasize but that many readers often fail to appreciate (Goldsmith, 1991). Heritability estimates *do not* provide an absolute index of the degree to which a given characteristic is influenced by the genes. It is nonsense to think, for example, that Joe's aggressiveness is made up of 30% genetic influence and 70% environmental influences or that Susan's ballet skills are 20% genetic and 80% ballet school and practice. If all children took ballet lessons, then a greater portion of the differences among the children in ballet skills may be due to their variations in their genetic endowment. But if only some children took ballet lessons, then how well children can perform *pirouettes* may depend largely on the availability of ballet lessons. In general, the heritability index depends on the variations in the environment that exist within a given society in which the study is conducted. The more homogeneous the environments are, the greater is the heritability index. Thus the heritability index reflects characteristics of a population, rather than of an individual. If the psychological environments to which children are exposed become more homogeneous across different cultures, for example, due to global communication and media influences, the result would be an increase in the relative proportion of the genetic influences in the observed variations among people.

Heritability estimates *do* index the portion of the individual *variability* related to the genetic *variability* that exists in the population. If the characteristic is so important that any variation in the genes that affect it can reduce the evolutionary fitness of the individual, the heritability index would be close to zero. That happens because all individuals are likely to be identical with regard to that gene, and any variability observed in that characteristic is likely to come from environmental differences. For example, most humans have two legs, and when legs are missing it's typically from accidents or injuries. The heritability index for the number of legs is therefore practically zero. That's the case, although legs are obviously grown through instructions in the human genome.

- Second, even when identical twins are reared apart, their similarities on personality measures are not necessarily due to their genes for personality itself. For example, similar interests and values in identical twins may in part reflect their similar physiques and appearance, constitutions, abilities, skills, and physical characteristics rather than any genes for personality. These physical qualities may lead other people to treat them similarly even when the twins live in different environments. A shared interest in becoming a fashion model, for example, may say more about the inheritance of faces than of personality. Their similar physical qualities also may lead each twin to see him- or herself in a somewhat similar way, for example, as highly attractive or unattractive, or as physically strong and skilled and competent or as weak and ineffective. This in turn could influence such aspects of personality as self-concepts and self-confidence and a host of related characteristics.
- Third, as mentioned earlier, many studies that compare the similarity of identical and fraternal twins who grow up together draw mostly on their answers on self-report personality questionnaires (the measure most often used). On these tests the identical twins might give more similar answers not just because they have the same genes but also because they might identify more closely with each other and emulate each other more, or might be treated more alike by parents and other people, and therefore become more alike in all sorts of ways. For example, they might often wear more similar clothes and share more activities and time together. Just as greater similarity in dress among identical twins does not necessarily imply that clothing tastes are genetically determined, it is important also to be cautious before concluding that similarity in answers to self-report questionnaires about an attribute necessarily implies the specific genetic heritability of that attribute.
- Fourth, high heritability coefficients do *not* imply that the particular characteristic cannot be changed significantly. Even when genetics importantly influence individual differences in a trait, the trait may be modified by environmental influences. For example, substantial genetic influence for height means that height differences among the sampled individuals are largely due to genetic differences. But even when a trait is highly heritable it may be influenced importantly by the environment. The average height of Europeans has climbed more than 20 cm in the past 150 years (Usher, 1996). Thus, although height is highly heritable, such environmental interventions as improving children's nutrition and health can affect it. Indeed, environmental factors seem to account for the average increase in height across generations, although within each generation individual differences in height are highly heritable. As another example, consider the role of inheritance in intelligence. Research with twins raised in various environments (either together or apart) suggests that intelligence measured on standard tests tends to be increasingly similar to the degree that the individuals have an increasing proportion of genes in common (Cartwright, 1978; Plomin et al., 1997; Vandenberg, 1971). But whereas a person's genetic endowment may set an upper limit or ceiling on the degree to which his or her intelligence can be developed (Royce, 1973), it is the environment that may help or hinder achievement of that ceiling (e.g., Cantor & Kihlstrom, 1987).
- Finally, the heritability index itself does not address the mechanisms through which the genetic influences on personality operate and exert their effects on the individual.

Heredity versus Environment: Another False Dichotomy

Debates about heredity and environment have raged for years. Unfortunately, they readily turn into either/or competitions to see which one is more important. As a leader in research on the role of inheritance in behavior points out: ". . . evidence for significant genetic influence is often implicitly interpreted as if heritability were 100%, whereas heritabilities of behavior seldom exceed 50%" (Plomin, 1990, p. 187). Plomin (1990) notes that this should make it clear that "non-genetic sources of variance" are also of self-evident importance. Indeed, Bouchard and colleagues, in their studies of identical twins, raised apart, acknowledge that in their own results, "in individual cases environmental factors have been highly significant" (1990, p. 225), as with the case, for example, of a 29-point difference in the IQs of two identical twins.

In short, regardless of the exact percent used to estimate the influence of genetic factors, clearly their influence is considerable, especially given that few findings in personality account for as much as 20% of the variance. Just as noteworthy, however, is the other side of that finding: namely, the fact that the same data show that at least half of the variance of personality is *not* due to genetic factors and thus also attest to the importance of the environment for personality. The recurrent theme throughout this research is clear: unquestionably one's genetic endowment has extensive influences on one's life and personality development, and so also does the environment. The challenge will be to untangle the mechanisms through which both genes and experience interact throughout the life course to influence what we become. That will require specifying the mechanisms that produce these effects and clarifying the nature of the characteristics that are heritable and the specific aspects of the environment that are important.

Summary

Taken collectively, the findings support the view that genetic factors play a significant role in personality, both in broad traits as measured by the Big Five, and in *if . . . then* . . . behavioral signatures (person × situation interactions), in attitudes and values, as well as in self-esteem (e.g., McGuire et al., 1994). In some cases, genetic influences seem to account for as much as half of the individual differences observed. The size of these effects may be exaggerated, however, particularly when the findings are based on self-reports. Plomin and colleagues, critically reviewing twin studies of personality based on self-reports, point out certain method problems in these studies that may systematically overestimate the role of genetics. They believe the biases can be corrected if results from adoption studies are appropriately taken into account. When corrections are made for the erroneous inflation of the heritability estimates (see the section, "Stress Is Bad for Your Brain"): "The true heritability estimate for self-reported personality is closer to the adoption study estimate of 20% than to the twin study estimate of 40%" (Plomin et al., 1990, p. 233). It is also clear, however, that even when one goes beyond self-reports the role of genetics in personality is still significant and has to be taken seriously. The task ahead is to understand the mechanisms through which these effects play out.

5.13 Compare heritability estimates derived from twin studies with those obtained in adoption studies.

▶ GENE–ENVIRONMENT INTERACTION

Assuming that both nature (genetics) and nurture (environment) are important influences on personality, the next step is to understand their interplay. This interplay is seen in the course of life as the personality of the person, partly influenced by genetics, interacts with and to some degree selects and shapes the situations in his or her psychological world. The causal relations go in both directions because those situations over time, in turn, exert their impact on what the person becomes. Let's examine this interplay and its implications for personality.

The Unique (Nonshared) Psychological Environment of Each Family Member

Twin studies have inquired into the environmental influences that make genetically identical "clones"—identical twins—different from one another. For many years, it was widely thought that children growing up in the same family would be similar to one another in personality for environmental reasons because they shared the "same" family situation. Genetic researchers now believe that this assumption is false. They contend that family members resemble each other in personality largely because of genetic influences, and that the environment seems to make members of a family different (e.g., Plomin et al., 1997). Their reasoning is based on two findings. First, twins reared apart are only somewhat less similar in personality than twins who grew up in the same family. In addition, in studies of adoptive families that have more than one adopted child, the genetically unrelated children show little similarity in personality even though they had the same **shared environment**, that is, they were raised within the same family (Plomin, Chipuer, & Neiderhiser, 1994).

5.14 Differentiate between shared and unshared environmental influences within the family.

Note that the **shared** or **family environment** in the twin studies was treated as a global entity, as if families treat all the siblings in them the same way. The psychological environments experienced by each member of the family, however, may be quite different and each may receive distinctively different treatments within the same family. Each parent may relate differently to each child. In fact, findings of birth order effects suggest that children in the same family encounter quite different psychological environments (Sulloway, 1996). Moreover, much of the psychological environment experienced by individuals involves continuing significant encounters outside the family (with peers, school and teachers, spouse, and in the broader group and culture), the nature and effects of which may change with different phases of development.

Nonshared Environmental Influences within the Family

The **nonshared** or **unique environment** exerts its effects on each person through many routes, beginning in prenatal development and birth order effects. It includes biological events such as illness and nutrition, as well as psychosocial events such as interpersonal experiences that may range from parental reactions to peer influences, romantic partners, and mates (see Table 5.6). For example, earlier-born children are larger, more powerful, and more privileged than later-born children and that, in turn, may affect their personality development (Sulloway, 1996). From the start, each child

TABLE 5.6 Some Environmental Influences that Siblings in the Family Do Not Share Equally

Position in the family
Parental reactions
Accidents
Prenatal events, illness
Peer group reactions and support
Other interpersonal experiences (e.g., mates)
Educational and occupational experiences

is born into a slightly different family psychologically and structurally because parents treat siblings differently, and siblings treat each other differently.

It is understandable that most parents find it hard to admit that they treat their children differently, given the social norms that press for them to treat each one the same. But children correctly believe that their parents do treat them differently—an impression confirmed by observational studies (Reiss, Neiderhiser, Hetherington, & Plomin, 2000). So, for example, parents are likely to react differently to their first and their fifth child, perhaps hovering over their first baby and swamped by the time the fifth one arrives. On close examination, children growing up in the same family lead remarkably separate lives (Dunn & Plomin, 1990). Even such variables as parental divorce tend to affect children within the family differently, depending, for example, on the child's age and role in the family as well as many other variables (Hetherington & Clingempeel, 1992). In short, siblings growing up in the "same" family experience it differently so that psychologically it is not the same.

Research that traces how differences in such experiences lead to differences in outcomes is still just beginning, but some links have already been shown (Reiss et al., 2000). Most of these associations connect negative aspects of parenting (such as conflict) with such negative outcomes as antisocial behavior later in development. It is especially interesting that some associations (of modest strength) have been reported between differences in parental negativity toward identical twins and their adolescent maladjustment on such indices as depression and antisocial behavior (Reiss et al., 2000). Obviously such differences cannot be due to genetic factors and thus must be due to the nonshared environment (Pike, Reiss, Hetherington, & Plomin, 1996). Generally weaker correlations are found between positive aspects of parenting (such as affection) and positive outcomes.

The correlations between measures of the children's nonshared environment and their personality also raise the old chicken and the egg question, that is, the direction of the effects: Does parental negativity cause negative outcomes in personality? Or do parents treat some of their children more negatively than others in reaction to the child's personality, responding more harshly, for instance, to siblings who are more difficult to deal with? If the latter holds, the differential treatment siblings receive may be due in part to each child's distinctive genetics (Plomin, 1994). In other words, differential parental treatment of siblings may be due to genetically influenced differences between the siblings, including in their personality.

5.15 Why is it difficult to interpret the causal influences between environmental and genetic factors?

Nonshared Environmental Influences Outside the Family

The nonshared environment includes, but goes far beyond, differences in siblings' unique experiences within the family (see Table 5.6). Some of the most important aspects of the nonshared environment unfold in the experiences children have outside the family as they interact with their expanding worlds, most notably in relationships with peers and in school and play contexts. If you reflect on your own life, you will not find it difficult to come up with examples of relationships and experiences outside the immediate family that influenced your development. In these interactions even siblings living in the same family form quite different relations with peers, encounter different types of social support, build different lives with different educational, occupational, and interpersonal experiences and events along the route (Plomin, 1994). Further, such factors as accidents and illnesses, as well as chance encounters and experiences, may initiate significant differences between siblings (Dunn & Plomin, 1990). While such events initially may be relatively minor, they can snowball and become compounded over time into large outcome differences years later.

To recapitulate, we saw that environmental influences that affect personality development do not seem to operate on a family-by-family, "on the whole" basis, but rather on an individual-by-individual basis. That suggests that environmental effects on personality are specific to each child rather than general for all children in a given family. It makes the unit of analysis of each child as he or she distinctively interacts with relevant specific environmental situations, including with particular family members. Environmental influences on personality development seem to operate mostly in a nonshared manner, making children growing up in the same family different from one another. As was discussed, attempts to identify specific sources of nonshared environment indicate that many sibling experiences differ substantially. Even such seemingly shared variables as parental attitudes about childrearing and parents' marital relationship might not be experienced the same way and might, in fact, be subtly different for each sibling.

Interactions among Nature–Nurture Influences

5.16 What research results suggest genetic effects on experience within the family?

There are continuous, complex interactions between the expressions of genetic influences and the situations and events that the person experiences (e.g., Rutter, 2006; Rutter et al., 1997). These interactions make it difficult to isolate the contribution of genetics versus environmental influences because their interplay becomes virtually indivisible.

For example, adult twins reared apart rated the family environments in which they grew up more similarly than did fraternal twins reared apart (Rowe, 1981, 1983). Presumably this happened for at least two possible reasons. First, identical twins even reared apart may be more alike in how they perceive and interpret their experiences. Second but equally important, they may have been treated more similarly due to their genetically influenced shared characteristics such as their more similar physical appearance, abilities, skills, and temperaments (Plomin, McClearn, Pedersen, Nesselroade, & Bergeman, 1988). Likewise, beyond the family environment, genetic similarity may lead to greater similarity in the experienced environments in peer groups (e.g., Manke, McGuire, Reiss, Hetherington, & Plomin, 1995), in the classroom (Jang, 1993), and in work environments (Hershberger, Lichteinstein, & Knox, 1994). It may also influence such other life events as proneness to childhood accidents or illness (Phillips & Mathews, 1995), exposure to trauma (Lyons et al., 1993), or to drugs (Tsuang et al., 1992).

Perhaps the clearest evidence for genetic effects on experience comes from observational studies that also show such genetic effects (although often of lower magnitude), making it plain that they do not just depend on self-reports and questionnaires. For example, the Home Observation for Measurement of the Environment, or HOME, is a widely used measure of the home environment that combines observations and interviews (Caldwell & Bradley, 1978). It assesses aspects of the home environment such as parental responsiveness and encouraging developmental advance. In an adoption study with this measure, the home environment of each sibling was assessed when the child was 1 year old and again when each child was 2 years old (Braungart, Fulker, & Plomin, 1992). HOME correlations for genetically unrelated children adopted into the same home (adoptive siblings) were compared to those for genetically related siblings in nonadoptive homes (nonadoptive siblings). HOME scores were more similar for nonadoptive siblings than for adoptive siblings at both 1 and 2 years, suggesting genetic influence on this measure (see Table 5.7).

In another observational study, O'Connor and associates (1995) obtained videotaped observations of adolescents' interactions with their mothers or their fathers in 10-minute discussions of problems and conflicts within each parent–adolescent dyad.

TABLE 5.7 HOME Score Correlations for Nonadoptive and Adoptive Siblings at Ages 1 and 2 Years

	Sibling Correlations	
Environmental Measure	Nonadoptive	Adoptive
1 year	.58	.35
2 years	.57	.40

Note: *Adoptive*, genetically unrelated, adopted into same home; *Nonadoptive*, genetically related in nonadoptive homes.

Source: Braungart, J. M., Fulker, D. W., & Plomin, R. (1992). Genetic influence of the home environment during infancy: A sibling adoption study of the HOME. *Developmental Psychology, 28*, 1048–1055.

The adolescent participants included six groups of siblings: identical twins, fraternal twins, full siblings in nondivorced families, and full siblings, half siblings, and unrelated siblings in stepfamilies. Using sophisticated estimates of heritability the researchers found some significant genetic influences both on the positive and negative interaction with both the mothers and fathers. Collectively these studies suggest that what the child brings to the world genetically unsurprisingly but importantly influences the treatment received by the social environment, for example, in the form of how parents interact with him or her (see *In Focus 5.4*).

5.17 How did a study with brave and scared mice prove the important role of environmental factors in development?

IN FOCUS 5.4

NATURE *AND (NOT VERSUS)* NURTURE: BOTH MATTER

In an important experiment, Francis and colleagues (2003) studied mice to examine how the maternal environment can affect the inhibitory behavior of pups. The advantage of working with mice is that while the mouse genome has enormous overlap with the human genome, mice experiments on nature and nurture are possible, but human experiments obviously are not.

The researchers worked with two strains of mice with different social behavioral patterns: B6 and BALB mice. B6 mice genetically are significantly higher in novelty seeking and lower in fearfulness than the BALB mice. The researchers tested how genetically identical brave, novelty-seeking (B6) mice behave when placed in an environment with a fearful (BALB) mother. Some were transferred as embryos shortly after conception and others were transferred just after birth. These mice were then compared to B6 and BALB mice who were raised by their biological mothers.

Even though all of the B6 mice in the experimental groups were genetically identical to one another, the B6 mice who were transferred to BALB mothers as embryos and remained with the BALB mothers after birth behaved in ways much more similar to the BALB mice in the control group. Although these mice came from the same, genetically brave strain of mice, their behavior became much more inhibited and fearful when carried and raised by scared, BALB mothers. On the other hand, B6 mice who were placed with a B6 mother either before or after birth acted much more like the B6 mice in the control group—that is, exploratory and more fearless. This study makes two important points: (1) Genetic endowment can be a very powerful determinant of an individual's behavior and (2) the maternal environment in which that individual develops can have a significant impact on how that behavior is expressed.

Source: Francis, D. D., Szegda, K., Campbell, G., Martin, W. D., & Insel, T. R. (2003). Epigenetic sources of behavioral differences in mice. *Nature Neuroscience, 6*, 445–446.

Genes Also Influence Environments

5.18 Describe some ways in which genetic factors influence nonshared aspects of the environment.

Genetic factors may contribute to the experienced environment in several ways (Plomin et al., 1997; Rutter et al., 1997). First, people encounter the environments that their genetic relatives, in part, make for them. Take activity level, for example, which seems to have a heritable component and is thus shared to some degree between the child and the parents (Saudino & Plomin, 1996). From the start, parents construct aspects of their child's early environment, and tend to make it more (or less) stimulating and activity-filled in a way that is consistent with both their own and their child's genetic propensities. Thus highly active children are likely to have active parents who model and reward high activity and who also provide them with both genes and an environment conducive to the development of high activity.

Second, the individual's genetically influenced characteristics affect how other people will react to him or her. For example, highly active children might receive more positive reactions from their peers or, in the opposite direction, more negative reactions from their schoolteachers.

Third, and most important, individuals actively seek and create situations and social environments in ways congruent with their genetically influenced dispositions and qualities. Whereas extremely active children are likely to create a high-energy environment by actively selecting highly active friends and activities, less active children are apt to make their environment less energy demanding. This self-directed process of selecting and creating one's own situations is the most central for personality; it is literally the seat of the sort of dynamic person–situation interactions through which dispositions and the environment reciprocally influence each other.

Given the multiple paths through which genetic influences impact on the environment, it is understandable that genetic factors often contribute substantially to measures of the environment in research. But while it is clear that genetic factors influence the environments we experience and select, the effects are complex and the direct genetic influence is only one part of the variance, and does not account for most of it.

These findings suggest that researchers need to move away from passive models of how the environment or the genes separately affect individuals and turn to models of person–environment interaction. These interaction models recognize the active role that persons play in selecting, modifying, and creating their own environments. In this process there is a continuous interaction between dispositions (partly influenced by genetics, partly by environmental influences) and situations as the individual deals with his or her world in the course of development. Such interaction implies that some of the most important questions in genetic research will involve the environment and some of the most important questions for environment research will involve genetics (Rutter et al., 1997).

A good example of how such interactions play out comes from a study of genetic and environmental influences in a sample of more than 9,000 twin pairs studied at ages 3, 4, and 7 (Knafo & Plomin, 2006). Children's genetically influenced characteristics importantly influenced parental feelings and disciplinary practices, which in turn affected how "prosocial" (caring of others vs. selfish) the child becomes (Knafo & Plomin, 2006). The researchers found that children who are seen as having empathy and who behave in prosocial ways tend to have parents who have positive feelings about them. These parents also relate to them with greater warmth, reasoning, and respect for the child's autonomy, as opposed to disciplining them by asserting their power. Findings like these suggest

The child's characteristics and the parent's child-rearing practices mutually influence each other.

that the child's characteristics, and the feelings and childrearing attitudes and practices of the parents, all interact and mutually influence each other reciprocally, reflecting the close interplay of multiple genetic and social influences in the development of personality.

The interplay of biological and psychological processes is evident at every level of analysis. It is apparent even at the molecular level: the synapses in the brain change physically when new learning occurs. In this interaction, genes are switched on to make new proteins that are crucial in long-term memory, wherein the person's history resides. Furthermore, even relatively small heritable differences in qualities of temperament, such as activity and energy levels, emotionality, and sociability, which appear to be visible in early childhood (Buss & Plomin, 1984), can be biological foundations for diverse enduring behavioral tendencies that may develop from these roots (Kagan, 2003).

For example, temperamentally more active, energetic children tend to explore and interact more vigorously and forcefully with their environments, rapidly encountering its challenges and gratifications as well as its dangers and frustrations. In time they also are likely to become more aggressive than children who are temperamentally inhibited from exploring the unfamiliar and thus inclined toward shyness (e.g., Daniels, Dunn, Furstenberg, & Plomin, 1985). Heritable variations in arousal thresholds in certain loci of the brain also could influence such behaviors as shyness (e.g., Kagan, Reznick, & Snidman, 1988). Heritable differences in sensitivity and physiological reactivity in response to sensory stimulation partly predispose people to become introverted rather than extroverted (Stelmack, 1990). In turn, introverts may be more disposed to avoid the types of social stimulation that extroverts desire and actively select for themselves (Plomin, Manke, & Pike, 1996).

Search for Specific Gene–Behavior Connections

Given the evidence for genetic influence on personality traits that has been found in recent years, researchers in the vanguard of the field are now trying to become more precise and to identify specific genes that might connect to specific characteristics. They are beginning to go much beyond demonstrations that genetic influences are important for personality.

In earlier research, specific genetic defects have been linked to various abnormalities such as mental deficiencies. PKU is a case in point (see Table 5.8). **PKU (*phenylketonuria*)** disease is an inherited disorder in which a genetic abnormality results in the lack of an enzyme necessary for normal metabolism. Because of this enzyme deficiency, a toxic chemical accumulates in the body and results in central nervous system damage and mental retardation. Diagnosis of PKU disease is now possible immediately after birth, and highly successful treatment has been devised. The child is placed on a special diet that prevents the toxic substance from building up in the bloodstream. When the biological mechanisms underlying other forms of mental deficiency are known, equally effective cures may be possible.

Some psychological characteristics are determined by an individual's specific genetic structure. For example, when the 21st chromosome in the body cell of an individual has a third member instead of occurring as a pair, the individual will have **Down syndrome**, a form of mental retardation. A technique for drawing amniotic fluid from the uterus of the pregnant mother enables doctors and prospective parents to know in advance if the developing fetus has this chromosome abnormality. This procedure is performed routinely for pregnant women 35 years of age or older because women in this age group are more likely to give birth to children with Down syndrome.

To link genes to personality, promising examples include the report that a gene for a dopamine receptor was correlated with novelty-seeking in two studies (Benjamin et al., 1996; Ebstein et al., 1996), with other researchers finding that the same gene was related to hyperactivity (LaHoste et al., 1996). While such findings are exciting for genetic researchers, they must be interpreted with much caution and still be treated as tentative and suggestive rather than conclusive.

These reservations are necessary because findings of associations between personality and specific genes in the past have failed to replicate. That happened, for example, for the reported correlation between neuroticism and a gene important in the functioning of the chemical neurotransmitter serotonin (Lesch, Bengel, Heils, & Sabol, 1996),

TABLE 5.8 Effects of Some Genetic Abnormalities: Two Examples

Name of Disorder	Description	Cause
Down syndrome	Severe mental retardation Physical appearance: small skull, sparse hair, flat nose, fissured tongue, a fold over the eyelids, short neck	A third, extra chromosome in the 21st chromosome pair Appears to be associated with advanced age in the mother
PKU (phenylketonuria)	Results in mental retardation if not treated soon after birth	A gene that produces a critical enzyme is missing

5.19 Have researchers been able to link specific genes to personality variables?

which two other studies could not reproduce (Ball et al., 1997; Ebstein et al., 1997). Perhaps even more important, personality traits involve extremely complex patterns of characteristics and behaviors such that an association with any specific gene probably will have only a small effect (Plomin, Owen, & McGuffin, 1994). That is, genetic influence on personality involves the action of many genes, each of which has a small effect rather than the direct effect of any single major gene.

Given this great but unsurprising complexity, it can be valuable to use the sorts of promising methods for identifying genes in lower animals that cannot be employed with people (Plomin & Saudino, 1994). For example, in such animal studies it is possible to use powerful techniques that alter specific genes, called knockouts, to test just how they influence behavior (Capecchi, 1994). In mice, for instance, several genes that, if disrupted, would result in fearfulness have been located (Flint et al., 1995). As predicted, mice display greater aggression when the researchers knock out the genes for an important neurotransmitter (Saudou et al., 1994) or enzyme (Nelson et al., 1995). The limitation of course is that it is difficult to generalize results from studies with mice to humans. But there are exciting prospects for discoveries in molecular genetics that do speak to the human condition and will prove generalizable to personality (Hamer & Copeland, 1998). However, that is the story that is not yet written but that should unfold in the next few years.

Causal Mechanisms: The Role of Neurotransmitter Systems

As discussed above, genetic and environmental influences are always in close interaction. The question then becomes: What are the causal mechanisms that underlie this interaction? To address that question at the molecular biological level of analysis, researchers now try to examine how genetic variability underlying neurotransmitter systems can be linked to variability in personality traits and behavioral patterns (e.g., Grigorenko, 2002).

Neurotransmitter systems are the physiological pathways that communicate and carry out the functions of signal detection and response via chemical receptors (neurotransmitters). The variability of each of these neurotransmitters is dictated by the variants of its corresponding gene. There are nine neurotransmitter systems, but based on their biochemical functions, some are more relevant to the carrying out of psychological functions than others. In general, personality psychologists have focused on three primary systems involved in behavioral functions (the dopaminergic, seritonergic, and GABAergic systems).

Researchers have been analyzing how certain behavioral patterns correlate with specific genetic variants. Originally, researchers aimed to show direct, one-to-one correlations between specific traits or behavioral attributes and specific genetic mutations. So far these studies have provided mixed results. Many of the experiments that seemed to exhibit this kind of direct correlation could not be replicated. Though it is clear that neurotransmitter systems are linked to the expression of behavioral patterns, it is also evident that these neurotransmitter systems do not necessarily act alone in producing their effect on behavioral attributes. In fact, recent studies have revealed that the various neurotransmitter systems work together very closely, and many of the behavioral functions originally attributed to specific neurotransmitter systems are actually a function of the interaction of more than one of these systems.

As we begin to understand more about these neurotransmitter systems and the genetic variations that affect their functioning, it is clear that the task of correlating genes to behavior is not as simple as was originally believed. The interaction between genetic expression and the phenotypic expression of personality is complex. Specifically, researchers must take into account that the genetic variability that underlies human behavior is influenced not only by the additive and interactive factors on the genetic level, but also by characteristics in the surrounding environment.

Let us look in detail at a comprehensive review of research on genes and personality (Grigorenko, 2002). The results challenge some of the basic, commonly accepted assumptions of recent years. Take the claim that genetic factors contribute extensively to the similarity of MZ twins, whereas the shared family–environment plays no serious role, discussed earlier in this chapter. Elena Grigorenko's (2002) review and research makes it clear that it really all depends. She reports a recent behavior–genetic analysis conducted with more than 700 Russian families in which shared family–environment factors contributed significantly to variation in the majority of the traits studied. Note that this contrasts with the fact that in a large subsample of the population (218 families in which at least one parent had a criminal record), genetic factors did *not* contribute significantly to variation in 13 of 15 traits. Why?

5.20 What were the results of Grigorenko's review of genetics and personality? What conclusions did she reach?

There are good biological reasons for these puzzling results. The main point here is that neurotransmitter systems interact with one another. Consequently, personality characteristics will not reflect the action of a single neurotransmitter system. The complexities get even greater because gene expression and surface-level behavioral characteristics are not stable, and instead tend to fluctuate across development in interaction with environmental conditions.

The fundamental message from all this for the student of personality is that the links between our biochemistry and our personality characteristics reflect interactions both within and between systems. These are not simple one-way causal influences—a message very much like the one that emerged in our review of the "person versus situation" debate at the trait level of analysis (Chapter 4). One specific implication is that it is unlikely that there will be either simple or direct relationships between particular genetic factors and very broad categories of personality traits like those represented by the Big Five. Thus, any expectation that a few genes might account for qualities like "open-mindedness" is probably unjustified. On the other hand, there are exciting studies that show how our genetic makeup interacts with environmental influences in the course of development to determine such important personality-relevant outcomes as depression and suicidal tendencies, as illustrated in *In Focus 5.5*.

Genetic and Environmental Influences on Person × Situation Interactions

The interplay of genes as well as the environment also is reflected in the kinds of **person × situation interaction patterns** and *if . . . then . . .* personality signatures, discussed in earlier chapters. These signatures may reflect both genetic and environmental influences, depending on the specific type of behavior involved. An early study using an adult twin sample showed, for example, that the person–situation interaction patterns for anxiety were influenced significantly by genetics, whereas for dominance shared

5.21 How might genetic factors influence person × situation interactions?

IN FOCUS 5.5

INTERACTION OF BIOLOGY AND ENVIRONMENTAL STRESS IN THE DEVELOPMENT OF DEPRESSION

In response to the same kind of stress, why do some people exhibit more depression and suicidal behaviors than others? Caspi and colleagues (2003) examined the possible biological basis for individual differences in this variability. Previous research has shown that stressful life events involving, for example, loss, humiliation, and threat can increase the chances of depression (e.g., Brown, 1998; Kendler, Karkowski, & Prescott, 1999; Kessler, 1997; Pine, Cohen, Johnson, & Brook, 2002). In addition, an individual's genetic makeup can affect his or her susceptibility to depression (e.g., Kendler et al., 1995). Considering those findings, Caspi and his co-researchers tried to determine the specific genetic difference that could affect an individual's propensity for depression when under stress.

The researchers decided to focus on the 5-HTT gene, which transports serotonin, a neurotransmitter that tends to keep an individual calm and content. In some individuals, this gene transports serotonin less efficiently than in others. The different versions or **alleles** of the gene vary in length, and on this gene, the shorter allele has been found to transport serotonin less efficiently than the longer allele (Lesch et al., 1996). Perhaps individuals with a less effective gene remain anxious or fearful in times of stress, increasing their risk for future depression. Guided by that hypothesis, the researchers predicted an interaction between the effectiveness of this gene and environment (stress) on depression. Specifically, those with a less effective 5-HTT gene (shorter alleles) would be more likely to exhibit depression symptoms than those with a more effective one.

In a prospective study of development from the ages of 3 years to 26 years, participants were measured periodically on a variety of life stressors and behaviors. A life-history calendar (a reliable measure of life-event histories) was used to assess stressful events that occurred after the 21st and before the 26th birthday. The events measured included employment and financial struggles, as well as housing, health, and relationship stressors. The number of stressful life events reported was unrelated to differences in the gene. However, as predicted, among individuals who had experienced similar stressful life events, those with a less efficient gene had depression symptoms, diagnosable depression, and suicidal behaviors much more frequently than those with a more efficient gene. Further analyses of the gene × environment interaction also showed that among carriers of the less effective gene stressful life events occurring after their 21st birthdays predicted diagnosed depression at age 26. Although the authors wisely caution that more research and replications are needed, their study provided preliminary evidence that a person's reaction to life stressors "is moderated by his or her genetic make-up" (Caspi et al., 2003, p. 386).

In a related study in 2002, the researchers asked whether a deficiency in certain genes also moderate the effect of stressful life events that happened not just in adulthood but in earlier developmental periods as well (Caspi et al., 2002). They found that the interaction between a genetic deficiency on the MAOA gene and childhood maltreatment that had occurred during the first decade of life predicted adult aggressive and antisocial behavior. This gene, when functioning efficiently, inactivates neurotransmitters commonly associated with increased human excitement and aggression (e.g., norepinephrine, dopamine), causing the individual to feel less excited and as a result, less likely, for example, to act violently. The interaction showed that maltreatment in early childhood predicted adult violent and antisocial behavior, but only among people who carried the less efficient gene.

5.22 Explain how researchers studied the role of the 5-HTT gene on depression and suicidal behaviors in young adults.

sibling–environmental influences were found (Dworkin, 1979). The results supported the general conclusion that an individual's behavior shows characteristic, meaningful patterns across situations that partly reflect genetic influences.

More recent studies with larger samples and other methods provide further and even stronger evidence for the same basic point (Cherney et al., 1994; Plomin et al., 1997, p. 202). An important implication is that genetic influences may be expressed not simply in how much of a given trait a person "has." Genetics also may influence the characteristic pattern in which that trait-relevant behavior is typically expressed in relation to particular types of situations (Borkenau et al., 2006; Mischel & Shoda, 1995; Wright & Mischel, 1987, 1988).

Social Environments Change the Expression of Genes, the Brain, and Personality

Researchers pursuing the genetic approach to personality readily acknowledge that even highly heritable traits can be constrained or limited in their full expression. We see that, for example, when the person's growth and ultimate height is affected by nutrition or disease in development. But although they refer to the interplay of genes and environment, often they do *not* see this interplay as a two-way reciprocal or mutual influence process. Obviously social environments and the experiences in the world (barring extreme radiation or other biochemical effects on the genes directly) cannot affect the structure of your DNA. So in that sense the interplay between genes and environment in these analyses refers to a one-way influence process from genes to environment, in which genetic influences impact through various routes on the environments experienced with no modification of the genetic structure itself.

5.23 Can the environment change genes? Cite results from stress research.

But it is also the case that social-psychological environmental influences can and do affect the expression of the genes: just by reading this paragraph you increase DNA transcription rates of certain neurotransmitters. And environmental influences also change the hardwiring of the brain—the neuronal structures themselves—and thus produce stable changes within the person at an organic level, even though they do not alter the structure of the DNA. This is evident, for example, in the finding that stress actually shrinks the size of the hippocampus—a brain structure basic for higher-order mental functions (e.g., Sapolsky, 1996).

Stress Is Bad for Your Brain

Sapolsky reviewed studies showing that sustained stress increases glucocorticoids (GCs), a chemical substance that at high rates can have negative effects on health. Consistent with this finding, Sapolsky (1996) reports research with rodents showing that exposure to excessive amounts of GCs can impair the brain, with particularly unfortunate effects on the hippocampus, a brain structure crucial for learning and memory. Studies with depressed patients (as summarized in Figure 5.2) also showed that the volume of this brain structure was significantly reduced, and the longer the depression the greater the amount of brain atrophy (Sapolsky, 1996). Furthermore, combat veterans suffering from posttraumatic stress reactions (e.g., after terrifying war experiences) also displayed not only greater exposure to GCs but also substantial reduction in their hippocampi on both sides of the brain.

In short, although the social environment does not influence the structure of the genes, it can influence their expression, the brain, and the person's personality. As other sections of the text discuss, situations and environments importantly influence what people experience and do in stable relationship to those contexts. When the situations remain stable, so does their characteristic pattern of social behavior; when the situations change, the behavior pattern also does so predictably (e.g., Mischel & Shoda, 1995, 1998). And as was just noted, such environmental events as stress levels not only impact dramatically on behavior and experience, but also change the hardwiring (i.e., the structures) in the brain. Person–environment interactions are two-way interactions in which the person's characteristics show some change over time, just as the characteristics also in part change the environment (Rutter et al., 1997).

In sum, environmental, genetic, and brain influences are in continuous interaction. These interactions affect what we feel and do, which, in turn, produces further changes.

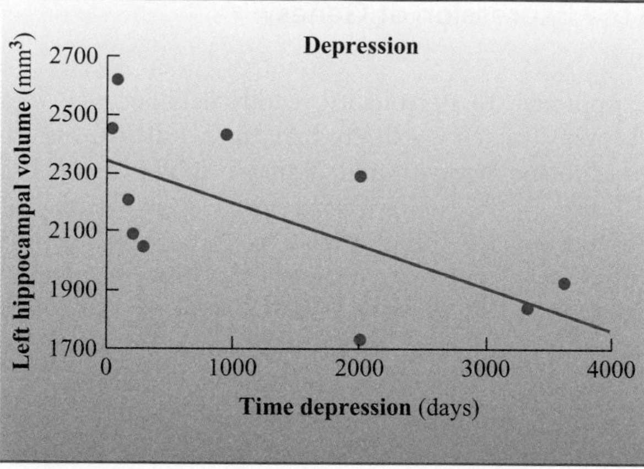

Figure 5.2 Relation between hippocampal volume and duration of depression among individuals with a history of major depression.

Reported in: Sapolsky, R. M. (1996). Why stress is bad for your brain. *Science, 273*, 749–750. Figure is referenced as adapted from Sheline, Y., Wang, P. W., Gado, M. H., Csernansky, J. G., & Vannier, M. W. (1996). Hippocampal atrophy in recurrent major depression. *Proceedings of the National Academy of Sciences of the United States of America, 93*(9):3908–13.

The challenge in future research on the interplay of genes, brain, and environment will be to clarify the complex and dynamic processes that lie between genes, brain, and behavior.

SUMMARY

GENETIC BASES OF PERSONALITY

- Many studies have shown evidence that genes play a larger role in influencing one's personality than previously thought, particularly for such temperaments as emotionality, activity level, and sociability.
- Twin studies examine the separate role of genetics and environment by comparing the similarities between identical and fraternal twins raised together and raised apart.
- In these studies, answers on self-report personality questionnaires typically yield correlations of about .50 for the similarity of identical twins reared together and about .25 for fraternal twins reared together. For identical twins reared apart, correlations are only slightly lower. About 40–50% of the self-reported personality differences among individuals may be accounted for by their genetic differences.
- Most twin data on personality come from self-report personality questionnaires and are open to criticism. However, in recent twin studies such measures as ratings by peers or observational measures also indicate a strong genetic influence.
- The meaning of heritability estimates and their uses and misuses were discussed.

GENE–ENVIRONMENT INTERPLAY

- Nonshared environmental influences on personality development are substantial, and children growing up in the same family experience it differently.
- Individual differences in what is experienced and in the environments one encounters are partly influenced by genetic factors that exert their impact through several routes. One's personality, itself influenced by genetics as well as environment, also affects the situations that one selects, influences, and creates in the course of development.
- Even highly heritable traits can be constrained or limited by aspects of their social environment. Although the social environment does not influence the structure of the genes, it can change the brain and thus produce stable changes within the person at an organic level.
- Stable person × situation interaction patterns also reflect both genetic and environmental influences.

▶ KEY TERMS

activity 102
alleles 120
behavior genetics 95
dizygotic (DZ) 100
Down syndrome 117
emotional reactivity 102
emotionality 102
gene 98
heritability estimates 108
human genome 96
inhibition 104
monozygotic (MZ) 100
neurotransmitter systems 118
nonshared (or unique) environment 111
person × situation interaction patterns 119
PKU (*phenylketonuria*) 117
shared (or family) environment 111
sociability 102
twin method 100
temperaments 101

CHAPTER 6

BRAIN, EVOLUTION, AND PERSONALITY

▸ BRAIN–PERSONALITY LINKS

Over millions of years, our species has accumulated genes that have proven useful for individual survival and reproductive success, passing them from generation to generation. The result is the set of what is currently estimated to be about 30,000 genes that make up the human genome. As noted in the last chapter, some of these genes are so important to an individual's basic functions that their DNA sequence is believed to be identical for all individuals. Any deviations from the optimal sequence perfected through evolution are likely to reduce adaptability. For other genes, there are variations. For example, there are variations in the genes that influence eye color, and individuals differ in the particular variations they have of those genes. Heritable differences in personality of the kind described in Chapter 5 reflect such variations.

But genes do not directly influence behavior. They influence behavior through their effects in shaping our body, particularly our brain, and the large number of specialized chemical components that regulate their functioning, such as enzymes, hormones, and neurotransmitters. (For an early attempt to link body–mind connections to personality, see *In Focus 6.1*.) We experience the world with distinctive brains. In the rest of this chapter, we explore theories and findings about how our biological structures and processes influence our thoughts, feelings, and behavior, giving rise to the distinctive personalities that characterize each of us.

Biological Bases of Extraversion–Introversion (H. J. Eysenck)

6.1 According to Eysenck, what biological differences underlie extraversion and introversion?

You already learned about the work at the trait level by Hans Eysenck (1916–1997), an outstanding English personality theorist, in Chapter 3. Eysenck also was a pioneer in trying to connect psychological dispositions to their biological foundations, focusing on the characteristics of extraverts versus introverts. Recall that extraverts are

IN FOCUS 6.1

AN EARLY EFFORT: PHYSIQUE AND PERSONALITY?

Attempts to connect the physical-biological aspects of individuals to their personality are hardly new. People since ancient times have noticed the dramatic differences in the kinds of bodies that different personalities seem to live in, and speculated about the possible connections between physical makeup and personality. In ancient Greece, Hippocrates described four types of personality—choleric, sanguine, phlegmatic, and melancholy—each thought to be caused by excessive amounts of bodily "humors" (yellow bile, blood, mucus, and black bile, respectively).

In early versions of personality work at the biological level, formal classifications of the possible connections between mental disorders and body type were developed by the German psychiatrist Kretschmer a century ago. In 1942, William H. Sheldon, an American physician, suggested three dimensions of physique and their corresponding temperaments. These are summarized in Figure 6.1 and for many years received much attention. As Figure (6.1) suggests, according to Sheldon the **endomorph** is obese, the **mesomorph** has an athletic build, and the **ectomorph** is tall, thin, and stoop-shouldered. Rather than dividing people into three distinct types, Sheldon considered every individual's status on each dimension. He developed a seven-point rating system for measuring body types. For example, a 7-3-1 would be high on endomorphy, moderate on mesomorphy, and low on ectomorphy, presumably with corresponding levels of the associated temperaments. Sheldon's typology thus was quite sophisticated, especially by comparison with earlier attempts.

Sheldon's ideas about the association between body build and temperament get some support when untrained people rate the personality characteristics of others. In part these findings may reflect the fact that stereotyped ideas about the characteristics of fat, athletic, and skinny people are shared by the raters. For example, if raters think most fat people are jolly and thin people are sensitive, they may base their judgments of the individuals they rate on these stereotypes rather than on observed behavior. Thus they may rate a fat person as jolly, no matter how he or she behaves. Studies of behavior that avoid such stereotypes generally provide less evidence for the value of this system (Tyler, 1956) and leave Sheldon's theory largely unsupported (Herman, 1992).

In addition to such effects from the stereotypes of others, people perceive and interpret their own body types. The thoughts and feelings we develop about our bodies may influence our behavior and who we become, increasing the connections between body types and personality. Thus, physical appearance and physical characteristics certainly affect the ways in which others perceive us, and ultimately even what we feel and experience about ourselves.

Physical characteristics such as strength, height, and muscularity also affect what we can and cannot do easily and thus also influence the situations we select, the work and avocations we pursue, and the interests and values that develop. In short, many different indirect causes may underlie the relations between physique and particular personality characteristics. The links between the two turned out to be much more complex and indirect than the early typologies suggested, and they are difficult to unscramble. Consequently, interest in these connections has gone down, particularly as better routes have opened for exploring the relations between biology and personality scientifically and with increasing precision, as discussed throughout this chapter.

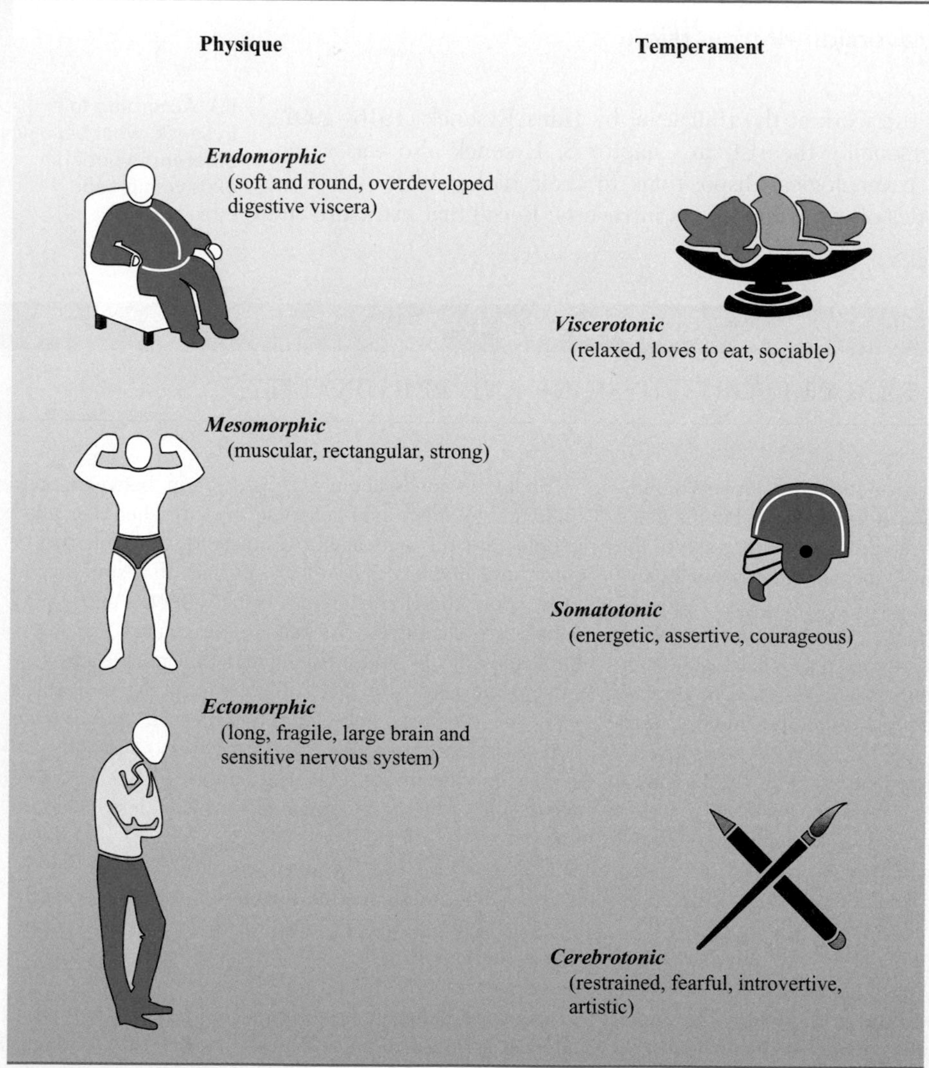

Figure 6.1 Sheldon's physique dimensions and their associated temperaments.

6.2 Describe and discuss the links Sheldon proposed between physique and personality.

characterized as active, outgoing, and venturesome, whereas introverts are defined as the opposite: withdrawn, quiet, introspective, with a preference for being alone or with a good friend or two, but an aversion for large groups. According to Eysenck's theory (Eysenck, 1990; Eysenck & Eysenck, 1985, 1995), extraverts differ from introverts because of differences in their physiological **level of arousal (LOA)** in the brain. Specifically, he proposed that these differences are influenced by the **ascending reticular activation system (ARAS)** of the brain, the system believed to regulate overall arousal in the cortex.

When Eysenck (1967) first developed his theory in the 1960s, the ARAS was viewed as a gateway that controls the level of stimulation into the cortex. In Eysenck's theory, introverts need only small amounts of stimulation to overstimulate them physiologically, which then leads them to become distressed and withdrawn in their behavior. In extraverts, in contrast, according to the theory, the ARAS is not easily stimulated, which leads them to seek activities that will increase the level of stimulation, for example, by socializing more actively and seeking activities—such as parties and adventures—more than introverts.

6.3 How did Eysenck test his theory? How are introverts and extraverts different physiologically?

To test this theory, Eysenck and colleagues conducted studies with extraverts and introverts and measured their brain wave activity and cardiovascular activity. Researchers found, for example, that introverts (compared to extraverts) show greater changes in their brain wave activity in response to low frequency tones, indicating their lower threshold for stimulation to the CNS (central nervous system), as the theory predicted (Stelmack & Michaud-Achorn, 1985). Overall, a good deal of research indicates that while extraverts and introverts don't differ in their level of brain activity at resting levels, for example while sleeping, they do differ as predicted by the theory in their physiological reactivity to stimulation. Many different types of studies suggest this conclusion (e.g., Eysenck, 1983).

The differences between extraverts and introverts in their reactivity to stimulation also should influence their performance under different arousal levels because different activities require different arousal levels to do them well. In earlier work, Hebb (1955) defined the **optimal level of arousal (OLA)** as the arousal level that is most appropriate for doing a given task effectively, and showed that too much or too little arousal undermines performance. This is intuitively familiar: as you know from your own experience, prepping for an important examination, for example, requires a higher level of arousal and alertness than you need when trying to relax or to go to sleep. The point is that to be able to perform effectively requires a good match between one's arousal level and the optimal arousal level needed for the particular task. Consequently, the differences between extraverts and introverts in their ease of arousal should have important implications for how well they do on many life tasks: they should do well on tasks that require arousal levels that match their own, but not on those where there is a major mismatch.

An extravert faced with monotonous work tasks such as closely monitoring control panels that remain generally stable, or proofreading, is likely to soon become bored and have trouble maintaining attention, becoming underaroused, and apt to tune out or even fall asleep. In this situation, an introvert will probably remain attentive and perform more effectively. Suppose, however, the job is that of a fireman or emergency room worker, and all the alarms and sirens suddenly are ringing, the emergency lights are flashing, the scene is chaotic. Now the situation is reversed in terms of the amount of arousal activated, and the introvert who is easily overaroused has the disadvantage, prone to becoming distressed and ineffective, whereas the extravert may be in his ideal element and functioning at his best.

This point was made in a classic, well-controlled experiment by Geen (1984) whose results supported the expectations from Eysenck's theory. Geen allowed extraverts and introverts to choose their preferred noise level of background stimulation while working on a potentially boring but difficult task (learning paired associations between words). As expected, extraverts chose higher levels of stimulation than did introverts. Under these conditions, according to the theory, both groups will be working under their preferred level of arousal and therefore should perform equally well—and they did. It also follows that when extraverts are given the lower levels of arousal preferred by introverts during the task, they should become underaroused and bored, and therefore do less well. Likewise, when introverts are given the higher arousal levels preferred by introverts, they should become overaroused and upset, and their performance should deteriorate. To test these expectations, Geen in fact reversed the preferred stimulation conditions on the work task, giving the introverts the noise levels chosen by the extraverts and vice versa. Again the results were as predicted: performance was poorer when extraverts worked under the lower stimulation conditions preferred by the introverts, and vice versa.

Brain Asymmetry and Personality Differences

Brain Asymmetry

People differ consistently in the degree to which the right versus the left sides of their brains are activated, and that difference is called **brain asymmetry**. To study these differences, the brain's electrical activity is assessed by the electroencephalograph (EEG) that was described in Chapter 2. To calculate differences in the brain's asymmetry, researchers subtract the level of EEG brain wave activity on the left side of the brain from the level of activity on the right side of the brain. A positive asymmetry measure indicates a relatively higher degree of activity on the right side of the brain; a negative measure indicates a relatively higher degree of activity on the left side of the brain (Sutton, 2002, p. 136). Stable individual differences have been found repeatedly in the brain's asymmetry in anterior (frontal) brain regions (e.g., Sutton & Davidson, 2000).

The Behavioral Inhibition and Activation Systems

6.4 Describe the BIS and BAS, as well as their functions.

One of these individual differences involves two neurological systems in the brain: the **behavioral inhibition system (BIS)** and the **behavioral activation system (BAS)**. The BIS causes individuals to withdraw from certain undesirable stimuli or punishments and thus inhibits behavior. You can think of it as a withdrawal–avoidance system that allows one to pause and then contemplate alternatives before taking action. Shakespeare's Hamlet probably would have scored high on measures of the strength of this system. This system enhances attention to threats and risks and possible punishment and is adaptive to humans because it is useful for avoiding danger and for surviving. In contrast, the BAS directs individuals toward certain desirable goals or incentives and thus activates approach behavior. You can think of it as an energizing system that activates and facilitates rapid action. Activity in this appetitive, positive-approach motivational system enhances attention to reward cues. It facilitates approach behaviors in the search for possible gratifications and positive outcomes in the pursuit of goals.

Brain Asymmetry and Emotional Reactivity

6.5 How are hemispheric activation differences related to types of emotions?

You can get a sense of these individual differences and their implications for personality from some experiments in which participants were exposed to videotapes depicting funny or aversive, fear-inducing, and disgusting themes. While they were watching these videos, their EEGs were recorded, their facial and behavioral reactions were filmed, and self-reports of their emotional reactions also were obtained. Individuals who had higher resting levels of activity in their left frontal area of the brain gave more positive responses to happy stimuli (Wheeler, Davidson, & Tomarken, 1993). They also showed higher levels of self-reported BAS sensitivity on questionnaires (Harmon-Jones & Allen,

1997; Sutton & Davidson, 1997). In contrast, higher resting levels of activity in the right frontal area of the brain were indicative of more negative feelings in response to aversive stimuli (Davidson, Ekman, Saron, Senulis, & Friesen, 1990), as well as higher levels of self-reported BIS sensitivity on the self-report measures of reactivity to threats.

Evidence for the stability of these individual differences in affective styles also comes from studies of very young children. For example, 10-month-old children were exposed to a brief separation from the mother while she left the playroom in an experimental situation. While some infants became greatly distressed, others remained much calmer. Those who cried and were more upset also tended to be the ones who characteristically have more brain wave activity on the right than on the left side, even when they were measured during the resting stage. Thus individual differences in this type of emotional reactivity seem to be a stable quality already seen in the young child (Fox, Bell, & Jones, 1992). Likewise in adults, brain asymmetry is sufficiently stable over time to suggest an enduring disposition that relates to how one deals with different kinds of emotion-inducing events and experiences (Davidson, 1993).

BIS, BAS, and Personality Traits

The degree of activity in these two systems also is linked to individual differences at the broad dispositional-trait level, as assessed, for example, by the NEO-PI-R and the Five Factor (Big Five) model. Specifically, greater activity in the BAS seems to be more characteristic of extraverts, and greater activity in the BIS is linked to introversion and anxiety, and to related measures of temperament beginning early in life (Derryberry & Rothbart, 1997; Gray, 1991). The BAS also seems to be associated with dominance/sensation seeking and impulsivity, and the BIS with conscientiousness/behavioral inhibition (MacDonald, 1998).

6.6 How do the BIS and BAS relate to introversion and extraversion?

Theoretically, because of their greater reactivity in the BAS, extraverts and those high in dominance/sensation seeking will focus more on rewards, especially immediate rewards, and look eagerly for situations in which they could get them. Think here of a person who loves adventures, gets easily involved, seizes opportunities, and often can be impulsive and indifferent to the long-term costs. In contrast, the greater reactivity in the BIS of introverts and anxiety-prone persons is related to their focus on threats and potential negative outcomes. The anxious introvert's tendency to be more passive and avoidant may reflect greater physiological sensitivity and alertness to all the possible things that could go wrong and produce trouble. Think here of the person who foregoes strong temptations and pleasures (from pizzas to potentially dangerous thrills and adventures) out of the fear of the delayed consequences (from upset stomachs to unwanted pregnancies and HIV infections).

It may be that because BAS is the more active system in extraverts, they tend to focus on rewards and seek situations in which they could find them to actively pursue their desires (Gray, 1991). This is in contrast to the more passive, avoidant behavior of introverts who may be physiologically more sensitized to punishment and threats (e.g., Bartussek, Diedrich, Naumann, & Collet, 1993). Gray's (1991) theory and related work also indicates that the BIS is linked to anxiety as a personality dimension, whereas the BAS is related to individual differences in impulsivity or the inability to inhibit and control one's immediate responses and urges.

The overall implication from this line of research for personality is clear. Individuals who are dominantly left-side active in their brains experience pleasant, positive emotions more easily when positive stimuli are encountered. People who are dominantly right-side active are more ready to respond with negative emotional reactions and distress when they face unpleasant or threatening events. Some people are more ready to feel and be happy than others; some people are more ready to feel and be distressed and to experience negative emotions than others.

In sum, although there still is considerable disagreement among theorists about the exact mechanisms and links to personality (e.g., Cloninger, 1988; Davidson, 1995; Depue & Collins, 1999), several tentative conclusions seem to be emerging. Individuals who are extremely reactive in the BIS tend to be especially sensitive to potential threat, punishment, and danger. They therefore may focus more on the potential negative outcomes rather than on the possible gains and rewards when considering alternative action possibilities. For example, they are likely to attend more to how much money they could lose from a business decision than to how much they might gain. They are more prone to anxiety and in the extreme even to panic, more tuned to negative outcomes and punishment, and less sensitive to possible rewards, incentives, and gratifications. On the other hand—or, more literally, on the other side of the brain—people who are highly reactive in the BAS are likely to show the opposite pattern: they are more responsive to incentives and possible positive outcomes, and more ready to experience positive emotions such as eagerness, hope, and excitement (see *In Focus 6.2*).

IN FOCUS 6.2

BIS/BAS AND EVERYDAY EMOTIONAL EXPERIENCES

Self-report measures of BIS and BAS reactivity (Carver & White, 1994) have been developed that correlate well with the brain measures (e.g., Gable, Reis, & Elliot, 2000). Table 6.1 lists items from the BIS/BAS self-report scales, and provides interesting brain-personality relationships.

For example, people who had higher resting levels of activity in their left frontal area of the brain (indicative of BAS activity) also self-reported higher BAS sensitivity on items like those shown in Table 6.1. In contrast, higher resting levels of activity in the right frontal area of the brain (indicative of BIS activity) were related to higher self-reported BIS sensitivity (Harmon-Jones & Allen, 1997; Sutton & Davidson, 1997).

Using these self-report measures, some researchers examined the impact of the two systems on college students' emotional experiences in everyday life. They explored the joint effects of dispositional differences in BIS and BAS sensitivities to cues of rewards and punishments on participants' daily experiences. These experiences included the emotions of undergraduate students, specifically, their positive affect (PA) and negative affect (NA), and the positive and negative events that they encountered in their daily lives at college (Gable, et al., 2000). According to BIS/BAS theory (e.g., Gray, 1991), as discussed in the text, individuals with high BIS dispositions will seek out and select negative cues and events in their environments. Those high in BAS dispositions will attend to and pursue positive events and possibilities for gratifications.

Dr. Gable and her research group wanted to test if people's BIS/BAS dispositions in fact influence their experiences and their daily emotional states (Gable et al., 2000). They hypothesized that because BAS increases sensitivity to positive events, individuals high in BAS will have stronger reactions to them. The reverse should be true for individuals high in BIS: people high in this disposition over time should have magnified reactions to negative events.

To test these ideas, participants were divided into BIS and BAS groups based on their scores on the BIS–BAS Scale (Carver & White, 1994). In a series of studies, they were then asked for daily reports of their positive or negative affect on a 20-item scale to rate how much "you feel from day to day" emotions described by words like happy, distressed, nervous, or enthusiastic (Watson, 1988). They also reported the occurrence of positive and negative daily events on a questionnaire consisting of 16 positive events (social and achievement) and 19 negative events (social and achievement), and indicated their frequency and importance for each.

These results show the important role of BIS/BAS as personality dispositions. Dispositional BAS sensitivity magnified peoples' reactions to positive events, and BIS sensitivity magnified their reactions to negative events. Furthermore, in their daily lives, on average, higher BAS people experienced more positive affect, more strongly.

Gable and colleagues also found that, as predicted, the number of positive events that occurred during the day on average was strongly related to participants' positive affect, and their negative affect was strongly related to the number of negative events. However, consistent with the BIS/BAS theory, on the whole, the two types of emotional reactions, positive and negative affect, seem to be functionally independent like the BAS and BIS systems themselves. This finding also fits with other data showing the independence of positive and negative affect (Cacioppo & Gardner, 1999; Watson, 1988).

TABLE 6.1 Some Items from the BIS/BAS Scale (Carver & White, 1994)

1	2	3	4
Strongly Agree		Strongly Disagree	

BIS

1. If I think something unpleasant is going to happen, I usually get pretty "worked up."
2. I worry about making mistakes.
3. I feel pretty worried or upset when I think or know somebody is angry at me.
4. Even if something bad is about to happen to me, I rarely experience fear or nervousness.

BAS Reward Responsiveness

1. When I get something I want, I feel excited and energized.
2. When I'm doing well at something, I love to keep at it.
3. When good things happen to me, it affects me strongly.
4. When I see an opportunity for something I like, I get excited right away.

BAS Drive

1. When I want something, I usually go all out to get it.
2. I go out of my way to get things I want.
3. If I see a chance to get something I want, I move on it right away.
4. When I go after something, I use a "no holds barred" approach.

BAS Fun Seeking

1. I will often do things for no other reason than that they might be fun.
2. I crave excitement and new sensations.
3. I'm always willing to try something new if I think it will be fun.
4. I often act on the spur of the moment.

Source: Carver, C. S., & White, T. L. Behavioral inhibition, behavioral activation, and affective responses to impending reward and punishment: The BIS/BAS scales. *Journal of Personality and Social Psychology*, 67, 319–333. © 1994, American Psychological Association.

Summary and Implications

6.7 Explain how the BIS and BAS are related to how people experience negative and positive events.

In sum, findings on the BAS and BIS and on brain asymmetry suggest that these are specific and distinct incentive and threat systems in the brain that are responsive, respectively, to environmental signals of reward and threat, and that are related, respectively, to positive and negative mood (e.g., Gable et al., 2000). This is important for understanding individual differences in personality because people differ in stable ways in their levels of reactivity in these two brain systems. These differences link to their behavioral dispositions with regard to active positive approach tendencies versus fearful behavioral inhibition and avoidance tendencies. These differences are reflected on measures of the relevant personality dispositions (extraversion, impulsivity for the BAS; inhibition, withdrawal, anxiety, or neuroticism for the BIS). In short, there are clear and meaningful specific links between peoples' characteristic brain activities and their characteristic emotional and behavioral reaction patterns to different types of positive and negative stimulation.

It is also noteworthy that brain systems such as BIS and BAS are linked to personality in context-specific ways that again reflect the importance of taking account of the relationship between the expressions of personality and the characteristics of the stimulus situation. You see this in the finding that high BIS reactivity relates to more sensitivity and attention to possible punishments, less to possible rewards, and is essentially diagnosed by the difference between the two. The distinctive dispositional pattern of people high in BIS activity takes the form: *if* threats-punishments are encountered, *then* inhibition, high anxiety-distress, negative emotions. The opposite *if . . . then . . .* pattern or personality signature seems to characterize those high in BAS. For them, *if* rewards, incentives, *then* approach, eagerness, positive emotions. While the two types also link to broad dispositions like extraversion, their behavioral expressions are especially evident when the relevant "ifs" are present. Once again, we find that the expressions of personality are seen in person–situation interactions as well as in overall behavioral tendencies.

6.8 How is the action of biological systems influenced by situational factors?

Probing the Biology of Neuroticism

New insights about personality dispositions are coming from studies that probe the relationships that do—and that don't—exist between individual differences with regard to various types of relatively broad trait categories like neuroticism on the one hand, and biological processes on the other. For example, Heller and colleagues (2002) find that anxious emotional arousal and worry may reflect two separate neural networks in the brain. Specifically, these networks are in the left versus right hemispheres, and in the frontal versus posterior regions, as measured by EEG and blood flow indices of cortical activity. Their research suggests that psychological conditions that have long been grouped under the term "neuroticism" may actually consist of two distinct mechanisms that need to be understood separately. These two systems thus may involve different mechanisms that lead to different experiences and life problems, and that require different treatment. This kind of research illustrates how discoveries at the biological level utilizing modern brain assessment techniques are allowing a greater level of precision in the analysis of broad dispositions like neuroticism. The ability to distinguish the different phenomena covered by a broad term like neuroticism makes it possible to examine their different causes. Then one also can develop distinctive therapies targeted to treat these different disorders more effectively.

Sensation Seeking: A Trait with a Specific Biological Basis?

6.9 How do high and low scorers on the sensation seeking scale differ behaviorally?

Why do some people go parachuting and drive fast, whereas others prefer TV and rarely exceed the speed limit? According to one researcher, Marvin Zuckerman, the answer may lie in a trait called **sensation seeking**. Of particular interest is that this trait also seems to have clear connections with findings from the biological level that point both to the role of brain chemicals and of genetics as determinants. First, let us consider the nature of individual differences in this characteristic. These differences are measured with a **Sensation Seeking Scale (SSS)**, which taps into four different aspects: Thrill and Adventure Seeking (engaging in risky sports and fast driving, for example), Experience Seeking (seeking novelty), Disinhibition (seeking sensation through social stimulation and activities), and Boredom Susceptibility (lack of tolerance for repetitive events).

This scale has helped to predict how people cope with situations in which there is a lack of stimulation: in this context, the sensation seekers get more restless and upset. It also predicts reactions to the opposite experience, as when one is placed in

TABLE 6.2 Characteristics of High Sensation Seekers

Risk-Taking Behaviors
- More varied sexual experience
- Greater use and variety of illegal drugs
- Risky driving habits
- More risky sports, take risks within sports

Intellectual Preferences
- Prefer complexity
- Have a high tolerance for ambiguity
- Are more original and creative
- Rich imagery and dreams

Interests and Attitudes
- Liberal, permissive, and nonconforming attitudes and choice
- Prefer high stimulation vocations (e.g., aircraft controllers, high-risk security officers, war-zone journalists, emergency room doctors)
- May view love more as a game and show less commitment to their relationships

close confinement with another person. In that situation, those low in sensation seeking become more stressed, both in their own reports of the experience and on biochemical measures (e.g., Zuckerman, Persky, Link, & Basu, 1968). Sensation seeking now has been related to a wide range of diverse behaviors (Zuckerman, 1979, 1983, 1984, 1994), as the examples in Table 6.2 summarize.

6.10 What is the hypothesized biological basis for differences in sensation seeking?

How does this personality characteristic connect to the Biological Level? As with extraversion, individual differences in sensation seeking also may arise in part from physiological differences in physical arousal, such as cortical activity in reaction to novel and familiar stimuli (Zuckerman, 1990). Hebb's (1955) ideas about optimal level of arousal (OLA) again are relevant here just as they were in our discussion of extraverts and introverts and their very different reactions to different types of situations that require a different arousal level for optimal performance. Consistent with Hebb, if individuals differ in their preferred optimal level of arousal, then those with a low optimal level of arousal will attempt to maintain a low level of arousal, which requires them to sometimes work toward reducing the stimulation in their environment. Those with a high OLA—the sensation seekers—will work toward increasing the stimulation they get in order to achieve and maintain their optimal level of arousal, and therefore they keep looking for change and searching for novel and complex sensations and experiences. Individuals who are high versus low on Zuckerman's measures of sensation seeking tend to choose occupations and display life patterns that are consistent with these expectations. High compared to low sensation seekers are more likely to be skydivers or police officers who prefer riot duty, to take greater risks in gambling situations, and to self-report having more diverse sexual experiences and partners (e.g., Zuckerman, 1978, 1984, 1991)—in other words, to behave in ways consistent with their needs for higher arousal states to obtain their "optimal" levels, as Table 6.2 indicated.

Sensation seeking also may be linked to impulsiveness. Impulsiveness is a quality that in extreme and unsocialized form characterizes people who are considered antisocial personalities, sometimes also called sociopaths or psychopaths. These are people who frequently engage in criminal and antisocial behavior, seem unable to control their own impulses or to show the type of conscientiousness and adherence to conventions generally expected in social interactions and relationships within the society and culture. Zuckerman (1993) suggests that these may be unsocialized, impulsive sensation seekers—individuals who have difficulty inhibiting their impulses for the sake of social adaptation. They seek sensation even when the long-term costs to them and society are high. Unsurprisingly, such individuals also tend to be low on measures of conscientiousness, and high on measures of aggression.

To find the biological bases for individual differences in sensation seeking, Zuckerman has paid particular attention to the role of the chemicals in the nerve cells of the brain that are crucial for transmitting nerve impulses from cell to cell across the slight space—the synapse—that separates them. The **neurotransmitters** are the chemicals that enable the nerve impulses to jump across the synapses. When their levels are appropriate, the transmission across cells continues, allowing signals to get to their destinations. As with most processes in nature, there is a system of checks and balances, of activation and inhibition. The proper level of neurotransmitters is maintained by **monoamine oxidase (MAO)**, enzymes that break down the neurotransmitters after they have passed along the route. The theory here is that high sensation seekers are the individuals who are low in their MAO levels, and therefore lack the chemical inhibitors required to keep their neurotransmitter levels down.

Some support for these ideas comes from moderate or low correlations found between sensation seeking on the sensation-seeking scale and lower MAO levels in the bloodstream (Zuckerman, 1993). Although the evidence is still limited, this work continues to stimulate exciting developments at the interface of personality and biology that seeks to connect personality characteristics to specific neurotransmitters. Some of these studies are using either pharmacological or psychophysiological techniques to examine the physiological correlates of social behaviors.

6.11 How might testosterone interact with socialization factors to influence antisocial personality development?

The hope of finding such simple and direct links is understandably appealing, but Zuckerman (1994) himself is cautious about the prospects, noting that there are likely to be extremely complex interactions between neurotransmitters, enzymes, and hormones that underlie the behavioral and psychological manifestations of personality (also see *In Focus 6.3*). Nevertheless, and beyond sensation seeking, there is

IN FOCUS 6.3

TESTOSTERONE AND THE ANTISOCIAL PERSONALITY

Research suggests that hormones, and specifically testosterone levels, may be a biological contributor to antisocial behaviors. High levels of the sex hormone testosterone relate to, and may possibly promote, such behaviors as assaulting others, going AWOL while on military duty, abusing drugs, having multiple sex partners, or encountering other social problems throughout development and adulthood (Dabbs & Morris, 1990). Also, the higher the levels of this hormone, the lower the level of education attained, and consequently the lower the ultimate socioeconomic level (Dabbs, 1992). The causal chain here, however, may be very complicated, influenced perhaps by a variety of socialization factors such as lower education rather than directly by testosterone.

The point here is like the one Zuckerman (1994) makes in his discussion of the biology of antisocial impulsivity: The interactions between neurotransmitters, enzymes, and hormones that underlie the behavioral and psychological manifestations of personality will probably turn out to be multiple and complex—and these biological factors are likely to also interact with a host of social and psychological factors. Thus, to adequately understand complex patterns of social behavior, whether antisocial or prosocial, one needs to consider determinants from every level of analysis discussed throughout this text.

promising pharmacological work, for example, indicating that the neurotransmitter serotonin and the neurohormone oxytocin may mediate social bonding and affiliation, as well as social dominance and aggression (e.g., Carter, 1998; Taylor et al., 2000). Likewise, there is interesting work suggesting correlations between testosterone levels and antisocial personality (see *In Focus* 6.3).

Recent research on sensation seeking is itself producing something of a sensation with reports of links to a specific gene and measures of novelty seeking, an aspect of the broader pattern of sensation seeking (Benjamin et al., 1996; Ebstein et al., 1996). Findings like these await much further research before conclusions can be reached, but they again point to the potentially exciting connections between aspects of behavior and their biological roots, which may well be found in the future. They make sensation seeking a particularly promising disposition for linking the biological and the dispositional-psychological levels of analysis.

▶ BIOLOGICAL ASSESSMENT AND CHANGE

Throughout this chapter and the last, you have seen that the interrelationships between biological processes and psychological processes central for personality, such as our emotions and motivations, are becoming increasingly visible. It has become possible to explore the relations between brain, evolution, and personality through the development of assessment methods that now enable researchers at the Biological Level to investigate these links systematically. In recent years, a revolution has occurred in such measurement that opens new routes for seeing brain–behavior connections.

New Windows on the Brain

Technological advances in brain imaging now allow researchers to use methods that capture even subtle nerve activity in the brain. As noted in Chapter 2, the technique of functional magnetic resonance imaging (fMRI) measures the magnetic fields created by the functioning nerve cells in the brain and with the aid of computers depicts these activities as images. These images enable researchers to see the brain areas that are most active as the person performs different kinds of mental tasks and experiences different kinds of perceptions, images, thoughts, and emotions, from fears to anticipated gratifications.

6.12 Describe fMRI and PET techniques for measuring brain processes.

Brain imaging makes it possible to trace the relations between activity at the Biological Level and what the person is doing, thinking, and feeling in different situations. The new windows on the brain allow a much more precise and detailed analysis of the links between activity in the brain and mental activity at the psychological levels reviewed throughout this text. For example, Kuhnen and Knutson (2005) measured brain activation with the fMRI while participants were making financial decisions that vary in risk-taking strategy. They found clear links between risky, nonoptimal financial decision-making strategies and activation of specific brain areas (the nucleus accumbens). Their results suggested that activities in "distinct neural circuits . . . promote different types of financial choices and indicate that excessive activation of these circuits may lead to investing mistakes" (Kuhnen & Knutsen, 2005, p. 763). Our brains may show we are making costly mistakes before we realize it ourselves or see the unfortunate consequences.

A second technique to link brain and behavior is the PET procedure, or positron emission tomography, which also was briefly introduced in Chapter 2. This technique creates images and maps of brain functioning by assessing metabolic activity in different

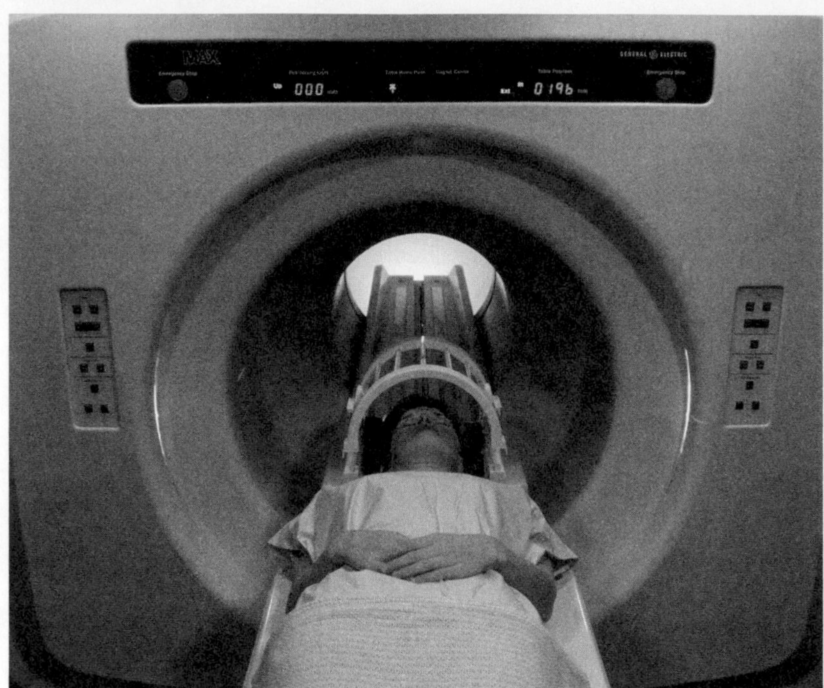

Woman entering an fMRI brain scanner.

(*Source*: Charles Thatcher/Stone/Getty Images)

areas. It records the radioactivity in the brain that occurs after the participant has been given a nontoxic but radioactively labeled form of glucose, which is the energy source for the brain's activity. These methods are being used by cognitive neuroscientists, increasingly working in collaboration with psychologists from the areas of social-personality and clinical psychology (e.g., Kosslyn et al., 2002; Ochsner & Lieberman, 2001).

Particularly exciting is the recognition that in these studies individual differences in personality are not "noise" that needs to be removed to decipher the mechanisms involved. On the contrary, attention to personality and the differences between individuals in responsiveness on these brain measures allows a much deeper and more complete understanding. For example, in studies of mental imagery using the amount of blood flow measurable in different areas of the brain, it was found that

> *monitoring individual differences in blood flow in relevant areas ... provides enormous power in predicting behavior ... individual differences not only can be used to establish that a particular type of representation is used during the task ... but also can help identify the neural underpinnings of such processing. (Kosslyn et al., 2002)*

The Amygdala and Personality

The new methods for examining brain activity and its links to mental and emotional reactions are proving to have major implications for personality psychology. To illustrate, a particularly important brain area for personality researchers is the **amygdala** (which means "almond" in Latin). This small almond-shaped region in the forebrain is buried deep under the prefrontal cortex (Figure 6.2). It is crucially important in fear learning (LeDoux, 1996). The central nucleus of this brain structure reacts almost instantly to

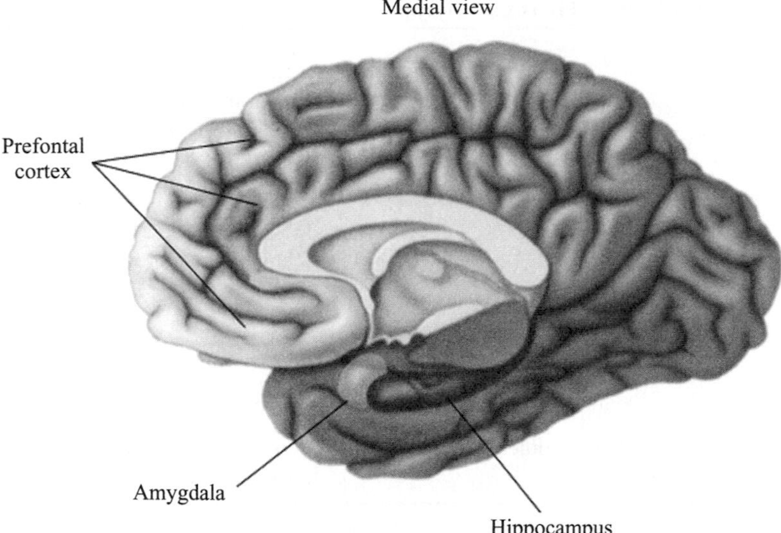

Figure 6.2 The amygdala is important in fear and emotional reactions.

signals that warn of danger, immediately sending out behavioral, physiological (autonomic), and endocrine responses. The amygdala mobilizes the body for action, readying it to flight or fight. It also seems to be involved in appetitive behaviors. Studies of individual differences in amygdala activation are casting new light on mind–brain connections in personality, as the following study illustrates.

Linking Inhibition to Amygdala Activation

6.13 In Kagan's study, how does amygdala activation differ between inhibited and uninhibited individuals?

In Kagan's work with inhibited, shy children (discussed in the previous chapter), researchers also examined how the childrens' inhibited behavior is related to biological processes and specifically to activation in the amygdala area of their brains (Schwartz, Wright, Shin, Kagan, & Rauch, 2003). Infants who were observed at 2 years of age in the lab to determine their level of inhibition were tested again when they were 22 years of age. That follow-up included assessing brain activity in a fMRI session while participants looked at either familiar faces (that they had been exposed to in an earlier session) or unfamiliar faces. The study examined how much activity was in the amygdala—the part of the brain that responds fast to threat and fear stimuli—for the 22-year-old participants while they completed the face task. The researchers found greater amygdala activation among the inhibited participants (compared to the uninhibited) while they were looking at unfamiliar faces. There were no significant differences in amygdala activation between inhibited and uninhibited participants in response to familiar faces. The findings made it clear that temperamental differences in inhibition and shyness are related to an overreactive amygdala when inhibited people are faced with novelty in the form of unfamiliar faces.

Biological Therapies

As we saw, some psychological dispositions have biological roots. If problematic behaviors, such as severe depression, in part reflect biological dispositions and biochemical problems, might they also respond to biological treatment? Researchers have actively pursued this question.

TABLE 6.3 Some Drugs Used in Pharmacotherapy

Type of Drug	Application	Therapeutic Effects
Antidepressants (cyclics, monoamine oxidase inhibitors)	Depression	Appear effective for elevating mood in some people
Antipsychotics (phenothiazines)	Schizophrenia	Well substantiated: get patients out of hospitals, have practically eliminated need for restraints in hospitals
Minor tranquilizers (benzodiazepines)	Anxiety, tension, milder forms of depression	Seem to slow down transmission of nerve impulses in the brain
Lithium	Manic behavior	Reduces mood swings
Methadone (a synthetic narcotic)	Heroin addiction	May eliminate craving for heroin; blocks "highs"

Note: These drugs are classified according to their effects on behavior, not according to their chemical composition. Chemically dissimilar drugs can produce similar effects.

Biological treatments attempt to change an individual's mood or behavior by direct intervention in bodily processes. Pharmacotherapy, or treatment with drugs, has so far proved to be the most promising biological therapy for psychological problems. The types of drugs used for specific purposes are summarized in Table 6.3.

Antidepressants

6.14 Describe the drugs commonly used for therapeutic purposes.

The antidepressants, or psychic energizers, are used to elevate the mood of depressed individuals. Two of the largest categories are the cyclics and the monoamine oxidase inhibitors, or MAOIs (Lader, 1980). Fluoxetine (trade name Prozac) is currently one of the most favored and widely used cyclic antidepressants, which increases the chemical neurotransmitter serotonin (Kramer, 1993). Excessively low serotonin levels seem to be related to such feelings as chronic pessimism, rejection sensitivity, and obsessive worry. Antidepressants have been shown to have varying degrees of efficacy and to produce various side effects (e.g., Davis, Klerman, & Schildkraut, 1967; Klein, Gittelman, Quitkin, & Rifkin, 1980; Levine, 1991). The MAOIs, for example, appear highly effective in certain types of depressed individuals, although their side effects can include a dangerous rise in blood pressure when foods high in tyramine, such as red wine and cheese, are consumed (Howland, 1991; Kayser et al., 1988; Potter, Rudorfer, & Manji, 1991). Lithium, an alkali metal in a drug category of its own, is used to stabilize mood swings and occasionally to treat severe depression (Grilly, 1989).

Antipsychotics

The phenothiazines (most notably chlorpromazine) have proved to be so useful in managing patients with schizophrenia that they are referred to as antipsychotic drugs. Their use in mental hospitals has been widespread since the 1950s and has changed the character of many hospitals, eliminating the need for locked wards and straitjackets. Discharged patients are often on maintenance dosages of these drugs and must occasionally return to the hospital for dose level adjustments.

The major tranquilizers have potentially serious side effects that may include motor disturbances, low blood pressure, and jaundice. There are also unpleasant subjective effects such as fatigue, blurred vision, and mouth dryness, which may explain why patients on their own may simply stop taking these drugs and often have to return to the hospital for an extended stay.

Tranquilizers

The barbiturates were the first widely used so-called "minor tranquilizers"—drugs that relieve relatively mild anxiety. However, these drugs were replaced by the benzodiazepines, which proved more effective with fewer side effects (Lader, 1980). For many years, the most widely used of these drugs was a synthetic chemical known by its trade name, Valium. It became the medicine most frequently prescribed in the United States for several years as Americans spent almost half a billion dollars a year on it.

Valium, like its predecessors the barbiturates, acts on the limbic system of the brain and is useful in the treatment of anxiety, panic disorder, and some convulsive disorders (Gitlin, 1990). Although Valium seemed less harmful than the barbiturates, it also proved to have side effects and to be potentially addictive. It can endanger a developing fetus and can have adverse effects of confusion and agitation, especially in the elderly. Now other benzodiazepines such as Xanax, Klonodin, and Ativan are popular alternatives, although their potentially severe side effects also require extremely cautious monitoring. The use of antidepressant medication in treatment of extreme anxiety or panic attacks also may be effective (Gitlin, 1990).

Other Common Drugs

Other widely used drugs include the psychostimulants, such as Ritalin, which are used in treating impulse disorders and severe attention deficits. Methadone, a drug that blocks the craving for heroin and prevents heroin "highs," is often used to overcome heroin addiction, either by weaning the person off it or by maintaining him or her on a fixed dose; however, methadone itself is addictive, and the process can take a long time (Lawson & Cooperrider, 1988).

As this brief survey suggests, some drugs appear to be positive contributors to a treatment program for some disorders. However, no drug by itself constitutes an adequate complete treatment for psychological problems. To the extent that the person's difficulties reflect problems of living, it would be naive to think that drugs can substitute completely for learning and practicing more effective ways to cope with the continuous challenges of life. And the fact that most drugs have negative side effects (Maricle, Kinzie, & Lewinsohn, 1988) makes it all the more important to seek psychological treatment for psychological problems whenever possible, often in conjunction with a medically supervised form of pharmacotherapy.

In spite of the problems encountered by efforts to treat psychological problems chemically, there is much exciting progress, and the new field of neuropharmacology is thriving (e.g., Cooper, Bloom, & Roth, 1996). For example, biological responses in panic disorders are becoming better understood and, in turn, the effects of various chemicals (such as sodium-lactate) on panic states are becoming known (e.g., Hollander et al., 1989). As a result, treatments for a wide range of anxiety and mood disorders are taking into account both biochemical and psychological processes (Barlow, 1988; Klein & Klein, 1989; Simons & Thase, 1992).

▶ EVOLUTIONARY THEORY AND PERSONALITY

In addition to the rapid growth of work linking genetic and brain processes to personality, evolutionary theory is greatly influencing research into personality differences. Both evolutionary theory and the genetics approach try to connect personality to its biological foundations, but there is a distinctive difference. The genetics approach focuses on the genetic influences that shape the specific biological processes and brain mechanisms underlying personality and social behavior. The evolutionary approach focuses on the processes that have shaped the genes over the long course of the species' development.

The Evolutionary Approach

6.15 How does the evolutionary approach differ from the genetics approach?

The evolutionary approach is based on Charles Darwin's well-established theory of the evolution of the species (e.g., Buss, 1991, 1997, 1999, 2001; Cosmides & Tooby, 1989). In this view, the important personality differences between people reflect the process of natural selection through which change takes place in all organic forms over the course of evolution. The processes of adaptation and selection help to explain the evolution of organisms and to understand *why* they become what they are (e.g., why kidneys, larynxes, feet, and keen sight develop). These attributes are in us now because, in the evolutionary view, they allowed our ancestors to survive and reproduce.

When Darwin's revolutionary theory, and the evidence for it, are discussed in textbooks, it's easy to miss the enormous power and personal as well as scientific implications for understanding the nature of life and indeed human nature itself. *In Focus 6.4* describes how one contemporary writer, Ian McEwan, sees this view of life.

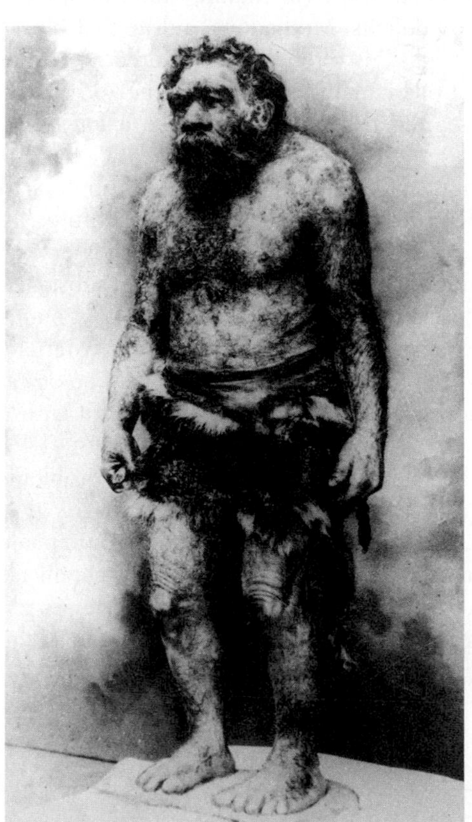

What personality attributes allowed our ancestors to survive and reproduce?

(*Source*: Mansell/Time Pix)

IN FOCUS 6.4

"THERE IS GRANDEUR IN THIS VIEW OF LIFE . . ."

Darwin, ending his great work on evolution, *On the Origin of Species (1859)*, after almost 500 sober scientific pages, quietly noted: "There is grandeur in this view of life . . ." (p. 469).

Ian McEwan (2005, p. 54), in his novel *Saturday*, comments on that grandeur:

> What better creation myth? An unimaginable sweep of time, numberless generations spawning by infinitesimal steps complex living beauty out of inert matter, driven by the blind furies of random mutation, natural selection, and environmental change, with the tragedy of forms continually dying, and lately the wonder of minds emerging and with them morality, love, art, cities—and the unprecedented bonus of this story happening to be demonstrably true.

The focus on reproduction and on passing forward one's own genes, rather than those of genetic competitors, has many implications for social life and personality. It suggests, for example, that such traits as dominance, conscientiousness, emotional stability, and sociability would have an especially significant role because they facilitate reproduction and survival (e.g., Kenrick, Sadalla, Groth, & Trost, 1990). Through the evolutionary process, people also should develop mechanisms that predispose them to be particularly fine-tuned to potential mates' indicators of health and various types of abilities, because they impact on their survival and reproductive success (McCrae & Costa, 1989, 1997; Wiggins, 1979, 1997). These mechanisms become stable and robust because of their evolutionary value (Buss, 1997).

In the evolutionary view, as language developed, many personality trait terms became established because they describe diverse, important features of the social world to which human beings have to adapt (Buss, 1989). People use these terms to try to answer questions about the status of others in the social hierarchy, their value for providing or sharing needed resources, their potential harmfulness or helpfulness, and so on. The lexicon contains thousands of trait terms that describe these features. These are the terms used in the psycholexical approach (discussed in Chapter 3), summarized in taxonomies like the Big Five. From an evolutionary perspective, it makes sense that the dimensions captured in such trait taxonomies are both highly evaluative and interpersonal, because such terms have adaptive functions and value. They seem intuitively to summarize the types of judgments people need to make as they try to know others within their "adaptive landscape." They provide a map of potential resources that identify, for example, who to go to for advice and help (those with high intellect, the open minded), or who to avoid (the unstable, the unconscientious, the hostile), or who to choose as a mate or partner.

6.16 What are the roles of directional selection and adaptation in evolutionary theory?

In evolutionary theory, the focus is not on the survival of the individual but on the fate of the gene pool that is distributed in groups across a population. The groups that survive, thrive, and rapidly reproduce will pass their genes forward into future generations. The characteristics that are passed on include many variations on which individuals differ—from height and weight through diverse abilities and social-personal traits. Over the course of many generations, the variations in characteristics that are transmitted are influenced by **directional selection**. Through directional selection, versions of the characteristics that enhance survival and reproduction gradually become increasingly represented, while those that handicap survival and reproduction tend to fade out. Such selection has a directional effect, leading ultimately to more adaptive qualities in future generations.

If that were the whole story, in time, individual differences would disappear and everyone in the surviving group would have the ideal qualities for survival. The script becomes complicated by the fact that the characteristics that may be highly adaptive in some contexts and environments may be dysfunctional and even catastrophic in others—and the species has to deal with all kinds of changing environments and challenges. Hence the maintenance of genetic variability and intermediate values of certain characteristics is often adaptive for functioning under ever-changing life conditions. When it is adaptive to have characteristics that are not at the extreme ends of dimensions, genetic variability may be maintained through a mechanism of **stabilizing selection** (Plomin, 1981).

Implications of Evolution for Personality

Evolutionary theory has great implications for personality (e.g., MacDonald, 1998). It provides provocative but often speculative insights and reinterpretations of everyday phenomena like human courtship and aggression among males. Consistently, its contributions are guided by the view that passing your genes or your group's genes—rather than those of your genetic competitor—forward to the next generation is much of what life is about.

Mate Selection

6.17 How do evolutionary psychologists explain such behaviors as male jealousy, mate selection, and altruism?

Evolutionary theory has a lot to say, particularly about mate selection and the competition for mates in humans. The theory predicts that in mate selection there will be important sex differences in the desired characteristics. To the degree that some genes predispose males to search for fertile partners, those genes are more likely to be passed on over the generations. If cues for fertility are youth and beauty, males may evolve to seek such features. In contrast, genes will be passed forward if they predispose females to seek partners who will have the resources, status, dominance, and power that provide for and protect their offspring.

Sexual Jealousy

Consider next the evolution of male sexual jealousy. From this perspective, male sexual jealousy evolved throughout the evolutionary past of the species. Anger, rage, and aggressive behavior against sexual competitors prevented the competition from sexual contact with the jealous individual's potential mates. As a result, jealous individuals increased their own reproductive success (Buss, 1997).

Likewise, the competition for mating and reproduction among males also may play a role in the violence and killing not infrequently seen among young males, and only very rarely among females. Male aggression is often provoked by disputes about respect, status, and dominance, and it may not be coincidental that the age at which the killing is highest is also the age at which the mating is highest (Wilson & Daly, 1996).

Sex Differences in Romantic and Sexual Regrets

Evolutionary theory (e.g., Buss & Schmitt, 1993) emphasizes the reproductive benefits for men to pursue romantic-sexual relationships because it increases the chances of passing on their genetic material. In contrast, for women, the finite number of pregnancies possible, and the needs to nurture the offspring for their survival, limits the amount of sexual activity required for maximal reproductive success. As a result, men may be more likely to wish they had been more active in pursuing females, and regret the opportunities they passed up.

Guided by this hypothesis, Roese and colleagues (2006) predicted a sex difference in what men and women look back on with regret. Men would more often regret the romantic-sexual activities and relationship they did *not* have, than the ones that they did have. That is, they would more often regret their sexual *inaction* (opportunities they did not take) than their actions. For women, the researchers predicted the two types of regret would be equal.

A series of studies supported these expectations. Thus with regard to romantic relationships and particularly sexual activity, men had significantly more regrets about what they did *not* do (their inaction), than about what they did do. For women, there were no differences in amount of regret about what they did do and what they did not do. This pattern of sex differences in regret was limited to the romantic-sexual domain, and especially to sexual activity, and was not found in regrets about academic choices, or friendship or familial relationships.

Consequently the results were consistent with the evolutionary hypothesis and the researchers' predictions. On the other hand, it is also consistent with many alternative interpretations. For example, there are good reasons to predict the same pattern of findings based on the differences for men and women in the psychological as well the social and economic costs and consequences of freely pursuing all possible sexual and romantic opportunities, such as the pregnancies and care-taking obligations to which they lead.

Explanations Are Not Justifications

At a theoretical level, evolutionary explanations may help one understand all sorts of behavior, at least in hindsight, but they do not justify it. Critics of the approach therefore are quick to note that today's abusive, violent, criminal behaviors, or hurtful macho attitudes and biases, cannot be excused by pointing to their possible origins in evolutionary struggles at the dawn of human life. Attitudes and behaviors that may have served prehistoric ancestors can be inappropriate and dysfunctional for many aspects of modern social life. Fortunately, human beings also have the capacity for self-regulation that enables them to modify their behavior adaptively without waiting for the species to evolve further over the eons of time (Bandura, 2001).

With these hedges in mind, the evolutionary approach nevertheless offers insights into social behavior today. Look through the lenses of evolutionary theory at human courtship on a weekend evening at a crowded urban singles bar. The males try to strut and impress with talk and demonstrations about their ambitions, virility, accomplishments, and possessions. In the same scene, the females display their distinctively different strategies for enhancing their appeal. And the motivations that drive the sexes in the courtship dance may also be quite different. The male is eager to mate and reproduce while the female is more motivated to delay reproduction until the resources and opportunities for long-term offspring protection and care are favorable.

Altruism

Evolutionary theory also speaks to human qualities that at first glance do not seem consistent with evolution, most notably altruism. Why should humans behave altruistically, taking risks that can kill them, as firemen and police officers do daily? Over the course of evolution, shouldn't such risk-taking and unselfishness fade out since it does nothing

Why do humans behave altruistically?

to increase the chance of passing your genes forward? The answer is again put in terms of the survival of the group, and not of the individual. To the degree that altruistic acts toward members of one's group facilitate their survival and reproduction, the genes from your gene pool will continue to be passed forward, even if you don't survive as an individual. Consistent with the theory, the most altruistic behaviors are often confined to one's own kin and kind, reflected in the phrase "charity begins at home." But the theory even sees an evolutionary basis for altruism toward strangers as a tendency acquired over the course of time as our ancestors discovered **reciprocal altruism**. This is the recognition that if we help others they are likely to reciprocate, in turn enhancing the potential for survival and reproduction (e.g., Trivers, 1971).

Evolutionary Theory and Inborn Constraints on Learning

6.18 How might innate factors affect organisms' learning capabilities? Why might humans differ from other animals in preparedness?

Evolutionary theory also has implications that need to be considered when thinking about the relations between learning and personality. For many years, psychologists searched for general laws of learning that they assumed would hold for all species and for all types of responses and stimuli. This assumption has been seriously challenged (Seligman, 1971) and the evidence against it has mounted (Marks, 1987; Marks & Nesse, 1994; Pinker, 1997). By now it will not surprise you that evolutionary theory proposes that the differences found between species in the types of associations they readily learn reflect differences in what it was necessary to learn in the evolutionary struggle for survival (Buss, 1996, 1997; Seligman, 1971; Seligman & Hager, 1972).

Biological Preparedness

Evolutionary theory also argues that people are disposed biologically to fear things that have threatened human survival throughout evolution (Buss, 1997; Seligman, 1971). For example, there are only a small number of common human fears, and they seem to be virtually universal. Fears of snakes, spiders, blood, storms, heights, darkness, and of strangers are typical, and they share a common theme: they endangered our evolutionary ancestors, and now we seem to be prewired to fear them. As Pinker (1997; p. 387) puts it: "Children are nervous about rats, and rats are nervous about bright rooms . . . and they easily associate them with danger." A wide range of data that in recent years increasingly point to prewired dispositions in the brain arose in the course of evolution. And these dispositions seem to yield the **biological preparedness** humans have not only for some fears rather than for others, but also for all sorts of high-level mental activities, from language acquisition to mathematical skills to music appreciation to space perception (Pinker, 1997).

Specificity of Psychological Mechanisms

Some of the most important challenges that required adaptive solutions and that created problems for human survival came not from the physical challenges of nature but from other hostile humans. As Buss (1997) points out, this recognition comes from studies on topics that range from group warfare to the evolution of language and higher mental functions (e.g., Pinker, 1997).

6.19 What is domain specificity? How is it explained by evolutionary theory?

To illustrate, consider the formation of dyadic alliances, such as lifelong mating relationships. These relationships pose problems that demand adaptive social solutions for reproduction and survival. To enable this, we need to accurately assess the resources and characteristics of potential friends and enemies as they initiate efforts to develop friendships and connections to enhance their adaptation and survival. Relevant to this function it has been suggested that humans have developed a **cheater detector**—a mechanism to detect cheaters who will seek the benefits of social exchange but refuse to reciprocate appropriately (Cosmides, 1989; Cosmides & Tooby, 1989).

The cheater detector mechanism also illustrates another key point of current evolutionary thinking: the concept of **domain specificity**. Because humans face a host of different types of social problems, each of which requires somewhat different strategies and solutions, evolutionary theory proposes that the mechanisms that emerge will be highly domain specific. Thus the psychological mechanisms that evolve were targeted to solve quite specific evolutionary problems like mate choice and mate retention (Buss, 1997). We saw that specificity in mate choice takes a somewhat different form for males and females. In turn, the psychological problem-solving mechanisms in mate choice are different from those needed in other social exchanges, for example, when dealing with potential enemies. Specificity appears to be a necessary requirement for achieving the enormous discriminativeness and flexibility in behavior that has been observed in most domains. In fact, specificity appears to be the rule, as seen in domains that range from the diversity of human motives to the specificity of learning, to the specificity of fears (Buss, 1997), to most patterns of interpersonal behavior (Cantor & Kihlstrom, 1987; Mischel, 1968, 1973; Mischel & Shoda, 1998).

Addressing the question of domain specificity, David Buss puts it this way: "A carpenter's flexibility comes not from having a single domain-general 'all purpose tool' that is used to cut, saw, screw, twist, wrench, plane, balance, and hammer, but rather from having many, more specialized tools each designed to perform a particular function" 1997, p. 325).

Evolutionary theory emphasizes that it is the "specificity, complexity, and numerosity of evolved psychological mechanisms" (Buss, 1999, p. 41) that enable the behavioral flexibility crucial for adaptation. The availability of many specific tools, not any single, highly elastic tool, gives the carpenter—and the human being—the flexibility required for the diverse challenges encountered.

Taking the analogy of the carpenter and his diverse, highly specialized toolkit a bit further, different carpenters are particularly skilled with some tools and less skilled with others and each has tools that vary in quality. Similarly, people differ in the domains in which they are likely to be especially vulnerable and those in which they excel: the pattern of each person is unique and domain specific in its behavioral expressions. These patterns are the stable *if* ... *then* ... behavioral signatures of personality discussed in Chapter 4.

The Value of Discriminativeness in Coping with Stress

6.20 How do coping flexibility and discriminitive facility relate to successful adaptation?

To illustrate domain specificity and the discriminative behavior and flexibility it demands, let's look at how people cope with stress effectively. An individual's ability to cope with daily stressors in the psychological and physical environment is fundamental to survival. Psychologists have distinguished two methods of coping with physical and psychological stress: problem-focused and emotion-focused coping (Chan, 1994; Lazarus & Folkman, 1984; Parker & Endler, 1996). The method that works best depends on the nature of the situation. Consequently, adaptive behavior ideally requires people to be flexible in the methods they use, and to discriminate among different types of situations so that they apply the method that best fits the particular context. For example, adaptive coping has to take into account whether or not the situation is controllable (Aldwin, 1994; Miller, 1992). If a situation is controllable, then it is more adaptive to respond in a problem-focused manner. In contrast, in an uncontrollable situation, problem-focused coping is ineffectual, and emotion-focused coping is more adaptive.

One of the important factors that influence an individual's ability to successfully cope with stressful situations is **discriminative facility** (Cheng, Hui, & Lam, 2000; Chiu, Hong, Mischel, & Shoda, 1995). Discriminative facility is the ability to appraise situations as they present themselves and to respond appropriately. Cecilia Cheng and her associates found that individuals who had more discriminative facility used more flexible coping strategies in an experimental setting, and they also showed decreased levels of anxiety (Cheng et al., 2000; Cheng, Chiu, Hong, & Cheung, 2001, Study 1; Roussi, Miller, & Shoda, 2000). In short, to cope well, one needs to discriminate carefully and identify the type of situation faced so that one can then use the problem-solving approach that fits it best. Like the carpenter, in addition to having the right specific tools available, people need to select the tool that fits the task.

In short, evolutionary theory emphasizes the adaptive value of flexibly allowing one's behavior to take into account the requirements of the particular context, and carefully discriminate among situations so that one can identify the specific requirements and act accordingly (e.g., MacDonald, 1998).

► SUMMARY

BRAIN–PERSONALITY LINKS

- William H. Sheldon was an American physician who classified individuals into three different body types and their corresponding temperaments.
- More recently, Hans J. Eysenck measured brain wave and cardiovascular activity in introverts and extraverts to further understand the physiological differences that underlie these types.
- The behavioral inhibition system (BIS) is the neurological system that may dispose individuals to withdraw from negative stimuli.
- The behavioral activation system (BAS) is the neurological system that may lead individuals to seek out positive stimuli or rewards.
- The BAS and BIS systems have been linked to the experience of positive and negative events and affect, respectively, and like PA and NA, they operate independently of one another.
- BAS and BIS research suggests that these are specific and distinct incentive and threat systems in the brain with important links to personality.
- Sensation-seeking behavior has been linked to several biological factors.
- The interactions between neurotransmitters, enzymes, and hormones that underlie the behavioral and psychological manifestations of personality seem to be multiple and complex and also interact with a host of social and psychological factors.

BIOLOGICAL ASSESSMENT AND CHANGE

- Personality psychologists utilize magnetic resonance imaging (MRI) and positron emission tomography (PET) scans to examine brain activity during various psychological experiences.
- The amygdala mobilizes the body for action, readying it to flight or fight.
- Biological treatments for psychological disorders favor pharmacotherapy, which makes use of a variety of drugs including antidepressants, antipsychotics, and minor tranquilizers.

EVOLUTIONARY THEORY AND PERSONALITY

- At the evolutionary level of analysis, personality traits and individual differences reflect the processes of natural selection and adaptation.
- For example, such traits as dominance, emotional stability, and sociability are seen as particularly robust because they have an especially significant role in mate selection and retention.
- The evolutionary perspective provides a fresh view of behaviors from mate selection and jealousy to altruism and the development of fears.
- Evolutionary theory emphasizes the adaptive value of flexibly allowing one's behavior to take into account the requirements of the particular context. This requires carefully discriminating among situations.

► KEY TERMS

amygdala 136
ascending reticular activation system (ARAS) 127
behavioral activation system (BAS) 128
behavioral inhibition system (BIS) 128
biological preparedness 145
brain asymmetry 128
cheater detector 145
directional selection 141
discriminative facility 146
domain specificity 145
ectomorph 125
endomorph 125
level of arousal (LOA) 127
mesomorph 125
monoamine oxidase (MAO) 134
neurotransmitters 134
optimal level of arousal 127
reciprocal altruism 144
sensation seeking 132
Sensation Seeking Scale (SSS) 132
stabilizing selection 142

TAKING STOCK

PART II

THE BIOLOGICAL LEVEL OF ANALYSIS

▶ OVERVIEW: FOCUS, CONCEPTS, METHODS

As summarized in the Overview table, work at the Biological Level in the last few decades is changing the conception of personality in many crucial ways. It has demonstrated the significant role of heredity in personality, particularly with regard to such qualities as emotionality, activity, sensation seeking, extraversion, and a host of psychosocial traits. It thus has called attention to the important role of biology and the genes in personality and social behavior as well as in human abilities. It has opened the way to studying the activity in the brain, and to linking biological processes to psychological processes—including the person's thoughts, feeling, and memories. The breakthroughs that are occurring rapidly in the tools available for studying these links are exciting, and they promise to pave the way for tracing the relationships between what goes on in the body and in the mind with increasing depth and precision.

Overview of Biological Level: Focus, Concepts, Methods

Basic units	Biological variables: genetics, brain and other biological systems; brain–behavior links; role of biology in social behavior
Causes of behavior	Biological and evolutionary processes; interactions between biological and environmental–social variables
Behavioral manifestations of personality	Social behavior, personality traits, mental-emotional states
Favored data	Physiological measures: PET scans, EEG, MRI; test responses; trait ratings; adaptive and maladaptive behavior patterns; brain–behavior links; interactions of genetic and environmental factors
Observed responses used as	Data for linking brain–behavior relations; behavior analyzed in terms of evolutionary theory
Research focus	Heritability of personality; analyzing brain–behavior relations; effects of biological variables on personality
Approach to personality change	Personality change is linked to brain/chemical changes; biological treatments for disorders (e.g., medications)
Role of the situation	Important for evolutionary analyses of social behavior

▶ ENDURING CONTRIBUTIONS OF THE BIOLOGICAL LEVEL

The Biological Level of analysis is justifiably creating great interest at present on many fronts. As you saw in the discussion in Chapter 5 on studies of identical twins, many qualities of personality, especially as assessed on standardized trait questionnaires, are substantially influenced by genetic-biological determinants. Humans are biological creatures, and personality is importantly influenced by biological processes, beginning with the genes that are our heritage. The findings that genes influence personality have become sufficiently clear and strong to avoid debates about whether or not they are important: they are very important—but so is the environment. Research now is going beyond demonstrations that genes have a substantial impact on personality to identify the specific biochemical and psychosocial processes and their interactions that underlie these effects. Fortunately, such studies are now being pursued vigorously and promise to yield increasingly precise answers.

By discovering new methods for viewing the activity in the brain, work at the Biological Level of analysis also has opened a new route for personality research. It makes it possible to study the relationship between the individual's psychological activities, such as thoughts, memories, and intense feelings experienced by the person, for example, when exposed to a feared stimulus, and the activation of specific brain areas and centers in the brain. Studies of brain systems like the BIS and BAS, and of brain asymmetry, are already yielding new insights into the biological processes that link to crucial aspects of personality. These features of personality are fundamental, influencing the approach and avoidance dispositions that characterize each person distinctively. They affect one's typical reactions to rewards and incentives versus punishments and threats, and the positive and negative emotions and moods that influence how we experience the world and relate to it.

The challenge ahead for this line of research will be to examine more fully how these biological systems relate to, and interact with, relevant aspects of personality assessed at the other levels of analysis, for example, in studies of human motivation, planning, and self-regulation. These new directions are already being pursued and are the topics of the final chapters in the text.

Questions for work at this level in the future will include the ways in which learning and therapeutic and educational experiences might be used to influence the level of activity in different brain areas in constructive directions. Such research ultimately may help liberate individuals from biological burdens of which they may not have to be the victims. The long-term yield from such research may help in the diagnosis and treatment of an array of human problems not yet imaginable in biochemical terms. If so, the approach also may make a great contribution to treatment and improvement of the human condition, but that possibility lies mostly in the years ahead. Concurrently, work on social evolution is providing new models, concepts, and methods for thinking in fresh ways about diverse aspects of social behavior—from mate selection and courtship to aggression, altruism, and human competencies. In the future, it will be important to try to link evolutionary processes to personality at the theoretical level in ways that allow empirical tests of the implications with increasing precision.

PART 

THE PSYCHODYNAMIC-MOTIVATIONAL LEVEL

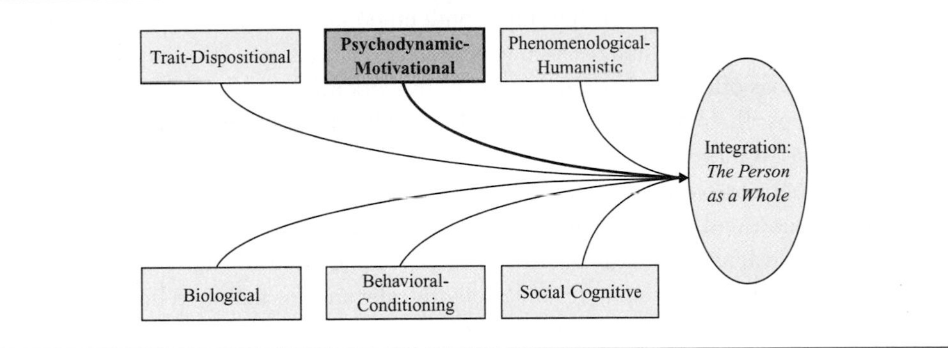

PRELUDE TO PART III: THE PSYCHODYNAMIC-MOTIVATIONAL LEVEL

We all know of people who are functioning reasonably well and then, often unexpectedly, show distressing changes in their behavior—depression, fears, anxieties, or other problems that change their daily lives. These changes are difficult to understand and explain because there seem to be no reasons for them in the rest of the person's life. What accounts for them? Early in the last century Sigmund Freud confronted this puzzle.

A hundred years ago in Vienna, a young woman sought help from her physician, Dr. Freud, because she suddenly could no longer see. In a careful examination, Freud found nothing physically wrong with her visual system, and there had been no accident or plausible incident to make her lose her sight. Another patient, while waiting for her appointment, could not resist once again scrubbing her already immaculate hands; that morning she had already washed them dozens of times. In other respects she seemed normal, rational, and was functioning well except for these new symptoms. Freud had to find a way to make sense of such problems and those of many of his other patients who needed help because their symptoms made no sense to them either and seemed to be in conflict with other aspects of their personalities. His struggles to meet these challenges and the brilliant theory he slowly formulated became the foundation for work at the Psychodynamic-Motivational Level of analysis.

Freud was guided by a hypothesis that he had formed early in his work with mental patients. Their behavior, he thought, simply could not be understood by looking only at the consistencies in what they did. The answers, he proposed, must be found by understanding their *inconsistencies*. For many years, he struggled to understand the ways in which those inconsistencies might reveal internal contradictions and motives of which the individual seemed to be unaware. If the causes were outside people's awareness, then the real meaning of their behavior could not be seen in what they said at the "surface level" of their self-descriptions.

The more deeply he probed, the more he became convinced that human behavior often is not rational and reflects unconscious motives, conflicts, and processes that are considered taboo by society and therefore condemned and avoided. To make sense of this, the theories that Freud and his followers proposed at first upset the world greatly, as revolutionary ideas often do. In time, however, his work influenced much of the agenda for personality psychology, and a good deal of it is still relevant today, although often in extensively revised forms.

Freud's theories were extremely broad. He tried to explain virtually everything about the human mind and its expressions in ways that he hoped would be universally true for all people across all cultures. His work has been debated and attacked, often with good reason, mostly for not being testable scientifically and for failing to be validated in many of the tests that have been attempted. Consequently many research psychologists have become skeptical about the long-term value of his work, giving Freud little credit for influencing current conceptualization in psychological science. Yet historically his contributions changed the view of human nature. He gave the world new insights into the self-defensive and often self-defeating characteristics of the human personality, as well as of the possibilities for transcendence and the creation of harmony and order within one's mind and life.

Freud addressed not just the development of abnormal problems but the ways in which essentially normal individuals may function to protect themselves from their own conflicts and anxieties beginning in early childhood, and to move beyond them. He also constructed what became the most sweeping, integrative, grand theory of personality structure, dynamics, development, mental illness, and health that had ever been developed within psychology, and revolutionized the conception of human nature.

Chapter 7 presents Freud's basic concepts. Chapter 8 examines applications for personality assessment and treatment, and illustrates research on mechanisms and processes central to Freud's ideas. Chapter 9 highlights the ideas and work he directly influenced at this level for many years, including in the study of motives such as competence and achievement that go much beyond those that Freud emphasized.

THE PERSONAL SIDE OF THE SCIENCE

Some questions at the Psychodynamic-Motivational Level you might ask about yourself:

- Does what I do sometimes puzzle me?
- How and why?
- What are the real motives that drive or underlie my behavior?
- How can I explain irrational fears and anxieties?
- How do I try to protect myself psychologically against getting hurt?
- How much of what I do is unconscious or done without awareness?
- What might be some unconscious influences on my behavior?
- Do I have motives that make me uncomfortable?
- If yes, what do I try to do about that?

CHAPTER 7

PSYCHODYNAMIC THEORIES: FREUD'S CONCEPTIONS

Sigmund Freud (1856–1939) started his career in medicine with research on cocaine. In 1884, the properties of this new drug intrigued him, partly because it helped him to get some relief from his own episodes of depression. When he became aware of cocaine's dangers, he soon gave it up, both for personal use and as a research problem. Studying for 6 months with the neurologist Jean Charcot in Paris in 1885, he became interested in the use of hypnosis to help patients deal with various nonorganic symptoms of "nervous disorders," particularly "hysteria."

Freud's breakthroughs began from his clinical observations of patients he was seeing in his private practice when he returned to Vienna. Imagine scenes like this one in his consulting room on a pleasant residential street in the Vienna of 1905. Freud is presented with a young girl who feels compelled to rinse out her wash basin over and over, dozens of times after each time she washes herself. Her habit becomes so intense and upsetting that her whole life revolves around it. Why? A young boy becomes terrified of horses, although he himself was never hurt by one. Why? It was puzzles like these that intrigued the Viennese physician Sigmund Freud, who invented psychoanalysis, reshaped the field of psychology, and influenced many later developments in all the social sciences and in Western concepts of human nature.

From these puzzles, Freud created a theory and a treatment method that changed our view of personality, health, and the mind itself. Working as a physician treating disturbed people in Vienna at the turn of the century, he formulated a theory that upset many cherished assumptions about human nature and startled the neo-Victorian world. Before Freud, people's behavior was believed to be under their conscious and rational control. Freud turned that conception upside down. Rather than seeing consciousness as the core of the mind, Freud compared personality to an iceberg: only the tip shows itself overtly, the rest lies below. Rather than viewing the person as a supremely rational being, he saw people as also driven by impulses and striving to satisfy deep and lasting sexual and aggressive urgings. Rather than relying on people's reports about themselves as accurate self-representations, he interpreted what they said and did as highly indirect, disguised, symbolic representations of unconscious, underlying forces.

7.1 How did Freud's views conflict with the prevailing beliefs of his time?

In the course of more than 40 years of writing and clinical research, Freud created a theory of personality structure and dynamics, a theory of personality development, as well as a theory of personality disturbances, and pioneered a new method for their treatment. Freud built both his theories and his psychoanalytic treatment on his wealth of clinical observations and therapeutic experiences with disturbed persons, as well as on his painful psychoanalyses of himself and many colleagues. In his patients he first noted certain **sensory anesthesias**, which are losses of sensory ability, as in blindness,

Sigmund Freud (1856–1939)

deafness, or loss of feeling in a body part, and others with motor paralyses, that seemed to have no neurological origin. He proposed that these symptoms expressed a way of defending against unacceptable, unconscious wishes. For example, a soldier who cannot admit his fear of facing battle develops a motor paralysis without a neurological basis. Or a young bride, unable to admit her hostility to her husband, becomes confined to her chair, although she shows no physical disease. All these examples illustrate **hysteria**. The fundamental feature of hysteria, according to Freud, is the presence of massive repression and the development of a symptom pattern that indirectly or symbolically expresses the repressed needs and wishes. On the basis of careful clinical observations, Freud gradually developed and progressively revised his theory of personality, continuously modifying his ideas in light of his growing clinical experiences and insights.

7.2 How did the study of hysteria influence Freud's views?

▶ BASIC ASSUMPTIONS: UNCONSCIOUS MENTAL DETERMINISM

Two key assumptions underlie much of Freud's conception:

7.3 What two major assumptions underlie Freud's ideas?

- First, his unique innovation was to propose that behavior is never accidental: it is psychologically determined by mental motivational causes. This is called the principle of **motivational determinism**.
- Second, these causes are outside of the person's complete consciousness or awareness.

The Unconscious

Freud the scientist wanted to try to explain the irrational behavior he witnessed in his patients. They seemed compelled to do things that they could not explain or sometimes even remember. Most puzzling, he could not attribute their symptoms to organic causes such as brain injuries or physical diseases: physically they were intact. They were consciously trying to stop their symptoms, desperate to relieve them, but they simply could not control them. Freud's insight was to propose that some unconscious, irrational force was behind the symptom psychologically. The battles between the conscious will and the unconscious became the war of mental life in his theory.

Around the year 1900, Freud first divided mental processes into conscious, preconscious, and unconscious (Freud, 1905/1953). We are instantly aware of our **conscious** thoughts. The immediately available level of consciousness refers to what is in one's attention at a given moment. The many events that we can bring into attention more or less easily, from the background music on the radio to memories of things experienced years ago, are **preconscious**. Thus, even though we are not aware of preconscious thoughts at a given moment, we can bring them into awareness voluntarily and fairly easily. In contrast, outside this range of the potentially available lies the **unconscious**. This third zone is not responsive to our deliberate efforts at recall, and it is the layer that was Freud's core concern. Because their content is threatening, unconscious mental activities are kept beyond awareness by a mechanism of repression that works actively to keep them away from our awareness, so that we simply are unable to raise them into consciousness.

7.4 Define and give an example of each of Freud's three levels of consciousness.

The Roads to the Unconscious

Freud was eager to find methods for his work that would make his ideas more than abstract claims or beliefs. It was through these methods that his conception achieved its richness and ultimately made its enormous impact. If the unconscious mind was so important for understanding psychological causes, then the challenge was how to get to it.

Dreams

7.5 Why do dreams occupy a position of importance in psychoanalytic theory? How are they related to neurotic symptoms?

Freud probed the unconscious most deeply through his explorations of dreams. He saw his 1899 book, *The Interpretation of Dreams*, like the adventures of a Columbus of the mind, a voyage into the darkest regions. The dream, Freud proposed, was the dreamer's unconscious effort to fulfill a wish that could not be expressed more directly. The analyst's task was to discover the hidden secrets underneath the surface content of the dream. To uncover those buried meanings, the analyst must overcome the dreamer's own resistance to facing him- or herself honestly, no matter how frightening or ugly the discoveries might prove to be.

In his voyage into the unconscious, Freud proceeded by scrutinizing his own dreams to try to face the motivations deep within his own personality. Unflattering self-revelation often resulted. For example, Freud is troubled by fears about plagiarizing, and he dreams about himself being treated as a thief stealing overcoats in lecture halls (Roazen, 1974, p. 99). Through self-analysis, Freud constructed his theory of the unconscious and the devious self-deceptions with which people try to disguise their own wishes from themselves.

In *The Interpretation of Dreams*, Freud built the case that in the dream we can find the hidden fulfillment of a desire that the person is trying to avoid experiencing consciously. Interestingly, this insight into the wish-fulfilling nature of dreams also led to the view that dreams, rather than disturbing sleep, actually function as the "guardians" of sleep. More than 50 years later, experiments discovered that in fact people need their dreams and become deeply troubled if their sleep is deprived of the phases in which dreaming naturally occurs (Roazen, 1974).

From his pioneering theory of dreams, Freud moved on to analyze the meaning of the disturbed behaviors and the anxieties his patients displayed and to develop a systematic theory about how to treat them. The main sources of anxiety, according to Freud, were the person's own unconscious sexual desires and aggressive impulses. He saw both sexual and aggressive urgings as basic human impulses or instincts, part of our heritage. He believed that sexuality does not begin with puberty but is visible early in childhood. It shows itself also in the young girl's affection for her father and the boy's infantile desires for his mother. Emotional attitudes, moreover, arise in these early relationships.

In the face of the objections and prudishness of the Victorian Age, he insisted that the route to self-acceptance was the honest recognition of one's instinctual sexuality and aggressiveness. Avoiding self-deception was the key. Making the unconscious impulses conscious was the road to health. The symptoms, Freud believed, were simply the indirect and sometimes symbolic expression of the unacceptable impulses that the person was unable to face consciously because of the anxiety they created.

Free Association

Much of Freud's thinking was built on the analysis of dreams, but that was not the only method he favored. His second road to the unconscious, sometimes called the "royal road," became the therapeutic method of **free association**. In this method, the patient, reclining on a couch, is encouraged to simply say anything and everything that comes to mind, no matter what it is or how irrational it might seem, without censoring it. *In Focus 7.1* discusses how free association is encouraged. In this way, the unconscious begins to become conscious. Although "resistance" to this process occurs often, it is gradually "worked through" until the unacceptable wishes can be faced. Then the patient is freed from having to manifest them indirectly through such symptoms as hysterical paralysis or other neurotic expressions.

IN FOCUS 7.1

ENCOURAGING FREE ASSOCIATION

Free association and the analysis of dreams are the methods of personality study that come most directly from Freud's work. Both methods are used in the context of patient–therapist meetings during psychoanalysis.

In free association, you are instructed to give your thoughts complete freedom and to report daydreams, feelings, and images, no matter how incoherent, illogical, or meaningless they might seem. This technique may be employed either with a little prompting or by offering brief phrases ("My mother . . ."; "I often . . .") as a stimulus to encourage associations.

Freud believed that dreams were similar to the patient's free associations. He thought the dream was an expression of the most primitive workings of the mind. Dreams were interpreted as fulfilling a wish or discharging tension by inducing an image of the desired goal. Freud felt that through the interpretation of dreams he was penetrating into the unconscious.

The following passages illustrate some typical instructions and responses in the process of encouraging free association during psychoanalytic interviews. The patient complains that she does not have any thoughts at the moment.

Therapist: It may seem that way to you at first, but there are always some thoughts there. Just as your heart is always beating, there's always some thought or other going through your mind.

Patient: Your mentioning the word "heart" reminds me that the doctor told my mother the other day she had a weak heart.

In a later interview the same woman became silent again and could not continue.

Therapist: Just say what comes to you.

Patient: Oh, odds and ends that aren't very important.

Therapist: Say them anyway.

Patient: I don't see how they could have much bearing. I was wondering what sort of books those are over there. But that hasn't anything to do with what I'm here for.

Therapist: One never can tell, and actually you're in no position to judge what has bearing and what hasn't. Let me decide that. You just report what comes into your mind regardless of whether you think it's important or not. (Colby, 1951, p. 153)

PSYCHIC STRUCTURE: ANATOMY OF THE MIND

To understand how we deal with unconscious wishes, Freud (1933) also developed an "anatomy" of the mind that occupied him in the early part of the 1920s. This led to the structural view of personality, consisting of three "institutions" or mental "agencies": the id, ego, and superego. These mental structures form sequentially in the course of early experience, with the superego, the last to emerge, crystallizing some time after the sixth year.

The three agencies or structures are closely linked to the three layers of consciousness. The id is in the unconscious layer, characterized by mental processes outside one's awareness; the ego is predominantly conscious; and the superego includes a mix of conscious and unconscious processes. Although the three parts interact intimately, each has its own characteristics, which are summarized in Table 7.1 and discussed next.

The Id: The Passions at the Core

The **id** is the mental agency or psychic structure that contains everything inherited, especially the instincts. It is the basis of personality, the energy source for the whole system, and the foundation from which the ego and superego later develop. The id, according to Freud, is the innermost core of personality, and it is closely linked to biological processes.

7.6 Describe the id and the process that governs its operation.

TABLE 7.1 The Freudian Conception of Mental Structure

Structure	Consciousness	Contents and Function
Id	Unconscious	Basic impulses (sex and aggression); seeks immediate gratification regardless of consequences; impervious to reason and logic; immediate, irrational, impulsive
Ego	Predominantly conscious	Executive mediating between id impulses and superego inhibitions; tests reality; seeks safety and survival; rational, logical, taking account of space and time
Superego	Both conscious and unconscious	Ideals and morals; strives for perfection; incorporated (internalized) from parents; observes, dictates, criticizes, and prohibits; imposes limitations on satisfactions; becomes the conscience of the individual

Life Instincts (Eros)

The id's instincts, Freud thought, have their source biologically within the excitation states of the body. They act like drives, pressing for discharge (release). For Freud (1933) the instincts are of two types. **Life** or **sexual instincts**, also called **Eros** (an ancient Greek term), are the life forces, the drives and passions that push for pleasure, reproduction, survival. Beyond the erotic and sex, the life instincts also deal with survival in different forms, for example, motivating hunger reduction and pain avoidance.

Libido

7.7 What is the libido, and with what part of the mind is it associated?

The life instincts generate **Libido**—the finite amount of energy that Freud assumed was within each person. In the course of development, Libido becomes attached to, or fixed on, aspects of the internal and external environment. The energy available to the organism is continuously transformed, fixed onto different "objects." Note that "objects" was a term that Freud and his followers used to refer to people and zones of the human body, not just inanimate things. Freud assumed that in spite of these transformations in where the energy is invested, the total amount of energy is conserved and stable. His energy system thus was consistent with the hydraulic models of 19th-century physics.

Id instincts are motivated, in the sense that their *aim* is to seek reduction, that is, to lower the state of excitation. Thus the tension that the build-up of the unexpressed drive creates has to be released, much like the build-up of steam in an overheating boiler has to be let out or the system explodes. Instinctual drives are biological and inborn, but the objects involved in attempts to reduce the drives depend on the individual's particular early experiences. The id was seen as a kind of dynamo, and the total mind (or psyche) was viewed as a closed system motivated to maintain equilibrium: any forces that were built up required discharge. The discharge could be indirect. Instinctual impulses could be displaced from one object to another, for instance, from one's parents to other authority figures or, more remotely, from the genitals, for example, to phallic symbols.

Death Instincts (Thanatos)

Although the life or sexual instincts are most important, as noted above, they constitute only one of two types of instincts Freud proposed. The second type consists of **death instincts**, also called by their Greek name, **Thanatos** (Freud, 1940). Psychologically, they reflect the unconscious human desire to return to the inanimate state, and are expressed in destructive aggressive behavior, including the self-aggressive and suicidal. This death drive also may be seen as a reflection in Freud's thinking of the fact that humans, like all organisms and all living cells, are, in a sense, fated to die. Broadly, it is a psychological parallel to the biological concept of metabolism—the biological term for the chemical processes and energy involved in the building up *(anabolism)* of protoplasm and living matter, and its wasting and destruction (*catabolism*). Analogous to cells undergoing catabolic processes, humans in Freud's view experience death instincts, and are in part driven by them. The psychological representations of both the life and death instincts are wishes, and they often are irrational and unconscious.

The Pleasure Principle

Increases in energy from internal or external stimulation produce tension and discomfort that the id cannot tolerate. The id therefore seeks immediate tension reduction, regardless of the consequences. Freud called this tendency toward immediate tension reduction the **pleasure principle**. The id obeys it, and seeks immediate satisfaction of its instinctual wishes and impulses, regardless of reason or logic or consequences.

Primary Process Thinking

To discharge tension, the id forms an internal image or hallucination of the desired object. The hungry infant, for example, may conjure up an internal representation of the mother's breast. The resulting image is considered a wish fulfillment, similar to the attempted wish fulfillment that Freud believed characterized normal dreams and the hallucinations of psychotics. **Primary process thinking** was Freud's term for such direct, irrational, reality-ignoring attempts to satisfy needs. Because mental images by themselves cannot reduce tension, the ego develops.

The Ego: In the Service of Reality, Reason, Order

7.8 How does the ego derive from the id, and what are its functions and operating principles?

The **ego** is a direct outgrowth of the id. Freud described its origin this way:

> *Under the influence of the real external world around us, one portion of the id has undergone a special development. From what was originally a cortical layer, equipped with the organs for receiving stimuli and with arrangements for acting as a protective shield against stimuli, a special organization has arisen which henceforward acts as an intermediary between the id and the external world. To this region of our mind we have given the name of* ego. *(1933, p. 2)*

The ego is in direct contact with the external world. It is governed by considerations of safety, and its task is preservation of the organism. The ego wages its battle for survival against both the external world and the internal instinctual demands of the id. In this task, it has to continuously differentiate between the mental representations of wish-fulfilling images and the actual outer world of reality. In its search for food or sexual release, for example, it must find the appropriate tension-reducing objects in the environment so that tension reduction can actually occur. That is, it must go from image to object, and get satisfaction for id impulses while simultaneously preserving itself.

The Reality Principle

The ego's function is governed by the **reality principle**, which requires it to test reality and to delay discharge of tension until the appropriate object and environmental conditions are found. The ego operates by means of a *secondary process* that involves realistic, logical thinking and planning through the use of the higher or cognitive mental processes. It allows reasoning, and takes account of time, space, and the nature of reality.

That is, while the id seeks immediate tension reduction by such primary process means as wish-fulfilling imagery and direct gratification of sexual and aggressive impulses, the ego is the executive, mediating between the id and the world, testing reality and making decisions about various courses of available action. For example, it delays impulses for immediate sexual gratification until the environmental conditions are appropriate.

Freud believed the ego was the only hope for the world, the part of the mind that would allow humans to emerge from the irrationality and primitivism of being driven wildly by their biological impulses. The ego was the way toward a life of reason, order, and harmony: "Where id was," Freud wrote, "there shall ego be," and psychoanalysis was the road for that transformation from the person's domination by impulsivity to reason, order, and insightfulness. The healthy, resilient ego functions like the conductor of an orchestra full of passionate players, leading them to create order together, rather than dissolve into a chaos of noise.

The Superego: High Court in Pursuit of Perfection, Ideals, Transcendence

7.9 How does the superego develop, and what are its functions?

Freud's third mental structure was the **superego**. He wrote:

> *The long period of childhood, during which the growing human being lives in dependence on his parents, leaves behind it as a precipitate the formation in his ego of a special agency in which this parental influence is prolonged. It has received the name of* superego. *In so far as this superego is differentiated from the ego or is opposed to it, it constitutes a third power which the ego must take into account. (1933, p. 2)*

Thus, the superego is the agency that internalizes the influence of the parents and their ideals. It represents the morals and standards of society that have become part of the internal world of the individual in the course of the development of personality. The superego is the conscience, the morality judge of right and wrong, of good and bad, in accord with the internalized standards of the parents and thus, indirectly, of society. The superego for Freud involved the internalization of parental control in the form of self-control. For example, the individual with a well-developed superego resists "bad" or "evil" temptations, such as stealing when hungry or killing when angry, even when there are no external constraints (in the form of police or other people) to stop him.

Freud thought the superego develops around age 5 out of the human infant's long period of helplessness and extreme dependency on caregivers. The young child desperately fears the possible loss of this early love; the threat of parents withdrawing protection and gratification is terrifying. At first this fear is rooted in the objective anxiety of losing love and satisfaction due to the child's own actions (being "bad"). In time, an active *identification* occurs as the child incorporates the parental images and commands into itself psychologically. As the parental wishes become incorporated through this process, the conscience becomes an internal voice rather than an external control.

Whereas the passion-filled id seeks pleasure and is irrational in its demands, the superego seeks perfection and the ideal. The superego, like the id, can become hugely demanding, operating in part at unconscious levels. It can torment the individual as mercilessly as the urgencies of the id, as seen in severe depressions characterized by extreme self-hatred and self-destructiveness. The tyranny of the superego is thus added to the demands of the id. But the superego is not only a conscience and moral judge, with rulings on right and wrong, and what to do and not to do, pulling the person away from vice. It also represents the ego ideals and higher values and goals that can inspire the individual to go beyond self-gratification and animal-like behavior, beyond the ego's concerns with practicality and survival, to strive toward ideals and higher goals, at least under some conditions. In this sense, the superego inspires transcendence, pushing the person toward virtuous behavior.

It is the burden and challenge of the ego—the executive, the conductor—of this passionate but potentially dissonant orchestra, to continuously coordinate and integrate these competing urgent voices and forces, while testing the waters of reality, to achieve harmony and order within the system.

Looking Back at Freud's Theory of Mental Structures and Their Biological Bases

Freud's id–ego–superego theory of three mental structures and their interactions proved to be highly useful for psychoanalytically oriented clinical work, greatly influencing clinical practice as well as views of human nature and personality. But in many ways it was more of a fruitful metaphor than an evidence-based scientific model of mental structure. Freud always hoped that the metaphor would turn out to have solid scientific value. Whereas he and his followers did much to ground the theory in empirical evidence, their evidence was based on clinical observation and inference, and therefore far from meeting the rigorous standards demanded in an advanced science. Consequently this model, even as a metaphor, was rejected by many academic psychologists and researchers, and in the middle of the last century, at the height of behaviorism, became out of favor and discredited as a loose fiction, in most American universities.

But science progresses in uneven steps, and sometimes the out of favor turns out to have had much value. Looking back at Freud's metaphor in the 21st century, some similarities, at least at a broad level, are emerging with findings from current work at the biological, brain, and evolutionary levels of analysis. Arguably, in the view of some psychologists, the id–ego–superego metaphor is turning out to be relevant to functions of some brain areas and their interconnections. To illustrate, consider brain areas like the amygdala, the small, almond-shaped primitive brain area tucked deep under the prefrontal cortex introduced in Chapter 6. This area seems to be basic in intense emotional reactions such as fear and fight or flight reactions in danger conditions, and in strong appetitive impulses and approach behaviors triggered by intense sexual and food temptations. Seen from an evolutionary perspective, these functions have quick survival value. In modern theories about mental functioning this area is part of what is called the "hot system" (e.g., Carlson & Beck, in press; Metcalfe & Mischel, 1999). This hot system has some family resemblance to Freud's id, although now defined on the basis of empirical findings and new discoveries about much more specific brain areas and mechanisms related to impulsivity (discussed in Chapter 17).

Like Freud's id, the hot system also does not provide long-term solutions to challenges that require problem solving, and in fact when it is highly activated it may seriously undermine reasoning and problem solving. Those functions require a rational or "cool" brain system, not unlike Freud's view of the ego and its functions. Such a "cool system" and its processes, now called "executive functions," are the focus of intense research at the cutting edge of cognitive neuroscience and the analysis of self-regulation (also discussed in Chapter 17).

Unlike lower animals on the evolutionary ladder, human beings have the capacity to take control with higher-level brain centers (the prefrontal cortex). This makes it possible for the person to start cool, rational thinking to try to solve the problem that the amygdala has already begun to respond to automatically and emotionally. How you think—hot or cool—can change the attention control centers activated, which in turn makes self-regulatory efforts either more or less difficult (e.g., Derryberry, 2002; Mischel et al., 1989; Posner & Rothbart, 1998). In short, humans have an emotional brain. But they also have other cognitive areas of the brain that are crucially important for the more rational, higher-level processes that make the species human, and that Freud conceptualized in terms of the ego structure and its functions. Thus while part of the brain is hot and emotional and virtually reflexive, reminiscent of Freud's instinct-filled id, there also is a thoughtful, cool part that can be rational with executive functions that can solve problems effectively, not unlike Freud's concept of the ego. And in current theories of mind–brain relations these areas are in continuous dynamic interaction, again reminding one of Freud's metaphor.

Finally, with regard to the superego, Alan Fiske (2002), an anthropologist-psychologist, argues from an evolutionary perspective that some human emotions have developed because they help enable the kind of self-regulation essential for social life and long-term relationships in human society universally (see Chapter 17). Feelings like empathy, affection, and loyalty are emotions necessary for human social life and presumably evolved because of their adaptive value for survival. Likewise, moral emotions, such as guilt and shame, also have adaptive value. They allow people to take account of the long-term consequences of their otherwise impulsive actions, to pause and curb their appetites, inhibiting relationship-destructive and community-destructive rash actions. This type of evolutionary approach provides a fresh view of Freud's superego. (For similar interpretations of the universality of morality and its evolutionary development and functions in social life, see also Marc D. Hauser [2006], *Moral Minds: How Nature Designed Our Universal Sense of Right and Wrong*.)

▶ CONFLICT, ANXIETY, AND PSYCHODYNAMICS

7.10 What three ego activities are involved in psychodynamic processes?

Psychodynamics are the processes through which personality works. In Freud's view, they concern three continuous tasks of the ego: (1) the control of unacceptable impulses from the id; (2) the avoidance of pain produced by internal conflict in the efforts to control and master those unacceptable impulses; and (3) the attainment of a harmonious integration among the diverse components of personality in conflict. Much of Freud's (1917/1955b) own energy was directed at understanding the **transformation of motives**: the basic impulses persist and press for discharge, but the objects at which they are directed and the manner in which they are expressed are transformed.

The idea that the original id impulses persist and are merely transformed in their expressions in the course of personality is fundamental in Freud's theory. But it was also a key point to which Gordon Allport strongly objected in his trait theory. That objection began in a meeting between Freud and Allport in Vienna early in the last century when Freud was already famous and Allport was still a young man who wanted to meet the founder of psychoanalysis, as discussed in *In Focus 7.2*. The meeting was personally deeply upsetting for Allport, and in his autobiography (Allport, 1967) he notes that the development of his own views on adult motivation as autonomous of their earlier roots began with this remarkable encounter.

Conflict

7.11 Describe the basic conflicts that characterize personality dynamics.

According to Freud (1915/1957a), the three parts of the mind—id, ego, and superego—are always in dynamic conflict. The term *dynamics* refers to this continuous interaction and clash between id impulses seeking release and inhibitions or restraining forces against them—an interplay between driving forces and forces that inhibit them. These forces and counterforces propel personality.

IN FOCUS 7.2

THE TRAUMATIC FREUD–ALLPORT MEETING

At the age of 22 Gordon Allport, who became the founder of American personality psychology and one of its most influential trait theorists (Chapter 3), was on a family trip to Vienna and boldly asked to see the already famous Dr. Sigmund Freud. Freud wrote back, inviting Allport to visit him, and when Allport arrived he was ushered into the inner office. "He did not speak to me but sat in expectant silence, waiting for me to state my mission"—an opening greeting standard for a psychoanalyst but one that Allport found distressingly uncomfortable (Allport, 1967, p. 8). Trying hard to "find a suitable conversational gambit" to break the silence, Allport told Freud about an episode he experienced in the tramcar on his way to the office. A 4-year-old boy had exhibited a "conspicuous dirt phobia," complaining to his mother about dirt being all around and not wanting to sit next to the "dirty man."

Freud undoubtedly noted that one of Allport's most conspicuous characteristics was his immaculate appearance, always impeccably freshly groomed and in starched white shirts. When the anecdote was finished, Allport recalls: "Freud fixed his kindly therapeutic eyes upon me and said, 'And was that little boy you?' Flabbergasted and feeling a bit guilty, I contrived to change the subject. While Freud's misunderstanding of my motivation was amusing, it also started a deep train of thought. . . . This experience taught me that depth psychology for all its merits, may plunge too deep, and that psychologists would do well to give full recognition to manifest motives before probing the unconscious." (1967, p. 8)

Allport himself realized that "Yes, my single encounter with Freud was traumatic" (1967, p. 22). This meeting was the beginning of Allport's ideas on the "functional autonomy" of motives and the need to attend to a person's contemporary motives, regardless of their possible original roots (see Chapter 12).

The Freud–Allport encounter speaks to a key theme in this textbook: the multiple levels of analysis in the study of personality each contribute to our understanding of the whole of personality. Both Freud and Allport may have been acutely perceptive in their observations and interpretations of their encounter, although each focused on a different level of the event. Freud saw Allport's choice of the anecdote about the little boy's concern with dirt as the opening conversation "ice breaker," and probably also his strikingly spotless, immaculate, dirt-free appearance, as indicators of underlying, unconscious infantile concerns and conflicts. In Freud's theory these are rooted in problems at the anal stage, and he immediately wanted to connect Allport's present behavior and interest to his early childhood. Allport, on the other hand, believed that peoples' adult motivations and interests should and could be understood in their own right. Consider, for example, an adult motivation to achieve order and a devotion to clarifying messy phenomena like the complexities of human personality. In Allport's case, such a motivation could be seen in his rigorous thinking about the nature and number of traits and the structure of human personality, as well as in his living an orderly, spotless, and exemplary professional and personal life, making contributions that inspired generations of students. In Allport's theory, adult motivations and values deserve to be treated and understood as functionally autonomous, regardless of speculations about their possible unconscious origins (discussed in Chapter 12). Indeed one of the many positive, constructive features of Allport's approach to personality is that he embraced many levels of analysis. While he believed that motives need to be taken seriously in their mature forms, he did not dismiss the possibility that their roots may have begun in much earlier experiences and motivations. But he did not want the possible early origins of motivations to undermine or distract from understanding the importance and value of their mature, autonomous nature. Both Freud and Allport may have been right.

The id's drive for immediate satisfaction of impulses reflects human nature: people are motivated to avoid pain and achieve immediate tension reduction. This drive for immediate satisfaction of instinctual demands leads to a clash between the individual and the environment. Conflict develops to the degree that the environment and its representatives in the form of other persons, notably the parents in childhood, and later the superego, punish or block immediate impulse expression.

Persons in time come to incorporate into their superegos the values by which they are raised, largely by internalizing parental characteristics, morals, values, and ideals. In

Freud's view, perpetual warfare and conflict exist between humans and environment. Insofar as societal values become internalized as part of the person, this warfare is waged internally between the id, ego, and superego, and it produces anxiety.

Anxiety is painful and therefore we automatically try to reduce the tension it produces. Freud first used defense as a psychoanalytic term (1899/1955a), but he focused primarily on one type of defense mechanism involving denial and repression. His daughter, Anna Freud, distinguished some of the other major defense mechanisms recognized today (A. Freud, 1936), which are discussed in the next chapter.

Psychodynamic theorists emphasize that when a threat becomes especially serious, it may lead to intense inhibitions and defenses. In the psychodynamic view, such defensive inhibition is desperate and primitive. It is a massive, generalized, inhibitory reaction rather than a specific response to the particular danger. This **denial** defense occurs when the person can neither escape nor attack the threat. If the panic is sufficient, the only possible alternative may be to deny it. Outright denial may be possible for the young child, who is not yet upset by violating the demands of reality testing. When the child becomes too mature to deny objective facts in the interests of defense, denial becomes a less plausible alternative and repression may occur.

Defense: Denial and Repression

7.12 How did Freud use his concept of repression to explain hysterical disorders?

In psychodynamic theory, **repression** usually refers to a particular type of denial: "... the forgetting, or ejection from consciousness, of memories of threat, and especially the ejection from awareness of impulses in oneself that might have objectionable consequences" (White, 1964, p. 214).

Repression was one of the initial concepts in Freud's theory and became one of its cornerstones. Freud (1920/1924) believed that the mechanisms of denial and repression were the most fundamental or primitive defenses and played a part in other defenses. Indeed, he thought that other defenses started with a massive inhibition of an impulse.

Freud based his ideas concerning repression and defense on his clinical observations of hysterical women at the turn of this century. Recall that he noted that some of these patients seemed to develop physical symptoms that did not make sense neurologically. For example, in a hysterical difficulty called "glove anesthesia," the patient showed an inability to feel in the hands—a symptom that is impossible neurologically. In their studies of hysteria, Freud and his associate Breuer hypnotized some of the patients and found, to their great surprise, that when the origins and meanings of hysterical symptoms were talked about under hypnosis, the symptoms tended to disappear. This finding proved beyond any doubt that the symptoms were not caused by organic damage or physical defects.

Partly to understand hysteria, Freud developed his theory of unconscious conflict and defense. In his view, such symptoms as hysterical blindness and **hysterical anesthesia** (loss of sensation) reflected defensive attempts to avoid painful thoughts and feelings by diversionary preoccupation with apparently physical symptoms. Freud thought that the key mechanism in this blocking was unconsciously motivated repression. Through repression, the basic impulses that are unacceptable to the person are rendered unconscious and thereby less frightening. Because such diversionary measures are inherently ineffective ways of dealing with anxiety-provoking impulses, these impulses persist. The impulses continue to press for release in disguised and distorted forms that are called "symptoms."

NEUROSIS

When Defenses Fail: Neurotic Anxiety and Conflict

Sometimes the defenses that disguise basic motives may become inadequate and denial and repression no longer work. Even under the usual circumstances of everyday life, the defenses are occasionally penetrated and the person betrays himself (Freud, 1901/1960). Such betrayals of underlying motives are seen when defenses are relaxed, as in dream life or in jokes and slips of the tongue. The defense process involves **distortion** and **displacement**, which occur when private meanings develop as objects and events become transformed into symbols representing things quite different from them. It is believed that these meanings are partially revealed by behavioral "signs" or symptoms that may symbolize disguised wishes and unconscious conflicts. For example, phobias such as the fear of snakes may reflect basic sexual conflicts; in this case, the feared snake has symbolic meaning.

Development of Neurotic Anxiety

It is now possible to consider the Freudian conception of how neurotic anxiety and problems may develop. The sequence here (depicted in Figure 7.1) begins with the child's aggressive or sexual impulses that seek direct release. These efforts at discharge may be strongly punished and blocked by dangers or threats (e.g., intense parental punishment such as withdrawal of love). Hence, they lead to objective anxiety. The child may become especially afraid that these impulses will lead to loss of parental love and in time, therefore, may come to fear his or her own impulses. Because this state is painful, the child tries to repress these impulses. If the ego is weak, the repression is only partly successful and the instinctual impulses persist. Unless expressed in some acceptable form, these impulses become increasingly "pent up," gradually building up to the point where they become hard to repress. Consequently, there may be a partial breakdown of repression, and some of the impulses may break through, producing some neurotic anxiety. Anxiety, in this view, functions as a danger signal, a warning to the individual that repressed impulses are starting to break through the defenses. Rather than emerging directly, however, the unacceptable impulses express themselves indirectly in disguised and symbolic ways.

7.13 What is neurotic anxiety, and what is its role in neurotic symptoms?

The Meaning of Neurotic Acts

Freud felt that the symbolic meaning of behavior was clearest in neurotic acts. He cited the case of a girl who compulsively rinsed out her washbasin many times after washing. Freud thought that the significance of this ceremony was expressed in the proverb, "Don't throw away dirty water until you have clean." He interpreted the girl's action as a warning to her sister, to whom she was very close, "not to separate from her unsatisfactory husband until she had established a relationship with a better man" (Freud, 1959a, vol. 2, p. 28).

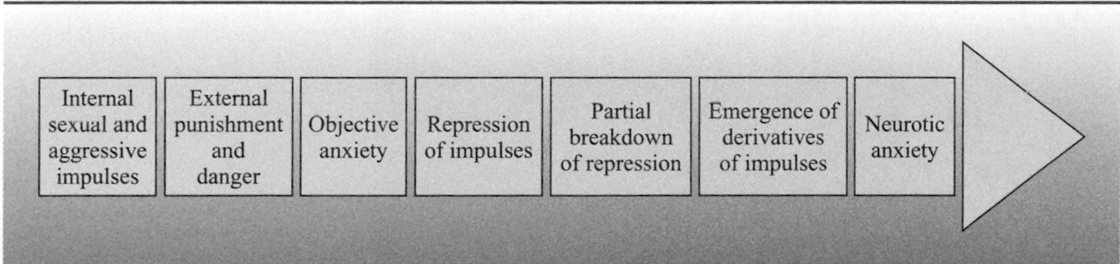

Figure 7.1 Sequence in Freudian conception of neurotic anxiety.

TABLE 7.2 Possible Meanings of Some Behavioral Signs in Freudian Theory

Behavioral Sign	Possible Underlying Meaning
Fear of snakes	Sexual conflict regarding genitals
Compulsive cleanliness	Reaction against anal impulses
Obsessive thought: "My mother is drowning"	Imperfectly repressed hostility toward mother
Paranoid jealousy	Homosexual wishes
Preoccupation with money	Problems around toilet training

Another patient was able to sit only in a particular chair and could leave it only with much difficulty. In Freud's analysis of her problem, the chair symbolized the husband to whom she remained faithful. Freud saw the symbolic meaning of her compulsion in her sentence "It is so hard to part from anything (chair or husband) in which one has once settled oneself" (Freud, 1959a, vol. 2, p. 29). Thus, the important object of conflict—the husband—was transformed into a trivial one—the chair. Freud cited these and many similar cases as evidence for the view that neurotic behaviors express unconscious motives and ideas symbolically.

The clinician's task, then, is to decipher the unconscious meaning of the patient's behavior and to discover the conflicts and dynamics that might underlie seemingly irrational behavior patterns (see Table 7.2).

Origins of Neuroses

7.14 At what developmental period do neuroses develop and what factors produce them?

In Freud's view, serious problems, such as the neuroses, and the roots of the symptoms that characterize them, begin in early childhood:

> It seems that neuroses are acquired only in early childhood (up to the age of six), even though their symptoms may not make their appearance till much later. The childhood neurosis may become manifest for a short time or may even be overlooked. In every case the later neurotic illness links up with the prelude in childhood.
>
> ... The neuroses are, as we know, disorders of the ego; and it is not to be wondered at if the ego, so long as it is feeble, immature and incapable of resistance, fails to deal with tasks, which it could cope with later on with the utmost ease. In these circumstances instinctual

Does a dream of a broken arm imply a desire to break one's wedding vows?

TABLE 7.3 Examples of Behaviors Motivated by Unconscious Wishes

Behavior Involved	Unconscious Wish	Transformation
Slip of the tongue: May I "insort" (instead of escort) you?	To insult	Condensation: (insult + escort = "insort")
Slip of the tongue: "Gentlemen, I declare a quorum present and herewith declare the session *closed*."	To close the meeting	Association of opposites: open = closed)
Dream of disappointment in quality of theater tickets, as a result of having gotten them too soon.	I married too soon; I could have gotten a better spouse by waiting.	Symbolism: (getting tickets too soon = marrying too soon)
Dream of breaking an arm	Desire to break marriage vows	Conversion into visual imagery: (breaking vows = breaking an arm)

Source: Freud, S. (1920). *A general introduction to psychoanalysis*. New York: Boni and Liveright.

> demands from within, no less than excitations from the external world, operate as "traumas," particularly if they are met halfway by certain innate dispositions. (1933, pp. 41–42)

As these quotations indicate, neuroses were seen as the products of early childhood traumas plus innate dispositions. But even the behavior of less disturbed persons was believed to reflect expressions of underlying unconscious motives and conflicts. These manifestations could be seen in the "psychopathology of everyday life"—the occurrence of meaningful but common unconscious expressions, as discussed next.

The Psychopathology of Everyday Life: "Mistakes" That Betray

Some of Freud's most fascinating—and controversial—ideas involved the elaboration of possible hidden meanings that might underlie such common occurrences as slips of the tongue, errors in writing, jokes, and dreams. In Freud's (1901/1960, 1920/1924) view, "mistakes" may be unconsciously motivated by impulses that the individual is afraid to express directly or openly. To show that mistakes may really be motivated by underlying wishes, Freud pointed out many instances in which even the attempt to "correct" the error appears to betray a hidden, unacceptable meaning. In one case, for example, an official introduced a general as "this battle-scared veteran" and tried to "correct" his mistake by saying "bottle-scarred veteran." Other examples are summarized in Table 7.3. Some common Freudian dream symbols are shown in Table 7.4.

7.15 How do everyday "slips" reveal the unconscious? Provide some examples.

TABLE 7.4 Some Freudian Dream Symbols and Their Meanings

Dream Symbol	Meaning
King, queen	Parents
Little animals, vermin	Siblings
Travel, journey	Dying
Clothes, uniforms	Nakedness
Flying	Sexual intercourse
Extraction of teeth	Castration

Source: Freud, S. (1920). *A general introduction to psychoanalysis*. New York: Boni and Liveright.

Motivational Determinism: Unconscious Causes

7.16 What is motivational determinism?

According to Freud's principle of motivational determinism, all behavior is motivated, and the causal chain that links wishes to actions can be complex and indirect.

Suppose, for example, a man fights with his wife about money, is personally fussy about his appearance, and becomes very upset when he loses his umbrella. These seemingly different bits of behavior might actually be motivated by a common cause. Much of psychoanalytic assessment and therapy is a search for such underlying causes. A psychodynamic explanation of behavior consists of finding the motives that produced it. The focus is not on behavior, but on the motivations that it serves and reflects. And usually these motives are disguised in their expressions and unconscious, rooted in early experiences.

▶ PERSONALITY DEVELOPMENT

Freud believed that every person normally progresses through five **psychosexual stages**. During the 5 five years of life, pleasure is successively focused on three zones of the body as the oral, anal, and phallic stages unfold. Then comes a quiet latency period of about 5 or 6 years. Finally, if progress through each stage has been successful, the person reaches the mature or genital stage after puberty. But special problems at any stage may retard or arrest (fixate) development and leave enduring marks on the person's character throughout life.

Stages of Development

7.17 Describe the five psychosexual stages and indicate how unresolved conflicts at the early stages create personality traits.

Oral

The **oral stage** occurs during the first year of life when pleasure is focused on the mouth and on the satisfactions of sucking, eating, and biting in the course of feeding (but see *In Focus 7.3*). The dependent, helpless person is said to be fixated at this stage, when the infant is totally dependent upon others for satisfaction of his or her needs.

IN FOCUS 7.3

HOW ORAL IS THE INFANT?

Although the feeding situation is a critical phase of early development, it is only one part of the total relationship between the growing organism and the world. Thus, the baby is more than an "oral" creature. Babies respond to stimulation of the mouth, lips, and tongue, but in addition, they see, hear, and feel, obtaining stimulation visually, aurally, and from being handled.

Professor Burton L. White of Harvard University in the 1960s carefully observed infants as they lay in their cribs. (The participants were physically normal infants in an orphanage.) He and his colleagues recorded the quantity and quality of visual–motor activity to study the babies' attention. On the basis of these observations, they plotted the development of the infants' tendency to explore the visual surroundings, as depicted in Figure 7.2. The findings surprised the investigators:

One important revelation for me which resulted from these weekly observations was that, contrary to my academically bred expectations, infants weren't really very oral during the first months of life. In fact, between two and six months, a far more appropriate description would be that they are visual-prehensory creatures. We observed subject after subject spend dozens of hours watching first his fists, then his fingers, and then the interactions between hands and fingers. Thumb-sucking and mouthing were rarely observed except for brief periods when the infant was either noticeably upset or unusually hungry. (White, 1967, p. 207)

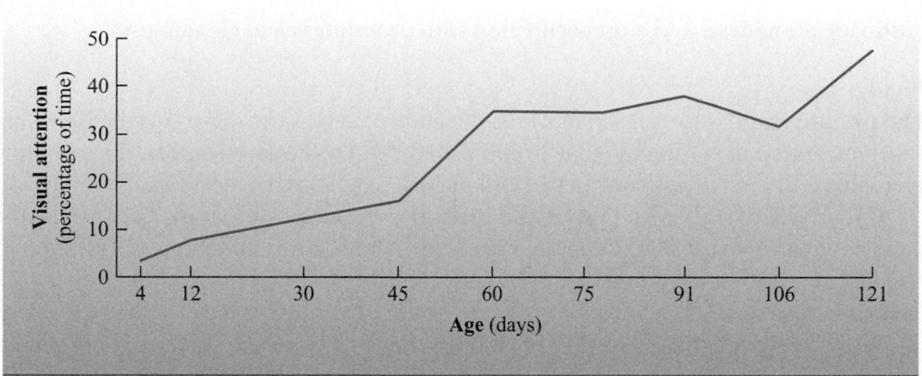

Figure 7.2 The development of the tendency to explore the surroundings.

Source: Adapted from White, B. L., & Held, R. (1966). Plasticity of sensorimotor development in the human infant. In J. F. Rosenblith & W. Allinsmith (Eds.), *The causes of behavior II* (pp. 60–70). Boston: Allyn & Bacon.

These observations were among the first to point out how much more we need to know about the details of the infant's perceptual and cognitive activities before we can reach conclusions about what goes on in early development. In fact, as this investigator's comments suggested, the "oral" infant is turning out to be much more attentive and cognitively active, and less oral and passive, than was believed in early formulations. More wakefulness and alertness, greater receptivity to stimulation, more directed attention, and less fussing begin to characterize the baby very early in life (Sroufe, 1977). Stimulation becomes less unsettling and may be sought out actively as the baby becomes more and more attentive, even to its own movements.

Indeed, in the last few decades, an explosion of research on early development, using close observation and ingenious experiments, suggests a dramatic increase in the infant's understanding, perceptual skills, and cognitive competence by the second or third month. Experiments by Elizbeth Spelke and her colleagues at Harvard University, for example, continue to probe the origins of human cognitive capacities. They are discovering the presence even at birth of remarkably rich and specialized "core knowledge" that soon enables all sorts of understanding within the infant. Included in such core knowledge, according to the researchers, is the capacity for understanding numbers and ultimately formal mathematics, for constructing and using symbolic representations, for categorizing objects, and for reasoning about other people and their mental states (e.g., Dehaene, Izard, Pica, & Spelke, 2006; Spelke, 2000). The findings are revolutionizing the understanding of the extraordinary richness of the infant mind. They are standing the earlier view of the newborn mind as a blank slate on its head (e.g., Talbot, 2006), and making it clear that the newborn is already much more than oral.

7.18 Does research support Freud's conception of the infant as primarily "oral"?

According to Freud, the oral stage is divided into two periods: (1) sucking and (2) biting and chewing. Later character traits develop from these earliest modes of oral pleasure. More specifically, oral incorporation (as in sucking and taking in milk in the first oral period) becomes the prototype of such pleasures as those gained from the acquisition of knowledge or possessions. In his view, the gullible person (who is "easily taken in") is fixated at the oral, incorporative level of personality. The sarcastic, bitingly argumentative person is fixated at the second oral period—the sadistic level associated with biting and chewing.

Anal

In the second year of life, the **anal stage** is marked by a shift in body pleasure to the anus and by a concern with the retention and expulsion of feces. According to Freud, during toilet training, the child has his first experience with imposed control. The manner in which toilet training is handled may influence later personal qualities and conflicts. For example, extremely harsh, repressive training might produce a person characterized by obstinacy, stinginess, and a preoccupation with orderliness and cleanliness.

Phallic

7.19 How does the *Oedipus complex* promote male sex role development?

The **phallic stage** is the period in which the child observes the difference between male and female and experiences what Freud called the **Oedipus complex**. This complex, symbolized in the father–son conflicts of ancient Greek myths, occurs at about age 5.

Freud thought that both boys and girls love their mother as the satisfier of their basic needs and resent their father as a rival for their mother's affections. In addition, the boy fears castration by the father as punishment for desiring his mother sexually. This **castration anxiety** is so terrifying that it results in the repression of the boy's sexual desire for his mother and hostility toward his father. To reduce the anxiety of possible castration by the father, the boy tries to become like him or to identify with him. In this identification, he gradually internalizes the father's standards and values as his own, becoming more like his father rather than battling him.

Identification with the father in turn helps the boy gain some indirect satisfaction of his sexual impulses toward his mother. In this last phase of the Oedipus complex of the male, the superego reaches its final development as the internalized standards of parents and society, and the opposition to incest and aggression becomes part of his own value system.

In the female, **penis envy**, resulting from the discovery that she lacks the male organ, is the impetus to exchange her original love object—the mother—for a new object—the father. Unlike the boy's Oedipus complex, which is repressed through fear, the girl—having nothing to lose—persists in her sexual desire for her father. This desire does, naturally, undergo some modification because of realistic barriers.

Latency

After the phallic stage, a **latency period** develops. Now there is less overt concern with sexuality; the child represses his or her memories of infantile sexuality and forbidden sexual activity by making them unconscious.

Genital

This is the final, mature stage of psychosexual development. Now the person is capable of genuine love for other people and can achieve adult sexual satisfactions. No longer characterized by the selfishness (narcissism) and mixed, conflicting feelings that marked the earlier stages, he or she can relate to others in a mature, heterosexual fashion. But before he or she reaches the **genital stage**, excessive stress or overindulgence may cause the person to become fixated at earlier levels of psychosexual development.

Fixation and Regression

7.20 How do fixation, regression, and identification enter into personality development?

The concepts of **fixation** and **regression** are closely connected with Freud's conceptualization of psychosexual stages of development. Fixation means that a sexual impulse is arrested at an early stage. Regression is reversion to an earlier stage in the face of unmanageable stress. Fixation occurs when conflict at a particular stage of psychosexual development is too great. Severe deprivation or overindulgence at a particular stage, or inconsistent alterations between indulgence and deprivation, also may lead to fixation.

In sum, personality is intimately related to the individual's mode of coping with problems at each stage of psychosexual development. The result is reflected in the nature of character formation, symptoms, and relations with other people. When individuals' resolution of problems at any stage of development is inadequate, later stress may cause them to regress to that earlier stage. They then display behavior typical of that less mature period.

Freud's Theory of Identification

Parts of Freud's theory of psychosexual stages have been modified and even rejected in recent years. Some of his closely related concepts regarding identification, however, have continued to be influential.

Early personality development occurs in the setting of the family. In that context, you saw Freud strongly emphasize the child's attachment to the mother and the rivalry between son and father for her attentions. This triangle of relations, called the Oedipal situation, is the basis for identification with the standards of the parent. This identification process Freud attributed to two mechanisms that operate during psychosexual development.

Anaclitic identification is based on the intense dependency of a child on the mother, beginning early in the course of the infant's development. Because of the helplessness of the infant, the dependency upon the caretaker is profound. Identification for girls is based mainly on this early love or dependency relation with the mother. In anaclitic identification, the child must first have developed a dependent love relationship with her caretaker (usually the mother). Later, when the mother begins to withdraw some of her nurturant attention, the child tries to recapture her by imitating and reproducing her in actions and fantasy.

For boys, dependency or anaclitic identification with the mother is followed later by **identification with the aggressor**. The "aggressor" is the father during the Oedipal phase of development. Identification with the aggressor is motivated by fear of harm and castration by the punitive father in retribution for the son's fantasies and his sexual wishes toward the mother. Freud described the situation vividly:

> When a boy (from the age of two or three) has entered the phallic phase of his libidinal [sexual] development, is feeling pleasurable sensations in his sexual organ and has learnt to procure these at will by manual stimulation, he becomes his mother's lover. He wishes to possess her physically in such ways as he has divined from his observations and intuitions about sexual life, and he tries to seduce her by showing her the male organ which he is proud to own. In a word, his early awakened masculinity seeks to take his father's place with her; his father has hitherto in any case been an envied model to the boy, owing to the physical strength he perceives in him and the authority with which he finds him clothed. His father now becomes a rival who stands in his way and whom he would like to get rid of. (1933, p. 46)

The hostile feelings that the boy experiences in the Oedipal situation create great anxiety in him; he desires the mother but fears castration from the father. To defend against the anxiety, he resolves the Oedipal conflict, repressing his aggressive wishes against his father and trying to become more like him. It is as though the boy believes that if he *"is"* the father, he cannot be hurt by him. Identification with the aggressor requires that the boy have a strong (but ambivalent) relation with the father. In this relationship, love for the father is mixed with hostility because the father possesses the mother and interferes with the son's urges. Freud thought that through identification with the aggressor, boys develop a stricter superego.

▶ IMPACT OF FREUD'S THEORIES

Image of the Person

7.21 Describe Freud's conception of the human being and relate it to your own beliefs.

Freud built a dramatic image of what a person might be, inventing a sweeping and novel theoretical system. Freud saw the person as struggling with himself and the world, blocked by anxieties, conflicted, and plagued by his own unacceptable wishes and unconscious secrets. This picture has captivated the imagination of many laymen as well as clinicians. Consequently, it has had an enormous impact on philosophical as well as psychological conceptions of human nature. In Freud's view, humans are not the unemotional, rational beings that Victorian society thought they were. Instead, people are torn by unconscious conflicts and wishes that push them in seemingly puzzling ways.

Freud believed that the environment is less important than inborn instincts in the dynamics of personality. He thought that external stimuli make fewer demands and, in any event, can always be avoided. In contrast, one's own impulses and needs cannot be escaped. Consequently, he made instinctual impulses the core of personality. Freud's emphasis on unconscious impulses as the most basic determinants of behavior is seen in an analogy in which the relation of the id and the ego is likened to that between a horse and its rider:

> The horse provides the locomotive energy, and the rider has the prerogative of determining the goal and of guiding the movements of his powerful mount towards it. But all too often in the relations between the ego and the id we find a picture of the less ideal situation in which the rider is obliged to guide his horse in the direction in which it itself wants to go. (1933, p. 108)

Thus, in Freud's psychology the id is stubborn and strong and often the ego cannot really control it effectively. The function of psychotherapy is to put the rider—the ego—in control. The resilient healthy ego becomes able to create harmony and integration that takes account of the passions of the id, the constraints and opportunities of reality, and the urgings and ideals of the superego. His metaphor for these dynamic interactions between id, ego, and super ego have long influenced psychotherapy, but have often been viewed critically by most of the scientific community. Yet you also saw that supporters of Freud's viewpoint believe it may be taking on new life in light of modern findings on mind–brain relationships that are examining the beautiful details of how some of the processes that Freud discussed abstractly play out specifically at the brain level.

The Healthy Personality

Psychodynamic theories also have shaped ideas about mental health, adaptation, deviance, and personality change, probably more than any other psychological approach.

7.22 What is Freud's conception of healthy personality functioning?

For Freud, a healthy personality showed itself in the ability to love and work and required a harmony among id, ego, and superego. Referring to the goal of psychotherapy, Freud wrote, "Where id was, there shall ego be." He meant that, for the healthy personality, rational choice and control replace irrational, impulse-driven compulsion. A healthy personality also required mature (genital) psychosexual development.

From the psychodynamic perspective, adequate adaptation requires insight into one's unconscious motives. Persons who can cope adequately are the ones who can face their impulses and conflicts without having to be extremely defensive. Symptoms represent the return of unsuccessfully repressed materials, reemerging to torture the person in disguised forms. Breakdowns reflect the inadequacy of defenses to deal with unconscious conflicts. Symptoms and mental problems develop when the ego does not have the strength to cope with the conflicting demands of external reality and the internal pressures of id and superego. In Freud's words (1940, pp. 62–63), when

> . . . the ego has been weakened by the internal conflict, we must come to its aid. The position is like a civil war which can only be decided by the help of an ally from without. The analytical physician and the weakened ego of the patient, basing themselves upon the real external world, are to combine against the enemies, the instinctual demands of the id, and the moral demands of the superego. We form a pact with each other. The patient's sick ego promises us the most candor, promises, that is, to put at our disposal all of the material which his self-perception provides; we, on the other hand, assure him of the strictest discretion and put at his service our experience in interpreting material that has been influenced by the unconscious. Our knowledge shall compensate for his ignorance and shall give his ego once more mastery over the lost provinces of his mental life. This pact constitutes the analytic situation.

The pact to which Freud refers above is also the basis for the close relationship between therapist and client that develops over the course of the analysis. It is called **transference**. The name reflects the view that the patient transfers onto the therapist many of the feelings experienced initially with the parents. In the course of the therapy, these feelings are examined closely and "worked through" until they become resolved.

Behaviors as Symptoms

The Freudian approach views an individual's problematic behavior as symptomatic (rather than of main interest in its own right). It searches for the possible causes of these symptoms by making inferences about the underlying personality dynamics. For example, an individual who has a bad stutter might be viewed as repressing hostility, one with asthma as suffering from dependency conflicts, and one with snake fears as victimized by unconscious sexual problems. This focus on the meaning of behavior as a symptom (sign) guides the psychodynamic strategy for understanding both normal and abnormal behavior. Thus, the psychodynamically oriented clinician seeks to infer unconscious conflicts, defense structure, problems in psychosexual development, and the symbolic meaning and functions of behavior.

7.23 How is behavior understood in Freudian theory?

SUMMARY

BASIC ASSUMPTIONS

- Freud's work was based on clinical observations of neurotic persons and self-analysis. This led him to posit the unconscious as a key component of personality.
- Freud used dreams and free association to tap into unconscious wishes.

PSYCHIC STRUCTURE

- The id, ego, and superego form the psychodynamic structure of the personality.
- The id is the primary, instinctual core, obeying the "pleasure principle."
- The ego mediates between the conflicting demands of the id and the superego, testing the outer world of reality, utilizing "secondary processes": logical thinking and rational planning to ensure survival.
- The superego represents the internalized moral standards, values, and ideals of society as conveyed by the parents.
- Recent empirical and theoretical research has shown evidence to support Freud's theory of psychic structure, despite it still being viewed often as archaic and unscientific.

CONFLICT, ANXIETY, AND PSYCHODYNAMICS

- Many of Allport's future views on adult motivation were shaped by a traumatic encounter with Freud at age 22.

- Personality dynamics involve a perpetual conflict between the id, ego, and superego.
- The desire for immediate gratification of sexual and aggressive instincts puts the person in conflict with the environment and ultimately the superego. This struggle produces anxiety.
- Defenses such as denial and repression may be used by the ego when it is unable to handle anxiety effectively. The person's unacceptable impulses and unconscious motives are transformed into "symptoms."
- The total mind (or psyche) is seen as a closed system motivated to maintain equilibrium: any forces that build up require discharge.

NEUROSIS

- When defenses fail, the conflicts may build up into neurotic anxiety, revealed indirectly through symbolic behavior.
- Neuroses are a product of early childhood trauma combined with innate predispositions.
- Small mistakes or slips of the tongue may reveal an unconscious need to express undesirable impulses.
- All behavior, even the seemingly insignificant or absurd, is motivated and significant.

PERSONALITY DEVELOPMENT

- Personality development includes a series of psychosexual stages: oral, anal, phallic, and genital.
- Later personality traits develop according to the individual's experience at each of these stages of maturation.
- In fixation, a sexual impulse is arrested at an early stage.
- Regression is a reversion to an earlier stage of development in the face of stress.
- Anaclitic identification and identification with the aggressor are two Freudian identification mechanisms.

IMPACT OF FREUD'S THEORIES

- Healthy individuals achieve a kind of truce and order within themselves by substituting rational choice and reason for raw id impulses to arrive at the final stage of psychosexual development.
- The Freudian approach views an individual's problematic behavior as symptomatic and searches for the unconscious causes of these symptoms.

▶ KEY TERMS

anaclitic identification 173
anal stage 171
castration anxiety 172
conscious 157
death instincts (Thanatos) 160
denial 166
displacement 167
distortion 167
ego 161
fixation 172
free association 158
genital stage 172
hysteria 157
hysterical anesthesia 166
id 159
identification with the aggressor 173
latency period 172
libido 160
life/sexual instincts (Eros) 160
motivational determinism 157
Oedipus complex 172
oral stage 170
penis envy 172
phallic stage 172
pleasure principle 161
preconscious 157
primary process thinking 161
psychodynamics 164
psychosexual stages 170
reality principle 161
regression 172
repression 166
sensory anesthesias 156
sexual instincts 160
superego 162
transference 175
transformation of motives 164
unconscious 157

CHAPTER 8

PSYCHODYNAMIC APPLICATIONS AND PROCESSES

Cynthia's best friends could not figure out what was going on with her. She and Jim had been seeing each other for years, and Jim was obviously wild about her. But they were shocked to hear that Cynthia had decided to marry him, suddenly talking nonstop about being in love, and sounding as if she was trying hard to convince herself rather than feeling it. Jim and Cynthia did get married. Three years later her friends were unsurprised when she announced she had filed for divorce.

Stories like these are familiar to everyone, and they reflect how often we are "Strangers to Ourselves," the title of a thoughtful book by psychologist Timothy Wilson (2002). It documents how much trouble human beings often have when they fail to know or recognize what they really feel and want. The voyage to uncover such self-knowledge can be extremely difficult. That voyage is the core mission of the psychodynamic level of analysis, and the topic of the present chapter. The ideas and research here tell an important story about personality psychology. Although many of the conclusions are different from original hypotheses, all of it has stimulated later developments throughout the field. Many of those ideas continue to influence how both professional psychologists and laypersons think about the nature of personality and the human mind, particularly the parts that are most difficult to reach and understand.

This chapter begins by looking at the applications of Freud's key ideas to how many clinicians working in this framework assess personality and try to make sense of the problems for which their clients and patients seek help. These assessments, in turn, help guide the treatment process, discussed next. There have been major changes in these applications in the last century, and while many of the original assumptions have not stood the test of time, some of the core ideas remain influential, even if often in modified forms. We conclude the chapter by examining research on psychodynamic processes and individual differences in patterns of defenses against anxiety fundamental for work at this level of analysis.

APPLICATIONS TO PERSONALITY ASSESSMENT

Freudian psychology was especially exciting because it promised a way to understand and to treat each complex individual with the depth that he or she deserves. In the Freudian approach, the goal of psychotherapy is to help the person to reveal unconscious motives, conflicts, and other dynamics. The objective is to uncover disguises and defenses, to read the symbolic meanings of behaviors, and to find the unconscious motives that underlie action. In this way, the clinician tries to find the distinctive qualities that characterize the individual.

The Core Beneath the Mask

8.1 How do psychodynamic clinicians explain intraindividual behavior differences?

Psychodynamic theorists recognized that a person's overt actions across seemingly similar situations often seem inconsistent. They felt, however, that these inconsistencies in behavior were merely superficial, because beneath them were underlying motives that actually drove the person consistently over the years. The basic motives persist across diverse settings, but their overt expressions are disguised. Therefore, the task is to find the person's fundamental motives and dynamics under the defensive distortions of the overt behavior. The challenge is to discover the basic core hidden behind the mask, to find the truth beneath the surface. But how?

Relying on the Clinician

Psychodynamic interpretations of a person's behavior depend more on the clinician's intuitions than on tests. The rules for relating behavioral signs to unconscious meanings are not spelled out and require clinicians to form their own judgments based on clinical experience and the "feel" of the case. The merit of such assessments depends on two things. First, it depends on the evidence supporting the techniques upon which the psychologist relies. Second, it depends on the value of clinical judgment itself. Because psychodynamic theories rest on the belief that the core of personality is revealed by highly indirect behavioral signs, evidence for the value of these indirect signs of personality is most important. We next review some of the main clinical methods that have been studied in the search for valuable signs of personality. Probably the most important of these methods are the projective techniques.

Projective Methods

8.2 What are the major features of projective tests, and the rationale underlying their use? Why are they favored by psychodynamic clinicians?

The main characteristic of **projective methods** is the open-ended way in which the testing situation is usually structured. Typically, the purpose of the test is disguised (Bell, 1948; Exner, 1993), and the person is given freedom to respond in any way that he or she likes. The assessor presents you with ambiguous stimuli and asks questions like "What might this be?" "What could this remind you of?" [while showing an inkblot] or say, "Create the most imaginative story that you can [showing a picture], including what the people are thinking and feeling, what led up to this situation, and how it all comes out." Or they read words ("I," "mother," "love") and ask you to "say the first thing that comes to mind."

Psychoanalytically oriented assessors favor projective techniques, because they assume that the "unconscious inner life" is at least partially "projected" and revealed in responses to the ambiguous projective test situation. The two most influential and popular projective techniques have been the Rorschach and the Thematic Apperception Test (TAT), described below. Both the reliability and the validity of the Rorschach have been heavily disputed and generally found to be problematic. In a comprehensive review, Kihlstrom (2003) concludes that even in the few cases in which projective techniques had some validity, there was no evidence that the findings reflected the person's *unconscious* mental states.

Nevertheless, a 1995 survey with replies from over 400 clinical psychologists across a variety of settings indicated that both the Rorschach and TAT still remain among the most commonly used personality assessment procedures in everyday clinical practice (Watkins, Campbell, Nieberding, & Hallmark, 1995).

The Rorschach

Developed by the psychiatrist Hermann Rorschach in 1921, the **Rorschach test** consists of a series of inkblots on 10 separate cards (Figure 8.1). Some of the blots are black and white, and some colored (Figure 8.2). The individual is instructed to look at the inkblots one at a time and to say everything that the inkblot could resemble or look like. The

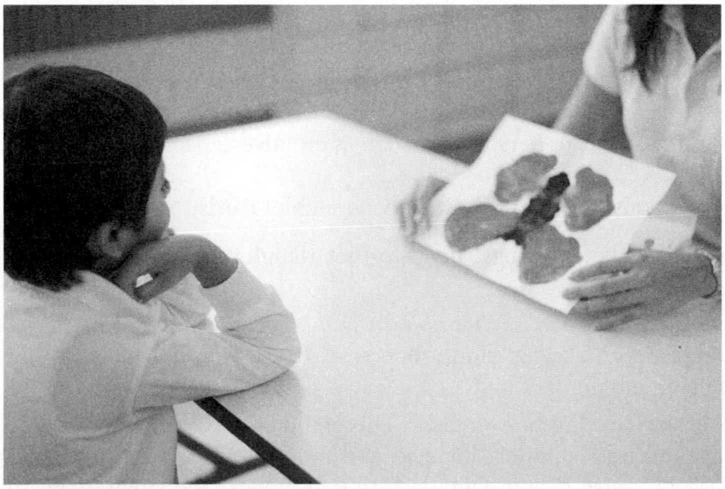

Figure 8.1 Taking a Rorschach test.

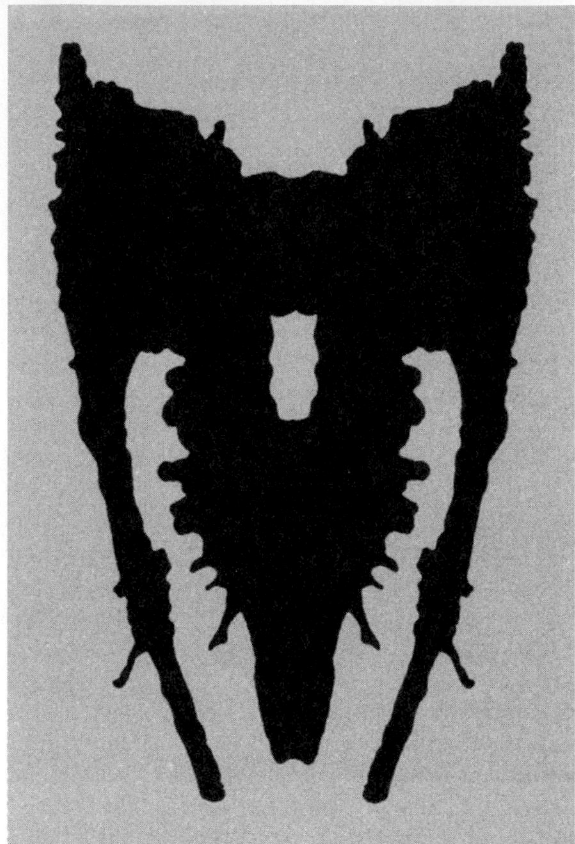

Figure 8.2 Inkblot similar to those in the Rorschach test.

8.3 How are responses to the Rorschach and TAT analyzed and used to inferpsycho-dynamics?

examiner then generally conducts an inquiry into the details of the person's interpretation of each blot.

Responses may be scored for location (the place on the card that the response refers to) and such determinants as the physical aspects of the blot, such as shape, color, shading, or an expression of movement (e.g., "The bat is flying right at him") that the patient notes. The originality of the responses, the content, and other characteristics also may be scored and compared to those of other people of similar age, and extensive manuals have been developed with rules for scoring (Exner, 1993). The interpreter may try to relate these scores to aspects of personality, such as creative capacity, contact with reality, and anxiety.

Here are Gary's reactions to two of the Rorschach inkblot cards:

Response: This looks like two dogs, head-to-foot (laughs), licking each other. That's about it, that's all.

Inquiry answers (to the question "What about the inkblot made you think of two dogs?"): They're sort of fuzzy . . . kinda shapeless. It was the dark skin and the furry effect that made me think of it.

Response: Didn't we have this one already? This could be an ogre laughing—his head thrown back and he's laughing, his eyes and mouth wide open. These over here look like insects, tsetse flies in fact, with tiny, tiny legs, and small, delicate, and rather beautiful wings. That's it, that's enough.

The Thematic Apperception Test (TAT)

The **Thematic Apperception Test (TAT)** was developed in the Harvard Psychological Clinic research program during the 1930s by Henry Murray in collaboration with Christina Morgan (Murray, Barnett, & Homburger, 1938). These researchers wanted measures that would get beyond direct self-reports to tap underlying needs of which the participant might not be aware, or which might be uncomfortable to acknowledge. With this goal, they developed a new projective test that examined the person's fantasies as revealed by stories told to a set of pictures.

The TAT consists of a series of pictures and one blank card (see Figure 8.3 with TAT-like card). Scenes show, for example, a mother and daughter, a man and a woman in the bedroom, a father and son. If you take this test, you will be told that it is a storytelling test and that you are to make up a story for each picture: "Tell what has led up to the event shown in the picture, describe what is happening at the moment, what the characters are feeling and thinking, and then give the outcome." You are encouraged to give free reign to your imagination and to say whatever comes to mind. It is expected that people will interpret the ambiguous pictures presented according to their individual readiness to perceive in a certain way ("apperception").

The themes that recur in these imaginative productions are thought to reflect the person's underlying needs, as well as potential conflicts and problems. Special scoring keys have been designed for use with the TAT (Bellack & Abrams, 1997; McClelland, Atkinson, Clark, & Lowell, 1953; Mussen & Naylor, 1954). In clinical work, the stories usually are not scored formally, and instead the clinician interprets the themes intuitively in accord with his or her particular theoretical orientation (Rossini & Moretti, 1997). But formal scoring is often used in research applications. Two of Gary's answers to TAT cards are shown in *In Focus 8.1*.

Applying Psychodynamic Clinical Inferences to Gary W.: A Freudian View

For an example of how the classic Freudian framework was applied in traditional psychodynamic assessment, let's look at one interpretation of the text's case, Gary W.

Figure 8.3 Picture similar to those in the TAT.

IN FOCUS 8.1

GARY'S TAT STORIES

Card depicting two men: Two men have gone on a hunting trip. It is dawn now and the younger one is still sound asleep. The older one is watching over him. Thinking how much he reminds him of when he was young and could sleep no matter what. Also, seeing the boy sleeping there makes him long for the son he never had. He's raising his hand, about to stroke him on the forehead. I think he'll be too embarrassed to go ahead with it. He'll start a fire and put on some coffee and wait for the younger man to wake up.

Card depicting young man and older woman: This depicts a mother–son relationship. The mother is a strong, stalwart person. Her son is hesitating at the doorway. He wants to ask her advice about something but isn't sure whether it's the right thing to do. Maybe he should make up his own mind. I think he'll just come in and have a chat with her. He won't ask her advice but will work things out for himself. Maybe it's a career choice, a girlfriend. I don't know what, but whatever it is, he'll decide himself. He'll make his own plans, figure out what the consequences will be, and work it out from there.

Oedipal themes abound in the case of Gary W., although he has grown a long way toward resolving them. W. emotionally describes his feeling that his father was his "severest critic" and that he is his mother's favorite. He says that he no longer sees adults as all-knowing, and he refers to his father as mellowed and "out of it." He reports warmth and affection for his mother, although these feelings are mixed.

In his own sibling relationships, Gary seems to have displaced much of his rivalry with his father onto his older brother. W. describes great outbursts of anger vented on Charles with obvious intent to injure. He compares Charles with their father and says that the two are alike in many respects. He is on better terms with Charles since the latter was in a car crash in which he was hurt. (This in some respects parallels his present hostile condescension, rather than competitive hostility, toward the father who has proved himself a failure in business.)

A recent revival of the Oedipal situation occurred when Gary's girlfriend left him for his roommate. She may well have symbolized his mother to him more than is usual: She is older, was married before, and has a child from the previous marriage. After he had confessed his love to her, she told him that she had been seeing his roommate. W. felt humiliated and "wounded in my vanity," because these events went on "behind my back." His feelings are reminiscent of the chagrin felt by the little boy when he realizes his father's role vis-à-vis his mother. W. attempted to resolve his anger by recognizing that he was not in a position financially to marry her, whereas his roommate was. His apparent satisfaction that his roommate after all has not married her, and that they may have broken up, also is consistent with the conceptualization that this relationship was filled with Oedipal themes.

The incomplete resolution of the Oedipal conflict is further evident in W.'s fear of injury and physical illness, in the depression that has followed a motorcycle accident (castration anxiety), and in the distinction he makes between girlfriends ("good girls") and sex objects ("easy girls"). Incomplete identification with his father, whether a cause or a result of this unresolved situation, is apparent. His search for a strong male figure is evident in his reactions to the headmaster and teacher at boarding school, described respectively as "a very definite, determined sort of person" and "not the sort of man you could push around." He is quite openly disparaging of his father, albeit on intellectual grounds. (This tends to be W.'s typical style.)

According to Gary, his mother sees sex as something bad and nasty. This report, as well as his suggestion that his mother has undermined his father's masculinity, may represent wishes that his mother may not be responsive to his father. He himself may regard sexuality ambivalently—his sexual experiences seem to involve much parental rebellion, and he keeps his sex objects separate from his affections. When he speaks about sex, he talks crudely of "scoring."

Gary's anxiety in social situations in general, and his fear of public speaking in particular, are further indices of his basic insecurity and his brittle defenses. He is concerned that he will be found lacking. The underlying castration anxiety is expressed symbolically in his comment that when he stands up to speak in public, he is afraid "the audience is ready to chop my head off," and when there is a possibility of debate, that he will be "caught with my pants down."

Gary shows some concern about homosexuality. He mentions it spontaneously when talking about friendship, and his descriptions of living in close proximity with other males include tension, friction, and annoyance. This anxiety is illustrated in his uncomfortable relationship with his current roommate.

The battle being waged between impulses, reality, and conscience are evidenced by Gary's concern with control and his obsessive–compulsive traits. W. makes a tenuous distinction between passion and reason, rejecting the former and clinging to the latter. He extends this distinction to interpersonal relations, drawing a line between "companionship" and "love." He reports an inability to empathize and form good object-relations. An example of repression of affect is W.'s difficulty in expressing anger. In this area, as in others, he tends to intellectualize as a way to systematize and control anxiety. His problems in expressing anger may also be reflected in his speech difficulties and in his verbal blocks, especially in public and social situations.

Instinctual elements arise to disturb the tenuous control gained by secondary processes. He complains that he sometimes gets drunk when he should be accomplishing things. He says he admires people with enough self-discipline not to drink, smoke, and sleep late. He speaks of trying to force himself not to do the things that he knows are bad for him and that interfere with his long-range objectives.

The need to control is also apparent in his performance and behavior on many of the psychological tests, where his approach is analytic rather than imaginative, and his expressive movements are tight and controlled. (His attention to detail and his constant intellectualization of real feelings, his hobby of insect study, and his admission that often "trivialities" bother him for a long time add up to a picture of restriction and repression in the service of anxiety reduction.) There is an anal retentive aspect of this need to control, which comes out rather clearly in his interaction with the assessor when he says testily, "Didn't you show that to me already—are you trying to squeeze more out of me?" A further compulsive trait is W.'s frequent counting, and the way he rigidly breaks his ability self-ratings down into component parts, and strives to ensure complete accuracy and coverage of whatever he is discussing about himself.

The need for control may circle back to castration anxiety. The two themes come together in W.'s fear of physical injury and in his fear of losing his brain capacity. The culmination of these two fears occurred when W.'s motorcycle failed him, and he is still preoccupied with this incident. He relates these fears more directly to the Oedipal conflict when, in the phrase association test, he links anger at his brother with fear of losing his mind.

8.4 What are the main Freudian themes in Gary W.'s case?

Note that the focus in this report is on hypothesized underlying dynamics. It implicitly assumes that sexual and aggressive motives and unconscious conflicts widely affect many behaviors. Statements about behavior tend to be relatively global and undifferentiated. The emphasis is on unacceptable impulses and defenses for coping with the anxiety they arouse. The report also tries to link current sexual and aggressive problems to relations with the parents and to Oedipal problems in early childhood.

This report provides a way of seeing meaning and unity throughout Gary's diverse behaviors. For example, his relations with his brother and with women became part of his larger efforts to cope with Oedipal problems. Indeed, a main attraction of psychodynamic theory is that it offers a systematic, unified view of the individual. It views him as an integrated, dynamic creature: when his underlying core personality is revealed, his seemingly diverse, discrepant behaviors become meaningful, and all fit into the total whole.

But the key question for scientifically oriented students is: Do psychodynamic reports of the kind made about Gary provide accurate and useful insights? Answers to this question reflect great individual differences, and depend on which clinician one might ask. It is clear, however, that over the years many psychologists, even if heavily influenced by the ideas and contributions of Freud, have become increasingly skeptical about the value of reports like the one about Gary. Instead, many psychologists have become more broad and eclectic in their clinical work, and draw liberally on contributions from many of the levels of analysis discussed throughout this text, trying to integrate them in their own ways.

▶ MURRAY, THE HARVARD PERSONOLOGISTS, AND HIGHER MOTIVES

The psychodynamic approach stimulated many innovations in personality theory and assessment. One of the most extensive and imaginative efforts unfolded under the leadership of Henry A. Murray, Robert W. White, and their many colleagues at the Harvard Psychological Clinic in the middle years of the last century, beginning in the late 1930s. This influential group, which became known as the **Harvard personologists**, provided a new model called **personology** for the intensive psychodynamic study of individual lives, and devoted itself to the portrayal of persons in depth. The Harvard personologists were influenced strongly by Freud and the post-Freudian ego psychologists, but they went much beyond Freud's work. They also were influenced, for example, by "biosocial" organismic views that emphasized the wholeness, integration, and adaptiveness of personality. In turn, they trained and influenced a group of students who went on to study a variety of important human motives that are useful for understanding the goals that different people enduringly pursue with varying degrees of intensity.

Studying Lives in Depth

The Harvard group focused on intensive long-term studies of relatively small samples of people. In one classic project (Murray et al., 1938), called *Exploration in Personality*, researchers studied Harvard college undergraduates over a period of many years and gathered data on their personality development and maturation at many points in their lives. They administered tests of many kinds, obtained extensive autobiographical sketches, observed participants' behavior directly, and interviewed them in great detail. These methods probed thoroughly into many topics and most facets of their lives. They included, for example, inquiries into the individuals' personal history and development, school and college, major life experiences, family relations, childhood memories, and sexual development (e.g., earliest recollections, first experiences, masturbation). They also assessed abilities and interests. A sampling of these topics is summarized in Table 8.1. The results often provided rich narrative accounts of life histories, as in Robert White's *Lives in Progress* (1952), which traced several lives over many years.

TABLE 8.1 Examples of Topics Included in the Study of Lives by the Harvard Psychologists

Personal history (early development, school and college, major experiences)
Family relations and childhood memories (including school relations, reactions to authority)
Sexual development (earliest recollections, first experiences, masturbation)
Present dilemmas (discussion of current problems)
Abilities and interests (physical, mechanical, social, economic, erotic)
Aesthetic preferences (judgments, attitudes, tastes regarding art)
Level of aspiration (goal setting, reactions to success and failure)
Ethical standards (cheating to succeed, resistance to temptation)
Imaginal productivity (reactions to inkblots)
Musical reveries (report of images evoked by phonograph music)
Dramatic productions (constructing a dramatic scene with toys)

Source: Based on Murray, H. A., Barrett, W. G., & Homburger, E. (1938). *Explorations in personality*. New York: Oxford University Press.

Assessment Strategy: Diagnostic Council

The researchers in the Harvard clinical studies were experienced psychologists who interpreted their data clinically. Usually a group of several assessors studied each individual participant. The assessors formed their impressions of the person from performance on various projective and objective tests, the autobiography and total personal history, and reactions to thorough interviews. Several assessors would study the same person and each generated his or her own clinical impressions. To share their insights, they pooled their overall impressions at a staff conference or "diagnostic council." These councils became a model for clinical practice. In them, a case conference was conducted in detail and in depth about each individual. On the basis of the council's discussions, inferences were generated about each participant's personality. They inferred basic needs, motives, conflicts, and dynamics; attitudes and values; and main character strengths and liabilities. This global assessment model is schematized in Figure 8.4. It depicts the strategy of using test behavior to generate inferences about the underlying personality. The prediction of future behavior is based on judgments of how a person with that particular personality would probably act. The test behavior itself is used as a sign of the underlying personality. See *In Focus* 8.2 for an example of this strategy for selecting American spies in World War II.

8.5 How was the diagnostic council used by Harvard psychologists in the in-depth study of individuals over time?

Higher-Order Motives

Perhaps most important for the advancement of personality theory and research, Henry Murray called attention to the finding that sex and aggression were by no means the only basic motives revealed by the in-depth study of fantasies with methods that he helped to develop. He was trained originally in medicine and chemistry, became deeply interested in the work of Freud and his many followers, and soon abandoned his medical training to adopt psychology as his research specialty. Murray became an enormously influential personality psychologist, who taught for many years at Harvard University. His innovative ideas and unconventional thinking about deep issues in personality made him an inspiration and a model for the many psychologists he trained. His influential investigation, *Explorations in Personality* (1938), conducted over many years with a large group of his students and collaborators, became a classic for many personality psychologists and a model for studying lives in depth.

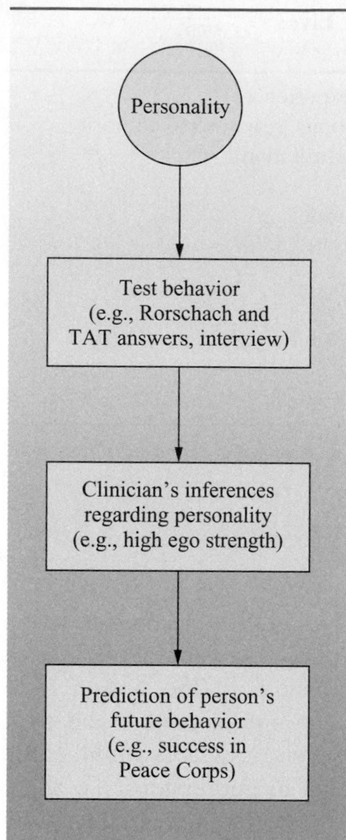

Figure 8.4 Global psychodynamic assessment. The clinician infers the participant's personality from his or her test behavior and predicts future behavior by judging how a person with that personality would probably react to specific future situations.

8.6 How do Murray's higher-order needs differ from biological drives? How do needs and presses conform to a person × situation perspective?

In-depth studies of lives revealed many human needs and motives. Although sex and aggression have retained an important place among the human motivations recognized by Freud's successors, Murray believed additional motives and needs have to be hypothesized to capture the complexity of personality. He and the Harvard personologists advanced the modern study of personality dynamics by identifying a wide range of such human motives that go far beyond the id impulses of classic Freudian theory, and providing methods like the TAT for trying to measure them.

The motives that the Murray group identified are called **higher-order motives**. They used that name because unlike such basic biological needs as hunger and thirst and sex, they do not involve specific physiological changes (such as increased salivation or stomach contraction). Instead, they are psychological desires (wishes) for particular goals or outcomes that the person values. Table 8.2 shows examples of the diverse needs inferred by Henry Murray and associates (1938) in their classical listing. Many of these motives have been investigated in detail (e.g., Emmons, 1997; Koestner & McClelland, 1990).

Motives, in Murray's view, do not operate regardless of the context or situation and its pressures, which he called **environmental presses**. Because Murray theorized that these situational presses influenced personality and its expressions, he and his colleagues developed intensive observational techniques that tried to assess them and take them into account.

The Harvard model for studying personality stimulated many research programs that helped clarify and specify the types of nonbiological higher needs that Murray's

IN FOCUS 8.2

SELECTING U.S. SPIES: THE OSS ASSESSMENT PROJECT

One of the important applied projects of the Harvard psychologists was to select officers for the supersensitive Office of Strategic Services (OSS) during World War II. These officers had to perform critical and difficult secret intelligence assignments, often behind enemy lines and under great stress. The researchers obviously could not devote the same lengthy time to studying OSS candidates that they had given to Harvard undergraduates in the relaxed prewar days in Cambridge. Nevertheless, they attempted to use the same general strategy of global clinical assessment. For this purpose, teams of assessors studied small groups of OSS candidates intensively, usually for a few days or a weekend, in special secret retreats or "stations" located in various parts of the country. Many different measures were obtained on each candidate.

One of the most interesting innovations was the **situational test**. In this procedure, participants were required to perform stressful, lifelike tasks under extremely difficult conditions. For example, "The Bridge" task required building a wooden bridge under simulated dangerous field conditions and under high stress and anxiety. But such situational tests were not used to obtain a sample of their bridge-building skills. Instead, the clinicians made deep inferences, based on the behavior observed during the task, about each person's underlying personality. It was these inferences of unobserved attributes or dispositions, rather than the behavior actually observed in the sampled situation, that entered into the assessment report and became the bases for clinical predictions. In this fashion, behavior samples and situational tests were transformed into inferences about underlying dispositions and motives.

To illustrate, in the *Assessment of Men* by the OSS staff (1948), the bridge-building situation was used to answer questions like these (p. 326): Who took the lead in finally crossing the chasm? And why did he do it? Was it to show his superiority? Why did each of the others fall back from the trip? Did they fear failure?

It is obvious that the chief value of this situation was to raise questions about personality dynamics that required an explanation on the basis of the personality trends already explored. If these could not supply a reasonable explanation, then new information had to be sought, new deductions made. Note that in the situational test, just as on the projective test, behavior was interpreted as a clue revealing personality. Although behavior was sampled and observed, the observations served mainly as signs from which the researchers inferred the motives that prompted the behaviors.

TABLE 8.2 Some Nonphysiological Human Needs Hypothesized by Henry Murray

Abasement (to comply and accept punishment)	Humiliation avoidance
Achievement (to strive and reach goals quickly and well)	Nurturance (to air or protect the helpless)
Affiliation (to form friendships)	Order (to achieve order and cleanliness)
Aggression (to hurt another)	Play (to relax)
Autonomy (to strive for independence)	Rejection (to reject disliked others)
Counteraction (to overcome defeat)	Seclusion (to be distant from others)
Defendance (to defend and justify)	Sentience (to obtain sensual gratification)
Deference (to serve gladly)	Sex (to form an erotic relationship)
Dominance (to control or influence others)	Succorance (to ask for nourishment, love, aid)
Exhibition (to excite, shock, self-dramatize)	Superiority (to overcome obstacles)
Harm avoidance (to avoid pain and injury)	Understanding (to question and think)

Source: Based on Murray, H. A., Barrett, W. G., & Homburger, E. (1938). *Explorations in personality*. New York: Oxford University Press.

8.7 How were situational tests used by diagnostic councils in the OSS Assessment Project?

group identified. One good example was the motivation for competence—the need to be effective in its own right—described first by Robert White.

Competence Motivation

A variety of higher-order motives such as curiosity, the need for stimulation, and the desire for play and adventure all may be seen as parts of a more basic motive: the desire for competence (White, 1959). According to Robert White, who also was a Harvard personologist working with Murray, everyday activities such as a child's exploring, playing, talking, and even crawling and walking reflect the desire for mastery and effective functioning; they are satisfying for their own sake (intrinsically) and create in the person a feeling of efficacy. White argues the point in these words:

8.8 What is the origin of competence motivation? How does it influence behavior?

> If in our thinking about motives we do not include this overall tendency toward active dealing, we draw the picture of a creature that is helpless in the grip of its fears, drives, and passions; too helpless perhaps even to survive, certainly too helpless to have been the creator of civilization. It is in connection with strivings to attain competence that the activity inherent in living organisms is given its clearest representation—the power of initiative and exertion that we experience as a sense of being an agent in the living of our lives. This experience may be called a feeling of efficacy. (1972, p. 209)

Competence motivation is a desire for mastery of a task for its own sake and may apply to such diverse tasks as running, piano playing, juggling, chess, or the mastery of a new surgical procedure. According to White, the desire for mastery arises independently of other biological drives (such as hunger and sex) and is not derived from them. Moreover, people engage in activities that satisfy competence needs for the sake of the activity, not for the sake of any external reward such as the praise, attention, or money to which it may lead. The concept of competence motivation is valuable in emphasizing the enormous range of creative activities that humans pursue and appear to enjoy in their own right, and it has played a major role in research on motivation and adaptive problem solving (e.g., Dweck, 1990). It is, however, only one of many motives that influence human behavior.

Diverse other higher-order nonphysiological motives and needs have been identified in personality research. These include the need for achievement (McClelland, 1985; McClelland et al., 1953), the need for affiliation (McAdams & Constantin, 1983), the need for control (Glass, 1977), and the need to endow experience with meaning, called need for cognition (Cacioppo & Petty, 1982). In addition, researchers are examining individual differences in a large array of other goals, motives, and personal projects that motivate behavior (e.g., Emmons, 1997).

Need for Achievement

David C. McClelland and his colleagues (1953), also working at Harvard University, used the TAT to explore the **need for achievement (n Ach)**. They defined this need as *competition with a standard of excellence*. To study it, they examined fantasies from stories told on the TAT by systematically scoring the occurrence of achievement imagery in the stories. They assumed that the more the stories told involved achievement themes and concerns, the higher the level of the achievement motive.

8.9 How has the TAT been used to understand the need for achievement?

McClelland (1961) found intriguing relations between TAT achievement themes and many economic and social measures of achievement orientation in different cultures. He devised special TAT cards showing work-relevant themes (see Figure 8.5) to assess the achievement motive. If, for example, the person creates stories in which the hero is studying hard for a profession and strives to improve, to compete against standards

Figure 8.5 A TAT card developed by David C. McClelland for measuring the "Need to Achieve."

of excellence, and to advance far in a career, the story gets high n Ach scores. This technique has become an important way of measuring the motive to achieve in an indirect or implicit way that avoids simple self-report and its potential biases. It has been used often in research for many years beginning in the 1950s (Atkinson, 1958) and yielded a rich network of meaningful relationships (McClelland, 1985).

For example, the level of achievement motivation exhibited by unemployed blue-collar workers was related to how they dealt with their unemployment situation and tried to find work again. Those higher in measured achievement motivation used more strategies in their job search, and began to look for a job sooner after being laid off than did those lower in this motive (Koestner & McClelland, 1990).

It is also noteworthy that achievement motivation, like most other motivations, is influenced by socialization experiences, especially those in childhood. Parents who set standards that challenge their children to compete and excel, who make their expectations clear, provide goals and standards that the child can meet, and who offer support along the work route toward attaining those goals, also tend to have children whose achievement motivation is higher.

Need for Power

Achievement motivation may be the most extensively researched motive, but it is only one of many that has received attention and yielded interesting findings. David Winter (1973), influenced by the work and methods of McClelland, focused on the **need for power**, defined in terms of the impact one wants to have on people. Individual differences are measured by scoring the power themes that appear in the stories people tell to the TAT (e.g., expressed concern with the status of the characters and the strength and impact of their actions). An extensive network of personal qualities and preferences—from greater risk-taking and more leadership activity to more visible indicators of status—is associated with this motive. People high on power motivation express more concern with impact on others, status, and reputation in their stories. To get the image that engages and reflects the power motive, think here of glossy advertisements for luxury automobiles shown glistening in the driveways of elegant mansions. As the image suggests, the advertisement industry is fully aware of the power motive, and seeks to engage it effectively in those who are likely to be responsive to it.

8.10 Based on research, how is need for power related to behavior?

Research on the power motive has found connections between power imagery in political communications, such as the speeches and writings of political leaders, and the warfare that follows at various points in history (Winter, 1993). Winter examined power images in the leaders' communication, for example between Britain and Germany at the time of World War I. These images also were analyzed in leaders' communications between the United States and the Soviet Union during the Cuban missile crisis in the 1960s. These analyses showed that power images increase before military action and threat erupts. In contrast, power images tend to decrease preceding a decrease in actual threat levels and warfare. The analysis of these images promises to have practical value for predicting important political events.

Need for Intimacy

The **need for intimacy** was examined by Dan McAdams (1990) and revealed a common human desire: people are motivated to warmly and closely connect, share, and communicate with other people in their everyday life. Also a student of McClelland, and like him, using the TAT, McAdams found that individuals who are high in this motive make more eye contact, and laugh and smile more (McAdams, Jackson, & Kirshnit, 1984). In social and group interactions, rather than dominating they tend to be oriented to the communal in their focus and goals (McAdams & Powers, 1981). They prefer close interactions with a few friends with whom they can communicate intimately, and they are not the typical extravert life-of-the party. Consequently, they are more likely to be seen as caring, loving, and sincere, rather than dominant (McAdams, 1990).

Implicit and Explicit Motives

The needs discussed here—from competence and achievement to power and intimacy—merely illustrate the diverse array that continues to be studied in the search for important individual differences. A common theme runs through them all: as Freud first noted, people often are unaware of all of their motivations, particularly when they are driven by motives that they do not like to see in themselves. Recognizing this, Barbara Woike (1995, in preparation) points out that people have two levels of motivation: explicit and implicit. **Explicit motives** are comprised of an individual's more consciously recognized goals, whereas **implicit motives** are associated with a person's less conscious, more emotional, and affect-related desires and drives. While explicit motives can be assessed with direct self-reports simply by asking people about their goals, to get at implicit motives, *indirect* and projective methods—like the TAT—are used rather than relying on simple self-reports. Sometimes called **implicit methods**, they provide a glimpse into human motives that bypasses the problems found on explicit self-report measures that are subject to distortions when people try to make their responses more socially desirable and appropriate. Unsurprisingly, the two types of measures, implicit and explicit, often are not closely related so that responses on one do not predict responses on the other (e.g., Greenwald et al, 2002).

Explicit and implicit motives may influence in different ways both what we remember about our lives and how it is remembered. Woike (1995) asked participants to complete measures of explicit and implicit motives and to report their most memorable experiences (MMEs) for 60 days. She expected, and found, that implicit motives tended to be related to affective, emotional MMEs associated with them, whereas explicit motives were connected with more affect-free daily routines and experiences. For example, individuals who had a stronger implicit motive for achievement recalled more emotional aspects of their achievement experiences, such as excitement about success on an important test. Likewise, those with strong implicit motives for intimacy recalled more intense emotional memories about close interpersonal encounters, such as feeling good after a long self-revealing talk with a close friend. In sharp contrast, for people with stronger explicit motives, for example for achievement, more routine and affect-free experiences and events were recalled, such as doing a term paper. The patterning of explicit and implicit motives also varied for different people. Thus those who measured high in explicit motives for intimacy, for example, could at the same time have high implicit motives for other goals, such as achievement, whereas others might exhibit the reverse pattern.

▶ TREATMENT AND CHANGE

8.11 What is the basic goal in psychoanalytic treatment? What methods are used to achieve positive outcomes?

The psychodynamic approach to treatment has had an enormous influence on American psychiatry and clinical psychology. Its major original version is **psychoanalysis** or psychoanalytic therapy, a form of psychotherapy developed by Freud and practiced by psychoanalysts.

Traditionally in psychoanalysis, several weekly meetings, each about an hour long, are held between the therapist and client (or "patient"), often for a period of many years. The treatment is based on the premise that neurotic conflict and anxiety are the result of repressed (unconscious) impulses. The aim is to remove the repression and resolve the conflict by helping patients achieve insight into their unconscious impulses.

The Beginnings: Free Association and Dream Interpretation

To uncover unconscious material (or lift the repression), the techniques of **free association** and **dream interpretation** were used in traditional psychoanalysis, and were dominant in Freud's time. As was noted before, in free association the patient, usually reclining on a couch, is instructed to report whatever comes to mind without screening or censoring his or her thoughts in any way. Here is a fragment of free association from a psychotherapy session as an example:

> *I wonder how my mother is getting along. You know how she and I don't get along. Once when I was about twelve, she and I were having an argument—I can't remember what it was about—argument 1001. Anyway, the phone rang and one of her darling friends offered her two tickets to the matinee performance of a ballet that day. What a day. She refused*

them to punish me. For a change! I don't think I even saw a ballet until I was grown up and married. Joe took me. I still get sad when I think about it. I could cry. All blue. It reminds me of all the times when I felt. . . .

Any difficulties or blocks in free association are considered as important as the material that is easily produced. These difficulties are interpreted as **resistance**, caused by unconscious defenses blocking access to material central to the patient's problems, and the person is encouraged to continue with the free association.

According to psychoanalytic theory, the ego's defense mechanisms are relaxed during sleep, making dreams an avenue to express repressed material. But the defenses still operate to distort the content of dreams, so interpretation is necessary to unravel their meaning. In treatment, the interpretations of blocks in association, and dreams, are done carefully so that the patient continues to relax the defenses. The therapeutic goal is to make the unconscious conscious as the patient gradually relaxes and overcomes resistances to facing unconscious conflicts and motives. Although free association and dream interpretation played a major role in the first few decades of clinical practice at the psychodynamic level of analysis, in modern applications they have mostly become just one of many different methods for probing into conflicts and defenses in psychotherapy.

Today's View of Freud's Theory of Trauma

Freud's theory of trauma and neurosis illustrates how some of his much-disputed ideas have remained influential, but only with substantial modifications. Freud's theory of the origin of neurosis emphasized the importance of childhood traumas—intense emotional experiences that the person cannot deal with and that "exert a disintegrating effect on the mind" (Spiegel, Koopman, & Classen, 1994, p. 11). Freud held that traumatic experiences can induce not only severe anxiety but also dissociative states of the sort he reported in his clinical observations of hysterical patients who developed physical symptoms (like "glove anesthesia") that made no sense neurologically.

8.12 In what ways do contemporary studies on trauma support Freud's views and suggest more effective methods of treatment?

Although these ideas continue to be controversial, and are rejected by many research psychologists today, they also have stimulated extensive contemporary research, for example, on reactions to acute stress, called **traumatic experiences**. These are experiences that abruptly and severely disrupt the person's normal daily routine, threatening him or her with physical injury or death, as happens under war conditions, in earthquakes, or to victims of violent crimes or terrorism. In contemporary research, it has been possible to document and study these experiences systematically. The results of these new studies in part support some of Freud's insights, although they also reject or completely revise many others. Most important, they serve to modify and improve the treatment procedures to help the victims deal with their traumas more effectively (e.g., Foa & Kozak, 1986; Kross, Ayduk, & Mischel, 2005; Roth & Newman, 1990; Spiegel & Cardena, 1990, 1991).

In the contemporary view, consistent with Freud, when traumas profoundly endanger the victim's core beliefs about oneself and the world, dissociative reactions may occur to keep the threat outside full awareness, split off from the rest of one's experience. Consequently, treatment is aimed at helping the person to integrate the experience and to manage the painful emotions. Freud originally emphasized simply helping the person to reexperience and repeat the event and its emotions and to express them in the therapy relationship.

Extreme events, like wars or terrorist attacks, may induce traumatic experiences.

(*Source*: AP/Wide World Photos)

Current approaches take another step called **cognitive restructuring**, the focus is on reinterpreting the meaning of the event in a way that allows the person to deal with it. It involves helping the person to give up the sense of control over the event that often creates inappropriate guilt:

> A soldier who survived a rocket attack may feel he traded his safety for that of a comrade who died. . . . Therapy is aimed at helping the victim acknowledge and bear the emotional distress which comes with traumatic memories, grieving the loss of control which occurred at the time and thereby admitting the uncomfortable sense of helplessness. (Spiegel et al., 1994, p. 18)

In short, in contemporary applications of Freud's ideas about traumas and disassociation, the focus is on helping the person to acknowledge the trauma itself; bear and reinterpret the memories of the traumatic events; and cast them into a more meaningful perspective with less self-blame. Support is given and encouraged, for example, by strengthening interpersonal relationships. These treatment features are characteristic of the "ego psychology" that grew out of, and built upon, Freud's work, and remain influential in some types of current clinical practice.

The Transference Relationship and Working Through

The therapist in traditional psychoanalysis is supposed to create an atmosphere of safety by remaining accepting and noncritical. Therapists deliberately reveal little about themselves and remain shadowy figures who often sit behind the patient and outside his view in order to facilitate a **transference** relationship. Transference is said to occur when the patient responds to the therapist as if he or she were the patient's father, mother, or some other important childhood figure. Feelings and problems initially experienced in childhood relations with these figures are transferred to the relationship with the

8.13 Why is the transference relationship so important in psychoanalytic treatment? What is involved in the working-through process?

therapist. Transference is regarded as inevitable and essential by most psychoanalysts. It is a concept that has been revitalized in current research on memory that shows how early feelings about a person can be reactivated later in life by other people who are perceived to be similar (Andersen & Chen, 2002), as discussed later in the text. In the transference, the therapist demonstrates to patients the childhood origins of their conflicts and helps them to work through and face these problems. Here in the words of a distinguished psychoanalyst (Colby, 1951) is an example of how the transference is used and interpreted:

> The manner in which a patient acts and feels about his therapist is a bonanza of psychological information. In subtracting the inappropriate from appropriate responses the therapist has a first-hand, immediately observable illustration of the patient's psychodynamics in an interpersonal relationship. . . .
>
> A woman from an old Southern family broke away in late adolescence from family ties and values. She became a nomadic Bohemian vigorously opposed to all authority. She expressed her feelings by zealous work in Anarchist societies and other radical movements. In therapy she often told of fearlessly challenging policemen and openly sneering at successful businessmen.
>
> Yet her behavior toward the therapist was in marked contrast to this. She was very respectful, non-aggressive and acquiescent—all attitudes she faintly remembers having as a child toward her parents until adolescence. The therapist's concept was that the patient unconsciously saw him as a feared and loved parent who must not be antagonized. She really feared authority as a source of punishment. (p. 113)

The insight to be achieved by the patient in psychoanalysis is not a detached, rational, intellectual understanding. People must work through their problems in the transference relationship. **Working through** involves repeated reexamination of basic problems in different contexts until one learns to handle them more appropriately and understands their emotional roots.

Alternative Psychodynamic Interpretations of Gary W.

The psychodynamic meaning of the same information may be interpreted quite differently depending on the specific theory and biases of the particular psychologist. This is especially likely when broad inferences are made about a person's deep, unobservable psychodynamics. For example, if a disciple of Alfred Adler assesses Gary W., he may find evidence for an inferiority complex and sibling rivalry from the same observations that lead a Freudian to infer castration anxiety and an Oedipal complex. Likewise, in the same set of responses, another psychologist may see Gary's fragmented self and his cry for empathic mirroring of his feelings.

Many psychologists now see such alternative views as a welcome development. It encourages the frank recognition that the same "facts" about a person are indeed open to multiple interpretations from different perspectives and levels of analysis. Each view may contribute a somewhat different vision of the individual from a different angle, and no one view is necessarily exclusively correct or absolute. Critics of this approach, however, are understandably concerned that there are no clear standards for selecting among alternative interpretations. There also is no strong evidence to help decide how to select those that might be most useful for different goals. Fortunately, work at the various levels of analyses that are presented in the subsequent parts of this text have helped to overcome these limitations.

▶ PSYCHODYNAMIC PROCESSES: ANXIETY AND THE UNCONSCIOUS

8.14 What three elements typically occur in anxiety responses? How can internal processes produce them and defend against them?

In this section we turn to research on the nature of psychodynamic processes and the unconscious that are central for the psychodynamic level of analysis. The psychodynamic view, beginning with Freud, originally saw **anxiety** as the emotional fear triggered when unacceptable impulses begin to push themselves into consciousness. Other theorists have liberalized the definition and recognize that anxiety can be experienced for many different reasons. In spite of the many varieties of anxiety that people experience, the following three elements are often found (Maher, 1966):

- A conscious feeling of fear and danger, without the ability to identify immediate objective threats that could account for these feelings.
- A pattern of physiological arousal and bodily distress that may include miscellaneous physical changes and complaints (Cacioppo et al., 1996). Common examples include *cardiovascular* symptoms (heart palpitations, faintness, increased blood pressure, pulse changes); *respiratory* complaints (breathlessness, feeling of suffocation); and *gastrointestinal* symptoms (diarrhea, nausea, vomiting). If the anxiety persists, the prolonged physical reactions to it may have chronic effects on each of these bodily systems. In addition, the person's agitation may be reflected in sleeplessness, frequent urination, perspiration, muscular tension, fatigue, and other signs of upset and distress.
- A disruption or disorganization of effective problem solving and cognitive (mental) control, including difficulty in thinking clearly and coping effectively with environmental demands.

An outstanding characteristic of human beings, emphasized in psychodynamic theories, is that they can create great anxiety in themselves even when they are not in any immediate external danger. A man may be seated comfortably in his favorite chair, well fed and luxuriously sheltered, seemingly safe from outside threats. And yet he may torture himself with anxiety-provoking memories of old events, with terrifying thoughts, or with imagined dangers in years to come. He also can try to end such internally cued anxiety within his own mind without altering his external environment, by avoiding or changing his painful thoughts or memories.

Does such avoidance of anxiety also occur unconsciously, outside the range of one's awareness? Is it in the service of our trying to hide from our own deeper feelings? A core assumption of the psychodynamic view is that the answer to these questions is clearly affirmative. After years of empirical research, however, that answer still remains controversial.

Defense mechanisms are attempts to cope mentally (cognitively) with internal anxiety-arousing cues. Usually it has also been assumed, in line with Freudian theory, that these efforts are at least partly unconscious—that is, they occur without the person's awareness. Because this assumption is so basic, research in the psychodynamic approach has tried to clarify this process. Especially important have been studies of unconscious processes and mechanisms of defense, which are a focus of this chapter. The greatest attention has been devoted to repression, probably because it is the most important one for Freud's theory.

The Psychoanalytic Concept of Unconscious Repression

Most people sometimes feel that they actively try to avoid painful memories and ideas and struggle to "put out of mind" thoughts that are aversive to them. Common examples are trying not to think about a forthcoming surgical operation and trying to prevent yourself from thinking about the unknown results of an important test. Psychologists often call such efforts to avoid painful thoughts "cognitive avoidance."

Cognitive avoidance obviously exists and everyone is familiar with it. No one doubts that thoughts may be inhibited. However, the mechanisms underlying cognitive avoidance have been controversial. The basic controversy is whether or not cognitive avoidance includes an unconscious defense mechanism of "repression" that forces unacceptable material into an unconscious region without the person's awareness.

Repression versus Suppression

8.15 Differentiate between suppression and repression of anxiety-producing thoughts.

The psychoanalytic concept of **repression** as a defense mechanism is closely linked to the Freudian idea of an unconscious mind. The early Freudians saw the unconscious mind as a supersensitive entity whose perceptual alertness and memory exceeded the conscious mind (Blum, 1955). A chief function of the unconscious mind was to screen and monitor memories and the inputs to the senses. This screening served to inhibit the breakthrough of anxiety-arousing stimuli from the unconscious mind to the conscious, or from the outside world to consciousness. Just as the conscious mind was believed capable of deliberately (consciously) inhibiting events by **suppression**, so the unconscious was considered capable of inhibition or cognitive avoidance at the unconscious level by repression.

Suppression occurs when one voluntarily and consciously withholds a response or turns attention away from it deliberately. Unconscious repression, in contrast, may function as an automatic guardian against anxiety, a safety mechanism that prevents threatening material from entering consciousness. Psychoanalysts have offered clinical evidence for the existence of repression in the form of cases in which slips of the tongue, jokes, dreams, or free associations seemed to momentarily bypass the defenses and betray the person, revealing a brief glimpse of repressed unconscious impulses.

Studying Repression

Repression has remained a cornerstone for most psychoanalysts (Erdelyi, 1985; Grunbaum, 1984), and it has been the subject of a great deal of research for many years. The early efforts to assess whether or not particular findings demonstrated the truth of Freud's concepts created more controversy than clarity. In more recent years, it has been recognized that well-designed experiments on the topic of cognitive avoidance can provide useful information about cognitive processes and personality regardless of their direct relevance to the Freudian theory of repression (Kihlstrom, 1999; Westen & Gabbard, 1999).

8.16 Summarize some of the challenges in studying repression experimentally and in attributing results to repression.

Early experiments on repression studied the recall of pleasant and unpleasant experiences (Jersild, 1931; Meltzer, 1930). These investigators assumed that repression showed itself in a tendency to selectively forget negative or unpleasant experiences rather than positive ones. Critics soon pointed out, however, that the Freudian theory of repression does not imply that experiences associated with unpleasant affective tone are repressed (Rosenzweig & Mason, 1934; Sears, 1936). Freudian repression, instead, depends on the presence of an "ego threat" (e.g., a basic threat to self-esteem) and not on mere unpleasantness.

Later researchers also recognized that to study repression adequately they should be able to demonstrate that when the cause of the repression (the ego threat) is removed, the repressed material is restored to consciousness (Zeller, 1950). This assumption was consistent with the psychoanalytic belief that when the cause of a repression is discovered by insight in psychotherapy, the repressed material rapidly emerges into the patient's consciousness. In other words, if the threat is eliminated, it becomes safe for the repressed material to return to awareness. Psychoanalysts often have cited cases in which a sudden insight supposedly lifted a long-standing amnesia (memory loss).

Experiments to show repression effects have been inconclusive. For example, when college students were threatened by taking a test described as measuring their unacceptable unconscious sexual conflicts, they tended to recall anxiety-arousing words less well. When the threat was removed (by revealing that the test was really not an index for such conflicts), recall improved (D'Zurilla, 1965). Does this mean that repression occurred? After much debate, it has become clear that the answer is "not necessarily"; other interpretations are at least equally plausible.

Reduced recall for threat-provoking information may simply reflect that the person is upset. Therefore, other thoughts, produced by the anxiety as the person worries, may interfere with recall. If the recall improves later when the threat is removed, it may only mean that the competing, anxious thoughts now no longer interfere with recall. It does not necessarily mean either that unconscious repression occurred or that awareness returned when the threat was removed (Holmes & Schallow, 1969; Kihlstrom, 2003; Tudor & Holmes, 1973).

Perceptual Defense

If unconscious repression is a mechanism that keeps painful material out of consciousness, one might also expect it to screen and block threatening perceptual inputs to the eyes and ears. Indeed, clinical reports from psychoanalysts suggest that in some cases of hysteria, massive repression may prevent the individual from perceiving (consciously registering) threatening stimuli such as sexual scenes or symbols.

One very severe instance of this would be hysterical blindness. In these cases, the individual seems to lose his or her vision, although no physical damage to the eyes or to the perceptual system can be detected. Case reports have suggested that such psychological failures to see might be linked to traumatic sexual experiences with resulting repression of stimuli that might unleash anxiety. Although clinical case reports often provide suggestive evidence, they are never conclusive. To go beyond clinical impressions, researchers have tried to study possible anxiety-reducing distortions in perception experimentally. Because it was obviously both unfeasible and unethical to induce sexual traumas in human participants, considerable ingenuity was needed to find ways to study perceptual defense in experiments.

The Long History of Perceptual Defense

8.17 What methods were used in perceptual defense research, what results were obtained, and what alternative explanations were offered?

In the 1940s and 1950s researchers reasoned that persons who did not give sexual or aggressive responses to ambiguous stimuli must be defending against this type of ideation, especially if the same stimuli generally elicited many such responses from most normal people. Consequently, if a person fails to identify potentially threatening inputs to the senses, such as anxiety-arousing sexual words or threatening scenes, it might indicate perceptual inhibition or defense.

To study this process, researchers presented threatening perceptual stimuli in decreasing degrees of ambiguity. They began at a point at which participants could tell what the words were and could reasonably interpret them in many ways, to a point of definiteness that permitted only one clearly correct interpretation. A helpful device for this purpose was the **tachistoscope**, a machine through which potentially threatening words (e.g., "penis," "whore") and neutral words (e.g., "house," "flowers") could be flashed at varying speeds. These stimulus words were presented on a screen very rapidly at first and then gradually exposed for increasingly long durations. The length of time required before each person correctly recognized the stimulus served as the "defensiveness" score; the longer the time required to recognize threatening stimuli, the greater the individual's defensive avoidance tendencies were assumed to be.

In one classic study, college students viewed words presented tachistoscopically so rapidly that they could not perceive them consciously. The words were either emotional or neutral in meaning (McGinnies, 1949). Each student was asked what word had been seen after each exposure. If the answer was wrong, the same word was presented again at a slightly longer exposure time, and the participant again tried to recognize it. It was predicted that such "taboo" words as "penis" or "raped" would be anxiety laden and therefore more readily inhibited than neutral words such as "apple." The results confirmed this prediction, showing greater perceptual defense (longer recognition times) for taboo words than for neutral words.

But these results also can be interpreted quite differently. As was noted long ago (Howes & Solomon, 1951), the perceptual situation places the participant in an embarrassing predicament. In the typical procedure, an undergraduate was brought to the laboratory by a professor or an assistant and then exposed to brief and unclear stimulus presentations by the tachistoscope. The task is essentially a guessing game in which the participant tries to discern the correct word from fleeting fragments. On the first trial of a word, for example, something like an "r" and "p" may be seen and the participant may guess "rope." On the next trial, the participant may think "good grief, that looked something like 'rape'!" But rather than make this guess to a professor or an assistant in the academic atmosphere of a scientific laboratory, the participant may deliberately suppress the response. Instead of saying "rape," "rope" is offered again, and the taboo word is withheld until the participant is absolutely sure that this perception is correct.

In sum, a major problem in interpreting results from such studies is that it is extremely difficult to know whether individuals are slower to report some stimuli because they are unconsciously screening them from awareness. Even without such an unconscious mechanism, they may be inhibited about reporting such stimuli until they are absolutely sure, just to avoid embarrassment.

Limitations of Early Laboratory Studies

Psychoanalytically oriented critics have been quite skeptical of the relevance of many of these studies for their theory (Erdelyi, 1993; Erdelyi & Goldberg, 1979). They argue that it is confusing and misleading to study single processes (such as repression) in isolation, outside the context of the person's total psychic functioning. They see these experimental studies at best as suggestive, but clinically irrelevant. They doubt that long-term psychodynamic processes like unconscious reactions to traumatic events in early childhood can be studied under the artificial conditions of the typical laboratory experiment (e.g., Erdelyi, 1993; Madison, 1960). It is also risky to generalize from college sophomores in a laboratory to clinical populations and clinical problems. The mild anxiety induced by experimental threats to college students may have little relevance for understanding the traumas experienced by the young child trying to cope with Oedipal fantasies or the severely disturbed patient in the clinic. On the other hand, the clinician's judgments and intuitive procedures for inferring unconscious dynamics, for example, from projective tests, also have serious limitations (Kihlstrom, 2003; Rorer, 1990). There have been many studies of unconscious repression and unconscious perception, but the conclusions that may be drawn from them have long remained controversial.

8.18 Psychoanalysts have been critical of experimental studies of unconscious processes. What are their major criticisms?

Although research on the Freudian unconscious remains controversial, some clear themes have emerged (e.g., Kihlstrom, 1999). The old experiments that try to demonstrate repression and unconscious perception were difficult to interpret (D'Zurilla, 1965; Erdelyi, 1985; Kihlstrom, 1999). After many decades of research, for example, one influential review of experimental research on repression concluded that "there is no evidence to support the predictions generated by the theory of repression" (Holmes, 1974, p. 651). Two decades later, another review led him to the same conclusion (Holmes, 1992). But it is just as easy to conclude that all these studies were flawed.

After a flood of studies, the two main ways of looking at the research results on the Freudian view of the unconscious are well summarized by Erdelyi (1985, pp. 104–105):

> One may begin to understand why experimental psychology, in contrast to dynamic clinical psychology, has taken such a different stance on phenomena such as repression. Experimental psychology, in the service of simplification and control, has studied manifest events, specific memory episodes, or percepts (as in perceptual defense). It is not typical, however, for a normal college subject to resort in the laboratory to such drastic defenses as to block out a clear memory episode or perceptual experience. Consequently, experimental psychology has had great difficulty in demonstrating repression in the laboratory and has understandably taken a skeptical attitude towards this phenomenon. Clinicians, on the other hand, deal continually with latent (hidden) contents, and in this realm the selective blocking or distortion of information through context manipulation is utterly commonplace. The clinician shakes his head in disbelief at the experimental psychologist, whose paltry methodology cannot even demonstrate a phenomenon as obvious and ubiquitous as repression. The experimentalist similarly shakes his head at the credulity of the psychodynamic clinician, who embraces notions unproven in the laboratory and which, moreover, rest on the presumed existence of unconscious, indeed, physically non-existent, latent contents.

In short, many clinicians remain convinced that evidence for the Freudian unconscious is almost everywhere; in contrast, many experimental researchers have had trouble finding it anywhere.

CURRENT VIEW OF UNCONSCIOUS PROCESSES: THE ADAPTIVE UNCONSCIOUS

Bottom line, what can be said about the role of the unconscious in modern personality psychology? To answer this, research experts in the area reviewed what is known about the nature of the unconscious (e.g., Bruner, 1992; Erdelyi, 1992; Greenwald, 1992; Wilson, 2002). Although there was no consistent agreement about how to characterize unconscious processes in terms of their precise role and significance, there was ". . . absolute agreement that exciting times, both in research and theory, are ahead for the unconscious" (Loftus & Klinger, 1992, p. 764). This optimism has turned out to be justified because methods and concepts in the research on this topic are becoming more sophisticated (e.g., Lewicki, Hill, & Czyzewska, 1992). Further, there is also growing attention to how motivational factors, such as the person's goals and needs, influence memory (e.g., Kihlstrom, 1999, 2003; Kunda, 1990, 1999; Singer & Salovey, 1993). The basic conclusion here is that while the psychoanalytic view of the unconscious is seriously questioned, the importance of unconscious processes has become even more clear with time. For example, modern research by social psychologists into the **automatic processing** of social information shows that our minds to a large extent operate at levels that are at least partly, and often completely, outside our awareness (e.g., Bargh, 1997; Bargh & Ferguson, 2000; Chartrand & Bargh, 1996). To illustrate, information related to racial and sexual stereotypes can affect our judgments and actions even when we are not aware of ever having seen that information (Bargh, Chen, & Burrows, 1996; Gladwell, 2005; Kunda, 1999). After reviewing the extensive evidence rapidly accumulating on the topic of information processing outside of awareness, Kunda (1999, pp. 287–288) concludes: "... there is considerable evidence that our judgments, feelings, and behaviors can be influenced by factors that we have never been aware of, by factors that we were aware of at one time but can no longer recall, and by factors that we can still recall but whose influence we are unaware of."

8.19 How does automatic processing differ from the Freudian view of unconscious processing?

As Wilson (2002) notes, Freud's contribution in pointing to the importance of unconscious processes was of enormous importance. But much of the unconscious is adaptive rather than defensive. It lets us process the huge flood of information we have to deal with in ways that are efficient and outside awareness. You see this, for example, when children learn their native language effortlessly and automatically. This adaptive unconscious allows us to function effectively, and much of it has little or nothing to do with unconscious defenses against hidden feared impulses. That in no way diminishes the importance of nonconscious feeling, thinking, and motivation. For many purposes—like figuring out what one really feels and wants and thinks—it is extremely important to develop self-insight into what happens within us largely outside our awareness. What is less clear, and a topic to which we will often return in this text, is how to best accomplish that. While the psychodynamic approach offers one route for trying to do so, it is by no means the only one, as you will see throughout this text, and usually it is the most costly one.

The Repressed Memory Debate: False Memories of Abuse?

8.20 What evidence is there that long-forgotten memories of abuse that suddenly reappear may in some cases be "false" memories? What is the risk of concluding that all are false?

Based on the Freudian premise that the human mind purposefully but unconsciously hides frightening or potentially damaging memories, repression is seen by many clinicians and researchers as a major root of psychological dysfunction. But skeptics see it more as a fiction created by a biased theoretical perspective through which therapists may unwittingly damage their patients and their families (Loftus, 1993, 1994; Ofshe & Watters, 1993). While repressed memory continues to remain a controversial academic topic in psychology, it now also has become the center of a public debate that has spread into the media.

Return of the Repressed

The public debate began in recent years when many people claimed that they had been the victims of childhood abuse. They asserted that they had been unaware of these abuses until their repressed memories for the traumatic event were recovered, usually in the course of psychotherapy. Often they then tried to bring criminal charges against the alleged perpetrators of these abuses. The question raised then was: are these recovered memories accurate or might they be **false memories**?

The reported recovered memories of abuse have often produced great personal pain and been the bases for lawsuits and punishment of the alleged abusers. As the defense lawyers are quick to point out, however, the existence of repression itself remains controversial. On the one hand, a review of over 60 years of research led Holmes (1992) to still conclude that "... at the present time there is no controlled laboratory evidence supporting the concept of repression" (p. 95). Likewise, in a study of children (ages 5–10) who witnessed the murder of one of their parents, Malmquist (1986) reported that none of the children seemed to repress the memory; instead, they frequently focused on it.

Nevertheless, most sophisticated and highly experienced clinicians still remain convinced that case studies compellingly document the existence of repression (Erdelyi, 1993). Supporting that view, some researchers make the case that memories for traumatic events from the early years of life, even after they have been forgotten, may reappear in adulthood under conditions of high stress (Jacobs & Nadel, 1985; Schooler, 1994, 1997; Schooler, Bendiksen, & Ambadar, 1997).

Did It Really Happen?

But even assuming that a defensive mechanism of repression occurs and in some cases is activated as a way of coping with traumatic events such as sexual abuse, there is a major problem in determining accurately whether a particular memory for a traumatic event is accurate or instead invented or grossly distorted. Modern memory research makes it clear that memories are not stored like videotapes on a shelf and later replayed. Rather, they are reconstructions of the past, and they are subject to being influenced by suggestions and cues from the outside world and the inside of one's mind, including one's own fantasies and speculations (e.g., Loftus, 1993, 1994; Ofshe, 1992). In short, memories can be created in people by suggestion and self-suggestion, or by suggesting to them that something occurred, often in ways that can even give the person confidence that they are based on reality. For example, when children are asked questions to probe the possibility of their having been abused, their answers are easily influenced by just how the question is asked. It is easy to have the young child become explicit about sexual misconduct that never occurred if the questions are posed inappropriately and suggestively, and that was made clear in the courtroom in many abuse trials.

The Power of Suggestion

One worry is that false memories may be unwittingly strengthened by therapists, particularly if they believe, as Freud did, that problems tend to stem from the abuse that the patient suffered as a child. Guided by that belief, some therapists may too easily encourage their patients to explore their unconscious minds, searching for repressed memories that may not exist. In this search, they may do what is sometimes called "memory work," using hypnosis, suggestive questioning, guided visualization, and dream interpretation (Loftus, 1994). Such exploration risks coming up with memories of traumatic events that may have been imagined or fantasized but that did not actually occur. In that case, instead of helping victims to reclaim lost pieces of their lives, they may hurt innocent people and create rather than reduce distress.

The Value of Self-Disclosure

The debate about repressed memory raised important questions but also may have risked creating excessive skepticism, leading people to doubt all reports about repressed memories that become accessible. The danger is that by making the topic so controversial, many victims of abuse and trauma in childhood and later life may be ignored or undermined in their efforts to find and express the truth. Relevant here is the discovery that when people have had traumatic experiences, it can greatly help them to discuss those memories candidly, rather than to try to hide or suppress them. The process of talking or writing about these traumatic experiences not only helps one feel better by "getting it off your chest," as folk wisdom has long suggested, but also can profoundly improve one's health. For example, by simply writing about their traumatic experiences during a period of 4 days, essentially healthy college students improved their health following the study, with fewer visits to the health center and improved blood pressure and immune system functioning (Pennebaker, 1993; Pennebaker, Kiecolt-Glaser, & Glaser, 1988). It would therefore be unfortunate if trauma victims failed to use opportunities to appropriately air rather than conceal their experience.

PATTERNS OF DEFENSE: INDIVIDUAL DIFFERENCES IN COGNITIVE AVOIDANCE

Cognitive avoidance of anxiety-provoking information is not only a basic process, it also is a dimension of personality on which people differ substantially and interestingly. Some people react to stimuli that arouse anxiety by avoiding them cognitively, but other people do not. For many years, individual differences in "defensive" patterns have been found (Bruner & Postman, 1947; Lazarus, 1976; Miller, 1987; Paulhus, Fridhandler, & Hayes, 1997).

Repression–Sensitization

8.21 What is meant by repression and sensitization? What research evidence exists that this is a meaningful personality dimension that relates to other behaviors?

The dimension on which these differences seemed to fall was a continuum of behaviors ranging from avoiding the anxiety-arousing stimuli to approaching them more readily and being extra vigilant or supersensitized to them. The former end of the continuum included behaviors similar to the defensive mechanisms that psychoanalysts called denial and repression; the latter pattern—vigilance or sensitization to anxiety-provoking cues—seemed more like obsessive worrying. This dimension has become known now as the **repression–sensitization** continuum. Repression–sensitization became the focus of much research both as a dynamic process and as a personality dimension on which individuals might show consistent patterns.

In general, individuals show some consistency in their cognitive avoidance of anxiety-provoking cues such as threatening words (Eriksen, 1952; Eriksen & Kuethe, 1956). In one study, reaction time and other measures of avoidance were obtained in the auditory recognition of poorly audible sentences that had sexual and aggressive content. People who were slow to recognize such sentences also tended to avoid sexual and aggressive materials in a sentence completion test (Lazarus, Eriksen, & Fonda, 1951). People who more readily recalled stimuli associated with a painful shock also tended to recall their failures; those who forgot one were more likely to forget the other (Lazarus & Longo, 1953). A tendency for some consistency in cognitive avoidance may exist at least when extremely high and low groups are selected (Eriksen, 1966). Correlations between cognitive avoidance on experimental tasks and various other measures of repression–sensitization also imply some consistency in these patterns (Byrne, 1964; McFarland & Buehler, 1997; Weinberger, 2002).

In short, in spite of disagreement about the concept and role of repression, there now is agreement that people do use a mechanism of mentally distancing themselves from awareness of threatening and negative thoughts or emotions. In modern research, the term repression often refers to that meaning.

Selective Attention

Individual differences in repression–sensitization have often been measured on a self-report questionnaire (Byrne, 1964). On this scale, **repressors** are people who describe themselves as having few problems or difficulties. They do not report themselves as highly sensitive to everyday stress and anxieties, whereas those with an opposite pattern are called **sensitizers**. Individual differences on this scale can predict selective attention to important personal information about the self. In one study, college students were exposed to personal information about themselves supposedly based on their own performance on personality tests they had taken earlier (Mischel, Ebbesen, & Zeiss, 1973). The results were made available to students in individual sessions in which each was left alone to look at descriptions of his or her personal liabilities (in one computer file) and personal assets (in another file). For example, the personality assets included such feedback as, "Affiliative, capable of cooperating and reciprocating deeply in relations with others. . . ." In contrast, the personality liabilities information included such descriptions as, "Nonperseverative, procrastination, and distractibility . . . resultant failures lead to greater and greater apathy. . . ." (Actually, all students received the same feedback, but in the debriefing session in which they were told the truth, it became clear that they had been convinced that the test results really described them; in fact, they believed the information had captured much about their personalities.)

The question was: Would repressors and sensitizers (as measured on the self-report questionnaire) exhibit different attentional patterns for the positive, self-enhancing information versus the negative, threatening information about themselves? There were clear differences.

These results are summarized in Figure 8.6. Sensitizers attended more to their liabilities and spent little time on their assets; in sharp contrast, repressors attended as much to their assets as to their liabilities. Later research suggests that repressors may

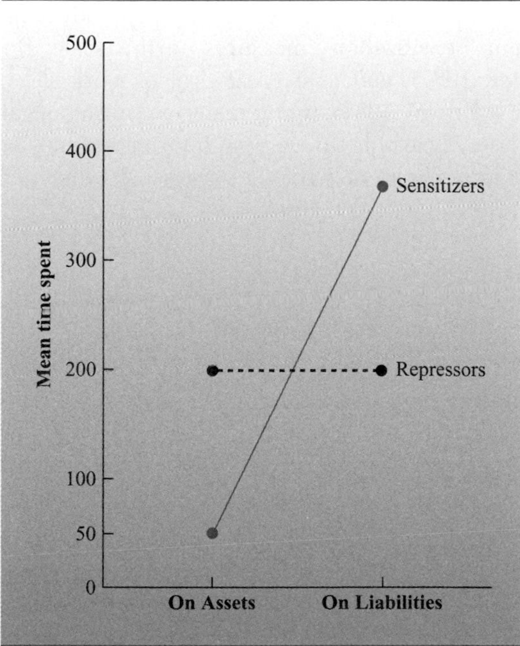

Figure 8.6 Attention deployment by sensitizers and repressors. Mean amount of time (in seconds) spent on assets and liabilities by sensitizers and by repressors.

Source: Based on data in the control condition from Mischel, W., Ebbesen, W. B., & Zeiss, A. R. (1973). Selective attention to the self: Situational and dispositional determinants. *Journal of Personality and Social Psychology*, 27, 129–142. (Figs. 1 and 2, p. 136.)

be people who are especially sensitive to criticism and threat, and use their defense to protect themselves against this vulnerability (Baumeister & Cairns, 1992).

In sum, the repressors and the sensitizers differed in how they dealt with positive and negative ego-relevant information. But these differences seem linked to their attentional strategies, not to unconscious distortions in their memory: both groups are able to recall threatening information about themselves with equal accuracy if they are made to attend equally to that information (Mischel et al., 1976). Normally, however, the sensitizers tended to focus on negative self-relevant information, whereas the repressors tended to avoid it and preferred to think about happier things. When the situation prevents repressors from simply ignoring the threat, they do begin to attend to it and worry anxiously about it (Baumeister & Cairns, 1992).

The two groups also differed in their self-descriptions: while repressors described themselves in positive, socially desirable terms, representing themselves consistently in a more favorable light, sensitizers painted a much more critical and negative self-portrait (Alicke, 1985; Joy, 1963). Most interesting, however, is that it is the repressor, not the sensitizer, who better fits the picture of the optimistic personality with a good mental and physical health prognosis.

This is surprising for psychodynamic theory, which has long assumed that accurate self-awareness and being in touch with one's personal limitations, anxieties, and flaws (i.e., sensitization) were important ingredients of the healthy personality. In contrast, repression and cognitive avoidance of negative information and threat were the hallmark of the brittle, vulnerable personality. It is, of course, likely that the massive emotional repression to which Freudians refer is quite different from the self-enhancing positive bias that seems to characterize repressors as identified on this scale. Likewise, the growth of self-awareness and accessibility of personal anxieties to which psychodynamic theory refers may also be different from "sensitization" measures on this scale. But as the next section also suggests (Miller, 1987), and as a great deal of work shows (Bonanno, 2001; Seligman, 1990; Taylor & Brown, 1988), under many circumstances an attitude of emotional blunting that deliberately avoids threatening information may be highly adaptive, a sign of mental health rather than of a fragile personality in need of insight.

Blunting versus Monitoring Styles

In a related direction, it has been shown that people differ considerably in their disposition to blunt and distract themselves or to monitor for (be alert to) danger signals (Miller, 1996). One promising scale tries to identify information avoiders and information seekers as two distinct coping styles. The **Miller Behavioral Style Scale (MBSS)** consists of four hypothetical stress-evoking scenes of an uncontrollable nature (Miller, 1981, 1987; Miller & Mangan, 1983). On this measure, people are asked to imagine vividly scenes like "you are afraid of the dentist and have to get some dental work done"; or "you are being held hostage by a group of armed terrorists in a public building"; or "you are on an airplane, 30 minutes from your destination, when the plane unexpectedly goes into a deep dive and then suddenly levels off. After a short time, the pilot announces that nothing is wrong, although the rest of the ride may be rough. You, however, are not convinced that all is well."

8.22 Distinguish monitoring versus blunting responses to threatening events. How are MBSS scores related to information search under anxiety-arousing conditions?

Each scene is followed by statements that represent ways of coping with the situation, either by **monitoring** or by **blunting**. Half of the statements for each scene are of a monitoring variety. For example, in the hostage situation: "If there was a radio present,

Some people cope with unpleasant events by mentally "blunting" (distracting themselves).
(*Source*: © AP/Wide World Photos)

I would stay near it and listen to the bulletins about what the police were doing"; or, in the airplane situation: "I would listen carefully to the engines for unusual noises and would watch the crew to see if their behavior was out of the ordinary." The other half of the statements are of the blunting type. For example, in the dental situation: "I would do mental puzzles in my head"; or, in the airplane situation: "I would watch the end of the movie, even if I had seen it before." The individual simply marks all the statements following each scene that might apply to him.

College students were threatened with a low probability shock and allowed to choose whether they wanted to monitor for information or distract themselves with music (Miller, 1981). As expected, the amount of time spent on information rather than on music was predicted reasonably well by an individual's MBSS score. In particular, the more blunting items endorsed on the scale, the less time the person spent listening to the information and the more time listening to the music. In sum, individuals differed in the extent to which they chose to monitor or distract themselves when faced with aversive events (possible electric shocks) in the experiment. These differences in coping style were related to their questionnaire scores, supporting the validity of the MBSS.

The Role of Control: When Don't You Want to Know?

Whether or not persons react to negative stimuli by avoiding them "defensively" in their cognitions and perceptions may depend on whether or not they believe that they can somehow cope with them by problem solving and action. If adaptive action seems impossible, cognitive avoidance attempts become more likely. But if the painful cues can be controlled by the person's actions, then greater attention and vigilance to them may occur. This point is illustrated in the same blunting–monitoring study just discussed that gave individuals a choice between stress-relevant information or distraction (Miller, 1979). The information was a warning signal for when an electric shock would come; the distraction was listening to music. Half the participants were led to believe the shock was potentially avoidable; the rest believed it was unavoidable. As Table 8.3 shows, when participants believed avoidance was possible, they preferred information;

TABLE 8.3 Number of Participants Who Seek Information (Warning Signal) or Distraction (Listen to Music) When Avoidance Is or Is Not Possible

	Information-Seeking	Distraction Seeking
Avoidance Possible	24	10
Avoidance Not Possible	11	23

Source: Based on Miller, S. M. (1979). Coping with impending stress: Physiological and cognitive correlates of choice. *Psychopathology, 16*, 572–581.

8.23 How does the controllability of aversive stimuli influence the adaptiveness of approach–avoidance tendencies?

when they thought it was unavoidable, they preferred distraction. Other research has documented the many circumstances under which coping with problems is improved by the selective avoidance of threatening information (Janis, 1971; Lazarus, 1976, 1990; Lazarus & Folkman, 1984).

Matching the Medical Information to the Patient's Style

In a real-life application to a medical situation, Miller and Mangan (1983) gave the MBSS to gynecologic patients about to undergo colposcopy, a diagnostic procedure to check for the presence of abnormal (cancerous) cells in the uterus. Based on scale scores, patients were first divided into monitors or blunters. Half the women in each group were then given extensive information about the forthcoming procedure, and half were given (the usual) minimal information. Psychophysiological reactions (like heart rate), subjective reports, and observer ratings of arousal and discomfort were taken before, during, and after the procedures. The results revealed, again as expected, that monitors showed more arousal overall than blunters (e.g., see Figure 8.7 for the physician's rating of patients' tension during the exam).

Most interesting, physiological arousal was reduced when the level of preparatory information was consistent with the patients' coping style. That is, physiological arousal was reduced for blunters who received minimal information and for monitors who received extensive information. The total results clearly show strong individual differences in informational preferences during the coping process when people are faced with threats. Most important, they showed that when monitors are told more, and blunters are told less, about an impending stress, each type is likely to cope with it best: matching the information to the style can reduce the stress experienced and enhance resources.

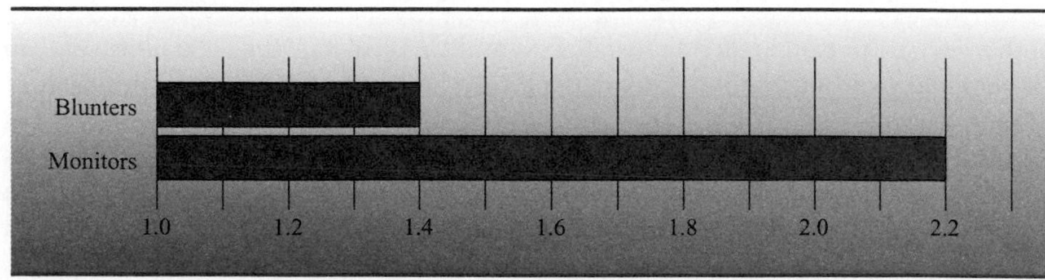

Figure 8.7 Doctor's report—Tension during exam.

Source: Miller, S. M., & Mangan, C. E. (1983). Cognition and psychopathology. In K. Dobson & P. C. Kendall (Eds.), *Cognition, stress, and health*. Reprinted with permission from Elsevier.

▶ SUMMARY

APPLICATIONS TO PERSONALITY ASSESSMENT

- Psychodynamic assessment tries to find the person's fundamental motives and dynamics, and relies on the clinician's intuition more than on personality tests.
- Projective methods such as the TAT (Thematic Apperception Test) or the Rorschach test are used often in psychodynamic assessment.
- In the Rorschach test, the individual is shown a series of inkblots and is asked to say what the inkblots resemble.
- The TAT consists of a series of ambiguous pictures for which the test-taker is asked to make up a story.
- Harvard personality psychologists, led by Henry Murray, provided a model for the intensive clinical study of individuals.
- A classic Freudian framework was applied in the example of Gary W.'s psychodynamic assessment.

MURRAY AND MOTIVES

- Henry Murray and the Harvard personologists focused on the intensive psychodynamic study of individual lives.
- The OSS Assessment project analyzed individuals while they performed tasks under highly stressful situations to infer each person's personality.
- Murray proposed that there are higher-order needs and motives, such as for competence motivation, achievement, power, and intimacy, which have no specific physiological basis.
- Current research distinguishes explicit and implicit motives.

TREATMENT AND CHANGE

- Psychoanalytic treatment aims to reduce unconscious defenses and conflicts by helping patients gain insight into their unconscious motivations, using methods like free association and dream interpretation.
- Traumatic experiences at any point in the life span may be reinterpreted and integrated into the person's life in a more meaningful, less distressing way through cognitive restructuring.
- Patients "work through" their problems in the transference relationship with the therapist.

PSYCHODYNAMIC PROCESSES: ANXIETY AND UNCONSCIOUS DEFENSES

- Conscious and unconscious defense mechanisms can be used to cope with anxiety-arousing stimuli.
- The nature and mechanisms of unconscious repression remain controversial.
- Nevertheless, there is compelling evidence that unconscious processes and events influence us massively.
- Many psychoanalysts warn against generalizing from experiments with college students to clinical populations and problems.

CURRENT VIEW OF UNCONSCIOUS PROCESSES: THE ADAPTIVE UNCONSCIOUS

- Modern research suggests that social information may be largely processed outside of our awareness.
- It is difficult to determine whether a particular memory for a traumatic event is accurate or invented or grossly distorted.

PATTERNS OF DEFENSE: INDIVIDUAL DIFFERENCES IN COGNITIVE AVOIDANCE

- Individuals tend to respond to stress in one of two ways: either avoidance or hypersensitization. This is the repression–sensitization personality dimension.
- These two types do not differ in their recall for threatening information.
- Repressors attend more to positive feedback, see themselves more favorably, and are more mentally and physically healthy, whereas sensitizers are preoccupied with negative feedback and are often self critical.
- There are individual differences in the tendency toward blunting (self-distraction) versus monitoring (increased alertness) in stressful situations.
- If adaptive action in the face of a threat seems impossible, cognitive avoidance or blunting may be more likely. If the potentially painful events are thought to be controlled by the person's actions, then greater attention and vigilance to them may be found.
- Matching the amount of information a person receives with their monitoring–blunting style can help reduce stress for medical patients.

▶ KEY TERMS

anxiety 195
automatic processing 199
blunting 204
cognitive restructuring 193
competence motivation 188
dream interpretation 191
environmental presses 186
explicit motives 190
false memories 200
free association 191

CHAPTER 9

POST-FREUDIAN PSYCHODYNAMICS

"Psychoanalysis was a well-guarded fortress, and most psychologists had little interest in scaling its walls . . . [in contrast] . . . 'pluralism' characterizes contemporary psychoanalysis" (Westen, 1990, p.21).

The Psychodynamic Level of analysis has expanded and diversified in the many years since Freud's original concepts were first expressed, increasingly speaking to the changes that characterize society and the issues and life challenges that are most important for people in the modern Western world. This chapter presents some of the main ideas of theorists who were influenced by Freud and retained much of Freud's psychodynamic orientation, but transformed its focus and shape in crucial ways. These "neo-Freudians" or "post-Freudians" or "ego psychologists" represent a wide range of innovations, and have been given many different labels. They began with Freud's own followers, including his daughter Anna Freud, at the start of the 20th century, and moved on to some radical departures from his ideas. Their unifying theme is that they retained a focus on the Psychodynamic-Motivational Level of analysis. But they went on to call attention to the diversity of human motives and to mental and emotional processes in personality development after early childhood that had been neglected before.

▶ TOWARD EGO PSYCHOLOGY AND THE SELF

9.1 Describe four changes in emphasis from classical psychoanalysis that occurred among neo-Freudian theorists.

Although each neo-Freudian writer has made a distinctive contribution, certain common themes emerge, especially in recent years. These themes suggest a gradual shift in focus, summarized in Table 9.1. Less attention is paid to Freud's ideas about the basic sexual and aggressive instincts of the id, and the id itself is given a less dominant role. More attention is on the concept and functions of ego and "self," to the point where the newer theoretical trends have been named **ego psychology** and its practitioners often are called **ego psychologists**.

Ego psychologists recognize that the ego has crucial functions that may be relatively independent of underlying unconscious motivations. The ego deals often with "higher-order," more cognitive motives and goals, such as the striving for competence, for achievement, and for power, to name a few of the many motives that may drive human behavior, illustrated in the work of Henry Murray and his followers discussed in the last chapter. The ego psychologists see these motives are part of normal ego functions as people form and pursue their life goals. In short, with this growth of the role of ego, and expansion of the range of human motives, the person is viewed as a more competent, potentially creative problem solver, engaged in much more than the management of instincts that press for discharge.

The neo-Freudians, as Table 9.1 suggests, also saw human development as a more continuous process that extends throughout the life span. More than the product of early psychosexual experiences, personality began to be viewed as a lifelong development. Personality is rooted in social and interpersonal relations and in the context of culture and society. It is not isolated within the psyche of the individual and in the drama of the relations with the immediate family in the first few years of life.

Let us now consider some of the major relevant theorists at this level of analysis to illustrate the range and nature of their ideas about personality.

Anna Freud and the Ego Defense Mechanisms

As noted in the last chapter, it was Freud who identified and focused on the mechanism of denial and repression. But it was another psychoanalyst, his own daughter,

TABLE 9.1 Post-Freudian Developments: Some Characteristics of the Neo-Freudians

Less Attention to	More Attention to
Id and instincts	Ego and self; ego defenses; higher-order motives
Purely intrapsychic causes and conflicts	Social, interpersonal causes; relationship issues
Earliest childhood	Later developments throughout the life span; adult functioning
Psychosexual stages	Social forces and positive strivings; the role of the culture and society

Anna Freud (1895–1982)

(*Source*: Bettman/Corbis Images)

Anna Freud, who provided important analyses of the various forms of defense mechanisms that the ego uses. Anna Freud's contributions have had an enduring influence on how we think about personality and human nature. Her personal development and struggle to emerge as a major psychoanalyst and theorist in her own right tells a story not only about her own life and mind but also of her father, and of psychoanalysis, as discussed in *In Focus 9.1*.

The Freud father–daughter relationship (*In Focus 9.1*) underlines the importance of understanding defense mechanisms, including one's own. Interestingly, it was Anna Freud who took the lead in helping to identify them, as summarized in Table 9.2.

Most analysts now view the defense mechanisms as the core of psychodynamics. These are the processes through which the ego does much of its peacekeeping work. They are the mechanisms through which the ego tries to subordinate the impulses, test reality, and accommodate the demands of the superego in the lifelong war within the psyche. The process of defense involves a continuous conflict between impulses seeking discharge and defenses designed to transform these wishes into an acceptable form for the ego. In the course of these transformations, energy is exchanged and directed toward different objects, mediated by the mechanisms of defense.

9.2 How are defense mechanisms involved in the energy exchanges that occur in psychodynamic processes?

Transformation of Motives

For example, if sadistic aggressive impulses cannot be repressed but still are too threatening to self-acceptance, they might be transformed into a more socially sanctioned form, such as an interest in surgery (see Figure 9.1). Likewise, sexual wishes toward the mother might be displaced into a career of painting madonnas, as some Freudians think happened among certain Renaissance painters. Freud (1909/1957b) himself suggested such dynamics in the case of Leonardo da Vinci. After reading *In Focus 9.1*, you might wonder what unconscious motive might have been underneath Freud's decision to analyze Anna on his couch for many years, and ask yourself what Freud might have inferred if an analytic colleague were to break the rule to not psychoanalyze the people who are closest to you.

IN FOCUS 9.1

"LITTLE ANNA" AND SIGMUND: A FREUDIAN SLIP?

You don't have to be a psychoanalyst to see that the Sigmund and Anna Freud father–daughter relationship revealed much more about both people than either one realized. It also tells us a good deal about psychoanalysis. According to Peter Gay, Freud's distinguished biographer, Sigmund unwittingly but systematically fostered in his daughter what Freud himself later called her "father complex" (Gay, 1988, p. 439). As a young girl Anna was frail, often sent to health resorts, and her father interpreted most of her problems, such as her back pains, as psychosomatic. Their relationship was always close and very special for both. Although on the one hand Freud encouraged "Little Anna" to grow up, on the other hand, according to Gay, "it was quite another (thing) to *let* her grow up" (p. 432). Freud supported Anna's professional ambitions and plans, including to become an analyst herself. He was proud of her achievements and intellectual development. But he consistently tried to block any romantic relationships with men. To divert them he even schemed to set her up with women friends for attachments and companionship, and interfered whenever Anna became interested in romantic relationships with men. Although Freud was "a consummate student of family politics, he failed to appreciate fully how much he must have contributed to his daughter's reluctance to marry" (p. 439).

Perhaps the "most irregular proceeding," Gay notes (p. 439), was Freud's decision to psychoanalyze his own daughter for more than 3 years, beginning in 1918, and restarted in 1924 for another year. "His decision to put (Anna) on the couch appears like a calculated flouting of the rules he had laid down with such force and precision—for others" (p. 440).

This Freudian "slip" tells us something about the history and nature of classic Freudian psychoanalysis. For critics of the approach, it's an example of the method's lack of scientific rigor and objectivity. But it also is an example of how both Sigmund and Anna Freud's discoveries and insights grew out of the painful laboratory of their own lives, with great emotional costs to both, but great gains for psychology. And it illustrates one of Freud's own main points: it's much easier to have insights about the motivations and behaviors of other people than about oneself.

TABLE 9.2 Definitions and Examples of Some Defense Mechanisms

Mechanisms	Definition	Example
Repression	Massive inhibition of a threatening impulse or event by rendering it unconscious (beyond awareness)	Guilt-producing sexual wishes are "forgotten"
Projection	Unacceptable aspects of oneself are attributed to someone else	Projecting one's own unacceptable sexual impulses by attributing them to one's boss
Reaction formation	Anxiety-producing impulse is replaced by its opposite in consciousness	Unacceptable feelings of hate are converted into "love"
Rationalization	Making something more acceptable by attributing it to more acceptable causes	Blaming an aggressive act on "being overworked" rather than on feeling angry
Sublimation	Expression of a socially unacceptable impulse in socially acceptable ways	Becoming a soldier to hurt others; becoming a plumber due to anal preoccupations

Freud in his original work was concerned with extreme examples of the mechanism of repression, but its workings also may be seen in many mild forms, as in the following illustration. Jim, a 13-year-old, has a girlfriend with whom he has had a few happy "dates," but she fails to show up at the movie after having promised to be there. Jim

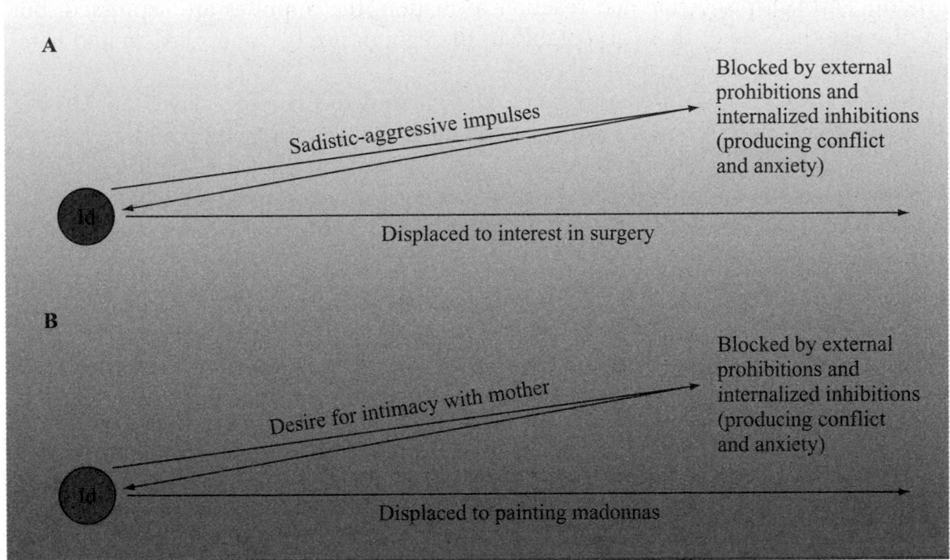

Figure 9.1 The psychodynamic transformation of motives: Examples of displacement in the form of sublimation.

says that he feels no anger, is not annoyed, and just "doesn't care." Yet he explodes later at dinner with his family and gets into a squabble with his little sister. Is Jim using repression? If Jim privately knows he is just trying to cover his irritation and upset, then repression is not a relevant explanation for what he is doing. On the other hand, if his anger is evident to those who know him well, but truly hidden from his own awareness, then repression may be at work as a defense. This hypothesis is strengthened if Jim also shows resistance to efforts by his mother to suggest, for example, that he may be upset by the broken date. In genuine repression, if you push the person to face the underlying feelings that are being avoided unconsciously, it may only increase the defensive attempts to reject the interpretation and avoid the emotion. That tends to make the defense more elaborate and even irrational. In this type of example, when the person is no longer a young child and the threat is relatively mild, repression is unlikely to be very deep. The depth and desperation of the defenses tend to be much greater in early childhood, or when the threats are profoundly frightening and the individual is highly vulnerable.

9.3 What are the major signs that repression is occurring?

Projection

In **projection**, the person's own unacceptable impulses are inhibited and the source of the anxiety is attributed to another person. For example, one's own angry feelings are attributed to one's innocent friend. Or a man who is attracted to his brother's wife sincerely believes she is trying to seduce him at a family gathering. Projection presumably gives relief because it reduces anxiety.

9.4 How are unacceptable impulses masked by projection, reaction formation, rationalization, and sublimation?

Reaction Formation

Another defense, termed **reaction formation**, occurs when a person transforms an anxiety-producing impulse into its opposite. For example, people frightened by their own sexual impulses and desires for unusual sexual adventures may become actively involved in a "ban the filth" vigilante group. They use their energy to vigorously censor books and movies they consider obscene, while secretly and unconsciously are attracted to them. Through projection and reaction formation, the impulses are expressed, but in a disguise that makes them acceptable to the ego: desire becomes disdain and hate. Sometimes this may involve unusual twists.

In the United States a congressman who chaired the House Caucus on Missing and Exploited Children was a leading opponent of child pornography and a vigorous proponent of a bill to make websites with sexually explicit photos of children illegal. In 2006 this same individual had to resign in a famous scandal in which he was accused by diverse sources of sending sexually explicit messages to young, male former Congressional pages.

In another notable headlines case, an American evangelical preacher, founder of the New Life Church, and leader of the National Association of Evangelicals, preached passionately against homosexuality and same-sex marriage, citing the bible. As a result of persistent allegations about homosexuality and drug use on his part, he ultimately resigned from his various positions.

A mother who was a leading psychoanalyst in the 1950s described reaction formation as a mechanism shown by her own children in their early development (Monro, 1955). As a psychoanalyst, she was especially sensitive to the possible problems faced in the anal stage and the impulses activated then. She therefore allowed her children considerable freedom to express their infantile anal interests with few inhibitions about when and where they relieved themselves. After experiencing that early phase of freedom, however, the children seemed to spontaneously develop an opposite pattern. Now they began to exhibit overcleanliness to the point of finickiness, wanting everything to be "super clean," orderly, and neat. They found dishwater disgusting, for example, and insisted on refilling the sink with clean water repeatedly in spite of an extreme water shortage in the county. Likewise, they refused to clean up the puppy's "mistakes," and, as their insightful mother put it, "The reaction of finicking disgust, very genuinely experienced, was clearly related to the positive pleasures recently renounced. Housekeeping became much smoother as reaction formation involving an extreme if somewhat spotty orderliness also gave way to advancing maturity" (Monro, 1955, p. 252).

Reaction formation is one of the defense mechanisms for which more than clinical and anecdotal support has been found, as the example in *In Focus 9.2* describes.

IN FOCUS 9.2

TESTING REACTION FORMATION IN THE LAB

According to the defense mechanism of reaction formation, people hate in others the most what they cannot accept about themselves. In a rare example of an experiment to test defense mechanisms, findings from a laboratory study provide indirect support for the use of reaction formation as a defense mechanism (Adams, Wright, & Lohr, 1996). The participants in this study were two groups of heterosexual men—one group was high on **homophobia** (they felt uncomfortable and could not really talk about homosexuality when asked to do so in the lab) and the other was low in homophobia (i.e., they were able to talk about homosexuality easily). Both groups of men watched three types of movies: heterosexual activity, lesbian activity, and gay activity. Prior to watching the movies, experimenters placed electrodes on the men's bodies that allowed them to measure increase in penile circumference as a measure of sexual arousal. Their findings showed that high and low homophobic men were equally aroused while watching the heterosexual and the lesbian movies. When watching the gay sexual activity movie, however, it was only the high homophobic group who experienced sexual arousal. The findings therefore suggest to the researchers that men who are highly homophobic may be so because they themselves have homophobic tendencies that they cannot accept.

Rationalization

Rationalization is a defense that involves trying to deceive oneself by making rational excuses for unconscious impulses that are unacceptable. For example, a man who has unconscious, deeply hostile impulses toward his wife might invent elaborate excuses that serve to disrupt and even destroy their relationship without ever admitting his true feelings. He might invoke explanations such as "pressures at the office," "a hectic schedule," or "worrying about inflation and politics" as reasons for staying away from home. In doing so, he experiences little guilt over (and might even feel justified in) ignoring, avoiding, and frustrating his wife.

Sublimation

Sublimation is an ego defense that is particularly significant in the development of culture. It consists of a redirection of impulses from an object (or target) that is sexual or aggressive to one that is social in character. Suppose that aggressive urges become too threatening to the young boy, for example the desire to kill the father while struggling with the Oedipus complex. He (or she) may sublimate (or transform) these impulses into socially acceptable forms that in the course of development evolve into the choice of surgery as a career.

Carl Jung

While Anna Freud remained basically loyal to the ideas proposed by her father, Carl Jung was a much more controversial figure who initiated a different form of the psychodynamic approach. Born in 1875, Carl Jung was raised in Basel, Switzerland, the son of a pastor in the Swiss Reformed Church. Upon earning his medical degree from the University of Basel, he began his career in psychology at the Psychiatric Institute in Zurich. Jung began as an admirer and associate of Freud but later became a dissenter and developed his own theory of psychoanalysis and his own method of psychotherapy. His approach became known as **analytical psychology**. Although it retains Freud's unconscious processes, it claims a **collective unconscious**—an inherited foundation of personality. Thus

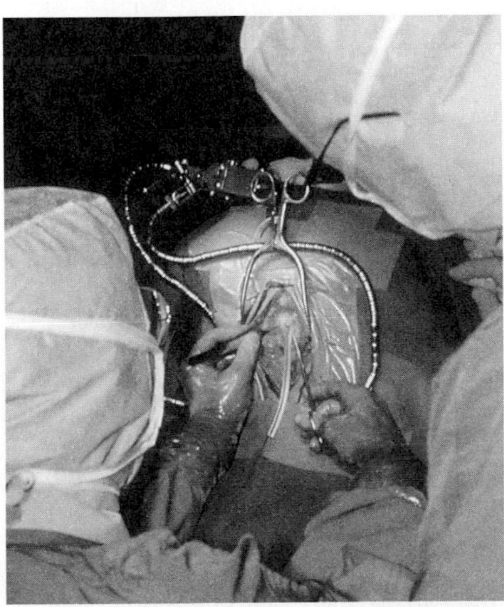

The concept of sublimation suggests that sexual and aggressive impulses may be redirected from their original objects and displaced to socially acceptable activities and careers.

(*Source*: Gregory G. Dimijian/Photo Researchers)

Carl Gustav Jung (1875–1961)
(*Source*: Corbis-Bettmann)

Jung believed the human mind contains not only a personal unconscious, but also an inherited collective unconscious; it contains unconscious images and patterns that reflect the human history of the species. The contents of the collective unconscious are **archetypes** or "primordial images." Unlike the personal unconscious, whose contents were once conscious but have been forgotten or repressed, the contents of the collective unconscious have never been in consciousness. Examples of archetypes include God, the young potent hero, the wise old man, the Earth Mother, the Fairy Godmother, and the hostile brethren. They occur in myths, art, and the dreams of all mankind.

9.5 How did Jung's notion of the unconscious mind differ from Freud's conception?

Jung often dwelled on the multiple, contradictory forces in life: "I see in all that happens the play of opposites" (1963, p. 235). In his view, the psyche included not only a conscious side but also a covert or **shadow aspect** that is unconscious. Personal growth involves an unfolding of this shadow and its gradual integration with the rest of the personality into a meaningful, coherent life pattern. The unconscious of every female includes a masculine, assertive element (the **animus**). The unconscious of every male includes a feminine, passive element (the **anima**). To be constructively masculine or feminine, individuals of each sex must recognize and integrate these opposite sex elements within themselves (see Table 9.3).

Jung described four basic ways of experiencing the world: *sensing, intuition, feeling*, and *thinking*, summarized in Table 9.4. According to Jung, people differ consistently in the degree to which they emphasize each way of experiencing. One person, for example, might typically prefer intuition to abstract thinking, choosing to become a psychoanalyst rather than a mathematician. Another might know the world mostly through his or her senses with little use of either intuition or reason.

9.6 Describe Jung's four basic ways of experiencing the world.

In addition, Jung was concerned with extraversion–introversion. Like the four ways of experiencing, extraversion–introversion for Jung are divided: one side is dominant in the conscious life while the other influences the unconscious side of the personality.

TABLE 9.3 Examples of Jungian Concepts

The Collective Unconscious	Found in everyone and said to contain inherited memories and ancestral behavior patterns
Archetypes	Basic elements or primordial images forming the collective unconscious, manifested in dreams and myths (e.g., Earth Mother, the wise old man)
The Animus	The masculine, assertive element in the unconscious of every woman
The Anima	The feminine, soft, passive element in the unconscious of every man
The Mandala	Usually a circular shape, symbolizing the self, containing designs often divided into four parts

Jung broadened the concept of psychic energy. He did not exclude the sexual instinct of Freudian theory but thought it was only one among many instincts. For Jung, the meaning of behavior became fully intelligible only in terms of its end products or final effects; we need to understand humans not only in terms of their past but also in light of their purposes and goal strivings.

Jung, like Freud, emphasized symbolic meanings. He believed, for example, that "abnormal behaviors" are expressions of the unconscious mind. Also like Freud, Jung thought that abnormal behaviors were merely one way in which the contents of the unconscious may reveal themselves. More often, he felt, they are expressed in dreams. Jung went beyond Freud, however, in his increasing fascination with dreams as unconscious expressions of great interest in their own right. This contrasts with their use merely as starting points for saying whatever comes to mind, that is, "free associations" in Freud's own approach (discussed in Chapter 7). As Jung put it: ". . . I came increasingly to disagree with free association as Freud first employed it; I wanted to keep as close as possible to the dream itself, and to exclude all the irrelevant ideas and associations that it might evoke" (1964, p. 28).

In the same direction, Jung became intrigued by the unconscious for its own sake. He viewed the unconscious not just as the source of instincts. For him it was a vital, rich part of everyone's life, more significant than the conscious world, full of symbols communicated through dreams. The focus of Jungian psychology became the study of people's relations to their unconscious, both personal and collective. Jung's method taught individuals to become more receptive to their own dreams and to let their unconscious serve as a guide for how to live.

9.7 How did Jung's conception and use of dreams differ from Freud's?

Jung's conception of personality is complex, more a set of fascinating observations than a coherent theory. He was one of the first to conceptualize a *self* that actively strives for oneness and unity. Jung saw the self (the striving for wholeness) as an archetype

TABLE 9.4 Jung's Four Ways of Experiencing the World

Ways of Experiencing	Characteristics
Sensing	Knowing through sensory systems
Intuition	Quick guessing about what underlies sensory inputs
Feeling	Focus on the emotional aspects of beauty or ugliness, pleasantness or unpleasantness
Thinking	Abstract thought, reasoning

that is expressed in many ways. The expressions of the striving for wholeness include the **mandala** (a magic circle archetype shown in Figure 9.2) and various religious and transcendental experiences. He devoted much of his life to the study of these expressions in primitive societies, alchemy, mythology, dreams, and symbols.

To achieve unity and wholeness, the individual must become increasingly aware of the wisdom available in his or her personal and collective unconscious and must learn to live in harmony with it. His ideas continue to fascinate many psychologists and are being applied to topics that range from "feminist consciousness" (Lyons, 1997) to the role of the spiritual in healing (Molina, 1996). However, his ideas remain difficult to study with the methods most psychologists favor, and may be having their greatest impact on artists who often cite him as a major influence, as well as on many individuals who feel they benefit from psychotherapists trained within the Jungian framework and from learning Jung's ideas.

Alfred Adler

Like Freud, Alfred Adler also was born in Austria, 14 years after Freud—in 1870. He earned his degree as doctor of medicine in 1895. After a brief period as an ophthalmologist, he practiced psychiatry, joining Freud's Vienna circle of associates at the turn of the century. A highly independent, even rebellious person, Adler broke from Freud after 10 years and began his own psychoanalytic movement, ultimately as a founder of the Society for Individual Psychology.

Adler's contributions have suffered an ironic fate. Much of what he said has become so widely accepted, and seems so plausible, that it has been incorporated into the everyday ideas and terms, the ordinary wisdom that we intuitively have about psychology. Some of these concepts are so common as to risk becoming cliches. Nevertheless, while the

Figure 9.2 A mandala.

popularity of Adler's ideas makes them less distinctive, they remain important even in contemporary thinking about personality.

It is often said that every personality theory captures best the personality of the theorist who created it. Adler's own childhood was marked by chronic illness and hostile relations with his five siblings. Interestingly, both these themes—physical weakness, or **organ inferiority**, and **sibling rivalry**—became central concepts in his theory. Adler's theory begins with a recognition of the infant's profound *helplessness*, a state that makes him or her especially vulnerable to any biological *organ inferiority* or weakness. This biological vulnerability becomes the root for a psychological state that endures in the person and that has central importance in Adler's theory: feelings of inferiority.

9.8 How are Adler's own life experiences reflected in his theory?

It is the struggle to overcome these inferiority feelings that provides the underlying motivation for lifelong compensatory strivings. Throughout the life course, the person tries to make up for this perceived deficit by striving for perfection and superiority. The particular attitude the person adopts toward the inevitable state of inferiority, rather than the deficit itself, was most important for Adler; given a courageous attitude, a perceived deficit can become a positive asset. We all know dramatic examples of personal victories in overcoming biological deficits. Demosthenes was the ancient Greek who achieved fame as a great orator, overcoming a childhood stutter, and more than one great athlete reached the Olympics after long efforts to compensate for early concerns with physical weakness or illness. This **compensatory motivation** contrasts sharply with the id impulses, sexual and aggressive in nature, featured as the driving forces in Freud's theory. It is a much more social psychological view of motivation. It is rooted in the person's feelings about a biological deficit but goes much beyond that origin. The striving to compensate can have many constructive healthy outcomes when pursued with courage. If compensatory efforts fail, however, the person may develop an **inferiority complex**, continuing to feel extremely inadequate about the perceived inferiority and failing to grow beyond it.

Adler also showed a more social orientation in other parts of his theory in which he is alert to cultural influences and social, interpersonal situations. He saw the rivalry between

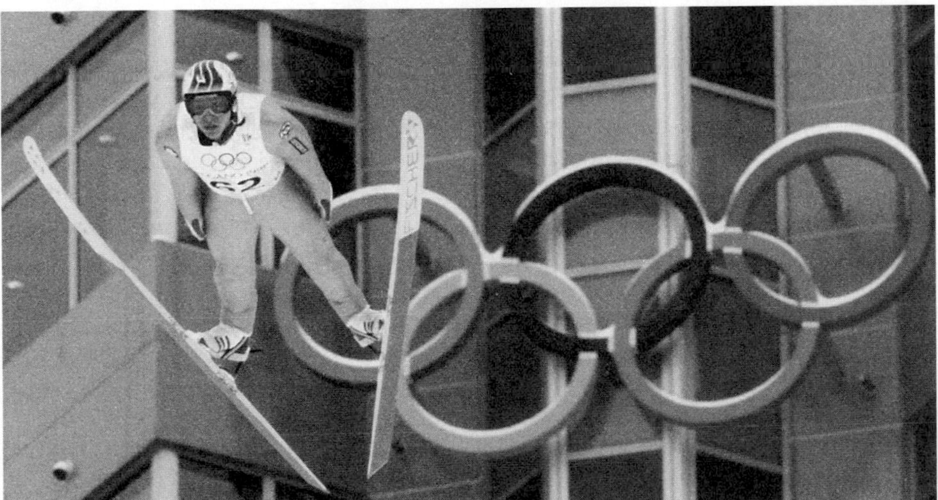

In Adler's view of compensatory motivation, the striving to excel may be a way of overcoming early feelings of inferiority.

(*Source*: © AP/Wide World Photos)

siblings within the family as an important part of development. Thus he viewed the family as the context for significant relationships and conflicts beyond those captured in the Oedipal triangle of mother–father–child that was central for Freud. Indeed, Adler's ideas were notable as a major break from concern with inborn impulses and hereditary causes to focus on the environmental forces and the social world as determinants of personality development. Although the individual functions with consistency and unity, the pattern that makes up the style of life, can be modified. This happens when the person changes the goals toward which the whole pattern of striving is directed.

9.9 Which concepts in Adler's theory reflect his positive view of human nature?

The striving for perfection plays a great role for Adler, but it is matched by his concern for the individual's social feeling or *social interest*. This focus on the positive, adaptive aspects of personality development is also seen in two other Adlerian concepts: courage and common sense. Taken together, social feeling, courage, and common sense constitute the set of characteristics that mark well-functioning, healthy persons.

Such persons cope with the realities of life, including their inevitable helplessness and inferiority, with confidence and constructive strivings, without excessive fear but also without unrealistic fantasies. In contrast, the unhealthy personality abandons appropriate effort and avoids facing realistic difficulties by a retreat into increasingly grandiose fantasies. These fantasies are maladaptive if they widen the gap to reality and provide an unrealistic avoidance of failure.

The positive qualities of social feeling, courage, and common sense are natural states: every person is capable of having them spontaneously unless they are blocked or frustrated in the course of development. For example, the excessively *pampered child* may develop a style of life characterized by being extremely demanding, while the severely *rejected child* may live life in a world seen as dangerous and hostile.

To help overcome this type of damage, the therapist in the Adlerian approach provides the encouragement and sympathetic understanding that allows the patient to face life more realistically and effectively. In this supportive atmosphere, the patient can abandon "mistaken" strivings for fantastic superiority and stop the retreat from reality to begin to face life with common sense, courage, and social feeling.

Erich Fromm

Erich Fromm (1941, 1947) helped to expand Freudian concepts to take account of the important role of society in the development and expression of personality. At the time this was a major step, making Freud's ideas relevant to understanding how people are connected—or disconnected—from the social system and other people.

For Fromm, people are primarily social beings to be understood in terms of their relations to others. According to Fromm, individual psychology is fundamentally social psychology. People have psychological qualities, such as tendencies to grow, develop, and realize their potentialities. These basic tendencies lead them to freedom and to want to strive for justice. Thus, human nature has a force of its own that influences social processes.

Fromm's explanation of character traits illustrates the difference between Freud's biological orientation and Fromm's social orientation. Fromm criticized Freud's idea that fixation at certain pleasure-giving stages is the cause of later character traits. According to Fromm, personality and character are importantly influenced by social and interpersonal processes: Character traits develop from experiences with others. Psychosexual problems are the body's expressions of an attitude toward the world that is socially conditioned. According to Freud, culture is the result of society's efforts to suppress instinctual drives. For Fromm, culture is molded by the structure, values, and substance of a given society.

Erich Fromm (1900–1980)

(*Source*: Corbis-Bettmann)

Another major point of departure from Freud is Fromm's belief that ideals like truth, justice, and freedom can be genuine strivings and not simply rationalizations of biological motives. Freud's psychology is a psychology of instinctual drives that defines pleasure in terms of tension reduction. Fromm's psychology, while still influenced by Freud, was among the first to try to make a place for positive attributes, such as tenderness and the human ability to love, and the desire for freedom, as basic aspects of human nature, adding a more positive side to Freud's view of the human condition.

9.10 Contrast Fromm's views on the origin of character traits and positive ideals with those of Freud.

► ERIK ERIKSON'S PSYCHOSOCIAL THEORY OF PERSONALITY DEVELOPMENT

Born in 1902 in Frankfurt Germany, Erik Homburger Erikson became one of the most influential ego psychologists of the last century. His work changed the conception of personality development, and eloquently addressed the concerns of every person who struggles to answer questions like: Who am I? Who do I want to be? Who can I become? What is my real identity? Early in his own life, he found these questions compelling but difficult to answer. According to his biographer (Friedman, 1999), Erikson grew up in Germany, the biological son of Danish parents. His father abandoned the family before Erik's birth and his mother married a Jewish pediatrician. Erik thus faced the dilemma of being a tall, blue-eyed Scandinavian growing up as a Jew in Germany, who felt accepted neither by his Jewish nor his non-Jewish peers. Thus he viewed himself as an "outsider" and the seeds were sown for an enduring concern with questions of identity, which ultimately became the focus of his work.

In his early 20s, Erikson briefly studied art in Europe, but experienced intense anxiety and occasional panic attacks that made it difficult for him to work effectively. He moved to Vienna in 1927 where he taught children at a small school and met a number of Viennese psychoanalysts, most notably Anna Freud. Anna Freud became Erikson's

Erik H. Erikson (1902–1994)

(*Source*: Corbis-Bettmann)

personal analyst and in time he proceeded to be trained in psychoanalysis himself. In 1933, with Hitler's ascent to power in Nazi Germany, he immigrated to the United States. Here he practiced his own innovative version of psychoanalysis with children for many years, and wrote a series of books and papers that importantly influenced both clinical practice and theory, as well as popular thinking about personality development and the search for personal identity in the course of personality development. Erikson's contributions are deeply rooted in Freud's, but extend and modernize them significantly, as he put it, with a psychoanalytic examination of the "relation of the ego to society" (1963, p. 16).

Stages of Psychosocial Development

9.11 Describe Erikson's psychosocial stages and the psychosocial crisis expressed at each stage.

Like Freud, Erikson (1950, 1963) proposed stages of development, specifically eight **psychosocial stages** that unfold over the course of the entire life cycle. While Freud's stages dealt with psychosexual development, and end soon after adolescence, for Erikson development is a life-long process of interpersonal adaptation, consistent with the neo-Freudian emphasis on broad interpersonal, social, and cultural influences, rather than instinctual drives alone. Development for Erikson thus is a process that plays out not only at the psychosexual and biological level but also at the level of ego development and interpersonal relations with family and society.

Trust versus Mistrust

Each stage has its distinctive **psychosocial crisis** and raises at least implicitly a core question the person has to deal with (see Table 9.5). For example, in the first stage of life (the "oral-sensory" stage of the first year), the crisis involves **trust versus mistrust**. At this stage the child's relation to the mother forms basic attitudes about "getting" and

TABLE 9.5 Erikson's Stages of Psychosocial Development

Stage and Age	Psychosocial Crisis	Optimal Outcome
I. Oral-sensory (First year of life)	Trust vs. Mistrust	Basic trust and optimism
II. Muscular-anal (Second year)	Autonomy vs. Shame	Sense of control over oneself and the environment
III. Locomotor-genital (Third through Fifth year)	Initiative vs. Guilt	Goal-directedness and purpose
IV. Latency (Sixth year to start of puberty)	Industry vs. Inferiority	Competence
V. Puberty and Adolescence	Identity vs. Role Confusion	Reintegration of past with present and future goals, fidelity
VI. Early Adulthood	Intimacy vs. Isolation	Commitment, sharing, closeness, and love
VII. Young and Middle Adult	Generativity vs. Self-Absorption	Production and concern with the world and future generations
VIII. Mature Adult	Integrity vs. Despair	Perspective, satisfaction with one's past life, wisdom

Source: Adapted from Erikson, E. (1963). *Childhood and society*. New York: Norton.

"giving." The basic question here is nonverbal but experiential, confronting the infant with the problem "Am I loved?", "Am I good?", and "Are others good?". If the crisis is properly resolved, the experiences at this stage lay the groundwork for later trust, drive, and hope. If it is not, the person may develop a sense of badness, pessimism, and distrust, including self-distrust.

Autonomy versus Shame and Doubt

In the second stage, early childhood, paralleling Freud's anal stage in time, the issue faced concerns **autonomy versus shame and doubt**, and the implicit questions confronted are "Can I have some control over my world?" and "Can I be effective?". The challenges faced at age 2–3 years deal with the struggle to gain some mastery, autonomy, and freedom, while avoiding shame and humiliation, not an easy balancing act for a small child in a big world. In Erikson's theory, toilet training struggles, for example, are not so much about redirecting libidinal expressions as about gaining some mastery and independence without humiliation. When the child gains some control over toilet functions, the sense of control and mastery tends to increase. But the challenges extend much beyond the toilet to social interactions with adults and peers, as well as objects in the environment. If these interactions are effective, the feeling of competence and autonomy increases, and the foundations are built for a sense of will and efficacy. In contrast, when the child's early efforts are met by ridicule or harsh rebukes, anxiety and self-doubts, as well as self-conscious shame and rigid defenses, readily increase. The challenge both for the caretakers and for the child is to achieve a reasonable balance between discipline and freedom, to enhance the child's sense of autonomy while also becoming sensitive to responsibility and necessary self-constraints and situational limits.

Initiative versus Guilt

As the various stages meld into each other, the concerns shift from autonomy to power as the 4-year-old tries to take the initiative and experiments with attempts to make his world and not just be made by it. Here the optimal outcome is gaining a sense of goal-directedness and purpose in action-taking, and the crisis concerns issues of **initiative versus guilt**, as the child implicitly asks "How can I be powerful"? At preschool age this question becomes dominant. The balancing act in the conflict between initiative and guilt can be difficult. The 4-year-old who readily takes the initiative to break another child's toy, or to spoil the dinner of the adults at an adjoining restaurant table, may need to moderate the quest for power with some appropriate social restraints. When well managed, the optimal outcome at this stage is the development of a sense of purpose and goal-directedness, that allows the child to pursue a valued goal with a sense of courage, rather than becoming excessively inhibited by punishment fears and guilt.

Industry versus Inferiority

In the fourth stage (Table 9.5), as the child begins elementary school, the psychosocial crisis is the conflict of **industry versus inferiority**. The term "industry" in the industry–inferiority challenge covers a wide range of adult tools and subject matter that must be mastered, and the child's performance now is being judged and evaluated continuously by teachers, parents, peers, and the self. The challenges at this stage play out at many levels because children are expected to learn new social roles, as well as the basic skills required within the particular culture, ranging from academic and technical to moral and ethical contents that are needed for productive participation in the adult world. At this stage, the child's implicit questions may be "Am I effective?" and "Am I competent?" To make it through this stage adaptively the child needs to feel efficacious, and to develop a sense of being able to master the challenges in ways that meet the relevant standards valued by others, while avoiding feelings of inferiority that undermine performance. Effectively managing the conflicts in this stage leads to the personal quality that Erikson calls **competence**, in contrast to the feelings of inadequacy and inability to complete work that characterize poor adaptation at this stage.

Adolescence and the Struggle for Identity versus Role Confusion

With puberty's biological changes, the adolescent soon faces large questions of the identity and roles that will be required in the adult world. Now he or she needs to figure out who he or she is, and wants to become. In Erikson's model, the challenge and crisis at this crucial stage is the conflict between **identity versus role confusion**. At the heart of the struggle, one has to answer the "who am I" question, not just verbally but at the level of feelings and new social roles and behaviors. A dilemma for the adolescent often is that none of the roles that seem available or possible provide a good fit with the confusing and shifting sense of identity that may be experienced.

To manage one's way adaptively through this difficult, sometimes tumultuous, stage, according to Erikson, requires integrating personal self-conceptions of the private self with the expectations and conceptions of the social world, including with the family with which one may sometimes even feel at war. The sense of identity involves a synthesis of how individuals have come to see themselves and their awareness of what the important other people in their lives expect them to be. He believed that all young people must generate for themselves some central perspective that gives them a meaningful sense of unity and purpose. This perspective integrates the remnants of their childhood with the expectations and hopes of adulthood (Erikson, 1968). Achieving an **ego identity** that allows a coherent blending of self conceptions and social conceptions, an identity that is connected to one's society rather than totally alienated from it, is the major life task that confronts everyone, in Erikson's theory. In contrast, a failure to form an adequate identity results in discomfort with one's roles, a sense of artificiality, and no firm standards.

In Erikson's words on the integrations required for ego (or "self") identity:

> The integration . . . of ego identity is . . . more than the sum of the childhood identifications. It is the accrued experience of the ego's ability to integrate all identifications with the vicissitudes of the libido, with the aptitudes developed out of endowment, and with the opportunities offered in social roles. (1963, p. 261)

The underlying assumptions of his view of development are:

> (1) that the human personality in principle develops according to steps predetermined in the growing person's readiness to be driven toward, to be aware of, and to interact with, a widening social radius; and (2) that society, in principle, tends to be so constituted as to meet and invite this succession of potentialities for interaction and attempts to safeguard and to encourage the proper rate and the proper sequence of their enfolding. (1963, p. 270)

Intimacy versus Isolation

In the early stages of adulthood, conflicts are between **intimacy versus isolation**. Individuals differ in the intimacy of the relationships they develop, or the isolation they experience. Adaptation in this stage facilitates the sharing of feelings and thoughts with family, friends, and significant others, as well as mutuality and connection in work relationships. It also enhances a sense of continuity in oneself that strengthens over time, and an acceptance both of the successes and disappointments that life brings. It contrasts with the isolation from others, the experience of life as a grinding routine, the focus on past disappointments and future nothingness and death, that characterizes extreme failures to negotiate the psychosocial crises of this stage in Erikson's view.

Generativity versus Self-Absorption/Stagnation

Early adulthood in time becomes adulthood and gradually blends into the later years. The mature adult faces the crisis of **generativity versus self-absorption and stagnation**. A positive resolution is marked by the ability to remain absorbed, productive, and vital in one's work and relationships, and increasingly concerned with the world and future generations. This constructive pattern of adaptation contrasts with the loss of interest in work and other people, and disconnection with the larger world and the human future.

Integrity versus Despair

In the late years of life the key conflicts are between **integrity versus despair**. The challenge is to find or construct a sense of meaning and order in one's life, to gain a perspective and wisdom that allows one to be satisfied with one's life. The positive outcome is to feel whole and content, rather than succumb to despair and feelings of meaninglessness, filled with bitterness about life, and absorbed with fears of death.

The fact that Erikson's ideas about personality development continue to have widespread appeal decades after they were formulated suggests that they speak to issues that remain important for many people in many parts of our culture. His thoughts concerning the "identity crises" of adolescence, for example, are still discussed widely. Indeed the phrase **identity crisis** has become a part of everyday speech, as well as a continuing topic of empirical research (e.g., Berzonsky & Neimeyer, 1994; Marcia, 1966, 1980).

Erikson's Contributions

Erikson's ideas about life stages contribute more than a broad description of life phases and the conflicts and challenges they produce, and more than a portrait of the vast individual differences in how these conflicts are managed. His work is important for personality psychology because it (1) called attention to the psychosocial and not just the instinctual or biological psychosexual nature of human development, while also making it clear that (2) developmental challenges and personality changes unfold over the entire life cycle, and that (3) development reflects not just the past but also the ways in which the individual anticipates and represents the future. These themes continue to be echoed and expanded decades after Erikson proposed them. And they are enriched now by empirical investigations documenting changes in the developmental course throughout the life span (e.g., Baltes, Staudinger, & Lindenberger, 1999; Kagan, 2006).

Perhaps most important, Erikson was a psychoanalyst who in several significant ways influenced and modernized the Freudian view of human nature. Erikson appreciated the importance of the unconscious and the dark sides of human nature, but his view of the human condition was much more optimistic. Unlike Freud's tragic vision of the individual trapped by early life experiences and the unconscious id impulses, his view of development and determinism did not see persons as the inevitable victims of their first few years of life. For Freud the early determinants continued to drive the individual for life. For Erikson, reintegration of the past was possible in the present and could even be driven by how we think about the future. He believed it is not just that early childhood influences adulthood; what we do and think as adults, our adult personality structures, can change how that childhood is interpreted and experienced and its subsequent impact. In this sense, we can rethink and partially rework our childhood experiences mentally, and we also can influence our futures proactively by how we anticipate them. These ideas, while developed at the Psychodynamic Level, are echoed and amplified by work at the Phenomenological-Humanistic Level, as you will see in that part of the text. They also form a bridge to the development of object relations theory and a focus on the self, discussed next.

9.12 How is Erikson's perception of human nature less deterministic than Freud's view of human nature?

▶ OBJECT RELATIONS THEORY AND THE SELF

As Erikson's contributions illustrate, over many decades, psychodynamic theory and practice have undergone particularly important transformations. While many clinical psychologists remain within an essentially Freudian psychoanalytic framework, many have moved far beyond Freud and his immediate followers, and this shift applies especially to research psychologists in academic settings. These innovators further changed how they think about personality, the roots of mental health, and ways to help troubled people.

The basic orientation of this approach has emerged clearly in an integrative review of this movement (Cashdan, 1988; Greenberg & Mitchell, 1983). There have been different variations in this shift. Leaders include such psychoanalysts as Melanie Klein (one of the earliest innovators) in England and, more recently, Otto Kernberg (1976, 1984) and Heinz Kohut (1971, 1977) in the United States. In this section, we emphasize the common themes of change that seem to characterize this movement.

The approach is called **object relations theory** and therapy (Cashdan, 1988), and the first point to note is that the "objects" in the language of this theory are simply other human beings. The term "objects" is a leftover from classic psychoanalysis, and the phrase

The developing self is defined from the start in relational, interpersonal terms in Kohut's theory.

(*Source*: J. Nourok/Photo Researchers)

"significant others" essentially could substitute for it. The important shift from classic psychoanalysis to object relations theory is that while the former focused on the instinctual drives, the latter focuses on the relationships to significant other people (i.e., object relations).

9.13 What is the central emphasis within object relations theories?

The most important object for the developing child generally, and unsurprisingly, is the mother. It is in the young child's relationship with the mother that the **relational self**—the self that becomes linked closely with the person's relationships to significant other people—begins to originate and emerge. Note that the self is defined from the start in relational or interpersonal terms.

"Good–Bad Splitting"

Within psychodynamic theory, one of the first to address the mother–child relationship in great depth was Melanie Klein, a British psychoanalyst who was Freud's contemporary. A theme that still persists from Klein's work is her clinical observation that the young child tends to divide the world into good and bad. Klein saw the core conflict throughout life as a struggle between positive feelings of love and negative feelings of hate. Her insight that in this conflict people tend to "split" the world into benevolent and malevolent components has been integrated into much current relational theorizing about personality structure and development.

Klein spoke of a nourishing good breast and an empty bad breast in the child's conflict-ridden representation of the mother as both good and bad. This notion has remained in a variety of contemporary psychodynamic ideas about "good" and "bad" self-representations, internal representations of the self and of other people. It is part of the belief that from infancy on there is a tendency to somehow "split" or partition experiences and objects (people) in good–bad, gratifying–frustrating terms (Cashdan, 1988), fragmenting rather than integrating them into a coherent whole. When these splits are severe, therapy seeks to help the person to integrate them.

The Development of Self

9.14 How is splitting involved in the development of the self concept and in a person's level of self-esteem?

Briefly, development is seen as a process in which the newborn begins in a world that is experienced as split into good (gratifications) and bad (tensions) feelings. In this early world, other people, including the mother, are not yet differentiated in the child's mind. Emotional splitting of experiences and people (initially primarily the mother) in good–bad, positive–negative terms continues throughout later life.

The most important "object," the mother, soon begins to be represented by the young child internally as an image. With cognitive development and the growth of language skills, the child can start to internalize not only a maternal image but also maternal conversation in the form of an inner dialogue. Some of these early conversations are audible. You know this if you have ever heard the conversations youngsters sometimes have with themselves as they praise or scold their own performance, saying "good boy" or "no, no" aloud to themselves. This internal dialogue is especially evident during toilet training and other early exercises in the development of self-regulation.

In time, the internalizations of maternal images and conversations become the foundations of the developing self. You can see this development, for example, in the increasing use of "I" in the child's speech. The child's utterance changes from "Jane wants ice cream" to the personal pronoun in which "I" want it, "I" eat it, "I" am bad.

In this conception, emotional splitting continues as an aspect of the developing self: "Just as early splitting of the mother creates a split in the maternal presence, so the split in the inner maternal presence creates a split in the self. Early splits give birth to later splits" (Cashdan, 1988, p. 48). In time, individuals come to view themselves as good or bad depending on their earlier good–bad emotional experiences of splitting. The sense of self-esteem that ultimately emerges characterizes how persons feel about themselves. It is both the consequence of the earlier experiences and the determinant of much of what is experienced later in the course of life.

As the splitting process continues, a variety of identity splits occur. They yield such important categories as one's sexual identity, career identity, identity as a parent, and so on. Each is colored emotionally in good–bad terms. The emotional splitting represented by the enduring concern with goodness–badness never ends. When it is tilted toward a badness imbalance, it continues to corrode the person's relationships and is not adaptive. The therapeutic process, in turn, is viewed as the method for undoing the imbalance, recognizing and overcoming inner conflicts, and developing a more integrated and positive image of the self.

ATTACHMENT: THE ROOTS OF OBJECT RELATIONS

Like Freud, object relations theorists focus on the importance of the early years. Unlike Freud's emphasis on how the instinctual drives are expressed and managed in the first few years, however, these theorists stress the type of relationship that develops with the early caretaker, usually the mother. This early relationship becomes the basic framework for the perception and experience of later relationships. The details of this developmental process have received increasing research attention by child psychologists. They study the quality and varieties of early attachment relations between mother and child (Ainsworth, Blehar, Waters, & Wall, 1978) and trace how these early relationships link to subsequent development (Sroufe & Fleeson, 1986). Much of this work was influenced by the attachment theory proposed by a British psychiatrist, John Bowlby, discussed next.

Attachment Theory

Bowlby was seeing a 3-year-old boy in psychotherapy. It was half a century ago, and he was being supervised by the psychoanalyst Melanie Klein, who refused to allow him to meet with the boy's mother. Frustrated by this experience, as well as by the unscientific nature of psychoanalytic theorizing, Dr. Bowlby developed his now-famous attachment theory (Holmes, 1993). This theory is consistent with object relations theory, giving center stage to the relationship between the young child and the **primary caregiver**—the mother, or whoever is the main early life caregiver for the child (Bowlby, 1982). For Bowlby, the psychological characteristics of the primary caregiver were crucial, and he emphasized the experienced relationship between the child and this person.

According to Bowlby, based on experiences in this relationship, the child develops **internal working models**. These are mental representations of others, of the self, or of relationships that guide subsequent experience and behavior. Children who have had positive, gratifying experiences with the primary caregiver in their environment will develop internal working models of others as responsive and giving, and of themselves as competent and worthy of affection; those who have painful or unsatisfying experiences develop internal models that reflect those troubled relationships. The basic message in attachment theory is that caregivers who are responsive to the infant's needs provide a **secure base**, a safe haven of dependable comfort in the young child's life from which the world can then begin to be explored with trust, without fear of abandonment. Attachment figures, like the primary caregiver, also serve a **safe haven** function in this theory: They are the people to whom the young child turns for support and comfort in times of threat, sickness, and need.

9.15 What is the role of working models in Bowlby's theory? How do these develop?

Bowlby developed his theory in part because he wanted to understand the intense reactions of distress experienced by infants when they were separated from their primary caregiver or attachment figure. He noted that separated infants would be visibly distressed (crying and clinging) and search visually for that person to prevent separation or to reestablish proximity. Bowlby reasoned that attachment behavior (e.g., visible distress and protest maintain proximity) was an adaptive strategy from an evolutionary perspective: it increased the likelihood that the infant would survive to reproduce. He also recognized that such attachment behaviors were evident not just in humans but in other mammals whose young had a long period of dependency. Consequently, attachment theory proposes that the attachment behavioral system evolved to maintain proximity to attachment figures, which in turn promoted survival and reproductive success.

Early Attachment Relations: Secure/Insecure Attachment Patterns

Mary Ainsworth (1989) developed the "Strange Situation" to examine patterns of infant–parent attachment in young children (e.g., Ainsworth et al., 1978; Stayton & Ainsworth, 1973). Her **Strange Situation** assesses individual differences in the young toddler's relationship with the primary caregiver.

9.16 Describe the *Strange Situation* and what it has revealed about children's attachment patterns. How are these patterns related to childhood behavior?

In this situation, the toddler (about age 18 months) is introduced to a novel playroom environment with the mother (assuming she is the primary caregiver) and a stranger. Then the toddler is exposed to different levels of availability of the mother, from present and involved with the child, to present and mildly preoccupied, to absent. The child is separated from the mother twice during the Strange Situation; once left with the stranger and once left alone, creating a stressful situation. After a brief separation the mother returns.

Three main patterns of behavior have been identified in this situation. Toddlers who avoided the mother throughout the procedure, as well as on reunion, were considered **insecure–avoidant**, or A babies. Some were able to greet the mother positively upon reunion, and then return to play, and they attended to the mother and desired interaction with her throughout the procedure. These were termed **securely attached**, or B babies. Those whose reunion behavior combined contact-seeking and anger, and who were difficult to comfort upon reunion, were classified as the C or **insecure–ambivalent** (also referred to as resistant) babies.

Note that both securely attached and insecure–ambivalent babies cry when their mothers leave, but they cry for different reasons according to this model. Crying is part of the protest response and the secure babies cry because it's an instrumental behavior that usually brings the mother back. The ambivalent babies presumably cry out of anger and despair because the mother has once again left. The bigger difference is that the secure babies are immediately comforted by the arrival of the mother and readily turn back to exploring the environment in her presence. The ambivalent ones just don't get comforted by the mother's presence—they cling to her and keep on crying. Because they are unsure of her availability, they simply cannot return to play and exploration. Home visits revealed that the different types of babies experienced different patterns of maternal responsiveness. For example, mothers of infants rated as securely attached were most responsive toward their babies. Mothers of resistant babies were inconsistent in their responsiveness. The responsiveness of mothers of avoidant children varied with the context: they were unresponsive to bids for contact and comfort, but they were controlling and intrusive in response to their children's attempts at independent play.

Secure children were more likely to remain confident and flexibly organized when faced with an insurmountable task as preschoolers (Arend et al., 1979). And when they became 6-year-olds they were able to generate adaptive strategies for coping with the temporary absence of a parent (Main, Kaplan, & Cassidy, 1985). Additionally, 5-year-olds with a history of a secure relationship with the mother were less likely to exhibit negative interactions with a peer (Youngblade & Belsky, 1992). Likewise, toddlers who at 18 months were able to cope effectively with separation from the mother in the Strange Situation, for example by distracting themselves and exploring the toys in the environment to reduce distress, were also more likely to become able to cope effectively with frustration in later childhood, when trying to delay gratification for valued but immediately unavailable rewards (Sethi, Mischel, Aber, Shoda, & Rodriguez, 2000).

Attachment in Adult Relationships

In addition to examining attachment behavior in the young child, attachment theory also has been applied to study adult attachment relations, as discussed in *In Focus 9.3*.

Studies of adult attachment styles generally classify participants into one of three categories, based on their self-reports: secure, avoidant, and ambivalent. Participants also are asked about their childhood experiences within the family, and their past and current romantic relationship history and satisfaction. Studies try to link the self-reported attachment styles to the participants' reports about their personal relationships. Table 9.6 gives examples of the kinds of relationships found.

As the table indicates, adults who see themselves as secure about relationships also report themselves to have had happier, more positive relationship histories, including in their families as children, and in their past and current relationships with romantic partners. Unsurprisingly, these differences are seen particularly when the secure adults are compared to those who describe themselves as avoidant in relationships. A study of adults

IN FOCUS 9.3

SECURE–INSECURE ATTACHMENT AND PERCEIVED SOCIAL SUPPORT IN CLOSE ADULT RELATIONSHIPS

Just home from work, Jane tells her husband she had an awful day at the office. He says, "Don't worry about it. I'm sure you did the best you could under the circumstances." Will Jane see these comments as supportive—or as evidence that she has an uncaring husband? *Perceived available support*—a person's perception of being loved and valued—is strongly related to one's health and well-being. On what does this perception depend? According to attachment theory, the person's "working model of attachment" is an especially important determinant. According to the theory, it is automatically activated by stressful events: it then filters or screens how the person appraises and experiences interactions with significant others in one's life (e.g., Collins & Feeney, 2000; Pierce, Baldwin, & Lydon, 1997).

Two laboratory studies explored whether working models of attachment are related to perceptions of social support in adult intimate relationships. In these studies, the researchers created a stressful task in the laboratory. They then manipulated (Study 1) or observed (in Study 2) the social support that participants received from their romantic partners. The research goal was to see how the individuals' secure or insecure levels of attachment influenced their perceptions of the support they received from their partners (Collins & Feeney, 2004).

Compared to secure adults, insecure adults tended to perceive their partners' messages as less helpful and less well intended. But note that that this happened only when the support message was ambiguous and therefore more open to subjective interpretation by the recipient. Under such ambiguous conditions, the more insecurely attached person's vulnerabilities became activated and influenced the interpretation of the situation. As the researchers note, unfortunately in real life, support providers often lack the skills and motivation to provide the effective clear support the insecure person needs (Collins & Feeney, 2000; Feeney & Collins, 2001, 2003). Overall, these studies do indicate links between the individual's working models of attachment and the subjective perceptions of social support.

Is early attachment the preface to adult romantic love?

(*Source*: (left) Joe Gemignani/Corbis Images; (right) Royalty-Free/Corbis Images)

at age 52 also used a more objective measure of relationship success, namely marriage and divorce statistics. It found the adults who were secure (self-described) also were almost all married (95%), whereas only 72% of the avoidant adults were married and half of them had been previously divorced (Klohnen & Bera, 1998). As the table also indicates, the three groups differ in their beliefs about romantic love, with the secure being believers, the avoidant more cynical, and the ambivalent thinking it comes easily but does not last.

TABLE 9.6 Some Correlates of Adult Relationship Style

Relationship Style	Associated with
Secure	Report they had supportive families; trusting, warm, happy parents; can tolerate separations from partners without high anxiety; have partners who tend to be satisfied with the relationship; able to give partners emotional support when they need it; generally construct positive romantic relationships; believe romantic love is real and can last.
Avoidant	Report they had aloof, emotionally distant parents, did not feel warmth, closeness or trust in family; tend to fear intimacy, find emotional commitment difficult; unable to be highly emotionally supportive of partner; cynical about romantic love and doubt that it lasts.
Ambivalent	Report they have many romantic relationships that don't last long; anxiously fearful of losing partners; ready and eager to change self to please partner; stressed by separations from partner. Believe falling in love is easy but does not last.

Source: Based on Hazan & Shaver (1987, 1994).

What conclusions do these diverse findings allow? On the one hand, people clearly differ in how secure they feel themselves to be in close relationships, both currently and in the past, and how they feel about those relationships. These feelings are associated also with what they expect to find in relationships, and what they are likely to experience within them, and how their partners will feel about them. As seen in *In Focus 9.3*, there are many links between self-reported adult attachment style and self-reports of current relationship satisfaction. For example, people who self-report more attachment avoidance in general (e.g.,"I don't feel comfortable opening up to romantic partners") also tend to be less positive about their current relationship quality on self-ratings of their satisfaction, commitment passion, and love (Noftle & Shaver, 2006).

Further, a study by Zayas and Shoda (2005) found that in individuals with secure adult attachment (compared to those with insecure adult attachment), thoughts about their romantic partner automatically elicited stronger automatic positive emotional reactions. Most interesting, in the Zayas and Shoda study, the researchers also found that in individuals with a secure attachment with their adult romantic partner, thoughts about their *mother* also automatically elicited stronger positive (e.g., supportiveness) reactions. These findings are consistent with Bowlby's (1969) attachment theory. They are notable because reactions to one's mother, as well as to one's partner, were assessed using the Implicit Association Test (IAT; e.g., Greenwald et al., 2002). Similar to priming techniques (Chapter 2), measures such as the IAT do not depend on what people say (e.g., via self-reports). Instead, these measures typically involve some type of categorization task that is administered on a computer. These tasks allow researchers to tap into how concepts in a person's mind are associated. For example, in the Zayas and Shoda study, the IAT assessed how strongly thoughts of one's mother were automatically associated with positive responses (e.g., "loving," "caring," "helpful").

9.17 Describe the three adult attachment patterns found in self-report studies. How do these patterns relate to measures of adjustment?

Some studies of adult attachment suggest that individuals may carry specific attachment styles with them in relationships throughout life (e.g., Fraley & Shaver, 1997; Hazan & Shaver, 1987; Klohnen & Bera, 1998; Kobak & Sceery, 1988). However, the degree to which adult attachment patterns are directly linked to those observed in toddlers and young children remains unclear. Although object relations theory generally assumes that the adult patterns are a direct outgrowth and continuation of those found in early life, the data are open to alternative interpretations and have been strongly questioned (e.g., Lewis, 1999, 2002).

9.18 How much temporal stability did Lewis find in attachment styles from childhood through adulthood? What are the implications of his findings?

For example, after an extensive and detailed review of the massive research on this topic, Lewis (1999, p. 341) concludes that attachment patterns do not show continuity over long periods of time (e.g., from 1 year of age to age 18 years) in the course of development. As was discussed above, at any given period of time, there are links between current attachment patterns and important indicators of functioning. But it is still not clear if—and how—the attachment styles of infancy become the model for all that follows. To the many people in the world whose early childhood was not a picture of ideally experienced security, this may be good news, even though it is disturbing to the classic theory of object relations and makes their assumptions of continuity still tentative.

Kohut's Theory

> *. . . man can no more survive psychologically in a psychological milieu that does not respond empathically to him, than he can survive physically in an atmosphere that contains no oxygen.*
>
> (Kohut, 1977, p. 85)

The object relations theorists share several themes, as the last section showed. One leader in this movement, Heinz Kohut, is selected in this section for further attention, because his work is seen as especially influential for changing views of the healthy and the disturbed personality. Kohut, a psychiatrist who received his medical training at the University of Vienna, went on to psychoanalytic training and teaching in Chicago where he gained recognition as a theorist and clinician in the 1970s.

9.19 According to Kohut, what changes in family life have occurred since Freud's era, and how have they influenced the nature of psychological problems?

In Kohut's view, throughout the century profound changes in the family and culture have occurred: psychoanalysis and psychodynamic theory must be responsive to them. An important change, he believes, is that Freud's patients typically came from a Western civilization in which life was concentrated in the home and family unit. Families tended

Heinz Kohut (1913–1981)

(*Source*: From The Restoration of Self by Heinz Kohut, International Edit)

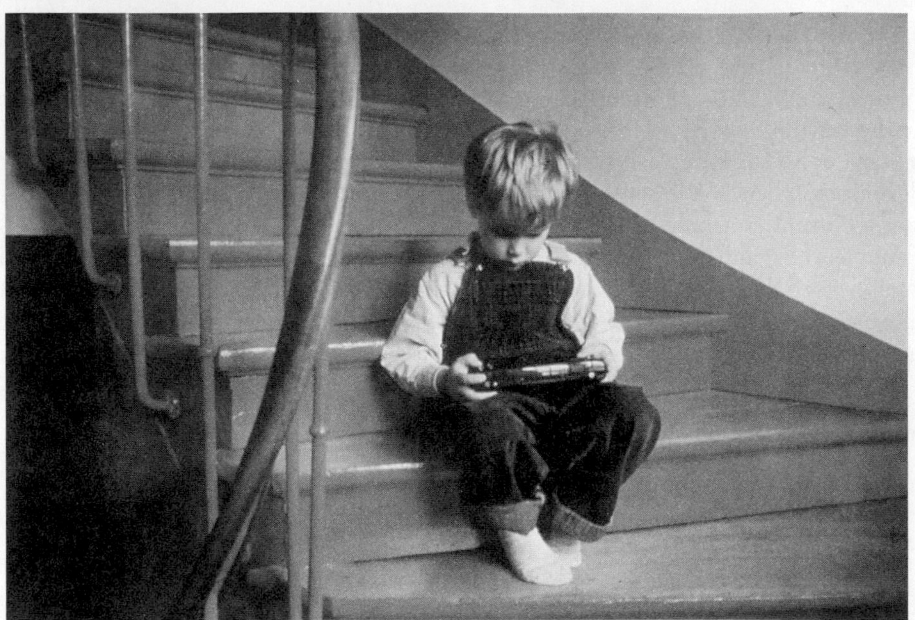

For Kohut, the modern child's life is characterized not by too much parenting and intimacy but by loneliness.

(*Source*: Jerome Tisne/Stone/Getty Images)

to expose their children to **emotional overcloseness** (Kohut, 1977, p. 269), and these intense emotional relations in turn often produced neurotic problems involving internal conflicts such as those in the Oedipus complex. The developing child was likely to be trapped in too much intimacy, too much stimulation, too much intrusiveness.

In contrast, children now are more likely to see parents at most in leisure hours and to develop much less clear role definitions and models: "The environment which used to be experienced as threateningly close, is now experienced more and more as threateningly distant . . ." (Kohut, 1977, p. 271). While personal problems used to arise from being too stimulated emotionally by parents (Freud, 1963), now youngsters tend to be *under*stimulated and may search for erotic sensations and other strong experiences to fill the emotional emptiness of their lives and to try to escape loneliness and depression.

Kohut's thinking has led the way for a new psychoanalytic interest in the self and for the treatment of problems such as disorders of the self. Rather than being driven by unconscious conflicts and impulses, Kohut sees patients today as often deprived of **empathic mirroring** and ideal "objects" (people) for identification. Because their parents were walled off from them emotionally, or too involved with their own narcissistic needs, they did not provide the necessary models for healthy development of the self and for the formation of meaningful, responsive relationships in adulthood.

People fear the destruction of the self when they don't feel the empathic human responses from the important others ("self objects") in their lives. Kohut compares this state to being deprived of **psychological oxygen**. The availability of empathic reactions from self objects is as vital to the survival of the self as the presence of oxygen is to the survival of the body: "What leads to the human self's destruction is its exposure to the coldness, the indifference of the nonhuman, the nonempathical responding world" (Kohut, 1984, p. 18).

What is feared most is not so much physical death, but a world in which our humanness would end forever (Kohut, 1980, 1984). In the same vein, Kohut does not see

Freud's castration anxiety as the ultimate human anxiety: "... the little boy's manifest horror at the sight of the female genitals is not the deepest layer of this experience ... behind it and covered by it lies a deeper and even more dreadful experience—the experience of the faceless mother, that is, the mother whose face does not light up at the sight of her child" (Kohut, 1984, p. 21).

This type of anxiety about being in a totally uncaring, unresponsive world is experienced in a dream that one of Kohut's patients had (1984, p. 19). In his "stainless steel world" dream, Mr. U. was in an ice tunnel with walls from which large, glistening strands of ice went down to the ground and up to the ceiling. It was like an enormous model of the human heart, large enough to be walked around in (like one in a museum the patient knew well). Walking within this icy heart, Mr. U. felt the anxiety of an oncoming but unnamed danger to which he was exposed, all alone, except for a shadowy figure to whom he appealed but who was unresponsive. In a flash, he was pulled through a crack in the wall into a cityscape that was blindingly bright—a landscape that was utterly unreal, with busy but completely unapproachable people all around: a "stainless steel world" in the patient's own words, in a science fiction scene with no escape, no communication, trapped forever, unreachable in a world of cold-heartedness.

Kohut's theory also leads to a reinterpretation of such Freudian constructs as the "Oedipal period." In his view, during this period the boy fears confrontation from a mother who is nonempathic and sexually seductive rather than affectionate and accepting of him. He also fears confrontation from a father who is competitive and hostile with him rather than pleased and proud. In parallel fashion, during the same period the girl fears confrontation from a father who is nonempathic and sexually seductive instead of affectionate and accepting. At the same time, she also fears a mother who is competitive and hostile rather than reflecting that she is proud of the child and pleased by her.

In Kohut's theory, if parents fail to respond empathically and healthily to their child in this phase of development, it sets up a defect in the self. As a result, the child develops a tendency to experience sexual fantasies and the fragments of love rather than love. Likewise, the child with a defective self also tends to experience hostile fantasies and only the fragments of assertiveness rather than appropriate assertiveness. The individual's typical internal reaction to these experiences becomes great anxiety. These characteristics of the defective self contrast with those of a healthy, normal personality, which, instead of anxiety and fragmented experiences, feels the glow of appropriate sexual functioning and assertiveness, as summarized in Table 9.7.

Relational Therapy and Restoration of the Self

Led by theorists like Kohut, **relational therapy** (also called "object relations therapy") has emerged as a coherent approach to treating personality problems. It is a psychodynamic approach in the sense that its roots are in earlier psychoanalytic theories. Like

TABLE 9.7 Kohut's Characteristics of the Self and Mental Health

Defective Self	Healthy Personality
Fragmented experience of love (sexual fantasies)	Feels glow of healthy pleasure in appropriate sexual functioning
Fragmented assertiveness (hostile in fantasies)	Able to be self-confidently assertive in pursuit of goals

them, its focus is on the individual's often unconscious, long-standing conflicts and defenses. It is distinctive, however, in three ways. It sees the history of these problems in early relationships, especially with the mother. It sees their expression in current relationships. Finally, it treats them by focusing on the interpersonal relationship within the therapy context.

9.20 Describe how relational therapy differs from traditional Freudian therapy.

In this approach, the therapist actively and empathically "engages" the patient to build a close therapeutic relationship. Interpretation and confrontation of basic relational problems occur in this supportive context. Note that this focus on the carefully nurtured empathic relationship contrasts with the "blank screen" image of the traditional Freudian analyst. The classic Freudian patient free associates while reclining on a couch, with the therapist sitting behind the patient. In relational therapy, the two face each other and interact actively, as the therapist provides empathic support as well as gradual confrontation.

▶ SUMMARY

TOWARD EGO PSYCHOLOGY AND THE SELF

- The psychoanalytic followers of Freud deemphasized the role of instincts and psychosexual stages.
- They concerned themselves more with the social milieu and the ego.
- Anna Freud described defense mechanisms that may serve the ego in coping with anxiety and life tasks. These mechanisms include repression, projection, reaction formation, rationalization, and sublimation.
- Jung emphasized the collective unconscious and its symbolic and mystical expressions. He focused on dreams and on the need to achieve unity through awareness of the collective and personal unconscious.
- Adler saw individuals as struggling from birth to overcome profound feelings of helplessness and inferiority by striving for perfection.
- According to Adler, people are social beings who are influenced more by cultural influences and personal relations than by sexual instincts.
- Fromm likewise saw people primarily as social beings who can be understood best in relation to others. Culture does not exist to stifle instinctual drives; instead, it is a product of the people in the society.

ERIKSON'S PSYCHOSOCIAL THEORY OF PERSONALITY DEVELOPMENT

- Erikson views social adaptation, not unconscious sexual urges, as the key force underlying development that takes place over an entire lifetime.
- Each of Erikson's developmental stages are characterized by psychosocial crises: trust versus mistrust, autonomy versus shame, initiative versus guilt, industry versus inferiority, identity versus role confusion, intimacy versus isolation, generativity versus self-absorption, and integrity versus despair.
- Most critical during this development is the evolution of "ego identity."

OBJECT RELATIONS THEORY AND THE SELF

- In object relations theory, the developing self is defined in relation to other "objects" or human beings.
- Klein observed that the young child splits the world into "good" and "bad" components.
- Kernberg and Kohut emphasize the mental representation of the self and other persons that develop in the early relationship with the primary caregiver.

ATTACHMENT: THE ROOTS OF OBJECT RELATIONS

- In attachment theory, the early relationship between the individual and his or her caregiver becomes the basic framework for the perception and experience of later relationships.
- Ainsworth's "Strange Situation" study assessed individual differences in attachment relations (insecure–avoidant, securely attached, or insecure–resistant) by putting the toddler in an unfamiliar setting with different levels of exposure to his or her mother.
- Kohut theorized that in Freud's time, families tended to expose their children to excessive emotional closeness, whereas children in the 21st century are more likely to have less parental exposure and emotional support, hence they may lack "empathic mirroring."
- Psychotherapy in this framework, called relational therapy, utilizes a close, empathic relationship between the therapist and the client to gradually confront conflicts and defenses. In this view, these problems developed out of difficulties in early relationships with primary caretakers, often the mother.

▶ KEY TERMS

analytical psychology 215
anima 216
animus 216
archetypes 216
autonomy versus shame and doubt 223
collective unconscious 215
compensatory motivation 219
competence 224
ego identity 224
ego psychology 210
ego psychologists 210
emotional overcloseness 234
empathic mirroring 234
generativity versus self-absorption and stagnation 225
homophobia 214
identity crisis 225
identity versus role confusion 224
industry versus inferiority 224
inferiority complex 219
initiative versus guilt 224
insecure–ambivalent 230
insecure–avoidant 230
integrity versus despair 225
internal working models 229
intimacy versus isolation 225
mandala 218
object relations theory 226
organ inferiority 219
primary caregiver 229
projection 213
psychological oxygen 234
psychosocial crisis 222
psychosocial stages 222
rationalization 215
reaction formation 213
relational self 227
relational therapy 235
safe haven 229
secure base 229
securely attached 230
shadow aspect 216
sibling rivalry 219
Strange Situation 229
sublimation 215
trust versus mistrust 222

TAKING STOCK

PART III

THE PSYCHODYNAMIC LEVEL

▶ OVERVIEW: FOCUS, CONCEPTS, METHODS

Some of the essentials of work at the Psychodynamic Level are summarized in the Overview table. The table reminds you that unconscious motives and psychodynamics within persons are viewed as the basic causes of their behavior, including their feelings, conflicts, and problems. Clinicians working at this level of analysis try to infer and interpret these causes from their overt "symptom-like" expressions in the individual's behaviors. Dreams, free associations, and responses to unstructured situations such as projective stimuli (e.g., the Rorschach inkblots), are especially favored sources of information. The responses from the person serve as indirect signs whose meaning and significance the clinician interprets. The role of the situation is deliberately minimized, guided by the belief that the more ambiguous the situation, the more likely it is that the individual's basic, underlying psychodynamics will be projected in how he or she interprets it and reacts.

Overview of Focus, Concepts, Methods: The Psychodynamic-Motivational Level

Basic units	Inferred motives and psychodynamics
Causes of behavior	Underlying stable motives and their unconscious transformations and conflicts
Behavioral manifestations of personality	Symptoms and "irrational" patterns of behavior (including dreams, "mistakes," and fantasies)
Favored data	Interpretations by expert judges (clinicians)
Observed responses used as	Indirect signs
Research focus	Personality dynamics and psychopathology; unconscious processes; defense mechanisms; the fragmented self
Approach to personality change	By insight into the motives and conflicts underlying behavior, by making the unconscious conscious
Role of situation	Deliberately minimized or ambiguous

In Freud's classic work, the focus of research, like the focus of personality assessment and of psychotherapy at this level of analysis, was on the person's unconscious psychodynamics and defenses. Those defenses disguise the underlying motives and conflicts that must be revealed and confronted in order for the individual to function well. Personality change requires insight into the disguised (unacceptable to the person) unconscious motives and dynamics that underlie the behavioral symptoms, so that they can be made conscious, accepted, and managed more rationally. When that occurs, the symptoms should diminish. In more recent work, however, increasing attention is being given to such concepts as the self, self-perception, and interpersonal relationship problems with significant others. In work over the last century by post-Freudians, the focus shifted to a greater concern with psychosocial, not just psychosexual development and life crises, extending over the entire life cycle, rather than just focused on the first few years of life. The ego psychologists and object relations theorists and clinicians called attention to the cognitive and ego processes essential for adaptive behavior, to the importance of attachment experiences rooted in the first few years of life but extending over the life cycle, and to the development of the self as an active agent. These revisions and extensions of Freud's contributions lead to a more optimistic view of human nature and the capacity of individuals to take account of the future, and to reconstrue the past, rather than to be the victims of their early history.

ENDURING CONTRIBUTIONS OF THE PSYCHODYNAMIC LEVEL

Freud and subsequent psychodynamic theorists and clinicians working at this level of analysis have had a profound impact on society and on philosophy, literature, and the arts, as well as on the social sciences. Freud's monumental contributions have been widely acknowledged. He opened the topic of childhood sexuality, revolutionized conceptions of the human psyche, provided strikingly powerful metaphors for the mind and human condition, and pioneered 20th-century psychiatry with his approach to the treatment of psychological problems. The evidence relevant to Freud's theory as a scientific psychological system, however, has been questioned persistently (e.g., Grunbaum, 1984).

Although Freud attempted to create a general psychology, his main work was with conflict-ridden persons caught up in personal crises. Freud observed these tortured individuals only under extremely artificial conditions: lying on a couch during the psychotherapy hour in an environment deliberately made as nonsocial as possible. This drastically restricted observational base helped to foster a theory that originally was almost entirely a theory of anxiety and internal conflict. It paid little attention to the social environment and to the interpersonal context of behavior. We have already seen that many of Freud's own followers greatly modified that initial emphasis and crafted a more ego-oriented and social, interpersonal approach. That trend is continuing.

This newer "ego psychology" and more "cognitive clinical psychology" is characterized by a greater focus on development beyond early childhood to include the entire life span. It attends more to the role of interpersonal relations and society and to the nature and functions of the concepts of ego and self and how the person thinks rather than to the id and its impulses. Freud's ideas thus have been going through a continuing revolution that goes beyond his own writings to the extensions introduced by his many followers over the years. The object relations theories of analysts such as Kohut and Kernberg are especially important innovations that seem to be changing psychodynamic theories substantially. They emphasize the self (rather than the instincts and the unconscious defenses against their expression) and thus have some similarity to the self theories discussed in later parts of this text.

One of the main criticisms of Freud's theory is that it is hard to test. Unfortunately, this criticism also applies (although to a lesser degree) to most of the later psychodynamic thinkers. That is true in part because psychodynamic constructs tend to have both the richness and the ambiguity of metaphors; while they may seem compelling intuitively, they are hard to quantify. Rooted in clinical experience and clinical language, the terms often are loose and metaphoric and convey different meanings in different contexts. The theory also requires the user to have available a clinical background with much experience and training as the framework and language on which the constructs draw.

These criticisms notwithstanding, many of the key concepts from the theory are still central in different areas of contemporary psychology, psychiatry, and clinical practice, and some of these have been modified and extensively researched, leading to many new insights and discoveries (e.g., Andersen, Chen, & Miranda, 2002; Bargh, 1997; Kihlstrom, 1999; Miller et al., 1996; Wilson, 2002). Especially vigorous efforts have been made to deal with defense mechanisms and conflict, and to submit them to experimental study (e.g., Blum, 1953; Erdelyi, 1985; Holmes, 1974; Sears, 1943, 1944; Silverman, 1976; Westen & Gabbard, 1999). Likewise, much modern work on the nature and development of human attachment, in the view of some of its leaders, is bringing "psychodynamic psychology back to life" (Shaver & Mikulincer, 2005, p. 22). You already saw some of the research that psychoanalytic ideas have influenced, and you will see many more examples throughout the text.

Particularly exciting in recent years is the renewed interest in psychodynamic concepts such as the unconscious, in light of new discoveries about mental processes (e.g., attention, thinking, and memory) emerging from the study of cognitive psychology. There are many interesting parallels, and people certainly are not aware of all the things that happen in their minds. Modern cognitive psychology has understandably stimulated a sympathetic reexamination of the nature of unconscious processes and their adaptive value for many aspects of human functioning (e.g., Kihlstrom, 1999; Wilson, 2002).

There is much evidence that unconscious processes and events influence us massively. For example, individuals with amnesia continue to be affected by previous experiences, although they cannot remember them (Kihlstrom, Barnhardt, & Tataryn, 1992). All sorts of information that influences how different individuals encode (interpret) and evaluate their social environments is acquired unconsciously (e.g., Lewicki et al., 1992). And most of what we feel and believe and do may be elicited or triggered automatically without conscious control or awareness (e.g., Bargh, 1997). Thus, the reality of unconscious processes is now accepted as a fact. However, their nature has been reconceptualized, with the recognition that many of the processes that function outside awareness are adaptive and efficient rather than defensive and maladaptive (e.g., Wilson, 2002).

In sum, when these contributions are put in perspective, they are most impressive. Especially notable is the continued recognition of the importance of motives and conflicts often operating at levels outside the person's full awareness. Likewise, work at this level called attention to the self-protective nature of the mind, and the diverse defense operations people use to reduce anxiety and to try to make themselves feel better about themselves. Unfortunately, while these defenses may reduce anxiety in the short term, they often come with substantial long-term costs to the self and to others. This list merely hints at the enormous contributions made by a genius and his colleagues and followers, beginning more than a hundred years ago, and still being vigorously pursued in current thinking, theory, research, and clinical applications.

PART 

THE BEHAVIORAL-CONDITIONING LEVEL

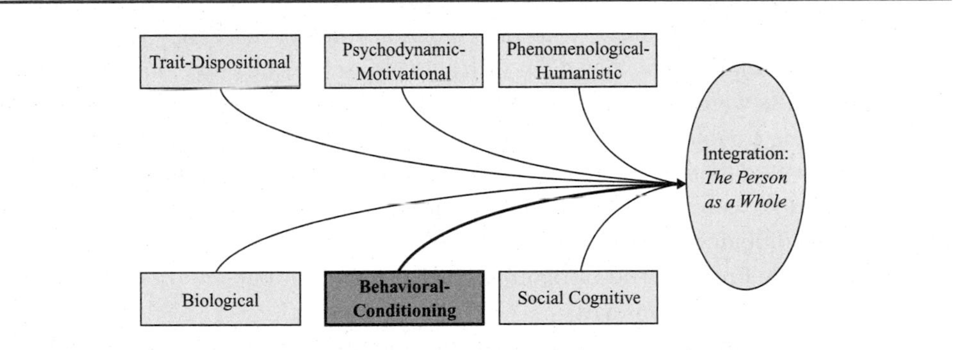

PRELUDE TO PART IV: THE BEHAVIORAL-CONDITIONING LEVEL

Mr. Z. was institutionalized in a large midwestern state mental hospital for psychotic patients in the 1950s. Pacing in a day-room with broken chairs and filled with the screams of disturbed people, he was a portrait of distress and isolation. At the center of this huge, bleak room was a glassed-in, walled nursing station, behind which the staff and occasional visiting physician took shelter. The ward was high security, with bars on the windows and locked doors everywhere. Medications for helping to deal with psychotic outbursts and aggressive rages were still in their infancy. In this kind of bedlam, some psychologists formed a hypothesis. They thought that the patients' wild behavior might in part be a function of the fact that the only time staff emerged to have any contact with them was when they began to act up. Might there be a relationship between the display of disturbed behavior and the conditions under which they received any kind of human attention? Might psychotic behavior actually be inadvertently strengthened by the hospital conditions under which they lived and the contingencies under which they received attention? Systematic studies over the years showed that even under less extreme conditions in human relationships, people often unintentionally reinforced and strengthened in each other the very behaviors that they were trying to control.

In Europe, in the first half of the last century, Freud's followers were capturing the attention of the clinical world with their psychoanalytic approaches to the treatment of personality problems. At the same time in the United States, psychologists were committing themselves to the scientific, experimental study of behavior under well-controlled laboratory conditions. Often they used animals as subjects so that intrusive experimental manipulations could be done (e.g., on how fears are learned) that were not possible to conduct with human beings. Committed to building a science of personality, they wanted to only study events that they could observe directly and objectively. Therefore, they deliberately avoided asking questions about anything that they felt they could not test experimentally. So they did not want to deal with questions about what people are like (Trait-Dispositional Level), or what their unconscious conflicts might be (Psychodynamic-Motivational Level), or what their "real" selves and internal experiences could be (Phenomenological-Humanistic Level).

Instead, they insisted on studying what organisms—whether rats or pigeons or people—actually *do*, and linking it to the conditions under which they do it. If they could not do this with people, they did it with animals. At the same time, however, some of these scientists were personally intrigued by Freud's clinical work, and its potential value for helping troubled people. Two pioneers, Neal Miller and John Dollard at Yale University, devoted themselves to make his ideas testable in experiments. As a first step, they translated the core ideas about conflict and anxiety into the language of learning theory and conditioning in ways that could be tested in experiments with animals. Their attempts to study Freud's ideas in rigorous experiments with rats are presented at the start of the first chapter in this part.

To apply the principles of learning to the study of personality, researchers also drew on earlier work in experimental psychology. That work, beginning with Pavlov in Russia, had shown how emotional reactions, both positive and negative, to previously neutral stimuli may be acquired through simple conditioning principles. The excitement here was that the analysis of learning promised to become a more scientific way of understanding some of the complex phenomena that had been discovered by Freud and his followers.

Learning, of course, occurs in various ways, and another breakthrough came in the contributions of the behaviorist B.F. Skinner and his many disciples. Not unlike Freud, Skinner also was often attacked, and often with good reason. Nevertheless, he provided a novel way for thinking about personality and above all, for applying the principles of learning to improve the human condition, as described in this part of the text.

Because of the intense focus on behavior in the work done at this level, one may ask: The Behavioral Level seems to be all about *behavior*, but what about personality? For researchers at this level, the route to changing anything on the "inside"—feelings, cognitions, personality—is by understanding the person's behavior and the "conditions that control it," and then using that knowledge to help the individual to behave in more adaptive, functional ways (e.g., O'Donohue, Henderson, Hayes, Fisher, & Hayes, 2001). They assume that if problematic behaviors like stutters, tics, debilitating fears, or inappropriate patterns of impulsive or overcontrolled behaviors are modified appropriately, then the internal states and stable qualities of the individual will essentially "catch up" and also change. A person who could not speak in public but now can is likely to feel and become less shy, for example.

Work at the Behavioral-Conditioning Level began in experimental psychology and remained isolated from mainstream work in personality research for many years. More recently, as part of the emerging integration among the various levels of analysis, these contributions are being connected to developments at the other levels of analyses, as you will see in subsequent parts of the text, particularly when we turn to the social cognitive level that builds directly on it.

THE PERSONAL SIDE OF THE SCIENCE

Some questions at the Behavioral-Conditioning Level you might ask about yourself:

- How are important behavior patterns, including emotions and fears, learned?
- How does what I do and feel depend on my earlier experiences?
- How can my behavior and feelings be modified by new learning experiences?
- Do aspects of my personality depend on the contexts in which I find myself?
- How am I different when with a good friend at school and when with my family at home for the holidays? Why?

CHAPTER 10

BEHAVIORAL CONCEPTIONS

Within the boundaries set by human genes and biological predispositions, what people become is influenced importantly by learning. Through learning, things that attract one person may come to repel another, just as one individual's passions may become another's nightmares. Much is known about human learning, and it can be harnessed to influence people for good or for ill.

In this chapter and in the next, you will find some approaches to personality that focus on the level of learning through conditioning. These approaches are called behavioral theories, or learning-conditioning theories, and several different varieties have been formulated. In this chapter, we consider some of the original classic concepts of this approach; in later chapters, we examine its more recent developments and applications.

Work relevant to personality conducted at this level has been done primarily by psychologists dedicated to the rigorous, scientific study of psychology, who were heavily influenced by research on the nature of the learning process. In work that began early in the last century, they devoted themselves to the development of an experimental methodology. Their goal was to conduct research that was experimental and yet relevant to understanding complex social behavior and individual differences. Guided by strategies in other natural sciences, they began with careful study of learning and performance in lower animals in highly controlled laboratory situations. While some were fascinated by the bold speculations about the mind that were coming at the same time from theorists like Sigmund Freud, most were skeptical about the use of informal clinical methods and case studies. Rather than probe the dreams and free associations of neurotic patients or theorize broadly about human nature and society, these researchers sought a system that would be objectively testable, preferably by laboratory techniques.

Psychologists working at this level studied the learning mechanisms through which certain events—"stimuli"—become associated with particular behaviors or responses. Like all scientific theorists, they wanted to understand causes—in this case, learning or the ways in which stimuli become associated with responses. The basic assumptions of the learning theories may appear at first glance quite different from those of psychodynamic theories. Yet they try to provide complementary accounts of many of the same basic personality phenomena. To illustrate this fundamental interrelatedness of these different levels of analyses, we begin this chapter with what may be the most systematic attempt to translate some of Freud's ideas into the concepts and language of learning.

10.1 What causal factors in personality are the focus of the behavioral level of analysis?

▶ THE BEHAVIORAL APPROACH TO PSYCHODYNAMICS: DOLLARD AND MILLER

In this section, we concentrate on the theory developed at Yale University in the late 1940s by John Dollard and Neal Miller, who were fascinated by Freud's bold speculations about the mind. But they were also skeptical about his informal clinical methods and were motivated to really test his ideas. We will call their orientation **psychodynamic behavior theory** because it is the major effort to integrate some of the fundamental ideas of Freudian psychodynamic theory with the concepts, language, and methods of experimental laboratory research on behavior and learning. Although this work began as a translation of Freud's core concepts into the language and ideas of theory, it went much beyond translation by also opening the way to extensive experimental research into the basic processes involved.

Neurotic Conflict: The Core

Freud conceptualized conflict and anxiety as fundamental for understanding personality, both normal and abnormal, and saw them as the core ingredients of neurotic behavior. In Freud's formulation, **neurotic conflict** involves a clash between id impulses seeking expression and internalized inhibitions that censor and restrain the expression of those impulses in accord with the culture's taboos. Dollard and Miller state the same basic ideas in the language of learning theory.

In their view of neurosis, strong fear (anxiety) is a learned drive that motivates a conflict concerning "goal responses" for other strong drives, such as sex or aggression—the impulses that also were basic for Freud. Specifically, when the neurotic person—or even the young child—begins to approach goals that might reduce such drives as sex or aggression, strong fear is elicited in him or her. Such fear may be elicited by thoughts relevant to the drive goals, as well as by any overt approach attempts. For example, sexual wishes or hostile feelings toward a parent may be frightening; hence a conflict ensues between the wishes and the fear triggered by their expression. These inhibitory fearful responses further prevent drive reduction, so that the blocked drives (such as sex and aggression) continue to "build up" to a higher level. The person is thus trapped in an unbearable neurotic conflict between frustrated, pent-up drives and the fear connected with approach responses relevant to their release.

10.2 How did Dollard and Miller translate Freud's concept of neurotic conflict into learning theory terms?

The neurotic person in this dilemma may be stimulated simultaneously by the frustrated drives and by the fear that they evoke. The high drive state connected with this conflict produces "misery" and interferes with clear thinking, discrimination, and effective problem solving. The "symptoms" shown arise from the buildup of the drives and of the fear that inhibits their release.

► RECASTING CONFLICT IN LEARNING TERMS

The study of approach–avoidance tendencies and the dilemmas that they can produce has been a core topic of personality psychology ever since Sigmund Freud made conflict the center of his theory a hundred years ago. Because these conflicts create anxiety, the individual, according to Freud, engages in massive unconscious efforts to reduce it, which in turn can produce all sorts of difficulties and symptoms. The problem for scientists early in the last century was that such conflicts were very difficult to study experimentally. To make approach–avoidance conflicts open to experimental research, John Dollard and Neal Miller (1950), working at the behavioral level of analysis years later, attempted to rethink psychodynamic conflicts in the language of learning. These were pioneering attempts to integrate the two levels of analysis in the study of goal pursuit. Given that there is much current interest in the approach and avoidance systems as key aspects of personality, the classic work of these pioneers has renewed relevance.

These researchers hypothesized approach and avoidance tendencies, and analyzed them in careful experiments with animals. In such conflicts, the organism, at least momentarily, is torn between two desirable goals. Just as conflict was central to Freud's conception of personality dynamics, so it was at the core of Dollard and Miller's theory. But whereas Freud developed his ideas about conflict from inferences regarding id–ego–superego clashes in his neurotic patients, Dollard and Miller tested their ideas in controlled experiments with rats. Their findings shed light on understanding some of the problems of Freud's patients in more objective terms.

Their original theory of conflict was based on a number of animal experiments (e.g., Brown, 1942, 1948; Miller, 1959). In one study, for example, hungry rats learned how to run down an alley to get food at a distinctive point in the maze. To generate **ambivalence** (approach–avoidance tendencies), the rats were given a quick electric shock while they were eating. To test the resulting conflict between approach to the food and avoidance of the shock, the rats were later placed again at the start of the alley. The hungry rat started toward the food but halted and hesitated before reaching it.

Dollard and Miller applied the concept of **goal gradients** to analyze these conflicts. Goal gradients are changes in response strengths as a function of distance from the goal object. To assess the strength of approach and avoidance tendencies at different points from the goal, a harness apparatus was devised to measure a rat's pull toward a positive reinforcement (food) or away from a negative reinforcement or punishment (shock). The harness enabled the experimenter to restrain the rat for a moment along the route to the goal and measure (in grams) the strength of the animal's pull on the harness at each test point (Brown, 1948). In this type of situation, the rats could be given different experiences that led the same response from them to become associated both with approach motivation (the food) and with avoidance motivation (the electric shock). First, the hungry rats learned to run the maze to get the food that was waiting for them at the end, thus developing **approach tendencies**. Then sometimes they also received the electric shock at the end of the maze, which led their maze-running response to also become associated with punishment, analogous to the dilemmas of

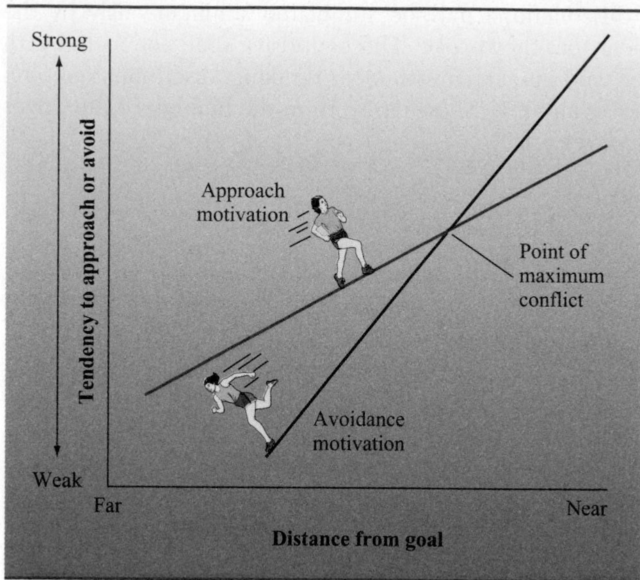

Figure 10.1 According to Neal Miller's analysis of approach–avoidance conflicts, both the tendency to approach and the tendency to avoid grow stronger as one moves closer to the goal. However, the tendency to avoid increases faster than the tendency to approach. Maximum conflict is experienced when the two gradients cross, because at this point the opposing motives are equal in strength.

Source: Smith, R.E. (1993). *Psychology*. St. Paul, MN: West. Reprinted with permission.

Freud's patients whose socially unacceptable desires also had become associated with fear of punishment.

After being shocked, the next time the rat is hungry and is in this maze, it faces an approach–avoidance conflict. This type of conflict is shown in Figure 10.1 (but illustrated with a human figure rather than a rat). Running toward the goal is associated with hunger reduction and induces approach tendencies. But it is also associated with getting electric shock, which makes running in the opposite direction a way to reduce the fear drive. As a result, the runner goes in both directions, first forward toward the food, and then away. Interestingly, the researchers found that when far from the goal, the approach tendency was stronger than the avoidance tendency, hence producing approach behavior. However, as the goal got nearer, the strength of the avoidance tendency increased sharply, leading to running in the opposite direction. The laboratory rats in the experiments stopped at the point where the approach and avoidance pulls became equalized, essentially torn equally in both directions. And at least by analogy, that is also the neurotic dilemma of persons afflicted with intense approach–avoidance conflicts (e.g., desiring sexual gratification but also fearful of it), and become psychologically paralyzed.

Primary Needs and Learning

In this learning reinterpretation, the newborn infant begins life with a set of *innate* or **primary biological needs**, such as the need for food and water, oxygen, and warmth. Satisfaction of these needs is essential for the organism's survival. But although these needs are innate, the behaviors required to satisfy them involve learning.

The most casual observation of other cultures quickly reveals that there are almost endless ways to fulfill even such primary needs as hunger and thirst. Through learning, great variability develops in the ways in which needs are fulfilled. Consider, for example, food preferences: The gourmet dishes of one culture may be the causes of nausea in another. The same learned variability seen in food preferences is also found in standards of shelter, clothing aesthetics, and values when one compares different cultures.

Most human behaviors involve goals and incentives whose relations to innate needs are extremely remote. People seem to strive for such exceedingly diverse goals as money, status, power, love, charity, competence, mastery, creativity, self-realization, and so on—as was discussed in earlier chapters. These and many more strivings have been characterized and classified as human motives. Neal Miller and John Dollard explored the learning processes through which such motives may evolve from primary needs.

Starting with the basic assumption that behavior is learned, Dollard and Miller (1950) constructed a learning theory to explain the wide range of behavior involved in normal personality, neurosis, and psychotherapy. In their view, the four important factors in the learning process are drive (motivation), cue (stimulus), response (act or thought), and reinforcement (reward). In its simplest form, their idea is that "In order to learn one must want something, notice something, do something, and get something" (Miller & Dollard, 1941, p. 2).

10.3 Describe the four central concepts in the learning process, according to Dollard and Miller.

These four events correspond respectively to "drive," "cue," "response," and "reward" ("reinforcement"). Learning, in their view, is the process through which a particular response and a cue stimulus become connected.

Think of an animal in the psychologist's laboratory. Motivated by the *drive* of hunger, the animal engages in diffuse activity. At one point, the animal happens to see a lever *(cue)*. Its *response*, at first accidental, is to press the lever, and this action releases food into his cup. The animal eats the food at once, thereby reducing tension of his hunger drive *(reward* or *reinforcement)*. Now in the future when the animal is hungry, it is more likely to press the lever again: The association between the cue stimulus (the lever) and the response (pressing it) has been strengthened. On subsequent trials, the hungry animal will press the lever sooner. Let us consider each of the four components separately.

Drive

For Dollard and Miller (1950), any strong stimuli may impel action and thus serve as drives. The stronger the stimulus, the greater its **drive** or motivating function. A mild stimulus (such as the faint sound of a distant horn) does not motivate behavior as much as a strong stimulus (the blare of the horn near one's ear). Examples of strong stimuli are hunger pangs and pain-inducing noise—they motivate behavior. While any stimulus may become strong enough to act as a drive, certain classes of stimuli (such as hunger, thirst, fatigue, pain, and sex) are the primary basis for most motivation. These stimuli are "primary" or innate drives. The strength of the primary drives varies with the **conditions of deprivation**: The greater the deprivation, the stronger the drive. Like Freud, Dollard and Miller's theory of drives was based on a "hydraulic" or steam boiler model. The buildup of a drive, like the steam in a boiler as the temperature rises, increasingly presses for release of discharge. When release occurs, the drive is reduced. Drive reduction is satisfying or "reinforcing" (as discussed further in the concept of "reinforcement" below).

Often the operation of primary drives is not easy to observe directly. Society generally protects its members from the unpleasant force of strong primary drives by providing for their reduction before they become overwhelming. Moreover, social

10.4 Differentiate between primary and secondary drives. In what sense is fear both a learned response and a learned drive that can result in reinforcement?

inhibitions—for example, in the area of sex—may further prevent the direct or complete public expression of primary drives. Consequently, much visible behavior is motivated by already altered "secondary" or **learned drives**. It is these learned drives (or motivations) that are most evident under conditions of modern society and that are important in civilized human behavior.

According to Dollard and Miller, learned drives are acquired on the basis of the primary (unlearned, innate) drives and are elaborations of them. The acquisition of fear as a learned drive has been studied carefully. (Some of the specific mechanisms of such learning are discussed in detail in the next chapter.) A fear is learned if it occurs in response to previously neutral cues (e.g., a white room). A learned fear is also a drive in the sense that it motivates behavior (e.g., escape from the room), and its reduction is reinforcing.

In one study, rats were exposed to electric shock in a white compartment and were permitted to escape to a black compartment where there was no shock (Miller, 1948). Eventually the rats responded with fear to the white compartment alone (i.e., without the shock). Even when the shock (primary drive stimulus) was no longer present, the animals learned new responses, such as pressing a lever or turning a wheel, in order to escape from the harmless white compartment. In commonsense terms, they behaved as if they were afraid of an objectively harmless stimulus. The motivation for this new learning lies, according to Miller and Dollard, in the learned fear of the white compartment. Thus, fear is conceptualized as both a learned response and a learned drive, and its reduction is considered to be a reinforcement.

Dollard and Miller's drives, both "primary" and "secondary," are like Freud's motives and impulses as the forces underlying behavior. While Freud's conceptualization stresses instinctual impulses, however, Dollard and Miller's makes room for many learned motives, whose roots are in primary drives.

Cue

"The drive impels a person to respond. Cues determine when he will respond, where he will respond and which response he will make" (Dollard & Miller, 1950, p. 32). The lunch bell, for example, functions as a **cue** for hungry schoolchildren to put away their books and get their lunchboxes. Cues may be auditory, visual, olfactory, and so on. They may vary in intensity, and various combinations of stimuli may function as cues. Changes, differences, and the direction and size of differences may be more distinctive cues than is an isolated stimulus. For example, a person may not know the absolute length of an unmarked line but yet be able to tell which of two lines is longer.

Response

Before a **response** to a cue can be rewarded and learned, it must of course occur. Dollard and Miller suggest ranking the organism's responses according to their probability of occurrence. They call this order the "initial hierarchy." Learning changes the order of responses in the hierarchy. An initially weak response, if properly rewarded, may come to occupy the dominant position. The new hierarchy produced by learning is termed the "resultant hierarchy." With learning and development, the hierarchy of responses becomes linked to language, and is heavily influenced by the culture in which social learning has occurred.

Reinforcement

A **reinforcement** is a specific event that strengthens the tendency for a response to be repeated. For Miller and Dollard, reinforcement involved **drive reduction** or tension reduction (e.g., when the hungry schoolchildren ate their lunch, their hunger drive was [temporarily] reduced). Miller and Dollard, guided by their hydraulic or boiler model of drives, believed that drives that are not released continue to build up like steam in the boiler, creating tension and pressing for discharge, as noted before. It is the reduction of tension—drive-reduction—that is the organism's goal: when it happens, it is reinforcing or rewarding.

10.5 According to Dollard and Miller, how do reinforcement and extinction occur?

A reduction of a drive reinforces any immediately preceding response. The reduction or avoidance of painful, aversive stimulation, and of learned fears or anxieties associated with pain and punishment, also may function as a reinforcement (Miller, 1948). If taking a Brand X headache pill quickly decreases a severe headache (aversive stimulation), the reduction of pain will reinforce the behavior of taking Brand X headache pills. Reinforcement is essential to the maintenance of a habit as well as to its learning. **Extinction** is the gradual elimination of a tendency to perform a response; it occurs when that response is repeated without reinforcement. You take Brand X headache pills but on many repeated occasions it is no longer followed by pain reduction. The time required to extinguish a habit depends on the habit's initial strength and on the conditions of the extinction situation. According to Dollard and Miller, extinction merely inhibits the old habit; it does not destroy it. If new responses performed during extinction are rewarded, they may be strengthened to the point where they supersede the old habit. For example, if a child is praised and rewarded for independent, autonomous play but consistently unrewarded (extinguished) when he or she dependently seeks help, the independent pattern will become predominant over the dependent one.

Conflict

Individuals may experience **conflict** when they want to pursue two or more goals that are mutually exclusive. For example, Shane may want to spend the evening with a friend but thinks he should prepare for an examination facing him the next morning; or Winnie may want to express her anger at her parents but also does not want to hurt them. When an individual must choose among incompatible alternatives, he or she may experience conflict.

10.6 What is the basis for conflicts? What major forms do they take?

Neal Miller's (1959) conceptualization of conflict, which is influenced by Lewin (1935), hypothesizes **approach** and **avoidance tendencies**. For example, in an **approach–approach conflict**, the person is torn, at least momentarily, between two desirable goals. Conversely, people often face **avoidance–avoidance conflicts** between two undesirable alternatives: to study tediously for a dull subject or flunk the examination, for example. The individual may wish to avoid both of these aversive events, but each time he starts to move away from his desk, he reminds himself how awful it would be to fail the test.

Some of the most difficult conflicts involve goals or incentives that are simultaneously positive and negative. These are the goals or incentives that elicit mixed feelings or ambivalent attitudes. For example, we may want the pleasure of a gourmet treat but not the calories, or we may desire the fun of a vacation spree but not the expense, or we may love certain aspects of a parent but hate others.

Recall that approach–avoidance conflicts had a predominant place in Freud's hypotheses regarding intrapsychic clashes—for example, between id impulses and inhibitory anxieties. Just as conflict is central to Freud's conception of personality dynamics, so it is the core of Dollard and Miller's theory. But whereas Freud developed his ideas about conflict from inferences regarding id–ego–superego clashes in his neurotic patients, Dollard and Miller tested their ideas in controlled experiments with rats (e.g., Brown, 1942, 1948; Miller, 1959).

Briefly, their model proposes the simultaneous existence of drive-like forces (approach tendencies) and of inhibitory forces (avoidance tendencies). Predictions about behavior in an approach–avoidance conflict involve inferences about the strength of the approach tendencies and of the inhibiting forces, the resulting behavior being a function of their net effect. Within this general framework of drive-conflict theory, many formulations have been advanced that are similar to the intrapsychic conflicts between id impulses and ego defenses that are crucial in Freud's theory.

Anxiety and Repression

10.7 How are anxiety and repression translated into learning theory terms? How does this approach explain repression?

Like Freud, but unlike most behaviorists, Dollard and Miller accept unconscious factors as critically important determinants of behavior, and, again like Freud, they give anxiety (or learned fear) a central place in dynamics. In their view, repression involves the learned response of **not-thinking** of something and is motivated by the drive of fear. That is, due to past experiences, certain thoughts may have come to arouse fear as a result of their associations with pain or punishment. By not-thinking these thoughts, the fear stimuli are reduced and the response (of not-thinking) is further reinforced. Eventually, not-thinking (inhibiting, stopping, repressing) becomes anticipatory, in the sense that the individual avoids particular thoughts before they can lead to painful outcomes. This formulation is similar to Freud's idea that repression is the result of anxiety caused when unacceptable material starts to emerge from the unconscious to the conscious but is repressed before it gets there.

Dollard and Miller's account thus serves as a clear translation of the psychodynamic formulation of anxiety, repression, and defense into the terms of reinforcement learning theory. Defenses and symptoms (e.g., phobias, hysterical blindness) are reinforced by the immediate reduction of the fear. While the temporary effect of the symptom is reduction of the fear drive and momentary relief, its long-range effects may be debilitating. For example, a phobic symptom may prevent a person from working effectively and hence create new dilemmas, fear, guilt, and other conditions of high drive conflict.

Reactions to Psychodynamic Behavior Theory

10.8 Summarize the major contributions and criticisms of psychodynamic learning theory.

Freud had constructed a theory of development without the benefit of learning concepts. He adopted a body of language and invented new terms that made it difficult to coordinate his theory with experimental psychology. Dollard and Miller demonstrated that this coordination could be achieved. They drew on laboratory research with animals to devise a personality theory in learning terms that closely paralleled, and in many respects translated, Freudian theory. The psychodynamic emphasis on motives, on unconscious processes, and on internal conflicts and defenses, such as repression, remained largely unchanged. Many psychologists found Freud's basic ideas more congenial and easier to adopt when they were put into the language of learning and experimental psychology. Consequently, these concepts stimulated much research.

Other psychologists were troubled because the research by Miller and his colleagues was based mainly on animal studies. Indeed, this fact has earned it some of its greatest criticism over the years. Careful investigation carried out with a lower species, such as the rat, whose behavior is far removed from human problems, may not hold up when extrapolations are made to people. Many critics have objected that human social behavior is fundamentally different than the behavior of animals in the laboratory and therefore requires a different methodology. Some critics were repelled by the analogies between rat and person and believed that in the transition from the clinic to the laboratory, some of the most exciting features of Freud's view of people were lost. Of course the real test of a position is not its appeal to friends and critics, but the research and conceptual advances it produces.

We now turn to the basic research that provided the foundation for Miller and Dollard's theory, and that still is a basis for understanding how some important aspects of personality may develop, are maintained, and sometimes can be changed dramatically. It also offered a way of making irrational fears and some of the other phenomena Freud identified less mysterious and more open to scientific testing.

▶ CLASSICAL CONDITIONING: LEARNING EMOTIONAL ASSOCIATIONS

Strong human positive and negative emotions, often complex and seemingly irrational, including negative feelings such as intense fears, and positive feelings, as in attraction, love, and patriotism, may be acquired through the simple processes of classical conditioning. It is therefore important to understand the basic rules of **conditioning** because they help to take the mystery out of many of the complex emotions we all experience. Knowing these rules is especially useful because we often experience strong negative emotions without awareness of why and how they originated, or how we might be able to change our feelings when they create serious problems for us—like being unable to take a desired job because it happens to be on a high floor.

Classical conditioning or **conditioned-response learning** is a type of learning, first demonstrated by the Russian psychologist Ivan Pavlov, in which a neutral stimulus (e.g., a bell) becomes conditioned by being paired or associated with an unconditioned stimulus (one that is naturally powerful).

Ivan Pavlov (1849–1936)

(*Source*: Corbis-Bettmann)

How Classical Conditioning Works

A dog automatically salivates when food is in its mouth. The response of salivation is a **reflex** or **unconditioned response (UCR)**: it is natural and does not have to be learned. Like most other reflexes, in humans and in animals alike, salivation helps the organism adjust or adapt: the saliva aids in digesting the food. Stimuli that elicit unconditioned responses are called **unconditioned stimuli (UCS)**. The unconditioned stimulus (food in this example) can elicit behavior without any prior learning.

10.9 Define UCS, UCR, CS, and CR. How are conditioned responses learned?

Any dog owner knows that a hungry dog may salivate at the mere sight of food, before it gets any in its mouth. The dog may even begin to salivate at the sight of the empty dish in which the food is usually served. Salivating at the sight of the empty dish that has been associated with food is an example of a learned or **conditioned response (CR)**. The stimulus that elicits a conditioned response is called a **conditioned** (learned) **stimulus (CS)**, in this case the dish: its impact on behavior is not automatic but depends on learning.

Pavlov discovered some of the ways in which such neutral stimuli as lights and metronome clicks could become conditioned stimuli capable of eliciting responses like salivating. His pioneering experiments with dogs began with his repeatedly making a certain sound whenever he gave his dogs their food. After a while he found that the dogs salivated to the sound even when it was no longer followed by food: conditioning had occurred. This type of learning is what we now call classical conditioning.

To sum up, in classical conditioning the participant is repeatedly exposed to a neutral stimulus (i.e., one that elicits no special response) presented closely in time preceding an unconditioned stimulus that elicits an unconditioned response. When this association becomes strong enough, the neutral stimulus by itself may begin to elicit a response similar to the one produced by the unconditioned stimulus. (See Tables 10.1 and 10.2 for basic definitions and examples.)

Higher-Order Conditioning

When a previously neutral stimulus, such as a light, a bell, or a face, has become a conditioned stimulus through its association with an unconditioned stimulus, such as food or pain, it can in turn modify one's reactions to another neutral stimulus

TABLE 10.1 The Language of Classical Conditioning

Term	Definition
Unconditioned stimulus (UCS)	A stimulus to which one automatically, naturally responds without learning to do so.
Unconditioned response (UCR)	The unlearned response one naturally makes to an unconditioned stimulus. The response may be positive or negative (e.g., salivating when food is placed in the mouth; jerking one's hand away from a hot stove).
Conditioned stimulus (CS)	A previously neutral stimulus to which one learns to respond after it has been paired or associated with an unconditioned stimulus.
Conditioned response (CR)	The learned response to a conditioned stimulus. This response was previously made only to an unconditioned stimulus, but now it is made to a conditioned stimulus as a result of the pairing of the two stimuli.

TABLE 10.2 Examples of Possible Effects of Classical Conditioning

Before Conditioning	After Conditioning
Dog knocks child over (UCS) Child cries (UCR)	Dog approaches (CS) Child cries (CR)
Mother feeds and cuddles baby (UCS) Baby relaxes (UCR)	Baby smells mother's perfume (CS) Baby relaxes (CR)
Car accident injures woman (UCS) Woman is afraid (UCR)	Woman thinks about getting in car (CS) Woman is afraid (CR)
Man drives across swaying bridge (UCS) Man is afraid (UCR)	Man approaches another bridge (CS) Man is afraid and avoids bridge (CR)
Mother discovers her daughter masturbating, scolds her, slaps her hands (UCS) Daughter is hurt and afraid (UCR)	Daughter looks at her nude body (CS) Daughter feels anxious and negative about her body, particularly her genitals (CR)

by being associated with it. This process is called **higher-order conditioning**. It was demonstrated when Pavlov found that after a metronome sound had become a conditioned stimulus (by being paired with food), it could itself be paired with a neutral stimulus (such as a red light) and, as a result of that association, the neutral stimulus would also elicit the unconditioned response of salivation. In people, words and other complex symbols can be conditioned stimuli capable of evoking powerful emotional responses through higher-order conditioning.

10.10 How does higher-order conditioning underlie many of our likes and dislikes?

A wide variety of stimuli, including activities, individuals, groups, and events, are valued according to their associations with positive or negative outcomes and even mere labels. For example, when neutral items are paired with words like "dirty" and "ugly," they take on negative valuations, but the same items become positively evaluated when they have been associated with words like "beautiful" and "happy" (Staats & Staats, 1957). Likewise, the names of countries and political parties and the sight of national flags or the sounds of national anthems can come to arouse intense positive or negative feelings depending on their earlier associations.

Most experiments in classical conditioning are performed in the laboratory, but the knowledge they have generated may help us to understand many things that happen outside the laboratory, such as the development of affections and attractions (Byrne, 1969; Lott & Lott, 1968). For example, a liking for particular people and things may depend on the degree to which they have been associated with positive or pleasant experiences (Griffitt & Guay, 1969). If so, one's affection for a friend may be directly related to the degree to which he or she has been associated with gratifications for oneself.

Now consider the development of fear. How do initially neutral (or even positive) stimuli acquire the power to evoke fear? Suppose, for example, a person repeatedly sees a light and experiences an electric shock simultaneously. In time, the light by itself may come to evoke some of the emotional reaction produced by the shock. Neutral stimuli that are closely associated in time with any pain-producing stimulus then become conditioned stimuli that may elicit fear and avoidance reactions. Thus, the seemingly irrational fears that some people have may reflect a conditioned association between previously neutral stimuli and painful events.

Classical conditioning may influence development throughout a person's life. If, for example, sexual curiosity and fear-producing experiences (such as severe punishment)

How much we like a person may depend on the degree to which he or she has been associated with gratification.

(*Source*: Miton Steinberg/Stock, Boston)

are closely associated for a child, fear may be generated by various aspects of the individual's sexual behavior even after there is no longer any danger of punishment. And conditioning can spread as well as persist: the child who is made to feel bad about touching the genitals may also become anxious about other forms of sexual expression and may even develop broader fears. In a classic study, following a strategy that would not be tolerated now because of the ethical issues it raises, Watson and Rayner (1920) induced a severe fear of rats in a little boy named Albert, who had not been afraid of rats before. This was done by classical conditioning: just as Albert would reach for the rat, the experimenters would make a loud noise that frightened him. After he had experienced the rat and the aversive noise several times in close association, he developed a strong fear of the rat.

Albert's fear generalized so that later, when shown a variety of new furry stimuli such as cats, cotton, fur coats, human hair, and wool, he responded with obvious fear to them as well. His fear had spread to these new objects even though they had never been paired with the noise. This is an example, using a human being, of the kind of learning found when rats who were shocked in a white compartment began to respond fearfully to the compartment itself even when the shock no longer occurred (Miller, 1948). The case of Little Albert has become one of the first bases for applications of classical conditioning to the analysis and treatment of human problems.

As the *In Focus 10.1* example illustrates, the behavioral view of neurosis is concerned with anxiety and avoidance no less than the psychodynamic view, but it tries to link them to external circumstances rather than to internal conflicts (Redd, 1995; Redd, Porterfield, & Anderson, 1978). Through direct or vicarious frightening experiences, people often develop anxiety in response to particular objects, persons, or situations. Not only encountering these events in reality but even just thinking about them may be upsetting. These emotional reactions may generalize and take many forms. Common examples include muscle tensions, fatigue, and intense fear reactions to seemingly neutral stimuli.

IN FOCUS 10.1

A BEHAVIORAL CHALLENGE TO THE PSYCHODYNAMIC THEORY OF NEUROSIS

Differences between theoretical approaches are seen most clearly when applied to the same case. Behavior theorists have strongly challenged Freud's theory of neurosis by reanalyzing in learning terms a case that he presented. Recall that Freud's view of how neuroses develop begins with the child's aggressive or sexual impulses, which seek direct, immediate release. Because expression of these impulses may be punished severely, the child may become anxious about his own impulses and try to repress them. But the impulses continue to seek release and become increasingly pent up. Eventually they may be impossible to repress, and components of them may break through, creating further anxiety. To reduce this anxiety, the person may attempt a variety of defense mechanisms. In neurosis, these defenses begin to break down: the unacceptable impulses start to express themselves indirectly and symbolically in various disguised forms, such as in phobias or obsessive–compulsive thoughts and actions. The roots of neurosis, in Freud's view, are always in childhood:

> It seems that neuroses are acquired only in early childhood (up to the age of six), even though their symptoms may not make their appearance till much later. The childhood neurosis may become manifest for a short time or may even be overlooked. In every case the later neurotic illness links up with the prelude in childhood. (1933, pp. 41–42)

An example from Freud's (1963) theory is his published case of Little Hans. Hans was a 5-year-old boy who developed a horse phobia. He was afraid of being bitten by a horse and, after seeing a horse hitched to a wagon slip and fall on a street near his home, began to dread going out. Freud interpreted the phobia as an expression of the child's psychodynamic conflicts. These conflicts included his desires to seduce his mother and replace his father. These desires, in turn, made him fear castration by the father; symbolically, the horse came to represent the dreaded father.

A behavioral analysis of this case, however, explains Hans's phobia without invoking any internal conflicts or symbolism (Wolpe, 1997; Wolpe & Rachman, 1960). Namely, the scene Hans witnessed of a horse falling down and bleeding on the street was sufficiently frightening to the young child to produce fear. In turn, the fear generalized to all horses and resulted in Hans's avoidance behavior. Thus, a simple conditioning process might explain a phobia: since the horse was part of an intensely frightening experience, it became a conditioned stimulus for anxiety, and the anxiety generalized to other horses. The process is the same as in the case of Little Albert whose fear was induced by conditioning, as discussed in the text.

10.11 Compare Freud's analysis of Little Hans with the behavioral reinterpretation of the case.

Psychodynamic and behavioral theorists do agree that the neurotic individual may make all sorts of efforts to escape and avoid painful feelings. Many of his avoidance attempts may be maintained persistently because they serve to terminate the pain. For example, such elaborate avoidance defenses as obsessive–compulsive rituals, in the form of handwashing for many hours, may be maintained because they reduce the person's anxiety (Wolpe, 1963). In addition, attention and sympathy from relatives and friends for being sick or relief from pressures and obligations can also serve to maintain the anxious person's avoidance patterns by providing reinforcement for them.

From Trauma to Anxiety

Some of the clearest examples of anxiety reactions occur after the individual has experienced a threatening danger or trauma. A near-fatal automobile accident, an almost catastrophic combat experience, an airplane crash—such intense episodes of stress are often followed by anxiety. After the actual dangers have passed, stimuli that remind the individual of those dangers, or signs that lead him or her to expect new dangers, may reactivate anxiety and distort perceptions (e.g., Rachman & Cuk, 1992).

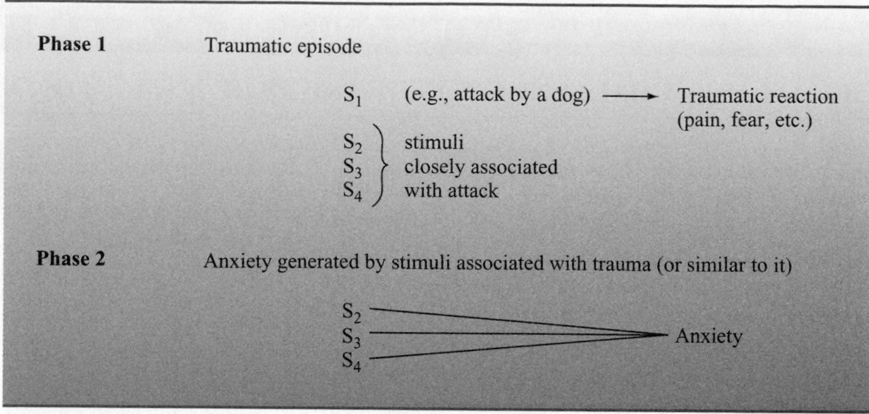

Figure 10.2 From trauma to anxiety.

After severe trauma, the victim is more likely to respond anxiously to other stress stimuli that occur later in life (Archibald & Tuddenham, 1965; Milgram, 1993). Surviving victims of Nazi concentration camps, for example, sometimes continued for years to be hypersensitive to threat stimuli and to react to stress readily with anxiety and sleep disturbances (Chodoff, 1963). These observations support the idea that anxiety involves a learned fear reaction that is highly resistant to extinction and that may be evoked by diverse stimuli similar to those that originally were traumatic. That is, the fear evoked by the traumatic stimuli may be reactivated and also may *generalize* to stimuli associated with the traumatic episode. For example, after a child has been attacked and bitten by a dog, her fear reaction may generalize to other dogs, animals, fur, places similar to the one in which the attack occurred, and so on (Figure 10.2). Moreover, if the generalization stimuli are very remote from the original traumatic stimulus, the person may be unable to see the connection between the two and the anxiety may appear (even to her) particularly irrational. Suppose, for example, that the child becomes afraid of the room in which the dog bit her and of similar rooms. If the connection between her new fear of rooms and the dog's attack is not recognized, the fear of rooms now may seem especially bizarre.

10.12 Why are trauma victims more reactive to later life stresses?

From a learning point of view, anxieties after traumas, like other learned fears, may be acquired through simple association or conditioning principles. If neutral stimuli have been associated with aversive events or outcomes, then they also may come to elicit anxiety in their own right. Such aversively conditioned emotional reactions may also generalize extensively to new stimuli (Figure 10.2). Clinical examples of aversive arousal and avoidance include many phobic and anxious reactions to objects, people, and social and interpersonal situations. Not only external events, but also their symbolic representations in the form of words or of thoughts and fantasies, may create painful emotions. In our example of the child traumatized by the dog, even thinking about the incident, or the room in which it occurred or similar rooms, may terrify the youngster.

Stimuli closer or more relevant to those associated with emotional arousal tend to elicit stronger reactions. In one study, novice sports parachutists and members of the control group took a specially constructed word association test (Epstein & Fenz, 1962; Fenz, 1964). The words contained four levels of relevance to parachuting. Throughout the word association tests, participants' physiological reactions, specifically their galvanic skin response, or GSR (which is a change in electrical activity of the skin due to sweating) were recorded to measure their emotional arousal in response to the various stimulus words. One testing occurred 2 weeks before the scheduled jump, another testing was done the day before the jump, and a final test was on the day of the parachute jump. The results showed more arousal in parachutists for parachute-relevant words. The effect was greatest for the words most relevant to parachuting, and their arousal was highest when the testing time was closer to the emotion-arousing parachute jump itself.

▶ OPERANT (INSTRUMENTAL) CONDITIONING: B.F. SKINNER'S CONTRIBUTIONS

The work of Pavlov and the many others who explored the implications of classical conditioning showed how emotional reactions, both positive and negative, to previously neutral stimuli may be acquired through the process of close association with unconditioned stimuli. But learning takes place in more than one form, and a second type, called instrumental or operant conditioning, provides another foundation for understanding the role of experience and learning for the development of personality. B.F. Skinner, arguably the most influential behaviorist of the last century, made operant conditioning the centerpiece of his approach. In numerous studies over the course of many decades he and his students and disciples illustrated its potential power for changing behavior dramatically and often surprisingly.

How Operant (Instrumental) Conditioning Works: Learning from Response Consequences

Behavior is modified by its consequences: the outcome of any response (or pattern of responses, often called **operants** for how the organism "operates" on the environment) determines how likely it is that similar responses will be performed in the future. If a response has favorable (reinforcing) consequences, the organism is more likely to perform it again in similar situations. Contrary to some widespread misconceptions, reinforcers or favorable outcomes are not restricted to such primitive rewards as food pellets or sexual satisfactions. Almost all events may serve as reinforcers, including such cognitive gratifications as information (Jones, 1966) or the achievement of competence. Such learning, based on the consequences produced by responses, is called **operant conditioning** (or, in earlier usage, trial-and-error or **instrumental learning**).

10.13 How does operant conditioning differ from classical conditioning?

When the consequences of a response pattern change, the probability of it and of similar response patterns occurring again also changes (Nemeroff & Karoly, 1991). If a little boy whines and clings to his mother and she drops everything in an attempt to appease him, the chances increase that he will behave in this way in the future. If she systematically ignores the behavior, however, and consistently fails to react to it, the chances decrease that the child will continue to behave this way.

Skinner's Basic Approach

Miller and Dollard's theory provided an account of human personality that gave motivation an important role. It also allowed a learning reinterpretation of many of the motivational concepts that Freud invoked in his psychoanalytic theory. But while the motivational focus of Miller and Dollard spoke to the interests of many clinical psychologists, Skinner rejected it completely. Skinner and his followers wanted to find a level of analysis that was entirely objective and required no inferences about underlying mental processes.

B. F. Skinner (1904–1990)
(*Source*: Corbis-Bettmann)

In Skinner's view of science, we can know people only by examining their behavior—the things they say and do. In a sense, all psychological approaches are based on the study of behavior, but they differ in how the behavior is used. For example, in analyses at the trait level, behaviors are used as signs for inferring the person's traits or attributes from the observable things the individual does. In the behavioral approach favored by B. F. Skinner, however, the observed behavior is the basic unit, and the interest is in specifying the conditions and stimuli or situations that "control" it. The concept that the stimulus controls the response is called **stimulus control**.

In this tradition, behaviorists tried to sample the individual's behaviors directly but generally were reluctant to interpret them as signs (indicators) of the person's motives or other attributes. For example, from this perspective one might try to sample Gary W.'s behaviors to find out just what he does before speeches, without drawing any inferences from them about his underlying anxiety, insecurity, or other personal qualities. To the degree that theorists limit themselves to behavior, their definition of personality itself becomes equated with the whole of an individual's behaviors: *the person "is" what the person "does."*

Importance of the Situation: The Role of Stimuli

Skinner and his followers give particular importance to the role of stimuli and situations in the regulation of behavior, including behaviors indicative of personality. Because the strategy used is often experimental, these stimuli are simply green or red lights or tones that have become associated with certain qualities through manipulated learning experiences. But evidence for the important role of the situation in social behavior and

10.14 What is meant by stimulus control of behavior?

even as a determinant of how we perceive other people also comes from more naturalistic social experiments by many other researchers working at the behavioral level.

Psychologists influenced by this approach point out that often behavior may be predicted simply from knowledge about relevant conditions. Consider, for example, studies that tried to predict the post-hospital adjustment of mental patients. Accurate predictions of post-hospital adjustment required knowledge of the environment in which the ex-patient would be living in the community—such as the availability of jobs and family support—rather than any measures of person variables or in-hospital behavior (e.g., Fairweather, 1967; Fairweather, Sanders, Cressler, & Maynard, 1969; Holahan & Moos, 1990).

Likewise, to predict intellectual achievement it helps to take into account the degree to which the child's environment supports (models and reinforces) intellectual development (Wolf, 1966). And to predict whether or not people respond to stress with illness, it helps to know the degree to which they have social supports (e.g., spouse, family) in their environments (Holahan & Moos, 1990; Nilson, Nilson, Olson, & McAllister, 1981). Finally, when powerful treatments are developed, predictions about outcomes may be useful when based simply on knowing the treatment to which the individual is assigned (e.g., Bandura, 1986; Bandura, Blanchard, & Ritter, 1969).

In daily life, different people are exposed to extremely different kinds of situations, often in stable ways. The life of a college student contains sets of situations that may importantly influence not only what the students do but also in time, through their interactions with those situations, what they become (Cantor, Kemmelmeier, Basten, & Prentice, 2002). Imagine a day in the life of a New York City taxi driver, or that of a monk, a professor, a company executive, or a hairdresser, and the differences in the kinds of situations they must encounter, day in and day out. Such differences are not limited to occupational and social role differences. A person with an irritating, defensive style of social interaction is likely to provoke different reactions from others compared to a person with a more agreeable style.

A dramatic illustration of the power of the situation and the social role it assigns to one is seen in a natural experiment that was considered shocking at the time (Rosenhan, 1973). Normal individuals (doctors, psychologists, and graduate students from Stanford University) admitted themselves to the local mental hospital by complaining of various psychiatric symptoms. Then, during their confinement, they proceeded to behave rationally, which they normally were. From the moment that they were admitted to the hospital, these individuals were consistently treated by the professional hospital staff (who did not know their true identity) as if they were insane, and labeled psychotic. The staff members erroneously seemed to assume that anyone committed to the mental hospital must in fact be psychotic, regardless of their rational, normal behavior. Just being there was enough to make normal people appear like mental patients in the eyes of the staff.

Rejection of Inferred Motives

To explain behavior, many earlier theorists hypothesized a wide range of human motives. Theories concerning motivation have helped to reveal the variety and complexity of human strivings, and also have contributed to the development of research about their causes. Investigators of motives originally were inspired by the model of experimental research on biological drives in animals. In animal studies of motivation, the hypothesized need of the animal (its hunger or sex drive, for example) has been linked clearly to observable conditions manipulated in the laboratory. For example, the strength of the hunger drive may be inferred in part from the amount of time that the animal has been deprived of food. When a dog has not been fed for 2 days, we may safely say that it has a high hunger drive. In such cases, references to drives and motives are straightforward. Likewise, some careful investigations of hypothesized higher-order motives in people have specified clearly the objective conditions that define the motive (e.g., Emmons, 1997; McClelland, 1992; McClelland et al., 1953).

10.15 Why did Skinner reject motives and inner conflicts as causes of behavior?

Less rigorous applications of motivational theory to personality, however, may use motives loosely (e.g., as "wishes" or "desires"), and their value as explanations of behavior is open to question—and Skinner took the lead in raising those questions for many years. In his view, the tendency to invoke motives as explanations of why people behave as they do is understandable, because that is how we "explain" behavior in commonsense terms. To explain why a child spent an unusual amount of time cleaning and grooming himself neatly, we easily might say "because he had strong cleanliness needs" or "because he had a compulsive desire for order."

Such hypotheses about motives may sound like explanations, but Skinner insisted that they tell us little unless the motive is defined objectively and unless the causes of the motive itself are established. What makes the child have "cleanliness needs?" What determines his "compulsive desires?" Why does she "wish" to be clean? These are the kinds of questions raised by B.F. Skinner, who worked for many years at Harvard University.

A pioneer in the behavioral approach, Skinner criticized many concepts regarding human needs as being no more than motivational labels attached to human activities. Thus, orderly behavior may be attributed to a motive for orderliness, submissive behavior to submissiveness needs, exploratory behavior to the need to explore, and so on. To avoid such circular reasoning and to untangle explaining from naming, behaviorally oriented psychologists like Skinner prefer to analyze behaviors in terms of the observable events and conditions that seem to vary with them. Hence, they refuse to posit specific motivations for behavior. Rather, they try to discover the external events that strengthen its future likelihood and that maintain or change it. This approach leads to questions like: When does that child's cleaning activity increase, and when does it decrease in relation to observable changes in the environment? For example, how do the reactions of the parents influence the behavior?

For Skinner, psychology is the science of behavior: inferences about unobservable states and motives are not adequate explanations, and they add nothing to a scientific account of the conditions controlling behavior. "Motivation" is simply the result of depriving or satiating an organism of some substance such as water or food for a given period of time. Thus, a "drive" is just a convenient way of referring to the observable effects of such deprivation or satiation. Likewise, Skinner avoids any inferences about internal "conflicts," preferring an experimental analysis of the stimulus conditions that seem to control the particular behavior in the situation. In his words:

> *Man, we once believed, was free to express himself in art, music, and literature, to inquire into nature, to seek salvation in his own way. He could initiate action and make spontaneous and capricious changes of course.... But science insists that action is initiated by forces impinging upon the individual, and that caprice is only another name for behavior for which we have not yet found a cause. (1955, pp. 52–53)*

The essence of Skinner's behavioristic view is the belief that our behavior is shaped by the external environment, not by motives, dispositions, or "selves" that are "in" the person.

Conditioned Generalized Reinforcers

Neutral stimuli may acquire value and become **conditioned reinforcers** when they become associated with other stimuli that already have reinforcing properties. Conditioned reinforcers become generalized when they are paired with more than one primary reinforcer. A good example of a conditioned generalized reinforcer is money, because it can provide so many different primary gratifications (food, shelter, comfort, medical help, and alleviation of pain). Gradually, generalized reinforcers may become quite potent even when the primary reinforcers upon which they were initially based do not accompany them anymore. Some people, for example, seem to learn to love money for its own sake and work to amass "paper profits" that they never trade in for primary rewards.

10.16 How are conditioned generalized reinforcers created?

Some generalized reinforcers are obvious—like money—but others are subtle and involve complex social relationships. Attention and social approval from people who are likely to supply reinforcement—such as parents, a loved one, or a teacher—often are especially strong **generalized reinforcers**.

Discrimination and Generalization in Everyday Life

Discriminative stimuli indicate when an operant response will or will not have favorable consequences. Without such signals we would not know in advance the outcomes to which different behaviors are likely to lead and life would be chaotic. With the help of discriminative stimuli we learn to stop the car when coming to a railroad crossing; to eat certain foods with forks and spoons and to continue to eat others with our fingers; to shout and cheer at football games, but not at course examinations; to wear warmer clothes when the temperature starts to drop and to shed them when it becomes hot; to stop at red traffic lights and to go when they turn green.

10.17 Define generalization and discrimination. Provide an example of a discriminative stimulus in your own life.

When a particular response or pattern of responses is reinforced in the presence of one stimulus but not in the presence of others, discrimination occurs. It may be all right to belch in your own room when alone or with close friends but less acceptable to do so when talking to a faculty advisor in her office, and people soon get feedback that makes this clear to them. Discrimination results from the reinforcement or condoning of behavior in some situations but not in others. The individual is more likely to display the behavior in those situations in which it will probably be reinforced than in those in which it is unlikely to be reinforced.

If a response pattern is uniformly rewarded in many conditions or situations, **generalization** occurs. For example, a child is likely to develop generalized aggressive patterns if he or she is encouraged or allowed to behave aggressively with his or her parents and teachers as well as with siblings and classmates both when he or she is at school and at home. Generalization depends on the similarity among stimulus situations. Stimuli that are physically similar or that have similar meanings result in the greatest generalization.

From the behavioral perspective, the socialization of children is based on discrimination training. For example, children must learn to control their bowel and bladder functions so that defecation and urination occur only in some situations and not in others. Active exploration of the toy box or the sandbox is permitted and encouraged, while forays into the medicine cabinet or mother's jewel box have quite different outcomes. As a result of such **discrimination training**, the child's behavior begins to depend on the specific conditions in which it unfolds.

When behavior yields similar consequences in a broad variety of settings, it can be expected to generalize from one situation to another. For example, if a little girl

"Generalized reinforcers" often are subtle and involve complex human relationships.

(*Source*: Bob Daemmrich Photography)

easily gets help in solving problems at home, at school, with parents, teachers, and siblings, she may develop widespread dependency. In contrast, when certain behaviors, such as curiosity, are punished in some situations but not in others, consistencies across the different situations should not be expected. A child becomes increasingly discriminating as the various roles of sibling, student, friend, and many more are learned. Each of these roles implies its own distinct set of appropriate behaviors in particular situations.

Shaping Behavior by Successive Approximations

Before a response can be reinforced, it must occur. Extremely complex responses, such as saying new words in a foreign language, are unlikely ever to be performed spontaneously by the learner. If you do not know how to say "How do you do?" in Greek, you are unlikely ever to come out with the right phrase spontaneously, no matter how many sounds you utter. To try to overcome this problem, and to help an organism form new responses, Skinnerians often use a procedure called "shaping."

10.18 How is shaping of behavior accomplished?

Shaping is a technique for producing successively closer approximations to a particular desired behavior. It consists of carefully observing and immediately rewarding any small variations of the behavior in the desired direction as they are spontaneously performed by the organism. At first, a large class of responses is reinforced; then gradually the class is narrowed, and reinforcement is given only for closer approximations to the final form of the desired behavior. For example, when teaching a pigeon to stand only in the center of a large bull's-eye target painted on the floor, one might reward the bird for standing increasingly close to the center.

The Patterning of Outcomes: Schedules of Reinforcement

The patterning, sequencing, or scheduling of reinforcement, that is, just when it does and does not occur in relation to the organism's behaviors affects the future occurrence and strength of the reinforced behavior (Ferster & Skinner, 1957). Sometimes the scheduling on which reinforcement is based may be even more important than the nature of the reinforcer (Morse & Kelleher, 1966). Different schedules have different influences on operant responses. Operant strength is measured by the rate of responses: the more frequently a response is made in a given period of time, the greater its rate (and inferred strength).

10.19 Describe the effects of schedules of reinforcement on learning and extinction of behaviors.

Continuous reinforcement (CRF) is a schedule on which a behavior is reinforced every time it occurs. Responses are usually learned most quickly with continuous reinforcement. A child would become toilet trained more quickly if he were praised and rewarded for each successful attempt. While continuous reinforcement is easy to create in a laboratory, in life it is a rare experience; a partial reinforcement or intermittent schedule, in which a response is reinforced only some of the time, is much more common. We see partial reinforcement when a child's bids for attention succeed only occasionally in getting the parent to attend, or when the same sales pitch produces a sale once in a while, or when the gambler hits the jackpot but only in between many losing bets.

Behavior that has received **partial reinforcement** or **intermittent reinforcement** often becomes hard to eliminate even when reinforcement is withdrawn altogether. A mother who intermittently and irregularly gives in to her child's nighttime bids for attention (crying, calling for a drink of water, or for just one more story) may find the child's behavior very durable and unresponsive to her attempts to stop it by ignoring it. Many potentially maladaptive behaviors (facial tics, physical aggression, immature dependency) are hard to eliminate because they are rewarded intermittently. For example, rewarding temper tantrums intermittently (e.g., by occasionally attending to them in an irregular pattern) may make them very durable. Since many potentially maladaptive behaviors, such as physical aggression and immature dependency, are rewarded intermittently, they can become very hard to eliminate (Plaud & Gaither, 1996).

The child with a speck of grit in her eye who successfully follows her father's instruction to blink to get it out may keep on blinking periodically long after the eye is clear of irritation. If her blinks are further reinforced by her parents' occasional attention (whether troubled concern or agitated pleas to "stop doing that!"), she may develop an unattractive facial tic that is extremely resistant to extinction. Likewise, as has often been noted, the gambler who hit a jackpot once may persist for a long time even when the payoff becomes zero. The persistence of behavior after partial reinforcement suggests that when one has experienced only occasional, irregular, and unpredictable reinforcement for a response, one continues to expect possible rewards for a long time after the rewards have totally stopped.

Superstitions: Getting Reinforced into Irrationality

The relationship between the occurrence of an operant response and the reinforcement that follows it is often causal. For example, turn the door knob and the door opens, the outcome reinforcing the action. Consequently, in the future, we are likely to turn door knobs to enter and leave rooms, and our behavior at the door seems rational. Often, however, the response–reinforcement relationship may be quite accidental, and then bizarre and seemingly superstitious behavior and false beliefs may be produced (Matute, 1994). For example, a primitive tribe may persist in offering human sacrifices to the gods to end severe droughts because occasionally a sacrifice has been followed by rain.

10.20 How are superstitious behaviors established? Why is it so difficult to abolish them?

The development of superstition, according to Skinner, may be demonstrated by giving a pigeon a bit of food at regular intervals—say every 15 seconds—regardless of what he is doing. Skinner (1953, p. 85) describes the strange rituals that may be conditioned in this way:

> When food is first given, the pigeon will be behaving in some way—if only standing still—and conditioning will take place. It is then more probable that the same behavior will be in progress when food is given again. If this proves to be the case, the "operant" will be further strengthened. If not, some other behavior will be strengthened. Eventually a given bit of behavior reaches a frequency at which it is often reinforced. It then becomes a permanent part of the repertoire of the bird, even though the food has been given by a clock which is unrelated to the bird's behavior. Conspicuous responses which have been established in this way include turning sharply to one side, hopping from one foot to the other and back, bowing and scraping, turning around, strutting, and raising the head. The topography of the behavior may continue to drift with further reinforcements, since slight modifications in the form of response may coincide with the receipt of food.

Punishment

In operant conditioning, reinforcement strengthens the operant, **punishment** weakens it. Skinner focused on the role of reinforcement, but punishment is also a powerful force in influencing behavior. Punishment can take two forms: in one form, "positive" punishment, **aversive stimulation** is given (e.g., an electric shock, a sharp slap to the face); in "negative" punishment, something desirable is removed (e.g., not being allowed to go to a party; removing a child's favorite toy).

Unsurprisingly, the influence of punishment on personality development in the course of socialization is both important and complex, and depends on many variables (Aronfreed, 1968, 1994). Often "aversive stimuli" in everyday life and childrearing may be conveyed subtly, by facial expressions and words rather than by brute force, and in extremely complicated patterns, by the same individuals who also nurture the child, giving love and other positive reinforcement. Moreover, the events that are punished often involve more than specific responses; they sometimes entail long sequences of overt and covert behavior (Aronfreed, 1994).

10.21 Describe advantages and possible disadvantages of punishment involving aversive stimulation.

The behaviors that are considered inappropriate and punishable in the course of socializing depend on such variables as the child's age and sex as well as the situation. Obviously the helplessness and passivity that are acceptable in a young child may be maladaptive in an older one, and the traits valued in a girl may not be valued in a boy. While the mother may deliberately encourage her son's dependency and discourage his aggressiveness, his school peers may do the reverse, ridiculing dependency at school and modeling and rewarding aggression and self-assertion.

A careful classic review of research on the effects of punishment upon children's behavior concluded, in part, that:

> . . . aversive stimulation, if well timed, consistent, and sufficiently intense, may create conditions that accelerate the socialization process, provided that the socialization agents also provide information concerning alternative prosocial behavior and positively reinforce any such behavior that occurs.
>
> (Walters & Parke, 1967, p. 218)

The important point to remember here is that when punishment is speedy and specific it may suppress undesirable behavior, but it cannot teach the child desirable alternatives. Therefore, parents should use positive techniques to show and reinforce appropriate behavior that the child can employ in place of the unacceptable response that has to be suppressed (Walters & Parke, 1967). In that way, the learner will develop a new response that can be made without getting punished. Without such a positive alternative, the child faces a dilemma in which total avoidance may seem the only possible route. Punishment may have very unfortunate effects when the child believes there is no way in which he or she can prevent further punishment and cope (Linscheid & Meinhold, 1990). If you become convinced that no potentially successful actions are open to you, that you can do nothing right, depression, hopelessness, and negative thinking may follow (Nolen-Hoeksema, 1997; Seligman, 1975).

Skinner's Own Behavior

Skinner's commitment to his methods of studying behavior was absolute. While his original interests were heavily in literature and the arts, his development and work as a scientist became his life mission, and he applied the findings to himself as much as to the animals he studied (see *In Focus 10.2*).

Summary of Two Types of Learning

As we conclude the chapter, Table 10.3 summarizes the two types of learning discussed: classical conditioning and operant conditioning. There is overlap between these types of learning, but each has some relatively distinct features, as indicated in the table, and each has a major place within current learning theory and research at this level of analysis. Taken together, they provide the foundations for many of the applications and therapeutic behavior modification methods discussed in the next chapter.

IN FOCUS 10.2

SKINNER ANALYZES HIMSELF

In his engaging personal autobiography, Skinner emphasizes that he views and analyzes his own behavior just like he does his rats and pigeons: "I have applied the same formulations, I have looked for the same kinds of causal relations, and I have manipulated behavior in the same way . . ." (1967, p. 407).

On the ways Skinner's environment shaped his own behavior:

> I was taught to fear God, the police, and what people will think. As a result I usually do what I have to do with no great struggle. I try not to let any day "slip useless away." I have studied when I did not feel like studying, taught when I did not want to teach. I have taken care of animals and run experiments as the animals dictated. (Some of my [laboratory] records are stamped December twenty-fifth and January first). (1967, p. 407)

Discussing his refusal to go much beyond direct rigorous observation and manipulation of behavior, and therefore struggling to avoid all kinds of speculation and theorizing, Skinner says:

> I have fought against deceiving myself. I avoid metaphors which are effective at the cost of obscuring issues. I avoid rhetorical devices which give unwarranted plausibility to an argument . . . I avoid the unwarranted prestige conferred by mathematics . . . I do not spin impressive physiological theories from my data, as I easily could do. (Skinner, 1967, p. 407)

And finally, on the topic of the "control of behavior" to which most of his own work was devoted: "I believe that man must now plan his own future and he must take every advantage of a science of behavior in solving the problems which will necessarily arise" (1967, p. 411).

TABLE 10.3 Summary of Two Types of Learning

Type	Arrangement	Effect	Example	Interpretation
Classical conditioning	A neutral stimulus (e.g., a bell) repeatedly and closely precedes a powerful unconditioned stimulus (e.g., food).	The originally neutral stimulus becomes a conditioned stimulus—that is, acquires some of the impact of the powerful unconditioned stimulus.	Bell begins to elicit a salivary response, even when not paired with food.	Organism learns that the conditioned stimulus (bell) signals (predicts) the occurrence of the unconditioned stimulus (food).
Operant (Instrumental) conditioning	A freely emitted response (operant) is repeatedly followed by a favorable outcome (reinforcement).	The operant increases in frequency.	If crying is followed by attention, its frequency is increased.	Organism learns that this response will produce that particular outcome.

▶ SUMMARY

THE BEHAVIORAL APPROACH TO PSYCHODYNAMICS: DOLLARD AND MILLER

- Dollard and Miller fused psychoanalytic concepts with the more objective language and methods of laboratory studies of animal learning.
- Dollard and Miller apply the concept of goal gradients to map approach and avoidance tendencies as a function of distance from the goal object.
- Their theory emphasizes drive, cue, response, and reinforcement as the basic components of learning. Events that reduce a drive serve as reinforcements.
- Neurotic conflict exists when two or more goals are mutually exclusive. This conflict can create anxiety and repression.

CLASSICAL CONDITIONING

- In classical conditioning, an unconditioned stimulus (UCS) is paired with a conditioned stimulus (CS), such that the former unconditioned response (UCR) may be enacted when only the CS is present, thus becoming a conditioned response (CR).
- Classical conditioning principles have been extended to explain some complex social phenomena and neurotic or abnormal behaviors, such as irrational fears.
- Traumatic fear may generalize so that events and cognitions closely associated with the original traumatic experiences may later evoke anxiety even after the objective danger is gone.

OPERANT CONDITIONING: B. F. SKINNER'S INFLUENCE ON PERSONALITY

- B.F. Skinner's work focused on operant conditioning, in which behavior patterns may be modified by changing the consequences (reinforcements) to which they lead. Information and attention, as well as food and sexual gratification, are among the many outcomes that can serve as reinforcers.
- In Skinner's conceptualization, analysis of the stimulus conditions controlling behavior (the "operants") replaces inferences about internal conflicts and underlying motives.
- In Skinner's view, discrimination in learning is fundamental in the socialization process. When behavior yields similar consequences under many conditions, generalization occurs, and the individual may display similar behavior patterns across diverse settings.
- Behavior may be shaped by reinforcing successively closer approximations to a particular desired behavior.
- While continuous reward or reinforcement for behavior may result in faster learning, irregular or intermittent reinforcement often produces more stable behavior that persists even when reinforcement is withdrawn. Many potentially maladaptive behaviors are rewarded irregularly and may therefore become very resistant to change.
- Irrational behavior may be created by accidental/noncausal pairings of behavior and response.
- The influence of punishment is complex and depends on many conditions, such as its timing.

▶ KEY TERMS

ambivalence (approach–avoidance tendencies) 247
approach tendencies 247
approach–approach conflict 251
aversive stimulation 266
avoidance tendencies 251
avoidance–avoidance conflicts 251
classical conditioning (conditioned-response learning) 253
conditioned reinforcers 263
conditioned response (CR) 254
conditioned stimulus (CS) 268
conditioning 253
conditions of deprivation 249
conflict 251
continuous reinforcement (CRF) 265
cue 250
discrimination training 263
discriminative stimuli 263
drive 249
drive reduction 250
extinction 251
generalization 263
generalized reinforcers 263
goal gradients 247
higher-order conditioning 255
intermittent (partial) reinforcement 265
learned drive 250
neurotic conflict 246
not-thinking 252
operant conditioning (instrumental learning) 259
operants 259
primary biological needs 248
psychodynamic behavior theory 246
punishment 266
reflex / unconditioned response (UCR) 254
reinforcement 250
response 250
shaping 264
stimulus control 260
unconditioned stimuli (UCS) 254

CHAPTER 11

ANALYZING AND MODIFYING BEHAVIOR

Many psychologists recognized that the principles of classical and operant conditioning, discussed in the last chapter, might be useful for treatment of at least some human behavioral problems, such as specific fears. Most psychologists, however, were concerned that the early behavioral work was based largely on studies with animals in artificial laboratory situations. Elegant experiments were done on the behavior of rats running in mazes and of pigeons pecking on levers as food pellets dropped down. But how could one extend the results from these studies to personality and the complex lives of people?

At the same time (before the 1970s), most clinicians saw behavioral concepts as too superficial for understanding the complexities of personality and irrelevant for helping people with personality problems. Partially in response to these challenges, behaviorally oriented workers tried to apply their ideas and methods to people and to issues relevant to personality and personality change. For several decades, they began to treat some of the most difficult behavioral and personality problems that had resisted other forms of therapy (e.g., O'Donohue et al., 2001). For example, they were allowed to try to treat hospitalized people who were so severely disturbed that there was little to lose by attempting experimental innovations with them after other available methods had proved to be unsuccessful. This chapter gives you a sense of their main strategies for assessment and change that are still relevant in various forms. By learning about some of these procedures, you will also get a better picture of the underlying philosophy that guides work at this level.

▶ CHARACTERISTICS OF BEHAVIORAL ASSESSMENTS

Rather than trying to infer the person's broad traits and motives, behavioral approaches focus on the specific external conditions and learning processes that might govern his or her behavior.

Keep in mind again that all scientific psychological approaches are based on behavioral observation: giving answers on personality inventories or saying what an inkblot looks like are behaviors just as much as crying or running or fighting. However, in most personality assessment, the observed behaviors (e.g., the check marks made on a trait rating scale, the responses to an inkblot) serve as highly indirect *signs* of the traits or motives that might underlie them. In contrast, in behavior assessments, the observed behavior is treated as a *sample*, and interest is focused on how the specific sampled behavior is affected by alterations in conditions (Mischel, 1968). For example, if the interest is in a child's physical and verbal aggression when relating to peers at preschool, then that is the type of behavior and situation that will be observed and assessed directly, rather than relying on teacher's or parent's reports, or scores on personality tests (O'Donohue et al., 2001).

11.1 How does behavioral assessment differ from trait measures of personality?

Case Example: Conditions "Controlling" Gary W.'s Anxiety

To illustrate the general strategy of behavior assessment, let's again consider the case of Gary W. An assessment of Gary at this level obviously would focus on his behavior in relation to stimulus conditions. But what behaviors, and in relation to which conditions? Rather than seek a portrait of Gary's personality and behavior "in general," or an estimate of his "average" or dominant attributes, the focus is much more specific at the behavioral level of analysis. The behavior patterns selected for study depend on the particular problem that requires investigation. In clinical situations, the client indicates the priorities; in research contexts, they are selected by the investigator.

During his first term of graduate school, Gary found himself troubled enough to seek help at the school's counseling center. As part of the behavioral assessment that followed, Gary was asked to list and rank in order of importance the three problems that he found most distressing in himself and that he wanted to change if possible. He listed "feeling anxious and losing my grip" as his greatest problem. To assess the behavioral referents for his felt "anxiety," Gary was asked to specify in more detail just what changes in himself indicated to him that he was or was not anxious and "losing his grip."

He indicated that when he became anxious he felt changes in his heart rate, became tense, perspired, and found it most difficult to speak coherently. Next, to explore the covariation between increases and decreases in this state and changes in stimulus conditions, Gary was asked to keep an hour-by-hour diary sampling most of the waking hours during the daytime for a period of 2 weeks and indicating the type of activity that occurred during each hour. Discussion with him of this record suggested that anxiety tended to occur primarily in connection with public speaking occasions—specifically, in classroom situations in which he was required to speak before a group. As indicated by the summary shown in Table 11.1, on only one occasion that was not close in time to

TABLE 11.1 Occurrence of Gary W.'s Self-Reported Anxiety Attacks in Relation to Public Speaking

Occurrence of Anxiety	Hours with Anxiety (10)	Hours without Anxiety (80)
Within 1 hour of public speaking	9 (90%)	0 (0%)
No public speaking within 1 hour	1 (10%)	80 (100%)

public speaking did Gary find himself highly anxious. That occasion turned out to be one in which he was brooding in his room, thinking about his public speaking failures in the classroom.

Having established a covariation between the occurrence of anxiety and public speaking in the social-evaluative conditions of the classroom, his assessors identified the specific components of the public speaking situation (e.g., when the audience is large and consists of important authorities, rather than a small group of friends) that led to relatively more and less anxiety. The purpose here was to establish a hierarchy of anxiety-evoking stimuli ranging from the mild to the exceedingly severe. This hierarchy then was used in a treatment designed to gradually desensitize Gary to these fear stimuli.

Note that this behavioral assessment of Gary is quite specific: It is not an effort to characterize his whole personality, to describe "what he is like," or to infer his motives and dynamics. Instead, the assessment restricts itself to some clearly described problems and tries to analyze them in objective terms without going beyond the observed relations. Moreover, the analysis focuses on the stimulus conditions in which Gary's behavior occurs and on the covariation between those conditions and his problem. Behavior assessment tends to be focused assessment, usually concentrating on those aspects of behavior that can be changed and that require change. Indeed, as you will see often in this chapter, behavior assessment and behavior change (treatment) are closely connected.

The assessment of Gary's anxiety illustrates one rather crude way to study stimulus–response covariations. Of course there are many different ways in which these covariations can be sampled. This chapter illustrates some of the main tactics developed for the measurement of human behavior at this level of analysis.

▶ DIRECT BEHAVIOR MEASUREMENT

For many purposes in personality study, it is important to sample and observe behavior in carefully structured, lifelike situations. In clinical applications, direct observation may give both client and assessor an opportunity to assess life problems and to select treatment objectives. Direct observation of behavior samples also may be used to assess the relative efficacy of various treatment procedures. Finally, behavior sampling has an important part in experimental research on personality.

The types of data collected in the behavioral approach include situational samples of both nonverbal and verbal behavior, as well as physiological measurements of emotional reactions. In addition, a comprehensive assessment often includes an analysis of effective rewards or reinforcing stimuli in the person's life. Examples of all of these measures are given in the following sections.

Situational Behavior Sampling

You already saw examples of **behavior sampling** in Chapter 2; such sampling is basic for much of the work at this level. Given the important role of fears and avoidance behavior, much attention has been given to assessing in detail the strength of diverse avoidance behaviors reliably in clinical situations. This was done, for example, by exposing fearful individuals to a series of real or symbolic fear-inducing stimuli. For example, fear of heights was assessed by measuring the distance that the phobic person could climb on a metal fire escape (Lazarus, 1961). The same people were assessed again after receiving therapy to reduce their fears. In this phase, they were invited to ascend eight stories by elevator to a roof garden and to count the passing cars below for 2 minutes. Claustrophobic behavior—fear of closed spaces—was measured by asking each person to sit in a cubicle containing large French windows opening onto a balcony. The assessor shut the windows and slowly moved a large screen nearer and nearer to the person, thus gradually constricting her space. Of course each person was free to open the windows, and thereby to terminate the procedure, whenever she wished, although she was instructed to persevere as long as possible. The measure of claustrophobia was the least distance at which the person could tolerate the screen. As another example, Table 11.2 shows a checklist for performance anxieties before making a public speech.

11.2 Describe how behavioral assessment has been used to assess anxieties and psychotic behavior.

Direct behavior sampling has also been used extensively in the analysis of psychotic behavior. One study, for instance, employed a time-sampling technique. At regular, 30-minute intervals, psychiatric nurses sought out and observed each hospitalized patient for periods of 1–3 minutes, without directly interacting with him (Ayllon & Haughton, 1964). The behavior observed in each sample was classified based on the occurrence of three experimenter-defined behaviors (e.g., psychotic talk), and the time-check recordings were used to compute the relative frequency of the various behaviors. This time-sampling technique was supplemented by recordings of all the

TABLE 11.2 Timed Behavioral Checklist for Performance Anxiety

	Time Period
Behavior Observed	1 2 3 4 5 6 7 8
1. Paces	
2. Sways	
3. Shuffles feet	
4. Knees tremble	
5. Extraneous arm and hand movement (swings, scratches, toys, etc.)	
6. Arms rigid	
7. Hands restrained (in pockets, behind back, clasped)	
8. Hand tremors	
9. No eye contact	
10. Face muscles tense (drawn, tics, grimaces)	
11. Face "deadpan"	
12. Face pale	
13. Face flushed (blushes)	
14. Moistens lips	
15. Swallows	
16. Clears throat	
17. Breathes heavily	
18. Perspires (face, hands, armpits)	
19. Voice quivers	
20. Speech blocks or stammers	

Source: Paul, Gordon. *Insight vs. desensitization in psychotherapy*. © 1966 by The Board of Trustees of the LeLand Stanford Jr. University, renewed 1994. With the permission of Stanford University Press, www.sup.org.

interactions between patient and nurses (such as each time the patient entered the nursing office). The resulting data served as a basis for designing and evaluating a treatment program. Similar ways of sampling and recording family interactions have been developed by others (Patterson, 1976; Ramsey, Patterson, & Walker, 1990). They studied highly aggressive children in the course of everyday family life, for example, at dinner. The attempt was to analyze the exact conditions under which aggression increased or decreased.

As illustrated in the assessment of Gary's public speaking anxieties, a daily record may provide another valuable first step in the identification of problem-producing stimuli. Many behaviorally oriented clinicians routinely ask their clients to keep specific records listing the exact conditions under which their anxieties and problems seem to increase or decrease (Wolpe & Lazarus, 1966). The person may be asked to prepare by himself lists of all the stimulus conditions or events that create discomfort, distress, or other painful emotional reactions.

Finding Effective Rewards

So far, we have considered the direct measurement of various responses. Behavior assessments, however, analyze not just what people do (and say and feel), but also the conditions that regulate or determine what they do. For that reason, behavior assessments have to find the rewards or reinforcers that may be influencing a person's behavior. If discovered, these reinforcers also can serve as incentives in therapy programs to help modify behavior in more positive or advantageous directions. Psychologists who emphasize the role of reinforcement in human behavior have devoted much attention to discovering and measuring effective reinforcers. People's actual choices in lifelike situations, as well as their verbal preferences or ratings, reveal some of the potent reinforcers that influence them. The reinforcement value of particular stimuli also may be assessed directly by observing their effects on the individual's performance (Daniels, 1994; Weir, 1965).

11.3 How can direct observation be used to identify reinforcers that control behavior? How have tokens been used to change behavior and to identify reinforcers?

Primary reinforcers such as food, and **generalized conditioned reinforcers** such as praise, social approval, and money, are effective for most people. For example, in one case study, researchers and teachers attempted to reduce the disruptive behaviors of a blind boy with a learning disability (Heitzman & Alimena, 1991). His behaviors were problematic because they disrupted the class and also prevented him from achieving optimal academic success. Differential reinforcement was used, reinforcing appropriate behavior but not inappropriate behavior, to reduce the latter to a socially acceptable level. In this procedure, the boy could not exceed a certain amount of disruptive or inappropriate behaviors in one day if he wanted to be rewarded. Examples of rewards were listening to a favorite tape, free time to talk to friends, and sitting in the teacher's car (he liked the feel of the velour seats). After 26 days, there was an 88% reduction in target behaviors.

Sometimes, however, it is difficult to find potent reinforcers that would be feasible to manipulate. With disturbed groups (such as hospitalized patients with schizophrenia), for example, many of the usual reinforcers prove to be ineffective, especially with people who have spent many years living in the back wards of a mental hospital. Ayllon and Azrin (1965) have shown how effective reinforcers can be discovered even for seemingly unmotivated psychotic patients. These reinforcers then can serve to motivate the patients to engage in more adaptive behavior.

As a first step, the patients were observed directly in the ward to discover their most frequent behaviors in situations that permitted them freedom to do what they wished.

TABLE 11.3 Mean Tokens Exchanged for Various Available Reinforcers (by eight Patients During 42 Days)

Reinforcers	Mean Tokens Paid	Number of Patients Paying Any Tokens
Privacy	1352.25	8
Commissary items	969.62	8
Leave from ward	616.37	8
Social interaction with staff	3.75	3
Recreational opportunities	2.37	5
Devotional opportunities	.62	3

Source: Based on Ayllon, T., & Azrin, N. H. (1965). The measurement and reinforcement of behavior of psychotics. *Journal of the Experimental Analysis of Behavior, 8,* 357–383.

Throughout the day, observers carefully recorded the things the patients did, or tried to do, without pressures from the staff. The frequency of these activities provided an index of their potential values as reinforcers.

Six categories of reinforcers were established on the basis of extensive observation. These categories were privacy, leave from the ward, social interactions with the staff, devotional opportunities, recreational opportunities, and items from the hospital canteen. "Privacy," for example, included such freedoms as choice of bedroom or of eating group, and getting a personal cabinet, a room-divider screen, or other means of preserving autonomy. "Recreational opportunities" included exclusive use of a radio or television set, attending movies and dances, and similar entertainment.

The patients could obtain each of the reinforcers with a specific number of **tokens**, which they earned by participating in such rehabilitative functions as self-care and job training. A sensitive index of the subjective reinforcement value of the available activities is obtained by considering the outcomes for which the patients later chose to exchange most of their tokens. Over 42 days, the mean tokens exchanged by eight patients for the available reinforcers are shown in Table 11.3. Note that chances to interact socially with the staff and opportunity for recreation and spiritual devotion are most unpopular. These results suggest that, with chronic hospitalized patients such as these, therapy programs that rely primarily on social motivations would not fare well. Instead, such reinforcers as privacy, autonomy, and freedom might be the most effective incentives.

▸ ASSESSING CONDITIONS CONTROLLING BEHAVIOR

To assess behavior fully, behavior theorists believe that we have to identify the conditions that control it. But how do we know whether or not a response pattern is really controlled or caused by a particular set of conditions? Behaviorally oriented psychologists test the conditions by introducing a change and observing whether or not it produces the expected modification in behavior. They ask: Does a systematic change in stimulus conditions (a "treatment") in fact change the particular response pattern that it supposedly controls? If we hypothesize that a child's reading problem is caused by poor vision, we would expect appropriate treatment (such as corrective eye glasses or corrective surgery) to be followed by a change in the behavior (i.e., an improvement in reading). The same should be true for psychological causes. For example, if we believe that the child's reading difficulty is caused by anxiety about pressure to read from her mother, we should try to show that if the mother reduces her pressure, it will yield the expected improvement in reading. That is, to understand behavior fully, we need to know the conditions that cause it. We can be most confident that we understand those conditions when we can show that a change in them yields the predicted change in the response pattern.

A rigid distinction between behavior assessment and treatment (i.e., behavior change) thus is neither meaningful nor possible. Indeed, some of the most important innovations in behavior assessment have grown out of therapeutic efforts to modify problematic behavior. A main characteristic of these assessment methods is that they are linked closely to behavior change and cannot really be separated from it.

The close connection between behavior assessment and behavior change is most evident in **functional analysis**—that is, analyses of the precise covariations between changes in stimulus conditions and changes in a selected behavior pattern. Such functional analyses are the foundations of behavior assessments, and they are illustrated most clearly in studies that try to change behavior systematically. The basic steps may be seen in a study that was designed to help a girl in nursery school, described later in the chapter.

Functional Analyses: Basic Method

11.4 What is involved in a functional analysis of behavior?

Skinner's work is based on the premise that a genuine science of human behavior is not only possible but desirable. In his view, science should try to predict and determine experimentally the behavior of the individual organism (Skinner, 1974).

Skinner proposed a functional analysis of the organism as a behaving system. Such an analysis tries to link the organism's behavior to the precise conditions that control or determine it. Skinner's approach therefore concentrates on the observable covariations between independent variables (stimulus events) and dependent variables (response patterns). The variables in a functional analysis, according to Skinner, must be external, observable, and described in physical and quantitative terms. It will not do to say that a child becomes concerned with cleanliness when she "fears her father's disapproval"; one must specify the exact ways that changes in the father's specific behavior (e.g., his praise) are related to specific changes in what the child does (e.g., how much she washes her hands per hour).

Skinner contends that the laboratory offers the best chance of obtaining a scientific analysis of behavior; in it, variables can be brought under the control of experimental manipulation. Furthermore, the experimental study of behavior has much to gain from dealing with the behavior of animals below the complex human level. Science, Skinner points out, advances from the simple to the complex and is constantly concerned with whether the processes and laws discovered at one stage are adequate for the next.

Skinner incorporated into his position many concepts regarding classical conditioning, but he concentrated on operant conditioning and showed its potential for powerful real-life applications. Skinner (1953) contends that most human social behavior consists of freely emitted response patterns, or operants. Even a little baby shows much spontaneous behavior: it reaches up to a mobile, turns its head, looks at objects, cries and gurgles, and moves its arms and legs. Through such operants, the organism operates on its environment, changing it and, in turn, being changed by it.

In research on operant conditioning, the typical experiment involves an animal or a person freely performing (emitting) operant responses. The experimenter has preselected a particular class of responses to reinforce (e.g., a young child successfully using a potty-training chair or an adult using personal pronouns in an interview). When the selected operant response is made (the child urinates in the potty or the adult says,

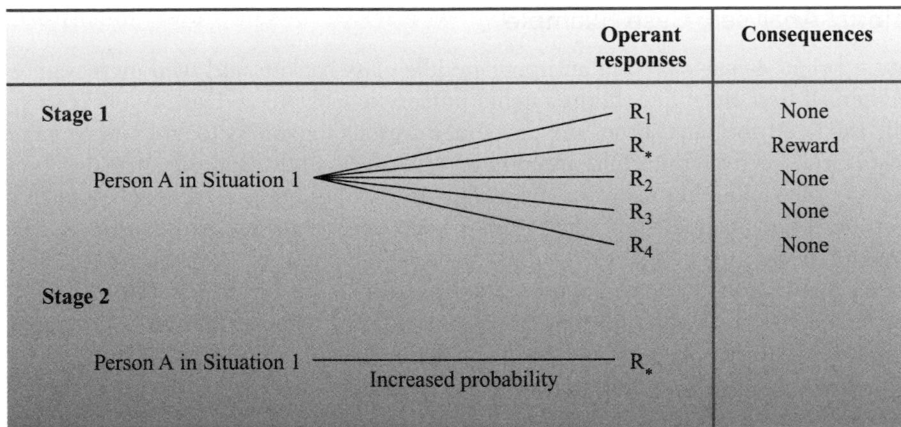

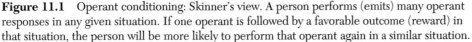

Figure 11.1 Operant conditioning: Skinner's view. A person performs (emits) many operant responses in any given situation. If one operant is followed by a favorable outcome (reward) in that situation, the person will be more likely to perform that operant again in a similar situation.

"I," "you," "she," and so on), the reinforcement occurs: the child gets a small toy; the interviewer nods or murmurs "good." Figure 11.1 illustrates what happens in operant conditioning.

The outcomes a person obtains for a particular behavior influence his or her future behavior. A child's refusal to eat may gain attention from a father usually too busy to pay the child much attention. Since the child's behavior is reinforced by the attention, she may refuse to eat again. If she is offered special treat foods in an effort to tempt her, she may quickly turn into a finicky eater with limited food preferences. By changing the outcomes of responses, reinforcing previously unreinforced behaviors or discontinuing reinforcement for other behaviors, even behavior patterns that seem deeply ingrained may be changed.

Influenced by Skinner, many psychologists have tried to modify maladaptive behavior by altering the consequences to which it leads. Working with people who have severe behavioral problems, they attempt to remove reinforcement for disadvantageous behavior and to make attention, praise, or other reinforcement contingent on the occurrence of more adaptive advantageous behavior. Learning programs of this type follow a set of definite steps. First, the problem behaviors are carefully defined and their frequency in a naturalistic context is measured. Next, one observes and records the reinforcing consequences that seem to maintain the behaviors. Guided by this analysis, the relearning program is designed and put into effect. Finally, the resulting changes are assessed over a period of time.

11.5 How are operant techniques used to change behavior?

For example, in one case, parents sought help because their 3-year-old daughter developed regressive behaviors and reverted to crawling rather than walking. This regression produced serious problems for the child and the family. An analysis of the girl's behavior suggested that her regressive, babyish actions were being encouraged and maintained unwittingly by the attention they brought her. Therefore, an effort was made to rearrange the response–reinforcement patterns so that crawling and infantile acts were not rewarded by the attention of worried adults. Instead, attention and other rewards were made contingent on more adaptive and age-appropriate behaviors, such as jumping, running, and walking, thereby increasing these desirable behaviors while the infantile ones decreased (Harris, Johnston, Kelley, & Wolf, 1964).

Functional Analyses: Case Example

11.6 What was the usefulness of a reversal design in the functional analysis of Ann's problem behaviors?

Ann was a bright 4-year-old from an upper-middle-class background who increasingly isolated herself from the other children in her nursery school (Allen, Hart, Buell, Harris, & Wolf, 1964). At the same time, she developed various ingenious techniques to gain prolonged attention from the adults around her. Ann successfully coerced attention from her teachers, who found her many mental and physical skills highly attractive. Gradually, however, her efforts to maintain adult attention led her to become extremely isolated from other children.

Soon Ann was isolating herself most of the time from other youngsters. This seemed to be happening because most of the attention that adults were giving her was contingent, quite unintentionally, upon behaviors that were incompatible with Ann's relating to other children. Precisely those activities that led Ann away from play with her own peers were being unwittingly reinforced by the attention that her teachers showered on her. The more distressing and problematic Ann's behavior became, the more it elicited interest and close attention from her deeply concerned teachers.

Ann was slipping into a vicious cycle that had to be interrupted. A therapeutic plan was formed where Ann no longer received adult attention for her withdrawal from peers and her attempts at solitary interactions with adults. At the same time, the adults gave her attention only when she played with other children. That is, attention from adults became contingent on her playing with her peers.

As part of the assessment, two observers continuously sampled and recorded Ann's proximity to and interactions with adults and children in school at regular 10-second intervals. The therapeutic plan was instituted after 5 days of baseline data had been recorded. Now, whenever Ann started to interact with children an adult quickly attended to her, rewarding her participation in the group's play activities. Even approximations to social play, such as standing or playing near another child, were followed promptly by attention from a teacher. This attention was designed to further encourage Ann's interactions with other children. For example: "You three girls have a cozy house. Here are some more cups, Ann, for your tea party." Whenever Ann began to leave the group or attempted to make solitary contacts with adults, the teachers stopped attending to her.

Figure 11.2 summarizes the effects of the change in the consequences to Ann for isolate behavior with her peers. Notice that in the baseline period before the new response–reinforcement contingencies were instituted, Ann was spending only about 10% of her school time interacting with other children and 40% with adults. For about half the time she was altogether solitary. As soon as the **contingencies of reinforcement** were changed and adults attended to Ann only when she was near other children, her behavior changed quickly in accord with the new contingencies. When adult–child interactions were no longer followed by attention, they quickly diminished to less than 20%. On the first day of this new arrangement (day 6), Ann spent almost 60% of her time with peers.

To assess the effects of reinforcement more precisely, the procedures were reversed on days 12–16. Adults again rewarded Ann with their attention for interacting with them and disregarded her interactions with children. Under these conditions (the "reversal" days in Figure 11.2), Ann's previous behavior reappeared immediately. In a final shift (beginning on day 17), in which attention from adults again became contingent upon Ann's interacting with children, her contact with peers increased to about 60%. After the end of the special reinforcement procedures (day 25), periodic postchecks indicated that Ann's increased play behavior with peers tended to remain fairly stable.

A complete analysis also must consider the total relations among stimulus conditions rather than focus on single aspects of reinforcement in isolation. These assessments

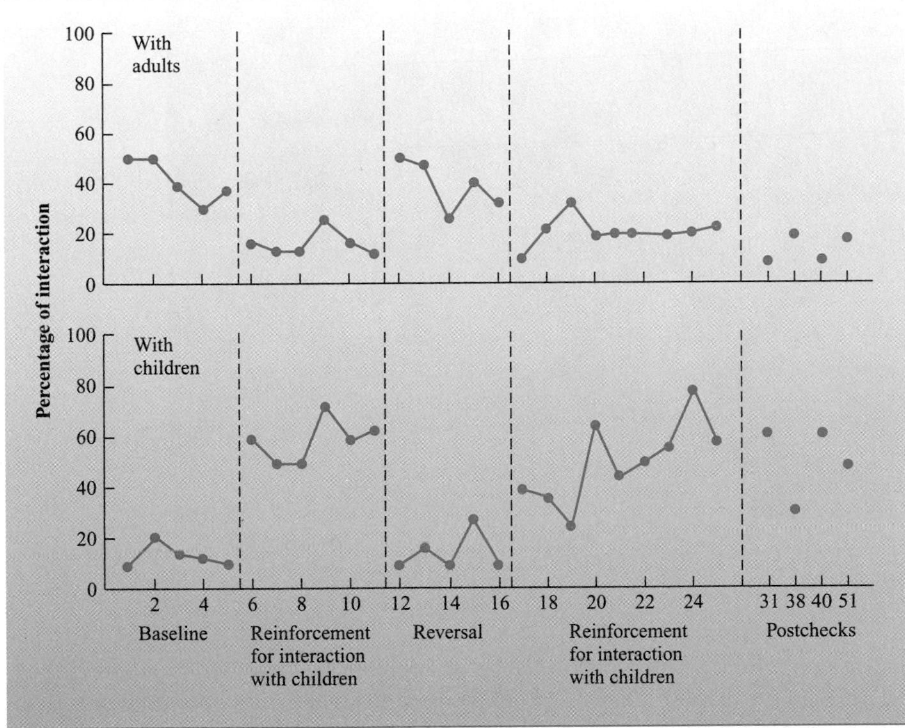

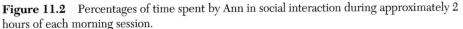

Figure 11.2 Percentages of time spent by Ann in social interaction during approximately 2 hours of each morning session.

Source: From Allen, E. K., Hart, B., Buell, J. S., Harris, F. R., & Wolf, M. M. (1964). Effects of social reinforcement on isolated behavior of a nursery school child. *Child Development, 35*, 515.

showed, for example, that this child was highly discriminating in the very particular times and circumstances during which she became self-destructive. For example, massive withdrawal of attention—as when the experimenter withheld attention from an entire session—did not affect her self-destructive behavior. In contrast, the removal of smiles and attention *only* for previously reinforced responses changed her behavior (also see Smith, Iwata, Vollmer, & Pace, 1992). Note that in this approach, assessment and behavior change become inextricably fused: the assessments guide the therapeutic program, and the efficacy of the treatment program is in turn continuously assessed (e.g., Frank & Hudson, 1990).

▶ CHANGING EMOTIONAL REACTIONS

Next we consider some of the main techniques and findings of behavior therapy based on the concepts of the classic learning-conditioning theories. First we focus on methods designed to change previously learned disadvantageous emotional reactions, such as anxiety.

Desensitization: Overcoming Anxiety

For many years, most therapists were afraid that symptom substitution would occur if they tried to remove the problematic behaviors. This concern stemmed from the

Systematic desensitization has been used effectively to treat anxiety about public speaking and many other fears.

Freudian assumption that attempts to change problematic behavior without first getting at the unconscious causes would lead to other problems that would be even worse than the original ones. This belief was based on the medical model of illness in which it is important to distinguish the observed behavior (e.g., pain in a leg) and its potential cause (e.g., a malignant tumor). Treating the symptoms with pain killers rather than the cancer of course would soon be disastrous. Joseph Wolpe, a psychiatrist who became skeptical about psychoanalytic theory, took the risk of attempting direct behavior modification with many of his patients. In 1958 he published a book describing a method of **systematic desensitization**, also referred to as **counterconditioning**, based on the principle of classical conditioning.

11.7 What behavior change principle underlies systematic desensitization? Describe the three procedural steps in the treatment.

Wolpe was impressed by the work of such early learning theorists as Pavlov and believed that neurosis involves maladaptive learned habits, especially anxiety (fear) responses. In neurotic behavior, he hypothesized, anxiety has become the conditioned response to stimuli that are not anxiety-provoking for other people. He reasoned that therapy might help the neurotic individual to reduce anxiety by counterconditioning him to make a competing (antagonistic) response to anxiety-eliciting stimuli. In his words, "If a response antagonistic to anxiety can be made to occur in the presence of anxiety-evoking stimuli so that it is accompanied by a complete or partial suppression of the anxiety responses, the bond between these stimuli and the anxiety response will be weakened" (Wolpe, 1958, p. 71). His attempt to desensitize the individual to anxiety-evoking stimuli includes three steps (summarized in Table 11.4):

1. *Establishing the anxiety stimulus hierarchy.* First the therapist helps the client identify the situations that evoke distressing emotional arousal and avoidance, usually in the course of interviews. Sometimes a person has many areas of anxiety, such as fear of failure, self-doubts, dating, guilt about sex, and so on. Regardless of how many areas or "themes" there are, each is treated separately.

TABLE 11.4 Three Basic Steps in the Desensitization of Anxiety

Step	Example
1. Establishing the anxiety stimulus hierarchy; anxiety-evoking situations ranked from least to most severe	*Low anxiety:* reading about speeches alone in your room *Intermediate anxiety:* getting dressed the morning on which you are to give a speech *High anxiety:* presenting a speech before an audience
2. Learning an incompatible response	Learning deep muscle relaxation by tensing and relaxing various muscle groups (head, shoulders, arms), deep breathing techniques, and similar methods
3. Counterconditioning: learning to make the incompatible response to items in the hierarchy	Practicing relaxation responses to the lowest item on the hierarchy and moving gradually to the higher items

Note: These items are examples from much longer hierarchies.

For each theme, the person grades or ranks the component stimuli on a **hierarchy of severity of anxiety** ranging from the most to the least intensely anxiety-provoking events (see Table 11.5). For example, a person who is terrified of public speaking might consider "reading about speeches while alone in my room," a mildly anxiety-provoking stimulus, while "walking up before the audience to present the speech" might create severe anxiety in him (Paul, 1966). In Gary W.'s case, "the minute before starting a formal speech" was the most anxiety-provoking, while "watching a friend practice a speech" and "taking notes in the library for a speech" were only moderately disturbing. As another example, a woman who sought treatment for sexual dysfunction indicated that

TABLE 11.5 Items of Different Severity from Four Anxiety Hierarchies*

	Anxiety Hierarchies (Themes)			
Severity (Degree of Anxiety)	1 Interpersonal Rejection	2 Guilt about Work	3 Test-Taking	4 Expressing Anger
Low	Thinking about calling Mary (a new girlfriend) tonight	Thinking "I still haven't answered all my mail"	Getting the reading list for the course	Watching strangers quarrel in street
Intermediate	Asking for a date on the telephone	Taking off an hour for lunch	Studying at my desk the night before the final	My brother shouting at his best friend
High	Trying a first kiss	Going to a movie instead of working	Sitting in the examination room waiting for the test to be handed out	Saying "No! I don't want to!" to mother

*These items are examples from much longer hierarchies.

"being kissed on cheeks and forehead" evoked merely mild anxiety but thinking about items like "having intercourse in the nude while sitting on husband's lap" produced the most intense anxiety in her (Lazarus, 1963).

2. *Training the incompatible response (relaxation).* After identifying and grading the stimuli that evoke anxiety, the person needs to learn responses that can be used later to inhibit anxiety. Wolpe prefers to use **relaxation responses** because they can be taught easily and are always inherently incompatible with anxiety: no one can be relaxed and anxious simultaneously. The therapist helps the client to learn relaxation by elaborate instructions that teach first to tense and then to relax parts of the body (arms, shoulders, neck, head) until gradually an almost hypnotic state of total calm and deep muscle relaxation is achieved. Most people can learn how to relax within a few sessions. The critical problem is to learn to relax to anxiety-evoking stimuli, and that task is attempted in the next phase.

3. *Associating anxiety stimuli and incompatible responses.* In the critical phase, counterconditioning, the client is helped to relax deeply, and then is presented with the least anxiety-arousing stimulus from the previously established hierarchy. Usually the stimulus event is described verbally or presented symbolically (in a picture) while the client is deeply relaxed and calm. As the therapist says the words for the item (e.g., "walking down a fire escape from the 6th floor") the client with a fear of heights tries to generate the most vivid image of it that his or her imagination can form. As soon as the client can concentrate on this item while remaining calm, the next, more severe item from the hierarchy is introduced until, step by step, the entire hierarchy is mastered (e.g.,"looking down from the roof of a skyscraper").

If at any point in the procedure the client begins to become anxious while presented with an anxiety stimulus, he or she signals the therapist. The client is promptly instructed to discontinue the image of the stimulus until calm again. Then a somewhat less severe item from the hierarchy is presented so that he or she can concentrate on it without anxiety. After that, the client is ready to advance to the next item in the anxiety hierarchy and the step-by-step progress up the list can be resumed.

In sum, the desensitization (counterconditioning) procedure attempts to have responses incompatible with anxiety (such as relaxation) occur in the presence of mildly anxiety-evoking stimuli. The incompatible response then will at least partially prevent the anxiety response. In that way, the association between the aversive stimulus and anxiety becomes reduced, while the association of the stimulus with the relaxation reaction becomes strengthened (Guthrie, 1935; Wolpe, 1958).

McClanahan (1995), for example, treated a woman who suffered from severe habitual nail-biting. McClanahan noted that the nail-biting was almost always precipitated by anxiety, which included feeling overwhelmed, apprehensive, nervous, and worried. The desensitization techniques used were deep muscle relaxation and Transcendental Meditation. Systematic desensitization reduced anxiety and decreased the frequency and duration of nail-biting significantly. Clinical reports of successful desensitization may be encouraging, but more conclusive evidence comes from controlled experiments, and many studies indicate that desensitization is a valuable method for modifying phobias and reducing anxiety (Kazdin & Wilson, 1978; Wilson & O'Leary, 1980).

Conditioned Aversion: Making Stimuli Unattractive

While some people suffer because they have learned to react negatively to certain situations, others are plagued because they become pleasurably aroused by, or even addicted to, stimuli that most people in the culture find neutral or even aversive. One example of this problem is fetishistic behavior, in which the person may become sexually excited by such objects as undergarments. In these cases, things that are neutral or even disgusting for most people have acquired the power to produce pleasurable emotional arousal. Another example is drug addiction for which the arousal may have a significant and necessary physiological component to it. Such reactions can provide the person with some immediate reduction of pain, but they often have severely negative and destructive long-term consequences (Baker, Piper, McCarthy, Majeskie, & Fiore, 2003).

11.8 What conditioning procedures are used in aversion therapy? What are some limitations of this approach?

A positively valued stimulus may be neutralized by counterconditioning if it is presented with stimuli that evoke extremely unpleasant reactions. Gradually, as a result of repeated pairings, the previously positive stimulus acquires some of the aversive emotional properties evoked by the noxious events with which it has been associated.

An Example: Treating Cocaine Dependency

Hundreds of thousands of Americans undergo treatment for substance abuse and dependence every year, and it has proved extremely difficult to help many of them. The dominant view in treatment efforts in much of the last century was influenced by psychoanalytic theory. It assumed that as a first step substance abusers had to overcome their defense mechanism of denial and their refusal to admit that they had a serious problem with potentially tragic consequences (as reviewed in Ksir, Hart, & Ray, 2005). Consequently it was believed that abusers could not really be helped until they "hit rock bottom" and let the reality of their problem sink in so that they become motivated to get help. As Ksir and colleagues (2005) point out, unfortunately often the consequences are extreme (e.g., death) before the abuser hits bottom and achieves insight.

Workers at the behavioral conditioning level were among the first to try to do research to find more effective treatments. In one example, chemical aversion therapy was used to treat cocaine addicts who volunteered to participate in a 2-week study (Frawley & Smith, 1990). The stimulus used to represent cocaine was a mixture of chemicals that tasted and smelled like "street cocaine." In the treatment room, there were pictures of paraphernalia for cocaine use, as well as the utensils used to snort cocaine. The patients were instructed to "snort" the "cocaine" in their normal fashion. They then were given an injection of nausea-inducing drugs and were instructed to continue to "snort" the "cocaine." Afterward, the patients were encouraged to focus on paraphernalia, pictures of cocaine, and to pair the cocaine use with negative consequences, all while experiencing nausea.

At 6 months' posttreatment, more than half of the cocaine addicts had totally abstained from cocaine since the treatment. As predicted, the pairing of the nausea with the cocaine use produced a conditioned aversion for the recovering addicts and helped them break their habit. Systematic counterconditioning has also been attempted with other addictions such as alcoholism (Bandura, 1969, 1986).

Psychologists are reluctant to use **aversion therapy** like this one because they inflict aversive experiences on a troubled person. However, aversion therapies usually are attempted only after other forms of help (such as interview therapies) have been tried unsuccessfully. In some cases, aversion treatments have come as a last resort in lieu of more drastic treatments, such as long imprisonment or irreversible brain surgery

(Rachman & Hodgeson, 1980; Raymond, 1956). And usually they are not imposed on the client: they are voluntary and the person submits to them with full knowledge and consent.

Indeed, it is this very dependence on the client's cooperation that limits the efficacy of the treatment. That is, after the initial counterconditioning trials, the client often may revert to his or her fetish without submitting voluntarily to further treatment. Since it becomes impractical to hospitalize him continuously or remove him from exposure to the problematic stimuli, he must learn to administer aversive stimulation to himself whenever necessary. For example, he may be taught to administer electric shock to himself from a small portable, battery-operated apparatus concealed in his clothing, or to induce aversive thoughts or imagery whenever he experiences the problematic urges. Thus, counterconditioning procedures ultimately provide the individual with a form of *self*-control. Whether or not he continues to practice and seek this self-control is up to him. And whether or not he practices self-control determines how effectively his new behavior will be maintained (Mischel, Cantor, & Feldman, 1996).

CHANGING BEHAVIOR

Many psychologists have tried to modify maladaptive behaviors by changing the consequences to which those behaviors lead. Guided to a large extent by B.F. Skinner's ideas about learning, they try to withdraw reinforcement for undesired behavior and to make attention, approval, or other reinforcement contingent on the occurrence of more appropriate, advantageous behavior (e.g., Haring & Breen, 1992). Their basic procedure is well illustrated in the work of Hawkins and his colleagues (1966).

Case Example: Hyperactivity

11.9 How have operant procedures been used to treat autistic children?

Hawkins's case was Peter, a young child of low intelligence. Peter was brought to a clinic by his mother because he was "hyperactive" and "unmanageable." Because the problems seemed to involve the relations between Peter and his mother, he was assessed and treated directly in his home. His mother served as a therapist under the guidance of the professional workers.

A first task was to specify the problematic behaviors. Direct observations of Peter in the home revealed the following problems to be among the most common and disturbing ones:

1. Biting his shirt or arm.
2. Sticking his tongue out.
3. Hitting and kicking himself, other people, or objects.
4. Using derogatory names.
5. Removing his clothing (and threatening to remove it).

The frequency of these and similar behaviors was carefully recorded at 10-second intervals during 1-hour observation sessions in the home. After the first assessments were completed, the researcher helped the mother to recognize the occurrence of Peter's nine most objectionable behaviors. Whenever these occurred during subsequent 1-hour sessions at home, she was taught to respond to them with definite steps. These steps involved signaling to Peter when his behavior became disruptive and, if a verbal warning failed, isolating him briefly in a separated, locked "time-out" room without toys and other attractions. Release from the room (and reinstatement of play, attention, and nurturance) was contingent on Peter's terminating the tantrum and showing more reasonable, less destructive behavior. This arrangement was opposite to the one the mother may have inadvertently used in the past, when she became increasingly concerned and attentive (even if distressed) as Peter became increasingly wild. Subsequent assessment revealed that the new regimen was effective in minimizing Peter's outbursts. While apparently helpful to Peter's development, reducing his tantrums may have been just one step toward the more extensive help he needed.

Using a combination of modeling and reinforcement procedures, Lovaas and his coworkers (1966, 1991) modified the deficient speech and social behaviors of severely disturbed ("autistic") children who were unable to talk. First, the therapist modeled the sounds himself. He rewarded the child only for vocalizing the modeled sounds within a specified time interval. As the child's proficiency increased, the therapist proceeded to utter more complicated verbal units. Gradually, training progressed from sounds to words and phrases. As the training continued, rewards from the therapist became contingent on the child's reproducing increasingly elaborate verbalizations more skillfully (i.e., more quickly and accurately). The combination of modeling and reinforcement procedures gradually helped the child to learn more complex meanings and complicated speech. Research like this shows the value of wisely used reinforcement; but rewards also may be hazardous, as discussed in *In Focus 11.1*.

11.10 How can overjustification effects be avoided in behavior change attempts involving the use of positive reinforcers?

IN FOCUS 11.1

REWARDS MAY BACKFIRE

Rewards are important for effective behavior, but they can be used unwisely. A major purpose of effective therapy (and socialization) is to wean the individual away from external controls and rewards so that his behavior becomes increasingly guided and supported by intrinsic gratifications—that is, satisfactions closely connected with the activity itself. Therefore, it is essential to use rewards or incentives only to the extent necessary to initiate and sustain prosocial (adaptive, desirable) behavior.

External incentives may be important in order to encourage a person to try activities that have not yet become attractive for him or her. When rewards are used to call attention to a good job, or to an individual's competence at an activity, they may actually bolster interest. They provide positive performance feedback and supply tangible evidence of excellence (Harackiewicz, Manderlink, & Sansone, 1984). Approval and praise from parents for trying to play a violin, for example, may be helpful first steps in encouraging the child's earliest musical interest. But when the youngster begins to experience activity-generated satisfactions (e.g. from playing the music itself), it becomes important to avoid excessive external rewards. Too much reward would be unnecessary and possibly harmful, leading the child to play for the wrong reasons and making him or her prone to lose interest easily when the external rewards are reduced or stopped altogether (Lepper, Greene, & Nisbett, 1973). Likewise, children need to be encouraged to develop a sense of fairness, empathy, and helpful responsiveness to the needs of other people. To become a social being requires attention to the long-term consequences of one's behavior and not just to its immediate payoffs. While such sensitivities might initially be encouraged by external rewards, ultimately they need to be sustained by gratification from the activities themselves.

In sum, **overjustification** of an activity by excessive external rewards may interfere with the satisfactions (intrinsic interests) that would otherwise be generated by the activity itself. Excessive external rewards may even have boomerang effects and lead the recipient to devalue and resist the rewarded activity. Children who get paid to do their homework may develop a feeling that schoolwork is an aversive chore rather than a route to learning and self-development.

People often are judged to be maladjusted mainly because they have not learned how to perform the behavior patterns necessary to effectively meet the social or vocational demands they encounter. They cannot behave appropriately because they lack the skills required for successful functioning. For example, the socially deprived, economically underprivileged person may suffer because he or she never has acquired the response patterns and competencies needed to obtain success in vocational and interpersonal situations. Similarly, the high school dropout in our culture does indeed carry an enduring handicap. Such **behavioral deficits**, if widespread, may lead to many other problems, including severe emotional distress and avoidance patterns to escape the unhappy consequences of failure and incompetence. Many special learning programs have been designed to teach people a variety of problem-solving strategies and cognitive skills (Bijou, 1965), and to help them achieve many other positive changes in behavior (e.g., Kamps et al., 1992; Karoly, 1980).

Contingency Management: Contracting to Control Drug Abuse

A promising behavioral approach to treating substance abuse is **contingency management**. The continuing interest in contingency management reflects the finding that this approach has produced consistent reductions in substance-using behaviors among diverse substance-abusing populations (Higgins, Heil, & Lussier, 2004). In one version, the person receives immediate rewards for providing drug-free urine samples. The value of the rewards is increased progressively with consecutive drug-free urine samples. However, rewards are withheld if the patient's urine sample is positive for an illicit drug. One problem with this approach is that it can quickly become too costly for most public treatment programs (Ksir et al. 2005).

A move to enroll the person more actively in his or her own behavior change program whenever possible is reflected in the use of **contingency contracting** (Rimm & Masters, 1974; Thoresen & Mahoney, 1974). In this procedure, the client makes a contract with himself and the therapist designed to help control his out of control behavior. An example was the treatment of "Miss X" for drug abuse as described by Boudin (1972). Miss X, a heavy user of amphetamines, made a contingency contract with her therapist. She gave him $500 (all of her money) in 10 signed checks of $50 each and committed him to send a check to the Ku Klux Klan (her least favorite organization) whenever she violated any step in a series of mutually agreed-upon specific actions for curbing her drug use. After applying the contract for 3 months, a follow-up for a 2-year period indicated that Miss X did not return to amphetamine use. The principle of contingency contracting can be extended to a wide variety of commitments in which the client explicitly authorizes the therapist to use rewards to encourage more advantageous behaviors in ways formally agreed upon in advance.

11.11 Describe the use and effectiveness of contingency contracting in self-control programs.

Experimental studies in laboratory situations have shown the value of operant conditioning principles for altering drug-taking behavior. For example, smoked cocaine self-administration by cocaine-dependent individuals can be decreased substantially when they get cash as the alternative reinforcer. Note that it has to be concrete and immediate, that is, cash; if merchandise vouchers were used instead they had little effect on cocaine self-administration (Hart, Haney, Foltin, & Fischman, 2000). Related research showed that stimulant abusers chose to self-administer methamphetamine on only about half of the choice opportunities they had when a monetary alternative was available to them (Hart, Ward, Haney, Foltin, & Fischman, 2001).

IN FOCUS 11.2

DEPRESSION AS INSUFFICIENT REINFORCEMENT

According to one influential behavioral theory, depression may be understood as a result of a persistent lack of gratification or positive outcomes (reinforcement) for the person's own behavior (Lewinsohn, 1975; Lewinsohn, Clarke, Hops, & Andrews, 1990). That is, depressed persons feel bad and withdraw from life because their environments are consistently unresponsive to them and fail to provide enough positive consequences for what they are doing. The situation is analogous to an **extinction schedule** in which reinforcement for a behavior is withdrawn until gradually the behavior itself stops. In the case of the depressed person, the only reinforcement that does continue tends to be in the form of attention and sympathy from relatives and friends for the very behaviors that are maladaptive: weeping, complaining, talking about suicide. These depressive behaviors are so unpleasant that they soon alienate most people in the depressed person's environment, thus producing further isolation, lack of reinforcement, and unhappiness in a vicious cycle of increasing misery and increasing withdrawal.

Behavioral View of Depression. Depressed people, according to this theory, may suffer from three basic problems. First, they tend to find relatively few events and activities gratifying. Second, they tend to live in environments in which reinforcement is not readily available for their adaptive behaviors. For example, they may live highly isolated lives, as often happens with older people living alone, or with younger people in large universities that make them feel lost. Third, they lack the skills and behaviors they need to get positive reactions and feedback from other people. For example, they may be shy and socially awkward, making gratifying relationships with others very difficult. It follows that they in turn develop feelings such as "I'm not likable," or even "I'm no good." The essentials of the theory are shown schematically in Figure 11.3.

Although the theory has not been tested conclusively, a good deal of evidence is consistent with it. For example, depressed people do seem to elicit fewer behaviors from other people and thus presumably get less social reinforcement from them. Depressed people also tend to engage in fewer pleasant activities and enjoy such events less than individuals who are not depressed (Lewinsohn, 1975).

This concept of depression immediately suggests a treatment strategy (Lewinsohn et al., 1990): increase the rate of positive reinforcement for the depressed person's adaptive efforts. Note that such a plan would require increasing the rate of positive outcomes received by depressed people contingent on their own behavior; it does not mean simply giving more rewards regardless of what the individual does.

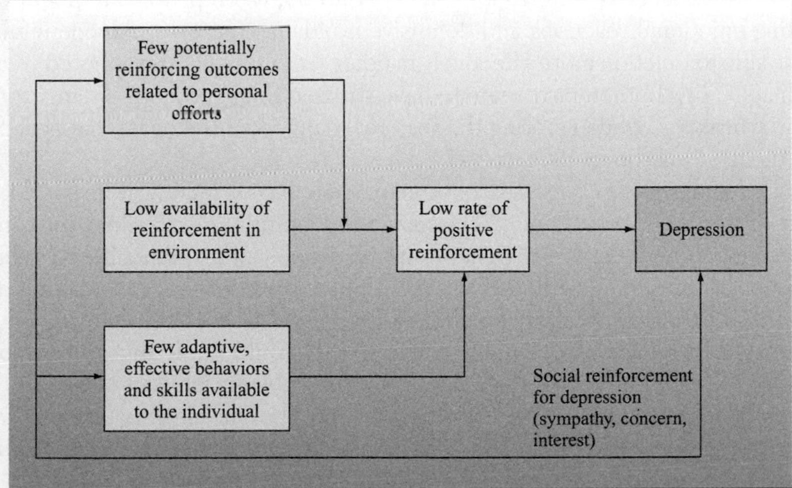

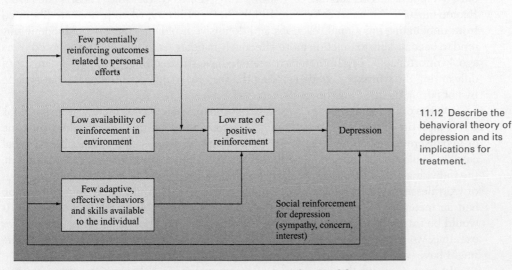

11.12 Describe the behavioral theory of depression and its implications for treatment.

Figure 11.3 Schematic representation of Lewinsohn's theory of depression.

Source: Based on Lewinsohn, P. M. (1975). The behavioral study and treatment of depression. In M. Hersen (Ed.), *Progress in behavior modification*. Reprinted with permission from Elsevier.

Symptom Substitution?

Do behavior therapies neglect the causes of the person's problematic behavior and thus leave the "roots" unchanged while modifying only the "superficial" or "symptomatic" behaviors? It is often charged that behavior therapists ignore the basic or underlying causes of problems. Advocates of behavior therapy insist that they do seek causes but that they search for *observable* causes controlling the current problem, not its historically distant antecedents or its hypothesized but unobservable psychodynamic mechanisms. Traditional, insight-oriented approaches have looked, instead, for historical roots in the person's past and for theoretical mechanisms in the form of psychodynamics. The difference between these two approaches thus is not that one looks for causes while the other does not: Both approaches search for causes but they disagree about what those causes really are.

11.13 What controversy gave rise to the concept of symptom substitution? What research evidence exists for symptom substitution?

> All analyses of behavior seek causes; the difference between social behavior and [psychodynamic] analyses is in whether current controlling causes or historically distant antecedents are invoked. Behavioral analyses seek the current variables and conditions controlling the behavior of interest. Traditional [psychodynamic] theories have looked, instead, for historical roots . . .
>
> (Mischel, 1968, p. 264)

Traditional approaches ask about the patient, "Why did she become this kind of person?" Behavioral approaches ask, "What is now causing her to behave as she does and what would have to be modified to change her behavior?"

Does a neglect in treatment of the psychodynamics hypothesized by traditional therapies produce **symptom substitution**? In spite of many initial fears about possible symptom substitution, behavior change programs of the kind discussed in the preceding sections tend to be the most effective methods presently available. Researchers have found that the changed behaviors are not automatically replaced by other problematic ones (Bandura, 1986; Kazdin & Wilson, 1978; Lang & Lazovik, 1963; Paul, 1966; Rachman, 1967; Rachman & Wilson, 1980). On the contrary, when people are liberated from debilitating emotional reactions and defensive avoidance patterns, they generally tend to become able to function more effectively in other areas as well. As was noted years ago: "Unfortunately, psychotherapists seem to have stressed the hypothetical dangers of only curing the symptoms, while ignoring the very real dangers of the harm that is done by not curing them" (Grossberg, 1964, p. 83).

On the other hand, some enthusiastic proponents of behavior modification overlook the complexity of the client's problems. They may oversimplify the difficulties into one or two discrete phobias when in fact the client may have many other difficulties. In that case, it would not be surprising to find that even after removal of the initial problem, the individual still is beset with such other psychological troubles as self-doubts, feelings of worthlessness, and so on. Such a condition, of course, would imply that the person had an incomplete treatment rather than that symptom substitution had occurred. It would be extremely naive to think that reducing Gary W.'s public speaking anxiety, for example, would make his life free of all other problems. Whatever other difficulties he might have would still require attention in their own right.

In sum, to avoid the emergence of disadvantageous behaviors, a comprehensive program must provide the person with more adaptive ways of dealing with life; such a program may have to go beyond merely reducing the most obvious problems. Behavior modification does not automatically produce generalized positive effects that remove all the person's troubles.

Evaluating the Consequences of Behavior, Not the Person

The behavioral approach avoids evaluating the health, adequacy, or abnormality of the person or personality as a whole. Instead, when judgments are made, they focus on evaluation of the individual's specific behaviors. Behaviors are evaluated on the basis of the kinds of consequences that they produce for the person who generates them and for other people who are around him or her. Evaluations about the positive or negative consequences of behavior are social and ethical judgments that depend on the values and standards of the community that makes them. Advantageous behaviors are those judged to have positive personal and interpersonal consequences (e.g., helping people "feel good," or increasing constructive, creative outcomes) without any aversive impact on others. Behaviors that have negative, life-threatening, destructive consequences, or those that endanger the full potentialities of the person or other people (e.g., debilitating fears, homicidal attempts), would be considered maladaptive.

The behavioral approach also implies a high value for the development of the individual's total competencies and skills so that he or she can maximize opportunities and options. Similarly, the person must be able to discern the important contingencies and rules of reinforcement in his or her life in order to maximize satisfactions and minimize aversive, disadvantageous outcomes. To be able to overcome unfavorable environments and life conditions, it is especially important to develop effective strategies for self-control.

Does Changing Behavior Change Personality?

11.14 Under what conditions can changes in specific behaviors foster personality change?

There is much controversy with regard to the depth and endurance of behavior change. Basically, the question is whether behavior change entails genuine, durable change or whether it is limited to relatively minor, specific behaviors that have little applicability to major life problems.

To facilitate transfer from treatment to life, workers at this level of analysis introduce into treatment stimulus conditions that are as similar as possible to the life situations in which the new behaviors will be used. For example, if the patient is afraid of going into elevators, the treatment may be conducted in elevators, not in the therapist's office.

The question remains: When fears and other emotional problems are reduced, and social competence improves through more adaptive, functional patterns of social behavior, does personality change? The answer depends on the definition of personality. There is considerable evidence that changing disadvantageous behaviors, such as a severe stutter or uncontrolled facial tics, and eliminating distressing, fear-producing emotional reactions, also improves how people feel about themselves, and their self-concepts (e.g., Bandura, 1997; Meichenbaum, 1995). Self-concepts, and self-esteem, tend to reflect at least in part the individual's actual competencies and how the person's behavior is seen by others (e.g., Leary & Downs, 1995). Our self-perceptions include the information that we get about the adequacy of our own behaviors, and if these self-perceptions are part of personality, then personality changes when behavior becomes more adaptive and gratifying. The individual who learns to perform more competently achieves more gratification and is also likely to develop a more positive attitude toward him- or herself. As a result of being able to overcome fears and anxieties, one should also become more confident. Reducing Gary W.'s fears of public speaking would not be a cure-all, but it might certainly help him to feel more positively about himself and would open alternatives (e.g., in his career opportunities) otherwise closed to him. Ultimately, if enough anxious behavior is brought under control, shyness may decrease, creating a cycle of improved behavior leading to improved confidence and positive expectations,

People's standards affect their reactions to performance outcomes. To some, an A$^-$ can feel like a failure.

leading to further personality change. At least, that is the rationale of much work at this level of analysis.

But while this may often be true, it does not always happen. Indeed, critics of behavior therapy note that people may suffer not because their behavior is inadequate but because they evaluate it improperly. That is, some people have problems with distorted self-concepts more than with performance. Often people label themselves and react to their own behaviors very differently than do the people around them and the rest of society. An esteemed financier, for example, may receive the rewards and praise of society while he is privately unhappy enough to commit suicide. Or a popular student who is the prom queen of her school might have secret doubts about her sexual adequacy and femininity and might be torturing herself with these fears.

Many personal problems involve inappropriate self-evaluations and self-reactions. In these cases, the difficulty often may be the person's appraisal of his or her performances and attributes rather than their actual quality and competence level. For example, a student may react self-punitively to his scholastic achievements even when their objective quality is high. The student who is badly upset with himself for an occasional grade less than an A may need help with self-assessment rather than with schoolwork. Fortunately, work at the phenomenological-humanistic level, reviewed in the next part of the text, goes on to address those issues.

▶ SUMMARY

CHARACTERISTICS OF BEHAVIORAL ASSESSMENTS

- Behavioral approaches to personality all carefully measure behavior in relation to specific stimulus conditions. They treat observed behavior as a sample, and the focus is on how the specific sample is affected by variations in the stimulus conditions.

DIRECT BEHAVIOR MEASUREMENT

- Behavior may be measured directly by sampling it, both verbally and in performance, and by measuring physiological and emotional reactions.
- The reinforcing value of stimuli may be assessed from an individual's choices in lifelike situations, verbal preferences, and ratings, or the observed effects of various stimuli on actual behavior.
- In clinical work, it may be especially important to discover rewards that are effective for the individual to facilitate therapeutic progress.

ASSESSING CONDITIONS CONTROLLING BEHAVIOR

- Functional analyses, the foundations of behavior assessments, require careful observation of behavior as it naturally occurs to ascertain the conditions that control or determine it.

- In behavioral interventions, systematic changes are made in controlling conditions until the problem behavior no longer occurs and more satisfying behaviors are substituted.
- An example of functional analyses was explored through the case study of 4-year-old Ann, whose teachers began to positively reinforce her interacting with peers to prevent her from social withdrawal.

CHANGING EMOTIONAL REACTIONS

- Systematic desensitization can help people overcome fears or anxieties. The individual is exposed cognitively (e.g., in imagination) to increasingly severe samples of aversive or fear-arousing stimuli; simultaneously she is helped to make responses incompatible with anxiety, such as muscle relaxation. Gradually the anxiety evoked by the aversive stimulus is reduced and the stimulus is neutralized.
- In conditional aversion, a positive-arousing stimulus (e.g., cocaine for a cocaine addict) may be neutralized by repeatedly pairing it with one that is very aversive (such as chemically induced nausea).

CHANGING BEHAVIOR

- Maladaptive behaviors such as hyperactivity may be modified by changing the consequences to which they lead. Attention, approval, or other positive consequences are withdrawn from the maladaptive behavior and rewards become contingent instead on the occurrence of more advantageous behavior.
- The overuse of external rewards may backfire.
- In contingency contracting, the person makes a contract with another individual to self-reward for increasing positive behaviors (or self-punish for performing negative behaviors), as specified in the contract.
- A promising theory of depression suggests that depressed people are caught in a vicious cycle of lack of reinforcement for their own efforts, leading to greater withdrawal from other people and, in turn, increased depression.
- To facilitate transfer from treatment to life, treatment samples the relevant situations and takes place in the same setting in which improvement is desired.

▶ KEY TERMS

aversion therapy 283
behavior sampling 272
behavioral deficits 286
contingencies of reinforcement 278
contingency contracting 286
contingency management 286
extinction schedule 287
functional analysis 276
generalized conditioned reinforcers 274
hierarchy of severity of anxiety 281
overjustification 285
primary reinforcers 274
relaxation responses 282
symptom substitution 288
systematic desensitization (counterconditioning) 280
tokens 275

TAKING STOCK

PART IV

THE BEHAVIORAL-CONDITONING LEVEL

▶ OVERVIEW: FOCUS, CONCEPTS, METHODS

The next table summarizes the main characteristics of work at the Behavioral-Conditioning Level of analysis. As the table indicates, these approaches focus on the individual's behavior in its context. Prior learning and cues in the situation are seen as important determinants of behavior. Preferred data consist of direct observations of behavior as it changes in relation to changing situations. Responses are used as samples of behavior, not as indirect indicators of hypothesized inner states, motives, or traits. Research seeks to analyze the conditions that influence or control the behavior of interest, including the conditions that allow persons to enhance and control their own behavior, for example, by rearranging their environments. To change the person's behavior, therapy is directed at identifying and modifying the consequences behavior produces or the outcomes associated with it. The situation is treated as an integral aspect of behavior; it provides cues and outcomes that impact the maintenance and modification of behavior. Thus, the situation cannot be removed from the assessment of behavior or from attempts to change behavior.

Overview of Focus, Concepts, Methods: The Behavioral-Conditioning Level

Basic units	Behavior-in-situation
Causes of behavior	Prior learning and cues in situation (including behavior of others); reinforcement contingencies
Behavioral manifestations of personality	Stable behavior equated with personality
Favored data	Direct observations of behavior in the target situation; behavior change as a function of changing the situation (stimulus conditions)
Observed responses used as	Behavior samples
Research focus	Behavior change; analysis of conditions controlling behavior
Approach to personality change	By changing conditions; by learning experiences that modify behavior
Role of situation	Extremely important: regulates much behavior, elicits emotional reactions and behavior patterns

▶ ENDURING CONTRIBUTIONS OF THE BEHAVIORAL-CONDITIONING LEVEL

The contributions of behavioral approaches for applied purposes were widely applauded for identifying many effective, if incomplete, ways to help think about and improve diverse problems in everyday life (O'Donohue et al., 2001). Dollard and Miller translated many key psychodynamic concepts into learning terms in ways that encouraged experimental research. Work at the behavioral level helped take the mystery out of many of the "abnormal" phenomena that had long puzzled earlier workers. Notably, it showed how seemingly inexplicable and irrational behaviors—such as intense anxieties and bizarre behavior patterns—may be shaped by the circumstances of life and the ways in which learning and reinforcement occur. Over the years, much of this work became the basis for current cognitive behavior therapies that directly address issues in personality change and the coping processes of normal individuals (Meichenbaum, 1993). Gradually, these therapies have integrated discoveries from the behavioral level with those from more recent work on social cognition and mental processes, which are discussed in later sections.

Likewise, findings from research at the behavioral level on the responses of animals in laboratory conditions became the basis of later studies of complex social learning and personality at the Social Cognitive Level. Recent breakthroughs at the biological level that identify brain centers involved in emotional reactions and those fundamental for other types of learning and memory functions also have given new life to work at the behavioral level. Brain processes and their links to behavior now can be studied experimentally, particularly in laboratory studies with animals. Consequently, the "black box" of the brain and the processes that occur within it, previously treated as "fictions" and off limits for a scientific psychology, have now become the arena for extensive research (e.g., LeDoux, 1996, 2001) at the vanguard of the science.

In the past, work at this level was faulted for overemphasizing the "stimulus" or "situation" and the role of rewards, and for missing much of the essentials of human personality, including the human potential for freedom and self-control: people are not just victims of their situations but also can actively create and change them, if not in the laboratory then certainly in real life. Critics saw behavioral work as reflecting a focus on the importance of the situation that minimizes the importance of dispositional or intrapsychic determinants such as traits and motives (Bowers, 1973; Carlson, 1971). A great deal of research in recent years has again demonstrated the power of stimuli to trigger automatically all sorts of cognitive, emotional, and behavioral reactions, leading practitioners to question the importance of the person's consciousness or internal thought processes (e.g., Bargh, 1996, 2001). The question of the degree to which the person can actually exert "agency" and intervene to change the ways in which stimuli impact on him or her remains one of the great open issues, actively pursued by a wide range of scientists and philosophers. We will revisit these big questions in the final sections of this text.

Historically, one of the persistent concerns about behavioral approaches is whether they really contribute to an understanding of the phenomena of interest to personality psychologists. An early worry about behavioral approaches was that they did not even try to study complex and distinctively human qualities, such as the emotions and internal states that seem so basic for understanding personality and appreciating its complexity. Indeed, some critics charged that behavioral psychologists only study what is easy to study with available methods. They accuse them of looking only under the light. Addressing this concern, researchers at the social cognitive level, discussed later in the text, introduced some of the important missing pieces.

PART 

THE PHENOMENOLOGICAL-HUMANISTIC LEVEL

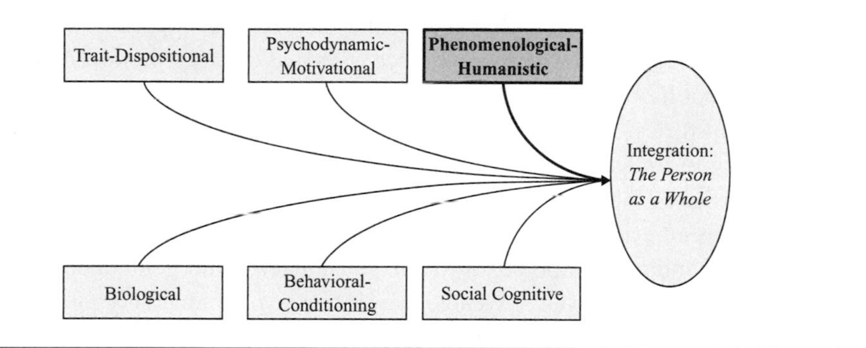

PRELUDE TO PART V: THE PHENOMENOLOGICAL-HUMANISTIC LEVEL

At the Phenomenological-Humanistic Level the goal is to connect with the individual's own inner psychological experiences as perceived and understood by that person. Questions here are: How do we see and experience ourselves, other people, and the social world? What are the implications and consequences of those perceptions? What is the nature of the self, and the relationship between self, other people, and the social world? How can we find or construct the "genuine self"—who one really is, and wants to be, apart from what other people want one to be? And how can people best realize or actualize their potential and experience their self-worth?

Work at this level began in the late 1940s and in the 1950s mostly as a passionate protest movement by psychologists who cared about personality, particularly by clinical psychologists working with disturbed and distressed people after the turmoil of World War II. The protest—almost a howl of objections—was against the two then-dominant forces in the field. On the one side it was against the psychoanalytic work of Freud and his followers that dominated clinical psychology and psychiatry at that time. The critique here was that the Freudian approach was too focused on the pathology and disordered aspects of personality, and too inattentive to its potential strengths. It also was driven by increasing doubts about the therapeutic efficacy and practical usefulness of psychoanalysis, as well as about its scientific validity. On the other side, the protest was directed against behaviorism and "rat psychology," which dominated most academic psychology departments in the United States.

Unlike the beginnings of the Freudian movement, there was no single leader. Instead, a number of different psychologists who cared about personality and psychotherapy began to raise questions that challenged the field's most basic assumptions at that time. Perhaps they were feeling about personality psychology what some readers might at this point in the text, wondering "is that all there is?" George Kelly, for example, proposed that what is most important about personality is exactly what had been left out: Each person views or "construes" the world in distinctly different ways, and it is these personal construals or appraisals that guide what people think, feel, do, and become. They may even lead the person to develop maladaptive, self-defeating, and self-destructive problems like those shown by Freud's patients. Most important, Kelly believed that people are free to change how they construe and appraise themselves and their world, and they can do so in constructive ways that enhance their freedom. In other words, we do not have to be victims of the past, of our traits and needs, of our genes, of our learning histories, and even of our life situations.

At the same time that Kelly was making his contributions and even in the same place—Ohio State University's Psychology Department—Carl Rogers, a former minister who also became a psychology professor, developed a new theory of personality that focused on the individual's potential for personal growth and genuineness and on the nature of the self. Collectively, psychologists at this level of analysis continue to add to the understanding of the self, mental processes, mental health, and the importance of interpersonal relationships for personality and personal growth. The contributions from this level also add greatly to the integrated view of personality that is emerging currently in the field.

THE PERSONAL SIDE OF THE SCIENCE

Some questions at the Phenomenological-Humanistic Level you might ask about yourself:

- What am I really feeling? How do I see myself? How do I see my parents?
- What do I feel about myself when I don't meet my parents' expectations?
- How is my real self different from the self I would ideally like to be?
- What is my ideal self?
- Am I happy? Fulfilled? Where am I going? What is my identity? Who do I want to become?

CHAPTER 12

PHENOMENOLOGICAL-HUMANISTIC CONCEPTIONS

Each person sees the world subjectively in his or her own personal way. To understand this privately experienced side of personality, we need to examine the nature of subjective experience and see how people perceive their world. For example, we cannot understand anxiety as an aspect of personality fully without understanding how the individual experiences it. We begin with a sample of such personal experience in the form of a self-description by a college student about to take a final examination:

> When I think about the exam, I really feel sick . . . so much depends on it. I know I'm not prepared, at least not as much as I should be, but I keep hoping that I can sort of snow my way through it. He [the professor] said we would get to choose two of three essay questions. I've heard about his questions . . . they sort of cover the whole course, but they're still pretty general. Maybe I'll be able to mention a few of the right names and places. He can't expect

us to put down everything in two hours . . . I keep trying to remember some of the things he said in class, but my mind keeps wandering. God, my folks—What will they think if I don't pass and can't graduate? Will they have a fit! Boy! I can see their faces. Worse yet, I can hear their voices: "And with all the money we spent on your education." Mom's going to be hurt. She'll let me know I let her down. She'll be a martyr: "Well, Roger, didn't you realize how this reflects on us? Didn't you know how much we worked and saved so you could get an education?. . .You were probably too busy with other things. I don't know what I'm going to tell your aunt and uncle. They were planning to come to the graduation you know." Hell! What about me? What'll I do if I don't graduate? How about the plans I made? I had a good job lined up with that company. They really sounded like they wanted me, like I was going to be somebody. . . . And what about the car? I had it all planned out. I was going to pay for it and still have enough left for fun. I've got to pass. Oh hell! What about Anne [girlfriend]? She's counting on my graduating. We had plans. What will she think? She knows I'm no brain, but . . . hell, I won't be anybody. I've got to find some way to remember those names. If I can just get him to think that I really know that material, but don't have time to put it all down. If I can just . . . if . . . too goddamn many ifs. Poor dad. He'll really be hurt. All the plans we made—all the . . . I was going to be somebody. What did he say? "People will respect you. People respect a college graduate. You'll be something more than a storekeeper." What am I going to do. God, I can't think. You know, I might just luck out. I've done it before. He could ask just the right questions. What could he ask? Boy! I feel like I want to vomit. Do you think others are as scared as I am? They probably know it all or don't give a damn. I'll bet you most of them have parents who can set them up whether they have college degrees or not. God, it means so much to me. I've got to pass. I've just got to. Dammit, what are those names? What could he ask? I can't think . . . I can't. . . . Maybe if I had a beer I'd be able to relax a little. Is there anybody around who wants to get a beer? God, I don't want to go alone. Who wants to go to the show? What the hell am I thinking about? I've got to study. . . . I can't. What's going to happen to me?. . .The whole damn world is coming apart.

(Fischer, 1970, pp. 121–122)

SOURCES OF PHENOMENOLOGICAL-HUMANISTIC PERSPECTIVES

Defining Humanistic Psychology, Phenomenology, Existentialism

Feelings and thoughts like those reported by this student are the raw materials of theories that deal with the person's subjective internal experiences, personal concepts, and the self, and these are the theories and ideas we examine in this chapter. Many of them were heavily influenced by two closely related movements within philosophy and literature in the middle of the last century: phenomenology and existentialism. At the outset, we briefly define each of these terms.

Humanistic psychology refers to the movement within personality psychology that grew beginning in the 1950s in the United States, mostly as a protest movement to the then dominant forces within the field. A group of psychologists, notably including Carl Rogers and Abraham Maslow, met and after a series of planning meetings, and a decade of effort, founded its own *Journal of Humanistic Psychology* in 1961. It was to be devoted to promoting a "holistic psychology" that would study the individual as a whole person, focusing on subjective experience and the self, rather than on subprocesses like learning or perceiving. This movement was being born often within the same universities that also were fortresses for the opposition, as the example in *In Focus 12.1* illustrates, resulting in some curious interpersonal relationships among the faculty members and students.

IN FOCUS 12.1

PIONEERS AT DIFFERENT LEVELS OF ANALYSIS AT WORK AND WAR IN THE SAME PLACE

In the middle of the last century, some of the main pioneers of ideas and research at different, and then seemingly competing, levels of analysis in personality were Gordon Allport, Henry Murray, and B.F. Skinner. They worked for more than 20 years as professors at Harvard University, almost within a stone's throw of each other. Not infrequently at least verbal stones did fly around, adding ferment and occasional turmoil, often stressing or amusing the students, but ultimately also energizing and enriching the field. In retrospect, each of these psychologists also played an important role in the history of the phenomenological-humanistic level. Allport and Murray did so by becoming two of the main champions of the internal or "experiential" view, as Murray called it, and Skinner by being the leader of the behaviorism against which much of the phenomenological-humanistic protest was aimed.

B.F. Skinner insisted that phenomena like human consciousness and internal experiences are outside the turf of scientific psychology (as discussed in Chapters 10 and 11). His Harvard colleague, Henry Murray, trained in medicine as well as in chemistry and psychoanalysis, had these reactions in his autobiography. Referring to himself on the faculty at Harvard, he writes: "A budding psychologist who was devoting fruitful hours listening to reports of the ongoing stream of consciousness—dreams, fantasies, memories, feelings, and thoughts of other people could scarcely have been disposed to adopt with zest the dogmas of those whose avowed purpose was to convince us that consciousness and purpose were nonexistent . . ." (Murray, 1967, p. 293). For Murray, the way personality psychology needed to go was best anticipated by one of the first great psychologists in America, William James, in 1903: "Individuality is founded in feeling, and the recesses of feeling, the darker, blinder strata of character, are the only places in the world in which we catch real fact in the making, and directly perceive how events happen and how (mental) work is actually done" (James, 1903, p. 501).

At Harvard, Skinner continued to refine and apply his views and methods, pushing work at the extreme behaviorist level as far as he could. Concurrently, in the same university, Murray was developing the TAT for the study of human motives, imagination, and fantasy, and launching his intensive study of lives and experience (discussed in Chapter 8). In another building not far away on the campus, Allport was further developing both his version of trait theory and his focus on the uniqueness of each individual, and the routes for assessing not just the person's external acts but also the inner motives and values and self that underlie them. None of them would have anticipated that in time history would prove that all their contributions turned out to be important, rather than in total conflict with each other, and that each would add a piece toward understanding the total complexities of personality and its expressions at many different levels.

Phenomenology refers to the study of consciousness and the appearances of things and events as the individual perceives and experiences them. Closely related to it is **existentialism**, a viewpoint that began with the philosopher Kierkegaard and was expanded by philosophers like Sartre, Merleau-Ponty, Heidegger, and many others, especially in Europe more than half a century ago. For personality psychologists, existentialism's central point was that human beings are completely free and responsible for their own behavior. Of particular interest was the view that this responsibility is at the root of the deep dread and anxiety that characterizes human beings. But, equally interesting and emphasized in humanistic psychology, it also gives the individual a greater degree of freedom and potential for self-change than had been recognized in most earlier personality theories.

12.1 What is the focus of the phenomenological level of analysis?

There are many variations in the orientation to personality presented in this chapter. In spite of these differences, however, a few fundamental themes emerge. The theories at this level of analysis are distinctive both in the concepts they reject and in the ones they emphasize. They tend to reject most of the dynamic and motivational concepts of the psychoanalytic level and also most of the assumptions of the trait and behavioral levels. Persons thus are viewed as experiencing beings in the "here and now" rather than as the victims of their unconscious psychodynamic conflicts, or of their traits, or of their reinforcement histories. Most of the approaches discussed in this chapter also stress people's positive strivings and their tendencies toward growth and self-actualization.

Most of the theories presented here focused on how the individual perceives, thinks, interprets, and experiences the world; that is, they tried to grasp the individual's point of view—the person's phenomenology or subjective experience. Ideally, they would like to look at the world through the "participant's" eyes and to stand in that person's shoes, to experience a bit of what it is to *be* that person. This phenomenological view is the main concern of the present chapter. We next consider some of its main versions, beginning with Gordon Allport.

Allport's Functional Autonomy

12.2 What did Allport mean by functional autonomy? How does this concept relate to a phenomenological approach to behavior?

Gordon Allport (1937) was one of the first voices, and most influential, to emphasize the uniqueness of the individual and of the integrated patterns that distinguish each person. He also noted the lack of motivational continuity during the individual's life and, probably influenced by his traumatic meeting with Freud in Vienna (Chapter 7), criticized the Freudian emphasis on the enduring role of sexual and aggressive motives.

According to Allport, behavior is motivated originally by instincts, but later it may sustain itself indefinitely without providing any biological gratifications. Allport saw most normal adult motives as no longer having a functional relation to their historical roots. "Motives are contemporary. . . . Whatever drives must drive now. . . . The character of motives alters so radically from infancy to maturity that we may speak of adult motives as *supplanting* the motives of infancy" (1940, p. 545). This idea has been called **functional autonomy** to indicate that a habit, say practicing the violin at a certain hour each day, need not be tied to any earlier motive of infancy. The extent to which an individual's motives are autonomous is a measure of maturity, according to Allport.

Allport thus stressed the **contemporaneity of motives** (1961): motives are to be understood in terms of their role in the present regardless of their origins in the past. In his view, the past is not important unless it can be shown to be active in the present. He believed that historical facts about a person's past, while helping to reveal the total course of the individual's life, do not adequately explain the person's conduct today. In his words, "Past motives explain nothing unless they are also present motives" (1961, p. 220). In sum, Allport emphasized that later motives do not necessarily depend on earlier ones. Although the life of a plant is continuous with that of its seed, the seed no longer feeds and sustains the mature plant. A pianist may have been spurred to mastery of the piano through the need to overcome inferiority feelings, but the pianist's later love of music is functionally autonomous from its origins. Allport focused on the individual's currently perceived experiences, his or her phenomenological self and unique pattern of adaptation. He also favored a holistic view of the individual as an integrated, biosocial organism, rather than as a bundle of traits and motives. Table 12.1 summarizes some of Allport's main ideas about individuality.

Lewin's Life Space

Still another important influence came from field theories (Lewin, 1936). These theories, developed in the context of social psychology, saw behavior as determined by the person's psychological life space—by the events that exist in the total psychological situation at the moment—rather than by past events or enduring, situation-free dispositions. The most elegant formulation of this position was Kurt Lewin's **field theory**. In field theory,

TABLE 12.1 Some Distinguishing Features of Individuality According to Allport (1961)

1. Motives become independent of their roots (*functional autonomy*).
2. A *proprium* or self develops, characterized by:
    - Bodily sense
    - Self-esteem
    - Self-identity
    - Rational thought
    - Self-image
3. A *unique*, integrated pattern of adaptation marks the person as a whole.

the way in which an object is perceived depends on the total context or configuration of its surroundings. What is perceived depends on the *relationships* among components of a perceptual field, rather than on the fixed characteristics of the individual components.

12.3 What are the major components of Lewin's life space? Describe his classic formula for the causes of behavior.

Lewin defined **life space** as the totality of facts that determine the behavior (B) of an individual at a certain moment. The life space includes the person (P) and the psychological environment (E), as shown in Figure 12.1. Behavior is a function of the person and the environment, as expressed in the formula

$$B = f(P, E)$$

Ordinary cause, based on the notion of causation in classical physics, assumes that something past is the cause of present events. Teleological theories assume that future events influence present events. Lewin's thesis is that neither past nor future, by definition, exists at the present moment and therefore neither can have an effect at the present. Past events have a position in the historical causal chains that create the present situation, but only those events that are functioning in the present situation need to be taken into account. Such events are, by definition, current or momentary. In other words, only present facts can cause present behavior.

To represent the life space, Lewin therefore took into account only that which is contemporary. He termed this the **principle of contemporaneity** (Lewin, 1936). This does not mean the field theorists are not interested in historical problems or in the effects of previous experience. As Lewin (1951) pointed out, field theorists have enlarged the psychological experiment to include situations that contain a history that is systematically created throughout hours or weeks. For example, college students in an experiment

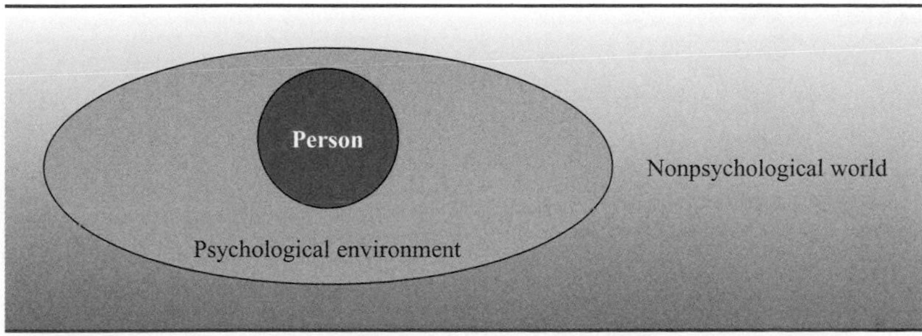

Figure 12.1 Lewin's life space. The life space contains the person in his or her psychological environment, which is delineated by a boundary (the ellipse) from the nonpsychological world.

might be given repeated failure experiences (on a series of achievement tasks) during several sessions. The effects of these experiences on the students' subsequent aspirations and expectations for success might then be measured.

The boundaries between the person and the psychological environment and between the life space and the physical world are **permeable boundaries**, that is, they can be crossed easily. That makes prediction difficult because one cannot be sure beforehand when and what facts will permeate a boundary and influence a fact from another region. Lewin asserts that the psychologist might therefore concentrate on describing and explaining the concrete psychological situation in terms of field theory rather than trying to predict the future.

Lewin (1935) rejected the notion of constant, entity-like personality characteristics such as unchanging traits. As a result of dynamic forces, psychological reality is always changing. The environment of the individual does not serve merely to facilitate tendencies that are permanent in the person's nature (Lewin, 1936). Habits are not frozen associations, but rather the result of forces in the organism and its life space.

Lewin was similarly dissatisfied with the usual concept of needs. In descriptions of psychological reality, Lewin said, the needs that are producing effects in the momentary situation are the only ones that have to be represented. A need in Lewin's theory corresponds to a tension system. Lewin was also interested in reward and punishment. He saw rewards as devices for controlling behavior in momentary situations by causing changes in the psychological environment and in the tension systems of the person.

For Lewin, behavior and development are functions of the same structural and dynamic factors. Both are a function of the person and the psychological environment. In general, with increasing maturity there is greater differentiation of the person and the psychological environment.

Kurt Lewin (1890–1947)

(*Source*: © AP/Wide World Photos)

Lewin's field theory had a major impact on experimental social psychology. His students extended his ideas and pursued them through ingenious experiments designed to alter the participant's life space—by altering perceptions about the self, about other people, about events. The effects of these alterations on attitudes, aspirations, and other indices were then examined carefully. Until recently Lewin's influence on personality psychology has been less extensive. There is, however, an increasing recognition of the importance of the psychological situation in studies of traits and motives (e.g., Magnusson, 1999; Mischel & Shoda, 1999).

Phenomenology and Existentialism: The Here and Now

Allport and Lewin's ideas, as discussed before, were valuable beginnings, but the two personality psychologists who most forcefully advanced the phenomenological-humanistic level of analysis were Carl Rogers and Abraham Maslow. Carl Rogers developed a view of personality in which private experiences, subjective perceptions, and the self all have an important part. Abraham Maslow, on the other hand, put his emphasis on human growth motivation. In his view, growth motivation moves the individual through hierarchically ordered degrees of health to ultimate self-actualization. "Every person is, in part, his own project, and makes himself" (Maslow, 1965, p. 308). Behavior is goal directed, striving, purposeful, and motivated by higher needs to realize or **self-actualize** one's human potential rather than by primary biological drives alone. Their ideas were most closely connected to the existential philosophical position developed by the European thinkers mentioned at the start of this chapter (e.g., Sartre), as well as by the Swiss psychiatrists Binswanger and Boss. The key features of their orientation are expressed by Rollo May, an American proponent of existential psychology. Thinking about a patient of his in psychotherapy, May recognizes that he has available all sorts of information about her, such as hypotheses from her Rorschach and diagnoses from her neurologist. He then comments (1961, p. 26):

> But if, as I sit here, I am chiefly thinking of these whys and hows of the way the problem came about, I will have grasped everything except the most important thing of all, the existing person. Indeed, I will have grasped everything except the only real source of data I have, namely, this experiencing human being, this person now emerging, becoming, "building world," as the existential psychologists put it, immediately in this room with me.

May's remarks illustrate the existentialist's focus on phenomenological experience, on the "here and now" rather than on distant historical causes in the person's early childhood. Furthermore, the existential orientation sees the human being as capable of choice and responsibility in the moment rather than as the victim of unconscious forces or of habits from the past.

12.4 What is the role of immediate experience in existential theories? Where are the true causes of behavior?

The Swiss existential psychiatrist Binswanger commented that Freudian theory pictured human beings not yet as people in the full sense, but only as creatures buffeted about by life. Binswanger believes that for a person to be fully himself—that is, to be truly realized or actualized as a human being—he must "look fate in the face." In his view, the fact that human life is determined by forces and conditions is only one side of the truth. The other side is that we ourselves "determine these forces as our fate" (cited in May, 1961, p. 252). Thus, in the phenomenological and existential orientation, humans are seen as beings whose actualization requires much more than the fulfillment of biological needs and of sexual and aggressive instincts.

The existentialists propose that we are inevitably the builders of our own lives and, more specifically, that each person is:

1. a *choosing* agent, unable to avoid choices throughout the course of life;
2. a *free* agent, who freely sets life goals;
3. a *responsible* agent, accountable personally for his or her life choices.

Our existence in life is given, but our essence is what we make of life, how meaningfully and responsibly we construct it. This is an often painful, isolated, agonizing enterprise. To find satisfying values, to guide our lives accordingly, to give life meaning—these goals are all part of the existential quest. They require the "courage to be"—the courage to break from blind conformity to the group and to strive instead for self-fulfillment by seeking greater self-definition and authenticity.

Finally, to grasp what it means to *be* also requires being in constant touch with the awareness of nonbeing, of alienation, of nothingness, and ultimately of the inevitability of death, everyone's unavoidable fate. The awareness of this inevitable fate and what that implies produces **existential anxiety**. The antidote for such anxiety is to face and live our lives responsibly, meaningfully, and with courage and awareness of our potential for continuous choice and growth.

12.5 What is meant by existential anxiety?

The phenomenological-humanistic approaches were influenced and motivated into action by all of these historical, philosophical, and scientific developments in the middle of the last century. To understand some of their main features more closely, we shall consider the ideas of one of its most articulate proponents in the next sections.

▶ CARL ROGERS'S SELF THEORY

Carl Rogers developed a theory of the self and the conditions that allow its optimal growth and fulfillment that has had an enduring impact on personality psychology and even more broadly on modern views of human nature.

Unique Experience: The Subjective World

Rogers's theory of personality emphasizes the unique, subjective experience of the person. He believed that the way you see and interpret the events in your life determines how you respond to them. Each person lives in a subjective world, and even the so-called objective world of the scientist is a product of subjective perceptions, purposes, and choices. Because no one else, no matter how hard he tries, can completely assume another person's "internal frame of reference," the person himself has the greatest potential for awareness of what reality is for him. In other words, each person potentially is the world's best expert on himself and has the best information about himself.

12.6 According to Rogers, how is behavior determined?

In Rogers's view, "behavior is typically the goal-directed attempt of the organism to satisfy its needs as experienced, in the field as perceived" (1951, p. 491). The emphasis is on the person's perceptions as the determinants of his or her actions: How one sees and interprets events determines how one reacts to them.

Self-Actualization

Like most phenomenologists, Rogers wanted to abandon specific motivational constructs and viewed the organism as functioning as an **organized whole**. He maintained that "there is one central source of energy in the human organism; that it is a function of the whole organism rather than some portion of it; and that it is perhaps best conceptualized

Carl Rogers (1902–1987)

(*Source*: Douglas A. Land, La Jolla, California)

as a tendency toward fulfillment, toward actualization, toward the maintenance and enhancement of the organism" (1963, p. 6). Thus the inherent tendency of the organism is to actualize itself. "Motivation" then becomes not a special construct but an overall characteristic of simply being alive.

12.7 What is meant by self-actualization? What does it imply about the nature of the human being, and how does this conception differ from Freud's?

In line with his essentially positive view of human nature, Rogers's theory asserts that emotions are beneficial to adjustment: "emotion accompanies and in general facilitates . . . goal-directed behavior, . . . the intensity of the emotion being related to the perceived significance of the behavior for the maintenance and enhancement of the organism" (1951, p. 493).

In the course of actualizing itself, the organism engages in a valuing process. Experiences that are perceived as enhancing it are valued positively (and approached), while experiences that are perceived as negating enhancement or maintenance of the organism are valued negatively (and avoided). "The organism has one basic tendency and striving—to actualize, maintain, and enhance the experiencing organism" (Rogers, 1951, p. 487). The idea and implications of self-actualization are discussed more fully in *In Focus 12.2*.

The Self

The self is a central concept for many phenomenological theories, and it also is basic for Rogers—as it was for many of the post-Freudians working at the psychodynamic level. Indeed, his theory is often referred to as a self theory of personality. The self or self-concept (the two terms mean the same thing for Rogers) is an organized, consistent whole. It consists of perceptions about oneself and one's relationships to others and to diverse aspects of life, and these all have values attached to them (Rogers, 1959, p. 200). As a result of interactions with the environment, a portion of the perceptual

IN FOCUS 12.2

SELF-ACTUALIZATION AS A NEED (MASLOW)

Abraham Maslow (1968, 1971) was one of the most influential spokespersons for the importance of becoming "in touch" with one's true feelings. He considered this a core ingredient of well-being and self-fulfillment. Maslow also emphasized human beings' vast positive potential for growth and fulfillment, and believed that the striving toward actualization of this potential is a basic quality of being human:

> Man demonstrates in his own nature a pressure toward fuller and fuller Being, more and more perfect actualization of his humanness in exactly the same naturalistic, scientific sense that an acorn may be said to be "pressing toward" being an oak tree, or that a tiger can be observed to "push toward" being tigerish, or a horse toward being equine. . .(1968, p. 160)

Maslow's commitment was to study optimal man and to discover the qualities of those people who seemed to be closest to realizing all their potentialities. In his view one has **higher growth needs**—needs for self-actualization fulfillment—that emerge when more primitive needs—physiological needs, safety needs, needs for belongingness and esteem—are satisfied (see Figure 12.2). Maslow wanted to focus on the qualities of feeling and experience that seem to distinguish self-actualizing, fully functioning people. Therefore, he searched for the attributes that seemed to mark such people as Beethoven, Einstein, Jefferson, Lincoln, Walt Whitman, as well as some of the individuals he knew personally and admired most. These positive qualities are an essential part of the humanistic view of the "healthy personality."

Maslow called the special state in which one experiences a moment of self-actualization a **peak experience**. It is a temporary experience of fulfillment and joy in which the person loses self-centeredness and (in varying degrees of intensity) feels a nonstriving happiness, a moment of perfection. Words that may be used to describe this state include "aliveness," "beauty," "ecstasy," "effortlessness," "uniqueness," and "wholeness." Such peak experiences have been reported in many contexts, including the aesthetic appreciation of nature and beauty, worship, intimate relationships with others, and creative activities.

In sum, in spite of its many different versions, the phenomenological-humanistic orientation tends to view "healthy people" as those who:

1. Become aware of themselves, their feelings, and their limits; accept themselves, their lives, and what they make of their lives as their own responsibility; have "the courage to be."
2. Experience the "here-and-now"; are not trapped to live in the past or to dwell in the future through anxious expectations and distorted defenses.

The peak experience is characterized by a feeling of fulfillment and joy.

(*Source*: David Young-Wolff/PhotoEdit)

3. Realize their potentialities; have autonomy and are not trapped by their own self-concepts or the expectations of others and society.

To help achieve these ideals, several avenues for constructive personality change have been favored by advocates of the phenomenological approach, as discussed next.

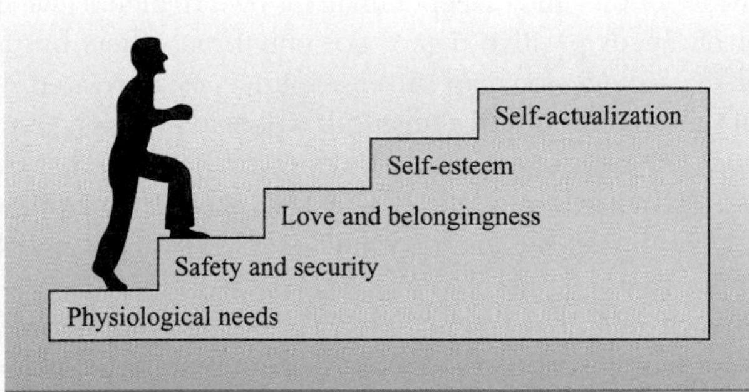

Figure 12.2 Maslow's hierarchy of needs. Maslow arranges motives in a hierarchy ascending from such basic physiological needs as hunger and thirst through safety and love needs to needs for esteem (e.g., feeling competent), and ultimately, self-actualization—the full realization of one's human potential, as in creativity. The lower needs are more powerful and demand satisfaction first. The higher needs have less influence on behavior but are more distinctly human. Generally, higher needs do not become a focus until lower ones have been at least partly satisfied.

field gradually becomes differentiated into the self. This perceived self (self-concept) influences perception and behavior. That is, the interpretation of the self—as strong or weak, for example—affects how one perceives the rest of one's world.

12.8 How did Maslow study optimal human functioning? What were the most notable characteristics of highly functioning people?

The experiences of the self become invested with values. These values are the result of direct experience with the environment, or they may be taken over from others. For example, a young child finds it organismically (intrinsically) enjoyable to relieve himself whenever he experiences physiological tension in the bowel or bladder. However, he may sometimes also experience parental words and actions indicating that such behavior is bad, and that he is not lovable when he does this. A conflict then develops that may result in distortion and denial of organismic experience. In this example, the satisfaction of defecating may start to be experienced as bad even though a more accurate symbolization would be that it is often experienced as organismically satisfying. Rogers goes on to suggest that in bowel training, denial or distortion of experience may be avoided if the parent is able genuinely to accept the child's feelings and at the same time accepts his or her own feelings.

Consistency and Positive Regard

12.9 What is the self? How does it develop, acquire values, and influence behavior?

Rogers proposes two systems: the **self** or **self-concept** and the actual experience of the organism itself. The two systems may be in opposition or in harmony. When these systems are in opposition or incongruence, the result is maladjustment, for then the self becomes rigidly organized, losing contact with actual organismic experience and filled with tensions. Perception is selective: We try to perceive experiences in ways consistent with the self-concept. The self-concept thus serves as a frame of reference for evaluating and monitoring the actual experiences of the organism. Experiences that are inconsistent with the self may be perceived as threats, and the more threat there is,

12.10 How does the need for positive regard cause inconsistencies between self-concept and experience?

the more rigid and defensive the self structure becomes to maintain itself. At the same time, the self-concept becomes less congruent with organismic reality and loses contact with the actual experiences of the organism.

Rogers (1959) assumed a universal **need for positive regard**. This need develops as the awareness of the self emerges and leads the person to desire acceptance and love from the important people in his life. Sometimes they may accept him conditionally (i.e., depending on his specific behavior), or they may accept him in his own right and give him unconditional regard. The person needs positive regard not only from others but also from his self. The need for self-regard develops out of self-experiences associated with the satisfaction or frustration of the need for positive regard. If a person experiences only unconditional positive regard, his self-regard also would be unconditional. In that case, the needs for positive regard and self-regard would never be at variance with **organismic evaluation**. Such a state would represent genuine psychological adjustment and full functioning.

Most people do not achieve such ideal adjustment. Often a self-experience is avoided or sought only because it is less (or more) worthy of self-regard. For example, a child may experience anger toward her mother but avoids accepting that feeling because she wants to be a "good girl." When that happens, Rogers speaks of the individual's having acquired a **condition of worth**. These are the conditions that other people, usually the parents, implicitly make a requirement for being loved and worthwhile. For example, a parent may lead a child to feel that to be worthy she has to get outstanding grades at school, or that the boy in the family has to be a robust athlete even if he is naturally inclined to become someone quite different. Experiences that are in accord with the individual's conditions of worth tend to be perceived accurately in awareness, but experiences that violate the conditions of worth may be denied to awareness and distorted grossly. When there is a significant amount of incongruence between the individual's self-concept and her evaluation of an experience, then defenses may become unable to work successfully. For example, if a young woman persistently experiences herself as painfully dissatisfied and "unhappy" in her efforts at schoolwork, but views herself as having to "succeed at college" in order to be an adequate person, she may experience great strain in her defensive efforts.

12.11 What role do conditions of worth play in anxiety and perception?

Rogers's theory, like Freud's, posits that accurate awareness of experiences may be threatening to the self. Anxiety in Rogers's theory might be interpreted as the tension exhibited by the organized concept of the self when it senses (without full awareness) that the recognition of certain experiences would be catastrophic to the self (1951). If a person's concept of the self has been built around his "masculinity," for example, experiences that might imply that he has some stereotypically feminine tendencies would threaten him severely. Anxiety thus involves a basic threat to the self, and defenses are erected to avoid it. Consistent with Rogers's theory, a great deal of research has demonstrated that people in fact engage in diverse strategies to protect their self-esteem when it is severely threatened. For example, they readily attribute important failures to chance rather than to themselves, but see success as due to their own abilities (Snyder & Uranowitz, 1978; Weiner, 1995).

Self-Determination

Rogers's ideas have turned out to be remarkably influential and continue to stimulate many directions of new research. One major line of continuing work builds on Rogers's theory about the individual's needs for autonomy and intrinsic organismic satisfactions that are independent of the external rewards and pressures imposed by others. In Deci and Ryan's theory of **self-determination**, for example, some actions are controlled by external pressures (e.g., from parents to do well, to satisfy conditions of worth) or to gain external rewards (e.g., payment for work one does not enjoy doing). But other actions have intrinsic value for the individual: they are *self-determined* (e.g., Deci, 1975; Deci & Ryan, 2000; Ryan & Deci, 2001). The perception that behavior is self-determined, rather than externally controlled, can make a big difference on how one feels about it and subsequent motivation. A good deal of evidence shows that a sense of self-determination about what one does and accomplishes enhances feelings of satisfaction as well as continued motivation, whereas external rewards and pressures, including those that are self-imposed, often can have the opposite effects (e.g., Grolnick & Ryan, 1989; Ryan, 1982).

Client-Centered Therapy

Rogers's work also led to a new and still influential form of thinking about personality change and conducting therapy to facilitate positive change. **Client-centered**, or **person-centered (Rogerian), therapy** seeks to bring about the harmonious interaction of the self and the organism. The warm and unconditionally accepting attitude of the counselor hopefully enables the client to perceive and examine experiences that are inconsistent with the current self-structure. The client can then revise this self-structure to permit it to assimilate these inconsistent experiences. According to Rogers, the client gradually reorganizes the self-concept to bring it into line with the reality of organismic experience: "He will *be*, in more unified fashion, what he organismically *is*, and this seems to be the essence of therapy" (1955, p. 269).

12.12 What is the objective in client (person)-centered therapy? Which therapist qualities contribute to a positive outcome?

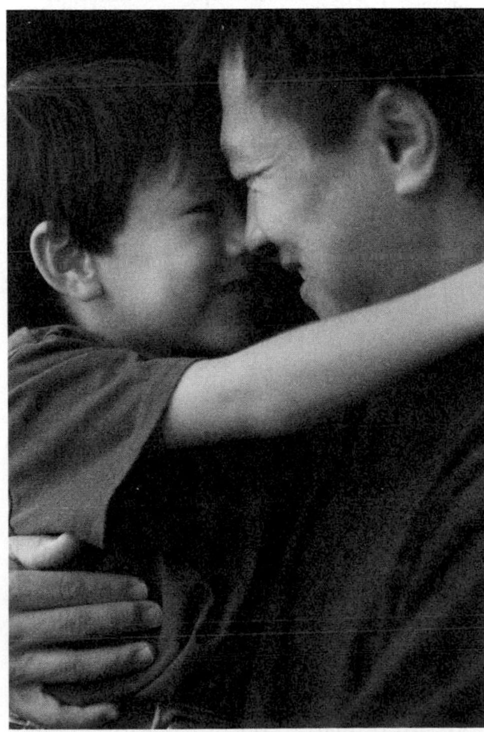

Rogers assumed a need for unconditional positive regard not only from others but from the self.

(*Source*: Mary Grace Long/Asia Images/Getty Images)

In his therapy, Rogers rejected most of Freud's concepts regarding the nature of psychodynamics and psychosexual development. He also avoided all diagnostic terms, refusing to put his labels on the client. He maintained, however, the interview format for psychotherapy (using a face-to-face arrangement rather than the orthodox psychoanalyst's couch for the client). Rogers and his students focused on the client–clinician relationship. Usually they required many fewer sessions than did psychoanalytic therapy, and they dealt more with current than with historical concerns in the client's life.

For Rogers (1959), the therapist's main task is to provide an atmosphere in which the client can be more fully open to her own **organismic experience**. To achieve a growth-conducive atmosphere, the clinician must view the client as intrinsically good and capable of self-development. The clinician's function is to be nonevaluative and to convey a sense of unconditional acceptance and regard for the client (Brazier, 1993). To reach the client effectively the clinician must be "genuine" and "congruent"—an open, trustworthy, warm person without a facade (Lietaer, 1993). The **congruent therapist**, according to Rogers, feels free to be him- or herself and to accept the client fully and immediately in the therapeutic encounter, and conveys this openness to the client. When a genuinely accepting, unconditional relationship is established, the client will become less afraid to face and accept his or her own feelings and experiences. Becoming open to the experience of herself as she is, she can reorganize her self-structure. Now, it is hoped, she will accept experiences that she had previously denied or distorted (because they did not fit her self-concept) and thus achieve greater internal congruity and self-actualization.

In sum, Rogers wanted to build an empathetic, interview-based relationship therapy that renounced the Freudian focus on psychodynamics and transference. Instead, he wanted to provide the client an unconditionally accepting relationship—an atmosphere conducive to "growth" (self-actualization). In this relationship, the focus is on empathic understanding and acceptance of feelings rather than interpretation, although the latter is not excluded. The clinician is relatively "nondirective"; the objective is to let the client direct the interview while the clinician attempts to accurately reflect and clarify the feelings that emerge.

In client-centered therapy, now also called person-centered therapy, permissiveness and unqualified acceptance on the part of the therapist provide an atmosphere favorable to personal honesty. Psychologists are urged to abandon their "objective" measurement orientation and their concern with tests. Instead, they should try to learn from the client how he or she thinks, understands, and feels. "The best vantage point for understanding behavior is from the internal frame of reference of the individual himself" (Rogers, 1951, p. 494). Although their focus is on empathy, the Rogerians have not neglected objective research into the relationship, as was noted earlier in this chapter in the context of interview research. As a result, Rogerians have helped to illuminate some of the processes that occur during client-centered therapy and also have provided considerable evidence concerning its effectiveness (e.g., Truax & Mitchell, 1971).

Rogers's client-centered psychotherapy differs in many ways from Freudian psychotherapy. Indeed, when Rogers first proposed his techniques, they were considered revolutionary. Sometimes his approach to psychotherapy is even described as the polar opposite of Freud's. While there are major differences between Freudian and Rogerian approaches to psychotherapy, on closer inspection there also are some fundamental similarities. Both approaches retain a verbal, interview format for psychotherapy; both focus on the client–clinician relationship; both are primarily concerned with feelings; both emphasize the importance of unconscious processes (defense, repression); and both consider increased awareness and acceptance of unconscious feelings to be major goals of psychotherapy.

12.13 Compare and contrast person-centered and psychoanalytic therapy.

To be sure, the two approaches differ in their focus. They differ in the specific content that they believe is repressed (e.g., id impulses vs. organismic experiences), in the motives they consider most important (e.g., sex and aggression vs. self-realization), and in the specific insights they hope will be achieved in psychotherapy (the unconscious becomes conscious and conflict is resolved vs. organismic experience is accepted and the self becomes congruent with it). But these differences should not obscure the fact that both approaches are forms of relationship treatment that emphasize awareness of hypothesized unconscious feelings and the need for the client to accept those feelings.

Rogers Reflects on His Own Work

Looking back at the almost 50 years of his contributions to psychology, Rogers (1974) tried to pinpoint the essence of his approach. In his view, his most fundamental idea was that

> the individual has within himself vast resources for self-understanding, for altering his self-concept, his attitudes, and his self-directed behavior—and that these resources can be tapped if only a definable climate of facilitative psychological attitudes can be provided. (p. 116)

Such a climate for growth requires an atmosphere in which feelings can be confronted, expressed, and accepted fully and freely. In his autobiography, Rogers openly discusses his own growth and relationships with others, noting that

> I have come to realize that if I can drop some of my defenses, let myself come forth as a vulnerable person, can express some of the attitudes which feel most personal, most private, most tentative and uncertain to me, then the response from others is deep and receptive and warming. (1967, p. 381)

Rogers notes that his emphasis on the person's potential freedom, the hallmark of a humanistic orientation, remains unchanged:

> My experience in therapy and in groups makes it impossible for me to deny the reality and significance of human choice. To me it is not an illusion that man is to some degree the architect of himself . . . for me the humanistic approach is the only possible one. It is for each person, however, to follow the pathway—behavioristic or humanistic—that he finds most congenial. (1974, p. 119)

In the same humanistic vein, Rogers regretted modern technology and called for autonomy and self-exploration:

> Our culture, increasingly based on the conquest of nature and the control of man, is in decline. Emerging through the ruins is the new person, highly aware, self-directing, an explorer of inner, perhaps more than outer, space, scornful of the conformity of institutions and the dogma of authority. He does not believe in being behaviorally shaped, or in shaping the behavior of others. He is most assuredly humanistic rather than technological. In my judgment he has a high probability of survival. (1974, p. 119)

In sum, Rogers's theory and the therapy he developed highlights many of the chief points of the phenomenological and humanistic approach to personality. It emphasizes the person's perceived reality, subjective experiences, organismic striving for actualization, the potential for growth, freedom, and self-determination (Rowan, 1992; Ryan & Deci, 2001). It rejects or deemphasizes specific biological drives. It focuses on the experienced self rather than on historical causes or stable trait structures. A unique feature of Rogers's position is his emphasis on unconditional acceptance as a requisite for self-regard.

▶ GEORGE KELLY'S PSYCHOLOGY OF PERSONAL CONSTRUCTS

> To the humanist every man is a scientist by disposition as well as by right, every subject is an incipient experimenter, and every person is by daily necessity a fellow psychologist.
>
> (G. A. Kelly, 1966, in B. A. Maher, 1979, p. 205)

The Person's Constructs and Personality

12.14 What are personal constructs? How does Kelly's orientation and measurement approach differ from the trait approach?

In the psychodynamic approach, the motive is the chief unit, unconscious conflicts are the processes of greatest interest, and the clinical judge is the favored instrument. George Kelly's (1955) personal construct theory, in contrast, seeks to illuminate the person's own constructs rather than the hypotheses of the psychologist. Its main units are personal constructs—the ways we represent or view our own experiences. Rather than seeing people as victimized by their impulses and defenses, this position views the human being as an active, ever-changing creator of hypotheses.

George A. Kelly (1905–1967)
(*Source*: Brandeis University)

According to Kelly, trait psychology tries to find the person's place on the *theorist's* personality dimension. **Personal construct theory** instead tries to see how the person sees and aligns events on *his or her own* dimensions (Fransella, 1995). It is Kelly's hope to discover the nature of the personal construct dimensions rather than to locate the individual's position on the dimensions of the psychologist's theory. If next week's test is important to you, Kelly wants to explore how you see it, what it means to you, not what your score is on a scale of test-taking anxiety.

Suppose that you see a person quietly letting herself be abused by someone else. You might conclude that the person is "submissive." Yet the same behavior might be construed by other observers as sensitive, cautious, intelligent, tactful, or polite. Thus Kelly emphasized that different people may construe the same event differently and that every event can be construed in alternative ways. The **personal construct** is the central unit of George Kelly's theory.

Characteristics of Personal Constructs

To illustrate, Kelly assumed that constructs are **bipolar**; each construct contains a pair of characteristics that are psychological opposites for the person, not necessarily logical opposites. The side of the construct that is applied in a characterization is called the **emergent pole**. For example, if I say "My father is aggressive," that is the emergent pole. Note that what I mean by "aggressive" may be quite different from what the term means for another person. Therefore for Kelly and his followers it's important to obtain an elaboration of the particular meanings the construct, in this case "aggressive," has for the individual. Equally important is the opposite end of the construct, the side that was not applied, called its **implicit pole**. Again it's important to elaborate what the psychological opposite of "aggressive" implies. Kelly insisted that it is a mistake to assume you know what such constructs and their opposites mean for a person unless the personal, subjective meaning is directly explored. He illustrated this dramatically for his students in his clinical work with clients. In one case the person indeed described his father as aggressive, and on elaboration the implicit pole turned out to be not the logical opposite *un*-aggressive, but *weak*. The point is: you can't know what another person means unless you find out; don't assume you know what only the construct's user knows.

12.15 Explain what Kelly means when he says that personal constructs are bipolar. In what way is a construct permeable?

Constructs also vary with regard to other characteristics. One of the most important is a construct's **permeability**: a highly permeable (vs. impermeable) construct is one into which a wide range of information can fit. For example, take the construct of "good versus immoral." If it is impermeable it implies that unless the person or behavior characterized fits a relatively narrow range (e.g., it must be consistent with one's own faith) it cannot be "good." If it is highly permeable, the construct can deal with and include a wide range of possibilities. For example, a person can be "good" regardless of their faith, or lack of faith, their sexual preferences, their family background, their socioeconomic level and status, and so on.

Constructs, according to Kelly, are used to make sense of the world, to try to predict events, and essentially to build one's terrain map of the world and how to function within it. When our construct systems do not allow us to adequately predict and interpret the events and people in our lives, feelings of uncertainty and helplessness may develop and anxiety is experienced. Especially when our most important or central constructs fail to function—as in major unexpected life crises and traumas—threat is experienced, and behavioral problems readily develop.

Exploring Personal Constructs

Kelly's operation for measuring a construct is best seen in his **Role Construct Repertory Test**, or **"Rep" Test**. On the Rep Test, you are asked to list many people or things that are important to you (e.g., self, mother, brother). After these items are listed (or the assessor lists them), you are asked to consider them in groups of three. In each triad you have to indicate how two items are similar to each other and different from the third. In this way the subjective dimensions of similarity among events, and the subjective opposites of those dimensions, may be evoked systematically. It is also possible to study the characteristics of the people's construct systems—for example, the number of different constructs they have in their construct repertory, and the characteristics of the constructs themselves.

The Rep Test is a flexible instrument that can be adapted for many different purposes, and it provides a convenient and fairly simple way to begin the exploration of personal constructs. Some examples, taken from the study of Gary W., are shown in Table 12.2 (which illustrates the general type of procedure that may be used to elaborate personal constructs).

Research on the temporal stability of personal constructs from Kelly's Rep Test indicates a good deal of consistency over time (Bonarius, 1965). For example, a high retest correlation (.79) was found for constructs after a 2-week interval (Landfield, Stern, & Fjeld, 1961), and factor analyses of the Rep Test suggest that its main factor is stable (Pederson, 1958), and thus that an individual's main constructs may be relatively permanent.

According to Kelly, the individuals' personal constructs gradually become elaborated through their answers on the Rep Test and through their behaviors in the interview and on other tests. To illustrate some features of the assessment of personal constructs, here is an analysis of our case based on how Gary spontaneously elaborates and contrasts the constructs with which he views the world. What follows are excerpts from an attempt by an assessor to summarize some of Gary's main conceptions.

A Personal Construct Conceptualization of Gary W.

Rationality–Emotionality

This is a construct dimension that seems to be of considerable importance for Gary. He elaborates what this construct means to him most clearly when he is discussing his interpersonal relationships. He describes a sexual relationship with a woman in such

TABLE 12.2 Elaboration of Personal Constructs: Examples from Gary W.

1. List the three most important people in your life:

   Me, my brother, my father

   How are any two of these alike and different from the third?

   My brother and I both know how to be tough and succeed, no matter what—my father is soft, knocked out, defeated by life.

2. Think of yourself now, 5 years ago, and 5 years from now. How are any two of these alike and different from the third?

   Five years ago I was warmer, more open and responsive to others than I am now. Now I'm mostly a scheming brain. Five years from now I hope to have recaptured some of that feeling and to be more like I was 5 years ago.

terms as "spiritual," "instinctive," "sublime," and "beyond rationality." It is characterized by intense feeling and the primacy of emotions, and it is based on physical attraction. Real friendships, in contrast, are based on rational grounds—such as interests and ways of thinking that are common to both parties.

The distinction between the rational and the emotional is echoed when Gary describes his worries in terms of those that are "rational" versus those that are "immediate and threatening." In discussing anger, he says that he has learned to cover up his feelings, but that his emotions sometimes "surface." He no longer gets violently angry, as he did when he was a child, but is "controlled," "stony," and "devious." He gives the most positive evaluation to reason, and contrasts what is reasonable with what is "worthless."

Transposed onto a time line, his distinction between reason and emotion forms part of the contrast between adults and children. After he was about 12 years old, Gary reconstrued his father, so the latter was no longer his "enemy" but instead became his "friendly, rational adviser." He also describes shifts in his relations with his mother and with his brother that apparently involve handling his feelings toward them in a less explosive way.

12.16 What did Kelly's approach reveal about Gary W.?

Power and Control versus Dependence and Weakness

In Gary's interview, descriptions of his childhood experiences, what parental figures require of a child, are typically the opposite of what the child wants. Gary describes life as a child as involving "denial, helplessness, nothing and nobody on my side." It was a time when he "couldn't control events," when he was being "manipulated" and "shamed." Gary contrasts foresight, and events that he can plan and control, with accidents, terror, and the unpredictable.

Security–Liberty

This is another major dimension for Gary. In describing jobs, acquaintances, and lifestyles, he talks in terms of "the ordinary 9 to 5 job complete with wife, kids, and mortgage," versus the "free and easy life." "Blind obedience" is contrasted to "judging the issues for oneself." Gary describes himself as being "uncertain," and contrasts being freewheeling with plodding determination. He sees himself as being currently without "acceptance" and "success" and he feels "cut off." His own "procrastination" hinders his "drive," but he hopes his "ambition will win out" and gain him both security and liberty.

Gary now sees his father as "emasculated" and "knocked out," although once he saw him as "a giant" and as his "enemy." The father seems to have moved along the conceptual continuum from "power and control" to a point where he is seen as inadequate and as being competition no longer. He dislikes his father for the middle-class values that he feels he represents and for his passivity. There is also the implication that he resents his father for not comparing favorably with his mother. The turning point in Gary's feelings for his brother, whom he disliked for sharing many of their father's qualities, came when his brother was badly hurt in a car crash. He now sees him as less conventional, more humorous, and self-examining.

Gary sees his mother, and ideal women in general, as "independent partners" rather than "devouring" sources of affection. Instead of making their families central in importance, they achieve success and recognition in work outside their home. They keep the male "alive" by providing stimulation through their competence, which extends even to athletics, rather than being dependent and "clinging." Gary sees himself as similar to his mother and says he loves her best, next to himself. On the more negative side, he sees his mother as frigid and incapable of expressing affection. However, in view of his own evaluation of emotionality, this criticism is a highly qualified one. He sees his mother as having in many ways been the cause of his father's defeat, but constantly adds that she did not intend this result and feels bad about it, that it was a byproduct of other admirable qualities she possesses.

His relationship with his mother is characterized by control of expression of both anger and love. He sees her dominating tendencies as dangerous, as evidenced by his childhood conception of her as omniscient and omnipotent. This fear seems to have generalized to his grandmother and to other women, as evidenced by his TAT stories.

In his relationships with women, there seems to be a general distinction between sex objects and companions. In describing a sexual relationship that he felt had no potentialities for friendship, Gary says, "If we hadn't been able to 'do it' we would have stopped seeing each other." He generally prefers women who are stimulating and challenging, though he fears all forms of domination, through either authority or emotional ties.

In his relationships with men outside his family, Gary prefers distance and respect and finds that closeness leads to friction, as with his present roommate. At school he found two older men whom he could look up to: a teacher to whom he was grateful for not being "wishy-washy" and another person whom he describes as being a "real man."

Behavioral Referents for Personal Constructs

12.17 How are behavioral referents used to clarify personal constructs? How does this differ from a psychodynamic approach?

Some of Gary's main personal constructs emerged from his self-descriptions and verbalizations. When people start to express their constructs, they usually begin with very diffuse, oversimplified, global terms. For example, Gary called himself "shrewd," "too shy," "too sharp." He also said he wanted to "feel more real," to "adjust better," and to "be happier."

What can the construct assessor do with these verbalizations? As we have seen in earlier chapters, psychodynamically oriented clinicians rely chiefly on their intuitive inferences about the symbolic and dynamic meanings of verbal behavior. Personal construct assessors recognize that talk about private experiences and feelings tends to be ambiguous. For example, statements of the kind commonly presented in clinical contexts, like "I feel so lost," generally are not clear. Instead of inquiring into why the person feels "lost," personal construct assessments try to discover referents for just what the statement means. An adequate personal construct assessment of what people say involves the analysis of what they mean. For this purpose, the assessor's initial task is like the one faced when we want to understand a foreign language. A personal construct analysis of language tries to decipher the content of what is being conveyed and to discover its meaning for the person. Its aim is not to translate what is said into signs of underlying motives, of unconscious processes, or of personality dimensions. Often it is hard to find the words for personal constructs. Just as the psychologist interested in such concepts as extraversion, identity, or anxiety must find behavioral referents to help specify what he or she means, so must the client find such referents for his or her private concepts, difficulties, and aspirations.

In sum, Kelly urged a specific and elaborate inquiry into personal constructs by obtaining numerous behavioral examples as referents for them. Kelly (1955) has described in detail many techniques to explore the conditions under which the individual's particular constructions about emotional reactions may emerge and change. His ideas still influence current work to explore the meanings that underlie puzzling behavior patterns and seeming inconsistencies in the expressions of personality.

Exploring the Meaning Underlying Puzzling Behavior Patterns

Contemporary work that was inspired by Kelly also tries to understand the personal meaning that may underlie puzzling patterns of behavior. Consider Mary, a senior attorney at an international corporate law firm, who is concerned about the performance of one of her new staff attorneys, John. Before becoming a corporate lawyer, Mary had done graduate work in psychology many years ago at Ohio State University where she was influenced by one of her professors, George Kelly.

Mary has been puzzled by the variability in John's work and wants to find a way to improve his sense of well-being and productivity. Is he always distracted, or does it depend on situations? What are the situations in which he's less distracted and can concentrate? In short, Mary is trying to assess the *if* ... *then* ... patterns that constitute his behavioral signature (Chapter 4) so that she can understand their meaning and implications. After she learns that John tends to be particularly distracted in meetings at the corporate headquarters but not when he travels to branch offices, she begins to wonder: What exactly is the important difference between the meetings at the headquarters and those at branch offices? In essence, Mary wants to know the personal meaning of the situations, seen from John's point of view. This is also one of the central questions for the science of personality. In particular, researchers have been asking: can personal meanings of situations be assessed in a systematic, objective fashion?

George Kelly anticipated this challenge, and in his personal construct theory offered a general strategy. Although his strategy was originally proposed for individual therapeutic settings, it is being extended to a method for systematically and objectively assessing the meaning of a situation to a given individual (e.g., Mischel & Shoda, 1995; Shoda, LeeTiernan, & Mischel, 2002). For example, meetings at company headquarters may be characterized by such features as the presence of the boss, the authority whose opinions directly influence promotion and salary decisions. Another feature might be the presence of highly competitive "career climbers" who focus only on advancement of their individual careers.

12.18 How does selective attention to psychologically meaningful features of situations provide information about a person's constructs?

The subjective meaning of the situations may be understood by a person's tendency to selectively attend to particular types of features. While some people may not even notice the career-advance focus of their colleagues at headquarters, for others, like John, it is highly salient. Individuals also may differ reliably in the psychological impact of attending to these features. In this example, John's perception of his colleagues' focus on selfish career advancement reminds him that he feels himself losing sight of the sense of purpose that initially attracted him to his career. Now suppose that John has a stable tendency to attend to and react to the presence of these features in distinctive ways, for example by becoming upset and less motivated in his own work. If so, it is important to identify the features that are influencing him if one wants to understand their meaning for him and the ways they are affecting what he is thinking, feeling, and doing.

People as Scientists

The psychology of personal constructs explores the maps that people generate in coping with the psychological terrain of their lives. Kelly emphasizes that, just like the scientist who studies them, human participants also construe behavior—categorizing, interpreting, labeling, and judging themselves and their world: Every person is a scientist.

12.19 In what sense is each individual a "personal scientist"? What are the "operational definitions" for personal constructs?

The individuals assessed by psychologists are themselves assessors who evaluate and construe their own behavior; they even assess the personality psychologists who try to assess them. Constructions and hypotheses about behavior are formulated by all persons regardless of their formal degrees and credentials as scientists. According to Kelly, it is these constructions, and not merely simple physical responses, that must be studied in an adequate approach to personality. Categorizing behavior is equally evident when a psychotic patient describes his personal, private ideas in therapy, and when a scientist discusses her favorite constructs and theories at a professional meeting. Both people represent the environment internally and express their representations and private experiences in their psychological constructions. Personal constructions, and not objective behavior descriptions on clear dimensions, confront the personality psychologist.

Kelly noted that most psychological scientists view themselves as motivated to achieve cognitive clarity and to understand phenomena, including their own lives. Yet the "subjects" of their theories, unlike the theorists themselves, are seen as unaware victims of psychic forces and traits that they can neither understand nor control. Kelly tries to remove this discrepancy between the theorist and the participant and to treat all people as if they were scientists.

Just like the scientist, participants generate constructs and hypotheses with which they try to anticipate and control events in their lives. Therefore, to understand the participant, one has to understand his or her constructs or private personality theory. To study an individual's constructs, one has to find behavioral examples or "referents" for them. We cannot know what another person means when she says, "I have too much ego," or "I am not a friendly person," or "I may be falling in love," unless she gives us behavioral examples. Examples (referents) are required whether the construct is personal, for example the way a patient construes herself "as a woman," or theoretical, as when a psychologist talks about "introversion" or "ego defenses." Constructs can become known only through behavior.

Constructive Alternativism: Many Ways to See

12.20 Define constructive alternativism. How do anticipations guide behavior?

If one adopts Kelly's approach to understanding people, then:

> Instead of making our own sense out of what others did we would try to understand what sense they made out of what they did. Instead of putting together the events in their lives in the most scientifically parsimonious way, we would ask how they put things together, regardless of whether their schemes were parsimonious or not.
>
> (Kelly, 1962, in B. A. Maher, 1979, p. 203)

The same events can be alternatively categorized. While people may not always be able to change events, they can always construe them differently (Fransella, 1995). That is what Kelly meant by **constructive alternativism**. To illustrate, consider this event: A boy drops his mother's favorite vase. What does it mean? The event is simply that the vase has been broken. Yet ask the child's psychoanalyst and he may point to the boy's unconscious hostility; ask the mother and she tells you how "mean" he is; his father says he is "spoiled"; the child's teacher may see the event as evidence of the child's "laziness" and chronic "clumsiness"; his grandmother calls it just an "accident"; and the child himself may construe the event as reflecting his "stupidity." While the event cannot be undone—the vase is broken—its interpretation is open to alternative constructions, and these may lead to different courses of action.

Kelly's theory began with this fundamental postulate: "A person's processes are psychologically channelized by the ways in which he anticipates events" (Kelly, 1955, p. 46). This means that a person's activities are guided by the constructs he or she uses to predict events. Like other phenomenological theories, this postulate emphasizes the person's subjective view, but it is more specific in its focus on how the individual predicts or anticipates events. Although the details of the theory need not concern us here, several of the main ideas require comment.

Kelly was concerned with the **convenience of constructs** rather than with their absolute truth. Rather than try to assess whether a particular construct is true, his approach attends to its convenience or utility for the construer. For example, rather than try to assess whether or not a client is "really getting depressed" or "really going crazy," one tries to discover the implications for the client's life of construing himself in that way. If the construction is not convenient, then the task is to find a better alternative—that is, one that predicts better and leads to better outcomes. Just as psychologists may get stuck with an inadequate theory, so their patients also may impale themselves on their constructions and construe themselves into a dilemma. Individuals may torture themselves into believing that "I am not worthy enough" or "I am not successful enough," as if these verdicts were matters of indisputable fact rather than constructions and hypotheses about behavior. The job of psychotherapy is to provide the conditions in which personal constructs can be elaborated, and tested for their implications. And, if they prove to be not helpful to the person, they then can be modified, just as a scientist can change a theory or idea that turns out not to work well. Like the scientist, every person needs the chance to test personal constructs and to validate or invalidate them, progressively modifying them in the light of new experience.

12.21 Why are constructs not evaluated in terms of truth or falsity? What did Kelly view as the goal for therapy?

Roles: Many Ways to Be

Rather than seeing humans as possessing fairly stable, broadly generalized traits, Kelly saw them as capable of enacting many different roles and of engaging in continuous change. A **role**, for Kelly, is an attempt to see another person through the other's glasses—that is, to look at a person through *his or her* constructs—and to structure one's actions in that light. To enact a role requires that behavior be guided by perception of the other person's viewpoint. Thus, to "role play" your mother, for example, you would have to try to see things (including yourself) as she does, "through her eyes," and to act in light of those perceptions. You would try to behave as if you really were your mother. Kelly used the technique of role playing extensively as a therapeutic procedure designed to help persons gain new perspectives and to generate more convenient ways of living.

12.22 What is a role as defined by Kelly? How was role-taking used therapeutically?

People Are What They Make of Themselves: Self-Determination

Like other phenomenologists, Kelly rejected the idea of specific motives. His view of human nature focuses on how people construe themselves and on what they do in light of those constructs (Fransella, 1995). Kelly (like Rogers) believed that no special concepts are required to understand why people are motivated and active: Every person is motivated "for no other reason than that he is alive" (Kelly, 1958, p. 49). Kelly's focus on how people view themselves and the world, and on self-determination and freedom, also contribute to modern efforts to enhance psychological strengths. This connection is seen especially in an influential movement called "Positive Psychology," discussed in the next chapter.

Finally, like many existentialists, Kelly believed that the individual *is* what he *does* and comes to know his nature by seeing what he is doing. Starting from his clinical experiences with troubled college students in Fort Hays, Kansas, where he taught for many years, Kelly independently reached a position that overlaps remarkably with the views of such European existential philosophers as Sartre. In Sartre's (1956) existentialist conception, "*existence precedes essence*": There is no human nature—man simply *is*, and he is nothing else but what he makes of himself.

▶ COMMON THEMES AND ISSUES

12.23 What major assumptions and commonalities characterize the various phenomenological approaches to personality?

The conceptions surveyed in this chapter are quite diverse and far more complex than a brief summary suggests. In spite of their diversity, they share a common focus.

The World as Perceived

Work at the Phenomenological-Humanistic Level of analysis focuses on the self as experienced, and the situations encountered as perceived by the individual. In a strong protest against the behaviorism dominant until the 1970s it brought personal constructs and feeling, including about oneself, into psychology. It led many researchers to develop methods that explore how people can see themselves more fully and honestly, as discussed in the next chapter. It opened a way toward building a science of what goes on inside the mind of the individual, including his or her self-conceptions and emotions. Perhaps most important, it broadened the vision of well-being and human nature, recognizing that self-awareness and self-acceptance are crucial aspects of personal growth and actualization (Spinelli, 1989).

Potential for Growth, Change, and Freedom

Theorists working at this level also were concerned with understanding the human potential for growth and change, and for alternative ways of construing and dealing with life's challenges. They proposed that people do not have to be victimized by their biographies (as George Kelly put it). While emphasizing the potential for freedom and choice, this perspective is also sensitive to the constraints and limitations of the human condition. Many who work at this level share the existential belief that "man is what he makes of himself."

Psychologists who appreciate the attractiveness of these beliefs, but who are committed to a deterministic view of science, also have to ask, however: What are the causes that govern what individuals make of themselves and conceive themselves to be? And how do individuals come to make themselves and conceive themselves in particular ways? While philosophers may put the springs of action and cognition into the will (as Sartre does), the scientifically oriented psychologist seeks to understand the psychological mechanisms that underlie the will (Mischel et al., 1989). Many psychologists accept the idea that individuals are what they make of themselves. However, as scientists they want to go further and search for the conditions and processes that make that possible. For example, they want to identify the influences that determine the person's self-conceptions and ability to choose. These challenges began to be addressed by work at the Phenomenological Level, as you will see in the next chapter, and it continues to be on the agenda of all levels in the rest of the text.

The existential idea that the person has potential control and responsibility for him- or herself, and that people are what they make of themselves, has profound implications for the study of personality. (For some unexpected similarities with behaviorism, see *In Focus 12.3*.) Instead of a search for where the individual stands with regard to the assessor's dimensions, the assessor's task is to help clarify what the individual is making of him- or herself, and the "projects" and goals and plans of that person (Cantor, 1990) as they unfold in the course of life (Emmons, 1997; Mischel et al., 1996; Seligman, 2002). The next chapter illustrates some of the main steps taken in this direction at the Phenomenological-Humanistic Level.

The early contributions at this level are diverse and significant and still remain vibrant in modified forms. For example, a great deal of current work is devoted to understanding the "self" and its role in personality (e.g., Leary & Tangney, 2003; McAdams, 2005b, 2006; Mischel & Morf, 2003). Likewise, as discussed in the next chapter, "positive psychology" (e.g. Duckworth et al., 2005), and work on the nature and measurement of well-being, fulfillment, and happiness, are all thriving (e.g., Diener & Lucas, 2000b; Lewis & Haviland-Jones, 2000). Collectively, psychologists at this level of analysis continue to add to the understanding of the self, mental health, and the importance of interpersonal relationships for personality and personal growth.

IN FOCUS 12.3

UNEXPECTED SIMILARITIES: BEHAVIOR THEORY AND EXISTENTIALISM

Work at the Phenomenological Level arose in part because its leaders wanted to protest against behavioral–learning–conditioning approaches. Ironically, after the heat of the battle cools, one can begin to see a surprising common theme. Thus, the behavioral focus on what the person is *doing*, rather than on attributes or motives, is compatible with the views of the famous existentialist thinker, Sartre, who was one of the inspirations for the phenomenological-humanistic movement. Sartre declared: "existence precedes essence." He meant by that phrase that:

> . . . man first of all exists, encounters himself, surges up in the world—and defines himself afterwards. If man as the existentialist sees him is not definable, it is because to begin with he is nothing. He will not be anything until later, . . . Thus, there is no human nature. . . . Man simply is (1965, p. 28)

A rejection of preconceptions about motives and traits was also true for George Kelly in his personal construct theory, and it is what he meant when he said, "I *am* what I *do*." He urged that to know what one is, one must look at what one does. Skinner, the arch behaviorist, would have agreed with him on this point at least. In fact, both approaches and levels of analysis may be similar to the degree that both share a focus on the here and now; both emphasize what the person is doing; both avoid distant historical reconstruction in favor of a concern with new action possibilities for the individual.

These commonalities violate many common stereotypes about both approaches. They suggest that each is enriched by taking account constructively of the other's work. The similarities, although only partial, are impressive, the more so because philosophically it is hard to imagine two positions that on the surface would seem more incompatible and opposed.

However, the two positions have one critical incompatibility. The existentialist takes the philosophical position that the individual is responsible and attributes to the person's choices the ultimate causes of behavior. In Sartre's phrase, a person "is what he wills to be" (1956, p. 291). A behavior theorist may share Sartre's desire to put "every man in possession of himself" rather than allow him to be possessed by unconscious psychic forces. But a behavioral analysis of causation cannot begin with the person's will as the fundamental cause of what he does, nor can it end with his constructs as a final explanation of his behavior.

The two positions differ in their focus of attention. The phenomenologist wants to know and understand the person's experience; the behaviorally oriented psychologist wants to clarify the conditions that control the ultimate behavior. The approaches to which we turn in the final part of the text seek to reconcile and integrate the two within a more comprehensive system that draws on contributions from each of the levels of analysis discussed throughout the text.

The contributions from this level also add greatly to the integrated view of personality that is emerging currently in the field.

▶ SUMMARY

SOURCES OF PHENOMENOLOGICAL PERSPECTIVES

- Phenomenological theories focus on the immediate perceived experience and concepts of individuals, and on their strivings toward growth and self-actualization.
- Allport stresses the functional autonomy of motives—current motives may be independent of their historical roots.
- Lewin's field theory introduces the notion of life space and the importance of the psychological environment. He stresses the immediate relationships between the person and the psychological environment.
- The existentialists focus on the "here and now." They emphasize that we build our own lives, and that each person is a choosing, free, responsible agent.

CARL ROGERS'S SELF THEORY

- Rogers's theory emphasizes the person's unique, subjective experience of reality. He proposes that the inherent tendency of the organism is to actualize itself.
- Maslow saw self-actualization as a basic human need.
- In Rogers's theory, the *self* (self-concept) develops as the result of direct experience with the environment and may also incorporate the perceptions of others. The experienced self in turn influences perception and behavior.
- Maladjustment occurs when the self-concept and a person's experiences are in opposition.
- Client-centered therapy seeks to bring about the harmonious interaction of the self and the organism through unqualified acceptance by the therapist.
- Rogers emphasizes unconditional acceptance as a requisite for self-regard.

GEORGE KELLY'S PSYCHOLOGY OF PERSONAL CONSTRUCTS

- George Kelly believes that constructs are bipolar, consisting of the psychologically opposite emergent pole and implicit pole.
- Kelly focuses on how the individual views his or her own experiences. His Role Construct Repertory (Rep) Test is used to study personal constructs.
- Kelly's personal construct theory has also inspired many to try and uncover meaning in puzzling behavior patterns.
- Kelly emphasizes that all individuals think much like the scientists who study them.
- "Constructive alternativism" refers to the individual's ability to construe the same event in different ways, leading to different courses of action.
- Role play may help the person to select more satisfactory modes of construing the world.

▶ KEY TERMS

bipolar 313
Client-centered/person-centered (Rogerian) therapy 309
condition of worth 308
congruent therapist 310
constructive alternativism 318
contemporaneity of motives 300
convenience of constructs 319
emergent pole 313
existential anxiety 304
existentialism 299
field theory 300
functional autonomy 300
higher growth needs 306
humanistic psychology 298
implicit pole 313
life space 301
need for positive regard 308
organismic evaluation 308
organismic experience 310
organized whole 304
peak experience 306
permeability 313
permeable boundaries 302
personal construct 313
Personal construct theory 313
phenomenology 299
principle of contemporaneity 301
role 319
Role Construct Repertory ("Rep") Test 314
self 307
self-actualize 303
self-concept 307
self-determination 309

CHAPTER 13

THE INTERNAL VIEW

The phenomenological theories discussed in Chapter 12 deeply influenced personality theory, assessment, and change. To be useful, these theories require ways to access the person's perceived internal experience. In Kelly's own words, if a person's private domain is ignored, "it becomes necessary to explain him as an inert object wafted about in a public domain by external forces, or as a solitary datum sitting on its own continuum" (1955, p. 39). On the other hand, if individuals are to be understood within the framework of scientific rules, methods have to be found to reach those private experiences and to bring them into view. In this chapter, we consider some of the methods used to examine the internal view of other people.

EXPLORING INTERNAL EXPERIENCE

Phenomenologists like Rogers and Kelly wanted to go beyond introspection and anchor their theories to scientific methods. In Rogers's (1947) view, for example, the therapist enters the internal world of the client's perceptions not by introspection but by observation and inference. The same concern with objective measurement of subjective experience characterized George Kelly's approach to assessment. This chapter considers some of the main efforts that have been made by psychologists working at this level to study experience objectively. Beyond finding such methods, they also have developed new strategies for personal growth and awareness. Although much of this work was begun more than 50 years ago, it has remained important (e.g., Deci & Ryan, 1980; Higgins, 1996a; Lamiell, 1997; Leary & Tangney, 2003; Ryan & Deci, 2001).

Why Self Matters: Consequences of Self-Discrepancies

The theories presented in Chapter 12 make a compelling case for the importance of subjective experience and of the self for personality. Going beyond theory to data, contemporary research is showing the powerful role of the individual's self-concepts, self-perceptions, and feelings about him- or herself (e.g., Hoyle, Kernis, Leary, & Baldwin, 1999; Leary & Tangney, 2003). The results show that the internal experiences on which the theorists in the last chapter focused change what people become and influence the types of problems and coping strategies they develop.

One of the most notable findings is that people experience different types of discrepancies between different aspects of the self, and these discrepancies influence their subsequent emotions and behaviors in predictable ways (see Table 13.1). It was Carl Rogers who first suggested that, beginning early in life, discrepancies develop between various mental representations of the self. For example, your **actual self**, that is, the representation of yourself as you are (e.g., a good basketball player) may be discrepant with your **ideal self**, the representation of who you would like to be (a great basketball player). Likewise, the actual self may be discrepant with the **ought self**, the representation of who you believe you should be (e.g., a doctor).

13.1 Describe three types of self-discrepancies and the emotions to which they give rise according to Higgins.

According to E. Tory Higgins (1987), building on Rogers's work, such discrepancies may be experienced not only from one's own vantage point, but also from that of significant others, such as a parent or an older sibling (see Table 13.2). An example of such a discrepancy would be a disagreement between the self you believe yourself to be (the actual self) and the "ought self" that you perceive your father thinks you should be. This could take a form like the thought: "I'm afraid my father will be angry with me because I didn't work as hard on my exams as he believes I should." That in turn can lead to feelings of agitation, such as fear and worry. In contrast, a perceived discrepancy between the actual self and ideal self makes an individual more vulnerable

TABLE 13.1 Types of Concepts about the Self

Self-Concept	Definition	Example
Actual	One's representation of oneself: the belief about the attributes one actually has	I am a caring and warm person, athletic and attractive
Ideal	One's representation of who one would hope, wish, or like to be: the beliefs about the attributes one would like to have ideally	I would love to be generous and giving, successful, popular, brilliant, and loved
Ought	One's representation of who one should be, or feels obligated to be: the beliefs about the attributes one is obligated to have, i.e., that are one's duty to possess	I should be more ambitious and tough, hardworking and disciplined

Note: In addition to one's own standpoint, each concept also can be represented from the viewpoint of a significant other. For example, your perception of who your father thinks you should be (e.g., strong-willed instead of caring) is an "ought/other" representation of the self.

Source: Based on Higgins, E. T. (1987). Self-discrepancy: A theory relating self and affect. *Psychological Review, 94*, 319–340.

E. Tory Higgins

to feelings of dejection, such as disappointment and dissatisfaction. In short, Higgins proposed and found evidence that various discrepancies like those shown in Table 13.2 have predictable emotional consequences.

Furthermore, different emotions lead to different patterns of coping with the perceived self-discrepancies (Higgins, 1987). Suppose, for example, that Gary W. experiences a discrepancy between the actual self and ought self and feels distressing negative

TABLE 13.2 Illustrative Self-Discrepancies

Types of Self-Discrepancies	Induced Feelings	Example
Actual/Own: Ideal/Own	Disappointment and dissatisfaction	I'm dejected because I'm not as attractive as I would like to be.
Actual/Own: Ideal/Other	Shame and embarrassment	I'm ashamed because I fail to be as kind a person as my parents wished me to be
Actual/Own: Ought/Own	Guilt and self-contempt	I hate myself because I should have more willpower
Actual/Own: Ought/Other	Fear or feeling threatened	I'm afraid my father will be angry with me because I didn't work as hard as he believes I should

Note: "Own" refers to the person's vantage point, "other" to the vantage point of another significant person (e.g., the father).

Source: Based on Higgins, E. T. (1987) Self-discrepancy: A theory relating self and affect. *Psychological Review, 94*, 319–340.

Actual–ideal self discrepancies can be painful.

emotions. If the discomfort associated with these negative feelings becomes too great, he may try to reduce or eliminate it in various ways. For example, to deal with a discrepancy between the perceived actual self and the own ideal self, one can reevaluate the negative interpretation of past painful events. Similarly, the high school student who feels rejected by others ("nobody likes me") because he was not elected class president then might think about the many close friends he has to reduce the negative feelings produced by the experienced actual–ought self-discrepancy.

13.2 What kinds of methods are used to cope with the various self-discrepancies?

Alternatively, to remove discrepancies people may change their actual behavior to match an important standard. Suppose an undergraduate studies very little for a midterm and receives a low grade on the exam. For the final, she may study very hard. In doing so, she relieves her guilt for not living up to what she herself perceives to be her responsibility to work diligently in college and receive exemplary grades. In this approach, regardless of the form the change actually takes, the motivation for the change arises from the conflicts each individual feels among his or her various representations of the self. These discrepancies, according to Higgins, cause specific types of emotional discomfort that individuals are motivated to reduce as best they can.

The key point from this is that the work on self-discrepancies makes clear that the self matters. It matters because the internal experiences that people have when they perceive such discrepancies are consequential for the emotions they experience and for the coping patterns they use to try to deal with them. For the scientist concerned with the experienced self and the internal view, the work by Higgins and colleagues also is interesting because it offers a way to study these experiences rigorously using the methods of the science. This work is also having practical applications for understanding serious personality problems, like eating disorders, as discussed in *In Focus 13.1*.

The View Through the Person's Eyes

Phenomenological study begins with the person's own viewpoint. To approach that viewpoint, one may begin with the individual's self-presentation, as expressed in the person's own self-description. Some of the raw data of phenomenology were illustrated in the self-description recorded by Gary W. when he was asked to describe himself as

IN FOCUS 13.1

EFFECTS OF SELF-DISCREPANCY: ANOREXIA

Alarmed by the growing number of cases of eating disorders, especially among adolescents and young adult women, researchers and clinical psychologists have been trying to understand this self-destructive, potentially fatal behavior. Explanations offered for eating disorders range from maladaptive interactions among family members to perceptual distortions in the way victims actually see their own bodies. Eating disorders also may reflect discrepancies among the individual's self-concepts, which impact his or her self-evaluation and can disturb self-regulation (Strauman, Vookles, Berenstein, Chaiken, & Higgins, 1991). This explanation stems from self-discrepancy theory (Higgins, 1987) in which different kinds of negative feelings typically are associated with particular kinds of perceived self-discrepancies. As discussed in the text, according to the theory, **actual/ideal discrepancies** make one vulnerable to feelings of dejection. In contrast, **actual/ought discrepancies** make an individual susceptible to feelings of agitation. In Higgins's theory, the person's **self-evaluative standards (self-guides)** are represented by the ideal self and the ought self. When the actual self falls short of these self-guides, the individual becomes prone to negative emotions and motivational states. These negative feelings, in turn, can produce distress and maladaptive behavior (Strauman et al., 1991). Some of the negative effects may be seen in eating disorders.

Thus, **anorexic behavior** (self-starvation) has been linked to actual/ought discrepancies (Strauman et al., 1991). According to Strauman and colleagues (1991), anorexic behaviors tend to be more characteristic of individuals whose actual self-concepts are discrepant from their representations of how significant others believe they ought to be. The anorexic behaviors seem to be part of a pattern of self-punitive, self-critical efforts to meet what these individuals see as the demands and expectations of significant others. In contrast, bulimic eating problems, such as binging, tend to be more associated with discrepancies between people's actual self-concept and their own ideal self-concepts. Emotionally, those suffering from bulimia experience dejection and related feelings as a reflection of the discrepancy between the body types they perceive themselves to have and their ideals. Interestingly, this seems to be the case irrespective of the person's actual body mass.

Self-discrepancy theory also suggests another insight into eating disorders. The fact that eating disorders are much more prevalent among adolescent girls than boys has led to speculation that women are more commonly socialized to derive feelings of self-worth from their physical appearance. Because modern society mainly considers thin women to be beautiful, many women feel compelled to constantly monitor their body weight and thus are more prone to eating disorders. An alternative explanation, however, is that girls typically are more restricted and controlled than boys. Consequently, prior to adolescence they develop more rigid self-guides, that is, more clearly defined ideal and ought selves. The stronger the self-guides, the more vulnerable the individual is to experience self-discrepancy and negative feelings (Strauman et al., 1991, p. 947). According to the theory, then, women are more likely than men to develop disordered eating habits.

a person, which was presented in Chapter 2, *In Focus 2.1*. If you look back at it, you will see that it gives at least a preliminary sense of Gary looking at himself and his world through his own eyes, using his own phrases, beginning to show some of his perceptions, thoughts, beliefs, and feelings.

13.3 How has self-discrepancy theory contributed to our understanding of anorexia?

How can we begin to interpret Gary's self-portrait? It is possible to proceed in terms of one's favorite theory, construing Gary's statements as reflections of his traits, or as signs of his dynamics, or as indicative of his social learning history, or as clues to the social forces that are molding him. But can one also make Gary's comments a bridge for understanding his private viewpoint, for glimpsing his own personality theory and for seeing his self-conceptions?

Because each of us is intimately familiar with his own conscious, perceived reality, it may seem deceptively simple to reach out and see another person's subjective world. In fact, we of course cannot "crawl into another person's skin and peer out at the world

13.4 What is the best way to find out about another person's internal experience?

through his eyes," but we can "start by making inferences based primarily upon what we see him doing rather than upon what we have seen other people doing" (Kelly, 1955, p. 42). That is, we can try to attend to him rather than to our stereotypes and theoretical constructs.

A most direct way to inquire about another person's experience is to ask him, just as Gary was asked, to depict himself. Virtually all approaches to personality have asked people for self-reports. Usually, these reports have served primarily as cues from which to infer the individual's underlying personality structure and dynamics. Perhaps because of the assumption that people engage in extensive unconscious distortion, the client's own reports generally have been used as a basis for the clinician (or the test) to generate inferences and predictions about him or her, rather than as a means of conveying the client's view of him- or herself.

Uses of Self-Assessments

Can people be "experts" about themselves? Can their reports serve as reliable and valid indices of their behavior? For example, in his self-appraisal Gary predicts that he can succeed in the job for which he is being considered. Is this self-assessment accurate, or is it a defensive hope?

13.5 What evidence exists that simple self-reports can have predictive validity that equals or exceeds that of more complex methods?

One way to address these questions is to examine whether people's self-assessments can predict their own future behavior. To establish the utility of a person's direct report about him- or herself, you must compare it with the predictions about him or her that can be made from other data sources. For example, you may compare the individual's self-reports with the statements drawn from sophisticated psychometric tests or from well-trained clinical judges who use such techniques as the interview and the projective test to infer the individual's attributes.

It has been a surprise for many psychologists to learn that simple self-reports may be as valid as, and sometimes better predictors than, more sophisticated, complex, and indirect tests designed to disclose underlying personality. In a pioneering study, researchers tried to predict future adjustment for schizophrenic patients (Marks, Stauffacher, & Lyle, 1963). They found that simple self-reports on attitude scales yielded better predictions than did psychometrically more sophisticated scales. Such attitude statements have also been one of the best predictors of success in the Peace Corps; they have been more accurate than far more costly personality inferences. Interviews and pooled global ratings from experts did not prove nearly as accurate as self-reports were (Mischel, 1965). In sum, useful information about people may be obtained most directly by simply asking them (e.g., Cantor & Kihlstrom, 1987; Emmons, 1997). These conclusions seem to hold for such diverse areas as college achievement, job and professional success, treatment outcomes in psychotherapy, rehospitalization for psychiatric patients, and parole violations for delinquent children (e.g., Emmons, 1997; Mischel, 1981b; Rorer, 1990).

In sum, under some conditions, people may be able to report and predict their own behavior at least as accurately as experts. Of course, people do not always predict their own behavior accurately. Sometimes individuals lack either the information or the motivation to foretell their own behavior, or are motivated to not reveal it even if they know it. If a criminal plans to steal again, we cannot expect him to say so to the examining prosecutor at his trial. Moreover, many future behaviors may be determined by variables not in the person's control (e.g., other people or accidents). The obtained findings do suggest that self-estimates and self-predictions are useful assessment tools.

The Q-Sort Technique

One problem with self-descriptions, however, is that different individuals may use different words, phrases, and expressions to describe the same experience, and therefore it becomes difficult to compare one person's self-description with another person's. To compare people, they need to use the same standard language to describe themselves. An especially useful technique for achieving this goal is the **Q-technique** or **Q-sort**, a tool that also has been used in work at other levels of analysis, including the trait-dispositional (Block, 1961, 1971). This technique consists of many cards, each with a printed statement such as "I am a submissive person," "I am likable," and "I am an impulsive person." Or the items might be "is a thoughtful person," "gets anxious easily," "works efficiently."

13.6 Describe the Q-sort technique, and the various aspects of the self that it can assess.

The Q-sort may be used for self-description, for describing how one would like to be (the ideal self), or even to describe a relationship. For a self-sort, clients would be instructed to sort the cards to describe themselves as they see themselves currently, placing cards in separate piles according to their applicability, ranging from those attributes that are least like them to those that are most like them. For example, the terms that Gary W. had indicated as most self-descriptive were "haughty, determined, ambitious, critical, logical, moody, uncertain." Or people might be instructed to use the cards to describe the person they would most like to be—their ideal person. To describe a relationship, they would sort the cards into piles ranging from those that are most characteristic of the relationship to those least characteristic. As these examples indicate, the method asks one to sort the cards into a distribution along a continuum from items that are least characteristic (or descriptive) to those that are most characteristic of what one is describing.

The Q-sort is also used to describe the characteristics associated with successful performance in a given task. For example, one can find the profile of qualities "most characteristic" of people who succeed in a particular situation. One can then search for those individuals who best match that profile when trying to predict who will or will not do well in that type of situation (Bem & Funder, 1978). Likewise, Q-sorts are often used to characterize changes in development, for example by comparing people's Q-sort profiles at different stages (Mischel, Shoda, & Peake, 1988).

At this level of analysis, for many psychologists, self-statements from Q-sorts may be of interest in themselves. The phenomenologist simply wants to see the person's self-characterization for its own sake. Unlike other measures that compare individuals with each other along a given dimension to obtain *between-person* differences, the goal of Q-sort assessment is the pattern of the various characteristics *within each person*.

Because the Q-sort requires arranging the cards into a predetermined distribution (e.g., 5 cards in the "least characteristic," 5 cards in the "most characteristic," and 20 cards in the "neither characteristic nor uncharacteristic" piles), if one averages across all the characteristics, everyone will have the same score. This is like giving different painters tubes of red, blue, green, and yellow watercolor paint, and they are asked to paint while making sure they use up all the paint they are given. If you "average" all the colors on each canvas, they will all be the same. What is different is the spatial configuration of the colors on the canvas. Similarly, what is different in the Q-sort depiction of an individual is the *arrangement* among the set of characteristics. With this focus on intraindividual arrangement or configuration, Q-sort has been used to determine how similar, or dissimilar, persons' descriptions are of themselves as they really view themselves ("real self") and as they would like to be ("ideal self"). For example, using a Q-sort that contains 100 cards, individuals can "paint" the picture of their real self. Using the same set of 100 cards, they also paint the picture of their ideal self. Now, the similarity between these two pictures of self can be indexed by the correlation between the two, because both real and ideal selves are described using the same 100 descriptors. As you'll see later, often the degree of similarity between these two descriptions is informative.

Interviews

Most modern phenomenologists have recognized that self-reports may not reveal everything important about behavior and may not give a complete picture of personality. Persons may be conscious of the reasons for their behavior but be unable or unwilling to report them, for example, if they are uncomfortable or ashamed about aspects of their own feelings, perceptions, and behaviors. Or they may not be conscious of all of their experiences, in which case they cannot communicate them no matter how hard they try. Rather than considering that as a limitation, phenomenologists such as Rogers focus on the person's frame of reference as an important vantage point for understanding him or her. To illustrate this point, imagine two people who, objectively, are both good singers. But while the first thinks she is a great singer, the second thinks he is often out of tune and believes that others are only being polite when they say he sings well. Obviously these differences in their subjective views of themselves make them quite different people even though both sing equally well.

13.7 How is the interview used to assess personality characteristics?

The psychologist's task, in Rogers's view, is to provide conditions that are conducive to growth and that facilitate free exploration of feelings and self in a therapeutic context. This is because one cannot expect people to be honest about themselves when they fear that their statements may incriminate them or lead to negative decisions about their future. In order to become more aware of and articulate private feelings, one needs an unthreatening atmosphere that reduces anxieties and inhibitions, and fosters self-disclosure (Jourard, 1967; Lietaer, 1993). Phenomenologically oriented psychologists therefore try to create conditions of acceptance, warmth, and empathy in which the individual may feel more at ease for open self-exploration (Vanaerschot, 1993). These conditions of acceptance are illustrated vividly in "client-centered" (Rogerian) therapy, discussed later in this chapter.

Rogerians have not only tried to create conditions conducive to personal growth, they also have studied these conditions through methods such as the interview (e.g., Rogers, 1942; Rogers & Dymond, 1954). They use the interview to observe how the individual interprets himself and his experiences, regardless of the validity of the data he provides. This is done in an atmosphere conducive to genuine self-disclosure in which self-revelation and honest self-reports are actively encouraged (e.g., Cantor, 1990; Fodor, 1987; Jourard, 1974).

The Semantic Differential

The **semantic differential** is used to study what different stimuli, events, or other experiences mean to the individual—that is, their personal significance. If you take the semantic differential you are asked to indicate the meanings of diverse words, phrases, and concepts by rating them on many scales (Osgood, Suci, & Tannenbaum, 1957). You are given a stimulus word like "feather," or "me," or "my father," or a phrase like "my ideal self," and are asked to rate each stimulus on a seven-point, bipolar scale. Polar adjectives like "rough–smooth" or "fair–unfair" are the extremes of each scale, and you

TABLE 13.3 Examples of Concepts and Rating Scales from the Semantic Differential

Concepts whose meanings are rated:

My Actual Self
My Ideal Self
Masculinity
Foreigner
Mother

Scales for rating the meaning of each concept:

Strong	___:	___:	___:	___:	___:	___:	___ Weak
Pleasant	___:	___:	___:	___:	___:	___:	___ Unpleasant
Hard	___:	___:	___:	___:	___:	___:	___ Soft
Safe	___:	___:	___:	___:	___:	___:	___ Dangerous
Fair	___:	___:	___:	___:	___:	___:	___ Unfair
Active	___:	___:	___:	___:	___:	___:	___ Passive

Note: As an exercise, provide these ratings yourself for each concept.

Source: Based on Osgood, C. E., Suci, G. J., & Tannenbaum, P. H. (1957). *The measurement of meaning.* Urbana: University of Illinois Press.

mark the point that most nearly indicates the meaning of the stimulus concept for you. For example, you might be asked to rate "my ideal self" on scales like those shown in Table 13.3. To see what that is like, you should try it for yourself, both for the concepts suggested and for any others you find interesting for yourself. The technique is both objective and flexible. It permits investigation of how people describe themselves and others, as well as how special experiences (e.g., psychotherapy) affect them.

13.8 Describe the semantic differential method. What three underlying factors consistently emerge from such ratings?

A great deal of research has repeatedly indicated that three main factors tend to emerge when the results are analyzed. A primary **evaluative (good–bad) factor** seems to be the most important (Kim & Rosenberg, 1980). In other words, evaluations in such terms as "good–bad" enter most extensively into how people characterize themselves, their experiences, and other people (Ross & Nisbett, 1991). The two other factors are **potency**, represented by scale items like hard–soft, masculine–feminine, strong–weak, and **activity**, tapped by scales like active–passive, excitable–calm, and hot–cold (Mulaik, 1964; Vernon, 1964).

Nonverbal Communication

Techniques like the semantic differential and the Rep Test sample what people say—that is, their verbal behavior. But significant communication among people is often nonverbal—it can involve facial expressions, movements, and gestures. Nonverbal expressions have intrigued psychologists of many theoretical orientations who are interested in the individual's perceptions and inner states. Researchers explore the possible meanings and effects of such nonverbal expressions as eye contact and the stare.

13.9 What is the significance of nonverbal behavior in assessing inner experiences?

For example, when an interviewer evaluates participants positively, they increase eye contact with him but when he evaluates them negatively, they decrease eye contact with him (Exline & Winters, 1965). The effects of eye contact seem to interact with the verbal content conveyed in the relationship. One study varied whether an interviewer looked at the participant frequently or hardly at all, and whether the conversation was positive or threatening (Ellsworth & Carlsmith, 1968). When the verbal content was positive, more frequent eye contact on the part of the inteviewer produced more positive evaluations of the interviewer. In contrast, when the verbal content was negative, more frequent eye contact produced more negative evaluation.

Although much is still unknown about nonverbal communication, many results have been encouraging. It has been shown, for instance, that "when people look at the faces of other people, they can obtain information about happiness, surprise, fear, anger, disgust/contempt, interest, and sadness. Such information can be interpreted, without any special training, by those who see the face . . ." (Ekman, Friesen, & Ellsworth, 1972, pp. 176–177). In short, phenomenological, "inner" experiences may be visible in the form of nonverbal behaviors.

Studying Lives from the Inside: Psychobiography

13.10 How have the methods of psychobiography and personal narrative been used to study people's lives?

The phenomenological approach has many of its deepest roots in the psychotherapies of theorists like Rogers and Kelly, but it also has been extended in other directions. Most notably, the approach has been adapted and combined with other methods to study lives in depth and over long periods of time (Runyan, 1997). Called **psychobiography**, the intensive study of individual lives has become a specialty area in its own right. These studies attempt to provide a comprehensive psychological understanding of one person, often selecting public figures like Adolf Hitler or Ghandi. As its advocates note, personality psychology has many sides, and does not have to be confined to quantitative comparisons between people or groups (Lamiell, 1997; Runyan, 1997). Instead, the study of lives focuses on one person at a time, and tries to cover the whole of his or her life in all its complexity over the life course. The methods employed borrow from biography, history, and other social sciences as well as from psychology and the phenomenological approach. As one of its most enthusiastic practitioners put it, there is a "softer human science end of psychology" whose advice to students is "Learn all you can about people and lives, including yourself" (Runyan, 1997, p. 61).

Narrative Identity: Stories that Give Lives Meaning

In a closely related direction, but with its own guiding philosophy and methodology, Dan McAdams (1999) has developed an approach to understanding persons and the ways in which they construct their lives. His approach builds on Erik Erikson's **identity** concept (Chapter 9). McAdams focuses on the **personal narratives**—the stories—that people tell themselves as they try to make sense of their own lives and experiences. He proposes that "The I apprehends experience in narrative terms, casting the Me as one or more characters in an ongoing sequence of scenes" (1999, p. 488). The I is a storyteller, and the story each person tells—both to him- or herself and to other people—varies with time and circumstances. The stories you tell in a college application, a job interview, when building a relationship with a potential romantic partner, or in a private diary entry to yourself will vary. The contents and structure of the story will change, and as life is lived the stories of one's life are progressively edited, revised, rewritten, reconstructed. The core of this message is that regardless of their validity by any external standard, these stories people tell about themselves are worth hearing, and personality psychologists—as well as nonprofessionals—can benefit by listening closely.

According to McAdams (2006), as well as Erikson, adolescents in Western modern cultures face the problems of constructing a self and identity that gives their turbulent, confusing lives some sense of coherence, direction, and meaningfulness. These identity **self-constructions** are in the service of trying to answer basic questions about who one is, why one lives, and how one fits into—or needs to change—the existing social order of the adult world. The concept of **narrative identity** deals with the internal stories that evolve over time to make sense of the diverse, often conflicting aspects of oneself and one's behavior. They help to provide some coherence to an otherwise potentially chaotic life. Rough, primitive, fragmented, and even fantastic stories about one's life may begin to form early in childhood. But it's difficult to use these stories to organize and direct one's life trajectory, and to construct a meaningful, coherent life story over time until adolescence, according to Habermas and Bluck (2000). As the person develops and matures cognitively and personally, the life story becomes increasingly coherent and organized. By mid-adolescence the multiple events in one's life begin to become causally connected and to serve as explanations. The story evolves, for example, of how an important friendship developed, why it intensified or broke, the interests and goals that are emerging, the imagined future, who one is and wants to be and become. An autobiography, even if mostly implicit, is being constructed, and it is an evolving life story with a past, present, and future that are linked with interconnected themes. The contents of the explanations constructed depend not only on the individual but also on the culture and its meaning systems (McAdams, 2006; Shweder & Much, 1987). In time, the narrative identity that develops may itself influence how the individual develops his or her self-concepts and regulates his or her behaviors to make them consistent with that emerging self (e.g., Mischel & Morf, 2003; Morf & Rhodewalt, 2001b).

13.11 How does an individual use his or her narrative identity?

ENHANCING SELF-AWARENESS: ACCESSING ONE'S EXPERIENCES

Given that people's subjective experiences of the self have far-reaching implications for their emotions, behavior, and their well-being, it should not be surprising that changing the subjective views of the self can have significant impact on individuals' well-being. Probably the most dramatic and controversial manifestation of the effort to alter the subjective experience of self on a massive scale was by means of psychedelic drugs, and in some ways it created at least a short-term cultural revolution in much of the Western world. Initially, drugs such as psilocybin and LSD were advocated most energetically by Timothy Leary and Richard Alpert when they were psychologists at Harvard University in 1961 and 1962. In the 1960s, the "mind-expanding" movement through drug-induced "trips" or psychic "voyages" gained many enthusiastic participants throughout the Western world. Such drugs as LSD undoubtedly produce major alterations in subjective experience, including the intensification of feelings (Leary, Litwin, & Metzner, 1963), but enthusiasm for them was soon tempered by the recognition that they entail serious risks. The trend became to search for greater awareness without the aid of any drugs by means of psychological experiences and changes within the self and in how life is lived.

Historically, routes to increasing awareness that rely on psychological experiences rather than on drugs include meditation (Ornstein, 1972), encounter groups, and "marathons" of the type developed originally at the Esalen Institute in Big Sur, California (Schutz, 1967). While meditative techniques were based mainly on Eastern religious sources (Ornstein & Naranjo, 1971), the encounter or "sensitivity training" movement drew on various role-play and psychodrama techniques, existential philosophy, and Freudian psychodynamic theory.

The resulting syntheses were seen in the ideas of the **Gestalt therapy** of Fritz Perls (1969), in the efforts to expand human awareness and to achieve "joy" and true communication (Schutz, 1967), and in the pursuit of "peak experiences" and "self-actualization" (Maslow, 1971). In its early versions, Gestalt therapy included confrontations and "encounters" that quickly challenged the person's self-reported

13.12 Indicate how Gestalt therapy and T-groups are used to explore and alter internal experience? What anecdotal and scientific evidence is there for their effectiveness?

experiences, sometimes interpreting them as superficial and defensive. Often the "leader" tried rapidly and directly to stimulate and probe the deeper feelings that might underlie what the person disclosed (Polster & Polster, 1993). In more recent versions, there is less rapid and dramatic confrontation and a slower, more empathic attempt to explore the person's internal experiences in his or her own terms. The aim is to focus awareness on what is being felt fully and honestly. The process of enhancing both self-awareness and interpersonal awareness becomes the center of the therapeuticign relationship, encouraging the person to be more closely in touch with what is experienced and freer to experiment interpersonally (Fodor, 1987; Wheeler, 1991).

Group Experiences

As part of the search for growth and expanded awareness, in the 1960s and 1970s a variety of group experiences became popular. Encounter groups have had many different labels, such as **human-relations training group (T-group)**, and **sensitivity training group**, but in this discussion the focus is on their common qualities. Schutz (1967) in his book *Joy* noted that encounter group methods involve doing something, not just talking. In this quest, he advocated a host of group methods that include body exercises, wordless meetings, group fantasy, and physical "games." Elliot Aronson (1972, p. 238), a pioneer of experimental social psychology and a major contributor to the science, described what is learned in group experiences this way: ". . . in a psychology course I learn how people behave; in a T-group I learn how I behave. But I learn much more than that: I also learn how others see me, how my behavior affects them, and how I am affected by other people." Referring to the process through which such learning occurs, Aronson (p. 239) emphasizes learning-by-doing; ". . . people learn by trying things out, by getting in touch with their feelings and by expressing those feelings to other people, either verbally or nonverbally." Such a process requires an atmosphere of trust so that members learn not how they are "supposed" to behave but, rather, what they really feel and how others view them.

At a theoretical level, the encounter group movement involved a complex synthesis of both Freudian and Rogerian concepts with a focus on nonverbal experiences and self-discovery. The psychodynamic motivational framework was largely retained and was used in many of the interpretations, but it was implemented by direct "acting-out" procedures for expressing feelings through action in the group, by body contact designed to increase awareness of body feelings, and by games to encourage the expression of affection and aggression. Thus, many of Freud's and Rogers's ideas were transferred from the consulting room to the group encounter, and from verbal expression to body awareness and physical expression. Indeed, Carl Rogers (1970) developed and extended many of his theoretical concepts to the encounter experience, and he became one of its leading advocates. Rather than talking about impulses, feelings, and fantasies, the individual is encouraged to act them out in the group. For example, rather than talk about repressed feelings of anger toward his father, the individual enacts his feelings, pummeling a pillow while screaming "I hate you, Dad, I hate you!" Many people have reported positive changes as a result of group experiences. To illustrate, consider this testimonial cited by Rogers (1970, p. 129):

13.13 What are some of the benefits to group experiences over class or individual experiences?

> I still can't believe the experience that I had during the workshop. I have come to see myself in a completely new perspective. Before I was "the handsome" but cold person insofar as personal relationships go. People wanted to approach me but I was afraid to let them come close as it might endanger me and I would have to give a little of myself. Since the institute I have not been afraid to be human. I express myself quite well and also am likeable and also can love. I go out now and use these emotions as part of me.

While such reports were encouraging, they are not firm evidence, and they were offset in part by reports of negative experiences (Lieberman, Yalom, & Miles, 1973). Some behavior changes did seem to emerge, but their interpretation is beset by many methodological difficulties (Campbell & Dunnette, 1968). When careful control groups were used, doubt was raised if the gains from encounter experience reflect more than the enthusiastic expectancies of the group members. For example, people in weekend encounter groups showed more rated improvement than did those who remained in an at-home control group, but improvement in the encounter groups did not differ from that found in an on-site control group whose participants believed they were in an encounter group, although they only had recreational activities (McCardel & Murray, 1974).

Nevertheless, a number of experimental studies indicated specific changes that may occur in some types of groups. These changes include a decrease in ethnic prejudice (Rubin, 1967; Saley & Holdstock, 1993), an increase in empathy (Dunnette, 1969) and susceptibility to being hypnotized (Tart, 1970), and an increased belief by individuals that their behavior is under their own control (Diamond & Shapiro, 1973). This evidence is accompanied by a greater awareness on the part of therapeutic group enthusiasts that not all groups are for all people, that bad as well as good experiences may occur (Bates & Goodman, 1986), and that coerciveness in groups is a real hazard that needs to be avoided (Aronson, 1972).

Particularly important is the finding that **self-disclosure** and sharing of stressful, traumatic experiences, either in groups or in other forms (e.g., in diaries) can have dramatically beneficial effects on well-being and health (Pennebaker, 1993, 1997). An illustration of the value of sharing traumatic experiences comes from work with patients suffering from advanced breast cancer (Spiegel, Kraemer, Bloom, & Gottheil, 1989). The patients were divided into two conditions, both conditions receiving the usual medical care for cancer. However, people in the intervention received weekly supportive group therapy for a period of 1 year, sharing their experiences with others openly. The patients who had this experience survived almost twice as long (37 months) as those who did not.

Meditation

As Eastern cultures have long known, and as Western cultures have only recently learned, meditation can have powerful effects on subjective experience. The term "meditation" refers to a set of techniques that are the product of another type of psychology, one that aims at personal rather than intellectual knowledge. As such, the exercises are designed to produce an alteration in consciousness. It is a shift away from the active, outward-oriented mode and toward the receptive and quiescent mode. Usually it is a shift from an external focus of attention to an internal one (Ornstein, 1972, p. 107).

Students, businessmen, athletes, ministers, senators, and secretaries were among the more than 600,000 people in the United States alone who enthusiastically endorsed one version of meditation called **transcendental meditation (TM)**. Introduced into the United States in 1959 by Maharishi Mahesh Yogi, a Hindu monk, TM has changed over the years in the public's mind from counterculture fad to mainstream respectability. TM is defined as a state of restful alertness from which one is said to emerge with added energy and greater mind–body coordination. It is practiced during two daily periods of 20 minutes each. The meditator sits comfortably with eyes closed and mentally repeats a Sanskrit word called a **mantra**.

Maharishi, his movement, and more recent followers maintain that the technique of TM can be learned only from specially trained TM teachers who charge a substantial

TABLE 13.4 The Mechanics of Meditation

1. Sit in a comfortable position in a quiet environment, eyes closed.
2. Deeply relax all muscles.
3. Concentrate on breathing in and out through your nose. As you breathe out, repeat a single syllable, sound, or word such as "one" silently to yourself.
4. Disregard other thoughts, adopt a passive attitude, and do not try to "force" anything to happen.
5. Practice twice daily for 20-minute periods at least 2 hours after any meal. (The digestive process seems to interfere with the elicitation of the expected changes.)

Source: Adapted from Benson, H. (1975). *The relaxation response*. New York: Morrow.

fee. One of the pioneer researchers into the effects of TM, Herbert Benson, a Harvard cardiologist, disagreed (1975). He believed that the same kind of meditation can be self-taught with a one-page instruction sheet, achieving the same measurable results (see Table 13.4).

Scientific research indicates that there are direct physical responses to meditation (Alexander, Robinson, Orme-Johnson, Schneider, & Walton, 1994). These changes include decreased rate of metabolism (decreased oxygen consumption), and an increase in alpha waves (slow brain-wave patterns). Although meditation was initially introduced as a technique for expanding consciousness, the current emphasis is on reducing stress, lowering blood pressure, alleviating addictions (O'Connell & Alexander, 1994), and increasing energy and powers of concentration.

13.14 What physiological and psychological effects occur from meditation?

The research publicized by the TM movement is open to criticism. The fact that many of the researchers are dedicated meditators themselves makes it possible that their results and interpretations may be unintentionally biased. Perhaps most important, the characteristic brain-wave pattern that the TM movement claims to be a sign of, the "alert reverie" produced by meditation, does not appear to be unique to meditation (Pagano, Rose, Stivers, & Warrenburg, 1976). It can occur, for example, in hypnosis when a state of deep relaxation is suggested. And Benson's (1975) relaxation technique (see Table 13.4) produces the same reductions in oxygen consumption and respiration rate that are produced during transcendental meditation without the expense and the complex rituals of meditation training. In reply, those committed to the movement argue that TM produces a wide range of more fundamental changes than relaxation, including a tremendous improvement in the quality of life. Perhaps because the subjective experience produced by meditation may appear unique to the meditators, they often continue to claim that meditation is a distinct state of consciousness in spite of the contradictory physiological evidence.

The Person's Experience and the Unconscious

For many years, most psychologists did not consider subjective experiences as phenomena of interest in their own right. They preferred, instead, to infer what dispositions and motives might underlie the person's behavior. The historical neglect of the individual's viewpoint probably has many reasons. One was the belief that because of unconscious distortions and defenses, people's self-appraisals were biased and inaccurate. Some psychologists thus refrained from studying the person's perceptions, concepts, and intentions because they felt such data were not really scientific. But it is entirely legitimate philosophically and logically to take account of individuals' reported subjective

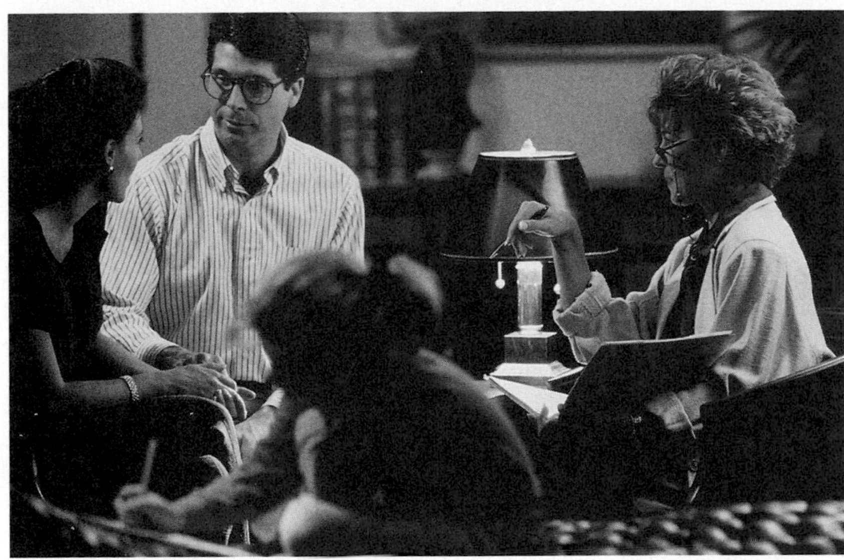

Family therapy analyzes the transactions in a relationship, helping each partner to see the viewpoint of the other.

(*Source*: Bruce Ayres/Stone/Getty Images)

perceptions—the rules they use and the reasons they give to explain their own actions (Lamiell, 1997; T. Mischel, 1964). It is not legitimate, however, to assume that these rules and reasons are useful bases for predicting what individuals will do—their behavior—in other situations. The links between persons' reported feelings and beliefs and their other behaviors have to be demonstrated empirically.

13.15 Why have some psychologists minimized the clinical and scientific value of subjective self-reports?

Although the phenomenological orientation focuses on the individual's viewpoint, in some of its variations it also seeks to infer his or her unconscious characteristics and conflicts. For example, Carl Rogers in some of his formulations (1963) has emphasized integration, unity, and achieving congruence with their "inner organismic processes." Rogers thought that these organismic processes were often unconscious. As a result of socialization procedures in our culture, persons often become dissociated, "consciously behaving in terms of static constructs and abstractions and unconsciously behaving in terms of the actualizing tendency" (Rogers, 1963, p. 20).

To the extent that psychologists accept the idea that unconscious processes are key determinants of personality, and rely on clinical judgment to infer them, they face all the challenges previously discussed in the context of psychodynamic theory. But methodological difficulties should not deter psychologists from listening more closely to what their "participants" can tell them; the caution applies to the interpretation process, not to the value of listening and empathizing. **Family therapies** have been influenced extensively by this perspective, and try to sensitize the members of a family to see each other's viewpoints and take them into account in their daily transactions within the family system.

Accessing Painful Emotions: Hypnotic Probing

In one direction, hypnosis is being used to help individuals access the painful feelings and memories that may become difficult to recall in the aftermath of traumatic experiences (Spiegel et al., 1994). Such mental avoidance may follow potentially life-threatening events and losses of the sort experienced by victims of disasters, violent crimes, or war.

13.16 How is hypnosis used to help people access dissociated experiences? What limitations of hypnotic probing have emerged?

But they may also occur in the course of everyday life, especially in early childhood when people have experiences and feelings that they may find traumatic and too difficult to deal with, as Freud stressed in his theory. The dissociated state itself is characterized by being out of touch with one's feelings, sometimes with amnesia, depression, a sense of numbing, detachment, and withdrawal.

In this type of therapy, hypnosis may be used within a highly supportive, structured setting to induce a trance state. While the person is in this state, memories of the painful events may be reexperienced in the safe therapeutic setting. Recall of the traumatic events is stimulated by the careful guidance and suggestions of the therapist, designed to elicit vivid images that make the memories more accessible (Spiegel, 1981, 1991). It may then become possible for the person to try to place the traumatic experience into perspective and to accept it emotionally. In this process, the person is encouraged to grieve for what has been lost rather than continue to "split off" the painful feelings and run away from them. According to this approach "... a loss not grieved leads to a life not lived—to a kind of numbing or withdrawal and depression ..." (Spiegel, 1981, p. 35).

While this approach has received much attention, in recent years its limitations and hazards also have become clear. Hypnosis is not a magic route to the truth: what is reexperienced and reported is subject to all sorts of influences, including implicit suggestions from the therapist and expectations about what will be revealed. As a result, the reports that follow are not at all above suspicion (Loftus, 1993, 1994).

Peering into Consciousness: Brain Images of Subjective Experiences

Interestingly, it was Freud who initially thought that hypnosis would provide a window into the unconscious, but who soon decided to abandon it in favor of other techniques—a choice that now seems like a mistake to some of his critics. Especially exciting is that new functional brain imaging techniques are helping to specify the brain locations that become activated during hypnotic concentration and that underlie different types of mental states and events (e.g., Schachter, 1995; Spiegel, 1991). For example, these imaging techniques show that the practice of meditation activates distinctive brain structures involved in attention and control of the autonomic nervous system (e.g., Lazar et al., 2000).

The Value of Self-Disclosure about Subjective Experiences

13.17 Summarize the research of Pennebaker on self-disclosure of painful events and its effects. How does Pennebaker account for the positive results?

Over the course of many years, Jamie Pennebaker and his colleagues have been studying how writing about stressful and traumatic experiences influences people's mental and physical well-being (Pennebaker & Graybeal, 2001). In Pennebaker's typical method, volunteer participants, usually college undergraduates, are brought into the laboratory and asked to write about either traumatic experiences from their past or superficial topics (for comparison purposes) for 15 minutes a day for 3 to 4 consecutive days.

As was noted in the discussion of psychodynamic process, these studies demonstrated that when people write about their traumatic and stressful experiences, they dramatically improve their well-being and health. Relative to people who are told to write about superficial topics, people who write about their emotional experiences subsequently make fewer visits to the doctor, at least in short-term follow-up studies (Pennebaker, Colder, & Sharp, 1990; Pennebaker et al., 1988; Smyth, 1998). They also show improved hormonal activity and immune function (Petrie, Booth, Pennebaker, Davison, & Thomas, 1995). In addition, people who self-disclose their subjective experiences by writing about them tend to show a number of other behavioral improvements. College students who

IN FOCUS 13.2

CAUTION: RUMINATION CAN INCREASE DEPRESSION

Being in touch with and expressing what you really think and feel, including with regard to painful emotions, may have considerable value, but thinking about the negative too much also has its hazards. Although many people believe that they should focus inward and attend in detail to their feelings, ruminating about the negative can become a pattern that makes depressive feelings even worse.

Going against the grain of popular wisdom, Susan Nolen-Hoeksema and colleagues have found that **rumination** tends to enhance angry and depressed moods rather than to foster improvements. People who ruminate are more likely to generate more negative memories, make more pessimistic predictions about the future, and interpret present situations more negatively than people who do not ruminate (Lyubomirsky & Nolen-Hoeksema, 1993, 1995). By ruminating about negative feelings, it can become more difficult to focus on and solve the problems that underlie one's distress and depression. In a study of people who lost a loved one to a terminal illness, those who ruminated more at the time of their loss were more depressed 18 months later than those who ruminated less (Nolen-Hoeksema, Parker, & Larson, 1994).

In moderation, the tendency to ruminate is a relatively common and stable coping style that is more prevalent among women than men (Butler & Nolen-Hoeskema, 1994; Nolen-Hoeksema et al., 1994). But chronic ruminators—people who reflexively ruminate in response to stress—experience more distressing thoughts and feelings compared to people who do not ruminate when under distress (Rusting & Nolen-Hoeksema, 1998). In fact, the tendency to ruminate may be an indicator that predicts future diagnoses of depression and anxiety (Nolen-Hoeksema, 2000).

self-disclosed improved their grades (Pennebaker et al., 1990), and unemployed workers got new jobs faster (Pennebaker, 1997).

13.18 How does rumination go beyond Pennebaker's approach? What negative effects result?

Contrary to classical psychoanalytical theory, Pennebaker does not believe that the power of writing is a function of catharsis or the release of pent-up negative feelings. Instead, he and his collaborators have evidence that writing about emotional experiences influences people's health and behavior by changing the way they think about their emotions and themselves. Writing allows them to construct mental narratives—literally stories—of their experiences. The specific psychological processes that make writing about emotional experiences lead to such positive outcomes still need more research and many studies are under way. Finally, note also that while it helps to write about one's negative feelings, brooding and ruminating about them can have the opposite effect, as discussed in *In Focus 13.2*.

► CHANGE AND WELL-BEING

The Meaningful Life, the Healthy Personality

The phenomenological orientation implies a "humanistic" view of adaptation, personal health, and "deviance." There are many variations, but in general, personal genuineness, honesty about one's own feelings, self-awareness, and self-acceptance are positively valued. **Self-realization**, the ultimate in fulfillment in this perspective, involves a continuous quest to know oneself and to actualize one's potentialities for full awareness and growth as a human being. Denouncing "adjustment" to society and to other people's values as the road to dehumanization, the quest is to know oneself deeply and to be true to one's own feelings without disguise or self-deception. Human problems are seen as rooted in distortions of one's own perceptions and experiences to please the expectations of society, including the demands of one's own self-concept (Chapter 12).

TABLE 13.5 Some Qualities of Maslow's "Self-Actualizing" People

1. Able to perceive reality accurately and efficiently.
2. Accepting of self, of others, and of the world.
3. Spontaneous and natural, particularly in thought and emotion.
4. Problem-centered: concerned with problems outside themselves and capable of retaining a broad perspective.
5. Need and desire solitude and privacy; can rely on their own potentialities and resources.
6. Autonomous: relatively independent of extrinsic satisfactions, for example, acceptance or popularity.
7. Capable of a continued freshness of appreciation of even the simplest, most commonplace experiences (e.g., a sunset, a flower, or another person).
8. Experience "mystic" or "oceanic" feelings in which they feel out of time and place and at one with nature.
9. Have a sense of identification with humankind as a whole.
10. Form their deepest ties with relatively few others.
11. Truly democratic; unprejudiced and respectful of all others.
12. Ethical, able to discriminate between means and ends.
13. Thoughtful, philosophical, unhostile sense of humor; laugh at the human condition, not at a particular individual.
14. Creative and inventive, not necessarily possessing great talents, but a naive and unspoiled freshness of approach.
15. Capable of some detachment from the culture in which they live, recognizing the necessity for change and improvement.

Source: Based on Maslow, A. H. (1968). *Toward a psychology of being*. New York: Van Nostrand.

13.19 What kinds of characteristics did Maslow identify in self-actualized people?

Maslow (1968) offered a description of the **healthy personality** from a humanistic viewpoint, and his view of the qualities of the **self-actualizing person** is summarized in Table 13.5.

Positive Psychology: Finding Human Strengths

Building on the work of psychologists like Maslow, but expanding it in new directions, in the 1990s, a group of psychologists in the United States, led by Martin Seligman, initiated a movement called **Positive Psychology**. Seligman (2002) pointed out that in the grim years after World War II psychology had become a science mostly aimed at healing deeply troubled human beings. He noted correctly that much of the thinking within psychology was guided by a disease model of human functioning and personality that focused on mental illness and pathology. In contrast, the aim of positive psychology is to change "psychology from a preoccupation only with repairing the worst things in life to also building the best qualities in life" (Seligman, 2002, p. 3). The field of positive psychology, according to Seligman, is directed at different levels, each with its own focus and goals, as summarized in Table 13.6.

Positive psychology developed as a movement in its own right, but its focus on subjective experience places it also within the phenomenological level of analysis, albeit on its positive or sunny side. The distinctive mission of positive psychology is to understand human strengths through research and to build therapeutic and educational interventions to enhance them. These strengths include such qualities as courage,

TABLE 13.6 Levels and Focus of Positive Psychology

Level 1: Subjective Experience
Focus: well-being and satisfaction with the past; flow, joy, sensual pleasures, and happiness in the present; constructive cognitions about the future—optimism, hope, faith.

Level 2: The Individual
Focus: positive personal traits, such as the capacity for love and vocation, courage, interpersonal skill, aesthetic sensibility, perseverance, forgiveness, originality, future-mindedness, talent, wisdom.

Level 3: The Group
Focus: civic virtues and the institutions that move individuals toward better citizenship: responsibility, nurturance, altruism, civility, moderation, tolerance, and work ethic

Source: Based on Seligman (2002).

interpersonal skills, rationality, insight, optimism and putting troubles into perspective, honesty, perseverance, realism, capacity for pleasure, future-mindedness, and finding purpose.

Just as Seligman predicted, since its founding positive psychology has evolved into a thriving area that connects well to other areas of psychology. It has many enthusiastic supporters (e.g., Aspinwall & Staudinger, 2003), and a rapidly growing supportive research literature. Duckworth, Steen, and Seligman (2005) document this progress, and further develop the conceptual framework for positive psychology. They identify three aspects or domains of happiness: *pleasure*, *engagement*, and *meaning*.

13.20 What are the three components of happiness according to the theory of positive psychology?

Valid assessment tools have been developed for each aspect. Most of these measures are in the form of self-reports to assess subjective experience. Many are closely connected to work on subjective emotional well-being, which is helping researchers to understand "the good life and happiness" (Diener & Lucas, 2000b, p. 334). Consistent with the work on narrative identity by McAdams (1995, 2006) and Csikszentmihalyi (1993), Seligman (2002) suggests that "narration"—story telling, as discussed earlier in this chapter—may be a particularly useful strategy for helping people toward the goals of positive psychology. Seligman notes that narration helps people to see their lives with a sense of agency rather than victimhood, and thus can become a powerful tool in a positively oriented, humanistic approach to psychotherapy.

Duckworth and colleagues find evidence that a variety of positive interventions can help to cultivate each of the three components of happiness. Nevertheless, the continuing challenge for positive psychology is to develop increasingly effective methods to enhance human strengths. In that search, George Kelly's (1955) contributions are likely to play a key role. As Kelly proposed in 1955, a key source of human strength and potential lies in people's ability to flexibly construe, transform, and interpret events to enhance their own well-being. In Kelly's phrases, no person has to "paint himself into a corner," no one has to be the "victim of his biography." And even when people victimize themselves with their own ideas, they can regain their freedom, Kelly insisted, by reconstruing their lives. Positive psychology's most constructive contribution may be its attempts to help people to view themselves in ways that can enhance their possibility for freedom and agency.

But as Kelly and the existentialists also recognized, life events often unfold in negative, distressing, and even catastrophic ways. If the psychology of human strengths remains sensitive to the dark sides and tragedies of human existence, it may be more effective in helping people to develop their potential to overcome them.

TABLE 13.7 Some Key Ingredients for Well-Being

- Finding meaning in life
- Optimism (vs. helplessness/hopelessness)
- Self-efficacy/agency (beliefs that one can do things effectively)
- Social support (relatedness: groups or friends that share experience caringly)

In recent years, research has identified many of the key psychosocial ingredients that enhance well-being (e.g., Aspinwall & Staudinger, 2002), summarized in Table 13.7. The results are generally consistent with the expectations of psychologists working at the phenomenological level. Namely, human resilience and strength—including physical well-being and health—in dealing with serious stressors is enhanced when the individual can find **meaning in life** and in the experience of living it. This is the case even when (or perhaps especially when) the experience is tragic, such as the loss of a life partner or the development of a life-threatening illness (O'Leary, 1997). A dramatic example is seen in how the actor Christopher Reeve, who had starred as Superman in the movies, dealt with his sudden paraplegic condition after an accident. He managed to construe this experience not as an occasion for self-pity but as an opportunity to make a contribution, becoming a dedicated spokesperson to increase research for spinal cord injury.

13.21 What psychosocial factors seem to contribute to physical and psychological well-being? Cite relevant research results.

Beyond such vivid single cases, there is a great deal of evidence that the ingredients of well-being, summarized in Table 13.7, significantly improve the biological response to illness (Ickovics, 1997). To illustrate, Shelly Taylor found that HIV-positive gay men who had lost a life partner but construed the experience as giving new meaning to their life maintained their level of immune functioning longer than did those who did not find meaning in the same experience (O'Leary, 1997; Taylor, 1995).

A second ingredient of resilience is an **optimistic orientation** (as contrasted to a pessimistic, hopeless, helpless orientation), and a focus on the positive in oneself and in human nature (e.g., Aspinwall & Staudinger, 2002). Scheier and colleagues compared optimists and pessimists (identified through a self-report measure) on a well-researched measure of coping styles in dealing with stress (Scheier & Carver, 1992). Optimists

The star of Superman became heroic also in real life.

(*Source*: Jerry Ohlinger/Corbis Sygma)

characteristically tend to use more active coping and planning, seek emotional support more, use religion, and attempt to grow constructively with the adverse experience they are having. They also are less likely than pessimists to use negative kinds of coping strategies. For example, when dealing with breast cancer, optimists are less likely to deny that they had cancer, tend to disengage less, and use generally positive ways of coping with their disease. In turn, such active coping styles and realistic acceptance of the illness tend to be predictive of survival. As the table indicates, beliefs that one can do things effectively, called **self-efficacy** (e.g., Bandura, 1986), and having relationships that provide support and connectedness also are important ingredients for effective coping and well-being.

▶ SUMMARY

EXPLORING INTERNAL EXPERIENCE

- Discrepancies develop between various mental representations of the self and they have emotional consequences. People use various strategies to reduce these discrepancies.
- Anorexia is an example of an actual/ought discrepancy, where individuals with anorexia believe there to be a large difference between the way they ought to be and the way they actually are.
- Research indicates that self-assessment sometimes can yield predictions as accurate as those from sophisticated personality tests.
- In the Q-sort procedure, participants are asked to sort attribute cards from most descriptive to least descriptive to describe, for example, the self, the ideal self, or a relationship.
- Phenomenologists use the interview to explore the person's feelings and self-concepts and to see the world from his or her framework and viewpoint.
- The "semantic differential" is a rating technique for the objective assessment of the meaning of the rater's words and concepts.
- Personal narratives and psychobiographies are other useful methods of exploring individuals at this level of analysis.
- People create narrative identities in order to make coherent sense of the events in their lives.

ENHANCING SELF-AWARENESS: ACCESSING ONE'S EXPERIENCES

- Methods to enhance self-awareness and interpersonal awareness include Gestalt therapy, meditation, and encounter groups, and generally emphasize emotional aspects of experience and existence.
- Researchers have also examined the effects of self-disclosure (e.g., by writing about traumatic experiences) and of rumination on diverse positive and negative outcomes.

CHANGE AND WELL-BEING

- In this perspective, the healthy personality is characterized by personal genuineness, honesty about one's own feelings, self-awareness, self-acceptance, and self-realization, without distorting one's self-perceptions.
- Positive psychology uses narrative restructuring to help people see themselves as agents in their own lives with the goal of helping people to increase their pleasure, meaning, and engagement in life.

▶ KEY TERMS

activity 331
actual self 324
actual/ideal discrepancies 327
actual/ought discrepancies 327
anorexic behavior 327
evaluative (good–bad) factor 331
family therapies 337
Gestalt therapy 333
healthy personality 340
human-relations training group (T-group) 334
ideal self 324
identity 332
mantra 335
meaning in life 342
narrative identity 333
optimistic orientation 342
ought self 324
personal narratives 332
Positive Psychology 340
potency 331
psychobiography 332
Q-technique (Q-Sort) 329
rumination 339
self-actualizing person 340
self-constructions 332
self-disclosure 335
self-efficacy 343
self-evaluative standards (self-guides) 327
self-realization 339
semantic differential 330
sensitivity training group 334
systems therapy 345
transcendental meditation (TM) 335

TAKING STOCK

PART V
THE PHENOMENOLOGICAL-HUMANISTIC LEVEL

▶ OVERVIEW: FOCUS, CONCEPTS, METHODS

As this part concludes, we again take stock and seek an overview of this level of analysis. Many psychologists welcome the emphasis on the person's cognitions, feelings, and personal interpretations of experience stressed by the contributors at this level of analysis. This concern with how individuals construe events and see themselves and the world has been a most influential force, and it has generated a great deal of research. The resulting contributions are widely acknowledged. Some of the main features of phenomenological-humanistic approaches are summarized in the next table, which shows some of their shared characteristics.

Overview of Focus, Concepts, Methods: The Phenomenological-Humanistic Level

Basic units	The experienced self; personal constructs and self-concepts; subjective feeling and perceptions; self-discrepancies
Causes of behavior	Self-concepts, personal construal (appraisal), feelings and conflicts, free choices
Manifestations of personality	Private internal experiences, perceptions, and interpretations, self-actualization
Favored data	Self-disclosure and personal constructs (about self and others); self-reports
Observed responses used as	Signs (of the person's inner states, perceptions, or emotions)
Research focus	Personal constructs; self-concepts, self-awareness and expression; human potential and self-actualization; emotion
Approach to personality change	By increased awareness, personal honesty, internal consistency, and self-acceptance; by modifying constructs; by alternative construals (appraisals)
Role of situation	As the context for experience and choice; focus on the situation as perceived

As the table indicates, the basic unit of personality is the experienced self and the personal concepts and feelings of the individual. These feelings and concepts and the conflicts experienced in relation to them are seen as basic causes of behavior, but the person has choice and responsibility for what he or she does. The favored data are people's reports and self-disclosures about their personal feelings and constructs. They provide the assessor with a glimpse of the person's inner states, perceptions, and emotions, and an empathic sense of what it is like to view the world through that person's eyes. The goal of research is to explore the individual's private feelings and concepts and examine their implications. It is assumed that by increasing self-awareness and "being in touch with" one's genuine experienced feelings, persons will enhance their perceived coherence, realize their potential for growth, and self-actualize. The effect of situations can be substantial but always depends on how they are perceived subjectively by the person.

▶ ENDURING CONTRIBUTIONS OF THE PHENOMENOLOGICAL-HUMANISTIC LEVEL

Work at this level, begun by pioneers in the middle of the 20th century, that focuses on how people construe or appraise themselves and their experiences, is still timely today. There is a renewed research interest in personal constructs and construal, the self, and the nature of selfhood (e.g., Hoyle et al., 1999; Leary & Tangney, 2003; Mischel & Morf, 2003), as discussed in Part VI and in the final chapters on the integration of levels.

Researchers at the Phenomenological Level looked beyond the individual's previous history, or early life traumas and conflicts, or traits, to offer a more positive, optimistic view of the human condition and the prospects for personal growth and constructive change. This focus also has encouraged movement toward a more positive psychology directed at enhancing human potential (Aspinwall & Staudinger, 2002). It proposed that people do not forever have to be victims of their past and can move beyond the less constructive aspects of their personalities toward much more positive ways of fulfilling themselves.

One enduring practical application from work at this level came in the form of family therapy or **systems therapy** (e.g., Minuchin, Lee, & Simon, 1996). These therapies try to understand how the problems of an adolescent, for example, are interpersonal and reflect conflicts and issues in the family system within which he or she lives. Treatment therefore needs to take account of what is going on in the family as a whole, not just in the adolescent's mind. It examines, for example, the role that was established for the "problem person" within the context of the larger system (e.g., "Anne's the one you can't count on"), and the ways in which that role feeds into the conflicts currently experienced. The goal is to help the family members to see each other more constructively. The hope is to reconstrue the "problem" to move beyond old stereotypes and essentially create new narratives that work better and fit the changing circumstances and the contexts of the family and all its members as they evolve and try to deal with each other. The same would be true if the case was one of an abused woman. Treatment would focus on understanding the abusive relationship and the ways in which it was maintained, not just on the personality of the abused person.

In sum, the applications of this approach have been broad, and have ranged from working to help overcome the psychological consequences of child abuse, battering, and incest to the trauma of HIV infection and AIDS (e.g., Walker, 1991; White & Epston, 1990) to modern family therapists (e.g., Minuchin et al., 1996), to help for women in abusive relationships with violent men (Goldner, Penn, Sheinberg, & Walker, 1990). These applications have made clear that many key phenomenological concepts can help in understanding and treating some of the most difficult problems of contemporary life.

They also illustrate how well the ideas of George Kelly and Carl Rogers, articulated half a century ago, have stood the test of time.

Theorists like Rogers and Kelly at first were lone voices calling for a new kind of personality psychology, and sketching some of its components and outlines. It is a tribute to the early theorists working at this level that many of the topics they championed are being built upon decades later with fresh and intense new interest, as seen, for example, in the vigorous Positive Psychology movement (Duckworth et al., 2005). Stimulated by the explosion of interest in cognitive approaches to personality, the self and its perceptions and cognitions are receiving unprecedented attention in personality psychology, as you will see in later chapters. In fact, they have become a centerpiece for current work at the Social Cognitive Level (Part VI).

PART 

THE SOCIAL COGNITIVE LEVEL

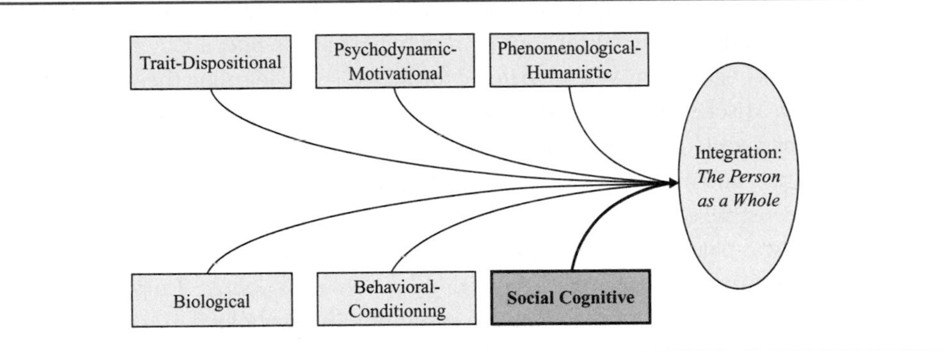

PRELUDE TO PART VI: THE SOCIAL COGNITIVE LEVEL

In the 1960s and 1970s, Albert Bandura and Walter Mischel were both young psychologists at Stanford University with offices across from each other. They both had been trained as researchers in approaches to personality that made learning and conditioning a cornerstone of personality development. Bandura was trained at Iowa State, Mischel at Ohio State, both in the middle of the last century when behaviorism was at its height. They both also had been trained as clinical psychologists who wanted to help people deal with their life problems. As clinicians working with people in real-life situations, as well as researchers eager to improve their science, they saw the limitations of the simple forms of behavioral conditioning that were based mostly on experiments with rats or pigeons in the laboratory. Consequently, they tried to connect findings from the behavioral approach with new insights starting to come from research on cognition and the extraordinary mental capacities of human beings. In time, their work and that of others (e.g., Kelly, 1955; Rotter, 1954) led to a radically different social and cognitive approach that was more directly relevant to personality and to clinical problems and treatment methods. It also addressed the specific mechanisms that enable people to use both social learning and cognitive principles to enhance their own abilities to self-regulate and to pursue their chosen life goals as effectively and happily as possible.

Currently, researchers at the social cognitive level are concerned with the links between what goes on in the mind of the person—their thoughts or cognitions, emotions, goals, and motivations—and their social behaviors. They try to understand both what people think and feel and want and what they actually do. With these broad goals, the social cognitive level tries to integrate contributions coming from the Behavioral Level, the Phenomenological-Humanistic Level, and from the study of social cognition, to form a more complete view of the person.

Thus, a distinctive feature of work at this level of analysis is that it is explicitly integrative: Rather than building a single unique theory or approach with distinct boundaries, its edges are deliberately fuzzy. Workers at the social cognitive level try to distill and integrate the findings that prove to be valid, reliable, and useful, regardless of the level of analysis at which they were initially explored. An overarching goal is to help make personality psychology a genuinely cumulative science that builds on its best results and concepts, regardless of their origins. Therefore, in this part, you will see numerous concepts that also are important in work at other levels of analysis, and that have been enriched and extended in new directions by researchers at the Social Cognitive Level.

These efforts began many years ago in the form of a "social learning theory" approach (Bandura, 1969; Mischel, 1968; Rotter, 1954), as theorists took from the Behavioral Level a focus on what people actually *do*, not just on what they say. Some also took from the phenomenologists and humanists, particularly from George Kelly, a focus on the ways in which people construe or appraise themselves and their experience (Mischel, 1973). And more attention was paid to the role of the person's expectancies, goals, and values in how information is interpreted and processed by different types of people. Further advances came rapidly with the onset of the cognitive revolution in psychology in the 1970s. It is stimulated in recent years by progress in the understanding of brain functions coming from related disciplines such as social cognitive neuroscience (e.g., Mischel, 2004).

The next chapter discusses the development and emergence of the social cognitive approach, its main theories and concepts, and some of its applications to personality assessment and therapy efforts. The second chapter in this part then illustrates the social cognitive processes studied and their implications for understanding personality.

THE PERSONAL SIDE OF THE SCIENCE

Some questions at the Social Cognitive Level you might ask about yourself:

- What is the role in personality of what people know, think, and feel?
- How does what I know, think, and feel about myself and the social world influence what I do and can become?
- What can I do to change how I think and feel?
- Will that change my personality and behavior?
- How much of who and what I am and do is "automatic"?
- How much is open to "willpower" and self-regulation?
- How do willpower and self-regulation work?
- How can I enhance my control over my life?

CHAPTER 14

SOCIAL COGNITIVE CONCEPTIONS

▶ DEVELOPMENT OF THE SOCIAL COGNITIVE LEVEL

Historical Roots

The social cognitive approach to personality began in the late 1960s. It was conceived by many psychologists who were in rebellion, frustrated by the limitations of earlier theories. At that time, the field of personality was divided into three theoretical camps. In one were enthusiastic Freudians guarding Freud's original work against anyone who sought to revise or criticize it. In a second camp were students of individual differences searching for broad personality trait dimensions. In the third camp were

14.1 How did George Kelly's contributions lay the groundwork down for theory development at the social cognitive level?

radical behaviorists concerned with conditioning and the relations between stimuli and responses, not with the internal ways an organism mediates between them. This third camp opposed any constructs that invoked the mind or mental activity in any form that could not be directly or simply measured. Except for occasional exchanges to attack each others' work, there was little communication among the camps. It was a milieu unresponsive to any "constructive alternatives." And it was much too early in the history of the field for workers at each level to see how much they had in common, and how the findings obtained at each level could enrich the others and add to the total conception of personality.

You have already seen one protest movement in response to this state of affairs in the ideas developed by theorists at the Phenomenological-Humanistic Level, such as Carl Rogers and George Kelly in their focus on the concepts and constructs of the individual, as perceived and understood by that person. This was especially the case with the contributions of George Kelly (see *In Focus 14.1*) whose work bridged the Phenomenological-Humanistic and the Social Cognitive Levels of analysis, to the benefit of both.

Linking Cognition and Social Behavior

As noted earlier, in the 1960s, personality psychologists who were attracted by the rigorous scientific emphasis of the behavioral level (Bandura, 1969; Mischel, 1968; Rotter, 1954) drew heavily on principles of learning established originally in experimental work with animals (reviewed in Chapters 10 and 11). Nevertheless, much as they tried to stretch those behavioral concepts, their own research findings forced a change in their views and led them soon to move beyond behaviorism.

Traditional behavioral approaches asserted that stimuli control behavior. But in fact, the perceiver's mental representations and **cognitive transformations** of the stimuli can determine and even reverse their impact. Although Kelly had argued this point theoretically, it had little clear empirical evidence. Such transformations were illustrated in research on the factors that influence how long preschool children will actually sit still alone in a chair waiting for a desired but delayed outcome (e.g., tempting pretzels or marshmallows) that has been placed in front them (Mischel et al., 1972). The question was: how long will children voluntarily continue to delay and what makes it hard or easy? It turned out that the answer depends importantly on how the children mentally represent the rewards (Mischel, 1974; Mischel et al., 1989, 1996).

14.2 How did delay of gratification research illustrate the important role of cognitive transformations?

For example, if a young child is left during the waiting period with the actual desired objects—the pretzels, for example—in front of her, it becomes extremely difficult to wait for more than a few moments. But through self-instructions they can cognitively transform the objects in ways that permit them to wait for long periods of time. If they think about the stick pretzels they want now as little logs, or think about the marshmallows as round white clouds or as cotton balls, they often can wait for the whole required time. In short, what is in the children's heads—not what is physically in front of them—determines their ability to delay (Mischel, 1974). Through self-instructions about what to imagine during the delay period, it is possible to completely alter (indeed, to reverse) the effects of the physically present temptations in the situation. This finding with little children made clear that it's what's in the head that is influencing behavior, not the external stimulus. Therefore, how people think and represent the world has to be taken into account to understand what they are doing and why they are doing it. George Kelly and Carl Rogers were right.

IN FOCUS 14.1

GEORGE KELLY: A BRIDGE TO THE SOCIAL COGNITIVE LEVEL

George Kelly taught psychology in the mid-1950s at Ohio State University and his influence on psychology still endures. He excited his many students (including Mischel, an author of the present text) about the possibilities for psychology—a psychology that was then at the height of extreme behaviorism. He criticized behaviorists by noting that they treated themselves as hypothesis-testing, wisdom-seeking scientists while they saw their "subjects" and "testees" as the reflexive victims of their reinforcement histories, "shaped" relentlessly by the external environment.

The fact that George Kelly was a very deep, original, refreshing voice was always clear to all who knew him. What has surprised many was not just his brilliance but how accurately he anticipated the directions into which psychology would move and continue to evolve over many decades. Almost every point of George Kelly's theorizing in the 1950s turned out to be a prophetic preface for the psychology of the next half century—and, it seems safe to now predict, it will continue to be for many years to come.

Long before "cognitive psychology" existed, Kelly (1955) created a cognitive theory of personality, a theory in which how people construe and think is at the core. The basics of that theory were described in Chapter 12, and were fundamental for the development of the Phenomenological-Humanistic Level. But Kelly's contributions were even broader. He anticipated the implications of cognition for personality theory. Perhaps most important was his focus on each person as a scientist who possesses a far greater freedom than psychologists previously allowed. This freedom, as discussed in Chapter 12, arose from the human capacity to test hypotheses and to recategorize and rethink events in alternative ways. By reconstruing themselves more conveniently, people, Kelly insisted, do not have to be the victims of their biographies; they can have volition and be *agentic*—that is, active agents who influence and change their lives.

The core of George Kelly's psychology was his belief that personal constructs are the basic units and that it is personal constructs, rather than stimuli, that are crucial. To make this point in one especially animated conversation in 1965, Kelly recalled vividly from his Navy experience during World War II how very differently he related to the same officer on different occasions depending on how, at the time, he construed that officer. He remembered that the captain seemed different to him in an informal role, chatting with his jacket off, from the way he seemed when he wore his officer's coat. "You see," Kelly said, "it is not the stimulus—the captain—but how I construed him that channelized my reactions to him."

Mischel jumped on Kelly's example, noting that a behaviorist like Skinner would find his story an excellent example, not of "construct control," but of "stimulus control": with his four stripes on, you see the captain one way; without his four stripes, you see him differently. To understand the construct change, he insisted, in the behavioral view, you have to include in your understanding how those four stripes came to control it and the exact conditions that now covary with it and with relevant behaviors. Kelly's calm, kind, unperturbed response to this argument made it plain that, as usual, he could see the other point of view—but was quite unmoved by it: The development of the person's constructs just did not interest him. Constructs were there, they channelized psychological processes, and just how they evolved or linked to "conditions" and specific action was not within his focus of concern. George Kelly did not want to elaborate his theory in those directions, just as he made a point of avoiding any methods or experimental studies intended to uncover "functional relations" or "controlling conditions": that was not his kind of psychology, and he wanted no part of it.

As a result, his theory remained exciting, provocative, but also incomplete. The greatest incompleteness of Kelly's thinking was that it provided a powerful theory of construing but gave few guides for linking peoples' constructions either to their past or to their future performance. To have the impact Kelly's theory deserves it also needed to have its methods expanded and enriched so that his always intriguing but sometimes difficult to specify constructs can be pinned down. Kelly's theory is a theory of how we categorize and what those categorizations do. It does not deal with how those categories arise nor with how changes in conditions may change our constructs. But a personality psychology that is purely ahistorical and relatively mute about performance, and about who is likely to do what when, is incomplete. It does not have to be, and much of the work at the social cognitive level begins with Kelly's ideas, and is built on the recognition that how you construe a situation guides how you deal with it. Thus while much of Kelly's contribution was fundamental for the Phenomenological-Humanistic Level of analysis, it also became a foundation for the development of theory and research at the Social Cognitive Level, as you will see in this chapter.

The Cognitive Revolution

The studies showing how what the child thinks about a stimulus, like an anticipated reward, and represents it mentally influences the impact of the stimulus, were part of an important development in the history of psychology that occurred beginning in the 1950s. It was the **cognitive revolution**, which started as a revolt against the then-dominant behaviorism but went on to literally transform psychology and all the behavioral sciences. As noted before, behaviorism insisted that scientific psychology is possible only by focusing on observable stimuli and responses; even discussion of mental states and processes was deemed unscientific because such states are not publicly observable. The cognitive revolution rejected this view. It gave birth to a new subfield of psychology called cognitive psychology. Its beginning is traced often to the publication of Ulric Neisser's book, *Cognitive Psychology*, in 1967.

Cognitive psychology developed rapidly in the 1970s and the 1980s, becoming a vibrant new field focused on how people represent knowledge about the world, how such representations develop, and are accessed in the processing of information. In the many years since its founding it has shown that the study of mental processes, such as thinking, knowledge, and memory, can provide a parsimonious, yet rigorous, scientific account of mental activity and its links to overt behavior, and it has opened the road to uncovering many mysteries of the human mind (e.g., Lemm, Shoda, & Mischel, 1995).

The effect of the cognitive revolution is still profound, and it importantly influenced both personality and social psychology. In personality psychology, it led to theories and research in personality psychology, referred to as "social cognitive" (and sometimes cognitive social), and they are the topic of the present chapter. In this chapter, we focus on some of the main conceptions in these theories. While they differed in important ways, their shared goal was to build a more comprehensive approach to personality that is both social and cognitive, drawing on findings from diverse areas of behavioral science, and from multiple levels of analysis within personality psychology. After describing these theories and their main concepts we examine some of the closely related developments in personality assessment and in therapy efforts to influence personality by researchers at the social cognitive level.

▶ ALBERT BANDURA: SOCIAL LEARNING THEORY

One of the early roots of social cognitive theories in personality psychology developed in the late 1960s when new discoveries by Albert Bandura (1969) and others in learning research revealed a third type of learning process that was independent both of classical conditioning and of reinforcement. Bandura recognized, of course, that reward or reinforcement has a powerful influence on behavior in a great variety of situations. But he also showed that people learn cognitively by observing others, not merely by experiencing rewards for what they do themselves. Much social learning occurs through observation without any direct reinforcement administered to the learner. Classical and operant conditioning remain important types of learning. However, it is now also clear that some of the most important human learning occurs through observation and other cognitive processes.

Learning Through Observation (Modeling)

Observational learning, sometimes called **modeling**, is learning that occurs without the learner's receiving direct external reinforcement. Such learning occurs even without

Albert Bandura

(*Source*: Courtesy Albert Bandura)

Children learn partly through observation and imitation.

(*Source*: F. Martinez/PhotoEdit)

the person's ever performing the learned response at all. You can learn a lot about how to kill people, for example, just by watching how it's done on television.

14.3 What is required for observational learning to occur?

Observational learning occurs when people watch others or when they attend to their surroundings, to physical events, or to symbols such as words or pictures. Albert Bandura (1969, 1986) for more than four decades has led the way in the analysis of observational learning and its relevance for personality. Much human learning, from table manners, interpersonal relations, including cooperation and aggression, to school and work, depends on observation of this kind rather than on direct reinforcement for a particular action. It is often indirect, and does not depend on actually observing an event, for example when others observe and then tell us about it. Likewise, the mass media, particularly films and television, are highly effective means of communicating experiences and observations, and contribute heavily to the enormous amount one learns about the social world. For example, after observing films of an aggressive model who punched, pummeled, and hurled a Bobodoll, children spontaneously imitated the model's aggressiveness when put in a similar situation (Bandura, 1965). (See Figure 14.1 for an illustration.) Similarly, after watching violent cartoons for some time, children became more assaultive toward their peers than did other youngsters who had viewed nonviolent cartoons for the same period of time (Steuer, Applefield, & Smith, 1971).

Completely new response patterns can be learned simply by observing others performing them. Observation is especially important for learning a language. Bandura (1977) emphasizes the advantages of observation for language learning compared to direct reinforcement for uttering the right sounds. He notes that exposure to models who speak the language leads to relatively rapid acquisition, while shaping would take much longer. If you don't know Polish it would take you a long time to learn how to say "thank you" in that language by blind trial and error or Skinnerian "shaping"; obviously it would be a lot quicker if you heard a Polish speaker say it. While this seems self-evident today, it did not seem that way in psychology at the height of behaviorism.

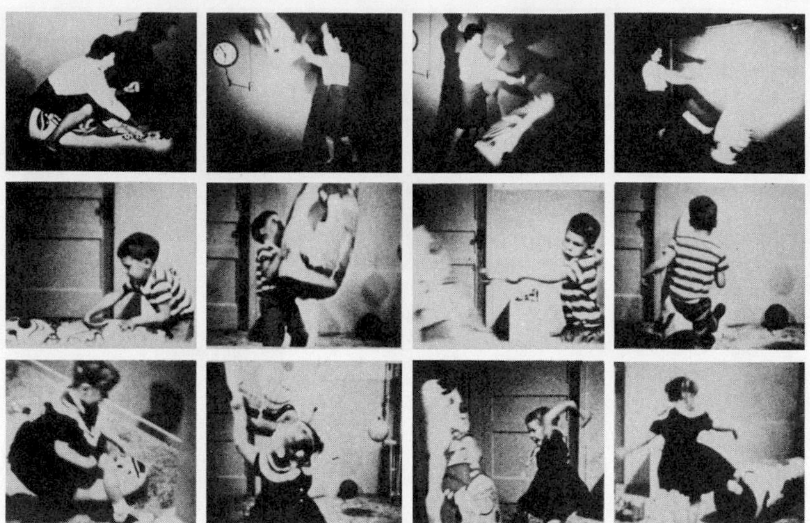

Figure 14.1 Photos depicting children spontaneously imitating a previously viewed model's aggressiveness.

Source: Bandura, A. (1965). Vicarious processes: A case of no-trial learning. In L. Berkowitz (Ed.), *Advances in experimental social psychology* (Vol. 2, pp. 1–55). New York: Academic Press.

Observing Other People's Outcomes: What Happens to Them Might Happen to You

14.4 How do observed consequences affect the likely occurrence of behaviors learned through modeling?

In short, and consistent with the findings from the cognitive revolution, people learn about the possible consequences of various behaviors from observing what happens to others when they engage in similar behaviors. Your expectations about the outcomes of a particular course of action depend not only on what has happened to you in the past, but also on what you have observed happening to others.

We are more likely to do something if we have observed another person (model) obtain positive consequences for a similar response. Seeing other children praised for cooperative play, for example, makes a child more likely to behave cooperatively in similar situations. If, on the other hand, models are punished for a particular pattern of behavior such as cooperation, observers are less likely to display similar behavior (Bandura, 1965).

Although laboratory studies offer clear demonstrations of the importance of expected consequences, examples from life are more dramatic. Consider, for instance, the role of modeling in the beginning of airline hijackings (Bandura, 1973). Air piracy was unknown in the United States until 1961. At that time, some successful hijackings of Cuban airliners to Miami were followed by a wave of hijackings, reaching a crest of 87 airplane piracies in 1969 that intermittently continued and, in tragically altered form, were seen again in the disaster of the September 11, 2001, terrorist attack on the United States.

In sum, you do not have to perform particular actions yourself in order to learn about them and their consequences; the observed as well as the directly experienced consequences of performances influence subsequent behavior. You do not have to rob a bank to learn that it is punishable, and you can even learn the techniques that help one do it by watching films; you do not have to be arrested for hijacking to learn about its consequences; and you do not have to rescue a burning child from a fire or return found money to discover that such acts are considered good. Models inform us of the probable consequences of particular behaviors and thus affect the likelihood that we will perform them.

Observation also influences the emotions we experience. By observing the emotional reactions of others to a stimulus, it is possible vicariously to learn an intense emotional response to that stimulus. Suppose you see someone wincing from a painful electric shock each time a red light goes on in the machine to which he is attached. Soon you will wince when the red light comes on. Thus, you may become "vicariously conditioned" when you observe repeatedly the close connection between a stimulus (red light on) and an emotional response (pain cues) exhibited by another person, and this happens without your receiving any direct aversive stimulation yourself.

14.5 What evidence exists that emotional responses can be acquired through observation alone?

This point was demonstrated in a study in which adults observed another person making fear responses in reaction to the sound of a buzzer supposedly associated with the onset of an electric shock. (Actually the person was a confederate of the experimenter and only feigned pain and fear without getting any shocks.) Gradually, after repeatedly watching the pairing of the buzzer and the responses made by the confederate, the observers themselves developed a measurable physiological fear response to the sound of the buzzer alone (Berger, 1962).

Importance of Rules and Symbolic Processes

Many studies that motivated the cognitive revolution showed that people did not seem to need trial by trial "shaping" but rather seemed to be helped most by the rules and self-instructions they use to link discrete bits of information meaningfully to learn and remember materials (Anderson & Bower, 1973). Likewise, studies with children indicated that it helps not only to reward appropriate behavior but also to specify the relevant underlying rules and principles so that children can more readily learn the standards that they are supposed to adopt (Aronfreed, 1966). When children understand that particular performance patterns are considered good and that others are unsatisfactory, they adopt the appropriate standards more easily than when there are no clear verbal rules (Liebert & Allen, 1967). Beginning early in life, the young child is an active thinker and perceiver who forms theories about the world, not a passive learner shaped by external rewards (Bruner, 1957; Flavell & Ross, 1981).

14.6 How are symbolic processes involved in learning?

Cognition plays a role even in classical conditioning. Suppose, for example, that a person has been conditioned in an experiment to fear a light because it is repeatedly paired with electric shock. Now if the experimenter simply informs her that the light (the conditioned stimulus) will not be connected again with the electric shock, her emotional reactions to it can quickly extinguish (Bandura, 1969, 1986). On later trials, she can see the light without becoming aroused. Findings like these forced both researchers and behavior therapists to pay more attention to the individual's mental processes. In the development of therapeutic methods to change behavior, they began to more directly engage the person's thought processes and social knowledge for therapeutic ends (Davison & Neale, 1990; Davison, Neale, & Kring, 2004).

These sorts of findings suggested that a more social cognitive approach to personality was required that takes into account how the individual characteristically deals mentally and emotionally with experiences. The search began within personality psychology for a theory of the cognitive–emotional–motivational processes that underlie the person's characteristic behavioral expressions and conflicts. As such, these efforts are in the tradition pioneered by Sigmund Freud, Henry Murray, and George Kelly, advanced over the century by many theorists reviewed in earlier chapters.

In the mid-1980s Bandura (1986), building on his earlier work on social modeling and observational learning, presented a broad social cognitive theory that addressed much in human social functioning, combining within it the contributions of diverse researchers and theorists. Bandura's writing covers a wide range, addressing how people acquire cognitive, social, emotional, and behavioral competences, and interact with—and create—their social worlds. He discusses in great detail how people motivate and regulate their behavior and create social systems that organize and structure their lives. He gives much attention to the importance of cognitive, vicarious, self-regulatory, and self-reflective processes in enabling human adaptive social behavior and change.

The Agentic, Proactive Person

Bandura emphasizes the human capacity to be **agentic** and exercise self-regulation and self-reflection as people generate behavior that, rather than being merely reflexive, is proactive and future-oriented. In this view, human functioning reflects the continuous interplay of personal, behavioral, and environmental influences, and Bandura shows in depth and detail, drawing on a vast range of research, the mechanisms that may underlie these complex interactions. His theory calls particular attention to the importance of the human ability to symbolize events and experiences and to anticipate consequences, plan events, and direct one's goals and activities purposefully through "forethought." The self-regulation and self-motivation of one's own behavior involves a process in which self-standards are adopted, and subsequent behavior is self-regulated by the positive and negative consequences they produce, including through self-reward and self-devaluative reactions. Bandura notes that the rapid informational, social, and technological changes in the modern world makes it more crucial than ever to enhance one's ability to flexibly self-regulate and work for one's own self-renewal to adaptively cope as social and economic demands change throughout the life course. In Bandura's broad theorizing, the most important and central construct is self-efficacy.

Self-Efficacy

Self-efficacy refers to the individual's belief that he or she can successfully execute the behaviors required by a particular situation. Perceptions of one's own efficacy importantly guide and direct one's behavior. The close connection between high self-efficacy expectations and effective performance is illustrated in studies of people who received various treatments to help reduce specific fears. A consistently high association was found between the degree to which persons improved from treatment (becoming able to handle snakes fearlessly) and their perceived self-efficacy (Bandura, 1977). If we assess perceived self-efficacy (asking people to specifically predict their ability to do a given act successfully), according to Bandura we can predict whether or not they will be able to perform it—for example, whether they now can pick up and play with the previously feared snake (Bandura & Adams, 1977). Results of this kind suggest some clear links between self-perceptions of one's competence and the ability to actually behave competently.

14.7 Describe the role of self-efficacy in overcoming one's fears.

Perceived self-efficacy influences the goals people set for themselves and the risks that they are willing to take: the greater their perceived self-efficacy, the higher the goals they choose and the stronger their commitment and perseverance in pursuing them (Bandura, 1997, 2001). Conversely, people who view themselves as lacking efficacy for coping with life tasks are vulnerable to anxiety and may develop avoidance patterns designed to reduce their fears. People who see themselves as lacking in essential efficacy also may become prone to depression. They may even show impairments in their immune system when coping with stressors that they believe they cannot control (Wiedenfeld et al., 1990).

The Role of Self-Efficacy in Personality and Behavior Change

Although many different therapy and change techniques may produce modifications in behavior, might they all work through the same basic mechanism? Bandura (1978, 1982) has proposed that there is such a common mechanism: people's expectations of self-efficacy. Behavior therapy and other forms of interventions work, according to Bandura, by increasing efficacy expectations and thus leading people to believe that they can cope with the difficult situations that threatened them before. In this view, individuals will try to overcome a particular fear, for example, to the extent that they expect they can do so successfully. Any methods that strengthen expectancies of personal efficacy will therefore help the person perform the relevant behavior. The best methods will be the ones that give the person the most direct, compelling success experiences in performing the particular behavior, thereby increasing efficacy expectancies most. For example, actually climbing a fire escape successfully is a better way to overcome a fear of heights than just thinking about it, because it provides a more complete success experience and a stronger expectation for future mastery.

In sum, different forms of behavior therapy in Bandura's view have positive effects mainly by enhancing the individual's sense of self-efficacy. Thus, he sees each of the major behavioral strategies for inducing change as sharing one crucial ingredient: They improve perceived self-efficacy, thereby freeing the individual to perform actions that previously were not possible. People with a sense of self-efficacy about their intended actions are more able to carry them out. High efficacy expectations thus help the individual to persist in the pursuit of goals, even in the face of adversities that would derail or depress persons who are less sure of their relevant personal competencies.

SOCIAL COGNITIVE RECONCEPTUALIZATION OF PERSONALITY: WALTER MISCHEL

In the first half of the last century many personality psychologists, following Gordon Allport's (1937) lead, had deliberately disconnected themselves from the larger field of psychology. That made good sense, and enabled the birth of the field, at a time when extreme behaviorism with its focus on animal learning and conditioning was dominant in American universities. Indeed, interest in the complexities of personality and the workings of the human mind was considered taboo in most psychology departments in the United States. But by the late 1960s the cognitive revolution was transforming psychology, and the outlines appeared for a different view of personality. It was a view that Mischel thought could help resolve the crisis in personality psychology that had been created by the 1968 critique of broad personality traits (discussed in Chapter 4).

With that goal, Mischel (1973) proposed the **social cognitive reconceptualization of personality**. It appeared at the height of the crisis in personality psychology precipitated by his 1968 book, *Personality and Assessment*. As discussed in Chapters 3 and 4, the 1968 book addressed the classic assumption of trait theory that people behave in highly consistent ways across different situations (e.g., conscientious people in situation A are also likely to be conscientious in situations X, Y, and Z). The book documented that this assumption was contradicted by the objective evidence and threw the field of personality psychology into turmoil. It raised the urgent question: How can this contradiction between the intuitive conviction of substantial consistency

14.8 What major controversy resulted from Mischel's 1968 critique of broad personality traits? What were some of the ways in which personality psychologists tried to resolve it?

Walter Mischel
(*Source*: Courtesy of Walter Mischel)

in personality and the evidence on low cross-situational consistency in behavior be reconciled?

Perhaps the assumption of consistency is wrong and people's behavior is determined mainly by situational influences. Perhaps the assumption is correct and the weak evidence reflects poor research methods and constructs. Each of these answers has had its proponents. Many social psychologists used Mischel's conclusion as license to treat individual differences as noise and to emphasize the power of context. Many personality psychologists used the findings as an impetus to search for methods and data analyses that could remove the effects of situations on the expression of personality, reflecting a view of situations as a source of noise.

Understanding Consistency in Personality: People as Meaning Makers

Mischel (1973) provided an alternative answer. He proposed that traditional personality psychology was looking for consistency in the wrong places. They were looking for consistency by stripping the effects of situations from people's behavior (by averaging the person's behavior regardless of the situation). Instead, he theorized that consistency could be found by analyzing behavior in its situational context. He predicted that such an analysis would reveal that people have consistent *if* ... *then* ... situation–behavior patterns, that they have contextualized personality signatures.

He arrived at this view by observing that cross-situational consistency does not make sense if one asks: How does the human mind work? What are people trying to do in particular situations? Proposing a view of the mind as dynamic and constructivist, he argued that people make meaning out of the situations they encounter and use this to adapt their behavior to each situation. Because such adaptability is vital to survival, humans could not possibly have evolved to behave consistently across situations that vary in the challenges they pose and the solutions they require from each individual. If, for example, a child that has been rewarded regularly in preschool for behaviors like "touching, holding, and being near" (a measure of dependency) with his teacher, but never with his father at home, and in fact expects his father to reprimand him for such behavior, it does not make sense to think there will be a high correlation in the child's "dependent" behavior across those two situations.

But where, then, does consistency come in? Mischel proposed that people behave in ways that are consistent with the meaning that situations have for them, meanings that reflect their individual biology and their history, including their social learning experiences. Thus, individual differences in personality emerge in the distinctive ways that people process and understand particular situations. This view locates the essential building blocks of personality in the cognitive and affective processes people use to mentally represent situations and to shape their efforts to behave adaptively and discriminatively in light of those psychological representations.

Social Cognitive Person Variables

14.9 Describe the five basic "person variables" in the social cognitive conception of personality.

To capture individual differences in these psychological representations, Mischel (1973) identified a basic set of psychological **social cognitive person variables**. Summarized in Table 14.1, these variables characterize the differences between people in how they interpret social stimuli and situations as they interact with them.

As the table shows, the person variables include the encodings or construal of the particular situations the person experiences, and the expectancies and beliefs, affects (feeling states and emotions), subjective values and goals, as well as competencies and self-regulatory strategies that then become activated. Each of these variables provides distinctive information about the individual, and collectively they interact to influence the behaviors that are generated in the particular situation. The analysis focused on how these person–situation transactions predictably generate the kind of contextualized *if ... then ...* patterns of variability in behavior that make up the second type of consistency in behavior described in Chapter 4 on the expressions of personality dispositions. As discussed in that chapter, you can see the consistency of personality

TABLE 14.1 Types of Person Variables

- *Encodings (Construals, Appraisals):* Categories (constructs) for the self, people, events, and the situations (external and internal).
- *Expectancies and Beliefs:* About the social world, about outcomes for behavior in particular situations, about self-efficacy, about the self.
- *Affects:* Feelings, emotions, and affective responses (including physiological reactions).
- *Goals and Values:* Desirable outcomes and affective states; aversive outcomes and affective states; goals, values, and life projects.
- *Competencies and Self-Regulatory Plans:* Potential behaviors and scripts that one can do, and plans and strategies for organizing action and for affecting outcomes and one's own behavior and internal states.

Source: Mischel, W., & Shoda, Y. (1995). A cognitive-affective system theory of personality: Reconceptualizing situations, dispositions, dynamics, and invariance in personality structure. *Psychological Review, 102*, 253.

not only in the individual's overall average behavioral tendencies but also in these more context-dependent *behavioral signatures of personality*. If Gary W. thinks he can attain acceptance from someone he values, he is overly nice to her, ingratiating himself, suppressing his own needs and desires to go along with the other person's preferences. But if Gary sees himself as being rejected, *then* he thinks about abandonment, feels panic, and erupts with anger, aggression, and insults against his partner. The pattern is self-defeating because his hostility in response to his own rejection fears is likely to lead to actual rejection even when there was none before, making his worst fears come true (Downey et al., 1998). The 1973 paper showed that such patterns, rather than threatening the construct of personality, attest to the complexity and adaptive discriminative flexibility and depth of human personality, and are essential for effective human functioning.

Encodings (Construals): How Do You See It?

We next consider each of the social cognitive person variables. Keep in mind that these variables become activated in relationship to the particular situations or psychological events that the person experiences from the situations encountered and created, or generates internally in thought and imagination. While each variable is described separately, they function together in interconnected patterns as the person interacts with the social world. As Bandura (1986) also emphasized, these person–situation interactions are not just passive or reflexive reactions to situations. They also are agentic and proactive: they influence and change, indeed in some ways they create, the situations the person subsequently experiences and ultimately his or her life space.

As George Kelly, Mischel's mentor in graduate school at Ohio State, had emphasized, people differ greatly in how they **encode** (represent, construe, appraise, interpret) themselves, other people and events, and their experiences. The same hot weather that upsets one person may be a joy for another who views it as a chance to go to the beach. The same stranger in the elevator who is perceived as dangerous by one person may be seen as interesting by another. Individuals differ stably in how they encode and categorize people and events, and these interpretations influence their subsequent reactions to them.

14.10 What is meant by encoding? How does encoding affect other thoughts, feelings, and behaviors?

Suppose Jack, a teenager, tends to encode (construe, perceive) peers in terms of their hostile threats, and is highly sensitive to their possible attempts to challenge, manipulate, and control him. If he cognitively represents his world in such terms, Jack

Different individuals may encode the same situation in different ways.

(*Source*: Sean Arbabi/Stone/Getty Images)

will be vigilant to threats and primed to defend himself. He therefore may see an innocent accident, such as having someone push against him in a crowded staircase, as a deliberate affront or violation (Cantor & Mischel, 1979; Dodge, 1986).

Different persons group and encode the same events and behaviors in different ways (Argyle & Little, 1972) and they selectively attend to and seek out different kinds of information (Bower, 1981; Miller, 1987). For example, some individuals tend to encode ambiguous negative events as instances of personal rejection (e.g., Downey & Feldman, 1996) and keep looking for clues that they are being rejected, which then makes them depressed and withdrawn. Other people, however, may easily feel disrespected and become angry and hostile even when they hear a mumbled greeting (e.g., Dodge, 1993).

How people encode and appraise events and selectively attend to what they observe also greatly influences what they learn. For example, people who have poor social skills tend to encode situations in terms of the degree to which they might feel self-conscious versus self-confident in them. In contrast, more socially skilled individuals encode the same situations in terms of other dimensions such as how interesting or pleasant they might be (Forgas, 1983).

Expectancies and Beliefs: What Will Happen?

14.11 Differentiate between self-efficacy and behavior–outcome expectancies. How do they affect goals, behavior, and behavior change?

This analysis of personality does not stop with a description of what people know and how they interpret events. It also seeks to predict and understand actual performance in specific situations. Research on learning made it clear that the actions people perform depend on the consequences they expect (Bandura, 1986; Rotter, 1954). To predict a specific behavior in a particular situation, one has to consider the individual's specific expectancies about the consequences of different behavioral possibilities in that situation (Mischel, 1973).

A particularly important type of expectancy consists of **self-efficacy expectations**: the person's belief that he or she *can* perform a particular behavior, like handling a snake or taking an exam, as discussed earlier in this chapter. Measures of these expectations predict with considerable accuracy the person's actual ability to perform the relevant acts. Efficacy expectancies guide the person's selection of behaviors from among the many that he or she is capable of constructing within any situation (Bandura, 1986).

Another type of expectancy concerns **behavior–outcome relations**. These behavior–outcome expectancies (hypotheses, contingency rules) represent the expected

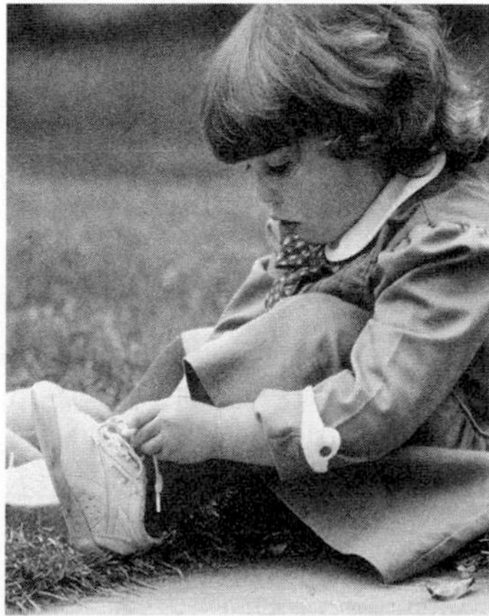

The development of self-efficacy takes many forms.

(*Source*: SUPERSTOCK)

if . . . then . . . relations between behavioral alternatives and expected probable outcomes in particular situations. In any given situation, we generate the response pattern that we expect is most likely to lead to the most subjectively valuable outcomes in that situation (Bandura, 1986; Mischel, 1973; Rotter, 1954). In the absence of new information about the behavior–outcome expectancies in any situation, behavior will depend on one's previous behavior–outcome expectancies in similar situations (Mischel & Staub, 1965). That is, if you do not know exactly what to expect in a new situation (a first job interview, for example), you are guided by your previous expectancies based on experiences in similar past situations.

For example, we generate behavior in light of our expectancies even when they are not in line with the objective conditions in the situation. If you expect to be attacked, you become vigilant even if your fears later turn out to have been unjustified. If you expect to succeed, you behave quite differently than if you are convinced you will fail. Indeed, we sometimes behave in ways that directly help to confirm our expectations, thus enacting self-fulfilling prophecies (Buss, 1987). The person who is easily suspicious, angry, and ready to aggress is likely to extract reciprocal hostility and defensiveness from others that will, in turn, confirm his beliefs about them.

Affects: Feelings and "Hot" Reactions

What we feel—our affects and emotions—profoundly influences other aspects of behavior (e.g., Contrada, Cather, & O'Leary, 1999; Smith & Lazarus, 1990; Zajonc, 1980). They also impact on the person's efforts at self-regulation and the pursuit goals (e.g., Mischel et al., 1996). It has long been known that such cognitions as beliefs about the self and one's personal future are themselves **hot cognitions**, that is, thoughts that also activate strong emotion (Ayduk & Mischel 2002; Metcalfe & Mischel, 1999; Ochsner & Gross, 2004, 2005). As Smith and Lazarus (1990) noted, anything that implies important consequences, harmful or beneficial, for the individual can trigger an emotional reaction. For example, when one is feeling bad or sad—what is called a negative affective state—and gets negative feedback about performance (e.g., a disappointing test score), it is easy to become demoralized and to overinterpret the feedback, resulting in depression (Wright & Mischel, 1982).

14.12 Why are "hot cognitions" so named?

Affective reactions to situation features (such as faces) may occur immediately and automatically (e.g., Murphy & Zajonc, 1993; Niedenthal, 1990), outside of awareness (Gollwitzer & Bargh, 1996). These emotional reactions in turn can trigger closely associated cognitions and behaviors (Chaiken & Bargh, 1993). The affective states and moods experienced are easily influenced by situational factors, even by such simple events as finding a coin on the street (e.g., Isen, Niedenthal, & Cantor, 1992; Schwarz, 1990). But what we feel also reflects stable individual differences, which may be related to temperament and biological variables (Rothbart et al., 1994).

Goals and Values: What Do You Want? What Is It Worth?

Goals and values drive and guide the long-term projects people pursue, the situations and outcomes they seek, and their reactions to them (e.g., Linville & Carlston, 1994; Martin & Tesser, 1989). They serve to organize and motivate the person's efforts, providing the direction and structure for the life tasks and projects they pursue (Grant & Dweck, 1999). Motives, such as achievement, power, intimacy, and others studied by the Harvard personologists, are also represented in the personality system by the person variable of goals.

14.13 Describe the organizational functions of goals and values. What is intrinsic motivation?

Goals influence what is valued, and values also influence performance. For example, even if two individuals have similar expectancies, they may act differently if the outcomes they expect have different personal values for them (Rotter, 1954, 1972) or if they are pursuing different goals (e.g., Cantor, 1994). If everyone in a group expects that approval from a teacher depends on saying certain things the teacher wants to hear, there may be differences in how often they are said due to differences in the perceived value of obtaining the teacher's approval. Praise from the teacher may be important for a student striving for grades, but not for a rebellious adolescent who rejects school. What delights one person may repel his or her neighbor. That makes it necessary to consider the individual's goals and the subjective value of particular classes of events, that is, his or her preferences and aversions. These goals and values are particularly important because much human behavior is driven by **intrinsic motivation**: the gratification the individual receives from the activity or task itself (Cantor, 1990; Deci & Ryan, 1987). Such motivation is reflected in the life goals that the person pursues, as will be discussed in detail in Chapter 17.

What Can You Do?: Overcoming Stimulus Control through Self-Regulation

People regulate their own behavior by self-imposed goals and self-produced consequences. Even in the absence of external constraints and social monitors, we set performance goals for ourselves. We react with self-criticism or self-satisfaction to our behavior depending on how well it matches our expectations and standards (Bandura, 1986; Higgins, 1990). The expert sprinter who falls below his past record may condemn himself bitterly; the same performance by a less experienced runner who has lower standards may produce self-congratulation and joy. To predict Mark's reaction to being pushed, for example, it helps to know the personal standards he uses to evaluate when and how to react aggressively. Will he react aggressively even if the peer who pushed him is much younger? Likewise, can he regulate his own response strategically, or will he react explosively and automatically?

14.14 How do self-regulation processes counteract external stimulus control of behavior?

People also differ in the types of plans that guide their behavior in the absence of, and sometimes in spite of, immediate external situational pressures. Such plans specify the kinds of behavior appropriate under particular conditions, the performance levels (standards, goals) that the behavior must achieve, and the consequences of attaining or failing to reach those standards (Mischel et al., 1996). Plans also specify the sequence and organization of behavior patterns (Gollwitzer & Moskowitz, 1996; Schank & Abelson, 1977). Individuals may differ with respect to each of the components of self-regulation (e.g., Baumeister & Heatherton, 1996).

Self-regulation provides a route through which we can influence our interpersonal and social environment substantially. We can actively *select* many of the situations to which we expose ourselves, in a sense creating our own environment, choosing to enter some settings but not others (Buss, 1987; Ross & Nisbett, 1991). Such active choice, rather than automatic responding, may be facilitated by thinking and planning and by rearranging the environment itself to make it more favorable for one's goals (e.g., Gollwitzer & Moskowitz, 1996). Even when the environment cannot be changed physically (by rearranging it or by leaving it altogether and entering another setting), it may be possible to *transform* it psychologically, as discussed in Chapter 17.

Self-observation plays an important role in the acquisition of skills and competencies. (*Source*: SUPERSTOCK)

Contributors to Person Variables: A Quick Look at a Long History

To see how the social cognitive person variables were developed, and based in part on earlier contributions, let's take a quick look at their long history. They were based on two quite different theoretical perspectives that at first may seem incompatible. One was the personal construct theory of George Kelly (discussed in Chapter 12) and the other was the social learning theory developed by Julian B. Rotter (1954). Both Rotter and Kelly were professors in the graduate training program in clinical psychology at Ohio State University in the early 1950s, and both were important mentors for Walter Mischel. In the early 1950s, Mischel did his doctoral dissertation with Rotter, but most of his clinical psychology training was with Kelly. For a personal view of Mischel's experience working with these two important mentors in graduate school, see *In Focus 14.2*.

Although Professor Kelly's and Professor Rotter's offices were across the hall from each other, the two men were as different as their theories. They had little direct contact, and little influence on each other, although they both greatly influenced any students who were at Ohio State in those years. Their ideas were expressed in two extremely important books, Rotter's *Social Learning and Clinical Psychology*, published in 1954, and Kelly's two-volume *The Psychology of Personal Constructs* (1955). Together, these two pioneers contributed much to modern personality and clinical psychology.

The person variable of "encoding strategies" explicitly reflected George Kelly's core point—the importance of how individuals construe their experience and themselves. This construal or appraisal characterizes the first phase of how people make sense of incoming social information and interpret its personal meaning. The conceptualization of

IN FOCUS 14.2

MISCHEL'S VIEW OF HIS MENTORS, JULIAN ROTTER AND GEORGE KELLY

The following is quoted from Walter Mischel's (2007) account of his graduate school years at Ohio State University, studying with both Julian Rotter and George Kelly in the Ohio State PhD program in clinical psychology from 1953 to 1956. In it, Mischel shows clearly how his work is rooted in that of his mentors. Mischel's work in psychology has been consistently devoted to building on his mentors' contributions in the new directions he considered essential:

> "The intellectual tension between the social learning theory just formulated by Julian B. Rotter and the personal construct theory newly developed by George A. Kelly, each full of fresh ideas, created an atmosphere of ferment and promise for clinical psychology and personality theory. Here the excitement was about finding evidence for what worked best and understanding the reasons for it, and building new conceptions for making sense of complex human behavior. Questioning the received wisdom of the field was welcomed, and ideas were wide open to revision and subject to empirical testing in the laboratory and in the clinic. Rotter's weekly evenings with his students modeled how vague notions can turn into incisive ideas that become experiments and showed me for the first time how exciting and generative a lab in psychology can be. . . .
>
> "Most students loyally aligned themselves unequivocally either with Kelly or with Rotter, the two major professors who had offices as far apart as possible and seemed to have little contact and zero cross-references either verbally or in their writings. I was impressed by both their ideas, and drawn strongly to both. Social learning theory seemed an appealing, refreshingly reasonable, data-based approach for designing research and suggested many potentially effective treatment and assessment strategies. Rotter's emphasis on expectancies and values in the analysis of action and prediction of individual differences was a major advance for bridging the gap between experimental and clinical psychology, and made it easy for his students to generate interesting experiments.
>
> "At the same time, personal construct theory, especially as illustrated in the masterful clinical approach that George Kelly modeled both with his clients and with his students, seemed an extraordinarily rich and original framework. Kelly's conviction (and he convinced many of us) that the "subjects" of psychology are no less capable of being scientists than the psychologists who study them, informed and guided everything in his approach. It made it possible, amazingly at a time when behaviorism was still predominant in psychology, to construe interpersonal problems and human characteristics in ways that respect the individual. It let us see the person as a thinking being rather than, as Kelly put it, 'a victim of his biography' or a point sitting fixed, stuck on the psychologist's trait continuum. When my life or work ran into a wall I often reminded myself of his definition of hostility, which he illustrated with the parable of the Procrustean bed. Hostility is when you keep forcing the data, whether about someone else or yourself, including your research results, to make them fit into your hypothesis or construct, even when they simply won't, rather than questioning the construct itself and maybe coming up with a better, more convenient one."

Source: History of Psychology Through Autobiography (pp. 236–237) *Vol.* 9, 2007.

personality in cognitive social terms, however, sought a personality theory that includes not only how people perceive and interpret but also what they actually choose and do (Mischel, 1973). For that purpose, it explicitly drew on expectancy-value concepts that had been given a central place by Rotter (1954). In Rotter's early social learning theory, the probability that a particular pattern of behavior will occur was a joint function of the individual's outcome expectancies and the subjective value of those outcomes.

Julian B. Rotter
(*Source*: Courtesy Julian B. Rotter)

In the late 1940s and early 1950s, Rotter introduced the expectancy construct to personality psychology and made it a centerpiece of his version of social learning. He had argued convincingly for the importance of both expectancies and values as basic building blocks for a theory of social learning that he wanted to speak more directly to the assessment and treatment of clinical problems. While his theory was extremely elegant, it was, like his colleague George Kelly's theory of personal constructs, apparently ahead of its time: the impact of both these theorists seems to be felt more decades later in indirect forms than when Rotter and Kelly first advanced their ideas.

14.15 Which of the five person variables were especially influenced by the theories of Rotter and Kelly?

▶ PERSONALITY ASSESSMENT

The social cognitive theories and research at this level of analysis substantially influenced both personality assessment and therapies aimed at personality change.

First, consistent with social cognitive theories, assessments at this level tend to be specific, focused on specific cognitions, feelings, and behavior in relation to particular types of situations, rather than on descriptions with situation-free, broad trait terms. Recall, for example, that self-efficacy refers to individuals' beliefs that they can do what is required in a particular type of situation or task (such as asking for a pay raise, or on a specific achievement task, or in approaching a dangerous object), not their overall efficacy expectations in general. This focus reflects the view that the expressions of the personality system and the person's goals and motivations are seen in *if . . . then . . .* personality signatures, not just in the overall levels of different types of behavior.

14.16 Describe three characteristics of social cognitive personality assessment. What kinds of measures are typically employed, and how do they differ from trait measures?

Second, assessments whenever possible also try to identify the implications for constructive personality change or treatment. They thus are aimed at identifying the psychological person variables that might be modified, for example by enhancing efficacy expectancies through exposure to relevant efficacy-building experiences. Such assessments, always closely linked to change or treatment programs, are being done effectively in areas that range from weight control in anorexic patients to recovery of sexual functioning after massive coronary problems, to overcoming debilitating fears.

Personality assessors in this approach also seek to identify the underlying person variables and processes that seem to account for the individual's stable behavior patterns. They tend to conceptualize these underlying variables in relatively specific (rather than global) terms.

Researchers and assessors therefore obtain self-reports, ratings, and other data to infer the particular person variable as directly and specifically as possible within these contexts. Some also try to sample and observe behavior as it occurs naturally. For example, they ask people to provide daily diary reports of what they actually did and experienced within specific situations (e.g., Ayduk, May, Downey, & Higgins, 2003; Bolger & Schilling, 1991; Cantor et al., 1991). There have been many applications, and we illustrate these with the example of the measurement of self-efficacy expectations.

Measuring Self-Efficacy Expectancies

Given the importance of the self-efficacy construct in social cognitive theories it is also a person variable that is used extensively in personality assessment at this level of analysis (Bandura, 1978, 1986; Cervone, Shadel, & Jencius, 2001; Merluzzi, Glass, & Genest, 1981). Self-efficacy is assessed by asking the person to indicate the degree of confidence that he or she can do a particular task. For example, Bandura and colleagues (1985) wanted to assess the recovery of patients who had suffered heart attacks. Many tasks were described to the patients. These included such potentially stressful things as driving a few blocks in the neighborhood, driving on a freeway, and driving on a narrow mountain road. They also included situations that would induce other kinds of emotional strain, as illustrated in Table 14.2. For each item the respondent indicates the confidence level for being able to do the task.

14.17 How is self-efficacy measured? How well do these measures predict behavior?

Self-efficacy measures are particularly useful because they tend to predict the relevant behaviors at high levels of accuracy. For example, a consistently strong association was found between rated self-efficacy and the degree to which people showed increased approach behavior toward previously feared objects after they had received treatment for their fears (Bandura, Adams, & Beyer, 1977). Note that a distinguishing feature of self-efficacy measurement is that it is always about a specific domain, such as the ability to approach a type of feared object, or to control your weight, or efficacy about college coursework in your major. This specificity contrasts with global measures, for example when you are asked to rate your "overall level of self-esteem." The focus on the context, situation, or contingency (e.g., *if ... then ...*) is of course a key characteristic of assessment at this level in which person qualities are directly linked to contexts and situations. It is also well illustrated in the work discussed next.

Individual Differences in *If ... Then ...* Signatures

Advances also are being made in assessments of individual differences that take close account of the situation. Iven Van Mechelen and his colleagues (Van Mechelen &

TABLE 14.2 Measuring Self-Efficacy Expectancies

Listed below are situations that can arouse anxiety, annoyance, and anger. Imagine the feelings you might have in each situation, such as your heart beats faster and your muscles tense. Indicate whether you could tolerate the emotional strain caused by each of the situations.

Under the column marked *Can Do*, check (√) the tasks or activities you expect you could do *now*. For the tasks you check under *Can Do*, indicate in the column marked *Confidence* how confident you are that you could do the tasks. Rate your degree of confidence using a number from 10 to 100 on the scale below.

10 20 30 40 50 60 70 80 90 100
Quite Uncertain   Moderately Certain   Certain

	Can do	Confidence
Attend a social gathering at which there is no one you know.	______	______
At a social gathering, approach a group of strangers, introduce yourself, and join in the conversation.	______	______
At a social gathering, discuss a controversial topic (politics, religion, philosophy of life, etc.) with people whose views differ greatly from yours.	______	______
Be served by a salesperson, receptionist, or waiter whose behavior you find irritating.	______	______
Complain about poor service to an unsympathetic sales or repair person.	______	______
When complaining about bad service, insist on seeing the manager if you are not satisfied.	______	______
In a public place, ask a stranger to stop doing something that annoys you, such as cutting in line, talking in a movie, or smoking in a non-smoking area.	______	______
Ask neighbors to correct a problem for which they are responsible, such as making noise at night, not controlling children or pets.	______	______
At work, reprimand an uncooperative subordinate.	______	______

Source: Examples reprinted from *American Journal of Cardiology, Vol. 55*, Bandura, A., Taylor, C. B., Ewart, C. K., Miller, N. M., & Debusk, R. F., "Exercise testing to enhance wives' confidence in their husbands' cardiac capability soon after clinically uncomplicated acute myocardial infarction," 635–638 (1985), with permission from Excerpta Medica Inc.

Kiers, 1999; Vansteelandt & Van Mechelen, 1998) are using the concept of *if . . . then . . .* signatures to classify people into different types based on the kind of responses they give in specific types of situations, such as those that are especially frustrating, as discussed in Chapter 4. The results are encouraging for building a classification system for types of people that is both theory-guided and specific enough to predict behavior in different contexts. Recall that the ultimate goal of such typologies is to predict the probability of certain types of individuals exhibiting certain types of behavior when faced with certain types of situations. The hope would be that this could allow a level of precision not possible with typologies based on characterizations in broad trait terms like "disagreeable" or "unsociable." In their recent work, these researchers took the additional step of linking their typology to measures of social cognitive person variables. Using a questionnaire that asked about the participant's encodings, expectancies, and whether they kept their anger in or let it out, they demonstrated meaningful links between such person variables and types of *if . . . then . . .* behavior signatures.

The Implicit Association Test (IAT)

Behavioral measures have the advantage of being objective, in that most people would agree that a child hit another child when they see the behavior in front of them. But what about assessing thoughts and feelings, especially those that are not within the person's awareness? We could, of course, ask people to tell us what's on their mind. But then we will learn what they *think* are their thoughts or feelings. What if these are not their *true* thoughts and feelings? And what exactly would one mean by "true" thoughts and feelings? These are the issues that are central for researchers at the Psychodynamic-Motivational Level of analysis, and they also are important for the Social Cognitive Level of analysis, which assumes that many of the person's thoughts and feelings may not be accessible to awareness. In recent years there have been important advances in assessing such aspects of personality outside awareness. Consider the following scenario:

14.18 What kinds of cognitive processes are implicit measures designed to assess?

> *A boy goes fishing with his father, but slips on a slippery rock and suffers a serious head injury. When the ambulance takes him to the ER, the doctor there turns pale, and exclaims, "Oh, my god, it's my son!"*

What's going on here? Is there something strange about this scenario? How do you explain this? Wasn't the boy's father with the boy when the accident occurred? In fact, nothing may be unusual with the scenario, and the most likely, and mundane, interpretation is that the doctor at the ER is the boy's mother. If you didn't think of that possibility right away, that may be because in your mind you may have associated doctors in emergency rooms more strongly with men than women, reflecting gender stereotypes in our society.

Such an association is *implicit* when people have no awareness of making it and being influenced by it as they process social information such as this scenario. It may be like a mental habit, not necessarily a motivated bias, which is applied automatically, without much awareness. Several ways to assess implicit associations have been developed (Greenwald et al., 2002). Here we describe one, called the **Implicit Association Test (IAT)**, for the assessment of **implicit self-esteem**, developed by Greenwald and Farnham (2000).

The IAT requires participants to make a series of judgments about each of the words presented to them briefly, one at a time, in quick succession.

Specifically, the words presented come from four distinct categories, and the participants' task is to indicate the category of the word presented, as quickly as possible, by pressing an appropriate computer key. One category of words refers to *self* such as "I," "me," and "mine." As soon as these words appear, participants press a particular computer key (e.g., the "A" key located on the left side of the keyboard). Another category represents "*not self*," and so when they see words such as "they," "theirs," and "it," they press a different computer key (e.g., the "5" key in the numerical keypad located on the right side of the keyboard). The remaining two categories refer to obviously good and obviously bad concepts. So when they see words such as *health, joy*, and *kindness*, they press one computer key, and when they see words such as *ugly, failure*, and *awful*, they press another.

If participants were given four separate keys to indicate each of the four categories, the task would be relatively simple. But the crucial innovation in the design of the IAT is that there are only two keys available to press on the keyboard. Therefore two concepts must "share" a key. This is done in one of two ways. In the "self = bad" condition, participants press the same key (e.g., "A") to indicate that the word they see refers to either "self" or "bad," and they press another key (e.g., "5") when the word refers either to "not self" or "good." Most participants find this combination of keys very difficult to master, and their responses are slow, in order to prevent making mistakes. In contrast, in the "self = good" condition, in which the concepts are combined in a different way, they find it much easier to do this task. Namely, when they use the same key to indicate they saw a word that referred to either "self" or "good," and the other key to indicate they saw a word that referred to either "not self" or "bad," they are much faster in completing the task.

The difference in the impact of these two ways of combining the concepts on the difficulty of the task, reflected in the time needed to complete it, is taken to indicate the strength of association between "self" and "good" (and "not self" and "bad"). This is a measure of self-esteem, because a central element of the concept of self-esteem is how positively or negatively one regards oneself. And it is an implicit measure because the associations being measured do not rely on people's own awareness and report of how strongly they associate self with good, but rather based on an automatic response that has been shown to be difficult to control consciously. In fact, the implicit and explicit measures of self-esteem were largely unrelated to each other. In the Greenwald and Farnham (2000) study, those who had a high implicit self-esteem as measured by IAT were no more likely than those who had low implicit self-esteem to describe themselves as "good" when they were asked to rate themselves on a "good"–"bad" continuum.

Because the self-report measures used in this study were well established in the field, one may be tempted to conclude that the implicit measure was not really needed. However, the measure of implicit self-esteem also was able to predict a phenomenon that has been well established as related to self-esteem (Brown & Dutton, 1995; Dodgson & Wood, 1998; Greenberg, Solomon, Pyszczynski, & Rosenblatt, 1992). Namely, people who were high in self-esteem, as determined by the implicit measure, were relatively unaffected by experience of failure, while those who were low in self-esteem by the implicit measure took the failure to heart (Greenwald & Farnham, 2000, Study 3).

Since its introduction in 1998, the IAT has become widely used to measure not only implicit self-esteem, but also implicit attitudes, beliefs, and values in a number of domains. One very interesting finding is that IAT measures of anti-Black prejudice predicted the White participants' behaviors toward Black people on indicators such as body openness, eye contact, and friendly laughter (McConnell & Leibold, 2001).

Incorporating the Psychological Situation into Personality Assessment

14.19 What is meant by the psychological situation? How does it relate to the *if...then...* situation–behavior signature at the Social Cognitive Level?

The discovery of the second type of behavioral consistency, the *if . . . then . . .* situation–behavior signatures, discussed in Chapter 4, has important implications for personality assessment. It makes it clear that assessments to predict what people will do and experience in different kinds of situations have to specify the "if"—the situations, and not just the behaviors—in order to see when the individual is and is not likely to exhibit characteristic behavior patterns. Further, the findings from work at the Phenomenological-Humanistic Level and the Social Cognitive Level showed that the effects of situations depend on how individuals subjectively perceive and construe or encode them. Therefore assessments need to incorporate the psychological situation as it is interpreted by the person. That is not an easy task, and it poses a major challenge for personality assessment efforts that seek greater predictive power. *In Focus 14.3*

IN FOCUS 14.3

IDENTIFYING PSYCHOLOGICAL SITUATIONS

A first challenge for researchers studying the consistency of behavior across different psychological situations was to identify the relevant situations. In the past, studies of behavior across situations usually focused on behavior settings or environments as the situations observed. Examples of such **nominal situations** within a school are the chemistry lab, the library, the playground, or the meeting with the instructor. In a summer camp, the nominal situations might be settings like the dining room, arts and crafts, cabin time, or at the waterfront (e.g., Newcomb, 1929). But the contributions from the Phenomenological and Social Cognitive Levels showed that the impact of such nominal situations depends on their meaning for the person, and people differ in the meaning that any given situation may have for them (Mischel, 1973; Shoda et al., 1994). It is the situation as encoded and construed by the individual—the **psychological situation**—that activate his or her distinctive reaction. The question then becomes: how can one identify psychological situations?

In the summer camp study of consistency in social behavior described in Chapter 4, researchers found that when people talked about the personality of individuals they knew well, they used **conditional hedges** to qualify their characterizations (Wright & Mischel, 1988). Statements like "Joe is always aggressive" often were contextualized after a few utterances with conditional hedges, such as "when kids tease him about his glasses." These findings gave clues about the kinds of psychological situations important in the setting studied. For example, psychological situations in the camp were identified as those in which individuals were "teased and provoked by peers," or "praised by adults" or "approached positively by peers." Because psychological situations occur across many physical settings (e.g., in the camp cabin, at arts and crafts, in the dining room), findings about a person's stable behavior within each type allow much broader generalizations. The psychological situations identified in the camp in turn became the ones in which behavior was systematically observed. The results (as discussed in Chapter 4), showed that individuals are characterized by stable *if* ... *then* ... patterns that form situation–behavior signatures of personality (Shoda et al., 1993b, 1994). When the psychological situations—the *"ifs"* for the person's distinctive behavior (e.g., having aggressive outbursts)—are identified, it becomes possible to predict when that behavior will and will not occur with greater precisions and insight into the underlying reasons (e.g., Shoda et al., 1994; Wright & Mischel, 1987).

gives an example of how researchers have tried to identify such psychological situations, drawing on the work in the camp studies in which the stable behavioral signatures were demonstrated originally.

PERSONALITY CHANGE AND THERAPY

The social cognitive approach to personality has influenced contemporary approaches to constructive educational and therapeutic change in many domains. They range from the treatment of all sorts of fears to the conduct of psychotherapy and the development of mass public education programs to improve health-enhancing behaviors, such as reduction of tobacco and other drug use, dieting, and reduction of high-risk sexual practices. These programs often use exposure to models who display the desired behaviors as part of their efforts to effect change, often combined with diverse other strategies (e.g., Bandura, 1986; Cervone et al., 2001).

14.20 What are the objectives of social cognitive approaches to therapeutic behavior change?

Overview of Approach

Therapists within this approach try to help clients to identify their disadvantageous ways of thinking about themselves, other people, and their problems. In the safety of the therapy situation, therapist and client interact to experiment with and explore alternative, more adaptive ways of thinking and reacting (emotionally and behaviorally) in situations that are problematic for the client (e.g., behaving in appropriately assertive but not aggressive ways when experiencing conflicts with authorities). A fundamental aim is to increase the client's perceived and real freedom to change in desired directions.

One route is to provide experiences that enhance efficacy expectations. Change becomes easier when clients begin to expect that they can cope more effectively and that they can face previously terrifying situations more calmly. Therapy includes a wide range of actual and imagined (symbolic) experiences designed to develop more effective strategies and plans for setting, and achieving, desired goals, for functioning more comfortably and effectively interpersonally, and for reducing anxiety, depression, and perceived stress.

Modeling has been used, for example, to help people overcome shyness and assert themselves more effectively when they feel they should. Assertiveness skills may be sought by anyone who wishes to be more effective with other people, whether roommates, a boss, spouse, or parent. People who are unable to be assertive, who cannot stand up for their rights, may not only be exploited and deprived by others but may feel ineffective and incompetent and lack self-esteem. Thus, **assertiveness training** may have many positive effects on one's life. The procedure may include observation of models who assert themselves effectively. This step may be followed by role playing with the therapist and by rehearsing more assertive responses, first in safe situations and ultimately in real life when the assertive responses are needed.

14.21 How are modeling and role playing used in social skills training?

Improvement in assertive behavior may be achieved by observation of models who display assertiveness. In **covert modeling**, this is done in imagination, as unassertive individuals visualize scenes in which a model performs assertively when it is appropriate. Here is a typical scene:

> *The person (model) is dining with friends in a restaurant. He (she) orders a steak, instructing the waiter that it be rare. The steak arrives and as the person cuts into it, it is apparent that something is wrong. He (she) signals the waiter, who comes to the table. The person says, "This steak is medium; I ordered it rare. Please take this back and bring me a rare one" (adapted from Kazdin, 1974, p. 242).*

Behavior Therapies Become Cognitive

Because so many behavioral approaches in clinical psychology and therapy have become cognitive, their more accurate new name within the profession is **cognitive behavior therapy** or **CBT**. Indeed they may more accurately be called "social cognitive behavioral therapy" except for the fact that it's much too cumbersome a label. Donald Meichenbaum (1995, p. 141), a CBT leader, describes how cognitive-behavioral therapists challenged the earlier behaviorists this way:

> They [cognitive-behavioral therapists] questioned the tenets of classical learning theories and psychoanalytic formulations, and caused the field to question how best to conceptualize the clients' thoughts and feelings. Moreover, they raised questions of how the clients' thoughts influence and, in turn, are influenced by their feelings, behaviors, resultant consequences, and physiological processes. They emphasized that individuals not only respond to their environments but are also the architects of those environments.

Donald Meichenbaum

(*Source*: University of Waterloo, Graphics Photo/Imaging)

Within the last four decades, the cognitive-behavioral model has evolved into a prominent force in psychology (Dobson & Craig, 1996). CBT is currently used to treat conditions such as depression, anxiety, phobias, obsessional disorders, aggression, and hypochondriasis (Dunford, 2000; Kendall & Panichelli-Mindel, 1995; Rachman, 1996). Its growth reflects many changes and reasons, as summarized in Table 14.3. It also gives increasing attention to the client's personal feelings, to experiences as seen by the client, and to developing as well a balanced, internally harmonious life. In that sense it shows similarity to many of the therapeutic values and practices first emphasized in the phenomenological–humanistic approaches, for example in the work of Carl Rogers and Abraham Maslow.

Conceptually and historically, CBT is rooted deeply within behavioral approaches. But its growth also was influenced by other contributions, and it now integrates work from the behavioral and social cognitive levels with insights and methods from most of the other levels of analysis. At a theoretical level it has considerable

TABLE 14.3 Some Reasons for the Growth of Cognitive Behavior Therapy

Recognition of problems that go beyond specific behaviors (e.g., career conflict, depression)
Helps people interpret and construe experiences constructively
Addresses affect (feelings and emotions) as well as action
Deals with interactions between thoughts, feelings, and action
Uses and combines diverse methods and concepts that prove useful

similarity to George Kelly's work on personal constructs, particularly for the treatment of depression.

Beck's Cognitive Therapy

The social-cognitive trend in therapeutic practice is reflected in their labels; for example, Aaron T. Beck's **cognitive restructuring**. Working as a psychiatrist in Philadelphia, Beck developed one of the most influential and well-articulated versions of cognitive therapy. His approach is directed at changing how people encode or construe their experiences and themselves, and he has applied it systematically to the treatment of depression (Young, Weinberger, & Beck, 2001). He defines cognitive therapy this way:

14.22 What are the goals and procedures in Beck's cognitive therapy?

> Cognitive therapy is an active, directive, time-limited, structured approach used to treat a variety of psychiatric disorders (for example, depression, anxiety, phobias, pain problems, etc.). It is based on an underlying theoretical rationale that an individual's affect and behavior are largely determined by the way in which he structures the world. His cognitions (verbal or pictorial "events" in his stream of consciousness) are based on attitudes or assumptions (schemas), developed from previous experiences. For example, if a person interprets all his experiences in terms of whether he is competent and adequate, his thinking may be dominated by the schema, "Unless I do everything perfectly, I'm a failure." Consequently, he reacts to situations in terms of adequacy even when they are unrelated to whether or not he is personally competent. (Beck, Rush, Shaw, & Emery, 1979, p. 3)

There are five basic steps in Beck's version of cognitive therapy:

1. Clients first learn to recognize and monitor their negative, automatic thoughts. These thoughts are "dysfunctional," that is, ineffective, and lead to serious dilemmas.
2. They are taught to recognize the connections between these negative thoughts (cognitions), the emotions they create, and their own actions. (See Figure 14.2 for examples of connections between thoughts and emotions.)
3. They learn to examine the evidence for and against their distorted automatic thoughts.

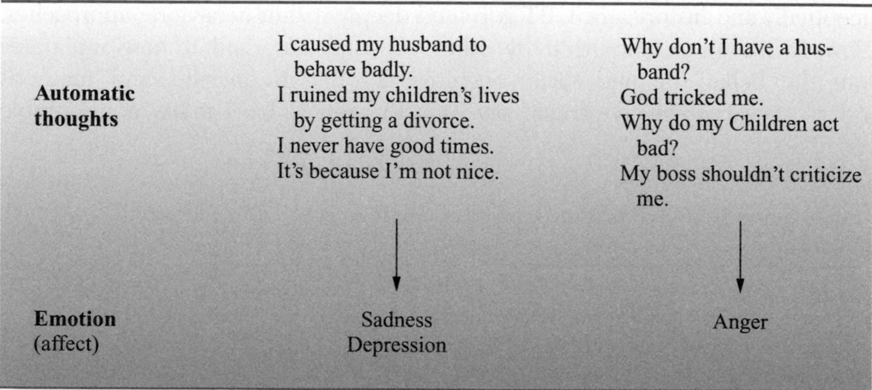

Figure 14.2 Examples of connections between negative automatic thoughts and emotion.

Source: Adapted from Beck, A. T., Rush, A. J., Shaw, B. F., & Emery, G. (1979). *Cognitive therapy of depression* (p. 250, fig. 3). New York: Guilford Press.

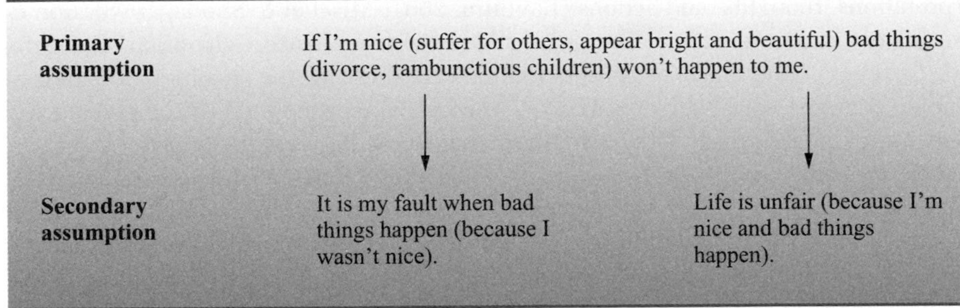

Primary assumption
If I'm nice (suffer for others, appear bright and beautiful) bad things (divorce, rambunctious children) won't happen to me.
Secondary assumption
It is my fault when bad things happen (because I wasn't nice).
Life is unfair (because I'm nice and bad things happen).

Figure 14.3 Examples of assumptions that encourage depression.

Source: Adapted from Beck, A. T., Rush, A. J., Shaw, B. F., & Emery, G. (1979). *Cognitive therapy of depression* (p. 250, fig. 3). New York: Guilford Press.

4. They substitute for these distorted negative thoughts more realistic interpretations.
5. They are taught to identify and change the inappropriate assumptions that predisposed them to distort their experiences. Examples of such assumptions are shown in Figure 14.3.

A variety of ingenious techniques have been developed to encourage people to undertake these five basic steps and to use them effectively to alter their actions, thoughts, and feelings. Cognitive therapy of this sort appears to be a promising part of treatment for depression and related emotional and behavioral problems. Its value has been explored in a large number of studies with subjects ranging from those with mild problems to hospitalized, severely depressive patients. The results seem to be consistently encouraging (Beck et al., 1979; Wright & Beck, 1996).

COMMON THEMES

The perspective that is illustrated at this level of analysis includes many different themes and variations. Some of the main shared features of this still-evolving approach are summarized below.

Work at this level of analysis is social in its concern with patterns of social behavior and the interpersonal aspects of life. It is cognitive in its emphasis on mental processes and on understanding how different people process incoming information (Higgins & Kruglanski, 1996). It examines how people process and use information about themselves and their social worlds, and studies the cognitive and emotional strategies they develop for coping with important life challenges. Research tries to see how individuals differ in their distinctive encoding (appraisal) of different features of situations. It also examines how those encodings activate and interact with other cognitions and affects in the personality system to generate the person's distinctive patterns of behavior.

The situation is important in work at this level because the personality system is in continuous interaction with situations: the behaviors that are generated depend on the situation involved in the particular interaction. But this is a two-way relationship: the effect of the situation also depends on the characteristics of the personality system. The personality system in part creates the situations themselves through its own interpretations, thoughts, and actions (Bandura, 2001; Mischel & Shoda, 1998). Sometimes this two-way interaction process is called **reciprocal interactionism** (Bandura, 1977), to refer to the chain of causes. In this causal chain, the qualities of a person (including cognitive social person variables), the behaviors generated by the person, and the environment all interact with each other, and each influences the others.

14.23 What is meant by the concept of reciprocal interactionism?

Many researchers at this level of analysis also hope that their ideas and work will help people to enhance their options and decrease their personal vulnerabilities. Put most simply, they would like their work to ultimately help optimize human well-being, freedom, and choice. Thus, they also emphasize human potential and assume that people can change constructively and extensively under appropriate conditions. With that goal in mind, often they study such real-life problems as overcoming anxious, depressive, and health-threatening mental states (Aspinwall & Taylor, 1997; Cantor & Kihlstrom, 1987; Taylor & Armor, 1996). Much of this work tries to improve people's sense of mastery and competence so they can better fulfill their potential, as discussed in the next chapter. The commitment is to enhancing the human potential for alternative, more constructive ways of coping, consistent with the phenomenological perspectives of such earlier theorists as George Kelly.

The emphasis on stimulus conditions in early behavioral approaches often implies a passive view of people—an image of organisms that are empty except for sets of automatic responses to external stimuli. In contrast, social cognitive approaches emphasize that people are active and agentic—that is, they actively shape their worlds and social environments. Consequently much of the research at this level deals with issues of self-regulation and self-control and is designed to see how people can more effectively regulate their behavior to "take charge" of their lives (e.g., Bandura, 2001; Mischel et al., 1996).

Recall that trait theories emphasize differences *between* people in their response to the same situation or even regardless of the situation. Social cognitive theories also address these differences. However, they go on to try to understand the unique ways an individual's behavior may change in response to even slight changes in conditions, as indicated in Figure 14.4. They focus on these enduring within-individual differences (intra-individual stability) as an important aspect of the difference between individuals. Understanding the psychological impact or meaning of particular events and conditions in the person's life requires observing how changes in those conditions alter what he or she expects, thinks, and feels.

Work at this level also draws on the behavioral level of analysis to the degree that it asks: Why and when will individuals *do* what they do? That is, it goes from

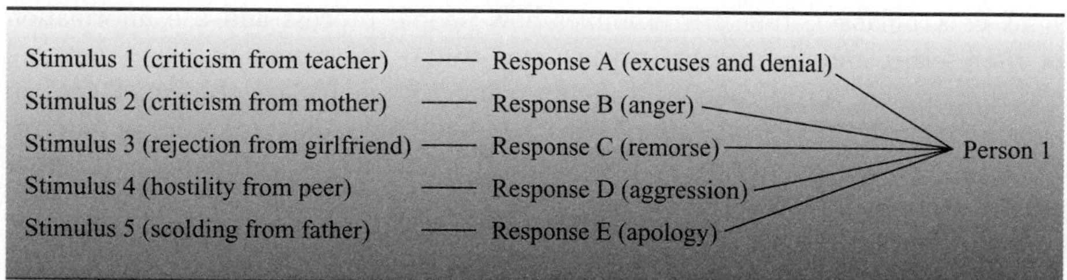

Figure 14.4 The same person behaves in distinctive but stable ways in response to various psychological situations.

social cognition, feelings, and motivation to a focus on human action (e.g., Gollwitzer & Bargh, 1996). But although the approach includes a focus on behavior, its primary goal is to clarify the psychological processes that underlie the particular behavior of interest.

▶ SUMMARY

DEVELOPMENT OF THE SOCIAL COGNITIVE PERSPECTIVE

- George Kelly's perception of the person as a scientist helped bridge the theoretical gap between behavioral explanations of personality and social cognitive theory.
- The social cognitive level was stimulated by the finding that the perceiver's mental representations and cognitive transformations of stimuli can determine their impact on the individual.
- The cognitive revolution rejected the ideas of behaviorism that focused only on observable stimuli and responses, and instead embraced the study of mental processes such as thinking, knowledge, and memory.

ALBERT BANDURA: SOCIAL LEARNING THEORY

- Albert Bandura called attention to the importance of observational learning for personality development and change.
- Observational learning can help create or remove fears and other strong emotional reactions.
- Human performance is dramatically improved by awareness of the rules or principles that influence the outcomes for behavior.
- Bandura's theory views people as agentic and proactive, able to influence their future through forethought and symbolic processes.
- Self-efficacy in this theory is a basic mechanism for enabling constructive change and self-regulation.

SOCIAL COGNITIVE PERSON VARIABLES: WALTER MISCHEL

- Mischel's (1973) reconceptualization of personality focuses on how the person's understanding of situations and their acquired psychological meanings guide his or her interactions with the situations encountered and self-generated. The expressions of these interactions play out in the stable *if* ... *then* ... behavioral signatures of personality that characterize how the individual predictably deals with different types of situations.
- The reconceptualization proposed a set of social cognitive person variables to characterize individual differences. They deal with how each person encodes (construes) different types of situations, and the expectancies and beliefs, affects, goals and values, and self-regulatory strategies and competencies that become activated in the interactions with those situations.
- Mischel's theory of social cognitive person variables was influenced by George Kelly's personal construct theory and Julien Rotter's social learning theory and helped to integrate the two.
- The assessment and functions of these person variables are illustrated with examples from Gary W.'s interactions with his social world.

PERSONALITY ASSESSMENT

- Assessments at the Social Cognitive Level of analysis tend to be specific and connected to treatment efforts, as exemplified in self-efficacy expectancy measures.
- The Implicit Association Test (IAT) uses a word-association task to evaluate participants' implicit level of self-esteem and diverse attitudes.

PERSONALITY CHANGE AND THERAPY

- Therapies at this level try to identify the person's disadvantageous ways of thinking and to encourage more adaptive ways of thinking, feeling, and solving problems.
- Aaron Beck's cognitive-behavioral therapy (CBT) treats personal problems and depression by changing the way people encode themselves and their experiences to find more constructive ways of thinking and behaving.

COMMON THEMES

- Social cognitive approaches focus on how individuals select, attend to, and process information about the self and the world and react to it.
- Reciprocal interactionism is a concept that recognizes that people's attributes and actions interact with the social environment continuously, each influencing the other.

▶ KEY TERMS

agentic 356
assertiveness training 372
behavior–outcome relations 361
cognitive behavior theraphy (CBT) 372
cognitive restructuring 374
cognitive revolution 352
cognitive transformations 350
conditional hedges 371
covert modeling 372
encode 360
hot cognitions 362
Implicit Association Test (IAT) 369
implicit self-esteem 369
intrinsic motivation 363
modeling 352
nominal situations 371
Observational learning 352
psychological situation 371
reciprocal interactionism 376
self-efficacy expectations 361
social cognitive person variables 359
social cognitive reconceptualization of personality 357

CHAPTER 15

SOCIAL COGNITIVE PROCESSES

PRINCIPLES OF SOCIAL COGNITION APPLIED TO PERSONALITY

In Chapter 14 we discussed the major social cognitive theories of personality. Research at this level of analysis is influenced by these theories, but it also is influenced importantly by work in the last few decades at the edges between personality and social psychology. You can see the close links between the two fields, and the fuzzy nature of the boundaries that somewhat artificially divide them, even in the title of their shared professional organization: *The Society of Personality and Social Psychology*. The psychologists who do this research often view themselves as hyphenated personality-social or social-personality psychologists. When one looks at research at the Social Cognitive Level, it's difficult to know where one field ends and the other begins. One of the basic ways in which these researchers are united is that they all draw heavily on principles and concepts about social cognition that have been discovered in the years since the cognitive revolution began.

Social Cognition and Personality

In the 1980s, as cognitive psychology matured, many social psychologists adopted the constructs and methodologies that had begun in cognitive psychology and proved to be fruitful. But while cognitive psychologists studied, for example, the mental structure of the concept of "bird" or "furniture" (Smith & Medin, 1981), social psychologists studied how people processed information about the social world, particularly the self and other people. The term **social cognition** refers to this large movement within social psychology, and it is increasingly active and influential, freely crossing the loose boundaries between personality and social psychology. This two-way intellectual traffic is generating the wealth of ideas and findings on social cognitive processes and personality that we discuss in the present chapter. You will see how some of the concepts and research methods developed within the social cognition movement in social psychology are being integrated into theory and research in personality psychology.

15.1 How does the research of cognitive psychologists and social psychologists compliment each other, and often intertwine, in the field of social cognition?

One of the most important of these concepts involves "schemas," seen in how we interpret the experiences of everyday life. These are our theories about what the personal world is all about. Given how key they are for understanding personality as studied at this level of analysis, we begin by considering them in detail. We then turn to how research on social cognition has helped illuminate our understanding of the self, coping processes, and social behavior.

Schemas

When Jana told her partner Rodolfo she had to spend the evening preparing for a work assignment due the next day, he became upset, and saw it as another sign of her increasingly uncaring attitude toward him. He felt rejected, and then quickly became irritated and angry, starting an argument. His interpretation of her behavior as rejecting him was of course only one way to encode it. Compare him with Mike who is less sensitive to rejection. When Mike heard a similar comment from his partner he took it at face value, respecting her need to concentrate on her work, and went to the movies.

To explain individual differences like Rodolfo and Mike's diverse reactions to similar behavior, personality researchers at the Social Cognitive Level of analysis begin by seeing how the different individuals construe and interpret its meaning and significance. The emotional and behavioral reactions that unfold are influenced by the mental representations, or **schemas**, with which people interpret the objects and social situations in their world, including themselves and their own psychological states, as well as other people. Schemas in social cognitive theories are important for understanding mental functioning because they are basic units for organizing information. They guide what we notice and what we remember.

Schemas are knowledge structures made up of collections of attributes or features that have a "family resemblance" to each other. People **categorize**, or group, information about ideas and experiences that have such resemblance or "go together" in order to organize and simplify vast amounts of information efficiently so that it can be used quickly to make inferences and decisions. These knowledge structures often have clear exemplars or best examples, called **prototypes**. A sparrow, for example, is a better or more prototypic example of a bird than an ostrich. Schemas help one to make sense of new events by recognizing what they are like in terms of their similarity to the cognitive structures that already exist. That happens, for example, when you see a flying object of a type you don't recall having seen before, but nevertheless have no trouble deciding it must have been a bird—not a plane, or a stone, or a balloon. It happened to Rodolfo in the chapter opening when he decided that Jana was uncaring and rejecting.

15.2 What are schemas? How do they develop?

Let's illustrate the concept of schemas more because they are basic in work at the Social Cognitive Level. Schemas include prototypes of types of people (Cantor & Mischel, 1979), such as "patron of the arts" and "comic joker," or social groups, such as "African American youth." Many schemas may be considered stereotypes, to emphasize the fact that these cognitive representations often are inaccurate. Schemas become activated when other thoughts that are associated with them become activated. For example, if a person thinks of herself as a patron of the arts, that self-concept is more activated when discussing whether or not the similarity between Georges Seurat's *Les Poseuses* (1888) and Pablo Picasso's *Quatre Baigneuses* (1921) goes beyond superficial resemblance (both images available at http://www.doubletakeexhibit.org/about/index.asp?pg=fp#3). In turn, when schemas are activated they can influence what people "see." For example, when you have been told someone is a comic joker, then a potentially ambiguous act (a person forgetting to tie her shoelace) may lead to inferences beyond the information given in the particular social situation (e.g., a readiness to interpret the behavior as an attempt to be funny).

Effects of Schemas

Directing Attention and Influencing Memory

Take a very quick glance at the photo below and then write down what you saw before reading on.

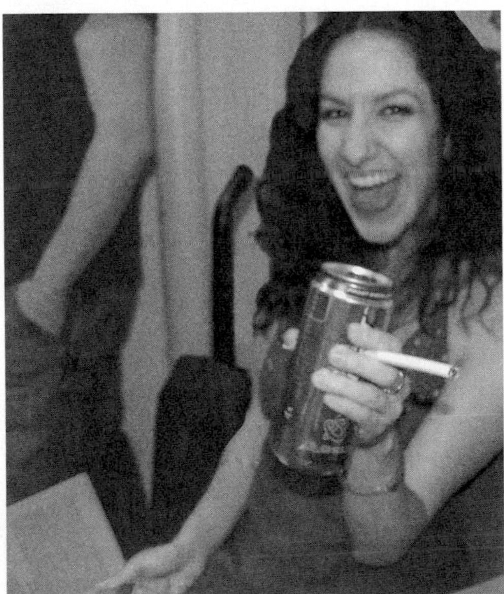

At first glance, what did you see in this photo?

Most people who were briefly shown this picture noticed neither the book nor the vacuum cleaner. That happened because when they look at this picture, typically they first see a young woman smoking a cigarette and holding a beer, and think of a wild party. A book and a vacuum cleaner do not fit with the wild party schema. In other words, the schema that is activated directs our attention, and affects our memory of events. While schemas make it possible for people to organize and function without becoming overwhelmed by a flood of information, they also can have unfortunate effects.

For example, research in social cognition has shown that an activated schema of a racial stereotype, primed (i.e., activated mentally) by the skin color of an individual, may lead to people "seeing things," sometimes with tragic consequences. That seems to have happened when a wallet held by a person of color was mistaken for a gun, leading to the shooting of Amadu Dialo by New York City police (Greenwald, Oakes, & Hoffman, 2003; Payne, 2001).

Making Inferences

Thus, schemas affect how we make inferences and form personality impressions, and they do so often in indirect and subtle ways. For example, in a recent classroom demonstration, one of the authors of this textbook showed a photo of a famous psychologist, with a phrase of trait terms under it. The right side of the class saw intelligent, creative, hardworking, *warm*, strong-willed, intellectual, and practical. The left side of the class read intelligent, creative, hardworking, *cold*, strong-willed, intellectual, and practical. Everything was identical except for the word *warm* or *cold*. When the class was asked, "Is this psychologist generous?" the right side of the class was more likely to say that he is generous rather than the left side of the class. In the study where this was first performed (Asch, 1946), 91% of the people who saw the *warm* schema said the person in the picture was generous, whereas 9% of the people who saw the *cold* schema thought the person was generous. There were no descriptions about generosity, but our schemas allow us to fill in the gap or make an inference.

Self-Fulfilling Prophecies

Schemas also can create self-fulfilling prophecies. That can happen when expectations created about others shape how one interacts with a person, which in turn causes that person to act in the way that was initially expected. The classic experiment on this point was done by Rosenthal and Jacobsen (1968). In the beginning of the school year, teachers were told that a randomly chosen set of students were on the verge of an intellectual spurt. This was not necessarily true. At the end of 8 months an IQ test was administered to the class and the students in the spurt sample scored higher on the exam than the rest of the class. Teachers' predictions about the randomly chosen spurt students made them act in a way that caused those students to excel academically. Perhaps they called on them more, spent more time with the students, and encouraged them more. In any case, the teacher's behavior caused a **self-fulfilling prophecy** whereby their expectations of success about the students led the students to actually perform better academically.

15.3 How can schemas about others actually affect the way we ourselves behave?

Activation of Schemas

Activation of schemas is determined by availability, accessibility, applicability, and salience (Higgins, 1996). A crayon analogy illustrates these concepts (Mendoza-Denton & Mischel, 2007). **Availability** refers to whether the schema exists or not. If the schema does not exist, then you will not use it. If I do not have a green crayon then I will not use it. **Accessibility** refers to how easy it is to access the schema. If the green crayon is in the back of the box, it is difficult to reach and I will rarely use it. If it is at the front of the box, it is easy to reach and I am likely to use it. **Applicability** refers to whether the schema is applicable to the situation. I will use my green crayon to color in the grass, but I will typically not use it to color snow or chocolate. **Salience** refers to the degree to which a particular social object stands out compared to other social objects in a situation. For example, if I have 19 green crayons in my box and only one black, the black crayon will have high salience. To illustrate salience in social perception, if you see one 20-year-old woman in a group of 70-year-old men, you are more likely to notice the young woman than the older men. And the schema of young people, and the schema of women, are likely to be activated.

15.4 What are the four main factors that determine the activation of schemas?

Priming refers to the process that increases temporary accessibility, for example, when a police officer in a dark subway car saw a dark skin color (the prime) and erroneously thought the person was carrying a gun rather than a wallet in his hand. Priming that activates one schema can also make related schemas more activated. So, if you have been listening to a radio story about the "glass ceiling" that women experience in their careers, schema of "women" are more likely to be activated than your schema of "youth." Thus when you see this group of people, you are more likely to think in terms of gender, and think to yourself, "Here she is, one woman in a group of almost all men." In an extreme case, you may not even notice that this woman also is the only young person in this group.

Salience and priming of course are not just events that occur when psychologists manipulate them in experiments in their laboratories. They occur every day in our heads, activated both by what we encounter in the social world, and what we experience in our own heads when we think and remember or ruminate or plan or even daydream.

What we now know about schemas and knowledge activation can shed light on important personality processes, as is illustrated in the remainder of this chapter.

THE SELF

Probably the most important schemas a person has are about the self, and it is the self that has become a focus of much social cognitive research and theorizing. This is a fairly new development within psychology in which the concept of the self has had many dramatic ups and downs historically. For many years at the height of behaviorism it was almost totally down if not taboo. There were, however, some notable exceptions, discussed earlier in this text. The self was important for the phenomenologists like Rogers, and likewise in the clinical work of some of the post-Freudians and object relations theorists like Kohut. But these remained lone voices for decades, muted by the dominance of behaviorists who judged the self to be a confusing fiction outside the realm of science. Currently, interest in the self is again extremely high (e.g., Leary & Tangney, 2003). After its long slumber, the self is attracting the attention of many theorists and researchers because new methods for studying social cognition have opened it to systematic study, and it has now become a core topic. In the remainder of this chapter we examine the self and self-relevant processes, focusing on concepts and research from the Social Cognitive Level of analysis.

At a commonsense level, everyone knows what the self is: we have a sense of ourselves, refer to ourselves, talk about ourselves, evaluate ourselves—sometimes blaming ourselves, sometimes praising ourselves—and we often try to control ourselves—with varying degrees of success. The "self" in personality psychology figures in concepts like "self-actualization," "self-evaluation," "self-regulation," and "self-control." For many researchers, the self now has become a prefix for practically every important process and function in a personality system.

Intuitively the "I," "me," or "self" is a basic reference point around which experiences and the sense of personal identity itself seem to be organized. At the Social Cognitive Level of analysis, the self is viewed not as a "thing" but as a set of schemas, a basic cognitive category, that serves as a vital frame of reference for processing and evaluating experiences (e.g., Baumeister, 1997; Markus, 1977; Markus & Cross, 1990; Markus, Kitayama, & Heiman, 1996).

Self-Schemas

15.5 In what two ways do we use the term "self"?

The **self-schemas** within an individual consist of interconnected knowledge structures of many different sorts based on a wide range of experiences in the course of development. In time, the child acquires an increasingly rich concept of him- or herself as an active agent, an "I" separate from other people and objects. A sense also develops of a "Me" that has defining features and qualities reflected in multiple self-concepts.

Self-schemas (Markus, 1977) include generalizations about the self, such as "I am an independent person" or "I tend to lean on people." These cognitions arise from past experiences and, once formed, guide how we deal with new information related to the self. To illustrate, if your self-schemas include being extremely dependent, passive, and conforming, you would process and remember information relevant to those schemas more quickly and effectively than do people for whom those schemas are not personally relevant because they would have high chronic accessibility (Markus, 1977). People have better recall for information about traits that they believe describe them than for traits that are not self-descriptive (Rogers, 1977; Rogers, Kuiper, & Kirker, 1977). Thus, we give information relevant to the self special cognitive treatment, for example, by being more attentive toward it.

15.6 Describe the meaning and functions of the self-schema.

Self-schemas are highly accessible personal constructs that a person is ready to use for encoding information. People differ stably in their self-schemas (Higgins, 1996b; Higgins, King, & Mavin, 1982). These self-concepts also have motivational implications. For example, most people desire to maintain positive views of themselves, are motivated to pursue self-knowledge, and want to enhance and improve themselves (Baumeister, 1996).

Each person develops a **self-theory** about his or her Me. This theory is a construction, a set of concepts about the self. It is created by the child from experience, but it in turn affects future experience (Epstein, 1973, 1983; Harter, 1983, 1999; Wiley, 1979). The individual's self-concepts are not a simple mirror-like reflection of some absolute reality. Self-concepts, like impressions of other people and of the world, involve an integration and organization of a tremendous amount of information. Self-concepts are not a mirror of reality, but they are correlated with the reactions and outcomes that the person has experienced throughout the past and expects to obtain in the future (Leary & Tangney, 2003; Wiley, 1979). Although the concepts change over time, their foundations form early in life, and they influence what that future becomes (Markus & Cross, 1990; Markus et al., 1996).

The Relational Self and Transference

In recent years, the self has been reconceptualized in light of current theory and findings on social cognition and specifically on how memory works.

The Relational Self

Self-knowledge (i.e., self-schemas) includes all the thoughts (cognitions) and feelings (affects) that develop about oneself. It consists of information that is stored and organized in memory as a cognitive–affective (mental and emotional) representation. This knowledge representation is closely connected in the memory system to knowledge representations about the significant other people in one's life (e.g., Andersen & Chen, 2002; Linville & Carlston, 1994), making these two types of information directly associated. Consequently, when the representation of a particular significant other is activated (e.g., you think about your mother), aspects of your own self-representation that have been mentally connected to that significant other also become activated mentally. These close connections in memory make the self intrinsically *relational* and interpersonal: in a sense, the significant others to whom one is close become part of one's personal identity. Thus, the self evolves from, and is linked to, the important relationships in one's life: in this sense, the self that emerges is intrinsically entangled with significant others.

15.7 In what sense is the self inherently relational? What do social cognition researchers mean by transference, and how does this compare with Freud's use of the term?

As the self develops in relation to a particular significant other person, expectations also develop about the most likely interactions that will occur with him or her. For example, an adolescent may come to expect that interactions with her mother about smoking are likely to play out along predictable lines (e.g., more hassles, more guilt, more avoidance). These scripts become reactivated in future interactions with the significant other or with other people who remind you of that person (Andersen, Reznik, & Chen, 1997).

Transference Reconsidered

The notion of the *relational self*, conceptualized in terms of memory representations that connect self-knowledge with representations of significant others, also allows a fresh view of the psychodynamic concept of transference. Transference, as discussed in earlier chapters, plays an important role in psychoanalytic theory and psychotherapy beginning with Freud, and in the ideas of Kohut and the object relations theorists. The

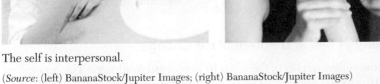

The self is interpersonal.

(*Source*: (left) BananaStock/Jupiter Images; (right) BananaStock/Jupiter Images)

Susan Andersen
(*Source*: Courtesy of Susan Andersen)

concept of transference has now been recast in social cognitive terms, and this is not just a renaming: it informs the process in light of findings from memory research. In the social cognitive reinterpretation by Susan Andersen and colleagues (2002), when one develops relationships with new people, transference readily occurs. This happens to the degree that representations of significant others in memory are activated by the newly encountered person.

Feeling attracted to—or repelled by—a newly encountered person, and easily making all sorts of inferences about his or her qualities (that may or may not turn out to be accurate), can be understood in terms of the particular significant other representation that is being triggered by, and applied to, the new person (Andersen et al., 1997; Chen & Andersen, 1999). If the psychiatrist's manner reminds the patient of her father, the cognitive—affective representation of the father, and of the patient's self in relation to him, also may become easily activated and brought to mind.

Note that this view of transference is compatible with Freud's (1912/1958) claim that the individual's mental representations of significant others, most notably the parents in early childhood, profoundly influence relationships to new people, including the psychoanalyst in the treatment process. It is different, however, because it sees this process in terms of social cognitive information processing rather than as a reflection of the psychosexual drives and conflicts favored in psychodynamic theory.

Perceived Stability of Self and Potential for Change

Perhaps the most compelling quality of the self is its perceived continuity. The experience of **subjective continuity** in oneself—of basic oneness and durability in the self—seems

15.8 What psychological mechanisms enable us to maintain consistency and continuity in the self-schema?

to be a fundamental feature of personality. Indeed, the loss of a feeling of consistency and identity may be a chief characteristic of personality disorganization, as is seen in patients with schizophrenia who sometimes report vividly experiencing two distinct selves, one of them disembodied (Laing, 1965).

Each person normally manages to reconcile seemingly diverse behaviors into one self-consistent whole. A man may steal on one occasion, lie on another, donate generously to charity on a third, cheat on a fourth, and still readily construe himself as "basically honest and moral." People often seem to be able to transform their seemingly discrepant behaviors into a constructed continuity, making unified wholes out of diverse actions. How does this integration work?

Many complex factors are involved (Harter, 1983; Markus & Cross, 1990). One answer to this question may be that people tend to reduce cognitive inconsistencies and, in general, simplify and integrate information so that they can deal with it (Ross & Nisbett, 1991; Tversky & Kahneman, 1974). The human mind may function like an extraordinarily effective reducing valve that creates and maintains the perception of continuity even in the face of perpetual observed changes in actual behavior (Festinger, 1957; Mischel, 1973). The striving for self-consistency that the phenomenologists emphasized (Rogers, 1951) has received support in the work of other researchers working on related topics (Aronson & Mettee, 1968; Cooper & Fazio, 1984).

Another basis for perceived consistency is that people often know a good deal about their own characteristic *if . . . then . . .* situation–behavior patterns (e.g., English & Chen, in press). There is a strong relationship between the intra-individual stability of those patterns and the person's self-perception of consistency. This finding was discussed in Chapter 4. It was found that college students who perceived themselves as consistent with regard to their "conscientiousness" had much more stable patterns of situation–behavior relations in their conscientious behavior than did those who saw themselves as not highly consistent (Mischel & Shoda, 1995). For example, students who always conscientiously prepared for tests but were not conscientious about keeping appointments on time would see themselves as consistent. Note that their consistency was in their stable *pattern*, rather than from one type of situation (test preparation) to another (punctuality).

In general, the self-concepts and personal constructs that people have seem to show a good deal of stability (Byrne, 1966; Gough, 1957; Mischel, 1968). Thus our personal theories about ourselves and the world tend to be relatively stable and resistant to change (Nisbett & Ross, 1980), as are our attitudes and values (E. L. Kelly, 1955). This perceived stability, however, coexists with the equally compelling fact that throughout the life course, people modify and transform their self-concepts as they envisage and construct "alternative future selves" (Cantor, 1990, p. 735) and strategically adapt to diverse life challenges (Mischel & Morf, 2003).

Multiple Self-Concepts: Possible Selves

The self traditionally has been viewed as unitary: a single self that is relatively consistent (Allport, 1955; Snygg & Combs, 1949). More recently, it is increasingly common to characterize the self as a multifaceted, dynamic set of concepts consisting of multiple selves. These different perceived selves reflect different aspects of an individual's total personality.

Consider a woman who seems hostile and fiercely independent some of the time but passive and dependent on other occasions. What is she really like? Which one of these two patterns reflects the woman that she really is? Must she be a really aggressive person with a facade of passivity—or is she a warm, passive-dependent woman with a surface defense of aggressiveness? In theory, at the Social Cognitive Level, it is possible for her to be all of these: a hostile, fiercely independent, passive, dependent, aggressive, warm person all in one (Mischel, 1969). Indeed, each of these aspects may constitute a different **possible self** or potential way of being, schemas that are all available and relatively accessible in memory (Markus & Cross, 1990). Of course, which of these selves she is at any particular moment would not be random; it would depend on which one is primed in any given situation. That is, it would depend on who she is with, when, and why, and most importantly on how she construes and interprets the situation, that is, its meaning to her. But each of these aspects of her self may be a quite genuine and real aspect of her total being, part of her own unique but stable patterning of person variables (Mischel & Morf, 2003).

15.9 What is meant by multiple self-concepts? How does it relate to the concept of possible selves?

The self-concepts that encode different aspects of the person vary, depending on particular contexts, on the type of behaviors that are self-assessed, and on the culture. As Hazel Markus and colleagues have noted, the beliefs and values of one's culture and group profoundly influence how individuals construe themselves and their future possibilities (e.g., Markus et al., 1996; Stigler, Shweder, & Herdt, 1990), and even the conception and definition of the "self" varies greatly across cultures. Thus, the self may be a more central concept for societies like ours that value self-enhancement and see the self as an entity than for societies like the Japanese that value the relations between the person and other people rather than oneself alone (e.g., Markus et al., 1996; Markus & Kitayama, 1991).

The concepts of the self that the person can access easily comprise what has been called the **working self-concept** (Markus & Nurius, 1986), which derives from various self-conceptions that are present in thought and memory. According to Markus and her

Hazel Markus

(*Source*. Courtesy Hazel Markus)

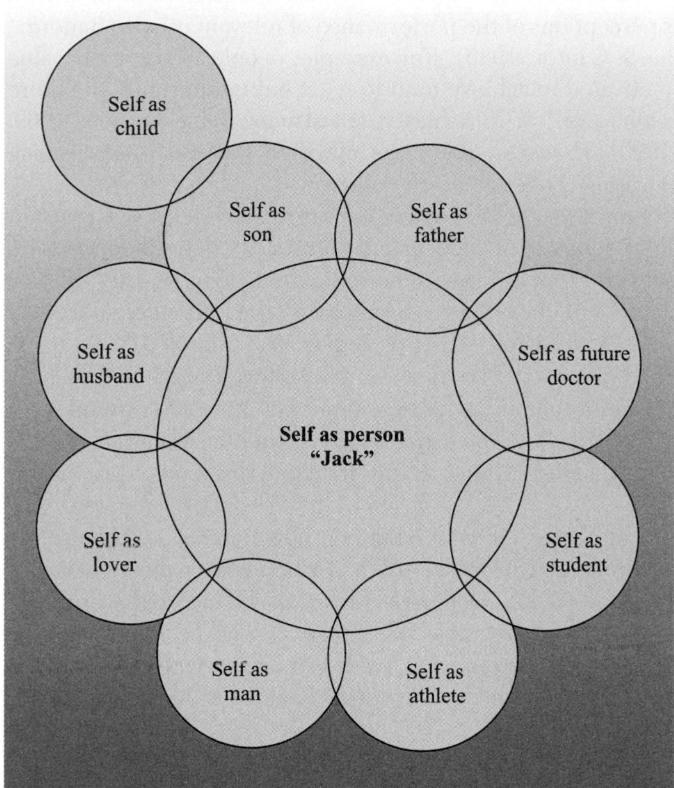

Figure 15.1 Schematic representation of a working self-concept. The working self-concept contains mental representations of diverse aspects of the self, from the present and the past, as well as imagined possible future selves.

colleagues, this working self-concept includes ever-changing combinations of *past selves* and *current selves*, as well as the imagined *possible selves* that we hope to become or are afraid of becoming. These possible selves serve as guides for behavior and can have significant impact on one's emotional and motivational states. A schematic representation of some components of a working self-concept is shown in Figure 15.1.

Self-Esteem and Self-Evaluation

One of the most critical aspects of the self-concept is **self-esteem** (Harter, 1983). Self-esteem refers to the individual's personal judgment of his or her own worth (Coopersmith, 1967; Epstein, 1973, 1990). Self-esteem is such an important aspect of the self-concept that the two terms are often used as if they were the same. Although self-esteem is sometimes discussed as if it were a single entity, persons may evaluate their functioning in different areas of life discriminatively (Crocker, 2002).

15.10 How does self-esteem develop and influence behavior?

Self-esteem and self-evaluations are influenced by the feedback that people continuously get from the environment as they learn about themselves, beginning in the early course of development (Leary, 2002; Leary & Downs, 1995). In their self-appraisal, individuals are guided by their memories and interpretations of earlier experiences, and by the framework of self-concepts, self-standards, and self-perceptions through which they view and filter their experiences. People compare themselves to their own standards, as well as to their perceptions of the performance of relevant others (Bandura, 1986; Higgins, 1996; Norem & Cantor, 1986). For example, people who greatly value achievement and who are motivated to achieve tend to react quite differently to failure experiences than do those who are low in achievement striving (Heckhausen, 1969; Koestner & McClelland, 1990). However, the same outcome that is a discouraging defeat for one may be a motivating challenge for the other.

People adopt many different strategies to cope with performance feedback relevant to self-esteem. For example, the impact of success and failure experiences depends on whether the person construes or "frames" the outcomes as reflecting on the self as a whole, or in terms that are more circumscribed and specific to the particular success or failure situation (Mendoza-Denton, Ayduk, Mischel, Shoda, & Testa, 2001). So if the experience of failure is framed in terms of being about the self as a whole without any situational qualifiers (e.g., "I am a failure"), the emotional fall-out and consequences generalize much more broadly than when the experience is framed in situation-specific *if . . . then . . .* terms (e.g., "I am a failure when it comes to taking this kind of test on this topic").

Self-evaluation processes are basic for understanding how people see themselves and respond to their own experiences. They reflect each person's compromises between the need for accurate perception of his or her performance in the real world and the self-protective desire to maintain a favorable self-image. Personality theorists have long recognized that in this self-evaluation process, we generally manage to combine a mix of "thorough realism" and "protective maneuvering" (Cantor & Kihlstrom, 1987, p. 152).

Costs of Self-Esteem Pursuit

People with high as compared to low overall levels of self-esteem generally seem to function better in many aspects of their lives, and to feel better about themselves in many domains (Hoyle et al., 1999). However, while having genuinely high self-esteem may have its substantial benefits, its active pursuit can have high costs (e.g., Crocker, 2002). The risk in the pursuit of self-esteem is that it can lead people to focus too much on themselves while neglectful of the feelings and needs of others. This can encourage competitiveness rather than cooperation (e.g., Carver & Scheier, 1998). It can lead to preoccupation with "how am I doing?" rather than attention to "how are you?"—and a neglect of other people while busily trying to build up one's own self-esteem. The costs of pursuing self-esteem tend to be especially high for people who see high self-esteem as essential for feeling that they are worthy. For them, threats to self-esteem may trigger anxiety followed by negative defensive reactions to reduce the discomfort. These defensive reactions can range from hostility and aggression to withdrawing from relationships or creating emotional distance that undermines important connections with other people (e.g., Baumeister, 1998).

15.11 How can the pursuit of high self-esteem create maladjustment?

Essential Features and Functions of the Self

The explosion of research on the self in the last few decades is leading to a consensus about its essential features (Hoyle et al., 1999; Mischel & Morf, 2003). In contemporary views on the self, the self is seen as having the following qualities:

- The self is essentially social and interpersonal—it arises out of social experiences with significant other people and is expressed in relation to them (e.g., Andersen & Chen, 2002).

In earlier forms this social view of the self was seen in the discussion particularly of Carl Rogers and the later work of Tory Higgins. It is seen clearly in current work, for example, on the relational self and the reinterpretation of transference in social cognitive terms.

- The self is important for understanding the processes of adaptation and coping—that is the doing or executive functions of personality (e.g., self-regulation, self-defense). In performing these functions it is a dynamic, motivated system (e.g., Baumeister, 2002; Derryberry, 2002; Leary, 2002).

Many of these qualities and functions were emphasized in earlier forms by the ego psychologists, stemming originally from the psychodynamic Freudian tradition. It was seen, for example, in Anna Freud's focus on ego defenses and in the theories and clinical practice of Alfred Adler and Carl Jung (Chapter 9).

- Closely related to the above is the view that the self has evaluative functions, and it is basic for the concept of identity (e.g., Crocker, 2002; Eisenberg, Spinrad, & Morris, 2002). It is motivated to protect self-esteem (Leary, 2002). These features were important in the theories of Erik Erikson, Heinz Kohut (1971), and Otto Kernberg (1976, 1984), which you already encountered in this text in Chapter 9. They are again being given new life in the work on self-regulation and goal pursuit discussed later in the text (e.g., Chapters 16 and 17).

15.12 Describe three important features of the self.

▶ PERCEIVED EFFICACY, HELPLESSNESS, AND MASTERY

Perceptions about one's adequacy and self-efficacy can have either self-enhancing or self-destructive consequences. In this section we consider how these positive and negative patterns develop and play out.

Self-Efficacy Expectancies

Expectancies and beliefs that one will be able to exert control and successfully execute necessary actions are essential for effective functioning and goal pursuit. They support one's efforts and guide whether, where, when, and how one should pursue relevant goals (Mischel et al., 1996). To even try to "take charge" in self-guided goal pursuit requires a representation of the self "as a causal agent of the intended action" (Kuhl, 1984, p. 127). Self-efficacy—the belief that "I can do it"—is a foundation for the successful pursuit of a difficult goal, or for changing and improving one's situation or oneself. Its psychological opposite, perceived helplessness, is the route to giving up, apathy, and depression (Bandura, 1986).

Learned Helplessness and Apathy

When people believe that there is nothing they can do to control negative or painful outcomes, they may come to expect that they are helpless (Seligman, 1975) and encode themselves in helpless terms. They expect that the aversive outcomes are uncontrollable, that there is nothing they can do. In this state, called **learned helplessness**, they also may become apathetic and despondent and that state may generalize and persist.

15.13 How does learned helplessness develop and affect behavior?

The concept of learned helplessness originally was based on findings from some experiments with animals exposed to extreme frustration. Consider, for example, a dog placed in a situation where he can do nothing to end or escape an electric shock delivered to his feet through an electrified grid on the floor. Later he may sit passively and endure the shocks even though he can escape them now by jumping to a nearby compartment (Seligman, 1975, 1978). These findings on learned helplessness with animals also were consistent with less rigorous observations of humans forced to face extreme and persistent frustration. Withdrawal, listlessness, and seeming emotional indifference are often found among war prisoners and inmates of concentration camps, for example. The victims seem to have given up totally, presumably overwhelmed by their inability to do anything that will change their desperate lot.

Dramatic examples of learned helplessness may be found among the children of America's migrant families whose plight was described by Coles (1970). He notes that unlike typical children in the middle class, migrant children soon discover that their shouts and screams will not necessarily bring any relief from their pains and frustrations. Consider this description by a migrant mother of her own helpless feelings in the face of her children's suffering:

> My children, they suffer, I know. They hurts, and I can't stop it. I just have to pray that they'll stay alive, somehow. They gets the colic, and I don't know what to do. One of them, he can't breathe right and his chest, it's in trouble. I can hear the noise inside when he takes his breaths. The worst thing, if you ask me, is the bites they get. It makes them unhappy, real unhappy. They itches and scratches and bleeds, and oh, it's the worst. They must want to tear all their skin off, but you can't do that. There'd still be mosquitoes and ants and rats and like that around and they'd be after your insides then, if the skin was all gone. That's what would happen then. But I say to myself it's life, the way living is, and there's not much to do but accept what happens. Do you have a choice but to accept? That's what I'd like to ask you, yes sir. Once, when I was little, I seem to recall asking my uncle if there wasn't something you could do, but he said no, there wasn't, and to hush up. So I did. Now I have to tell my kids the same, that you don't go around complaining—you just don't.
>
> (Coles, 1970, pp. 9–10)

In sum, a good deal of research now suggests that when people believe they cannot control events and outcomes, they gradually develop a sense of helplessness (Seligman, 1990; Wortman & Brehm, 1975) and even severe depression. In the extreme, when people feel they cannot tolerate the frustrations in their lives, they may lose interest in all activities and virtually stop behaving, often spending a great deal of time in bed. They tend to become very sad and feel worthless, often suffering a variety of physical complaints.

15.14 What two kinds of causal attributions do people make?

There is general agreement that the behaviors listed in Table 15.1 characterize depressed people as a group. Each depressed individual displays his or her own combination of any of these behaviors, often including deep unhappiness, emotional numbness and loss of interest, withdrawal from normal activities, and profoundly negative feelings about oneself and life. In contrast, when people believe that they can make an impact on their environment, that they can influence and control events, they become more alert, happier—and may even live longer (Seligman, 1990).

Causal Attributions Influence Emotions and Outcomes

Did I do it? Was it my fault? Did I really deserve it? Was it just luck? Did he spill the milk on me on purpose? Is she mean or just upset today? The different ways in which individuals answer these kinds of questions about causation reflect some extremely interesting individual differences. *Causal attributions* are the explanations people make of the causes of events, and they have predictable implications for how they feel about

TABLE 15.1 Some Indicators of Depression

Mood
Feel sad and blue most of the time
No longer enjoy things they used to
General loss of feeling
Fatigue, apathy, boredom
Loss of interest in eating, sex, and other activities
Physical symptoms
Headaches
Difficulty sleeping
Gastrointestinal symptoms (indigestion, constipation)
Weight loss—loss of appetite
Vague physical complaints
Behaviors
Unsociable—often alone
Unable to work, less sexual activity
Complaining, worrying, weeping
Neglect appearance
Speak little (speech is slow, monotonous, soft)
Ideation
Low self-esteem ("I'm no good")
Pessimism ("Things will always be bad for me")
Guilt, failure, self-blame, self-criticism
Feel isolated, powerless, helpless
Suicidal wishes ("I wish I were dead," "I want to kill myself")

Source: Based on "The behavioral study and treatment of depression," by P. M. Lewinsohn, 1975, in M. Hersen (Ed.), *Progress in behavior modification* (pp. 19–64). New York: Academic Press.

themselves and other people (Weiner, 1990). For example, we may see the same event—say, getting an A on an exam—as due to *internal causes* (such as high ability or hard work) or as due to *external causes* (such as the ease of the task or good luck). How we feel about the grade depends on whether we see it as due to internal or external causes (Phares, 1976; Rotter, 1966).

15.15 What four classes of symptoms characterize depression?

Pride and Shame

Generally, "pride and shame are maximized when achievement outcomes are ascribed internally, and minimized when success and failure are attributed to external causes" (Weiner, 1974, p. 11). In other words, a success that is perceived to be the result of one's ability or effort (internal causes) produces more positive feelings about oneself than does the same success when it is viewed as merely reflecting luck or an easy task (external causes). Similarly, we feel worse (e.g., experience "shame") when we perceive our failure as reflecting low ability or insufficient effort than when it is seen as due to bad luck or the difficulty of the particular task. For example, being fired from a job for one's incompetence has a different emotional impact than does being fired because the firm went bankrupt (see *In Focus 15.1* for discussion).

As noted in *In Focus 15.1*, in most people, perceptions of causes tend to be biased in self-enhancing ways (Greenwald, 1980; Harter, 1983; Leary, 2002). This bias can have beneficial effects, although in the extreme it can be self-deluding. But at the other

IN FOCUS 15.1

THE PERCEPTION OF CONTROL AND MEANINGFULNESS

There is a strong bias to see events and behavior as meaningful, orderly, and controllable even when they are random. You have seen this attributional bias if you have ever watched behavior in a casino. If you observed closely, you probably noticed how often gamblers act as if they can control chance by shaking the dice just right, or waiting to approach the roulette wheel at the perfect moment, or pulling the slot machine levers with a special little ritual. Gamblers are not unique in believing they can control chance events.

Even when something is clearly the result of chance (like the cards one draws in a poker game), people may see it as potentially controllable and not just luck. There is a deep human tendency to see the world as predictable and fair. We expect a "just world" (Heider, 1958), a world in which the things that happen to people are deserved and caused by them—even things like whether or not they win a lottery, get cancer, or are raped and murdered. Much research (reviewed by Langer, 1977) suggests that people often do not discriminate between objectively controllable and uncontrollable events. Instead they seem to have the "illusion of control," acting as if they can even control events that actually are pure chance.

In most people, this is part of a **self-enhancing bias**: We are more likely to see ourselves as causally responsible for our actions when they have positive rather than negative outcomes. When we do well or win, it is to our personal credit; when we do badly or lose, we could not help it (e.g., Fitch, 1970; Urban & Witt, 1990). Even when outcomes are negative, as in a tragic accident, we may find it hard to cope with events unless we somehow can see them as "just," meaningful, and orderly (e.g., Taylor & Armor, 1996; Taylor & Brown, 1988). Although this finding was first seen as evidence for a simple self-enhancing bias by perceivers, more recently it has been shown to have important, potentially beneficial and therapeutic effects for personality (e.g., Seligman, 1990; Seligman, Reivich, Jaycox, & Gillham, 1995; Taylor & Armor, 1996).

15.16 Define self-enhancing bias. How does this relate to our general expectation of a "just world"?

extreme, to lack the self-enhancing, self-protective bias completely may risk developing a depressive orientation (Lewinsohn, Mischel, Chaplin, & Barton, 1980).

Perceived Control and Predictability

Even when the particular task is something aversive that has to be endured and cannot be controlled—like a painful dental procedure—the belief that one can predict or control the event or the stress is an important ingredient for adaptive behavior. For example, in a classic study, college women were exposed to an aversive noise while they worked on a task. The noise either occurred at a predictable time or unpredictably (Glass, Singer, & Friedman, 1969). Their tolerance for frustration and the quality of their performance on the task were impaired only when the noise was unpredictable. Equally interesting, the negative effects were reduced considerably if during the stress period the participants believed they could do something to control the end of the stress. Generally, most people tend to become less upset when they think they can predict and control stressful or painful events (Staub, Tursky, & Schwartz, 1971), even if the perception is illusory (Taylor & Brown, 1988).

Reinterpreting Helplessness and Depression: Pessimistic Explanatory Styles

Persons are most vulnerable to perceiving themselves as helpless when they see the bad things that happen in life as due to their own internal qualities rather than to more momentary, external, or situational considerations (Abramson, Seligman, & Teasdale, 1978). They explain why they failed the test, for example, by thinking "I'm incompetent" rather than as due to the flu they had and the fact that they could hardly see the page.

People who do this consistently have a distinctive, essentially *pessimistic explanatory style*.

Pessimism is defined as an explanatory style that has three components: the person sees bad events as enduring, widespread, and due to the self. At an early age, this style can be a predictor of poor health for the future (Peterson, Seligman, & Vaillant, 1988). In one study, a group of healthy 25-year-old college graduates filled out questionnaires asking them to tell about difficult personal experiences in their lives. Researchers then analyzed the way the students explained the bad events that had occurred to determine whether or not their explanatory styles were generally pessimistic. Judges rated the explanations according to three criteria: the level of *stability* (seeing an event as having no end in sight; for example, "It won't ever be over for me"), *globality* (generalizing the event to many aspects of one's life), and *internality* (accepting one's self as causing or central to the problem rather than attributing it to some external factor or just plain circumstances). The more consistently stable, global, and internal the explanations, the higher the "pessimistic" style score.

15.17 Describe the three attributional elements of the pessimistic explanatory style. How does pessimism relate to physical well-being?

Over a span of 35 years, the group was followed up with health examinations, and measures of illnesses were recorded. For about 20 years after college, there were no significant differences in the health of the participants. By the time they reached the ages of 45 through 60, however, those who at age 25 had been more pessimistic in their responses were more likely to be suffering from illness.

Researchers of optimistic–pessimistic explanatory styles also studied newspaper interviews with ballplayers from the Baseball Hall of Fame, published throughout the first half of the century. The interviews quoted the players' explanations of good and bad events as they discussed how and why they won or lost games. Players who attributed their losses to their own personal, stable qualities and thus saw them as their own fault, but saw their wins as due to momentary external causes (e.g., "The wind was right that afternoon") tended to live less long than those who used more optimistic explanatory styles to construe their good and bad experiences (Peterson & Seligman, 1987).

Learned Optimism

The opposite of the learned helplessness pattern is a pattern of experience and thinking called **learned optimism** (Seligman, 1990). To develop this style the person is helped to encode the daily hassles and setbacks in life by deliberately using self-enhancing explanations. Now negative experiences become viewed as momentary, specific, and not due to one's one failings. This optimistic, positive way of interpreting experience tends to be associated with a wide range of positive outcomes, as assessed by self-reports of feeling happier and evidence of more effective functioning and work success (also see *In Focus 15.2*).

15.18 Contrast learned optimism with learned helplessness. How are optimism and self-enhancing illusions related to psychological adjustment?

Similar results were found with different measures based on self-reported optimism in one's orientation to, and interpretation of, life events. For example, the degree of optimism in the person's orientation to life predicts recovery from coronary bypass surgery in patients; it also predicts fewer physical symptoms in college students (Scheier & Carver, 1987). People with an optimistic orientation to life seem to face stressful situations by thinking about them constructively to deal with them as effectively as possible, essentially trying to make the best of the situation even if it is an extremely difficult one. In contrast, the pessimistic orientation is associated with withdrawal, which automatically prevents problem solutions or constructive reinterpretation (Scheier, Weintraub, & Carver, 1986).

IN FOCUS 15.2

THE ILLUSORY WARM GLOW OF OPTIMISM

Traditionally, psychologists have considered an accurate perception of self as essential for mental health (Jahoda, 1958). Researchers, however, have found that most psychologically healthy people have somewhat unrealistically positive illusory self-views, whereas those who perceive themselves more accurately tend to be the less mentally healthy (Armor & Taylor, 2002; Taylor & Brown, 1988). For example, people with realistic self-perceptions are more likely to experience low self-esteem and depression, while more stable individuals tend to see positive personality traits as being most descriptive of themselves (Alicke, 1985; Brown, 1986).

The exaggeratedly positive self-perceptions that most people have became apparent in a study comparing depressed patients with nondepressed psychiatric and normal controls (Lewinsohn et al., 1980). Patients who had interacted in small group situations were asked to rate both themselves and each other with regard to personality characteristics. Nondepressed individuals' self-ratings were considerably more favorable than the ratings others had given them. Self-ratings of depressed individuals were consistent with the ratings given them by others, suggesting that the nondepressed people had unrealistically positive self-views, seeing themselves through rose-colored glasses.

Individuals biased by such self-enhancing illusions also tend to feel they have an unrealistically large amount of control in pure chance situations, where in fact they cannot influence the outcome (Langer, 1975). In a study involving dice-throwing, for example, nondepressed participants felt that they would have greater control when throwing the dice themselves than when someone else did it for them (Fleming & Darley, 1986). The opposite state is found in depressed persons, who are likely to have a more realistic perception of the amount of control they have in chance situations—which in the case of dice-throwing is zero. Likewise, people in a depressed state tend to be reasonably accurate when predicting the future, while the nondepressed display an unrealistic optimism (Alloy & Ahrens, 1987). These results are clear, interesting, and consistent but, of course, they should not be misread as suggesting that gross distortions of reality characterize nondepressed individuals.

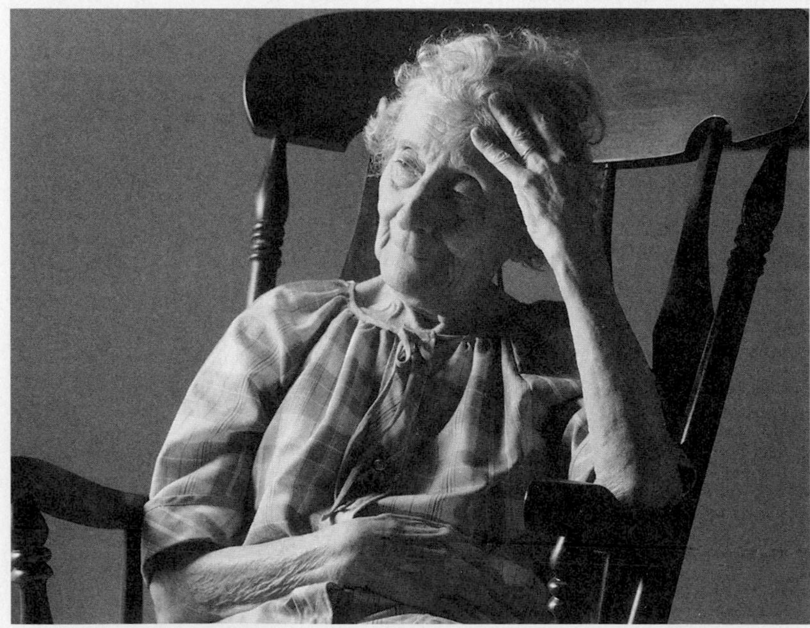

The depressed may perceive themselves *more* accurately than the nondepressed perceive themselves.

(*Source*: Robin Sachs)

Helpless versus Mastery-Oriented Children

15.19 Compare the attributional patterns of helpless and mastery-oriented children, and their effects on performance.

Following failure on a task, some individuals seem to fall apart and their performance deteriorates. But other people actually improve. What causes these two different types of responses to failure? The answer to this question again requires understanding how the person construes or interprets the reasons for the experience. Consistent with the work on learned helplessness, children who believe their failure is due to lack of ability (called *helpless children*) were found to perform more poorly after they experienced failure than did those who see their failure as due to lack of effort (called *mastery-oriented children*). Indeed, the **mastery-oriented** children often actually performed better after failure (Dweck, 1975).

When faced with failure, helpless children seem to have self-defeating thoughts that virtually guarantee further failure. This became clear when groups of helpless and mastery-oriented fifth-graders were instructed "to think out loud" while solving problems. When children in the two groups began to experience failure, they soon said very different things to themselves. The helpless children made statements reflecting their loss or lack of ability, such as "I'm getting confused" and "I never did have a good memory" (Diener & Dweck, 1978, p. 458). None of the mastery-oriented children made lack-of-ability statements. Instead, these children seemed to search for a remedy rather than for a cause for their failure. They gave themselves instructions that could improve their performance, such as "I should slow down and try to figure this out" and "The harder it gets, the harder I need to try."

The helpless children made many statements that were irrelevant to the solution and that usually were ineffective strategies for problem solving (see Table 15.2). For example, one helpless male repeatedly chose the brown-colored shape, saying "chocolate cake" in spite of the experimenter's repeated feedback of "wrong." Finally, the attitudes of the two groups toward the task differed markedly. Even after several failures, mastery-oriented children remained positive and optimistic about the possibility of success, while helpless children expressed negative feelings and resignation, declaring, for example, "I give up."

TABLE 15.2 Coping Strategies of Helpless and Mastery-Oriented Children

Helpless Children	Mastery-Oriented Children
Attributions for failure to self "I'm getting confused" "I'm not smart"	*Self-instructions to improve performance* "The harder it gets, the harder I need to try"
Solution irrelevant statements "There's a talent show this weekend, and I am going to be Shirley Temple"	*Self-monitoring statements* "I'm really concentrating now"
Statements of negative affect "This isn't fun anymore"	*Statements of positive affect* "I love a challenge"

Source: Based on Diener, C. I., & Dweck, C. S. (1978). In analysis of learned helplessness: Continuous changes in performance, strategy, and achievement cognitions following failure. *Journal of Personality and Social Psychology, 36*, 451–462.

Tuning In to the Wrong Thoughts: Anxiety

Effective goal pursuit is severely sabotaged by anxious, self-preoccupying thoughts (e.g., "I'm no good at this—I'll never be able to do it"). These anxious thoughts compete and interfere with task-relevant thoughts (e.g., "Now I have to recheck my answers"). The result is that performance (as well as the person) suffers (Sarason, 1979). Self-preoccupying thoughts interfere most when the task to be done is complex and requires many competing responses. One just cannot be full of anxious, negative thoughts about oneself and simultaneously concentrate effectively on difficult work, like preparation for a chemistry final exam. Likewise, as the motivation to do well increases (as when success on the task is especially important), the highly anxious person may become particularly self-defeating. That happens because under such highly motivating conditions, test-anxious people tend to catastrophize, imagining all the terrible things that could happen. They then become even more negatively self-preoccupied, dwelling on how poorly they are doing. In contrast, if one can become less anxious, then attention can be devoted to the task and the person can concentrate on how to master it effectively.

15.20 How does anxiety affect goal striving?

Enhancing Self-Efficacy When Expecting Failure

People who expect failure are likely to fulfill their prophecy. But if they are led to think they can do better, will their performance actually improve? One study of academically borderline college students examined just this question (Meichenbaum & Smart, 1971) and concluded that students who were led to expect success in fact became more successful in their schoolwork.

The power of positive thinking is shown even more dramatically through "mental practice." In one experiment, participants were instructed to imagine throwing darts at a target (Powell, 1973). Half of them were asked to imagine that their darts were hitting near the target's center; the other half imagined that their darts were striking outside the target area. Dart throwing improved significantly for people who had imagined successful performances during mental practice, but not for those who had imagined poor performances. Numerous studies to increase self-efficacy have shown similar effects (Bandura, 1986). The moral is plain: Think success! It is a moral, and an approach, completely consistent with the key mission and philosophy of positive psychology (Duckworth et al., 2005).

Incremental versus Entity Theories: Your Own Personality Theory Matters

Not just psychologists but everyone—including the young child—has theories. Often their theories are not spelled out and thus are implicit theories of personality, but they can have profound effects on daily life. Carol Dweck and colleagues have shown that people's implicit theories or beliefs about the malleability or fixedness of personality and character predict many of their reactions to others as well as to their own performance and feelings. This work began when Dweck and Leggett (1988) found that children who display the helpless pattern see their intelligence as a fixed trait or static entity that they cannot change or control. In contrast to such an entity interpretation, youngsters who are mastery-oriented tend to view their intelligence more flexibly as something they can increase and develop.

15.21 Compare entity with incremental theories. How do they affect the goals people choose and their achievement outcomes?

These different views or theories about intelligence also orient them toward different types of goals. The **entity theorists** seem to choose goals motivated by the desire to avoid unfavorable judgments and to gain approval about their competence. The

Carol Dweck

(*Source*: Courtesy of Carol Dweck)

incremental theorists choose goals motivated by the desire to increase their competence, for example, seeking opportunities to learn new things and enhance their mastery.

Children's theories about their intelligence also predict important real-life outcomes in their development. Children were tracked from sixth to seventh grade in their transition to junior high school (Henderson & Dweck, 1990). The most impressive gains in grades during this transition were found for the incremental theorists. In sharp contrast, children who saw their intelligence as fixed tended to remain low achievers if they had been low achievers before and, most distressing, among these entity theorists "... many of those who had been high achievers in sixth grade were now among the lowest achievers" (Dweck, 1990, p. 211). Clearly, our self-concepts and theories about our important qualities, our way of "encoding" or construing ourselves, impact our subsequent development (see *In Focus 15.2*).

Going further, Erdley and Dweck (1993) divided late grade school children into those who held entity versus incremental theories and showed them slides depicting some negative behaviors of a "new boy at school." For example, he lied about his family background, cheated from a classmate's paper, and stole a classmate's leftover art materials. They also received information about situational factors (the boy had moved in the middle of the school year to the new school) and about possible psychological mediators (the boy was nervous about making a good impression).

As predicted, entity theorists made significantly stronger judgments about the boy's global moral traits (e.g., bad, mean, nasty) than did incremental theorists. Furthermore, entity theorists did not revise their trait judgments of the boy when positive information was provided, whereas incremental theorists responded to the inconsistent information. Entity theorists also expected their first impression of the boy to remain valid forever, whereas incremental theorists predicted that the boy might act differently in the future. Once they have rendered a negative moral judgment, entity theorists generally recommend punishment for the transgressor (Chiu, Dweck, Tong, & Fu, 1997; Erdley &

Dweck, 1993), whereas incremental theorists recommend education or rehabilitation, consistent with their belief in the possibility of personality change even in wrongdoers.

The implications of these two types of theories for other attitudes and behaviors also have been explored across different cultures. For example, although Hong Kong college students were significantly more "collectivistic" than U.S. students, the entity theorists in both cultures made stronger dispositional inferences than did incremental theorists, apparently assuming that what people do even in a single instance reflects their stable fixed traits (Chiu, Hong, & Dweck, 1997). Entity theorists also showed less flexibility in their self-conceptions and orientation to other cultural groups than incremental theorists (Hong, Chan, Chiu, Wong, Hansen, Lee, Tong, & Fu, 2003). Likewise, entity theorists, in another study, endorsed both positive and negative stereotypes about ethnic groups (African Americans, Asians, Latinos) and occupational groups (lawyers, politicians) more strongly than did incremental theorists in studies with college students (Levy, Stroessner, & Dweck, 1998). In short, one's implicit personality theory shows itself in many forms, influencing how one judges people and interprets behavior.

Is the entity theory or the incremental theory better? Although an entity view has so far been linked with more maladaptive outcomes, neither view necessarily reflects the truth. And each theory has advocates convinced of its greater value.

▶ SUMMARY

PRINCIPLES OF SOCIAL COGNITION APPLIED TO PERSONALITY

- Research in the fields of personality and social psychology at the Social Cognitive Level is very closely linked, often focusing heavily on principles and concepts about social cognition discovered since the cognitive revolution.
- Schemas are mental representations with which individuals interpret objects and social situations in the world. They are developed by categorizing or grouping information about "objects," including people.
- Activation of schemas is determined by availability, accessibility, applicability, and salience.

THE SELF

- Self-concepts or self-schemas are knowledge structures developed from the person's perceived life experiences. They influence how new information relevant to the self will be processed.
- The relational self is a representation of the self that is connected to representations of the significant other people in one's life. In new relationships, representations of significant others may be activated by the newly encountered person.
- A fundamental feature of personality is the experience of subjective continuity, or the basic sense of oneness and durability in the self.
- The working self-concept comprises the most salient concepts of the self.
- Self-esteem refers to the individual's personal judgment of his or her own worth.
- Self-evaluation reflects the individual's performance, as well as earlier experiences and personal self-standards.

CAUSAL ATTRIBUTIONS, HELPLESSNESS, AND MASTERY

- Self-efficacy provides a foundation for the successful pursuit of difficult goals.
- People with learned helplessness believe they have no control over negative outcomes in their lives and may become apathetic and depressed.
- Causal attributions influence emotions and behavioral reactions. Events that are attributed to *internal causes* are more likely to produce pride or shame than are results attributed to *external causes*.
- Pessimism is an explanatory style in which bad life outcomes are attributed to one's own internal qualities. Learned optimism is an opposite, self-enhancing explanatory style that often has positive effects.
- *Helpless children*, who perceive their intelligence as unchanging, tend to perform poorly after failure. Conversely, *mastery-oriented children*, who feel they can improve their intelligence, cope better with failure.
- Entity theorists choose safe goals to avoid negative outcomes but incremental theorists prefer goals that enhance their competence.

▶ KEY TERMS

accessibility 382
applicability 383
availability 382
categorize 380
entity theorists 398
incremental theorists 399
learned helplessness 391
learned optimism 395
mastery-oriented 397
pessimism 395
possible self 388
priming 383
prototypes 380
salience 383
schemas 380
self-enhancing bias 394
self-esteem 389
self-fulfilling prophecy 382
self-schemas 384
self-theory 384
social cognition 380
subjective continuity 386
working self-concept 388

TAKING STOCK

PART VI
THE SOCIAL COGNITIVE LEVEL

▸ OVERVIEW: FOCUS, CONCEPTS, METHODS

As Part VI, the Social Cognitive Level of analysis, concludes, the next table summarizes its main characteristics and enduring contributions.

Overview of Focus, Concepts, Methods: The Social Cognitive Level

Basic units of personality	Underlying person variables and processes: Encoding (construing, including self-concepts and explanatory styles), expectancies and beliefs, affects, values and goals, self-regulatory competencies
Causes of behavior	Reciprocal interaction between person and situation, mediated by the person variables interacting within the personality system
Behavioral manifestations of personality	Stable patterns of person–situation interactions; distinctive signatures of *if* . . . *then* . . . relationships (she does *X* when *Y*, but she does *A* when *B*)
Favored data	Self-reports, diaries, ratings, and behavior samplings relevant to person variables; outcome information (such as symptoms, later school grades) within specific situations; findings from experiments
Observed responses used to	Infer underlying person variables and social cognitive, emotional, motivational processes; assess and predict behavior and outcomes (such as proneness to disease, well-being)
Research focus	Refining theories about underlying social cognitive processes, clinical implications (for health, for risk prevention in vulnerable individuals, for therapy, for enhancing self-efficacy)
Approach to personality change	By changing person variables and mediating processes (dynamics), modifying expectations, developing effective self-regulatory strategies and plans for goal attainment
Role of situation	Important; provides psychological cues and interacts with person variables

As the overview table indicates, the Social Cognitive Level focuses on the psychological variables that underlie the differences between individuals in their cognitions, emotions, and actions. For that purpose, psychologists study the diverse person variables discussed in this section of the text. They see these variables as basic units of personality and as important—but not exclusive—determinants of the patterns of behavior that characterize individuals distinctively and enduringly. They try to understand (1) the processes through which the variables operate and exert their effects, and (2) the unique patterns through which different persons manifest these variables in their behavior. These behavioral expressions of personality are found in stable patterns of *if* . . . *then* . . . , person–situation interaction.

► ENDURING CONTRIBUTIONS OF THE SOCIAL COGNITIVE LEVEL

Work on personality at the Social Cognitive Level began in the early 1970s by building on the foundations provided by earlier behaviorally oriented theorists, particularly social learning theory (e.g., Bandura, 1969; Rotter, 1954), and George Kelly's focus on personal constructs as guides for behavior and social perception. Going beyond the "stimulus–response" concepts developed in simple learning experiments with animals, more complex social learning was studied, and social cognitive theories of personality were expanded to include the role of both cognitive and social variables (e.g., Bandura, 1969, 1986; Mischel, 1973, 1990; Rotter, 1954). Work at this level moved away from a focus on external stimuli and rewards and explicitly rejected the idea that situations are the only (or even the main) determinants of behavior. Instead, personality was conceptualized in terms of cognitive and social person variables. The reciprocal (mutual) interaction between the person and the situation was emphasized, recognizing that people select, create, and change situations actively and are not merely passively "shaped" by them (Bandura, 1977, 1986; Mischel, 1973, 1984).

In the last few decades, social cognitive theories still include principles of social learning as a centerpiece for understanding many aspects of personality and social behavior. But they now give an even greater role to social cognition, emotion, and motivation, and address an increasingly wide range of personality and social phenomena. In one direction, work at this level of analysis is building on and revitalizing the contributions of phenomenological approaches and self-theorists, reopening many of the topics the self-theorists pioneered more than thirty years ago. This renewal has already proved to be fruitful. Decades ago, phenomenological approaches were criticized because they relied heavily on people's perceptions, which are subject to all sorts of biases and, therefore, are potentially inaccurate sources of information. Researchers at the Social Cognitive Level in recent years have turned this so-called problem into an exciting research topic. Instead of dismissing the individual's perceptions because of their possible biases, they have made those biases major topics in the study of social cognition, investigating how they influence social judgment and decisions.

The realization that how people perceive themselves and their experiences crucially influences their behavior, previously the distinctive hallmark of phenomenological approaches, has become also a central assumption within social cognitive approaches. Because researchers now use more sophisticated methods of measurement, difficult topics that previously resisted objective research are being opened. For example, the "self" in personality psychology has gone from an abstract concept about which theorists speculated to become an active research topic about which much has been learned. The same can be said for emotions, whose nature is becoming much clearer. Thus researchers at the Social Cognitive Level are seeking ways to link social cognition and social perception to other aspects of personality and social behavior. We saw, for example, some of the determinants of perceptions of personal control, and that changes in those perceptions can influence behavior for good or ill. The results ultimately should help clarify the relations between what people perceive and think and what they feel and do.

The classic humanistic commitment to enhance personal growth and the human potential has long been a key feature of phenomenological approaches. Now it also seems to be absorbed increasingly into some forms of cognitive behavior therapy. Personality psychologists within this framework devote much attention to the therapeutic implications of their work for both psychological and physical health and well-being (e.g., Contrada, Leventhal, & O'Leary, 1990; Taylor, Lerner, Sage, Lehman, & Seeman, 2004).

Traditionally, most approaches to personality have proposed certain basic assumptions about the nature and causes of personality (e.g., in terms of unconscious psychodynamics and motives). Their proponents have devoted themselves to trying to prove the truth and importance of those assumptions, usually ignoring findings from other approaches. As a science progresses, however, it tends to develop a more cumulative strategy in which concepts are modified, deleted, and incorporated in light of new research findings, regardless of the theoretical orientation that guided the original researchers. The field then matures into one in which the contributions of individual theorists become moments in a larger history of continuous change and evolution. In time, the best of what proves useful and valid is retained; the rest is left behind.

The Social Cognitive Level of analysis spans personality and social psychology, and is heavily influenced also by developments in cognitive psychology. Work at this level helps to provide a foundation for a cumulative science of individuals because it deliberately drew on earlier work that had proved promising rather than trying to emerge with a totally novel approach. A review of much of the work at the Social Cognitive Level suggests the emerging "convergence and complementarity of theoretical conceptions and empirical findings" that may be seen as a basic indicator of the field's progress (Cervone, 1991, p. 371). The degree to which the various levels of analysis do in fact complement and add to each other will become especially clear in the final part of the text that focuses on the integration among all the levels.

PART 

INTEGRATION OF LEVELS: THE PERSON AS A WHOLE

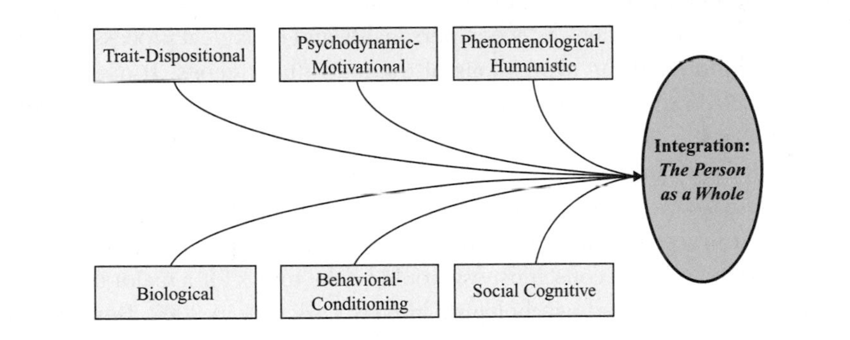

PRELUDE TO PART VII: INTEGRATION OF LEVELS

Historically, work at each level of analysis developed to address the limitations of existing theories and methods, and to highlight aspects of personality that had been ignored or inadequately treated in earlier theory and research. Thus, Freud's revolutionary view that much of human nature is essentially irrational and outside awareness startled and upset earlier conceptions, behaviorism developed in striking contrast to Freud's work, and the phenomenological approach arose as a passionate protest against both of them. Proponents of work at each level often were in intense competition, and the controversies became sharp and heated. But looking back after a century of personality psychology one can see the many ways the levels come together and connect. An integrative "big picture" view of the person that builds on the enduring contributions from all levels is becoming visible. In this final part of the text we examine this emerging view.

We begin with a review of the most basic contributions from each level. Even the short summary of these contributions below is a reminder that each level adds something significant to the others. Thus, far from being incompatible alternatives, the six levels provide insights on different aspects of the whole person. To reiterate a key theme in this text, when the levels are seen together and integrated, they enrich rather than fragment the view of the whole person.

OVERVIEW OF CONTRIBUTIONS FROM EACH LEVEL

Work at the **Trait-Dispositional Level** asks: (1) How can we best describe important, stable, consistent individual differences in personality over time and across many situations? and (2) What units do we need to capture the meaningful variation within an individual's personality?

An answer for the first question came, for example, with the Five Factor model (or Big Five) of traits. This work provides a useful map of broad individual differences. It demonstrated Type I consistency, which is seen in overall average differences between people in their levels of different behavioral dispositions. An answer to the second question came with the discovery of Type II consistency, seen in differences in people's stable *if* . . . *then* . . . situation–behavior patterns or personality signatures. These findings open the way for exploring how the stable patterns of variability in a person's behavior develop and the processes that might underlie them.

The **Biological Level** revealed the importance of the individual's biological heritage, and the close connections between personality and biological processes, including the role of evolution and the expressions of the individual's genes. It opened the way to studying mind–brain–behavior links and their connections to individual differences in personality. In the last few decades, work at the Biological Level and in cognitive science has vitalized and transformed psychological science and offers new insights for biologically based information-processing models of the personality system and its complex mental processes. In most of the last century, few psychologists would have anticipated that the self and consciousness would be the topics for a major conference of leading brain researchers and psychologists in New York City in 2002. Research now is probing into how what people think, feel, and do depends on their genes and their brains, neural networks, and biochemistry, all in continuous interactions with the environment. At the same time, it is becoming clear that what people think, feel, and do changes their brains, neural networks, and biochemistry.

The **Psychodynamic-Motivational Level** revolutionized the view of human nature by showing that much of what we feel, think, and do may be outside awareness, and self-defensive in its motivations. Much of it also may reflect conflicts (e.g., between competing motives or goals) within the personality system that play out at multiple levels, in indirect and complex patterns of seemingly paradoxical behaviors. You can see this, for example, when people show unexpected behaviors, surprising themselves, and sometimes even shocked, by their own actions or words. A comprehensive model of personality has to incorporate the puzzling and not just the obvious features of personality. Freud's was the first and most ambitious modern model of the personality system and still influences efforts to construct an integrative framework based on the state of psychological science a century later. His followers, the ego psychologists, went on to show the importance of higher-order ego functions and cognitive processes (e.g., competence motivation, self-regulatory abilities) and examined how they enable coping throughout the life cycle. Further, the self and object relations theorists working at this level recognized the central role of interpersonal relations, and of secure attachment, for mental health and adaptive functioning, and pioneered the analysis of these processes.

At the **Behavioral-Conditioning Level**, the focus was on the external stimulus or situation, objectively defined by observers, and on the ways in which external conditions and rewards influence and shape much of human behavior through learning processes.

This level showed that social behavior is readily influenced by specific situations, and by the consequences or reinforcers to which behavior leads; changes in those consequences in turn modify behavior in predictable ways. Likewise, a wide range of emotions, both positive and negative, are acquired through processes of conditioning, and can be modified by applying the same principles of conditioning in therapeutic efforts. Applications of the principles of learning to therapeutic efforts to modify problematic behavior (e.g., disabling fears, self-control difficulties, depression) have proved to be useful, particularly when used jointly with methods and insights found at other levels of analysis, as seen in cognitive behavior modification.

Researchers at the **Phenomenological-Humanistic Level** recognized that the effects of situations depend on how individuals subjectively perceive and construe or encode them. Therefore they emphasized the psychological situation as it is interpreted by the person, and opened the way to identify and assess such situations. Their contributions made it clear that a comprehensive model of the personality system has to deal with the role of psychological situations in the expression and organization of individual differences in personality. The Phenomenological-Humanistic Level also showed that personality involves more than the person's external behavior. It argued convincingly that personality is an organized system. It called attention to the importance of the self and self-concepts and showed that people are not just passively and reflexively responsive to external stimuli and rewards; the personality system can function in a proactive or future-oriented direction. It is "self-directed" and indeed much behavior is self-determined.

Taking the Phenomenological-Humanistic Level another step forward, the **Social Cognitive Level** showed the importance of peoples' mental representations of themselves, of other people, and of their experience. It called attention to the importance of learning through observation and modeling, and the key role of self-efficacy expectations and cognitive processes in social learning and behavior change. It identified individual differences in terms of such cognitive social variables as the person's schemas, expectancies, beliefs, goals, competencies, and other cognitions and affective states, and linked these variables to the social behavior the person generates in interaction with situations.

In sum, with all the levels in mind as background, this final part of the text illustrates a more integrated view of personality that is emerging, based on ideas, findings, and methods from all levels of analysis that have proved to be useful.

Chapter 16 shows how findings from the different levels contribute to an integrated view of the person. Drawing on these contributions, the chapter outlines the kind of integrative personality system needed to give a coherent "big picture" view of the functioning individual in the social world, and to understand the diverse expressions of personality. It is a view built on the basics of current personality science, and the enduring contributions of the field's rich history.

Chapter 17 applies this integrated view to understand how people with different personality structures and organizations characteristically self-regulate in pursuit of their important life goals and personal development.

Chapter 18 considers the person in the social interpersonal and cultural context. It examines the diverse aspects of personality and the multiple influences—from the biological to the social-cultural—that affect peoples' relationships, their personal and gender identities, and their links to their society and culture.

Will the insights and findings from current personality research and theory allow people to become more self-directed, effective, constructive, fulfilled, and happier? Cure-alls are unrealistic and unlikely. But what is known about how the personality system functions is sure to increase one's understanding of the nature and complexity of the human personality and its amazingly diverse behavioral expressions. And it may even help individuals to "take charge" of their own lives with more freedom to influence their future in the directions they choose for themselves.

CHAPTER 16

THE PERSONALITY SYSTEM: INTEGRATING THE LEVELS

So far this text showed how each level of analysis generated findings, insights, and concepts that enrich our understanding of the nature of personality and its diverse expressions. But do they really add up? Or are you left with this view, and that view, and still another view, and another, but no overall coherent conception, no take home message beyond the fact that there are many—maybe too many—different ways to study personality and to think about it?

This chapter examines how the various levels do indeed allow an integration if one focuses on the essentials of each of their contributions, rather than on their obvious differences. It discusses how after a century of vigorous personality science the outlines are becoming visible for a more coherent model or framework for conceptualizing personality. This view tries to integrate selectively the contributions from the past that have been supported empirically, with current advances at the cutting edge of cognitive, social, and brain science, to build an integrative working model of the personality system and the person as a whole. We begin with a brief summary of the types of consistency in the expressions of individual differences that have been found, and that a comprehensive model of the personality system has to account for and explain. We then look at how work at each level has identified essential requirements for such a system, and made enduring contributions that the system has to incorporate. We outline the essential assumptions and features of the emerging integrative model and discuss how it works, and how it tries to integrate and take account of the key established findings from all levels. Research examples and real-life applications illustrate the uses of this type of personality system.

WHAT HAS TO BE INTEGRATED?: CONTRIBUTIONS FROM EACH LEVEL

16.1 Describe the key contributions of each of the six levels of analysis.

Each level has yielded reliable and important findings that have to be taken into account in an integrative model of personality, summarized in Table 16.1. Let's look more closely into these discoveries and insights brought to light by each level of analyses.

Trait-Dispositional Level: Two Types of Consistency

As a first basic requirement, a comprehensive, integrative personality system has to be able to account for the consistencies in the behavioral expressions of individual

TABLE 16.1 Contributions of Each Level to an Integrated Personality System

Level of Analysis	Key Contributions	Role/Function in System
Psychodynamic-Motivational	Unconscious processing Defensive processing	Processing is often without awareness System is self-defensive, selective, biased
Trait-Dispositional	Broad traits/behavior tendencies; *if* ... *then* ... behavioral signatures	System generates individual differences in broad, stable behavior and *if* ... *then* ... behavioral signatures
Biological	Role of brain processes and genetics in personality; temperament; role of evolution	Interactions with all personality processes;
	Neural network models of brain organization	Metaphors and models for personality organization
Behavioral-Conditioning	Behavior connected to situations	System produces behavior linked closely to situations
	Emotional conditioning Response consequences	Influences system's emotional reactions Influence expectations and behavior scripts
Phenomenological-Humanistic	Subjective perception; cognitive appraisal Self-actualization; self-construction	Basic in system organization and function System is self-organizing, proactive
Social Cognitive	Social learning; social cognitive person variables	Basic in system organization and function, cognitive–affective units; social cognitive person variables

differences. Recall that research at the Trait-Dispositional Level has shown that these consistencies come in two types. To briefly recap:

Overall Average Differences in Types of Behavior (Broad Traits)

In Chapters 3 and 4 you saw that researchers at the Trait-Dispositional Level of analysis searched for, and found, meaningful ways in which people are different from each other "on the whole" (i.e., Type I consistency). They showed that when observers used broad personality trait terms they agree, for example, that some people are perceived as distinctly more sociable than others, some more conscientious than others, some more outgoing and extraverted, and so on for a variety of different characteristics. They also found that people differ reliably and stably from each other in their rated personality characteristics and overall levels of different kinds of behavior. The differences between people at this level have been described and classified systematically on many dimensions or factors, called *supertraits*. You saw this in the contributions of the Big Five, for example, and in research on various important human motives. These characterizations of stable individual differences are useful for many goals, because observers agree reasonably well with each other about peoples' personal qualities described at this level. The findings quantify and categorize individual differences on personality traits and motives that are relatively stable over time, often over many decades.

But as Chapter 4 also showed, and work at other levels confirms, situations are important influences on behavior: if you look closely there is much *within*-person variability in what a given person does, and thinks, and feels, across different situations. Recall that this variability was found first by researchers beginning in the 1920s (e.g., Hartshorne & May, 1928; Newcomb, 1929), who were focusing on behavior as it occurs in particular situations. When they studied behaviors for broad traits like sociability and conscientiousness, and observed what the same individual did across different situations (e.g., in different classes and activities at school, or from school to home to work), they found that a person who was one of the most conscientious at work could be one of the least conscientious at home, for example. Thus the consistency they were looking for turned out to be much less than they had expected and violated their basic assumptions. This surprise would not go away: similar findings kept being reported over many years (e.g., Mischel, 1968; Mischel & Peake, 1982; Pervin, 1994; Peterson, 1968; Shoda, 1990; Vernon, 1964).

If . . . Then . . . Situation–Behavior Signatures of Personality

16.2 What are the two types of personality consistency?

The finding that consistency across different types of situations generally turned out to be lower than expected greatly upset the field. It seemed shocking because the assumption that people are reasonably consistent and predictable, at least some of the time, is at the heart of the concept of personality. Consequently some researchers began to search for possible predictable regularities within the ever-changing stream of behaviors (discussed in detail in Chapter 4). However, to be effective that search requires quantitative studies of behavior of many individuals systematically observed across multiple situations and over time. Because extensive and repeated observation of social behavior as it unfolds in its natural context could not be done until video cameras and adequate computers became available, such research became possible only in the early 1980s when these tools became widely available (e.g., Mischel & Peake, 1982; Mischel & Shoda, 1995; Shoda, Mischel, & Wright, 1993a, 1994; Wright, Lindgren, & Zakriski, 2001). When it finally became possible to conduct, it revealed that such *if . . . then . . .* stable and distinctive patterns do in fact exist and are highly informative about the nature of personality and its expressions (e.g., Borkenau et al., 2006; Mischel & Shoda, 1995; Shoda et al., 1993a,

1994; Wright et al., 2001). These findings demonstrated that these patterns of variability are stable, and form Type II consistency (Mischel, 2004).

Biological Level

Work at this level showed that personality is linked to its biological bases and the human species' evolutionary history. It revealed possible connections between genes, brain, and behavior and focuses on their interactions in the genesis of individual differences. It also shows the value of applying concepts and methods from the study of human evolution and adaptation to understand a wide range of social phenomena, from mating practices to altruism to coping with threat and stress. Insights, findings, and methods from this level open the way to connecting biological processes with work at all the other levels, and to study mind–brain–behavior links in depth. For example, the feelings, thoughts, and personal constructs of interest to the phenomenologists now can be studied using fMRI, allowing one to trace how what we think and understand relates to our brain activities and to behavior. It is a sign of how far the field has moved that mental phenomena not long ago considered beyond the pale of scientific inquiry are now the central subject matter for brain research. An integrative view has to take full account of the biological bases of personality, and the processes through which the person's biological heritage interacts with experiences in the physical and psychological environment.

Psychodynamic-Motivational Level

This level of analysis discovered that people have motives and feelings that are threatening (anxiety-provoking) to them and to other people (e.g., parents) on whom they are dependent. Consequently, self-protective mechanisms and defenses may develop to reduce the anxiety and conflicts that these motives and feelings create. As a result, the expressions of socially unacceptable motives and feelings, such as sexual and aggressive impulses, may become indirect and at least partially outside awareness. The contributions from this level helped build a comprehensive view of personality. It is a view that includes the unconscious and self-protective aspects of personality and the dynamics through which they work. Freud's ideas and findings profoundly influenced clinical psychologists and other therapists, called attention to the importance of processes outside awareness, and provided methods and measures to help deal with a wide variety of personality problems and disorders. They also changed the conception of human nature and personality in much of the Western world. Freud's vision of human nature focused mostly on its dark, tragic side. In his revolutionary view, the person is the product of the conflicts and psychosexual experiences within the first few years of life, victimized by unconscious wishes and conflicts that undermined adaptive, rational behavior. This vision captured basic human qualities that were previously unrecognized.

In extensive expansions of Freud's ideas, but building directly on them, his followers, the ego psychologists, constructed a more optimistic conception of human personality, in which the person is an active agent and architect of his or her own future. Post-Freudians like Erik Erikson called attention to the psychosocial and not just the instinctual or biological psychosexual nature of human development. They recognized that developmental challenges, crises, and changes occur over the entire life span. The post-Freudians appreciated the importance of the unconscious but also incorporated a focus on ego development, cognitive processes, attachment and interpersonal relationships, and the construction of the self, into modern psychodynamic thinking and clinical practice. In these ways many of the developments at the psychodynamic level in the second half of the last century paralleled and enriched those occurring around the same time at the Phenomenological-Humanistic Level that, ironically, originally arose in part as a protest against Freud's conception.

Behavioral-Conditioning Level

The search for the regularities in the stream of behavior began at this level of analysis that focused on analyzing peoples' behavior in relationship to the specific situations in which it occurs, moment by moment. These researchers proposed that what we do is always linked to the particulars of the situations and therefore the specific situation had to be incorporated into the search for regularities in behavior.

Contributions at this level began early in the last century with discoveries about how simple processes of learning and conditioning can help make scientific sense of such phenomena as seemingly irrational fears and impulsive emotional reactions. It created methods for examining experimentally the relationship between changes in conditions and changes in social behavior, opening the way to research basic processes of learning. It demonstrated the importance of the environment in the development and modification of even extremely complex patterns of behavior. It insisted that the study of personality has to include what people do—it has to examine actual social behavior as it unfolds within particular contexts and interactions, not just what people say they do or what they say they are like. Thus, this level provided methods for closely observing and studying behavior and its links to the situations that preceded it and the consequences that followed. It opened the way for a more rigorous approach that went beyond self-reports and ratings to understand what people really do in relation to the situations they encounter and create. For many years, when behaviorism was at its height in the middle of the last century, workers at this level were unwilling to even consider the internal mental and emotional processes within the person because they lacked the methods for investigating them objectively. Since then, advances in ways of studying brain and hormonal processes and emotional reactions provided such methods and brought fresh life to work at this level.

Phenomenological-Humanistic Level

Research at this level went on to show that the effects of situations depend on how the perceiver construes them, that is, on the psychological situation as experienced. Work at this level made clear that the study of what goes on inside the person at the mental-emotional experiential level has to be included in personality psychology and can be investigated with its methods. It called attention to how the ways in which people view (construe, appraise) situations and themselves influence how they feel and how they cope with life challenges and stresses. It showed that individuals don't have to be the victims of their biology and their biography but can do much to change both their life course and their internal states and experiences by altering how they construe or interpret them. And it gave center stage to the experience of the self as both an object that "knows itself" and as an active agent that can act to influence the life course. In all these ways, the pioneers at this level were years ahead of the field. Their contributions have been the foundation for some of the most interesting developments in the evolution of personality psychology as a cumulative science.

Social Cognitive Level

Work at the Social Cognitive Level began by combining contributions from several of the other levels. First, it expanded the understanding of the role of social learning in personality development, noting the crucial importance of cognition and observation in the learning processes most relevant for personality. It showed that humans learn through what they see and observe and hear and read, and do so often even without making any external response or receiving any external rewards. It went on to integrate these insights with findings on work from other levels, including studies of the self, personal constructs, expectancies, values, and goals. It showed the importance of individual differences in these social cognitive person variables, and then investigated how individuals can self-regulate and modify the impact of situations on their own behavior in light of their long-term goals and values. Work at the Social Cognitive Level also provided a model for beginning to combine the contributions of multiple levels to build a more integrated science, closely linked to social psychology and other relevant areas of science, including the study of mind–brain–behavior connections.

A comprehensive and cumulative model of personality has to incorporate the essential contributions from all levels of analysis that we just reviewed into the characteristics of an integrative personality system. Before we go on to outline such a system, however, you also need to recall some basic principles about how the human mind processes social information about the world and the self, and how these principles can be applied to better understand social behavior and personality processes. As discussed in Chapter 15, these principles emerged out of the cognitive revolution. Beginning in the 1970s that revolution in turn led to the development of research on social cognition that spanned both social and personality psychology. Some of its most relevant discoveries for personality dealt with peoples' cognitive structures or schemas. This work showed how schemas influence the ways we interpret situations, other people, and ourselves, the inferences and decisions we make, the events we remember, and the social behaviors we enact in relation to the social world. Chapter 15 also illustrated applications of these principles to understanding such personality-relevant phenomena as how individuals conceptualize the self and significant other people, and the theories they form about themselves and the social world.

▶ TOWARD INTEGRATION: CHARACTERISTICS OF THE PERSONALITY SYSTEM

With this background in mind, we next examine the kind of framework needed to integrate the collective discoveries and principles from all levels of analysis discussed throughout this text.

Application of Neural Network Information-Processing Models to Personality

A large step toward building a comprehensive integrative personality model began with efforts to apply cognitive theories of social information processing to personality. Initially in the 1970s these efforts were based on, and limited by, analogs with information processing in the early computers available at that time (e.g., Carver & Scheier, 1981). Current models of personality as an information-processing system draw heavily, instead, on neural network models in contemporary cognitive neuroscience (e.g., Anderson & Lebiere, 1998; Thompson-Schill, Braver, & Jonides, 2005; Vallacher, Read, & Nowak, 2002; Wager et al., 2005). The metaphor for this network is not based on the digital computer but on biological systems, in particular the systems of connections within the human brain through which the neurons are interconnected and process information. These new models were developed when researchers realized that the ability of the human brain to perform complex information processing does not come from the reasoning that characterizes the digital computer's central processing unit (CPU). It comes instead from the pattern of interconnections among a number of simple units (i.e., neurons) in the human brain and the immense numbers of interconnections among them. Discoveries by visual neuroscientists, for example, have revealed how such networks can extract increasingly complex features from images projected on the retina. This type of neural network model goes far beyond early computer analogs, and promises to have some of the richness and complexity needed for understanding personality.

16.3 What kind of model is suggested that takes into account the contributions of each level?

Applied to personality psychology, a **network information-processing model** focuses not just on how much of a particular quality (e.g., of self-efficacy expectations) a person has. Rather, it emphasizes the way the person's internal mental representations or schemas are related to each other and interconnected to form a system that functions as an organized network structure. In the language of modern cognitive psychology and **connectionist theories**, the **nodes** in the network (conceptually similar to the neurons in the biological theories) are constructs, and their relationships or connections are represented by **links**.

For personality psychology, the technical details of these circuits and pathways in such network structures are not important but the basic overall idea is essential. There are **excitatory (activating) links** and **inhibitory (deactivating) links** in the networks. The more often concepts are activated in your mind, the stronger the excitatory link. When one construct or node gets activated, all of the constructs connected to it get activated. Swimsuits and beaches are closely associated via excitatory links. When I think of swimsuits, I also think of beaches. The less frequently two concepts are activated together, the stronger the inhibitory or deactivating links. Swimsuits and skiing in the snow are connected by an inhibitory link. There is a connection between swimsuits and skiing, but they rarely appear together in life so their relationship actually becomes inhibitory—when we think of one, we are less likely to think of the other. The retrieval of information is mediated by the spreading of activation among the interconnected nodes. Some nodes are only weakly connected with each other or unassociated.

An Application: The Cognitive-Affective Personality System (CAPS)

The **Cognitive–Affective Personality System**, abbreviated as **CAPS**, was developed with the goal of integrating many of the ideas from research on social cognition and cognitive neural network models of the mind into a framework for a comprehensive personality system (Mischel, 2004; Mischel & Shoda, 1995). Although some of the origins of CAPS are rooted in the social cognitive model of personality (e.g., Mischel, 1973) described in Chapter 14, it was designed to take account of the enduring contributions coming from all levels of analysis. Unlike most personality theories, CAPS thus is not a model that "belongs" to any particular theorist, nor to any one level of analysis in personality psychology. It is an evolving general framework for viewing personality in an integrated, comprehensive way. It is a "meta-theory"—a broad framework—that is kept open to change as new findings become available and the science continues to develop.

The label "cognitive–affective processing system" sounds cumbersome but is informative. As the "cognitive" label suggests, this is a framework for a system of personality that deals with knowledge representation. It is an information-processing system, but

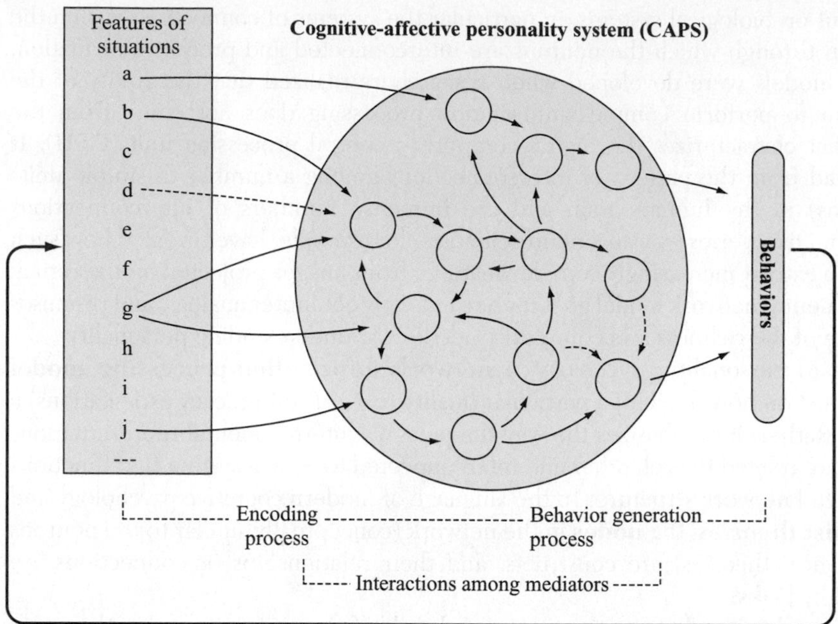

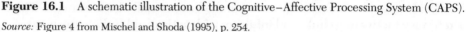

Figure 16.1 A schematic illustration of the Cognitive–Affective Processing System (CAPS).

Source: Figure 4 from Mischel and Shoda (1995), p. 254.

it is not just cognitive and unemotional or "cool." It is also an affective system that deals with how different individuals process "hot," emotion-laden events and feelings (e.g., Kahneman & Snell, 1990; Metcalfe & Mischel, 1999; Smith & Lazarus, 1990). An illustration of CAPS is shown in Figure 16.1.

16.4 What kind of units make up CAPS?

This type of personality system contains diverse mental representations called **cognitive–affective units**, or **CAU**s. Examples of CAUs are the mental representations or schemas of the social cognitive person variables identified at the start of the cognitive revolution in psychology (Mischel, 1973). As discussed in Chapter 14, they include the person's construal (encoding) and representations of the self, people, and situations, enduring goals, expectations-beliefs, and feeling states, as well as memories of people and past events, and diverse competencies, skills, and abilities, including plans and strategies for self-regulation in goal pursuit. CAUs, like all schemas, are activated following basic principles of knowledge activation, such as *accessibility*, as discussed in Chapter 15.

Two Basic Assumptions: Chronic Accessibility and Stable Organization

16.5 Based on the network information-processing system model, in what two ways do individuals differ?

To conceptualize individual differences in personality, this kind of information-processing system builds on just two basic assumptions (Mischel & Shoda, 1995):

1. Individuals differ in how readily and often they access or activate different types of CAUs (e.g., Cervone & Shoda, 1999; Higgins 1996a). Such differences in **chronic accessibility** are seen, for example, in the fact that in ambiguous interpersonal situations some people often encode negative events as instances of personal rejection (e.g., Downey & Feldman, 1996), whereas others tend to feel angry even when they hear a mumbled greeting (e.g., Dodge 1993).

Because people experience many ambiguous interpersonal situations that they can encode in their characteristic ways, large individual differences result in overall average levels of different types of behavior. This is the Type I consistency discussed in Chapter 4.

2. Individuals differ in the distinctive **stable organization of relationships** and pathways among the cognitions and affects (the CAUs) available in the personality system (Mischel & Shoda, 1995). Thus, the expectations, goals, affects, competencies, and behavioral tendencies within the individual's system are interconnected and organized in a relatively stable network structure. In CAPS this is the **personality structure**, and individual differences in personality reflect differences in these structures.

Expressions of Personality Structure: *If . . . Then . . .* Personality Signatures in CAPS

The behavioral expressions of a person's personality structure are seen particularly in his or her characteristic *if . . . then . . .* personality signatures (described in Chapter 4). For example, when Jack takes difficult math tests, he often leaves the exams before finishing. That is because in his personality structure these types of situations activate his anxious thoughts, and these are strongly connected to failure feelings that escalate into panic, avoidance, and withdrawal. In contrast, Maria's highly anxious thoughts on these exams quickly activate "cooling down" strategies that let her relax briefly and then renew her problem-solving efforts. So Jack and Maria may be the same overall in the anxiety that each experiences, but they differ in how their anxiety reactions in turn are connected to, and activate, a whole chain of the other CAUs in predictable patterns. For Jack it may lead to avoidance reactions, while for Maria it leads to cooling off and renewed effort, and for each the distinctive interconnections activated within the system play out in a characteristic *if . . . then . . .* personality signature.

16.6 How does the CAPS model account for individual differences in behavior?

As the person experiences situations that contain different psychological features, different CAUs interconnected within the system become activated in characteristic patterns. Therefore the activation of CAUs changes from one situation to another. This change occurs not only within the individual psychologically but also in what is expressed and enacted in behavior. For example, the "self" (technically, the self-schemas) activated in relation to mother when visiting the family for the holidays is different from the one experienced in relation to one's partner on the drive home, and each plays out in characteristic patterns of behavior (e.g., Andersen & Chen, 2002; Zayas, Shoda, & Ayduk, 2002). Thus, because the *ifs* are different (i.e., mother vs. partner) the *thens* (i.e., what one does in response to each person) are different. The result is a distinctive pattern of *if . . . then . . .* relations as the individual deals with different types of psychological situations, for example, more dependent and compliant with the mother at home, more assertive with the partner in the car. Consequently, the person's behavior changes predictably in relation to changes in situations, resulting in Type II consistency (Chapter 4).

Note that the CAUs that become activated within a person change depending on the situation, even though the personality structure—the organized network itself—does not (Mischel & Shoda, 1995; Shoda & Mischel, 1998). Each individual's personality structure is relatively stable, and is predisposed in distinctive ways, both by its biological bases (e.g., temperament, genetic predispositions), and by its psychosocial-developmental history (e.g., Cervone, 2004; Mischel, 2004; Mischel & Shoda 1995).

Personality Dispositions (Processing Dynamics)

Personality dispositions, also called **processing dynamics**, in CAPS are the person's characteristic patterns of CAUs—the thoughts, feelings, and behavior tendencies—that become activated in distinctive psychological situations, seen in the *if* ... *then* ... signatures of personality. A good example is the **rejection sensitivity (RS)** disposition or dynamic, defined by Geraldine Downey and colleagues as the tendency to expect and overreact anxiously to potential rejection cues (Downey & Feldman, 1996). This type of individual has high expectations of rejection (i.e., schemas) that get activated in situations that are applicable to rejection, for example, in a conflict with a romantic partner in which rejection by the partner is possible. These expectations are linked to a readiness to encode ambiguous interpersonal experiences as intentional rejection, which in turn activate hot affect, particularly anxiety, and maladaptive behavioral scripts, such as aggressive overreactions and withdrawal/avoidance. To unpack that abstract definition of personality dispositions and dynamics, and illustrate the concept concretely, let's look at what research has revealed about two different well-studied processing dispositions.

16.7 What differentiates traits from processing dispositions?

The Rejection Sensitivity (RS) Signature: Finding Both *If* ... *Then* ... and Trait Components

RS and Aggression

Figure 16.2 summarizes empirical findings that link high RS to aggression in social behavior. As you can see, high RS people are not overall more aggressive than low RS people in their mean level of aggressiveness. Instead they show a specific *if* ... *then* ... signature. High RS people's aggression is specifically elicited in situations in which they perceive rejection (Ayduk et al., 1999). In the absence of perceived rejection, however, high RS people are not any more aggressive than low RS people. In fact, they may even show a tendency to be lower in aggression. For example, high RS women tend to be especially solicitous, putting the other person's needs first in their relationships (e.g., Purdie & Downey, 2000). This is because high RS people care about preventing rejection and attaining acceptance and may behave in overly accommodating or even self-ingratiating ways when things in their relationships are going relatively well.

In short, then, when it comes to aggressive behavior, the behavioral signature of high RS people is that they are aggressive *when* they feel rejected but not aggressive

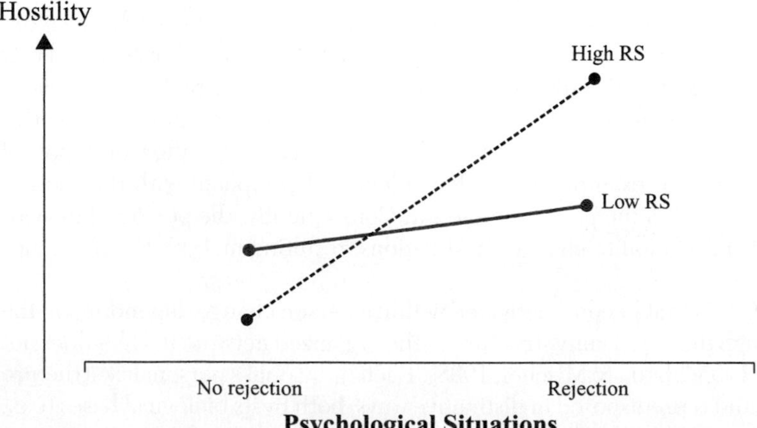

Figure 16.2 Situation–behavior profiles for rejection sensitivity and aggression.

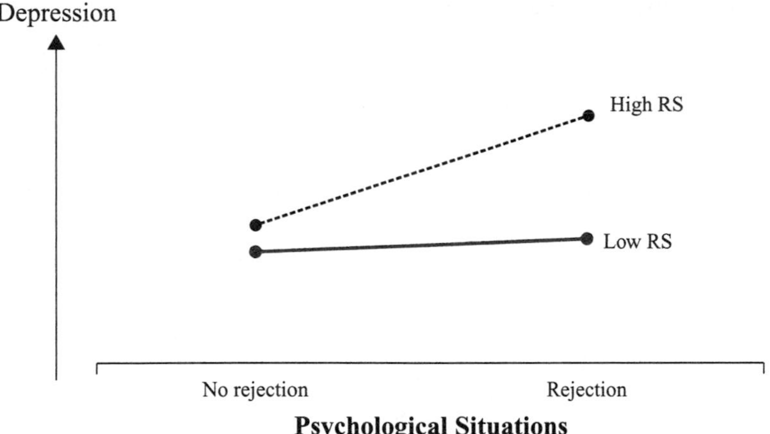

Figure 16.3 Situation–behavior profiles for rejection sensitivity and depression.

when they are in situations that do not communicate rejection. However, they are not overall more likely than others to express anger, disapproval, and coercive behaviors in certain types of intimate situations.

16.8 Describe the relationship between RS and aggression.

RS and Depression

Figure 16.3 summarizes findings on high RS people's depression. In contrast to aggression, we see mean level differences in depression between high and low RS individuals: the former shows higher levels of depressed affect and behavior across situations than the latter. This is an example of a broader, trait level manifestation of RS.

In addition, however, we also see they exhibit a behavioral signature for depression that is similar to the one for their aggression. Although high RS people are more depressed than low RS people overall, this difference is especially magnified in situations of rejection. For example, Ayduk, Downey, and Kim (2001) followed up college women in relationships across the course of a semester. They assessed whether during that time women experienced breakups initiated solely by their partners, by themselves, or by mutual agreement. The findings indicated that high RS women showed a significant increase in feelings of depression from the start to the end of the semester if in the interim they had experienced a partner-initiated breakup but not if the breakup was self- or mutually initiated. Given that partner-initiated breakup communicates rejection in particular, the *if . . . then . . .* profile displayed by high RS people is such that they get especially depressed when rejected. In contrast, low RS women showed the same low level of depression whether they were rejected or not.

The Narcissistic Signature

Narcissism is another well-studied example of a personality disposition conceptualized in a CAPS-like framework. Narcissists are people whom most of us have met, and when we do, we rarely forget them; although when we get to know them, we often find them extremely difficult to deal with and wish we had never met them. Think of the vain would-love-to-be a movie star type, deeply in love with himself, and ever-eager to prove how wonderful he is—almost desperately trying to convince himself as well as the world that he is really the greatest.

The **behavioral signature of narcissists** (Morf, 2006; Morf & Rhodewalt, 2001a, 2001b) has a striking key feature. Narcissists are vigilant for opportunities in which they can affirm and bolster their grandiose self-concepts (Morf, Ansara, & Shia, 2001; Morf, Weir, & Davidov, 2000; Rhodewalt & Eddings, 2002). They are characterized by the pattern of *if* opportunities to promote the self, *then* much effort is put out toward proving its superiority over everybody else. They have cynical views of other people, seem insensitive to their concerns, and lack empathy for them. Research shows, for example, that if they are in situations that usually call for modesty, as when others outperform them, they nevertheless readily derogate their competitors, belittling their achievements. Remarkably they tend to do so even when the long-term costs turn out to be self-defeating and destructive to the relationships that they are trying to build (Morf, 2006). They also protect themselves by reinterpreting their experiences in ways that ingeniously amplify any positive feedback they may have received while ignoring or discounting all the negative (Morf & Rhodewalt, 2001a, 2001b). In sum, their dynamics, both inside their heads and in their relationships to the social world, seem driven by their attempts to convince themselves and the world that everybody really loves them. They may, however, be struggling to convince themselves that they are in fact lovable.

16.9 What is the *if . . . then . . .* signature of someone who is narcissistic?

The behavioral signatures and processing dynamics of the narcissistic and the high rejection-sensitivity types share some characteristics but are meaningfully different in other ways, such as their underlying goals and motivations (Morf, 2006). Narcissists treat interpersonal situations as challenges for eagerly showing off how good they are by outdoing and outperforming other people and trying to be in the spotlight. In contrast, rejection-sensitive people in the same situations anxiously scan them for potential personal rejection, motivated to prevent getting hurt, and all set to magnify even a hint of criticism, and to quickly overreact to the prospect.

The model of narcissism developed by Morf and colleagues (Morf, 2006; Morf & Rhodewalt, 2001) connects the CAPS approach to personality dynamics with work on the self and identity. They propose that the motivation that underlies the narcissistic personality type, and other types as well, involves the person's efforts to regulate their own behavior to be consistent with the desired selves (or self-schemas) that they are trying to build and maintain. This dynamic self-construction process plays out not just internally, but in the person's relationships with other people. In this model, a grandiose, yet vulnerable, self-concept drives narcissists to seek continuous external self-affirmation in the social arena. But because narcissists are insensitive to other peoples' concerns and are often critical and confrontational, their self-construction efforts risk failing in the long run. Their behavior helps maintain their self-esteem in the short term, but undermines their interpersonal relationships in the long term and can be self-defeating, undermining the self and self-esteem they are struggling, perhaps too hard, to build, and never seem to attain. Morf's (2006) model and research program address a basic aim of personality psychology by simultaneously identifying trait-like individual differences and analyzing the psychological processes that generate them.

Personality Development and Change

Recall that a basic CAPS assumption is that each personality system is characterized by a distinctive relatively stable organization in the interconnections among its CAUs. As was discussed, it is this organization that makes up the personality structure. Where does it come from? How does it change in the course of development? What remains stable? What changes? What are the conditions that lead to stability versus change? These kinds of questions drive research on personality development within the CAPS framework, and you have seen some of the answers in previous chapters: they draw on findings from work at all levels of analysis.

Personality development and change involve both biochemical and social cognitive influences and processes in continuous interactions. For example, individual differences in temperament or reactivity, such as activity, irritability, tension, distress, and emotional lability, become visible early in life (Bates & Wachs, 1994). They interact with a host of other psychological and biochemical factors to influence the cognitive and affective structures and organization that evolves rapidly in the first few years of life (e.g., Rothbart et al., 1994). The personality system may change as a result of modification in the biological substrates or developmental changes and significant life events. The effects may be seen as a change in the personality structure, and in the situation–behavior signatures and dynamics that become activated in relation to different kinds of situations at different points in development.

Features and Findings Integrated from Each Level

Now let's look at how a model like CAPS incorporates, and takes account of, key contributions from the varying levels of analysis.

To recap, the Trait-Dispositional Level identified two types of behavioral consistency in the expressions of personality, and an adequate model of the personality system has to be able to take account of both types. CAPS has been shown to predict and generate both Type I and Type II consistencies in people's behavior (Shoda & Mischel, 1998). Computer simulations and empirical studies have demonstrated that this type of system generates unique and stable profiles of variability (Shoda, 2007), reflected in stable *if* ... *then* ... behavioral signatures (Mischel & Shoda, 1995; Shoda et al., 1993b, 1994). Different psychological situations trigger different processing dynamics (i.e., the particular CAUs that become activated) that result in behavioral signatures. So when the *if*s change, so do the person's behaviors. However, they do so in predictable patterns because the underlying personality structure—the network of interconnections among the CAUs—remains stable. CAPS also generates mean differences in the average levels of these profiles that are indicative of broader trait-level individual differences, reflecting stable individual differences in the chronic accessibility of different types of CAUs (Shoda & Mischel, 1998, 2000; Shoda et al., 2002).

16.10 How does the CAPS model incorporate all six levels of analysis?

In CAPS the contributions from the *Biological Level* are fundamental. Temperament and biological history and genetic endowment, just as much as psychosocial and learning history, underlie the development and organization of the personality structure in CAPS. This biological prewiring constrains and guides how that structure deals with different types of information. The biological level also showed that the way these biological structures are expressed and evolve depends on continuous two-way reciprocal interactions with the environment, from conception on, beginning in the womb and extending throughout the life course. In addition, current research influenced by CAPS focuses on mind–brain connections (and ultimately links to the genetic endowment), as in studies of self-control that relate how people think and appraise situations to their brain activity (e.g., Lieberman, 2007; Ochsner & Lieberman, 2001).

Consistent with the discovery at the *Psychodynamic–Motivational Level* that much if not most of the mind operates at levels outside awareness and plays out in automatic ways, CAPS is a neural network model that operates rapidly and functions at multiple levels, often outside conscious awareness (Kihlstrom, 1999, 2003). That happens in **automatic processing**; such processing relies on preexisting schemas and is usually involuntary, unconscious, and requires no motivation to be activated. There is a great deal of such automatic, uncontrolled processing in CAPS. But as the ego psychologists recognized, much that is important in personality and adaptive functioning also requires cognition and thinking. That plays out in **controlled processing** and conscious thought, as in planning, problem solving, future-oriented decision making, and self-control. It requires motivation, effort, and self-regulatory competencies, and often is essential for overcoming impulsive responding that could lead to unfortunate future consequences. When one first begins to drive it is a controlled process, but years later it becomes an automatic process that runs more or less on its own much of the time. The same is true for self-control patterns, as in control efforts to overcome eating or drug abuse problems; at first much effortful control may be required, but ultimately it can become mostly automatic.

Also consistent with discoveries at the psychodynamic level, CAPS is a "hot" emotion–driven, reflexive, affective personality system, just as much as it also is a cool, more reflective, cognitive system. The interactions among the hot system and the cool system within CAPS have at least a strong family resemblance to the Freudian id and ego systems. The way these subsystems interact is examined in the next chapter on processes in self-regulation within this type of model.

The focus both on the situation and on behavior—on what the person does—was a core contribution from the *Behavioral-Conditioning Level* and it is an integral part of CAPS. The connections activated in the personality system at any time depend on the particular situation with which the individual is interacting. Thus the CAPS personality structure continuously interacts with the situations experienced, and the processing of this information is played out at the behavioral level, expressed in the two types of consistency discussed previously. Likewise, the CAUs include expectations and other schemas that reflect the individual's social learning history and the consequences that different types of behavior have yielded in the past in similar situations. To the degree that experiences in the course of development change the activation level of different CAUs, and even the interconnections among them, the personality structure itself continues to evolve.

You can see the contributions of the *Phenomenological-Humanistic Level* to CAPS in the emphasis on the *psychological* situation, that is, the situation as perceived and appraised or construed by the individual, not just on the objective stimulus. Moreover, these psychological situations are not just external; they also are self-generated and internal, experienced in such processes as planning, thinking, remembering, daydreaming, and exercising effortful control in long-term goal pursuit and so on, and even created by one's own mood and affective states. These processes within CAPS integrate the phenomenological focus on the self and the ability of individuals to be agentic and proactive in influencing their own futures.

Likewise, key findings from the *Social Cognitive Level* are integrated into CAPS by incorporating such cognitive social person variables as the person's expectancies, goals, values, and self-regulatory competencies. All of these schemas are represented in the CAUs that are interconnected within the personality system. They play out in the personality signatures activated in different psychological situations that in turn account for the two types of consistency identified at the trait-dispositional level.

While far from complete, these examples point to the fact that a CAPS framework is responsive to, and takes account of, key findings from all levels of analysis. Most important, it does so not only by integrating the past, but also by being open to continuous modification, and if needed disconfirmation, in light of new insights and discoveries that are sure to come in the future.

In sum, CAPS was designed as an integrative neural network information-processing model, built to take account of the enduring contributions from all levels of analysis. CAPS is a dynamic social–cognitive–affective information system—a personality system that interacts with situations and generates the distinctive stable patterns of thoughts, feelings, and behaviors that characterize an individual. In this framework, individuals are potentially proactive social agents transacting with the specific challenges and constraints of their lives, rather than passive victims of their social and biological histories who simply act out their received traits and genetic predispositions. CAPS takes account situations but without depriving the person of agency: the personality system, and the person, within this model are *proactive* and "agentic" in the sense that it is the individual who not only selects and in part constructs many of the situations experienced, but who also can change their meaning and thus their impact.

16.11 In what ways are individuals considered to be proactive in the CAPS model?

THE PERSONALITY SYSTEM IN ACTION

The CAPS framework assumes that the impact or "power" of the external situation depends, at least in part, on how the person construes or encodes it, that is, on the internal psychological situation. The internal situation consists of the personal meanings that situations have acquired for the individual. Those meanings in turn activate the stream of thoughts, feelings, expectations, goals, and scripts that reflect the underlying coherent, organized structure of personality. This type of system is dynamic, self-generating, and not limited to "inside the head"; it is contextualized within the social world, and enacted in the transactions between the individual and the situations encountered and created. To illustrate the workings of the personality system in those interactions, we turn to an example from Gary W.'s life.

Figure 16.4 gives a glimpse of the multiple processes and interactions operating in this type of cognitive–affective personality system. It contains representations for a host of dispositions, internal characteristics, and person variables that have been identified and studied by researchers working at all levels of analysis. You saw these

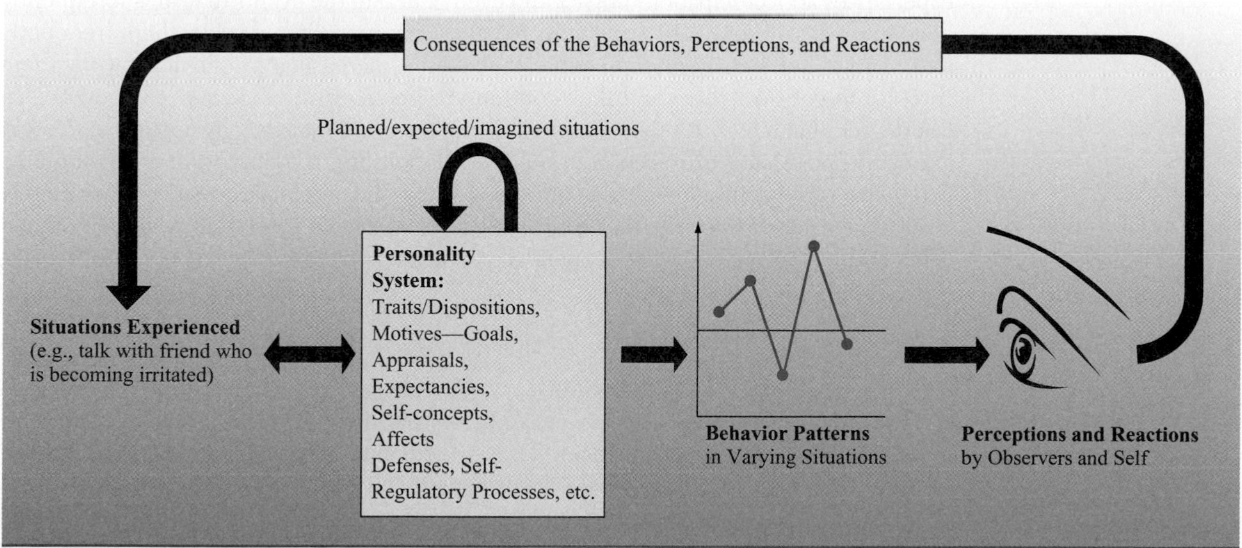

Figure 16.4 The personality system in context.

throughout the text, and they were applied concretely to the case of Gary in many earlier chapters. They include his biological dispositions (e.g., BIS/BAS), psychological traits, appraisals, expectancies, self-concepts, goals, self-protective defenses, and self-regulatory processes—and much more.

External and Internal Sources of Activation

The personality system is in a continuous state of activation, and the activations come from two sources. One source is *external activation* that comes from the situations encountered at a given moment in time. Consider, for example, a conversation Gary is having with his friend in which the friend is becoming irritated. The **active ingredients** are the features of those situations to which Gary is particularly attuned, such as potential rejection cues in an interpersonal context—in this case, the signs of the friend's irritation. These are the features—the psychological situations—for which Gary scans attentively and to which his personality system reacts distinctively and characteristically in stable patterns, that is, in terms of his personality dynamics. The two-way arrow from the situations to his personality system indicates that the two are in **reciprocal interaction**, each influencing the other. Gary's personality system selects and focuses on those active ingredients in the situations experienced, and it is also influenced by them, for example, leading him to an outburst of temper.

16.12 Explain what reciprocal interaction means in a personality system.

The second source is internal activation, in the form of Gary's own thoughts and feelings and plans, for example, as he ruminates about himself and his relationships or thinks and plans what to do tomorrow. Research has examined how people activate their own dynamics by thinking about situations, by ruminating about them (e.g., Nolen-Hoeksema et al., 1994), or through selective recall and reexperiences of past events and feelings, and selective attention to different aspects of the self, such as one's perceived strengths, resources, vulnerabilities, conflicts, ambivalences, and anticipated future (e.g., Bandura, 1986; Kross, Ayduk, & Mischel, 2005; Mischel, Ebbesen, & Zeiss, 1973, 1976; Norem & Cantor, 1986). Even in daydreaming, fantasies, and scenarios that are planned or imagined we create our own internal trigger stimuli that may activate our characteristic dynamics (e.g., Taylor & Schneider, 1989). These internal experiences and anticipations impact and even generate the events that we subsequently encounter. If you ruminate about your rejection experiences and relive them frequently and vividly and angrily in your mind, it makes it increasingly difficult to work them through to get over them and they continue to be reactivated (Kross et al., 2005). To the degree that a high RS person, for example, becomes increasingly anxious and angry about the possibility of rejection in a close relationship, the chance of a self-fulfilling prophecy—and getting rejected—increases. Thus, the personality system is not merely reactive: it is also proactive, that is, future-oriented, in the sense that what you do and think and feel influences what happens to you next.

Expressions of the System—and Their Consequences

At the behavioral level, the behaviors Gary generates are represented in the figure as an *if . . . then . . .* behavioral signature to indicate that they occur in particular distinctive situations (e.g., his temper outbursts occur *if* rejection is perceived) and play out over time in stable ways. This profile also has an overall level in terms of the total amount of the characteristic behavior (e.g., hostility, temper-anger) he tends to display on average.

Gary's behaviors influence the situations he encounters in the future. The eye that is seeing his behavior in Figure 16.4 indicates that what he does is also observed and experienced by perceivers. One of these perceivers is Gary himself: We not only generate behavior, we also perceive and interpret it. Obviously, how he sees and interprets his outburst may be quite different from how others, for example, his partner, will view it and in turn react. Those perceptions affect what happens next by changing how the people who observe Gary respond to his behavior. This is indicated in the figure by the large curved arrow that shows those perceptions and their behavioral consequences influencing the subsequent situations that Gary is likely to experience.

16.13 How does Gary's behavior influence the situations he experiences?

Over the course of time, the characteristics of the personality system change the stable psychological environment the individual tends to experience. Thus, people not only impose their own meanings on situations, but through their own behavior, they also select and create many of the situations they experience (e.g., Buss, 1996; Kenrick & Funder, 1988; Swann, 1983). Gary's case illustrates this process of how one can shape one's own situations. Because he dreads social-evaluative situations, he avoids them whenever he can, preferring to isolate himself. This further strengthens his inclination to withdraw and be a "loner" and isolates him even more. A side effect is that he never learns to confront and cope more effectively with the social encounters he fears most. This is painfully evident in public speaking situations that he simply cannot avoid, and in which he easily panics, especially when he feels himself being evaluated by respected male peers in business contexts. His panic response further elicits the disrespect and "snickers" of his peers, thereby intensifying his dread and avoidance pattern in a vicious cycle.

Gary's preference for isolation and withdrawal has by now become a well-established pattern. He even announces to acquaintances that he prefers his own company to meeting other people, which they perceive as a rejection by him or an expression of aloofness. Then they reciprocate by avoiding him, which isolates him even more and fuels his sense of alienation and distrust. In this way, personality variables influence the choice of the types of situations to which people expose themselves (e.g., Bolger & Schilling, 1991; Buss, 1987). For example, individuals who cooperate tend to elicit reciprocal cooperation from their partners on a task, which in turn confirms and strengthens their choice of a cooperative rather than a competitive strategy (Kelley & Stahelski, 1970).

The analysis of complex social interactions shows how each person continuously selects, changes, and generates conditions just as much as they are affected by them (e.g., Patterson, 1976, 1990). In classic studies, husband–wife interactions were observed as the couples coped with such conflicts as how to celebrate their first wedding anniversary when each had made different plans (Raush, Barry, Hertel, & Swain, 1974). For example, Bob has arranged and paid in advance for dinner at a restaurant, but Sue has spent half the day preparing for a special dinner at home. As the couple realize their conflict and try to resolve it, their interactions continuously reveal that each antecedent act (what Sue has just said to Bob) constrains each consequent act (how Bob responds).

The interpersonal strategy in such interactions depends both on the type of person and the type of situation. For example, in the context of getting along with a peer, a more dependent person is likely to use a self-denigrating strategy. On the other hand, when the situation focuses on pleasing an authority, the dependent person is apt to use a self-promoting strategy (Bornstein et al., 1996). Once more, we see the effects of person–situation interactions.

Shaping One's Own Future Situations: Selecting Dating Partners

The fact that individuals in part create the interpersonal situations they are likely to encounter has many nonobvious implications. A widespread belief in today's society is that some people may be recreating past relationship experiences, even if they are negative and potentially harmful, through the dating partners they select. A series of studies by Zayas and Shoda (2007) examined how people shape their close interpersonal environments, both actively (e.g., by the people they choose to interact with) and passively (e.g., by the people that they attract). To assess who people choose to interact with, the researchers developed a mock Internet dating service. Participants read descriptions of various dating partners (written by actual people) that differed systematically on key personal characteristics. After reading all the personal ads, participants then selected those individuals that they wanted to get to know better. The researchers found that women who had reported more instances of experiencing psychological abuse (e.g., partners called them names, yelled at them, were controlling and jealous) in their most recent romantic relationship were three times more likely to select a personal ad that had been judged by a separate group of women as potentially abusive.

The researchers further speculated that women with certain personal characteristics, such as an adult attachment style characterized by dependency and insecurity, may be preferred by abusive men. Consistent with this idea, men who had reported more instances of inflicting psychological abuse in a past romantic relationship were two times more likely (compared to men who had not) to prefer a female dating partner characterized by high insecurity and dependency. These studies highlight how people shape their environments through the people they choose to interact with as well as the people that they attract. The findings also suggest that characteristics of potential dating partners are "psychological ingredients" of situations that affect partner preferences. For example, aggressiveness and jealousy in potential male dating partners may be a "psychological ingredient" attracting women who have experienced psychological abuse in the past, and an anxious attachment style in potential female dating partners may be a salient psychological ingredient influencing the partner preference of men who have been abusive in the past. Thus, perhaps unwittingly, people may keep creating for themselves in the future more of the same problems that proved harmful to them in the past.

Regardless of the quality of the interactions, the close relationship among romantic partners may in time develop its own distinctive CAPS-like personality, as discussed in *In Focus 16.1*.

Applying CAPS to Real-Life Problems: Breast Self-Examination

16.14 How does the network information-processing system model help to explain why risk information can make some women more likely to perform breast self-examinations and others less likely to do so?

The CAPS model is being applied to understanding individual differences in dealing with a wide variety of important life problems. The first task, for the researcher, or the clinician, or anyone who wants to apply this kind of model to real-life situations, is to identify the particular problem that needs to be addressed and the specific goals. It all depends, for example, whether the purpose is to identify people likely to make good roommates for you, or a person likely to become a good life partner for you, or strategies likely to help you work toward important personal goals more effectively.

In one such study the specific goal was to understand why some women at risk for breast cancer adhere to recommendations to perform breast self-examination to detect breast cancer at an early stage, while others find it very difficult to do so, even when their objective medical situations and risks are the same. Figures 16.5 and 16.6 each depict a type of individual and their network of cognitions and affects relevant for the decision and actual performance of breast self-examination (BSE) (Miller et al., 1996). The formation of BSE-relevant choices, decisions, and intentions are illustrated on the

IN FOCUS 16.1

WHEN THE "SITUATION" IS ANOTHER PERSON: THE PERSONALITY OF CLOSE RELATIONSHIPS

CAPS is not only a model of the person but also of situations when they consist of other people. In a close relationship, one person's behavioral output becomes the other person's situational input, and vice versa, and the two form an interpersonal system. If each partner's personality is characterized by a stable *if* ... *then* ... behavioral signature, the interactions between them can be modeled to predict the "personality" of the interpersonal system they form. That system has its own distinctive relationship signature and dynamics, as discussed in a theoretical paper by Zayas, Shoda, and Ayduk (2002).

Intuitively, a long-term interpersonal relationship is sometimes said to have its own personality—a personality that becomes more than simply an average of the personalities within it. Think of the unlikely combinations of partners that may work best because their "chemistry" is right. The CAPS analysis allows one to model these emergent qualities of relationships, and their links to the personalities of the individuals as their interpersonal systems evolve.

In a CAPS demonstration study, each individual was modeled by a stable and distinct *if* ... *then* ... pattern or "behavioral signature," where "if" is the psychological features present in a situation, and "then" is the cognitions and affects that become activated by them (Shoda et al., 2002; Zayas et al., 2002). This conceptualization of an individual makes it possible to explicitly model in computer simulations the process by which the "personality" of relationships emerges out of the interactions among individuals.

Studies of the emergent qualities of interpersonal relationships ultimately may allow specific predictions about the cognitions, affects, and behaviors of an individual in a given relationship, based on information about the partner. In a loose analogy, the possibility is not unlike that of chemistry, in which the "behaviors" of substance A in reaction to substance B are predicted by knowing the molecular structures of both. Understanding and empirically assessing each individual's cognitive–affective system may be a step toward being able to predict the "chemistry" of interpersonal systems, as well as that of the individual in interaction with the important situations of life. A great deal has been learned about situations, making it possible to construct a taxonomy of them, as illustrated by Harold Kelley and colleagues (2003) in their *Atlas of Interpersonal Situations*. That taxonomy identifies more than two dozen situations that have been found to be important in social psychological research, classified in terms of the kinds of psychological challenges they present (e.g., delay of gratification, cooperation with a partner in difficult situations that create conflicts of interest).

16.15 How does CAPS account for "chemistry" in close, interpersonal relationships?

left half of the oval and their behavioral execution is illustrated on the right half. A solid arrow connecting one cognitive–affective unit to another indicates that the activation of the first increases the activation of the second (i.e., excitatory links). Broken arrows show that the activation of the first reduces or inhibits the activation of the second (i.e., inhibitory links). Individuals may differ in the strength with which this thought is activated. Such individual differences are shown by arrows of different thicknesses. For example, Arrow 1 in Figure 16.5 is thicker than Arrow 1 in Figure 16.6, indicating that for a woman whose network resembles Figure 16.5, the objective risk information strongly activates the thought "I may develop breast cancer." In contrast, for a woman whose network resembles Figure 16.6, the objective risk information does not activate this thought as strongly.

Research has also shown that women differ in the types of outcomes that they imagine, following the detection of a lump. For example, some may imagine a scenario in which early detection leads to a cure (Arrow 7), whereas for others, more negative outcomes will be salient (Arrow 8). Depending on whether a woman's cognitive–affective processing network resembles Figure 16.5 or Figure 16.6, the risk information can have potentially opposing effects. On the one hand, risk information is expected to strengthen the intention to perform a BSE, through Arrow 3, as well as through arrows 1, 6, 7,

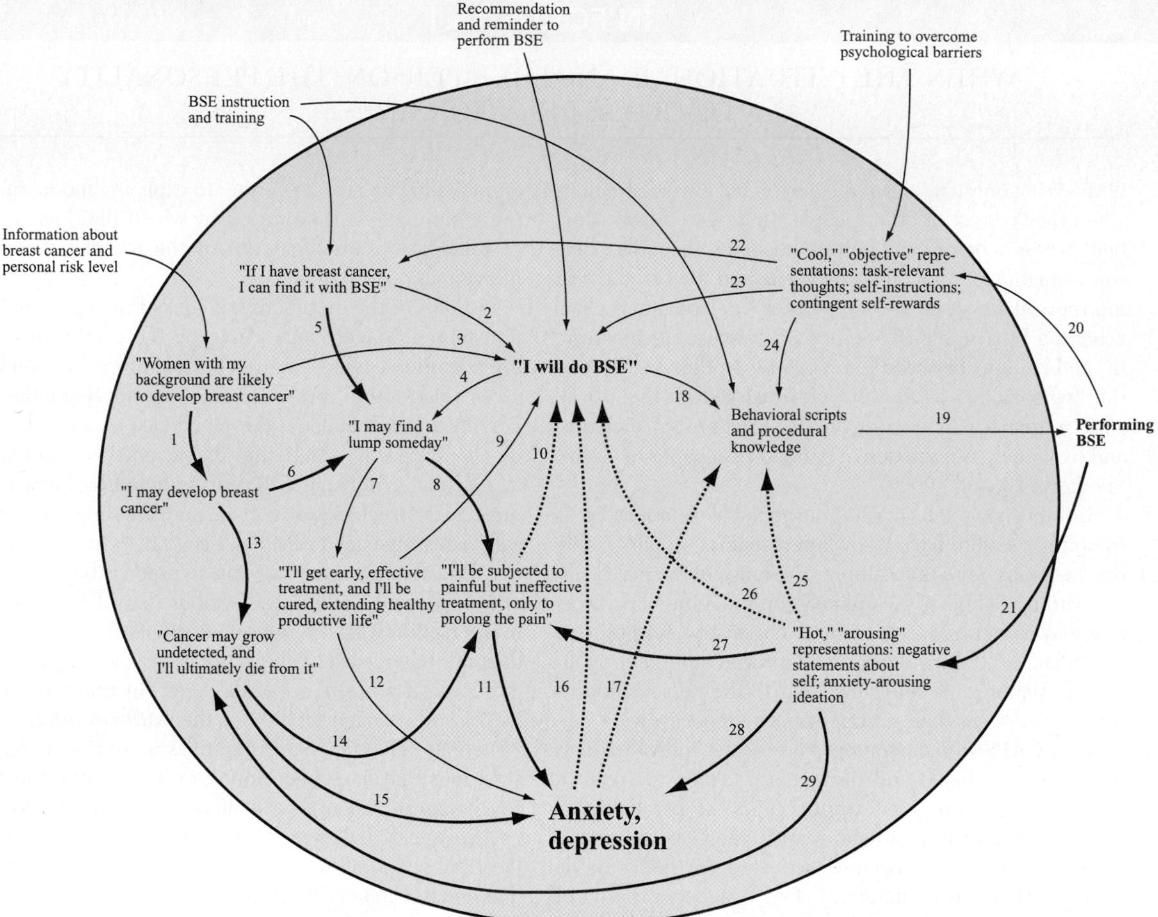

Figure 16.5 An illustrative CAPS network that undermines intention and performance of BSE. Situational features activate specific subsets of the mediating units, which in turn activate other mediating units. The networks of connections are considered stable and characterize the individual. Arrows indicate activation relationships, such that when one unit is activated, other units that receive solid arrows from it will receive activation proportional to the weight associated with each arrow. The weight may be positive (solid arrows) or negative (dashed arrows).

Source: Based on, and adapted from, Figure 5 of Miller, Shoda, and Hurley (1996), p. 83.

and 9. On the other hand, risk information also increases the negative affect and anxious arousal that become activated (Arrows 1, 13, and 15, as well as Arrows 1, 6, 8, and 11), which can become overwhelming and thereby activate avoidance (Arrow 16). This would lead a woman to avoid even confronting her situation (e.g., by denial of her breast cancer risk; Rippetoe & Rogers, 1987).

Getting "Under the Hood": What is the Person Thinking, Feeling, Doing in the Situation?

CAPS can also be applied to examine the psychological differences between individuals at the concrete level of everyday life and experience. In this illustration we do so, focusing on two young friends, Veronica and Martha, to see what they are thinking and

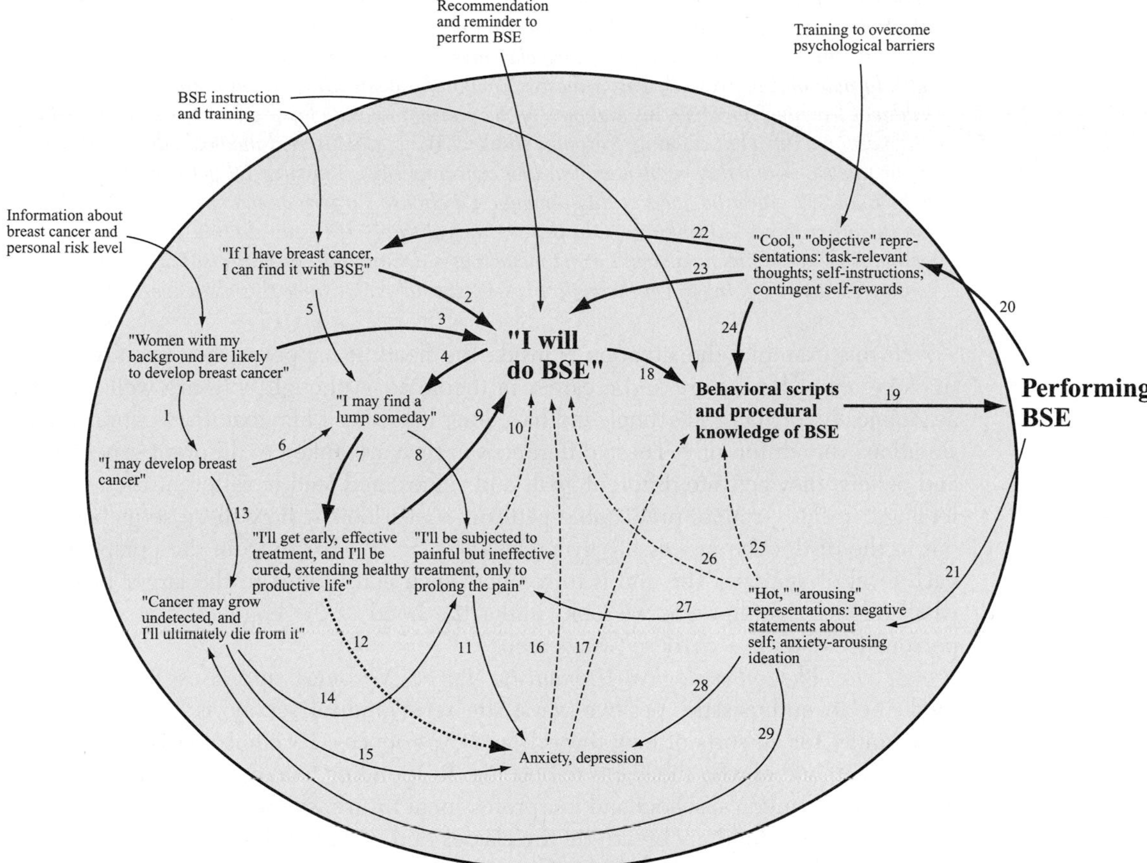

Figure 16.6 An illustrative CAPS network that enhances intention and performance of BSE.

Source: Based on, and adapted from, Figure 6 of Miller, Shoda, and Hurley (1996), p. 84.

feeling and doing in a stressful situation they both face. We use this illustration to show how CAPS integrates contributions from diverse levels of analysis to understand the life dilemmas individuals face, each in his or her distinctive ways.

A few years ago, Veronica and Martha were close college friends, although they could hardly be more different. Veronica "goes for the gold"—she is open to possibilities for new challenges and gratifications every day. This is true for her, whether in the sports world in which she excels, or in taking on academic challenges, or in her readiness for new weekend adventures. Her roommate Martha is at the opposite pole—she always "plays it safe." When Veronica says "Let's get pizza," Martha says, "But it's so full of calories!" But Martha is determined. Once she sets her mind on something, she diligently works toward it and almost always achieves her goal. When they were in college she typically tried out several classes before staying in any, and dropped those that looked like they could be too much for her. Although she often thought that most would be too difficult, usually she actually was able deal with them. In fact, to her own surprise, she turned out to be an excellent student even in difficult courses and on average her grades were better than Veronica's.

Now, four years later, Veronica and Martha are in their third year in medical school, a goal they long dreamed about. They both have successfully finished the grueling coursework in biochemistry, and today, on the first day of class in anatomy, they dissect a cadaver. With their shiny new dissecting kits, dissecting manuals, and scrub suits, each begins dissecting a real human body for the first time. Two classmates leave the lab 15 minutes into dissection, visibly pale and distressed. This semester, they will be spending many hours next to their cadaver learning the seven ins and outs of the pterygopalatine fossa and other structures in the nasal cavity. That evening, Veronica thinks: "Wow, finally, real medical education. I'm a bit uneasy about this right now, but like everyone says, I'm sure I'll get used to it, and who knows, I might be good at this—maybe I'll choose surgery as my specialty." Martha, on the other hand, is thinking: "OK, this is the real thing. If I can't do this, no matter how many A's I get in biochemistry, I won't make it as a doctor. But the truth is, I almost fainted today. How am I going to get through this semester when we have this class every week?"

In this example, the situation is inside the head: it happens when each woman is thinking about her future and a career in medicine. Although both are well qualified academically for medical school, and have long had it as a life goal, they appraise their situations very differently. These differences in turn are linked to different expectancies and beliefs, they activate different goals and values, and lead to different thoughts and feelings, in fairly stable, predictable patterns. Let's look at how these sequences play out in the distinctive processing dynamics for each. We do so from the perspective of each level of analysis. The aim is to see how each contributes to the larger picture of what might be going on as we look "under the hood of the engine"—the minds and personality systems—of these two women.

At the Phenomenological-Humanistic Level, Veronica appraises her future in medicine in enthusiastic, positive ways; she sees medical school as a challenge and opportunity for all sorts of new rewards and experiences. It seems consistent with her sense of self and of who she wants to become. Responding to a questionnaire asking her to think about medical school and her professional future, she writes: ". . . I know I will hardly be able to hold my breath till the classes end, at last, at last, and the real clinical work gets going—not with cadavers in anatomy lessons—struggling, sweating all night in the emergency room, fighting to save a life hanging in the balance—How do I feel? Proud! Proud and happy . . . and eager for more."

In sharp contrast, Martha construes the prospect as full of threats. She perceives her "imagined future in medicine" as a whole new set of possibilities for failure and distress, a "can of worms." Like Veronica, she feels committed to becoming a physician, and wanted it for herself since childhood and the doctor's kit was her favorite game. But she also sees many scary obstacles and dangers on a long, hard road ahead of her. In her answers on the same questionnaire she imagines herself failing, disappointing her father and herself, maybe winding up hurting a patient and being sued for malpractice. But her anticipations of dangers also activate scripts about how she might be able to plan to minimize and avoid the negative possibilities ("I could take extra time to practice those high-risk emergency routines, like intubation that looks like a nightmare on TV—the patient died in the episode I watched—but he didn't have to . . . if only . . ." Her other answers suggest she seems to feel relieved and recommitted to her goals as she realizes she has both the drive and the ability to ultimately master the skills she'll need to feel she "can do it right, without fouling up."

At the Social Cognitive Level, Veronica's appraisal and thinking reflects a strong **promotion focus**: attention is directed to potential accomplishments and rewards rather than to possible threats, risks, and losses (Higgins, 1997, 1998). Veronica not only focuses on the rewards and opportunities of the situation; she also expects and vividly anticipates the many good, exciting things that her career will bring. She even fantasizes discovering a new cure, and imagines herself collecting the awards for her breakthroughs, glowing already with how good it will feel. Consistent with her promotion focus, she believes her past success and positive prospects reflect her courage and willingness to take big chances for big opportunities and challenges (Higgins, 1998).

16.16 Explain how promotion focus and prevention focus can help different individuals succeed in a given field.

Martha's encoding, in contrast, is typical of a strong **prevention focus** (Higgins, 1998). She attends not to the possible rewards to be gained but to the possible threats, losses, negative outcomes, even disasters the future in medicine might hold for her. Consistent with her highly active prevention focus, Martha imagines and anticipates all the things that could go wrong. For her the appraised situation activates her beliefs that she has often succeeded because she pays strict attention to the rules and avoids potentially goal-threatening possibilities. In her dynamics, negative outcomes are anticipated, but they also activate her expectations that if she works vigilantly to avoid them she will be able to succeed.

Recall that research at the Social Cognitive Level showed the importance of *self-efficacy expectations*—beliefs that one will be able to exert control and successfully execute necessary actions essential for effective goal pursuit (e.g., Bandura, 1986; Kuhl, 1984; Mischel et al., 1996). Both Veronica and Martha may have equally high self-efficacy expectations about being able to pass the entry tests for getting into medical school—indeed Martha's self-efficacy expectancies may be higher than Veronica's. These expectancies may be good predictors of how well they actually will do on those tests, and perhaps even in medical school, in spite of the very different thoughts and feelings they have when they think about themselves as becoming physicians (Figures 16.7 and 16.8). But in terms of their distinctive processing dynamics, the important point is that their high self-efficacy expectancy play different roles within the organization of their systems. For Veronica they support her high risk-taking strategies; for Martha they allow her to persist in her vigilant threat-reduction and avoidance strategies.

At the Biological Level, Veronica's behavior suggests high activity in her Behavioral Activation System (BAS), the energizing biological system (discussed in Chapter 9). It is the appetitive, positive–approach motivational system in her brain that enhances

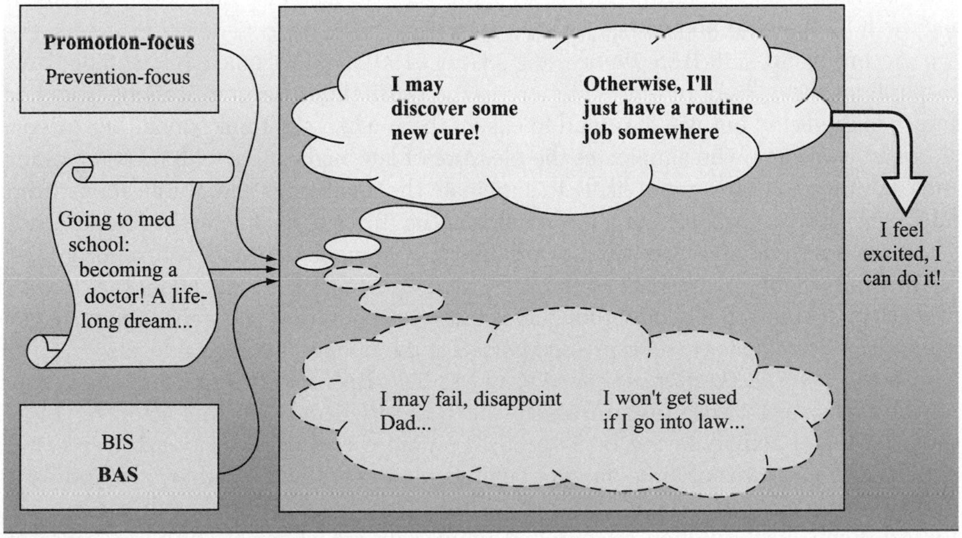

Figure 16.7 Veronica's processing dynamics in goal pursuit. Thinking about medical school activates promotion focus and BAS.

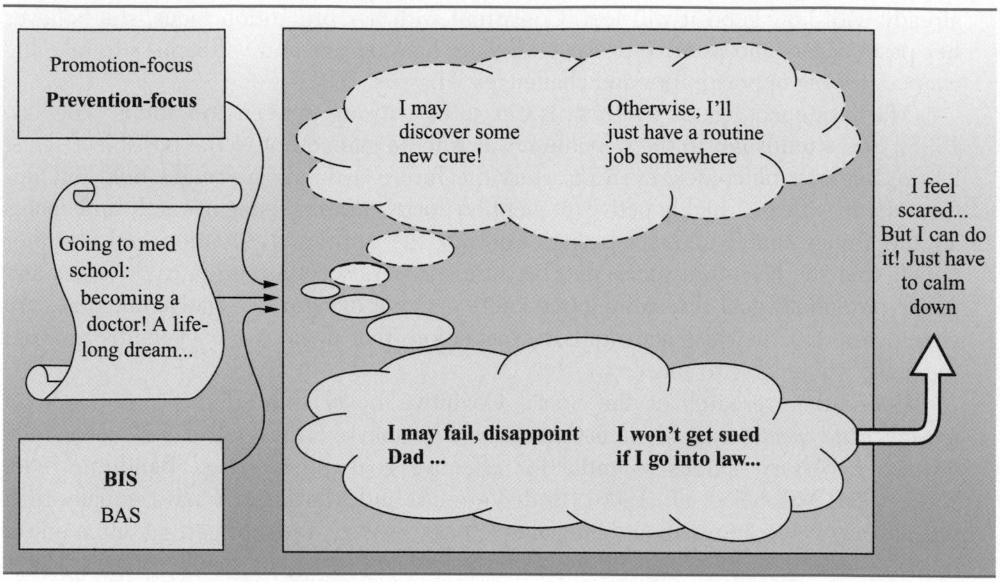

Figure 16.8 Martha's processing dynamics in goal pursuit. Thinking about medical school activates prevention focus and BIS.

attention to reward cues and facilitates approach behavior in goal pursuit, and it is a biological basis for the promotion system Higgins proposes at the Social Cognitive Level. The downside of high activity in the BAS system is that it does not sensitize the person to the potential long-term risks and negative consequences of tempting approach behaviors that can be dangerous. Martha, on the other hand, is high in BIS activity: in her the Behavioral Inhibition System is highly active. It enhances attention to risks, threats, dangers. Her high BIS level is also reflected in her psychological prevention focus as seen at the Social Cognitive Level. From an evolutionary perspective this system evolved because it enabled humans to survive by being alert to dangers. Like most systems in nature, it has benefits and costs.

According to BIS/BAS theory (e.g., Gray, 1991), if Veronica has a high BAS disposition, she will not only attend more to the possibilities for gratifications from her future in medicine but will also tend to expect them when she thinks about her career. Veronica is the one who anticipates the pleasure of late-night pizza with no concern for the calories. She also is more likely to anticipate the challenges and gratifications from late nights working in the emergency room, and the thrills of dealing with life-and-death situations—a prediction consistent with her phenomenology and self-reports. For Martha, for whom the prospect of pizza activated expectations mostly about the calories and an upset stomach all night, thoughts about working in the emergency room trigger the concerns and anxiety she expressed herself at the phenomenological level.

16.17 Describe Veronica's personality from the social cognitive level, the biological level, and the trait-dispositional level.

At the Trait-Dispositional Level, Veronica's high BAS activity implies that she may also be high on extraversion as measured by the NEO-PI-R and the Five Factor (Big Five) model. Greater activity in the BAS seems to be more characteristic of extraverts, and is related to measures of temperament beginning early in life (Derryberry & Rothbart, 1997; Gray, 1991). Her high BAS activity also may be associated with a tendency toward dominance/sensation seeking and impulsivity (MacDonald, 1998). Because of their greater reactivity in the BAS, extraverts and those high in dominance/sensation seeking will focus more on rewards, especially immediate rewards, and look eagerly for situations in which they could get them. They therefore also are more likely to be high in promotion focus.

In sum, at the broad trait level, Veronica might be described as a person who seizes opportunities, focuses on getting rewards rather than avoiding threats, may love adventures, and probably gets easily and enthusiastically involved with all sorts of possibilities. Martha provides a portrait of psychological opposites. High in BIS, she may also be high in introversion and perhaps more risk-averse. But keep in mind that these broad overall differences on the whole between Veronica and Martha coexist with the fact that on closer examination we would also see their stable *if ... then ...* behavioral signatures of personality, reflecting person × situation interactions. For example, while Veronica may be high on BAS activity when dealing with her career and work, she may become higher in BIS and feel easily rejected in romantic relationships, switching to a vigilant prevention focus, eager to not let any emotional entanglements undermine her work ambitions. And Martha might surprise us and show an opposite pattern, with more BAS and promotion focus, and less BIS, withdrawal, and inhibition when it comes to love and attachment. She might even show some surprisingly extraverted characteristics when relating to the people she loves, especially her boyfriend who she feels brings out another side of her that's confident, almost worry-free, and spontaneous. Human personality is much more complex than the broad generalizations that are so tempting and easy to make about it from any single level of analysis.

16.18 Given what we know about Veronica and Martha, can we predict how they will act with their friends at a movie?

The Psychodynamic-Motivational Level calls attention exactly to that complexity and the often subtle, conflicted, distorted, and indirect and variable expressions of personality. It reminds us, for example, that the appraisal/encoding process operates not just at a conscious level of self-awareness that can be tapped by self-reports or introspection. Situations are also appraised, encoded, and processed automatically and without awareness (Metcalfe & Mischel, 1999). Indeed, as work at the Behavioral-Conditioning Level also has long emphasized, and more recent work at the Social Cognitive Level demonstrates, much and probably most of what people think, feel, do, and even consciously experience is elicited automatically and reflexively (Bargh, 1996). That makes it important to use more indirect or "implicit" methods for their assessment, and work at the Psychodynamic-Motivational Level paved the way for current efforts at the social cognitive, brain, and other levels.

Finally, at *the Behavioral-Conditioning Level*, many of the Veronica–Martha appraisal differences reflect their learning and emotional conditioning histories, and are the product of those experiences. The focus would be on examining in detail how both their appraisals and their other related behaviors change in relation to different contingencies of reinforcement and situational variations. The goal would be to identify the specific stimuli that activate their different appraisals, particularly their conditioned positive and negative emotional responses.

To recapitulate, Veronica and Martha differ in their BIS/BAS reactivity and in their Big Five factor scores and profiles, especially with regard to extraversion, impulsivity, neuroticism, and anxiety. Both at the Phenomenological Level and at the Social Cognitive Level they experience their worlds in dramatically different ways. They contrast in typical moods and feeling states, and in how they mentally and emotionally represent their experiences and their possible futures as they imagine their possible careers in medicine. They use opposite strategies in their pursuit of goals—one "psyches" herself up, imagining the exciting possibilities; the other scares herself about the possible negatives and stressors along the route, using a strategy called **defensive pessimism** (Norem & Cantor, 1986; Showers & Cantor, 1984).

Putting It Together: Integrating the Levels

Research and theory in personality psychology was generated by psychologists working for more than a century at the different levels of analysis, but at the level of the individual the personality system functions as an integrated, distinctive whole. The ultimate goal of personality science since Gordon Allport (1937) founded the field has been to understand how such a system puts all the different pieces together to function in concert at the level of each individual's life. The core goal of an integrative personality model like CAPS therefore is to at least outline such a system at the level of the individual person. Martha and Veronica illustrate different CAPS personality systems, in the sense that their personality structures are put together distinctively and therefore are expressed differently in characteristic ways. Their personality systems differ in the chronic accessibility of CAUs: Veronica, for example, more readily encodes situations as opportunities for rewards, Martha focuses on their potential long-term hazards. But just as important, the women differ in how their CAUs are interconnected in their personality structures, and thus in the activation patterns in their heads and in their behavior that become triggered by different situations. You can see these differences in their processing dynamics at multiple levels of analysis, as described above: Taken together they begin to tell a more complete story about each person as a whole, functioning, thinking, feeling human being.

Although Martha focuses on failure possibilities, she also manages to deal with them vigilantly and effectively. Her goal pursuit is facilitated by her high self-efficacy expectations and strong goal commitment and self-control skills and competencies. Thus both women may succeed in their goal pursuit, but how they do it reflects their very different personality systems. Martha does it by being cautious and avoiding failure, activating effective coping behaviors, such as persistency and focused attention, for which she has high self-efficacy expectancies. Veronica does well by expecting success, and focusing on the rewards to be gotten rather than on the risks to be feared. Both patterns illustrate potential routes to success, although they are distinctively different strategic orientations and reflect their stable personality structures. Each has extremely different experiences, activates very different patterns of thoughts and feelings when facing similar stressors, and enact distinctive coping patterns, both in their controlled, conscious, and in their automatic coping patterns (Cantor & Kihlstrom, 1987; Higgins, 1998).

Self-Regulation for Purposeful Change

Just as a structural diagram of a complex system helps one to understand its functions, persons who have some understanding of their personality organization and processing dynamics may be able to better predict the events and conditions that will activate their *if ... then ...* patterns. Such understanding is important particularly as a first step in assessment if one wants to change them. Therapy is an approach that tries to help the person recognize some of the key internal or external stimuli that trigger distressing thoughts, feelings, and behaviors. With this knowledge, individuals may be better able to influence and regulate their own personality states and behaviors (e.g., Mischel & Mischel, 1983; Rodriguez, Mischel, & Shoda, 1989). That entails assessments to identify active ingredients of situations and explore the cognitive–affective processing dynamics that they activate. Therapeutically it requires developing alternative ways of encoding and learning to deal differently, cognitively, emotionally, and behaviorally, with the problem-producing situations that trigger dysfunctional or disadvantageous behavior patterns. The goal is to help the person to systematically change their meanings. Many of the relevant processes for such therapy and self-change efforts are discussed next in Chapter 17.

▶ SUMMARY

CONTRIBUTIONS FROM EACH LEVEL

- An integrative model of personality includes contributions from all six levels of analysis.
- The trait-dispositional level of analysis identified the two types of consistency: cross-situational consistency and *if* ... *then* ... situation–behavior consistency.
- The biological level of analysis has explored the importance of the individual's genetic and biological characteristics in the personality system as well as the evolutionary history of the human species.
- The psychodynamic-motivational level showed that our thoughts and behaviors can have unconscious, self-defensive motivations.
- The behavioral-conditioning level focused on analyzing people's behavior in relationship to the situations in which it occurs. It also showed the power of conditioning in the development of fears and other strong emotions.
- Workers at the phenomenological-humanistic level recognized that the behavioral and emotional effects of situations depend on how individuals subjectively perceive and construe them.
- The social cognitive level combined features of multiple levels of analysis to explain individual differences in personality and examined the role of social learning.

TOWARD INTEGRATION: CHARACTERISTICS OF THE PERSONALITY SYSTEM

- Neural network information-processing models applied to personality focus on how the person's internal mental representations—the specific cognitions and feelings that become activated—are related to each other to form an organized network structure.
- In the Cognitive–Affective Processing System (CAPS), individuals are characterized by the ease of accessibility for different types of cognitions and affects or cognitive–affective units (CAUs) and the distinctive organization of relationships among them in the system.
- CAUs include the person's self-representation, representations of others, situational construal, enduring goals, expectations-beliefs, and feeling states, and while the accessibility of each CAU fluctuates, the relationships between them remain stable.
- The stable structure of the personality system plays out in distinctive patterns of *if* ... *then* ... relationships between situations and behavior that characterize each individual distinctively.
- Rejection sensitivity (RS) is a processing disposition that consists of associations between expectations of rejection, readiness to encode ambiguous situations as rejection, hot affect, and maladaptive behavioral scripts.
- While they are not more likely to be aggressive in general, individuals who are high in RS tend to have an *if* ... *then* ... profile of increased aggression and increased depression in situations where they feel rejected.
- The narcissistic personality signature is characterized by a pattern of seeking out situations that allow for self-promotion and using these situations to prove one's superiority.
- Personality development and change involve both biochemical and social cognitive influences that continuously interact.
- CAPS integrates contributions from all levels of analysis.

PERSONALITY SYSTEM IN ACTION

- The personality system can be activated by internal (thoughts, feelings) and external (situations) cues.
- People's behavior becomes part of their personality system because it impacts how they are perceived by others, how they perceive themselves, and the kinds of situations that they experience.
- People shape their environments through the people they choose to interact with as well as the people that they attract.
- Because each person brings his or her own stable personality system to a relationship, CAPS may also be used to understand the dynamics of close interpersonal relationships, which, in a sense, develop their own personality.
- Understanding an individual's personality processing system can help to predict behavior in a relevant situation, as shown in the study on women's breast self-examinations.
- People may succeed in their goal pursuit by being cautious and avoiding failure (prevention focus) and/or by

eagerly pursuing their desires (promotion focus). Each focus has its advantages and disadvantages.

- The BIS and BAS biological systems influence how individuals appraise and respond to situations.
- In CAPS, the person is capable of being proactive, not only in the selection of situations but in the interpretation, transformation, and construction of situations. Therapy in this framework can help people recognize some of the key internal and external stimuli that trigger distressing thoughts, feelings, and behaviors.

▶ KEY TERMS

active ingredients 424
automatic processing 421
behavioral signature of narcissists 420
chronic accessibility 416
Cognitive–Affective Personality System 415
cognitive–affective units 416
connectionist theories 415
controlled processing 422
defensive pessimism 433
excitatory (activating) links 415
inhibitory (deactivating) links 415
links 415
network information-processing model 415
nodes 415
personality dispositions 418
personality structure 417
prevention focus 431
processing dynamics 418
promotion focus 430
reciprocal interaction 424
rejection sensitivity (RS) 418
stable organization of relationships 417

CHAPTER 17

SELF-REGULATION: FROM GOAL PURSUIT TO GOAL ATTAINMENT

On May 7, 2006, a column, "Marshmallows and Public Policy," by David Brooks, featured in the New York Times *reported an experiment done around 1970 at Stanford University. The researchers left 4-year-olds in a room with a bell and some marshmallows—one marshmallow on one part of a plate, two on the other. If the child rang the bell the adult would immediately return and they could eat the one marshmallow right away; but if they didn't ring the bell and waited for him to return by himself, they could have the two marshmallows. A video of the experiment showed the children fidgeting, squirming, hiding their eyes, kicking, struggling to control themselves and to keep waiting. Their behavior varied greatly. Some did not continue and quickly rang the bell, others endured the whole 15 minutes. A dozen years later, those who had waited longer tended to get on average higher SAT (Scholastic Aptitude Test) scores and better social and cognitive life outcomes in adulthood. Those who rang the bell sooner on average got worse parental and teacher evaluations in adolescence, and tended to have more drug and interpersonal problems at age 32. Why? How can we understand these differences and what do they tell us about personality?*

The last chapter showed how the contributions from all levels of analysis complement each other and, taken together, help to build an integrative view of the personality system and the functioning individual. You saw how each level contributes to understanding how and why individuals differ in their characteristic ways of thinking, feeling, and coping with different types of situations. In this chapter, you will see how the integration of work from multiple levels of analysis advances our understanding not only of a given individual or personality type, but also of a broad array of important self-regulatory behaviors essential for adaptive, effective functioning and goal attainment. An example of such behavior is seen in the "marshmallow experiment" described in the chapter opening.

This chapter illustrates how the integrative approach deals with a basic and enduring challenge for personality psychology and for a scientific understanding of human nature. It asks: How can people have "agency" and "willpower" to self-regulate, delay gratification, and attain their long-term goals, even in the face of strong internal and situational pressures, barriers, temptations, and constraints? And how do individual differences in self-regulation influence and predict personality development and consequential outcomes over the life course? Put most simply: What is "willpower" psychologically, and what makes it possible? Can these processes be harnessed to help the individual toward better self-actualization of his or her potential? We examine how work from all levels of analysis contributes toward answering these questions. And we see how these contributions help to clarify how people can protect themselves against their own dispositional vulnerabilities, and against external pressures and temptations, when they interfere with their long-term life goals, ideals, and well-being.

▶ OVERVIEW OF CONTRIBUTIONS TO SELF-REGULATION FROM EACH LEVEL

17.1 How does each level of analysis contribute to our understanding of self-regulation?

Table 17.1 summarizes some of the key contributions from each level of analysis to describing and understanding individual differences in self-regulation and goal pursuit.

As the table indicates, the *Trait-Dispositional Level* showed that people differ greatly in their self-regulatory behaviors. It documented in detail what even casual observation suggests: some people stick to stringent diets, or give up cigarettes after years of smoking them addictively, or keep struggling and waiting and working for distant goals even when tempted greatly to quit. But others fail in spite of affirming the same initial good intentions. The ancient Greeks considered a lack or a weakness of the will a character trait and called it **akrasia**—the deficiency of the will. In modern versions of the trait-dispositional approach these broad individual differences are described and measured objectively, for example, in terms of Conscientiousness in the Five Factor (Big Five) model.

Research at this level also has shown that people differ not only in their overall levels of self-regulation but also in the situations and conditions in which they do and

TABLE 17.1 Contributions of Each Level to an Integrative View of Self-Regulation

Level of Analysis	Key Contributions
Psychodynamic-Motivational	Self-regulation problems reflect internal conflicts between basic biological impulses (id) versus inhibiting influences (ego, super ego), often outside awareness; recognized importance of the ability to delay gratification and analyzed some of its mechanisms; examined insight and rational ego/cognitive control to overcome defensive, irrational, self-defeating automatic processing
Trait-Dispositional	Found and measured broad individual differences in conscientiousness and self-regulation, as well as distinctive *if . . . then . . .* behavioral signatures in self-regulation; examined constructs and dimensions of ego control and ego resilience; identified problems of undercontrol and overcontrol and their implications for personality development over the life course
Biological	Identifying brain centers, pathways, and interacting "hot" and "cool" systems in effortful control and delay of gratification; clarifying role of attention deployment in effective self-regulation and focused problem solving; found links to trait and temperament measures
Behavioral-Conditioning	Showed importance and power of situations and stimulus control. Found processes and determinants of behavior outside awareness (i.e., automatic rather than consciously controlled); analyzed how emotional conditioning and response consequences shape behavior (including irrational behavior) and make self-control and self-regulation difficult
Phenomenological-Humanistic	Perception is subjective; person's cognitive appraisals and construal of situations influence their impact on behavior; showed possibilities for self-determination; higher-order processes (e.g., self-actualization, self-construction) provide routes to enhance self-direction and overcome stimulus control. Constructive alternative ways of construing and thinking can help people from becoming victims of their social and biological history
Social Cognitive	Helped bridge the gap between construal and action; showed how the construal of the situation interacts with other mental representations (expectancies, beliefs, goals) to influence goal-directed effortful behavior; analyzed the mental mechanisms and strategies that enable delay of gratification and goal-directed self-control; demonstrated the consequences of this ability, visible in early life, for major long-term life outcomes; found new evidence that much self-regulation operates automatically outside awareness

do not self-regulate and self-control effectively. Individual differences in self-regulation include differences in stable *if . . . then . . .* signatures. The same student who consistently gives up sleep and socializing in order to study and work hard in schoolwork may be unable to forego the temptations of junk food even when determined to adhere to a rigorous diet. The same judge who is a model of morality and conscientiousness on the bench may become indicted for inappropriate and illegal sexual or financial behavior. That recognition raised the "why—how does that happen?" question—and it motivated much of the work at the Psychodynamic Level.

At the *Psychodynamic-Motivational Level*, a century ago Freud proposed that puzzling problems in self-regulation, including a wide variety of mental problems and physical symptoms, may reflect underlying conflicts within the person, and contributed a systematic dynamic view of the process. Indeed, he and his co-workers made the concept and psychodynamics of self-regulation the core of their personality system. Recall that Freud cast human self-regulation as a mostly unconscious battle between biological impulses, in his view primarily sexual and aggressive, pressing irrationally for immediate gratification, and the repressive counterpressures coming from the rational ego and the judgmental internalized high court or conscience, the super ego (Chapter 7). His contributions included an analysis of the mechanisms that enable delay of gratification early in life and contributed insights into the mechanisms that may enable the transition from impulsivity to reason, problem solving, and future-oriented rational behavior. His work showed the importance of insight to overcome unconscious defensive and self-defeating distortions and irrationality in one's own behavior, and to attain mature, rational control mechanisms.

At the *Biological Level*, a hundred years after Freud, researchers are finding neural bases in the brain for some of the processes underlying self-regulation. At least metaphorically, these findings at the cutting edge of the field today parallel some of the core ideas first proposed in the psychodynamic model. Using modern imaging methods, studies of the brain are revealing areas that are the seat of "hot" impulsive, automatic reactions, as in strong appetitive urges, fear, and aggressive responses. These "hot system" areas, deep under the prefrontal cortex, are basic in emotional reactions. They interact with higher-level brain centers that allow humans—at least sometimes and under some conditions—to inhibit those rapid, reflexive, automatic responses (fight, flight, grab) in favor of more future-oriented, cognitive, and reflective problem solving and self-regulation.

As Table 17.1 notes, the *Behavioral-Conditioning Level* demonstrated the power of "stimulus control," and identified the many conditions that can control peoples' emotions, as in classical conditioning, as well as manipulate their social and interpersonal behavior. These conditions control and shape much human behavior, often with little or no awareness on the part of the individual. In spite of their vast differences in approach, psychologists working at the Behavioral Level and the Psychodynamic Level share an emphasis on processes that influence behavior importantly in automatic ways outside consciousness. And both levels contributed to an understanding of those processes.

Work at the *Phenomenological-Humanistic Level* showed that how you construe and think about situations greatly influences what they do to you and what you can do to them. Research at this level made it clear that perception is subjective: how the person construes and appraises situations influences their impact. Through reconstrual and exploration of constructive alternatives individuals can overcome stimulus control and enable new behavioral and self-realization possibilities. This view argued powerfully that people are capable of self-determination. Higher-order processes and motivations (e.g., self-actualization) provide possible routes to enhance self-direction and to enable genuine self-construction. As George Kelly insisted, people don't have to become the victims of their social and biological history.

Work at the *Social Cognitive Level* went on to bridge the gap between construal and action. It showed how the person's construal of the situation interacts with other mental representations (expectancies, beliefs, goals) to influence goal-directed effortful behavior (e.g., Bandura, 1986; Mischel, 1973, 1984). In other words, it helped to fill in the psychological processes through which the person can move from construal of the situation to coping behavior and self-regulation in interactions with the social world. Partly inspired by Freud's work, it also analyzed in detail the mental mechanisms that make delay of gratification and goal-directed self-control possible. It also showed the consequences of this ability, visible in early life, for major life outcomes years later in development (e.g., Mischel & Ayduk, 2004; Mischel, et al., 1989). Likewise, researchers at this level now find that much if not most of what humans do and experience in self-regulation operates automatically at levels outside awareness (e.g., Bargh & Barndollar, 1996; Bargh, Gollwitzer, Lee-Chai, Barndollar, & Trätschel, 2001; Bargh & Williams, 2006).

The integrative approach to self-regulation that is emerging builds on the contributions from all these levels. A major challenge it faces is to unravel the links between what we think and what we do, at the levels of mind, brain, and self-regulatory behavior as people pursue their important life goals. As discussed in the rest of this chapter, there is good progress, with many exciting prospects.

► SELF-REGULATORY PROCESSES IN GOAL PURSUIT

Personal Goals and Projects

Much of life and human self-regulation is spent in the pursuit of goals. The goals an individual pursues are organized and coherent, and of central importance in the functioning of the personality system. Individuals differ in the goals they value, and within the individual, specific goals shift over the course of development. The goals of a college student, and the situations, challenges, and threats faced, are obviously different from those experienced in early childhood, or those that will be salient at mid-life and beyond. In this section, we focus on how the personality system plays out and the cognitive and emotional processes that become activated as individuals pursue their important life goals (e.g., Cantor, 1990; Cantor & Kihlstrom, 1987; Zirkel, 1992).

Life Tasks

Current **life tasks** are defined as projects to which individuals commit themselves during particular periods in their lives, such as in the transition from high school to college (Cantor & Kihlstrom, 1987, p. 168). These self-created tasks help give meaning to the individual's life and provide organization and direction for many more specific activities and goal pursuits that are in their service.

Common life tasks include "getting into college," "getting promoted," "finding the right person and getting married," "making myself more fit," and "taking off a couple of years to do something meaningful for needier people." Life tasks thus are significant long-term goals that are meaningful for the individual at a particular point in life. While they are typically experienced as personally urgent, they are also often ill-defined and loosely formulated, with limited self-awareness.

Many people share certain types of life tasks in the same phase of life. For example, first-year students in an honors college at the University of Michigan often had life tasks like the following in common: "Being on my own," "making friends," "establishing an identity," "getting good grades," and "establishing a future direction" (Cantor & Kihlstrom, 1987, p. 172). When the students were encouraged to elaborate their plans, feelings, and specific strategies, some common themes emerged. Concerns about achievement, intimacy, and gaining better self-control were widespread. Each student, however, also uniquely construed his or her tasks and focused on somewhat different aspects of the same common themes. For example, while "being on my own" meant learning to cope with personal failures without the help of parental hugs for one student, for another it meant working on how to manage money responsibly. These studies draw on the person's own expertise to articulate his or her personal constructs, plans, and problem-solving strategies for dealing with everyday real-life challenges (e.g., Cantor et al., 2002; Harlow & Cantor, 1996; Snyder & Cantor, 1998).

Goal Hierarchies

Goals are organized hierarchically in the personality system, with some—the **super ordinate goals**—more important than the **subordinate goals** (e.g., Carver & Scheier, 1998; Vallacher & Wegner, 1987). The goal to be and feel "safe and secure" is a higher-level goal than "finding a partner I can trust" or "getting a job I can count on." The latter goals are at a lower level than the superordinate one, but they are much higher than "making the apartment safer." Making the apartment safe is executed at the even more subordinate level of "going to the hardware store" or cleaning out potential fire hazards. Likewise, the goal of being "a worthy person" is higher in the organization of the system than a goal such as being "kind and caring." Being kind and caring connects to even lower-level goals like "helping the needy person cross the street."

17.2 Explain the concept of goal hierarchies and the factors that influence which goals are pursued.

When goal attainment at a given level (e.g., getting a job) is blocked and frustrated, people may continue to strive toward the higher-level goal (being safe and secure) toward which the lower-level activity was directed. They may try, for example, to focus more on building the relationship with the partner now and postponing the job search, as long as it still serves the same higher-level goal (Martin, Tesser, & McIntosh, 1993). Goals are central for understanding the personal and life goals that people pursue, but the processing dynamics of how they pursue them depend on their own standards and self-evaluations as they monitor their progress.

Standards and Self-Evaluation

In goal pursuit, beginning early in life, people evaluate their own behavior and perceived progress, and they reward and punish themselves accordingly, thereby further influencing how they progress—or fail to do so (e.g., Bandura, 1989; Carver & Scheier, 1990). They congratulate themselves for what they see as positive, and they feel good or bad or uncertain about their own achievements. They self-administer psychological, social, and material rewards and punishments. In short, people assess themselves and become their own internal judges and reward–punishment system, using the standards that they have developed for themselves (Bandura, 1986, 2001; Higgins, 1990, 1997). Self-praise and censure, self-imposed treats and punishments, self-indulgence and self-laceration are signs of this pervasive human tendency to congratulate and condemn oneself.

17.3 How do self-evaluative standards influence striving and emotional responses?

You see it when people celebrate their good test scores and their acceptance letters, or kick themselves for what they read as disappointments and setbacks. In this self-evaluation process, people compare their current state of performance with those standards. If they perceive a discrepancy, they tend to be motivated to reduce it or to reset their standards to a lower level (e.g., Carver & Scheier, 1981, 1990). As Bandura put it: "When people make self-satisfaction or tangible gratifications conditional upon certain accomplishments, they motivate themselves to expend the effort needed to attain the requisite performance" (Bandura, 1986, p. 350). By generating consequences for their own actions, individuals can bring them into line with their higher-order values and goals.

Why Self-Regulate?

Automaticity

17.4 How does self-regulation relate to the concept of automaticity?

Most of goal pursuit is automatic. You see automatic behavior in routine activities from attending classes and going to work or interacting with friends and family, to dealing with stress and coping with temptation and frustration. Most of the time, these processes seem to run on their own as if the person were on automatic pilot (e.g., Bargh, 1997, 2001).

These automatic mental–emotional processes activated in goal pursuit are adaptive for most life functions. But sometimes what runs off automatically may be exactly what the person is eager to *not* do—for example, to yield to the temptation of the dessert when trying to diet, or to head for the movies soon after deciding to spend the evening working. Examples of the difficulty of overcoming the usual automatic reactive tendencies are easy to find in daily life. Every dieter knows the quick failure of good intentions when the waiter flashes the chocolate pastry on the dessert tray. Strong motivation is not enough when the temptations are intense and "in your face."

Beyond Automaticity to Willpower?

The impressive power of the situation and stimulus control was shown in work at the Behavioral Level, and in more recent studies in social cognition (e.g., Bargh, 1997, 2001). John Bargh and his colleagues demonstrated that most of what people do runs off automatically without conscious intervention. It is elicited by the particular stimulus conditions in the situation, often without the person's awareness. In these situations it becomes easy for people to bypass their own evaluative self-standards and to exhibit reflexive, automatic, and often impulsive behavior—that they may later regret. These findings coexist with the intuitive conviction that human beings have the capacity to take control and exert willpower at least some of the time (e.g., Ayduk & Mischel, 2002; Derryberry, 2002). Often people do overcome obstacles and temptations along the way to achieving their valued long-term goals, and manage to resist the pull of even strong situational pressures. How do they do it?

Self-Regulation Requires Both Motivation and Competence

Effective self-regulation and self-control in goal pursuit depends both on the person's *motivation* and on his or her *competencies*. First let's consider the role of motivation. Take the motivation to refuse a slice of double-chocolate fudge cake. The motivational strength of this may depend, for example, on whether the individual construes the cake as "unhealthy and fattening" or as "a great treat." It also depends on how much the person values the long-term superordinate goals that are served by eating healthy and being fit. If these self-regulatory behaviors are serving a higher goal central to the self, like being a worthy, self-respecting person, their motivational significance will be high and they will be mentally more accessible.

17.5 What besides regulatory motivation is needed in order to manifest willpower?

It helps to distinguish between self-regulatory *motivation* and *competence*. Often people have one of these but not the other; a good example is a recent President of the United States. His adroit handling of political and foreign affairs showed that he had such skills, yet he either was unable or insufficiently motivated to apply them to himself when it came to his personal affairs, and he was disgraced and almost impeached as a result. Even

The same person can have high self-control in some situations but not in others.

(*Source*: (left) Reuters New Media/Corbis Images; (right) © AP/Wide World Photos)

when motivation is high, self-control in the face of temptations and frustrations requires more than good intentions. As William James (1890) noted more than a hundred years ago, the gap from "desiring and wanting" to "willing" cannot be bridged unless "certain preliminaries" are met. Even with high regulatory motivation, goal attainment depends critically on the availability and accessibility of effective self-regulatory competencies. **Self-regulatory competencies** refer to the cognitive and attentional mechanisms that help us execute goal-directed behavior. In the remainder of this chapter, we examine the processes that underlie these competencies, noting again how contributions from each level add to the total picture.

The Biological Level: Effortful Control

First, we consider the nature of these regulatory competencies and mechanisms at the biological-brain level. In the last few decades, much has been learned about the neural mechanisms that underlie and enable self-regulation and what brain researchers call "executive functions." Interestingly, a century earlier, Freud and his followers had used the same term to refer to the ways in which the ego enables delay of gratification and impulse control. Findings from cognitive neuroscience now indicate that at the Biological Level many of these inhibitory functions involve "executive systems" in the frontal cortex.

Brain Mechanisms in Effortful Control

17.6 Define executive functions. Which brain regions are involved?

Researchers have described an **anterior attentional system** that regulates the pathways involved in **executive function** (or **EF**) throughout the cortex (Derryberry, 2002; Eslinger, 1996; Miyake, Friedman, Emerson, Witzki, & Howerter, 2000; Posner & Rothbart, 1991, 1998; Stuss & Knight, 2002; Zelazo & Müller, 2002). EF is required for adaptive, goal-directed behaviors to solve novel problems, particularly those calling for the inhibition of automatic or established thoughts and responses (Casey, Tottenham, & Fossella, 2002).

These EF brain systems, and their associated psychological processes, enable **effortful control**, or in lay language, willpower, in goal pursuit. They do so by allowing people to regulate their attention. This attention regulation process includes the ability to focus attention in perception, to switch attention between tasks, to ignore or inhibit interfering responses, and to control thoughts flexibly. There has been a virtual flood of research into the details and pathways of these EF mechanisms in the brain, facilitated by the new brain imaging techniques. (Examples include studies by Carlson & Beck, in press; Casey et al., 1997, 2000; Derryberry & Reed, 2002; Durston et al., 2002; Eigsti et al., 2006; Nee, Wager, & Jonides, in press; Smith & Jonides, 1999; Wager, Sylvester, et al., 2005.) This is good news for an integrative approach to self-regulation because it paves the way for tracing the links between psychological processes within the personality system as they play out at the brain/Biological Level.

The Trait-Dispositional Level

At the Trait-Dispositional Level, self-report measures have been developed to identify individual differences in the attention control mechanisms that are basic for effortful control (see Table 17.2 for sample items) and that are correlated with the brain measures. Attention control scores are related positively to extraversion and negatively to anxiety and impulsivity (Derryberry, 2002; Derryberry & Reed, 2002; Eisenberg, Fabes, Guthrie, & Reiser, 2002) in findings that closely parallel those from work on the BAS/BIS discussed in Chapter 6.

TABLE 17.2 Items from the Attention Control Scale

Please read each item below and then indicate how often you experience it, using the following response scale:

1	2	3	4
almost never	sometimes	often	always

____ 1. It's very hard for me to concentrate on a difficult task when there are noises around.
____ 2. When I need to concentrate and solve a problem, I have trouble focusing my attention.
____ 3. When I am working hard on something, I still get distracted by events around me.
____ 4. My concentration is good even if there is music in the room around me.
____ 5. When concentrating, I can focus my attention so that I become unaware of what's going on in the room around me.
____ 6. When I am reading or studying, I am easily distracted if there are people talking in the same room.
____ 7. When trying to focus my attention on something, I have difficulty blocking out distracting thoughts.
____ 8. I have a hard time concentrating when I'm excited about something.
____ 9. When concentrating, I ignore feelings of hunger or thirst.
____ 10. I can quickly switch from one task to another.

Source: Derryberry, D., & Reed, M. A. (2002). Anxiety-related attentional biases and their regulation by attentional control. *Journal of Abnormal Psychology, 111,* 225–236.

Ego Control and Ego Resilience

Ego control refers to the degree of impulse control in such functions as inhibition of aggression and the ability to plan. A related construct, **ego resilience**, refers to the individual's ability to adapt to environmental demands by appropriately modifying his or her habitual level of ego control. Ego resiliency allows functioning with some "elasticity" and "permeability" (Block, 2001, p. 123). Together, these two constructs represent core qualities for adaptive functioning from an influential trait-dispositional perspective that also has been influenced by modern pychodynamic research (e.g., Block, 2001; Eisenberg et al., 2002).

Jack Block

As Jack Block (2001, pp. 123–124) notes: "The resilient person anticipates wisely when to stop something unfruitful (like repetitively hitting a large boulder with a tiny hammer) or to continue something that may ultimately prove fruitful (like shattering a small boulder with a repetitive sledge hammer). In its adaptiveness, resiliency well serves evolution." This illustration also highlights the importance of the ability to discriminate, and the flexibility that it allows—an emphasis now found in the evolutionary approach, in the social cognitive approach, and in findings from the Biological Level of analysis (e.g., Grigorenko, 2002).

17.7 How have ego control and ego resilience been measured in children? How are they related to adaptive behavior?

A number of tasks are used to measure the construct of ego control and ego resilience. In one classic study researchers rated children's tendency to inhibit impulses to infer their level of ego control and also observed their delay behavior in experimental situations (Block & Martin, 1955). They exposed the children to a frustration in which a barrier separated the child from desired and expected toys. The **undercontrolling** children (those who had been rated as not inhibiting their impulses) reacted more violently to the frustrating barrier than did **overcontrolling**, inhibited children. The undercontrolling youngsters also became less constructive in their play.

Individuals who are high (rather than low) on indices of ego control tend to be somewhat more able to control and inhibit their motor activity. For example, they may be able to sit still longer or draw a line more slowly without lifting their pencil. These are only a few examples from much larger networks of correlations that support the constructs of ego resiliency and ego control. Research has shown important differences in the life trajectories associated with individual differences on these dimensions (Block, 1971; Block & Block, 1980, 2006; Letzring, Block, & Funder, 2005; Mischel, 1984; Shoda, Mischel, & Peake, 1990).

In studies of the ego-resiliency construct, toddlers were evaluated for the degree to which they seemed secure and competent (in a problem-solving task). The toddlers who were secure and competent also scored higher on measures of ego resiliency when they reached the age of 4–5 years (Gove, Arend, & Sroufe, 1979; Matas, Arend, & Sroufe, 1978). Ego-resilient children at age 3 are also viewed as more popular, interesting, and attractive at later ages (Block & Block, 1980). Further, the resilience concept also is related to delay of immediate gratification for the sake of more valued but delayed outcomes (Shoda et al., 1990), discussed below.

In sum, both the concepts of ego control and ego resiliency help characterize important individual differences in self-regulation and self-control patterns (Eisenberg et al., 2002). These differences remain relatively stable over many years in the course of development (e.g., Caspi, 1987; Caspi & Bem, 1990; Mischel et al., 1989). To recapitulate, work at the Biological Level is identifying the brain centers that enable executive skills and self-regulation. Work at the Dispositional Level on characteristics like ego resilience provides useful descriptions of what a person with self-regulatory competence is like. What about the Social Cognitive and Phenomenological-Humanistic Levels?

The Social Cognitive and Phenomenological-Humanistic Levels

Work at these levels currently tries to understand the mental mechanisms—the thoughts and strategies—that enable self-regulatory competence and effortful control. Specifically: How does what you think, or where you focus your attention, enable or undermine your ability to self-regulate in emotion-arousing dilemmas? Applied to the dieter who has resolved to forego the double-chocolate cake tonight, how will what she thinks and how she deploys her attention make it possible for her to stick to her goal? To answer such questions, researchers at the Social Cognitive Level have examined how mental activities—cognition and attention—during goal pursuit influence the ability to persist and reach difficult but important long-term goals (e.g., Gross, 1998; Lazarus, 2006; Lazarus & Folkman, 1984; Mischel, 1974; Mischel & Ayduk, 2002; 2004). The following sections illustrate the ways in which these mental activities influence effortful behavior and self-control, depending on how the events are construed or mentally represented.

17.8 What questions about self-regulation are explored at the Social Cognitive Level of analysis?

▶ SELF-REGULATION IN APPROACH (APPETITIVE) DILEMMAS

This section examines how certain mental processes enable—or undermine—self-regulation and goal pursuit in approach or appetitive dilemmas, as in the dieter's struggles with dessert temptations. Then in the section that follows, we do the same with regard to avoidance and aversive dilemmas. In both types of dilemmas people need willpower, or rather, the mental processes that make willpower possible. One of the clearest examples of the need for willpower, or in scientific terms, effortful control, is seen when people try to defer immediate gratification for the sake of important but delayed consequences.

Delay of Gratification Ability

The ability to voluntarily delay immediate gratification, to tolerate self-imposed delays of reward, is at the core of most concepts of willpower, ego strength, and ego resilience. It is hard to imagine civilization without such self-imposed delays, and it was Freud who called attention to the great importance of this ability as a requirement for ego development a century ago. Learning to wait for desired outcomes and to behave in light of expected future consequences is essential for the successful achievement of long-term, distant goals.

17.9 Why is delay of gratification an essential self-regulation skill? Describe the methods used to study this ability in children.

Beginning with toilet training, impulses and urgent needs have to be delayed and fulfilled only under special conditions of time and place. In social relationships, the culture also requires delays, for example, the expectation that people should postpone sexual relations, marriage, and children until they are "ready for them." The importance of self-control patterns that require delay of gratification has been widely recognized. It is personally familiar to every student who has tried to persist with schoolwork due the next day when greater temptations were available at the moment. The challenge for self-regulation research is to answer the question: Given that one has chosen to wait or work for a larger deferred goal, how can the delay period be managed and the impulse to take the immediate reward be resisted?

The Goal-Directed Delay Situation: The Marshmallow Test

A simple method for the study of willpower in such "hot" approach–appetitive situations has proved to be the preschool delay of gratification paradigm (see Figure 17.1), now famously called the **marshmallow test**, briefly described in the chapter opening (Mischel, 1974; Mischel et al., 1989; Mischel & Ayduk, 2002). In this method, the experimenter creates a dilemma for the young child.

To recap, and provide more detail on the chapter opening description, typically a 4-year-old is shown some desired treats, for example, marshmallows or little pretzel sticks, or small cookies, or tiny toys. The child faces a conflict: wait until the experimenter returns and get two of the desired treats, or, ring a bell, and the experimenter will come back immediately—but then the child gets only one treat. After the child chooses to wait

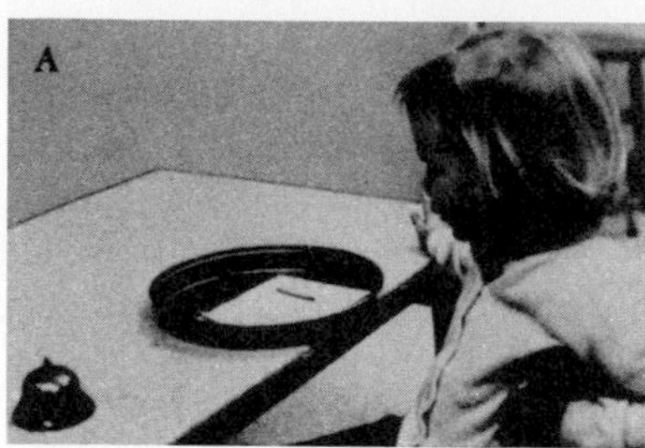

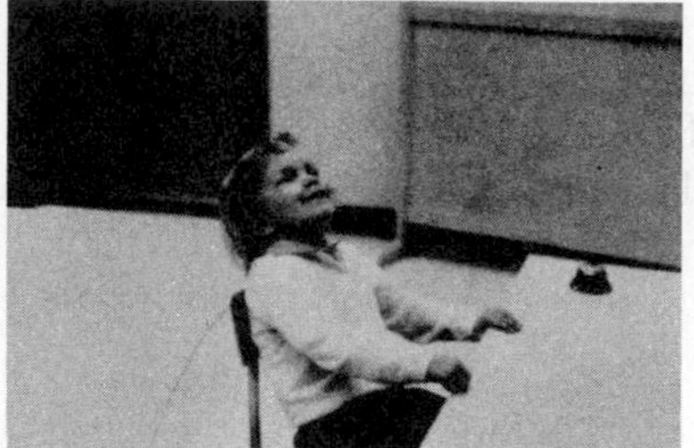

Figure 17.1 Waiting for delayed gratification.

Source: Based on Mischel, W., Ebbsen, E. B., & Zeiss, A. R. (1972). Cognitive and attentional mechanisms in delay of gratification. *Journal of Personality and Social Psychology, 21*, 204–219.

for the larger outcome, the delay soon becomes difficult and frustration grows quickly. This situation has become a prototype for studying the conflict between an immediate smaller temptation and a higher-order but delayed larger goal, the bigger treat that will come later (when the experimenter returns). In this type of situation, more than 500 preschoolers in the Stanford University community were studied through observation and experiments (e.g., Ayduk & Mischel, 2002; Mischel, 1984; Mischel et al., 1989; Mischel, Ebbesen, & Zeiss, 1972, 1973).

Research on delay of gratification illustrates how research in personality over time can build on work from all levels of analysis, ultimately yielding an integrative view based on the components that are validated by the research. When these studies began many years ago, the researchers were guided by the idea that delay becomes easier when the desired gratification can be visualized (Mischel et al., 1972). That hypothesis was based on Freud's (1911/1959b) classic idea that delay of gratification becomes possible when the young child creates a mental ("hallucinatory") image of the object of desire—the mental representation of the object, according to psychodynamic theory, allows mental "time binding" and enables delay and impulse inhibition (Rapaport, 1967). Using very different language a similar idea came from experiments at the Behavioral-Conditioning Level. They also suggested that delay ability requires an anticipatory representation of the reward or goal (reviewed in Mischel, 1974), or self-instructions to make them more salient and powerful (Bandura, 1986). The first experiments on delay with 4-year-olds examined these ideas, predicting that waiting would be longer if the rewards were made available for attention during the delay period.

Cooling Strategies: It's How You Think That Counts

Strategic Self-Distraction

17.10 What methods were used by children able to delay gratification? How was this strategy studied experimentally, and with what results?

Figure 17.2 shows results of an experiment that manipulated the extent to which children could attend to the reward objects while they were waiting (Mischel et al., 1972). In one condition, the children waited with both the immediate (less preferred) and the delayed (more preferred) reward facing them in the experimental room so that they could attend to both outcomes. In another group, neither reward was available for the child's attention, both having been removed from sight. In the remaining two groups, either the delayed reward only or the immediate reward only was available for attention while the child waited. As the figures shows, the child waited much longer when the rewards were not available for attention, directly contradicting the initial predictions. This was the study, however, that opened the way for a long-term research program that identified just what kinds of mental representations do, and don't, facilitate the ability to delay.

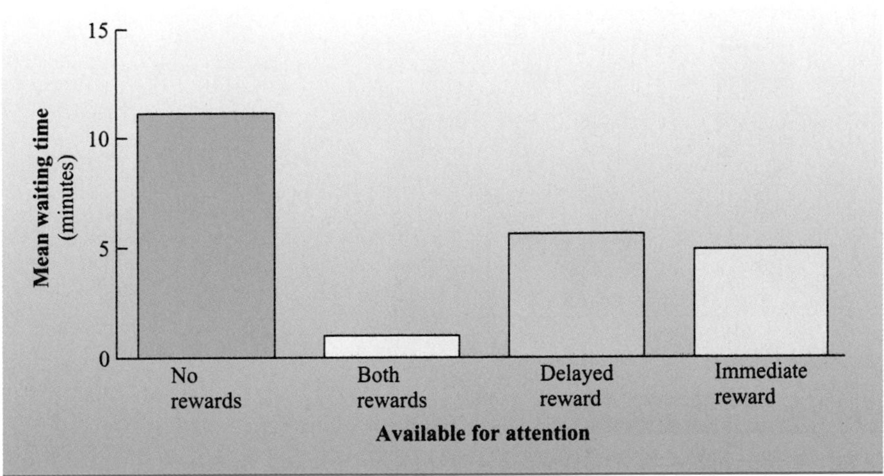

Figure 17.2 Effects of attention on delay of gratification.

Source: Based on data from Mischel, W., & Ebbsen, E. B. (1970). Attention in delay of gratification. *Journal of Personality and Social Psychology, 16,* 239–337.

In the first phase of these studies, a series of experiments demonstrated that delay of gratification is made easier by distracting attention from the rewards and thus from the aversiveness of wanting them but not having them. For example, children waited much longer for a preferred reward when they were distracted cognitively from the goal objects (e.g., by "thinking of fun things") than when they directly attended to them (Mischel et al., 1972, 1989), consistent with the old saying "Satan, get thee behind me."

These findings also were consistent with what the researchers observed the children doing spontaneously. Some youngsters used a strategy that was both simple and effective. They managed to wait for the preferred reward for long periods by converting the aversive waiting situation into a more pleasant, nonwaiting one. They used self-distraction techniques to spend their time psychologically doing something (almost anything) other than waiting. Rather than focusing prolonged attention on the treats for which they were waiting, they avoided looking at them. Some covered their eyes with their hands, turned away, or tried to reduce their frustration and temptation by generating their own diversions: they talked to themselves, sang little songs, invented games with their hands and feet, and when all other distractions seemed exhausted, even tried to fall asleep during the waiting situation—as one little girl successfully did.

The next experiments showed that rather than trying to maintain aversive activities such as delay of reward through stoic "acts of will" and focused attention, self-control is helped by mentally *transforming* the difficult into the easy, the aversive into the pleasant, and the boring into the interesting, while still maintaining the activity on which the ultimate reward depends. Rather than "willing" oneself to heroic bravery, one needs to enact the necessary "difficult" response while engaging in another, easier one, cognitively (Mischel et al., 1996; Peake, Hebl, & Mischel, 2002). The trick here is to turn the difficult (often impossible) into the easy by transforming it mentally, as discussed next.

Hot and Cool Construal

The outcomes or rewards in this type of situation may be construed in terms of their "hot," consummatory properties, or in terms of their "cool," informative properties

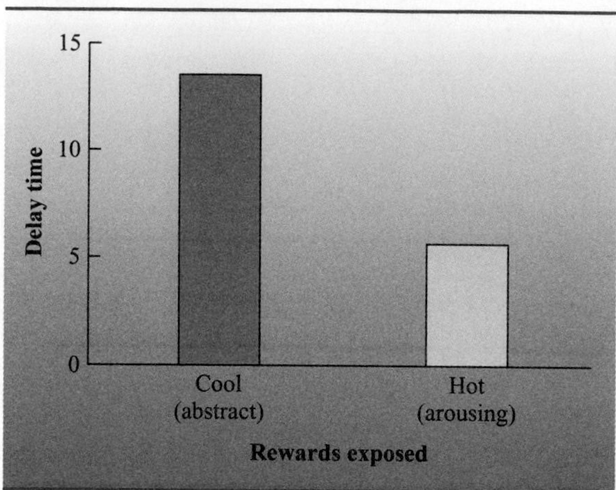

Figure 17.3 Effects of hot–cool thinking on delay time.

Source: Based on studies reported in Mischel, W., Shoda, Y., & Rodriguez, M. L. (1989). Delay of gratification in children. *Science, 244*, 933–938.

(e.g., Berlyne, 1960; Mischel, 1974). A hot representation of a reward such as a desired treat activates the behaviors associated with experiencing or consuming it. When young children look at the actual rewards, or think about them, they may focus spontaneously on these hot, arousing qualities. If they do this, they increase their own frustration and arousal, making it more difficult to continue to wait (e.g., Mischel & Ebbesen, 1970; Mischel et al., 1972; Toner, 1981). In contrast, a psychologically distant or cool, cognitive representation of the rewards has the opposite effect on self-regulation, enhancing goal-directed waiting (see Figure 17.3). Thus, presenting children with a picture of the rewards (e.g., in the form of life-size slide-projected images) or instructing them to cognitively transform them in their heads (e.g., by turning the pretzels into thin, brown logs in their imagination) actually facilitates waiting. In short, further experiments found that just how one thinks about the rewards (hot or cool) in the contingency crucially influences how long one can wait or work to attain them (Carlson, Davis, & Leach, 2005; Metcalfe & Mischel, 1999; Mischel & Baker, 1975; Mischel & Moore, 1973; Mischel et al., 1989; Peake et al., 2002).

17.11 How do hot and cool construals of rewards differ? How can they be used to resist immediate gratification?

Flexible Attention

Adaptive self-regulation in goal pursuit involves more than application of cooling strategies. It requires shifting attention flexibly rather than unconditional use of cooling strategies. Experiments confirm that some of the children who delay best seem to focus briefly on the hot features in the situation to sustain motivation but then quickly switch back to the cool features and self-distraction to avoid excessive arousal and frustration (Peake et al., 2002).

Effective self-regulation also requires sensitivity to the demands, constraints, and opportunities of the particular situation. Such **discriminative facility**—taking into account characteristics of each situation and responding accordingly—may play a central role in coping, self-regulation, and social-emotional competence in general (see Cheng, 2003; Chiu et al., 1995). Distraction, or cooling, then, is likely to be adaptive when applied to coping in aversive or frustrating situations that must be tolerated for goal attainment, but not in many other types of situations. The key is to know when to cool, when to stay warm, and to be able to do so when you need to. The mechanisms described underlie the kind of flexible, discriminative behaviors that Jack Block (2001), working at the Dispositional and Psychodynamic Levels, also saw as the essence of the resilient person.

Summary

In sum, in this section we have focused on voluntary delay of gratification when trying to control impulses in the process of waiting or working for a positive delayed outcome or goal. The bottom line of these findings is that they show that how the person construes and interprets the situation, and deploys attention while attempting effortful control, has clear effects on effortful control ability: hot construals hurt, cool construals help.

Life-Span Implications of Self-Regulatory Competence

So far, we examined the processes that make self-regulation possible and that underlie individual differences in this ability. But does this ability really matter, and do individual differences in it early in life predict anything long term that's important?

Stable Self-Regulatory Competence

Self-regulatory competence as assessed in the delay of gratification paradigm in early childhood turns out to be a reliable index of a stable competence basic for many aspects of personality. To illustrate, those who waited longer in this situation as preschoolers were described by their parents as more socially and cognitively competent teenagers. They were perceived as more able to manage stress and exert effective self-control in diverse frustrating situations in adolescence (Mischel et al., 1989). They also had substantially higher SAT scores than the children who could not wait (Shoda et al., 1990). In a follow-up when they reached their early 30s, correlations remained significant between their preschool delay behavior and adult-relevant measures of social-cognitive competence, goal-setting, planning, and self-regulatory abilities (Ayduk et al., 2000).

17.12 What is the evidence that self-regulatory competence is a stable personality factor that aids adjustment?

Long-Term Protective Effects

Especially exciting is the finding that this type of self-regulatory competence may have significant long-term protective effects on other aspects of personality. Self-regulatory competence can help to protect people from experiencing many of the negative consequences associated with their dispositional vulnerabilities. Consider again the tendency to be highly rejection-sensitive (RS) in interpersonal relationships. Often, highly rejection-sensitive people in time develop lower self-esteem and become either more aggressive or more depressed, which, in turn, undermines the quality of their lives (Downey & Feldman, 1996). But that is not necessarily their fate.

In an adult follow-up of the preschoolers who had participated in the original delay of gratification studies 20 years earlier, preschool delay ability predicted adult resiliency against the potentially destructive effects of RS (Ayduk et al., 2000, Study 1). Specifically, high RS people who were able to delay gratification longer in preschool were buffered in adulthood against low self-esteem and self-worth, were better able to cope with stress, and had greater ego resiliency. High RS people who were unable to delay gratification in preschool had lower academic achievement and more frequent cocaine/crack use than low RS people. As Figure 17.4 shows, high RS people who had high preschool delay ability were buffered against such negative outcomes.

A parallel study, conducted among low-income, urban, minority middle-school children who are at higher demographic risk for maladjustment, replicated these findings with population-appropriate measures (Ayduk et al., 2000, Study 2). Again, among

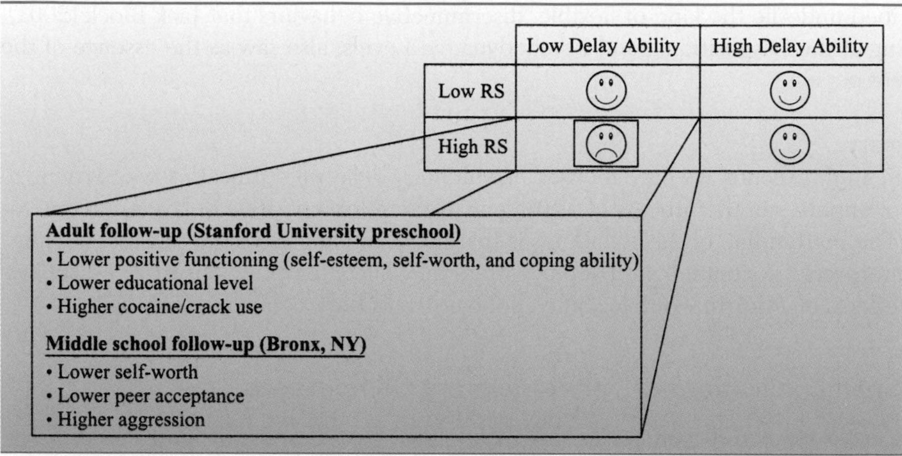

Figure 17.4 Chronic vulnerability (rejection sensitivity) is linked to negative outcomes when delay ability is low.

Note: Smiley faces show positive outcomes, frowning faces, negative outcomes. High delay ability protected even high rejection-sensitive people from the negative outcomes experienced by equally rejection-sensitive people who also were low in delay ability. Only the combination of High RS, Low Delay predicted significantly negative life outcomes.

Source: Based on studies in Ayduk, O., Mendoza-Denton, R., Mischel, W., Downey, G., Peake, P. K., & Rodriguez, M. (2000). Regulating the interpersonal self: Strategic self-regulation for coping with rejection sensitivity. *Journal of Personality and Social Psychology, 79*, 776–792.

children high in RS, delay of gratification ability was associated with lower aggression against peers, greater interpersonal acceptance, and higher levels of self-worth. Children who were low in delay ability but high in RS exhibited the negative behaviors typical of the RS dynamics. The overall findings support the idea that self-regulatory competencies restrain the influence of high RS on the behavior that is ultimately generated by the personality system.

Individual differences in attention control and self-regulation are visible already in the behavior of toddlers, and they predict self-regulatory competencies years later in development. In one study, mother–toddler interactions were observed as they unfolded at 19 months of age (Sethi et al., 2000). Some toddlers used effective attention deployment strategies, such as self-distraction, to cope with and "cool" distress while briefly separated from their mothers in a playroom experiment. They tended to become the preschoolers who also used more effective attention strategies to help themselves to delay gratification when tested in preschool $3\frac{1}{2}$ years later. When they were toddlers, they had actively directed attention away from the mother's absence, distracting themselves by exploring the room and playing with toys. In contrast, other toddlers were unable to activate such cooling strategies at 19 months. Instead, they stayed focused on the absence of the mother (e.g., clinging to the door) and became distressed. These tended to be the youngsters who also were less able to effectively self-distract during preschool delay and were unable to wait to get the bigger treat that they wanted.

In sum, individual differences in the use of effective attention strategies for reducing stress and making self-regulation easier are seen early in life and seem to endure. Stable individual differences in attention processes such as eye-gaze aversion and flexible attention shifting and focusing also have been found as early as in infancy. Further, effective attention control is related to having lower impulsivity and less negative affect later in life, as seen both in children and in adults (Derryberry, 2002; Derryberry & Rothbart, 1997). Thus, attention control is part of a generalized self-regulatory competency that enables effective cooling of arousal and self-control of impulsive behaviors. These skills have adaptive long-term benefits and can protect against dispositional vulnerabilities.

Multiple Interacting Influences in Self-Regulation

Table 17.3 summarizes examples of interactions between indices of self-regulatory competence and a variety of social stressors, and other determinants and influences in the course of early personality development. Overall, these studies, conducted at different levels of analysis, indicate that self-regulatory competence may help protect individuals against the negative impact of diverse disadvantages, social conditions, and experiences, such as lack of maternal guidance, maternal hostility, and other measures of uncaring parenting, as summarized in Table 17.3. But note also the study by Stams and colleagues (2002) of internationally adopted children followed from 6 months of age to 7 years of age. It found that ego control and cognitive development, considered markers of self-regulatory competence, are predicted jointly by the child's difficult temperament early in life and attachment insecurity with the adopted mother.

A note of caution needs to be remembered. The causal directions and pathways generally are uncertain in studies of personality development because the results are based on correlations indicating the associations among multiple influences and determinants. In such research it's difficult to tease out which influences lead to which outcomes. The findings on the whole indicate that many of these variables and influences are closely connected, but the exact nature of the connections remain somewhat uncertain. A conclusion that can be reached with confidence, however, is that the number of interacting factors in personality development that influence self-regulation is large. And self-regulatory competence in turn has multiple important positive influences on many aspects of the person's life. These multiple determinants and factors are found at many levels of analysis, and they are expressed in the personality system's continuous interactions with the social world over the course of development.

TABLE 17.3 Self-Regulation and Personality Development: Examples of Interacting Influences

Source	Finding
Rubin, Cheah, & Fox (2001)	Preschoolers' reticent and shy behavior was predicted by an interaction between child's emotional regulation and lack of maternal guidance. Children with emotional control problems were more likely to be shy and reticent only if they had mothers who were not responsive and did not give guidance, as assessed during stressful teaching task.
Morris et al. (2002)	Among first- and second-grade children, maternal hostility, a characteristic of negative parenting, was related to acting out (aggressive, externalizing) behavior problems, as reported by teachers. But this was true only in children with poor effortful control. It suggests, again, that the effect of negative parenting on social adjustment may depend on the child's regulatory control. And vice versa, the child's difficulties with self-regulation may lead to greater behavioral problems only in the presence of negative parenting.
Stams, Juffer, & van Ijzendoorn (2002)	In a sample of internationally adopted children followed from 6 months of age to 7 years of age, attachment insecurity (with the adopted mother) and difficult child temperament predicted lower levels of ego control and cognitive development.
Gunnar, Larson, Hertsgaard, Harris, & Brodersen (1992); see Gunnar & Donzella (2002), for review.	Child's temperamental negative affectivity (e.g., seen in temper tantrums) predicts increases in cortisol—a physiological marker of dysregulation—in the face of stress, but only when there also is poor, and unresponsive adult caretaking.

▶ SELF-REGULATION IN AVOIDANCE (AVERSIVE) DILEMMAS

Cognitive Appraisal of Stress: Dealing with Negative Emotions

17.13 Describe some advantages and undesirable consequences of cognitive detachment in aversive situations.

The way we encode or appraise situations influences self-regulation not just when the situation involves temptations but also when it is negative and aversive. The cognitive appraisal strategies that help people deal with the control of appetitive impulses as in the delay situation, also apply to emotional self-regulation for dealing with aversive emotions, fears, and stress-inducing situations. An example of such stressors is the anxiety-producing situation medical students confront in the anatomy room when it's time to dissect their first human cadaver (see *In Focus 17.1*).

Experimental research confirms that an attitude of detachment helps people react more calmly when exposed to gory scenes portraying bloody accidents and death (Koriat, Melkman, Averill, & Lazarus, 1972) or when expecting electric shock (Holmes & Houston, 1974). These results are consistent with reports showing that soldiers may immunize themselves against emotion by distancing themselves psychologically from their victims, for example, by calling them "gooks" and labeling them as subhumans. While highly effective for reducing feeling, a detachment strategy to reduce emotionality can be misused, producing callous, insensitive attitudes and cold-bloodedness toward others, in war, in medical practice, and in much of social life. On the other hand, in many life situations, detachment through cognitive reappraisal to attain emotional cooling provides a basic route for effective emotion regulation.

Cognitive Appraisal versus Hiding Negative Feelings

17.14 How did James Gross study the relative effectiveness of emotional suppression and cognitive reappraisal? What were the results?

When people are trying to hide their secret thoughts, or reduce the pain and fear of viewing a horrible event, what processes allow them to regulate their negative emotions? Stanford University psychologist James Gross and his colleagues have focused on two specific emotion regulation strategies. One is **cognitive reappraisal**, the other is hiding negative feelings or **suppression**.

In a typical study, Gross brings participants into the laboratory and informs them that they will be watching a movie. The film they will see shows detailed, close-up views of severe burn victims or of an arm amputation. The researchers then divide

IN FOCUS 17.1

OVERCOMING THE STRESS OF DISSECTING A CADAVER IN MEDICAL TRAINING

In a study that directly speaks to this type of self-regulatory dilemma, researchers interviewed medical students witnessing a medical autopsy for the first time (Lief & Fox, 1963). They found that many aspects of the autopsy procedure appear to have been designed as an institutionalized ritual to help students cope with their distress by making it easier for them to detach themselves emotionally. The autopsy room itself is arranged to provide a sterile, clinical, impersonal atmosphere. The face and genitalia of the corpse are kept covered unless they are being examined, and so on. But beyond the physical arrangements, it is a detached, emotionally distanced scientific stance that further helps to keep the whole procedure abstract and impersonal, helping to reduce emotional arousal. But as is always the case, adopting such a stance is easier for some people than for others.

participants into one of three different groups and give each different instructions before they view the film. In the cognitive reappraisal condition, they are asked to use a cooling strategy. Specifically, they are asked to try to think about the movie in a detached, unemotional way, objectively, and to focus attention on the technical details of the event, not feeling anything personally (e.g., pretend that you're a teacher in medical school). In the suppression condition, participants are asked to try to hide their emotional reactions to the film as they watch it so that anyone seeing them would not know that they were feeling anything at all. In the control condition, participants are simply asked to watch the movie.

This and similar studies find that cognitive reappraisal is an overwhelmingly more adaptive way to regulate negative emotions. It is much better than suppression in which people try to hide the feelings they are experiencing. These differences are seen in how the two strategies influence the intensity of people's experiences as well as their effect on the person's level of physiological autonomic nervous system arousal and distress. Specifically, people who are told to think about the movie in a way that cools the emotional content (reappraisal condition) experience fewer feelings of disgust and less physiological activation (evidenced by less blood vessel constriction) when compared to people who are asked to try to hide and suppress their emotional responses to the film so that no one could see their real feelings on their faces (Gross, 1998).

Cognitive reappraisal and suppression produce differences at the cognitive level of analysis as well. In a variation of the study described above, participants saw a slide show instead of a movie and were later asked how much of the information from the slide show they remembered. People who suppressed during the experiment performed more poorly on the memory task relative to people who engaged in cognitive reappraisal (Richards & Gross, 2000). In addition, people who have a chronic tendency to suppress perform more poorly on memory tasks than those who don't tend to suppress (Gross & John, 2003). Finally, note that the results from this work on emotion regulation are consistent with a psychodynamic level view of the relative ineffectiveness of emotional denial: trying to hide one's feelings is a poor defense mechanism (Chapters 8 and 9).

Seeing ghastly images and horrible scenes certainly is a strong stressor and it has provided a useful method for studying the power of cognitive appraisals in dealing with aversive situations (e.g., Lazarus, 2006). But much of human stress arises not when looking at photographs or films but in painful social interactions and upsetting emotional hassles and clashes inevitable in close relationships. In recent new directions, researchers are also clarifying the mental mechanisms that allow people to "get over" and work through such emotional stressors, as discussed in *In Focus 17.2*.

Cognitive Transformations to Deal with Stress

Not surprisingly, a good deal of related research leads to the conclusion that psychological distancing and strategic self-distraction, when possible, can be an excellent way to manage unavoidable stresses like unpleasant medical examinations (Miller, 1987; Miller & Green, 1985) and coping with severe life crises (Taylor & Brown, 1988). Self-distraction (e.g., watching travel slides or recalling pleasant memories) increases tolerance of experimentally induced physical pain (e.g., Berntzen, 1987; Chaves & Barber, 1974). Similarly, distracting and relaxation-inducing activities such as listening to music reduce anxiety in the face of uncontrollable shocks (Miller, 1979, 1996) helps people cope with the daily pain of rheumatoid arthritis (Affleck, Urrows, Tennen, & Higgins, 1992) and even with severe life crises (e.g., Taylor & Brown, 1988). "Cooling" strategies generally can help one to transform potentially stressful situations to make them less aversive.

IN FOCUS 17.2

WORKING THROUGH, AND GETTING OVER, EMOTIONAL HASSLES IN CLOSE RELATIONSHIPS

You get into an argument in a close relationship. Rather than "move on" after the argument is over, thoughts regarding the event stream through your mind, often against your will, leading you to become increasingly upset. Both common wisdom and research suggest that in order to "get over" such intense negative emotional experiences people need to work through and understand their feelings. However, people's attempts to do this are often counterproductive, leading to rumination that increases distress. So what is a person to do? This question is addressed by research into the psychological processes that enable people to adaptively confront and analyze negative feelings and experiences, in order to get over them, without leading them to become overwhelmed.

According to Kross and colleagues (2005), two conditions enhance such adaptive reflection. First, a person has to remain calm and "cool" when thinking about intense negative emotional experiences. In their research, the authors facilitate "emotional cooling" by instructing participants to adopt a *psychologically distanced* perspective (i.e., take a step back . . . watch the conflict happening to you from a distance) immediately after cueing them to recall an intense, anger-arousing experience. Second, when attempting to work through emotions it helps to focus specifically on the reasons underlying one's feelings (e.g., "Why did I feel that way?"), rather than on the specific chain of events and emotions experienced (e.g., "What did I feel?"; "What happened?"). The combination of these two mental operations (i.e., focusing on reasons from a self-distanced perspective) is important because they enable people to cognitively re-represent their experiences and the emotions they elicited in relatively cool, cognitive terms, making sense of them without overwhelming them with their aversiveness (Metcalfe & Mischel, 1999).

Kross and colleagues (2005) showed that participants who are instructed to *both* adopt a distanced perspective and focus specifically on the reasons underlying their feelings are most able to think about their experiences without increasing negative affect. In contrast, groups of participants who do not engage in both of these mental operations display elevated levels of distress. The overall findings help explain when people's attempts to understand their negative feelings are likely to be adaptive and when they are likely instead to trigger rumination.

17.15 What kind of cognitive transformations can help people "work through" an emotionally distressing situation?

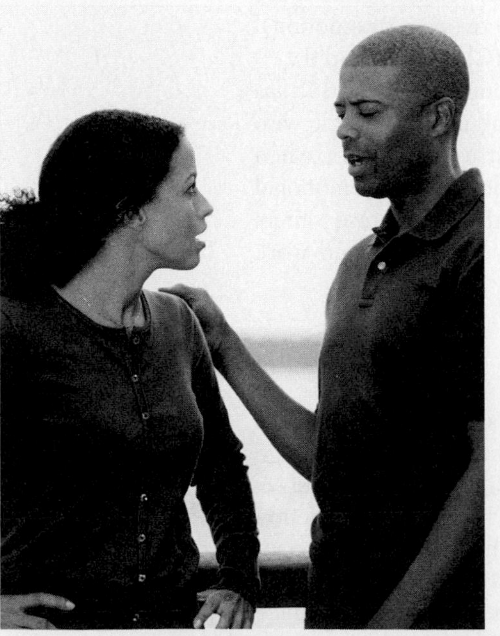

How can people decrease negative affect during emotional conflict?

(*Source*: Image Source/Getty Images)

For example, if surgical patients are encouraged to reconstrue their hospital stay as a vacation to relax a while from the stresses of daily life, they show better postoperative adjustment (Langer, Janis, & Wolfer, 1975), just as chronically ill patients who reinterpret their conditions more positively also show better adjustment (Carver et al., 1993). In sum, when stress and pain are inevitable, the adage to look for the silver lining and to "accentuate the positive" seems wise.

The type of cognitive strategy that helps one to deal best with stress also depends on the individual (Miller, 1987). Recall, for example, individual differences in the tendency to use distraction or "blunt" rather than to sensitize or "monitor," discussed in the chapter on repression as a mechanism of defense (Chapter 8). The point to remember is that such preferences in the type of information sought for dealing with stress affect how the person copes best with stress; while one strategy may help some people, the opposite strategy may help others. The task is to get the right match.

▶ INTERACTION OF HOT AND COOL SYSTEMS IN SELF-REGULATION

The biological brain system and the personality system of processing dynamics activated in any given situation are in a continuous, dynamic two-way interaction process. What the medical student thinks when dealing with the dissection, and where he or she focuses his or her attention (on the ghastly tortured expression on the face, on the intricate ways in which the capillary system is organized) influence what becomes activated in the brain, which influences what one next feels and thinks, on and on. To reiterate, the psychological system and the biological system interact: to understand them requires attention to how they play out jointly.

Specifically, with regard to both approach and avoidance dilemmas, the person's thoughts, cognitive appraisals, and attention deployment are related to, and influence, what happens in the relevant brain systems. That process, in turn, influences what is experienced emotionally and cognitively in continuous interaction. At the Social Cognitive Level, cooling operations make it easier to activate long-term goals and reduce the hot pull of the immediate emotion-producing triggers in the situation. Consequently, what becomes activated in the brain and at the neural level is modified as well. To understand this more deeply, we have to examine the relevant interactions.

The Emotional (Hot) Brain/The Rational (Cool) Brain

To reiterate, the situations in which people most need and want to control their impulses often are those in which it is most difficult for them to do so. These are the situations that elicit "hot" emotional reactions such as intense fear and anxiety, or strong appetites and cravings. These were seen in miniature form in the studies of little children trying so hard to wait for bigger treats but unable to hold out as the temptation to "get it now" becomes too strong. These kinds of hot situations tend to automatically trigger hot reactions—to eat the dessert, take the drug, grab the hundred-dollar bill dropped in your path. Such situations rapidly generate the associated feelings of fear or desire and the urge to respond impulsively. They lead people to bypass self-regulatory controls and self-standards just when they need them most. Why does that happen so easily?

17.16 What kinds of situations are the most difficult for impulse control?

Bodily Changes: Emotion in Stress

When an event triggers automatic fear reactions or is perceived as stressful, physiological reactions in the body are triggered at the Biological Level. Such feelings as "makes my heart race" and "choked up with rage" or "ready to vomit" are experienced psychologically in emotional states that involve bodily changes. It is the activation of the sympathetic division of the autonomic nervous system that produces many of the physiological changes that are experienced in reaction to perceived stress. They include a cascade of events such as channeling of the blood supply to the muscles and brain, slowing down of stomach and intestinal activity, increase in heart rate and blood pressure, and the pupils in the eyes widen. There is an increase in rates of metabolism and respiration, increase in sugar content of the blood, decrease in electrical resistance of the skin, increase in speed of the blood's ability to clot, and even "goose pimples" resulting from the erection of hairs on the skin.

Fight or Flight Reactions

These changes are referred to as parts of the automatic **fight or flight reaction**, because they are considered to be the body's emergency reaction system to threat and danger. At an evolutionary level, this automatic reaction pattern reflects an adaptive system developed over the course of the species' history for getting ready to cope with environmental challenges. These biological reactions enable the organism to cope rapidly and effectively with diverse environmental dangers, in part by providing the alertness and energy necessary for survival in the face of attack. This mechanism was crucial for survival in earlier ages in the species' history when physical dangers lurked everywhere.

17.17 How can stress responses have evolutionary value but be maladaptive in today's world?

Activation of this system can save your life when you face a real emergency—for example, when about to be assaulted in a dark alley, or in the midst of a sudden fire. However, in contemporary life, it is often elicited in response to situations that do not objectively endanger survival. When you face a French examination, or a cadaver you have to dissect in an anatomy class, or walk into the boss's office to ask for a raise, it may feel high risk; but adaptive behavior in dealing with such challenges requires more fine-grain reactions—like thinking and planning—rather than fight or flight. In these situations, automatic hot emotional reactions, particularly intense fears, become debilitating rather than adaptive (e.g., LeDoux, 1996, 2001). And when individuals have these experiences persistently over long periods of time, they can become dangerous to physical health and well-being. The Type A pattern used to illustrate a dispositional typology in Chapter 3 is an example.

In sum, hot reflexive reactions may be part of the overall arousal state that helps initiate quick adaptive action, as in an emergency response to sudden dangers that mobilize the body's resources like a fire alarm. In the course of human evolution they are sure to have had important adaptive advantages for survival. However, this alarm system can make reflection and self-regulation most difficult (Metcalfe & Mischel, 1999).

The Hot Amygdala

The amygdala, the small, primitive brain structure crucially important in emotional reactions like fear (LeDoux, 1996), reacts immediately to danger signals, preparing the body biologically to fight or flee as virtually reflexive reactions. As noted above, presumably this automatic emergency reaction was useful for adaptation. From an evolutionary perspective, it had survival value to be able to react fast to the snake in the grass without having to think about it, or to fight the opponent who is ready to strike when flight is not possible. The amygdala also seems to play an important role in strong appetitive behaviors, leading to impulsive approach behaviors, as when the sizzling pizza becomes irresistible to the hungry dieter, or the preschooler can't resist the tempting, immediately available treat in the delay experiments.

17.18 What brain areas underlie the hot and cool behavior regulation systems, and how do they interact with one another?

The Rational Cool Brain

But these automatic reactions are only a "quick fix" that actually doesn't work well for most situations people face in modern life (LeDoux, 1996, p. 176). Unlike lower animals on the evolutionary ladder, human beings have the capacity to take control with higher-level brain centers (the prefrontal cortex). This makes it possible for the person to start cool rational thinking to try to solve the problem that the amygdala has already begun to respond to automatically and emotionally. How you think—hot or cool—can change the attention control centers activated, which in turn makes self-regulatory efforts either more or less difficult (Derryberry, 2002; Posner & Rothbart, 1998). In short, humans have an emotional brain. But they also have other cognitive areas of the brain that are crucially important for the more rational, higher-level processes that make the species human. While part of the brain is emotional, there also is a thoughtful part that can be rational and used to solve problems effectively. Both areas of the brain interact in dealing with emotion-arousing dilemmas. The Hot System/Cool System Interaction model of self-regulation considered next was designed to understand these interactions.

Hot System/Cool System Interaction in Self-Regulation

To understand how the person's thoughts and feelings interact to enable or prevent self-control, a two-system biosocial model of willpower was developed to integrate findings on self-regulation from all levels of analysis. In this model, self-regulation is a function of a balance between two processing systems: the **emotional**, **hot system** and the **cognitive**, **cool system** (Metcalfe & Mischel, 1999). The emotional, hot system generates automatic approach–avoidance or fight-or-flight responses. Biologically it is based primarily in the amygdala. In contrast, the cognitive cool system, based in the **hippocampus** and frontal lobe, is the locus of cognitive thought processes, generating thoughtful reflective reactions and plans. At relatively low levels of stress, the two systems work in concert, but as stress levels and aversive arousal (e.g., frustration) increase, hot-system processing begins to dominate the cool system. Thus, effective self-regulation hinges on being able to access cooling mechanisms to reduce negative arousal and suppress hot system activation when needed (Carlson & Beck, in press; Metcalfe & Mischel, 1999).

The *cool cognitive system* is specialized for complex mental and spatial representation and thought. It is cognitive, emotionally neutral, contemplative, flexible, integrated, coherent, slow, strategic—the seat of self-regulation and self-control. The *hot system* is specialized for quick emotional processing and automatic responding to "hot" trigger stimuli, as when rejection cues elicit abusive behavior from highly rejection-sensitive people. It is quick and automatic, and is the basis of emotionality. It activates fears as well as passions, and it is impulsive and reflexive. This system is fundamental for emotional (classical) conditioning, but its activation undermines efforts at self-control, reflective thought, and planfulness.

IN FOCUS 17.3

NEURAL MECHANISMS IN IMPULSIVE VIOLENCE

Recent advances in brain imaging technology have allowed researchers to understand how impulsive "hot" behavioral tendencies, seen for example in outbursts of violence and impulsive aggression, play out in underlying neural processes at the brain level of analysis. Among the many scientists that are active in this area of research, University of Wisconsin psychologist Richard Davidson and his colleagues (2000) have been pinpointing specific patterns of brain activation that underlie the self-regulation of impulsive behavior.

Drawing on both animal and human brain research, Davidson and his colleagues (2000) have found that emotion is normally regulated in the human brain by a complex circuit of brain structures involving several interconnected regions. Brain imaging studies suggest that in a typical sequence of events, threatening behaviors (staring eyes, shouting, etc.) are conveyed to the amygdala, which then sends information to other higher regions of the brain that are responsible for initiating behavioral reactions.

In normal people, however, this pattern of events (threatening stimuli → amygdala activation → response) does not always lead to impulsive emotional responses. A number of prefrontal brain regions connect to the amygdala and interact to constrain the impulsive expression of emotional behavior. These connections provide people with the ability to self-regulate their emotional responses. It is the prefrontal brain regions that seem to constitute the core structures underlying the process of emotion regulation and are thus essential for achieving emotional restraint at the Biological Level. Consequently, functional or structural abnormalities in one or more of these regions, or in the interconnections among them, are believed to increase people's impulsive tendencies. Indeed, Davidson and his colleagues' research suggest that individuals who are predisposed to aggression and violence many suffer from an abnormality in this prefrontal circuitry.

The balance between the hot and cool systems is influenced both by stress and by the person's level of development. Stress—both chronic and situational—enhances the hot system and reduces activity in the cool system. With maturation beginning at about age 4 years, the cool system becomes more developed and active, and the hot system becomes more manageable (see *In Focus 17.3* for discussion of the brain mechanisms involved as maturation normally occurs).

Attention Control

How does all this translate into what people have to do for effective goal pursuit and resistance to temptations when dealing with the kinds of dilemmas discussed throughout this chapter? Extrapolating from the delay of gratification research and other studies on self-regulation (Derryberry, 2002; Mischel et al., 1996), when the person thinks of the rewards that can be obtained right away in a "hot" way, they become irresistible. But through mental transformations and strategic self-distractions, one can effectively continue to delay by "cooling" the hot pull of the immediate gratifications (Mischel et al., 1989). Parallel strategies can help to reduce the aversive arousal created for the medical student for the first time dissecting a human body, who has to control himself from automatically dashing out of the room or becoming ill. For that goal, he has to shift attention away from his distressing feelings and focus instead on the complex technical details of the brain structures on the cadaver he is working on to prevent messing up the dissection.

17.19 How can voluntary attentional control guide hot and cool systems in an adaptive fashion?

Cool cognitions focused on the technical details of the procedures allow him to regulate his feelings adaptively, and shift them away from his distress and empathy with a dead human on to the medical task that needs doing. But that can change in a millisecond if suddenly something in the face reminds him that it looks a little like his father when he died.

When people manage to cool their impulsive hot reactions by attention control, they can make use of the vast cognitive resources that give humans their evolutionary advantage (Metcalfe & Jacobs, 1998; Metcalfe & Mischel, 1999). In other words, the trick is to think cool when your impulse is to act hot, and reduce hot ideation so that automatic hot responses are not made. Then problems can be dealt with more rationally, allowing long-term goals to be pursued effectively even in the face of strong momentary temptations to forget them. The ability to use attention control effectively in this manner is related closely to mechanisms that are activated in the brain. The first chapter of this text described the case of Charles Whitman, the Texas Tower killer who suddenly massacred people on the college campus below him. Many years later it now is becoming possible to understand what may go wrong in such cases at the Biological Level, as discussed in *In Focus 17.3*.

Making Willpower Automatic: From Intentions to *If . . . Then . . .* Implementation

To make adaptive hot system/cool system interactions more accessible when they are needed most urgently takes more than good intentions and highly valued long-term goals. The process that makes it possible to go from good intentions to effective action control and goal attainment has been clarified by Gollwitzer and colleagues in research on the role of plans in self-regulation (see Gollwitzer, 1999; Patterson & Mischel, 1975). They find that to avoid succumbing to stimulus control it helps to plan out and rehearse specific *if . . . then . . .* **implementation intentions** or contingency plans. These plans specify the steps needed to protect the person from the obstacles, frustrations, and temptations likely to be encountered, keeping in mind and in awareness the demands of the current goal that is being pursued (Gollwitzer, 1999).

17.20 How are *if . . . then . . .* implementation intentions helpful in goal pursuit?

When planned and rehearsed, *if . . . then . . .* implementation intentions help self-control because goal-directed action is initiated relatively automatically when the relevant trigger cues become situationally salient. Implementation intentions help in a wide range of regulatory tasks, from action initiation (e.g., I will start writing the paper the day after Thanksgiving), to inhibition of unwanted habitual responses (e.g., When the dessert menu is served, I will not order the chocolate cake), and resistance to temptation (e.g., If the distraction arises, I will ignore it). This research indicates that some effortful, deliberative process of linking action plans to specific situational triggers (the "ifs") is necessary in the initial phases to begin to make self-control automatic. After this link has been established and sufficiently rehearsed, it is easier to self-regulate effectively because the essential cool system strategies become activated much more readily, even when stress is high, without conscious effort. If the specified situational cue is activated and encountered, the planned behavior runs off automatically (Gollwitzer, 1990, 1999). In this sense, implementation intentions also help to take the effort out of "effortful self-control."

Social Emotions Enable Self-Regulation: Links to Evolution

The discussion so far might easily create the impression that self-regulation always requires cooling one's emotions so that rational, problem-focused thinking can proceed effectively. In fact, it all depends on which emotions are involved. There are many social

17.21 Why are social emotions an important evolutionary mechanism for human life? What is their relation to Freud's superego?

emotions that activate feelings like loyalty to the group or a partner. Such emotions can support self-regulation by calling attention to the long-term consequences of behaving, for example, in selfish or disloyal ways. Observations of life in diverse cultures throughout the world lead anthropologists and other social scientists to that conclusion as well (e.g., Fiske, 2002; Nesse, 2001). Their analysis again draws on evolutionary theory.

For example, the anthropologist-psychologist Alan Fiske (2002) proposes that from an evolutionary perspective, certain emotions have developed and are universally experienced because they are useful for self-regulation and make social life and long-term relationships possible in human society everywhere. The emotions that are experienced, however, also are shaped by the local demands and structures of the particular culture. Fiske argues that people need to have emotions that represent their important relationships, reflected in such feelings as empathy, affection, and loyalty.

Further, because humans are naturally impulsive and self-serving creatures driven to immediate gratification, they need to experience these essentially social and moral emotions, including guilt and shame, that allow them to take account of the long-term consequences of their actions. Such emotions help people to curb their appetites and prevent themselves from acting in impulsive, relationship-destructive and community-destructive ways. They are experienced as quick internal signals that help activate rapidly the self-control necessary for cooperation, for resisting temptation, and for maintaining duties and obligations. In short, this evolutionary and anthropological view casts what Freud called the superego in a new light. It sees the social-moral emotions as reflecting adaptive evolutionary processes. The basic point is that humans have intense social and moral emotions because they motivate them to "curb their non-social appetites in the interest of the relationships that are so crucial to their survival, reproduction, and welfare" (Fiske, 2002, pp. 173–174). These ideas are still in need of much research before they allow for firm conclusions. However, they help make clear that self-regulation reflects a basic human process shaped by a wide range of interacting influences, and is central for understanding the nature of personality.

The Downside of Self-Regulation

On the one hand, cooling operations and effortful attention control seem to have significant value for the adaptive pursuit of life goals and effective functioning over time. On the other hand, these competencies may come with a cost, making some of these "high delay" individuals susceptible to other kinds of difficulties such as tendencies to become avoidant and withdrawn (Eisenberg et al., 2002). Likewise, whether or not one *should* or *should not* delay gratification or "exercise the will" in any particular choice is often everything but self-evident. Lionel Trilling, a distinguished humanist with much to say about psychology, captured the risks of too much self-control in a few words. After reminding us of the place of passion, he said "the will is not everything," and spoke of the "panic and emptiness which make their onset when the will is tired from its own excess" (Trilling, 1943, p. 139). An excess of will can certainly be as self-defeating as its absence. Postponing gratification can be an unwise—and even stifling—joyless choice. But unless people develop the competencies to sustain delay and continue to exercise their will when they want and need to do so, the choice itself is lost.

17.22 In what ways can excessive self-control be maladaptive?

Conclusions

Putting it together, "willpower" requires a combination of self-regulatory competencies and regulatory motivation: both desire (goals and motivations) and regulatory competencies (e.g., flexible attention deployment strategies) are needed. Both are necessary if one is to go from good but difficult intentions to their realization under frustrating, temptation-filled conditions. Even when regulatory competency is available, it will not be activated in the absence of regulatory motivation. Case studies and dramatic examples abound of individuals, including a recent U.S. president who exerted remarkable self-regulation in many areas of life—but did not do so in other areas, although the consequences were destructive. Presumably these individuals had the ability to control themselves but not sufficient motivation. Conversely, regulatory motivation is unlikely to sustain difficult, long-term goal pursuit unless regulatory competency is available and accessible to smooth the journey.

17.23 How does the social cognitive conception differ from the notion of willpower as an internal force that people either have or don't have?

The ingredients of willpower and particularly the processing dynamics that enable delay of gratification and self-regulatory competence have long been mysterious, but some of the essentials now seem clear. Individual differences in self-regulatory ability are visible early in life, and a good deal is also known about the basic attention control mechanisms that enable it. These mechanisms help to demystify willpower and identify some of its key ingredients. Attention control is important in dealing both with fear and with the regulation of appetitive-approach behaviors. The implications of regulatory ability for the self are straightforward. This ability influences self-concepts and self-esteem, interpersonal strategies (e.g., aggression), coping, and the ability to buffer or protect the self against the maladaptive consequences of chronic personal vulnerabilities such as rejection sensitivity.

Some of the core studies on self-regulation began years ago when researchers at the Social Cognitive Level wanted to test ideas about the mechanisms that enable delay first proposed at the Psychodynamic Level and also at the Behavioral Level. Both levels had suggested that a focus on the rewards or goals, and attention directed at them, should sustain the ability to wait or work for them. After many years of research, the results show that the predictions were partly right, partly wrong, or just importantly incomplete, as often happens in the growth of a science. Delay ability, and much self-regulation, does hinge, as Freud put it, on mental representations of the objects of desire. But the crucial feature is whether the mental representation is hot or cool.

Looking back, work inspired by insights from both the Psychodynamic and the Behavioral Level, conducted in a framework influenced by the Phenomenological and Social Cognitive Levels, gradually is emerging with a more integrative and complete view of delay ability based on different pieces of contributions from all the levels. This is noteworthy not just as a piece of the history of personality research, but because it documents a main thesis of this text: In the long view, personality research and ideas developed at the different levels of analysis don't leave you just with many alternative ways of thinking about personality. They also add up to give an increasingly cumulative and integrative picture of the growth of personality science that begins to demystify some of the complexities of human personality.

Potential for Self-Directed Change?

An important question remains about self-regulation: can it be taught to empower the self and improve resilience? We do know that attention control strategies can be briefly modified in experiments (Ayduk, Mischel, & Downey, 2002; Mischel et al., 1989). Moreover, when effective control strategies are modeled, they may be readily adopted and generalize to self-control behavior outside the lab for at least a few months (Bandura & Mischel, 1965). What is not yet known is whether effective attention control to reduce stress and frustration during goal pursuit can be increased long term via socialization, education, and therapy.

▶ SUMMARY

OVERVIEW OF CONTRIBUTIONS TO SELF-REGULATION FROM EACH LEVEL

- Each level of analysis contributes to our understanding of self-regulation processes.
- At the Trait-Dispositional Level self-regulatory behaviors are seen as evidence of dimensional constructs.
- At the Psychodynamic-Motivational Level self-regulation reflects internal conflicts between id, ego, and superego, while the Biological Level looks at physiological correlates of self-regulation.
- Theorists at the Behavioral-Conditioning Level look at how situations and stimuli affect self-regulatory ability, and those from the Phenomenological-Humanistic Level look at how the individual's construals impact his or her ability to self-regulate.
- The Social Cognitive Level examines how an individual's construal interacts with the situation and other mental representations to influence goal-directed behavior.

SELF-REGULATORY PROCESSES IN GOAL PURSUIT

- In goal hierarchies, when a lower-level goal (e.g., getting a job) is blocked and frustrated, people often continue to strive toward the higher-level goal (being safe and secure).
- In goal pursuit, people influence their own progress by rewarding and punishing themselves.
- Most goal pursuit is automatic.
- Effective self-regulatory behavior and self-control in goal pursuit depends both on motivation and on regulatory competencies. The latter require cognitive and attention control mechanisms that help execute goal-directed behavior.
- At the Biological Level, the anterior attentional system regulates executive function (EF) throughout the cortex.
- Ego control refers to individual differences in the degree of impulse control in such functions as inhibition of impulses.
- Ego resilience is a construct that refers to the individual's stable ability to adapt flexibly to environmental demands by appropriately modifying his or her habitual level of ego control.
- At the Social Cognitive Level, researchers have examined how cognition and attention effect goal pursuit.

SELF-REGULATION IN APPROACH (APPETITIVE) DILEMMAS

- The ability to voluntarily delay immediate gratification is at the core of most concepts of willpower and ego resilience.
- Successful delay of gratification in goal pursuit involves the ability to prevent oneself from focusing attention on the frustrating, emotion-arousing aspects of difficult situations, and instead strategically shifting attention elsewhere.
- When people are able to construe rewards in terms of their "cool," informative qualities instead of their "hot," consummatory properties, they are better able to delay gratification.
- The attention control mechanisms that underlie delay of gratification can help shield individuals against the negative consequences of their chronic personal vulnerabilities.

SELF-REGULATION IN AVOIDANCE (AVERSIVE) DILEMMAS

- To cope with aversive situations, individuals who practice cognitive reappraisal (cognitive "cooling" strategies) experience less negative feelings and physiological arousal than individuals who try to suppress their feelings.
- Psychological distancing in combination with a focus on the reasons underlying one's feelings can make it easier to think about distressing situations.
- People seem to cope better when they cognitively transform or redefine stressful situations in more positive ways.

INTERACTION AMONG HOT AND COOL SYSTEMS IN SELF-REGULATION

- The emotional, hot system, centered in the amygdala, underlies automatic approach–avoidance or fight-or-flight responses.
- The cognitive, cool processing system, based in higher brain centers, particularly the prefrontal cortex, enables thoughtful, reflective thinking and planning.
- The balance between the hot and cool systems is influenced both by stress and by the individual's level of development. To effectively self-regulate, the individual

must prevent or postpone automatic, hot, emotional, impulsive responses and activate cooling strategies by shifting attention and cognitions away from the hot features of the reward or the frustrating features of the conflict.

- In order to avoid stimulus control, people can rehearse specific *if . . . then . . .* implementation intentions.
- "Hot," automatic responses are necessary in some situations. For example, strong social emotions can help people to resist temptation and avoid shirking responsibilities.
- Always postponing gratification creates problems, but unless people develop the competencies to delay when they want and need to do so, they lose the choice itself.

▶ KEY TERMS

akrasia 438
anterior attentional system 444
cognitive, cool system 459
cognitive reappraisal 454
discriminative facility 450
effortful control 444
Ego control 445
ego resilience 445
emotional, hot system 459
executive function (EF) 444
fight or flight reaction 458
hippocampus 459
implementation intentions 461
life tasks 441
marshmallow test 447
overcontrolling 446
self-regulatory competencies 444
subordinate goals 441
super ordinate goals 441
suppression 454
undercontrolling 446

CHAPTER 18

PERSONALITY IN ITS SOCIAL CONTEXT AND CULTURE

In an integrative view that draws on all the levels of analysis, personality has many diverse aspects: cultural, social, psychological, and biological. This final chapter gives an overview of these aspects and influences on the person, and on the development of personality, gender roles, and sex differences within the particular culture and social context. We focus on how these multiple influences interact in the development of the personality system and play out in how the person functions within the social world.

CULTURE AND PERSONALITY

The culture in which a person is raised is an important part of the mix of social–environmental influences on personality. The enduring challenge for a cultural–psychological approach to personality is to understand the links between personality and culture.

Mapping Cultural Differences with the Big Five

Historically, much cross-cultural research, just as much personality research, has separated personality and the qualities of the individual from the social context, not just with regard to specific situations but also for the role of culture as a whole (Kitayama & Markus, 1999; Pervin, 1999; Poortinga & Hemert, 2001; Shweder, 1991). This traditional view "... construes skin as a special boundary that separates one set of 'causal forces' from another. On the sunny side of the epidermis are the external or situational forces that press inward on the person, and on the meaty side are the internal or personal forces that exert pressure outward" (Gilbert & Malone, 1995, p. 21).

In this tradition, attempts to explore the links between culture and personality have a long history. One of the first researchers to systematically examine the relationship between culture and personality was the anthropologist Ruth Benedict. In her 1934 book *Patterns of Culture*, Benedict described two personality types of the Southwest Pueblos of Mexico: the Apollonian and the Dionysian, based on a distinction used by the philosopher Nietzsche in his studies of Greek tragedy. Benedict characterized the Dionysian Pueblos as having a generalized love for excess, and the Apollonian Pueblos as sober and mistrustful of excessive behavior—qualities that, according to Benedict, were evident across a wide range of domains. Following Benedict, much subsequent research on culture and personality focused on identifying broad behavior trends in the national character or "dominant personality" of cultural groups (e.g., Kardiner, 1945; Linton, 1945).

In current studies of culture and personality, many researchers guided by the trait-dispositional approach try to show the universality of a personality trait structure, particularly the "Five Factor Model"—open-mindedness, conscientiousness, extraversion, agreeableness, and neuroticism—across cultures (e.g., McCrae & Allik, 2002). Their goal is to "map" the world across these five dimensions (Allik & McCrae, 2004; McCrae, 2004). They want not just to show that the French, for example, are lower on Agreeableness than Americans (McCrae, 2004), but rather that they can describe both Frenchmen and Americans in terms of the same Big Five factors. Researchers in this approach also cite evidence from animal studies (e.g. Gosling & John, 1999; Gosling, Kwan, & John, 2003) as well as heritability studies (Bouchard & Loehlin, 2001; Loehlin, McCrae, Costa, & John, 1998) as evidence for the biological basis of trait structure (see Triandis & Suh, 2002). As you also saw in earlier chapters, many believe that biological–genetic bases underlie differences in the Big Five. Some even argue that such biological differences cause cultural differences (McCrae, 2004).

18.1 How are some personality theorists using the Five Factor Model to understand different cultures?

Cross-Cultural and Intracultural Differences

There is support for this approach insofar as researchers have shown convincingly that there are differences among cultural groups in their overall trait levels on rating scales (Triandis & Suh, 2002). But just as in personality research, culture and personality researchers also found that for many classes of behavior, *within-culture variability* is greater than *between-culture variability* (Barnouw, 1985; Bock, 2000; Inkeles, 1996; Kaplan, 1954; Triandis, 1997; Wallace, 1961; Whiting & Child, 1953; Whiting & Whiting, 1975). As Gordon Allport (1961, p. 167) recognized half a century ago: "no individual is a mirror-image of the modal or average culture pattern. We are molded by real culture and not by the anthropologist's distilled image of it. To apply this image directly to people is to falsify the diversity of personality found within any single culture." Thus, despite the intuitive appeal of the culture and personality approach, it has long faced serious challenges. The most difficult problem is how to account for mounting evidence that cultural group members sometimes behave according to their culture's dominant personality—and sometimes do not.

Individualism versus Collectivism

Consider, for example, a well-studied typology that contrasts **individualism** and **collectivism**. Individualism involves a sense of the self as autonomous, devoted to the pursuit of personal goals, and relatively independent and self-focused. In contrast, collectivism is defined by closer connections to groups and family. People at this pole of the typology are sensitive to the goals of the family and groups with which they are connected, and devoted to fulfilling duties and obligations. Even as adults, they remain interdependent in their social relationships, values, and goal pursuits. Likewise, in the collectivist culture individuals focus less on the self and self-enhancement and more on relationships, social obligations, and roles in comparison with those in an individualistic culture (e.g., English & Chen, in press; Markus & Kitayama, 1998).

18.2 Distinguish between individualist and collectivist cultures.

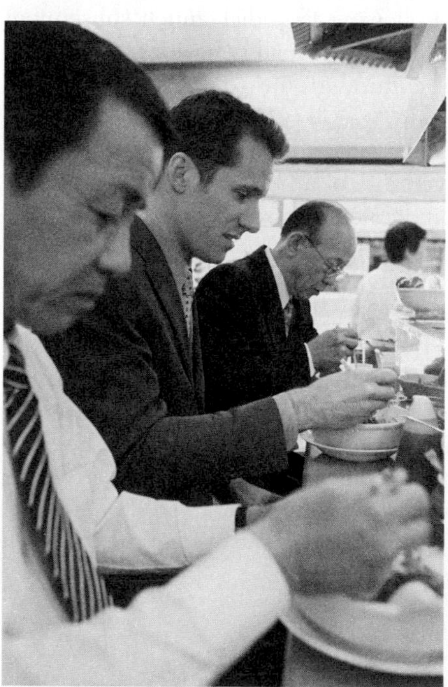

Behaviors appropriate in one culture may seem awkward in another.

The problem is that when cultures are described in broad trait terms like individualism versus collectivism, the fit tends to be imperfect. This is true because the terms capture something only about the average tendencies and characteristics of the majority of people within the culture. For example, rough estimates suggest that these descriptions may fit about 60% of the people in a culture (Triandis & Suh, 2002). That means that in a culture of individualism, 40% of the people don't show individualistic characteristics, and in a collectivist culture, 40% of the people cannot be characterized as collectivistic.

In sum, as you have seen throughout this text, the variability *within* a person or type is often as impressive as the differences *between* persons and types. Likewise, the variability within a culture is often as impressive as the differences between cultures. Nevertheless, as you saw also in earlier chapters, attention to the broad overall average differences can be valuable. It can give at least a rough map of what to expect in a given culture, and some of the outlines of its meaning system. It is certainly useful to know that in many situations in Asia, tactics that might be appropriate in New York City would be embarrassing, and vice versa. There is good reason that visitors come fortified with guides on what to expect and when and where to expect it. It is also useful to know that at a very broad level of trait description, in spite of cultural differences, there are important commonalities in the ways in which people characterize each other. You can see this in the finding that at least three or four of the factors in the Big Five factor structure can be found in most cultures, albeit not without exceptions. An important reservation to keep in mind here, however, is that even when the same factors appear in diverse cultures, the particular meanings and usage may be quite different (Triandis & Suh, 2002).

Culture as a Shared Meaning System

Starting in the 1990s, a new approach, influenced by the cognitive revolution and by work at the Social Cognitive Level, goes beyond descriptions of broad average cultural difference and wants to understand how cultural forces shape individual behavior (Hong & Mallorie, 2004; Kashima, 2001; Markus & Kitayama, 1998; Shweder, 1990). This approach views culture as a *shared meaning system*. The person's **cultural meaning system** includes distinctive views about what the world is like and what different situations and behaviors mean and call for (e.g., Markus & Kitayama, 1998). Much like the CAPS personality system, it contains concepts and feelings about the nature of the self and its ideals, and the relationships between self and other people. It includes basic goals-values, emotions, standards, self-regulatory rules, and scripts for appropriate and inappropriate interpersonal behavior and control strategies in goal pursuit. Like the cognitive–affective units in the personality system (Chapter 16), these **units of culture** are shared within the meaning system of the particular community (Betancourt & Lopez, 1993; Triandis, 1997). Every visitor to a different culture soon discovers how these differences are expressed—and unless one learns their meanings, life can be very confusing (see *In Focus 18.1*).

18.3 How are cultural and personal meaning systems related?

Cultural groups differ in the goals, values, and beliefs that are psychologically *available and chronically accessible*. For example, while one culture may teach its members beliefs about spirit possession, this notion may not be part of the explanatory repertoire for others' behavior among members of other groups. Likewise, a strong

IN FOCUS 18.1

CULTURAL DIFFERENCES IN EMOTIONAL MEANINGS: APPRAISING THE SITUATION

To appraise situations, you have to interpret their emotional meanings. Is your father really angry or teasing? Is your roommate being friendly or just polite? Usually these interpretations are made automatically, depending on previous experience and expectations. But the automatic appraisal *can* be inaccurate.

Anthropological reports of differences in cultural expressions of emotions make that clear. Visitors to an unfamiliar culture would make many mistakes if they tried to assess the meaning of emotional expressions in terms of their own past experience. A Masai warrior honors a young man who looks promising by spitting in his face; an Andaman Islander greets a visitor by sitting down on his lap and sobbing his salutation tearfully; a scolded Chinese schoolboy takes a reprimand with cheerful grinning as a sign of his respect; and to show anger, Navajo and Apache Indians lower the voice instead of raising it (Opler, 1967). Within each culture, people reach an agreement about the meaning of emotional cues. But certain facial expressions also may have universal meaning. The emotions of anger, happiness, disgust, sadness, fear, and surprise, shown in photographs of faces, tended to be correctly identified in a variety of extremely different cultures (Ekman, 1982).

On visits to extremely different cultures, people usually try to be careful not to misinterpret the emotional signals they observe and to avoid reacting inappropriately. A similar caution may be useful in carefully attending to the emotional signals that come from people in one's own personal life. Focused attention, rather than automatic responding, may allow one to see more clearly what is really going on both in another culture and in another person—and often also in oneself.

cultural norm of valuing others' welfare may make such a concern more chronically accessible—and thus easily activated—to individuals of that culture (e.g., Markus & Kitayama, 1991). Stigmatized group members in a culture also often have shared experiences that more readily activate their concerns about discrimination compared to nonstigmatized group members (Mendoza-Denton et al., 1997; Mendoza-Denton & Mischel, 2007).

Finally, of the diverse beliefs, goals, values, encodings, and feelings that one can potentially experience at any given time, only those that are relevant or "applicable" in a given situation become activated and influence subsequent behavior (Hong, Benet-Martinez, Chiu, & Morris, 2003). For example, one cultural difference identified in prior research has been a tendency toward self-enhancement in the United States as opposed to Japan (Heine, Lehman, Markus, & Kitayama, 1999), but this cultural difference is expressed in particular culturally defined situations and contexts. Another example comes from demonstrations that European Americans are highly self-enhancing, and this is especially true for situations that European Americans spontaneously nominate as being relevant to their self-esteem (Kitayama, Markus, Matsumoto, & Norasakkunkit, 1997). Japanese, in contrast, were more self-critical, but again especially in situations identified by their in-group as relevant to self-esteem. Thus, culture influences personality hugely—not only in terms of the goals and important beliefs, but also in the way that situations are represented and their particular psychological features. At the same time, these units are only activated and guide behavior in relation to specific situations (Mischel & Shoda, 1995). Consequently, while people who share a culture and its meaning units may converge in their experiences and behavior in some situations, such convergence will not occur in situations that do not activate culturally shared cognitions

(Mendoza-Denton, Shoda, Ayduk, & Mischel, 1999; Mendoza-Denton & Mischel, 2007).

Cultural Differences in the Organization of Personality?: *If ... then ...* Cultural Signatures

Kitayama (2002) points out that cultures differ not only in terms of how much particular qualities (e.g., agreeableness) tend to be found but also in how their meaning system is organized and expressed. Life experiences shared by members of a group—the teachings of elders, the experiences shared with others, the values imposed by society—generate a mental organization and network of psychological meanings that is immersed in and reflects the surrounding culture. If features of a situation activate this culturally shared subnetwork, individuals may generate similar reactions to that situation. On the other hand, in situations that don't activate a culturally shared psychological feature, group members' responses may not be alike, and in fact may be similar to those of another group.

18.4 Give an example of how situations can interact with cultural meaning systems to create *if ... then ...* cultural signatures.

In other words, cultural differences, like personality differences, are expressed in stable ***if ... then ...*** **cultural signatures** that are activated in some situations but not in others (e.g., Oishi, 2004; Oishi, Diener, Napa Scollon, & Biswas-Diener, 2004). For example, in one large study, researchers closely examined intra-individual variation in moods across various situations, sampled in Japan, India, and the United States (Oishi et al., 2004). They studied the relationship between situation (e.g., alone, with a stranger) and mood at the individual as well as at cultural levels by having each participant record the mood experienced in various situations when signaled at random moments over time. They thus were able to examine each individual's "*if ... then ...*" patterns of stable situation–mood relations. Consistent with Mischel and Shoda (1995), they found that even when two people from two different cultures have the same average level of positive moods, they show distinctive, highly individualized patterns in when they do or do not experience positive moods.

English and Chen (*in press*) gave Asian-Americans and European-Americans measures of how they viewed themselves and their self-concepts in different contexts and relationships (e.g., "I often change the way I am, depending on who I am with"; "I am the same around my family as I am around my friends"), and examined in detail the variations in their self-views in a series of studies. The researchers found that Asian-Americans not only elaborate, but also maintain, stable "relationship-specific selves" in ways that depend on who they are with and the particular context, and did so much more than European-Americans. For example, Asian-Americans saw themselves as being very different people when they were with a close friend and when they were with their mother. In contrast, European-Americans viewed themselves in more globally consistent terms, essentially as having and being the same kind of self regardless of who they were relating with. Thus while self-conceptions in European-Americans tended to be more global in their self-concepts regardless of context, the Asian-Americans were characterized as more contextualized but temporally stable in their *if ... then ...* relationship signatures.

Diverse differences in meaning systems and *if ... then ...* signatures can even be observed among subgroups (which can be defined on status characteristics including but not limited to race, ethnicity, and gender) that live within the same larger culture. A striking example of differences in cultural signatures and meaning systems within the United States was seen in the reactions to the famous 1995 verdict of the criminal

Opinions about O.J. Simpson's guilt were sharply split.

(*Source*: AP/Wide World Photos)

murder trial of O.J. Simpson, the African American former football star and celebrity. Opinions about O.J.'s guilt were sharply split along racial lines. An analysis of reactions to the verdict, however, showed that this split was only part of the story (Mendoza-Denton et al., 1997). The deeper analysis showed that among African Americans certain key features of the case—for example, the Los Angeles detective who planted evidence to influence a conviction—activated their widely shared cognitions about historically unfair police treatment toward African Americans. In turn, these cognitions inhibited other thoughts such as "there is a lot of evidence against the defendant." For European Americans, in contrast, the realities of race-based discrimination are less available and strong. They focused instead on the evidence, which supported their belief that he was guilty and should have been convicted of the crime. It was these differences between the racial groups that accounted for (or "mediated") the effect of race on their reactions to the verdict. Further, the fact that reactions to verdicts in other high-profile trials have not been split along racial lines indicates that while members of cultural groups share certain subnetworks in their mental systems and personality organization, these are activated in some situations, but not necessarily in others.

An Integrated System View of Culture and Person Dynamics

A *system view of culture* avoids treating cultures as causal entities that "account" for group differences (e.g., Betancourt & Lopez, 1993). It recognizes that cultural values and belief systems shape the institutions and everyday practices of a cultural group, which then themselves lead to particular **cultural affordances** (Kitayama, 2002; Kitayama & Markus, 1999) or opportunities for the practice, expression, and reinforcement of these cultural values. A core cultural belief system such as the Protestant Work Ethic (Levy, West, Ramirez, & Karafantis, 2006), for example, can foster institutions that reinforce its expressions, and influence the contexts and situations that people navigate in their daily lives (Vandello & Cohen, 2004). Likewise, a belief in personal mastery over the environment or over nature can lead to the valuation, and construction, of gymnasiums and sports centers where such mastery and discipline become practiced and customary and in a sense create a "physical culture" (Triandis et al., 1980). These broad influences lead to differences in the psychological availability of certain constructs (e.g., belief in mastery over aging), and in the value, importance, and accessibility of these belief systems through social institutions.

18.5 How does the system view of culture explain cultural differences in behavior?

A shared meaning systems approach to culture and personality is illustrated in research on the *culture of honor*. It analyzes how historical forces shape cultural practices and norms (cultural affordances), which in turn influence the way individuals behave in particular situations (Cohen, 1998, 2007; Nisbett & Cohen, 1996). Cohen and colleagues (1996) note that the American South has long been seen as more violent than the North, and in fact argument-related homicide rates in the South and West are higher than they are in the North (Nisbett & Cohen, 1996). But Southerners also have a reputation for being charming and polite (e.g., "that ol' Southern charm"). The culture of honor hypothesis tried to reconcile the view of a violent South with a view of a charming and genteel South. It proposes that strong vigilance to disrespect and ready use of violence to protect property and name have over time affected social practices and norms. This is symbolized both in games that amount to tests of "manhood" (e.g., "chicken" games, or kicking each other in the shins), as well as in legal lenience toward violence instigated by affronts to honor (Cohen & Nisbett, 1994, 1997). Thus, some distinctive *if* ... *then* ... patterns seem to characterize the behavior of people sharing a culture of honor (Cohen, Vandello, Puente, & Rantilla, 1999). A laboratory experiment that provides some support for the culture of honor hypothesis is described in *In Focus 18.2*.

IN FOCUS 18.2

USING THE GAME OF CHICKEN TO STUDY THE CULTURE OF HONOR

A laboratory-based experiment offers some evidence for the culture of honor *if* ... *then* ... profile. Northern and southern White men participated in a laboratory study generally described to be about personality (Cohen et al., 1996). In the lab, they were asked to fill out questionnaires, and then drop them off at the end of a long, narrow hallway. The researcher then subjected half of the southern and half of the northern participants to an affront. As they walked down the hallway, they had to squeeze past an assistant (a confederate of the researchers) who was taking something out of a cabinet. Pretending annoyance, the confederate slammed the cabinet shut, insulted the participant under his breath, and deliberately bumped him on his way out of the hallway. The participant still had to make his way to the end of the hallway, but at this point another confederate started walking toward him down the narrow hallway, setting the stage for a potential game of "chicken" to see who would step out of the way first.

As the researchers predicted, compared to northern men, the southerners who had been bumped waited longer before they stepped aside to let the second confederate through, indicating a more aggressive response to restore honor characterized by southern men. They also were rated by observers as more aggressive and dominant, and gave a firmer handshake compared to northern participants. But among participants who had not been bumped, the southerners were rated as more "polite" and less aggressive than the northerners. The point is that the findings are consistent both with the belief that southerners are more polite *and* more aggressive than northerners. They displayed a clear *if* ... *then* ... pattern, reflecting a culture of honor in which both types of behavior are predicted but each is expected in different situations, and each makes sense when one sees their underlying meaning and dynamics.

Summary: The Link between the Cultural and the Personal Meaning Systems

In short, the culture in which a person is socialized importantly influences how personality develops and is expressed. As you saw in the previous sections, the cultural meaning system includes distinctive views about what the world is like and what different situations mean and call for (e.g., Markus & Kitayama, 1998). Much like the personality system, it contains concepts and feelings about the nature of the self and its ideals, and the relationships between self and other people. It includes basic goals-values, emotions, standards, self-regulatory rules, and scripts for appropriate and inappropriate interpersonal behavior and control strategies in goal pursuit. The significant people in the life of the child model and communicate the meaning system of their culture just as they communicate the vocabulary and grammar of the language. In time, each individual develops a **personal meaning system** that incorporates some components from the shared cultural meaning system while other components reflect unique life experiences.

Culturally Specific Personality Dispositions

Current research is beginning to illustrate how culturally specific personality dispositions can arise from differences in the socialization and learning experiences that are specific to members of a cultural group. Mendoza-Denton et al. (2002), for example, have proposed that because African Americans in the United States are especially likely to be socially excluded, marginalized, or mistreated on the basis of their race, members of this group in particular may develop race-based rejection sensitivity. This processing dynamic is similar to rejection sensitivity in personal relationships (Downey & Feldman, 1996). However, its antecedents (prior experiences of discrimination), situational trigger features (situations where racism is possible), and consequences (mistrust in historically White institutions) make it a processing dynamic that is more likely to occur among African Americans than European Americans.

18.6 Describe research on race-based rejection sensitivity and the situations that evoke it.

Importantly, this processing dynamic, while stable over time, is relevant and activated only in situations where discrimination on the basis of race is applicable, and does not necessarily characterize the individual's responses and behavior in other contexts. As such, the approach allows for an analysis of how shared cultural experience can lead to similar behavior by members of cultural groups when they are in certain situations. At the same time, it still allows for diversity in group members' behavior in many other contexts. This approach takes into account individual differences as well as commonality among members of cultural groups. It also avoids having to rely on global cultural stereotypes that limited earlier efforts to understand the impact of culture on personality. The approach is illustrated with studies of race-based rejection sensitivity in *In Focus 18.3*.

Summary: Interacting Influences in Culture-Personality Links

In sum, culture may influence the situations that people tend to experience, the ways they interpret these situations, and thus how they respond to them. This happens both within the personality system—that is, internally in the person's mental and emotional experience—and in the characteristic behavioral patterns that are generated. Culture also influences personality by affecting the ways in which other people, as well as the self, react to those behaviors, in turn changing the subsequent situations the person is likely to encounter. This interplay of personality and culture over time involves continuous dynamic interactions between the inside and the outside, the individual and the social world, as the two influence each other reciprocally.

IN FOCUS 18.3

STUDYING RACE-BASED REJECTION SENSITIVITY

Researchers have stressed that to understand the psychology of minority group members one has to take account of the group's life experiences and historical background. An important part of that experience is a history of stigmatization and continuing discrimination (Sellers, Caldwell, Schmeelk-Cone, & Zimmerman, 2003; Shelton, 2000). This history, as well as the individual's own earlier experiences, can profoundly affect one's sense of self (Humphreys & Kashima, 2002; Kashima et al., 2004; Mischel & Morf, 2003), as well as his or her responses to discrimination. Research on *sensitivity to race-based rejection* (RS-race; Mendoza-Denton et al., 2002; Mendoza-Denton, Page-Gould, & Pietrzak, 2005) helps to spell out some of the relevant mechanisms.

The construct of sensitivity to race-based rejection grew out of research on personal rejection sensitivity discussed in earlier chapters (Downey & Feldman, 1996; Levy, Ayduk, & Downey, 2001). The essence of this concept is that when people experience rejection from parents, peers, or other important figures in the form of abuse or neglect, they become vulnerable to developing anxious expectations of rejection—namely, a "hot," affectively laden expectation that future rejection lies in store in similar kinds of situations. These anxious expectations lower the threshold for perceiving rejection, and once the rejection is perceived, activate intense, "hot" reactions to the perceived rejection. Applying this construct and dynamic to the domain of discrimination, Mendoza-Denton and colleagues (2002, 2005) explored the idea that rejection sensitivity also can develop on the basis of a devalued group membership—such as gender, sexual orientation, or race.

Cultural influences come into play at several levels. First, as has been widely recognized, stigma is context-specific—an attribute or personal characteristic that is devalued in one domain may be valued (or be neutrally valenced) in another context (Crocker, Major, & Steele, 1998). As such, the context within which a person operates can dictate the type of interpersonal experiences—and stable dynamics that develop—as a result. Second, even when two groups might be negatively stigmatized, the nature of the stigma depends on the assumptions that a given stigma carries about one's group. In the United States, for example, being African American carries a suspicion of academic inability (Steele, 1997), but not about athletic ability, whereas the reverse is true of Asian Americans (Chan & Mendoza-Denton, 2004). As such, then, although two people may be equally apprehensive concerning their status, the situations in which their rejection concerns are going to be activated are going to be different. Finally, the coping mechanisms marshaled in response to the rejection may be different—again, one's cultural group provides one with culture-specific appropriate strategies in response to rejection.

Mendoza-Denton et al. (2002) conducted focus groups to identify the situations that activate race-based rejection concerns among African Americans, and used those situations to develop a questionnaire. The situations included such scenarios as being stopped during a random traffic stop, or being passed over for an opportunity to answer a difficult question in class. These are the kinds of situations that contain "active ingredients" that readily activate feelings of discrimination among relevant minority groups. This questionnaire was given to a sample of African American, European American, and Asian American undergraduates. As the researchers expected, African Americans scored highest on the measure, whereas European American and Asian American participants scored low on the measure and did not differ from each other. Individual differences in the measure predicted spontaneous attributions to race in these situations among African Americans but not among European Americans or among Asian Americans (Mendoza-Denton et al., 2002).

Among African Americans, individual differences in anxious expectations of race-based rejection subsequently predicted, over a 3-week period, reports of rejection, and more intense feelings of alienation and rejection following the rejection. Most informative, individual differences in RS-race among African Americans predicted students' GPA over the course of five semesters. This finding illustrates how culture is both "in the head" and "out there"—people enact self-protective mechanisms in response to discrimination. At a systems level, discrimination is maintained by the broader culture and social structures. What the culture and the social world do, and what individuals experience and do in their responses to those social influences, involves continuous reciprocal interactions, each influencing the other, often with unfortunate consequences (Mendoza-Denton et al., 2002; Mendoza-Denton & Mischel, 2007).

▶ GENDER AND SEX DIFFERENCES

18.7 Differentiate between sex and gender.

Established at birth, biological sex soon begins to direct much of one's psychological and social development. It influences self-concepts and identity, as well as goals, roles, and values, and continues to have a dominant influence throughout life.

Gender is a concept that refers to the social meaning of being a male or a female. Almost universally, gender is one of the most powerful determinants of how people view themselves and how other people treat them. Gender is probably one of the most important psychological categorizations that people make, and one that has become increasingly controversial. The controversy is based on many challenges to conventional, rigid **gender stereotypes** about what it means to be a man or a woman within a particular culture or society (e.g., Deaux & Major, 1987).

Overview and Issues

Neonatal Sex Differences

Some researchers have concentrated on sex differences in newborns (neonates) in order to study possible innate sex differences before socialization practices exert their huge effects. Human neonatal behavior indicates some sex differences in activity level and in reactivity to a variety of stimuli. For example, sex differences occur in infants' responses to facial stimuli during the first year of life (Lewis, 1969, 1990). Girls vocalized and smiled more and showed greater differential expression to the facial stimuli, although boys looked longer. At age 2–3 months, girls are more sensitive to skin exposure than boys (Wolff, 1966). Newborn females seem to react more to the removal of a covering blanket, and show lower thresholds to air-jet stimulation of the abdomen (Bell & Costello, 1964). Newborn boys raise their heads higher than newborn girls do (Bell & Darling, 1965), and there are also sex differences in infant play behavior (Goldberg & Lewis, 1969). The interpretation sometimes drawn from these early sex differences in response to stimulation is that they are innate. But as in other domains of personality, nature and nurture—heredity and environment—tend to be deeply and often inextricably entwined.

18.8 What behavioral sex differences exist in infants?

Gender Concepts

Gender concepts—beliefs about the types of behavior more appropriate for one sex than for the other—are widely shared within a particular culture and to some extent across cultures (D'Andrade, 1966). Individuals differ in the sanctioned sex-role standards that they adopt or reject. Some modern Western cultures or subcultures have been shifting toward greater flexibility in the range that tends to be explored by individuals and tolerated by others, although signs in opposite directions also can be seen in other cultures throughout the world. The concept of **sex-role identity** refers to the "degree to which an individual regards himself as masculine or feminine" (Kagan, 1964, p. 144). The degree of match or mismatch between the sex-role standards of the culture and the individuals' assessment of his or her own attributes can have far-reaching implications on the personality that each develops and the social world in which he or she functions.

Expression of Gender-Relevant Behavior

As Deaux and Major (1987) note, sex and gender are constructs that deeply influence social relations. Gender-linked behaviors are expressed by males and females often at automatic levels and play out as almost reflexive scripts. Both sexes respond to the gender-relevant cues in their social interactions in ways that activate their conceptions

IN FOCUS 18.4

ADULT SEX DIFFERENCES AND THEIR IMPLICATIONS

For half a century, the nature and extent of sex differences in personality have been topics of extensive research and passionate debates (e.g., Gilligan, 1982; Maccoby & Jacklin, 1974; Mischel & Mischel, 1973). In adults, a variety of sex differences have been reported over the years. For example, the physical fight response to stress and threat shows higher levels for males than for females in humans, primates, and rats (e.g. Archer, 1990; Eagly & Steffen, 1986). Distinct sex differences also are reported in nonverbal behavior, such as facial expressiveness and body expressiveness (reviewed by Eagly, 1987) and greater rough and tumble play and physical aggressive tendencies in boys than girls (Collaer & Hines, 1995). Possible sex differences also have been found in some aspects of cognitive functioning, but taken as a whole, the largest differences, unsurprisingly, have been shown for physical abilities (e.g., Eagly & Crowley, 1986; Eagly & Steffen, 1986).

Differences in mental and social abilities and in behaviors are considerably more modest, although a few minor differences between the sexes "are sprinkled across all domains" (Ashmore, 1990, p. 500). The exception may be physical aggression, in which fairly large differences tend to be found even when diverse measures are used. In most other domains, however, some argue that the more attention that is paid to avoiding sex bias in the research, the fewer the gender differences that are actually found (e.g., Riger, 1992).

Nevertheless, there is evidence for a number of nontrivial sex differences, although their interpretation has been extensively debated (Eagly, 1995). For example, sex differences have been reported on measures of the Big Five Factor model that use trait ratings (e.g., Hoyenga & Hoyenga, 1993). Examples include moderately greater rated assertiveness in males, and greater trust, tender-mindedness, and anxiety in women. These data may reflect widely shared social perceptions and possible gender stereotypes, but they may or may not speak to differences in the actual social behavior of the sexes when it is studied by direct observation.

What is the conclusion one can reasonably draw when all the findings are looked at together? To some critics, the most impressive finding about sex differences in psychological characteristics is how unimpressive they generally seem to be and how much smaller they are than had been assumed in earlier years. They note that it is important to keep in mind that the variability *within* each sex on these measures is often more impressive than the differences found on average *between* the sexes. To others, it seems that the differences found are large enough to be taken seriously and that the reasons they are minimized are mostly political. In that view, sex differences are significant but they are being trivialized because of a "feminist commitment to gender similarity as a route to political equality" (Eagly, 1995, p. 155). Both interpretations have validity. Compared to within-sex differences, the differences between the sexes on most variables are probably not significant enough for practical purposes. Nevertheless, they may be reliable enough to provide clues as to how biological differences that exist at birth interact with culture to result in sex differences that are observed in adults. How the data are read depends on one's philosophy and politics on the topic, as well as on the methods used to estimate the size and meaning of the statistical differences that are reported.

18.9 In which areas do adult sex differences exist? Why is it difficult to interpret their causes?

about themselves as males and females. These gender-relevant conceptions include a host of expectations and values that guide the behavior they think appropriate to the context (see *In Focus 18.4*).

As an example of the influence of gender roles in the automatic processing of social information, consider a study conducted by Sadalla, Kenrick, and Vershure (1987). Students were asked to watch films of men in high or low dominance conditions. To create a condition of low dominance, an actor engaged in conversation with another male, repeatedly nodding his head, looking down often, and speaking little. To establish the reverse condition, the actor was more relaxed, nodded less, and made more assertive gestures. Students of both sexes rated those in the higher-dominance condition as more attractive. When shown films of women in similar conditions, however, no relationship was found. Thus the person's sex determined whether assertiveness-dominance led to perceived attractiveness—behaviors that made the male more attractive did not increase the perceived attractiveness of the female in this situation. Results like these lead many researchers to the conclusion that gender "is something we enact . . . a pattern of social organization that structures the relations, especially the power relations, between women and men" (Riger, 1992, p. 737).

If . . . then . . . Patterns in Sex Differences

Sex differences are not just expressed as average overall differences in different types of behavior, but also in distinctive *if . . . then . . .* patterns that may form distinctive behavioral gender signatures. These are revealed in significant interactions in how males and females deal differently with particular contexts or situations. Such interactions were shown in a fine-grain study of boys and girls in a summer camp observed over many situations for the whole summer (Zakriski, Wright, & Underwood, 2005).

For example, girls were less likely than boys to be aggressive in response to provocation from their peers, and were more likely to withdraw when they were provoked by them. But close examination also showed that girls were more likely than boys to be aggressive in response to direct efforts by adults to control them. When the adult counselors in a residential camp setting warned or punished them for inappropriate behavior, they responded with more verbal aggression than boys did.

As the researchers point out, these sex differences in the interpersonal situations in which each sex is more or less aggressive than the other would never have been found if one looked just for overall average levels in sex differences. The lesson here is there may be many gender differences in the expressions of personality in all sorts of behaviors but they depend on context, and can't be found unless context is taken into account.

This study also showed informative differences between the sexes in the types of interpersonal situations they experienced during the summer. The older girls, for example, were less likely than older boys to be teased or bossed around by peers, and were less often warned by adults, which in turn may have influenced their own levels of aggression. It's therefore important to look at sex differences not just in levels of different types of behavior, and in the situations or contexts in which behavior occurs, but also in the rates at which the sexes experience different types of interpersonal encounters and situations.

Interactions of Biology, Sex, and Culture in Response to Threat

When thinking about the influence of biological and social–cultural influences on personality, it is easy to fall into "either–or" ways of casting the question, and to want to know, "bottom line, which one is more important?" We saw this clearly in the discussion of the influence of nature and nurture—genetics and social experience—on personality (Chapter 5). The same issues and the same answers apply in the present discussion of genetics, heredity, and social–cultural influences. To make sense of the whole story of sex differences in social behavior and personality, for example, the answer has to take into account the importance *both* of social factors, as discussed above, *and* of biological–evolutionary factors. Above all, one has to look at how the two influences *interact* so that what emerges depends critically on both. This point is made convincingly in a theory developed by University of California Los Angeles psychologist Shelley E. Taylor and her colleagues (2000). They reached a radical conclusion that challenged much of the work on how humans, and particularly females, respond to threat and stress.

18.10 What difference in behavioral responses to stress does Taylor propose? What biological differences might underlie this difference?

Shelley Taylor

(*Source*: Courtesy Shelley Taylor)

It has long been assumed that in response to stress people react with fight-or-flight patterns, and this was assumed to be the universal human and animal reaction when severely threatened, for example, by animal predators or natural disasters. Taylor and colleagues note that the widely accepted belief (beginning with Cannon, 1932) that humans respond to high stress and threat with automatic fight-or-flight responses is based on thousands of studies, but almost all were conducted with males, especially male rats. For females, the biobehavioral response to threat may be very different than it is for males, and for many good reasons.

Men Fight or Flee: Women Tend and Befriend

The theory Taylor and colleagues propose builds on recently discovered biological differences between human males and females, particularly in their neuroendocrine responses to threat. At the biological level, females are less likely to make a physical fight response to stress because they lack **androgens**, the hormones that in many species "act to develop the male brain for aggression ... and then activate aggressive behavior in specific threatening contexts (such as responses to territorial establishment and defense)" (Taylor et al., 2000, p. 413). The role of testosterone, the male sex hormone, in aggression is controversial, but its level in humans increases with acute stress and is associated with hostility. In contrast, according to Taylor, in female humans, aggressive responses are not organized by testosterone or androgens and therefore do not involve the same automatic reaction patterns in response to stress.

Taylor integrates these findings with insights from the evolutionary level of analysis. According to her theory, the aggressive response to threat and stress from an evolutionary perspective may have been adaptive for men when dealing with danger (e.g., when on the hunt in the wilderness) but not for the challenges that females faced as the mothers of offspring. Females of most species, including humans until relatively recently, were pregnant, nursing, or caring for their young offspring, during their fertile lives. For these functions, a female fight-or-flight response to stress may have been strikingly nonadaptive for survival and hence became inhibited. The theory suggests that instead, females developed a **tending response to stress** that involved caretaking and grew out of the attachment system in humans. Many studies support this argument by showing that nurturing behaviors, such as touching the infant and carrying it close on the chest, benefit both mothers and offspring under high stress conditions (Taylor et al., 2000). A similar argument, based both on biology and evolution, is made for the value of **befriending**, for example, through group living and activities, as a highly adaptive way for females to cope with stress.

For the student of personality, a clear message comes from the analysis by Shelley Taylor and colleagues:

> Rather than viewing social roles and biology as alternative accounts of human behavior, a more productive theoretical and empirical strategy will be to recognize how biology and social roles are inextricably interwoven to account for the remarkable flexibility of human behavior. (2000, p. 423)

Interactions in the Genesis of Gender Roles

Cross-cultural studies of gender roles by anthropologists show the wide range of gender roles across different cultures (Gilmore, 1990). This diversity in sex roles spans "from marked stereotypic male and female patterns to extremely muted, even quite difficult-to-detect gender differences" (Nisbett, 1990, p. 258). For example, a highly stereotypic pattern of machismo, characterized by pride in male sexual prowess, courage in the face of physical danger, and economic dominance, is extremely common throughout the world, but even in this pattern there are striking exceptions. Analyses of these **macho patterns** by Gilmore and other anthropologists indicate that they reflect an adaptation process to extreme risks. These adaptations seem to be commonly connected with the economic role of males, for example, as hunters in the wild, or as protectors of vulnerable animal herds.

18.11 What cultural differences in male "macho" behavior did Gilmore find? What did he conclude?

Gilmore's (1990) comparisons of Truk and Tahiti, two tropical "paradise" islands in the South Pacific, make the case convincingly. Trukese males became violent fighters who personified macho qualities—competitive and eager to show their physical prowess, accumulating many love affairs beginning early in life, while the women of their culture were expected to personify submissiveness. In contrast, Tahitian males did not compete with each other for material possessions. They were expected to be submissive, and allowed their women free and open sexual activity, for example, with Westerners, almost as soon as they landed. Why? As Nisbett (1990, p. 260) notes in his review of this work:

> The Tahitians fish in a lagoon at no risk to themselves and food is quite plentiful. The Trukese must obtain their fish in the open sea. When a Trukese male leaves for a day of fishing, there is a genuine possibility he will not return. Thus the fearless, aggressive macho style is an adaptation to danger. Males are taught to fear unmanliness more than death because this is the only way to encourage men to produce when there is great danger . . . a muting of gender differences and surcease from the crushing requirements of assertive masculinity are a privilege of those societies that can put food on the table without great risk.

The fact that at least in some societies men as a whole are gentle (the Tahitians) and even timid (the Semai people of central Malaysia) has serious implications for understanding both gender roles and culture. According to Gilmore (1990, p. 230), these exceptions to the norm for macho aggressive masculinity suggest that "… manliness is a symbolic script, a cultural construct, endlessly variable and not always necessary." In the course of evolution, when there was dangerous work to be done, men were more likely to do it because of their anatomy and greater physical strength. But now that more of the "high risk–high glory" jobs do not depend on physical strength, one may well ask Gilmore's (p. 231) searching question: "Why should only males be permitted to be 'real men' and earn the glory of a risk successfully taken?"

▶ INTERACTING INFLUENCES ON PERSONALITY DEVELOPMENT

Where does personality come from? What shapes the various aspects of personality? What influences the accessibility of various thoughts and feelings, and the network of connections among them?

The individual's personality system develops from a foundation that is both biochemical and psychosocial; it is guided by the genes in interaction with the environment, as well as reflecting the influences of social learning and culture. As indicated in Figure 18.1, these processes interact in the course of development, influencing the personality system and the social world the person experiences. They impact, for example, on such person variables as how the person construes—and shapes—the situations encountered, as well as how the individual is perceived (Mischel & Shoda, 1998; Saudino & Plomin, 1996).

If individuals are genetically and temperamentally disposed toward greater aggressiveness, for example, they soon become more likely to interpret the motives of other people as aggressive and to anticipate aggression from others (Dodge, 1986). They also may confirm these expectations and beliefs by behaving more aggressively, thereby evoking more aggressive reactions. Likewise, as aggressiveness becomes an established pattern, it also may be incorporated into the values and self-standards and goals of the individual. Each time the aggressive pattern is activated, it becomes more easily accessible in the system as a dominant response tendency, triggered even by minor frustrations

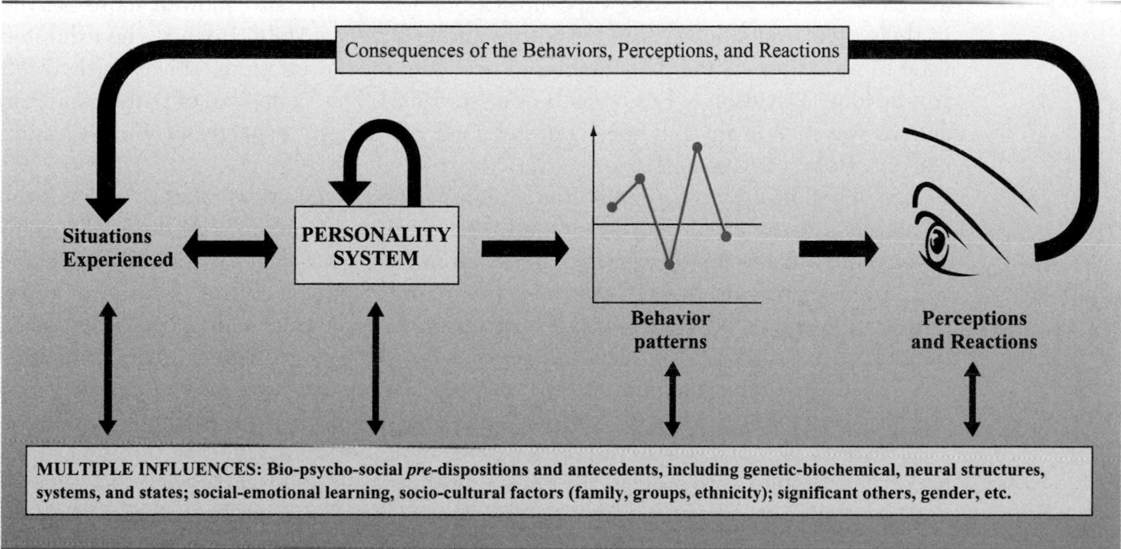

Figure 18.1 Influences on the personality system.

and stress. Increasingly the person also may seek out peers and groups likely to further support this type of behavior and to strengthen it as a source both for self-esteem and peer approval. A common example is when aggressively inclined adolescents are drawn to like-minded peers in aggressive groups and gangs that then collectively and mutually further support their aggressive tendencies (e.g., Bandura & Walters, 1959).

In sum, as the example suggests, the early behavioral tendencies and temperamental and personality characteristics of the individual interact with the psychological environment over the course of time as personality develops and becomes expressed in relatively stable ways (e.g., Caspi, 1998, 2000; Caspi et al., 2005; Contrada et al., 1990). The above example shows how a dispositional tendency like aggression may be reinforced early in life by the social environment and then becomes well established. But your dispositional tendencies are not necessarily determinants of your fate in life. For example, the studies described next show that socialization experiences can help infants who are temperamentally shy to develop into people who are not shy: because social experiences can modify temperament, and biology does not have to be destiny (Schmidt & Fox, 2002).

Biology–Trait–Socialization Interactions: Shyness

18.12 How has shyness research illuminated biological–environmental interactions in personality development?

Shyness is a problem that plagues many people. Researchers have been examining how shyness as a trait in children and young adults manifests itself, and how biological and social factors might jointly influence what happens ultimately to the development of temperamentally shy young children (Schmidt & Fox, 1999, 2002). Their question was: Must the temperamentally shy infant and young child become a shy person in the course of development?

Their first goal was to understand the biological basis for childhood shyness and to identify features that may predict childhood shyness in infancy. Initial studies showed that when new stimuli were presented to infants, a distressed reaction was indicative of shyness likely to develop in preschool and in later childhood, as discussed in earlier chapters with Kagan's work on inhibited children (Kagan & Snidman, 1991). To understand how and why this correlation existed, researchers monitored brain activity via electroencephalograph (EEG) during exposure to new stimuli. Infants who exhibited a high degree of stress during exposure to the new stimuli also showed more activity in their right frontal lobe during exposure and in a resting state. Infants who exhibited little to no distress at the presentation of new stimuli showed more activity in their left frontal lobe (Davidson & Fox, 1989; Fox et al., 1992). This same kind of pattern of brain activity was seen in shy and nonshy preschool-age children, respectively (Fox, Schmidt, Calkins, Rubin, & Copan, 1996).

In a follow-up, researchers tried to understand why some of the infants who displayed distress in the first study and thus were temperamentally disposed toward shyness did not develop shyness as older children. The answer, in part, is in their specific socialization experiences. As noted also in Chapter 5, many of the children who did not develop childhood shyness had less overprotective mothers and/or had been placed in social situations (such as daycare) more often (Fox et al., 2001). The researchers concluded that initial temperamental tendencies toward shyness in childhood can be modified and may be overcome by parenting practices and social experiences.

Shyness, like many broad dispositions such as neuroticism, comes in different forms and types. Studies with college students as well as with children suggest that shyness and sociability are not part of a single dimension (Schmidt & Fox, 2002). They are distinguishable on measures of electrical activity in the cortex as well as on indices such as EEG, and heart rate measured both when at rest and when experiencing a social stressor. So the individual who is highly shy but also highly sociable will be characterized by both biological and psychological–behavioral features that are quite different from an equally shy person who is low on the sociability dimension. Again it is the interaction of multiple variables and processes that determine how temperament and biology play out in personality development.

▶ WHAT DEVELOPS?: THE EVOLVING SELF

In this chapter we have considered the multiple aspects of personality and the diverse influences—from cultural to biological—that help answer the question; Where does personality come from? But what is it that emerges from all these influences? As Carlson (1971) put it years ago: Where is the *person* in personality research? Unsurprisingly, this big question has more than one answer.

The personality system generates patterns of behavior that are perceived and reacted to in the social world in ways that change the situations subsequently experienced. Looked at from the outside, the person can be studied and understood at many levels of analysis, and when the levels are combined the view is enriched. That has been a main message of this concluding part of the text.

But there also is another answer to the questions "where is the person?" and "what emerges?" Namely, throughout the life course it is the self or self-system that evolves and continues to construct itself (e.g., Hoyle et al., 1999; Leary & Tangney, 2003; Mischel & Morf, 2003; Morf, 2006). Then what is this "self" about which so many different claims have been made? So far in this text, although the self was discussed as a concept with many different meanings at each level of analysis, there is also a common theme that does emerge. As one modern summary puts it:

> The self is a dynamic psychological system, a tapestry of thoughts, feelings, and motives that define and direct—even destroy—us. Minus the self, there is little more to human beings than meets the eye: frail, relatively hairless creatures ruled by instinct and circumstance.
>
> (Hoyle et al., 1999, p. 1)

The term used in current work to capture the essence of the self is **selfhood**. First introduced in a presidential address by Brewster Smith to the American Psychological Association in 1978, the term was used to talk about what it means to be human. In its scientific use it refers to the *"thoughts, feelings and behaviors that arise from the awareness of self as an object and agent"* (Hoyle et al., 1999, p. 2).

18.13 What is meant by "selfhood"?

The point here is that each person has the experience of self-awareness, of consciousness of him- or herself as a coherent entity, a distinct whole person. This is the sense of **self as "object"**. And each person tries to pursue these actively in the process of self-construction to continue to build a self and a life within the interpersonal world (Tesser, 2002). This is the sense of **self as "agent**."

Taking Charge: Human Agency

The Self-Construction Process

This text has attempted a scientific account of personality and the personality system in its context. Such an account can easily sound as if the personality is a machine-like system that simply reacts almost reflexively to the many influences that formed it and that now push and pull it around. But that interpretation misses one of the most essential features of personality and of selfhood: namely, the individual has the potential to behave in ways that are forward-looking and to actively change the situations of his or her life, rather than just reacting to them passively. In short, selfhood involves a process of self-construction (e.g., Hoyle et al., 1999; Mischel & Morf, 2003; Morf, 2006; Morf & Rhodewalt, 2001). It is a process in which individuals actively pursue life goals central for the self as they try to build their lives. To reiterate, you saw this concretely in the discussion of how individuals pursue life goals. Most importantly, in Chapter 17 you saw that the process of self-regulation allows people to influence their own life course, to transform and change at least some of the situations they experience, and to actively take charge of their life trajectory.

The same chapter also noted that toddlers already show individual differences in their ability to regulate their attention, and that these differences predict how well they can delay gratification, which in turn predicts many outcomes in their lives as adults. These outcomes ranged from their SAT scores to their educational attainments, to their long-term goal-setting, to their sense of self-worth and ability to cope with life stresses. So is the toddler's future more or less sealed by the time the diaper stage of life is over? The answer of course is emphatically "no."

The Self as an Active Agent

Self-Direction/Agency

First it's important to remember that when findings "predict" outcomes, they are based on correlations. When these correlations are statistically significant, as they are in most of the research discussed here, they still always leave much of the variance in the outcome unaccounted for. It is highly unusual for any single variable to account for more than 25% of the variance. Even when multiple variables are considered together, research in most areas indicates that at least 50% of the "variance" in behavior remains unexplained, open, and unpredicted.

A key question for each person then becomes: "what can I do to influence those outcomes—and myself—in ways that I would like my life and myself to develop?" In psychological terms, this is the question of **human agency** (e.g., Bandura, 2001), and the role of the self as a potentially active agent. To the degree that people have agency—and perceive themselves to have such agency—they may influence proactively the course of their personal experience, their views of the world, and their life paths (e.g., Mischel & Morf, 2003).

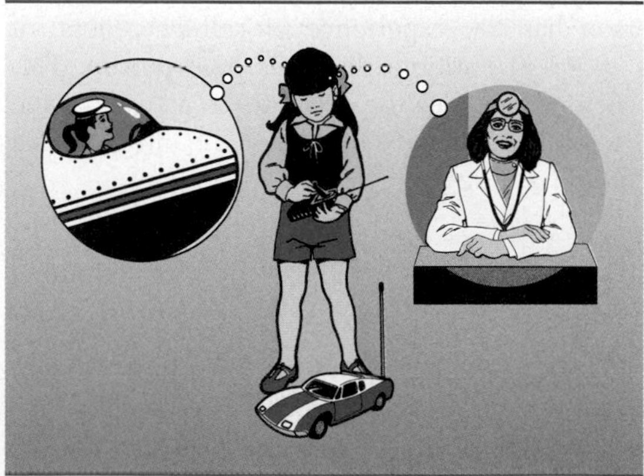

The agentic self: People can influence who and what they become.

The Relational Self

Discussions about agency and self-direction can risk sounding as if one is advocating a self-centered person seeking to advance in the world as an autonomous agent indifferent to others. But on closer examination, the self, as we have seen, is relational in nature (Chapter 15). People are not self-sufficient agents; they need each other, and to thrive requires connection as much as self-direction and agency. This recognition is seen especially in cultures characterized by collectivism, but it is not absent in cultures that focus on individualism.

18.14 Need human agency be self-centered?

For example, effective coping with long-term stress generally depends not just on what the person does inside the head but also on the psychological support environment. People deal better with stress, and are less likely to respond to it with illness, when they have social ties and supports, such as spouses, relatives, close friends, and groups to which they belong (Antonovsky, 1979; Holahan & Moos, 1990). Coping is also better when people can share their stressful experience with others (Nilson et al., 1981). When people are members of a group to which they "belong," they can receive emotional support, help with problems, and even a boost in self-esteem (Cantor et al., 2002; Cobb, 1976; Cohen & McKay, 1984). When they have a spouse to whom they feel they can talk, they tend to thrive, but having a spouse to whom one feels unable to talk makes the risk of depression considerably greater (Coyne & Downey, 1991). The self is relational and thrives with social support and connectedness, not in isolation (Leary & Tangney, 2003).

What Do People Need to Thrive?: The View from Multiple Levels

If people have the capacity to take charge of what they become and their own life course, one has to also ask questions about the psychological qualities of the life one wants to live. While, of course, people differ in the specific goals they pursue in their lives, it may be reasonable to assume that they strive to have mental health, experience personal growth, and in general, *thrive*. But what does it mean to thrive? Work at several of the levels has had something to say about the essentials for personal growth, mental health, and thriving as a human being. Let's review some of the main examples to see the view of well-being that emerges when they are considered together. Table 18.1 summarizes some of the key ingredients identified.

18.15 Summarize what is required for psychological health from different levels of analysis. What five "bottom-line" requisites emerge?

TABLE 18.1 Overview of Ingredients for Psychological Thriving, Well-Being, and Mental Health

Level of Analysis	Key Ingredients
Trait-Dispositional	Positive traits (emotional stability, conscientiousness, agreeableness)
Psychodynamic-Motivational (Freud)	Insight into unconscious; able to love (unambivalent relationships) and work
Phenomenological-Humanistic (Existential)	Self-acceptance; responsible for self and choices: agentic
Social Cognitive	Competence/self-efficacy, relatedness (interpersonal connectedness); able to self-regulate: agentic

At the *Trait-Dispositional Level*, it is easy to identify the negative traits, for example, emotional instability or neuroticism, excessive impulsivity and anxiety, disagreeableness-hostility, lack of conscientiousness. Likewise, the positive qualities are clear since they are at the opposite ends of each of these dimensions. While it is informative to have descriptions of positive and negative qualities, this level focuses on describing the current and ideal functioning, and does not really address change possibilities in psychological terms.

The good news is that other levels of analysis do directly address the possibilities for constructive change. At the *Psychodynamic-Motivational Level*, Freud's answer to the question was stated simply in his hope for the outcome of successful therapy: *Where id was there ego shall be*, was the phrase he used. Philosophically, for Freud that meant having to recognize and accept one's unconscious, animal-like biological urges, but to live life without enacting them. In his view, psychoanalysis helped people gain deep emotional insight into unconscious wishes and conflicts, and ultimately accept them without either having to act on them or deny them. The healthy person for Freud was one who becomes able to *love*, which is seen in the ability to have unambivalent close relationships, and to *work*. For Freud's followers, the answers shifted toward the need for a healthy ego and self. In Kohut's words (Chapter 9), each person needs, above all, a self that feels empathic human responses from significant others. The healthy self feels the glow of pleasure in appropriate mature sexual functioning, as well as self-confident assertiveness in the pursuit of goals.

At the *Phenomenological-Humanistic Level*, the focus was not on recognizing and accepting that people are animals but rather that they are humans and as such have distinctive qualities. Most notably, a person has higher-order needs that go beyond the biological, and a self that has its own distinctive characteristics. For Carl Rogers, the essential point for thriving was to allow yourself to be genuine and to grow as you really are. That requires, in his view, that one listen to and accept one's organismic true self without distorting it to reduce anxiety or to please other people. For the existentialists and humanists also working at the Phenomenological Level, attention was on the combination of freedom and responsibility in making choices in life (e.g., May, 1961). The commonly used terms for these ingredients currently are autonomy or agency—namely a sense that one is at least partly causing one's own behavior, thus responsible and in charge of oneself or agentic.

This conception has been renewed and expanded in recent years in the *positive psychology* movement, dedicated to turning psychology away from its earlier focus on "repairing the worst things in life to also building the best qualities in life" (Seligman, 2002, p. 3). The field of positive psychology now calls attention to the conditions that allow people to thrive—to personally experience feelings of well-being and satisfaction with the past, happiness in the present, and optimism and faith in the future (Chapter 13). Beyond the personal, positive psychology also seeks to cultivate a society that is responsible, altruistic, values a work ethic and tolerance, recognizing the fact that the individual's well-being and the conditions of the social world are bound together.

Closely related to these ideas are those used at the *Social Cognitive Level* to describe the essentials for well-being. Here the focus is on self-perceived competence, and agency as reflected in Bandura's concept of self-efficacy, and in Dweck's concern with mastery and a belief that one is able to change and improve. Researchers who work on the self, selfhood, and self-determination (Deci & Ryan, 1995, 2000) also see competence as essential for thriving, but they include an additional important component: **relatedness**. Because the self is intrinsically relational or interpersonal, people require the support and connection with others with whom they can feel close and mutually supported—they need relatedness as well as a sense of agency, competence, and efficacy, as was also noted earlier in this text. Finally, a common denominator that is seen at most levels is the importance of appropriate self-regulation, since that is an essential component for attaining the goals that one is pursuing (as discussed in detail in the previous chapter), and enables the person to be agentic.

Taken together, there is a clear consensus in the ingredients for well-being identified by these very different levels over the course of a century of work. To function well psychologically, people need to:

- Understand and accept themselves
- Have a sense of competence
- Feel positive, agentic, and responsible for their behavior and choices
- Be connected to other people and society
- Self-regulate appropriately

Potential for Change

18.16 To what extent do biological factors limit capacity for self-change?

Given what is known so far about personality, how great is the individual's potential for change and self-direction?

The Role of Genetics

On the one hand, the findings of behavior geneticists underline the role of the DNA and the person's genetic heritage (Wright, 1998). Recall, for example, that identical twins reared apart often display amazing similarities in what they do and become. But as a counterexample, mate choice, for instance, although it is extensively influenced by the evolutionary history of the species, seems exempt from genetic influences (Chapter 5), and surely these choices are important expressions of the self. As one writer noted: "Are we not defined in a profound sense by the relationships we forge with others . . . ?" (Angier, 1998, p. 9). And again you have to remind yourself that even the strongest correlations in the heritability studies usually leave more than half the variance unexplained. Most of that unexplained variance is attributable to the environment—and that includes most importantly what the person does within that environment in the course of life.

The Role of the Brain

The same question now also is often raised about the role of the brain: Doesn't the brain we inherit pretty much dictate the rest of the script that unfolds? Isn't biology destiny? A clear answer comes from the work of Eric Kandel, a recent Nobel Prize–winning scientist who studied the well-mapped nervous system of Aplysia, a lowly sea slug.

In elegant studies, Dr. Kandel showed that learning leads the organism to produce new proteins that, in turn, remodel the neurons in the nervous system. The sea slugs that were put into controlled learning conditions that led to long-term memory also developed two times as many neuronal connections as the control group of slugs who were untrained. The implication for humans was clear: learning changes the structures and functions of the brain. And if the simple learning that slugs can do profoundly changes their nervous system, given the human capacities for learning, we have the potential to alter what happens in our brains dramatically.

Eric Kandel
(*Source*: AFP/Corbis)

In this text, you have seen much evidence about how individuals can construe and reinterpret themselves and explain events in ways that help to empower them and make their lives better and more constructive. Learning about the personality processes that allow change and emotional growth, as well as those that provide stability and coherence, also provides a potentially powerful route for self-direction. It can allow one perhaps to have more agency and to become thoughtful and wise about one's future. As George Kelly argued (Chapter 14), every person is a scientist, and in that sense can use what is known to form and test hypotheses about what might be possible.

The exciting possibilities for freedom and growth that each person has are not limitless. People may constructively rethink and reappraise their possible selves and expand their efficacy to a great degree, but their DNA influences the tools with which they do so. In addition to biology, cultural and social forces in part influence and limit both the events that people can control and their perceptions of their own possibilities (e.g., Kunda, 1999; Nisbett, Peng, Choi, & Norenzayan, 2001; Stigler et al., 1990). Within these boundaries, people have the potential to gain substantial control over their own lives, shaping their futures in ways whose limits remain to be seen.

A few hundred years ago the French philosopher Descartes wrote his famous phrase "cogito ergo sum"—I think, therefore I am—and opened the way to modern psychology. With what is becoming known about personality, we can modify his assertion to say: "I think, therefore I can change what I am." Because by changing how I think, I can change what I feel, do, and become.

SUMMARY

CULTURE AND PERSONALITY

- Cultures may differ in the typology of individualism versus collectivism, but this typology represents an average cultural tendency that may not fit many people within the culture.
- The cultural meaning system contains basic goals-values, emotions, standards, self-regulatory rules, interpersonal scripts, and control strategies that are activated only in certain situations.
- Culture influences the situations that people tend to experience and the ways they interpret these experiences and respond.
- Each individual develops a personal meaning system that incorporates some components from the shared cultural meanings system and others from their own unique life experiences.
- Researchers have found that race-based rejection sensitivity (RS) is related to experiences of rejection and academic performance in African American students.
- Culture influences personality by affecting the ways in which other people, as well as the self, react to the individual's behavior.

GENDER AND SEX DIFFERENCES

- Gender influences the views the individual develops about him- or herself as well as how other people treat the person.
- There are significant psychological differences in behavior both between the sexes and within the same sex.
- Gender differences are found not just in overall sex differences in levels of behavior but also in the *if . . . then . . .* patterns in which personality is expressed.
- Females may respond to stress by tending and befriending instead of by fight or flight.
- There are distinct cultural differences in the way that gender roles are interpreted.

INTERACTING INFLUENCES ON PERSONALITY DEVELOPMENT

- The multiple influences on the personality system include the interactive effects of biological determinants, learning, and social and cultural influences.

WHAT DEVELOPS?: THE EVOLVING SELF

- In self-construction, individuals actively pursue life goals central for the self as they build their lives.
- The self is relational: it thrives on social support and connectedness, not in isolation.
- People have the potential to learn and thus alter the structures and functions of their own brains.
- Ideal qualities of a well-functioning personality include self-understanding and self-acceptance, a sense of competence, responsibility, agency, connection to other people, and the ability to self-regulate appropriately.

KEY TERMS

androgens 479
befriending 480
collectivism 468
cultural affordances 472
cultural meaning system 469
gender 476
gender concepts 476
gender stereotypes 476
human agency 484
if . . . then . . . cultural signatures 471
individualism 468
macho patterns 480
personal meaning system 474
relatedness 486
self as "agent" 483
self as "object" 483
selfhood 483
sex-role identity 476
tending response to stress 480
units of culture 469

TAKING STOCK

PART VII

INTEGRATION OF LEVELS: THE PERSON AS A WHOLE

Personality psychology is evolving toward becoming an increasingly cumulative science that is based on promising ideas, findings, and methods from all areas of the field and all levels of analysis. The last three chapters in this text illustrated a more integrative approach to personality. It builds on concepts and findings from diverse levels of analysis that historically were considered incompatible but that, in fact, can enrich each other.

▶ PROSPECTS FOR PERSONALITY PSYCHOLOGY

Of course, integration for its own sake is not useful if the result is a conglomeration of concepts and findings with no clear criteria for inclusion or exclusion. Genuine differences in theory and research are often a necessary step in scientific progress. Not everyone can win, and not every idea will survive. The challenge is to gain breadth and perspective, but without indiscriminate inclusion, and with rigorous testing of the ideas, fine-tuning the survivors progressively as the state of knowledge changes. By including useful concepts and discarding those that are not useful from all areas and levels of analysis, a solid integration begins to emerge.

▶ PERSONOLOGY REVISITED

More than 50 years ago, Henry Murray and his colleagues at Harvard University's Social Relations Department wanted to create a science of persons as individuals. To describe their ambitious work, they created a new term, "personology," for the study of persons and lives in depth (Chapter 8). While this term is no longer widely used, the goal that these pioneers pursued remains, and it is more timely now than ever before. Innovative as Murray and his colleagues were, they still lacked the methods to do their work as effectively as they wished. Fortunately, half a century later, advances in the science, for example, in biological approaches to personality and in the study of mental and emotional processes, are making it feasible to study individuals in increasing depth as Murray and his colleagues had hoped to do. For example, and as noted in the text, it is now possible to study what happens in the brain of an individual at the same time that his or her thoughts and feelings are studied. And it is possible to link these levels of analysis to intensive direct observations of how the person's behavior patterns interact with diverse situations sampled over extensive periods of time, either directly recorded or sampled through diaries. Valid, reliable, and useful tests and methods are available at each level of analysis, and all can be brought together to study personality with the depth and detail that this formidable task requires, and that makes personality an exciting field for now and for the future.

Personality psychology always has had two goals—description of individual differences and analysis of the processes that underlie them. By studying both together it becomes possible to build an increasingly cumulative and precise science of personality and human nature. The pursuit of both goals together provides an increasingly rich and clear view not just of personality constructs (e.g., neuroticism, self-regulatory competence) but also of the persons described with those terms and their distinctive characteristics. When the beautiful details begin to be put together, the coherent whole person emerges.

GLOSSARY

Ability traits Cattell's term for traits that are concerned with effectiveness in gaining the goal.

Act trends General behavioral trends; Buss and Craik view traits as descriptions of individual differences in *act trends* instead of underlying internal causes.

Active ingredient Features of situations that activate certain psychological processes in the perceiver.

Activity Temperament that effects the vigor or intensity of responses; also refers to individual differences on a dimension that ranges from hyperactivity to extreme inactivity.

Actual self The representation of oneself as one is.

Actual/ideal discrepancies The differences between the self one perceives oneself to be and the self one would like to be.

Actual/ought discrepancies The differences between the self one perceives oneself to be and the self one thinks one should be.

Affect Feelings and emotions.

Agentic To be at least partly responsible and in charge of oneself and one's behavior.

Aggression Any behavior intended to harm or injure another living being who is motivated to avoid such treatment.

Agreeableness (A) Good-natured, helpful, trusting, lenient; opposite of antagonism.

Akrasia An ancient Greek term for the character trait marked by a deficiency of the will.

Alleles Different versions of a gene.

Ambivalence Simultaneous attraction and aversion toward someone or something.

Amygdala A small, almond-shaped region in the forebrain that is crucially important in emotional reactions, particularly fear.

Anaclitic identification Hypothesized by Freud as the earliest form of identification based on the infant's intense dependency on the mother.

Anal stage The second of Freud's psychosexual stages, it occurs during the child's second year; pleasure is focused on the anus and on the retention and expulsion of feces.

Analytical psychology Carl Jung's theory of personality; humans are viewed as purposive and striving toward self-actualization; the unconscious includes a collective as well as a personal unconscious and is a healthy force.

Androgens Hormones related to aggression, found in the male brain in many species.

Anima In Jung's theory, the feminine, passive element in the unconscious of every male.

Animus In Jung's theory, the masculine, assertive element in the unconscious of every female.

Anorexic behavior Self-starvation; has been linked to *actual/ought discrepancies*.

Anorexia nervosa A disorder in which the individual (usually an adolescent female) refuses to eat, without any apparent cause, sometimes starving to death.

Anterior attentional systems Area of the frontal cortex that regulates the pathways involved in executive functions (or EF).

Antidepressants Drugs used to elevate the mood of depressed individuals.

Antipsychotic drugs Drugs used in the treatment of major psychosis, notably schizophrenia.

Anxiety A state of emotional arousal which may be experienced as a diffuse fear; in Freud's theory, the result of a struggle between an impulse and an inhibition.

Applicability In social cognition, refers to whether the schema or mental representation a person has available is applicable to the situation.

Approach Behavior that is directed toward actively achieving a goal or positive reward; commonly associated with the *behavioral activation system (BAS)*.

Approach (appetitive) dilemma When an individual faces an approach temptation that threatens to interfere with another more important, higher-order goal.

Approach tendencies Individual's tendency to approach desired stimuli.

Approach-approach conflict Conflict that occurs when a person must choose one of several desirable alternatives.

Approach-avoidance conflict A conflict that occurs when a person confronts an object or situation that has both positive and negative elements.

Archetypes Jung's term for the contents of the collective unconscious—images or symbols expressing the inherited patterns for the organization of experience (e.g., mother archetype).

Ascending reticular activation system (ARAS) The system in the brain that is believed to regulate overall arousal in the cortex.

Assertiveness training Training usually involving modeling and practice in developing and using effective assertive skills; a type of behavior therapy.

Automatic processing Mental operations that occur outside of our awareness.

Automaticity Responses made automatically with little or no control, thought, or awareness.

Autonomy versus shame and doubt Erikson's psychosocial stage at age 2-3 years dealing with the struggle to gain some mastery, autonomy, and freedom, while avoiding shame and humiliation.

Availability In social cognition, refers to whether a schema or mental representation exists within the person or not.

Availability heuristic A cognitive rule or principle suggesting that the more easily we can think of something, the more likely we are to believe it to be in reality.

Aversion therapy Procedures that pair attractive, arousing, but problem-producing stimuli with another stimulus that evokes extremely negative reactions; the positive stimulus comes to evoke some of the negative or aversive reactions or is at least neutralized; for example, alcohol may be combined with nausea-producing drugs.

Aversive stimulation Punishment for a given response.

Avoidance Impulse to flee from a person or situation.

Avoidance (aversive) dilemma When an impulse to flee threatens to interfere with the pursuit of a higher-order goal.

Avoidance tendencies Individual's tendency to avoid undesirable stimuli.

Avoidance-avoidance conflict A conflict that occurs when a person must choose one of several undesirable alternatives.

Befriending (response to stress) Responding to stressful situations by making friends and offering assistance.

Behavior genetics Study of the role of genes in social behavior and personality.

Behavior modification Techniques used in behavior therapy which are derived from learning principles and intended to change behavior predictably for therapeutic goals.

Behavior sampling Method of selecting representative behaviors from an individual's daily life; can be done through self-reports, diary studies, and behavioral observation.

Behavioral activation system (BAS) Neurological system in the brain that activates approach behavior.

Behavioral deficits Lack of skills required for successful functioning.

Behavioral inhibition system (BIS) Neurological system in the brain that activates withdrawal from certain stimuli and inhibits behavior.

Behavioral-Conditioning Level Approach to psychology emphasizing observable, objectively measurable behaviors and the relationships between these behaviors and specific events or stimuli in the environment.

Behavior-outcome relations The relationship between possible behavior patterns and expected outcomes in particular situations; an aspect of the expectancies that constitute one of the person variables in the Social Cognitive Level of analysis.

Behavioral signatures of narcissists Behavioral signature characterized by the pattern of *if* there is an opportunity to promote the self, *then* much effort is put out toward proving superiority over everybody else.

Benzodiazepines Minor tranquilizers that replaced the barbiturates as primary pharmacologic treatment for anxiety; an example is Valium.

Big Five Structure A popular taxonomy for characterizing individuals in terms of five major traits based on factor analysis of bipolar trait ratings and questionnaires.

Biological Level Approach to personality that deals with genetic, hereditary, and evolutionary influences on personality.

Biological preparedness Biological predisposition to learn some associations more readily than others.

Bipolar representations According to object relations theorists, the combination of an individual's perception of self, his or her perception of another individual significant to him or her, and the emotions produced in him or her as a result of interaction between them; they become the templates through which the individual perceives ensuing relationships.

Blunting Ignoring anxiety-arousing stimuli as a means of coping with them; a style of information processing designed for dealing with stress.

Brain asymmetry The degree to which the right versus the left sides of the brain are activated.

CAPS The psychological processing system that distinctively characterizes the individual (See *Cognitive-Affective Personality System*).

Cardinal traits Allport's term for highly generalized dispositions or characteristics that influence most aspects of an individual's behavior throughout life.

Castration anxiety A male's fear of losing his penis; Freud believed this anxiety was central in the resolution of the Oedipus complex and the boy's identification with the father.

Categorize To group information about ideas and experiences that have such resemblance or "go together" in order to organize and simplify vast amounts of information efficiently so that it can be used quickly to make inferences and decisions.

Causal attribution Perception (judgment) of the causes of behavior, either to internal or external causes.

Central traits Allport's term for traits that are less important and pervasive than cardinal traits but that still influence much of a person's behavior.

Cheater detector A mechanism that humans have developed to detect individuals who seek the benefits of social exchange without reciprocating appropriately.

Chronic accessibility The ease with which particular cognitive-affective units or internal mental representations become activated or "come to mind."

Classical conditioning (conditioned-response learning) A type of learning, emphasized by Pavlov, in which the response to an unconditioned stimulus (e.g., food) becomes conditioned to a neutral stimulus (e.g., a bell) by being paired or associated with it.

Client-centered (person-centered) therapy Approach to therapy developed by Carl Rogers; emphasizes a nonevaluative, accepting atmosphere conducive to honesty and concentrates on present relationships and feelings.

Cognition Thought; mental activity.

Cognitive Pertaining to thoughts; mental.

Cognitive behavioral therapy (CBT) Therapy aimed at changing problematic behavior by thinking about one's problems and oneself more constructively and less irrationally (e.g., by modifying one's assumptions).

Cognitive cool system Processing system that generates cognitive thought processes and thoughtful, reflective reactions and plans; based in the hippocampus and frontal lobe.

Cognitive learning See *modeling* and *observational learning*.

Cognitive reappraisal Changing the way that one thinks about an experience in order to maintain self-regulation.

Cognitive restructuring Therapeutic technique aimed at learning to think about one's problems more constructively and less irrationally; Albert Ellis's *rational emotive therapy* is a form of cognitive restructuring.

Cognitive revolution A rejection of behaviorism and a focus instead on mental (cognitive) processes, leading to the development of cognitive psychology.

Cognitive social competence (social and cognitive competencies) Person variable referring to an individual's abilities to cognitively process and use social information.

Cognitive social theories Approaches to personality that focus on the cognitive processes and structures underlying personal differences.

Cognitive transformations (of stimuli) Cognitively changing the mental representation of a stimulus by focusing on selected aspects of it or imagining it differently.

Cognitive-Affective Personality System (CAPS) The personality system as conceptualized within the social cognitive framework (see Mischel & Shoda, 1995).

Cognitive-affective units Mental-emotional representations—the cognitions and affects or feelings—that are available to the person.

Collective unconscious Inherited portion of the unconscious, as postulated by Jung; consists of ancestral memories and archetypes that are part of each person's unconscious.

Collectivism A cultural typology defined by closer connections to groups and family in one's self-conception, used especially to characterize Asian cultures.

Common traits According to Allport, traits that are shared in different degrees by many people.

Compensatory motivation Motivation for the individual to compensate for early concerns with physical weakness or illness.

Competence Ability to perform a given task or types of tasks; related to self-efficacy.

Competence motivation Desire to acquire mastery of a task for its own sake.

Concurrent validity Degree of correlation between a measure and another behavior/measure recorded at about the same point in time.

Condition of worth Conditions that other people, usually parents, implicitly make as a requirement for being loved and worthwhile.

Conditional hedges Qualifying or contextualizing characterizations of others (e.g., "Joe is aggressive when people tease him about his glasses.")

Conditioned reinforcers Neutral stimuli that have acquired value by becoming associated with other stimuli that already have reinforcing power.

Conditioned response (CR) A learned response to a conditioned stimulus; a response previously made to an unconditioned stimulus is now made to a conditioned stimulus as the result of pairing the two stimuli.

Conditioned stimulus (CS) A previously neutral stimulus to which one begins to respond distinctly after it has been paired with an unconditioned stimulus.

Conditioning A basic form of learning (see also *classical conditioning*; *operant conditioning*).

Conditions of deprivation Length of time an organism has been deprived of relief from an innate drive (e.g., hunger, thirst, sex).

Conflict Occurs when motivated to pursue two or more goals that are mutually exclusive.

Congruent therapist Therapist who feels free to "be himself" and to accept himself and the client fully and immediately in the therapeutic encounter.

Connectionist theories Theories that emphasize the way the person's internal mental representations or schemas are related to each other and interconnected to form a system that functions as an organized network structure.

Conscientiousness (C) Careful, self-reliant, goal-directed, scrupulous; opposite of undirectedness.

Conscious Within awareness.

Constitutional traits Those source traits that reflect constitutional factors.

Construct Any class of behavior, thoughts, emotions, and situations.

Construct validity The process of establishing that the theory about what accounts for behaviors on a particular test is valid; it involves validation of both the test and the theory that underlies it.

Constructive alternativism Recategorization of individuals or events to facilitate problem solving; a concept in George Kelly's theory.

Constructivist view of science Theory of science that there is no single, absolute Truth awaiting discovery, merely different ways of viewing and conceptualizing phenomena that are more or less useful and valid for particular purposes and contexts.

Contemporaneity of motives Motives are understood in terms of their role in the present regardless of their origins in the past.

Content validity The demonstration that the items on a test adequately represent a defined broader class of behavior.

Contingencies of reinforcement Conditions that must be present in order for a response to be rewarded.

Contingency contracting Self-imposed regulations that guide a person's behavior in the absence of immediate external pressures.

Contingency management The use of rewards or *contingency contracting* to guide a person's behavior.

Continuous reinforcement Schedule of reinforcement in which a response is reinforced every time it occurs.

Control group The group of participants that does not receive the experimental treatment but is otherwise comparable to the experimental group; responses by this group can be compared with those by the experimental group to measure any differences.

Controlled processing Conscious thought, e.g., planning, problem solving, and future-oriented decision-making and self-control, in contrast to automatic processing.

Convenience of constructs According to Kelly, the utility or convenience of a construct for the individual.

Correlation The relationship between two variables or sets of measures; may be either positive or negative, and is expressed in a correlation coefficient.

Correlation coefficient Quantitative expression of a correlation; ranges from 0 to +1 or −1.

Counterconditioning (desensitization) Replacement of a response to a stimulus by a new response in behavior therapy.

Covert modeling A type of behavior therapy in which the individual imagines a model performing the desirable behavior in an appropriate situation (see also *modeling*).

Criterion validity Correlation between scores on a given test and the scores on other measures that serve as referents or standards.

Cross-situational consistency The individual's consistency across different types of situations (e.g., from home to school to work).

Cue Stimulus that directs behavior, determining when, where, and how the response (behavior) will occur.

Cultural meaning system Culturally distinctive views about what the world is like; contains concepts and feelings about the self and its relation to others.

Current life tasks Long-term projects to which individuals commit themselves during designated periods of their lives.

Death instincts See *Thanatos*.

Defense mechanisms According to Freud, ways in which the ego unconsciously tries to cope with unacceptable, anxiety-producing id impulses or feelings and events, as in repression, projection, reaction formation, sublimation, or rationalization.

Defensive pessimism Using worrying about the possible negatives and stressors in goal pursuit as a defensive strategy.

Denial In Freudian theory, a primitive defense mechanism in which a person denies a threatening impulse or event even though reality confirms it; the basis for development of repression.

Dependent variable Aspect of the person's behavior that is measured after the independent variable has been manipulated.

Directional selection Selection process in which versions of characteristics that enhance survival and reproduction gradually become increasingly represented, while those that handicap survival and reproduction tend to fade out.

Discrimination training Conditioning that involves reinforcement in the presence of one stimulus but not in the presence of others.

Discriminative facility The ability to appraise situations as they present themselves and to respond accordingly.

Discriminative stimuli Stimuli that indicate when a response will or will not have favorable consequences.

Distortion/Displacement Occurs when private meanings develop as objects and events become symbols representing things quite different from themselves.

Dizygotic twins Fraternal twins; two organisms that develop in the uterus at the same time but from two egg and two sperm cells; not genetically identical.

Domain of interpersonal behavior According to Wiggins, a comprehensive taxonomy of personality dimensions discovered through factor analysis.

Domain specific knowledge and expertise The group of competencies essential for everyday problem-solving and coping behaviors.

Domain specificity Specific psychological problem-solving strategies that facilitated reproduction, adaptation, and survival in the course of evolution.

Double-blind experiment Experimental procedure in which neither participants nor experimenters know whether participants are in experimental or control conditions.

Down syndrome Genetic abnormality consisting of a third chromosome in the 21st chromosome pair; causes severe mental retardation and a distinctive appearance.

Dream interpretation A method used in psychoanalysis to better understand the unconscious fears and desires of the patient through an analysis of the patient's dreams.

Drive Any strong stimuli (internal or external) that impels action.

Drive reduction Reduction of tension caused by the fulfillment of a drive.

Dynamic traits Cattell's term for traits that are relevant to the individuals being "set into action" with respect to some goal.

Ectomorph According to Sheldon, an individual who has a tall, thin, and stoop-shouldered figure and has an artistic, restrained, and introvertive temperament.

Effortful control "Willpower" or active, strategic effort in goal pursuit and self-regulation.

Ego In Freudian theory, the conscious part of the personality that mediates between the demands of the id and the demands of the world; operates on the reality principle.

Ego control Degree of impulse control; important in delay of gratification, planfulness, and aggression inhibition (see also *ego resilience*).

Ego identity The ego's ability to integrate changes in the libido with developmental aptitudes and social opportunities.

Ego psychology A variety of psychoanalytic theory that stresses ego functions and de-emphasizes instinctual drives.

Ego resilience Refers to the individual's ability to adapt to environmental demands by appropriately modifying his or her habitual level of ego control, thus functioning with some flexibility.

Electrocardiogram (EKG) A polygraph that measures the patterns of electricity produced by muscular contractions of the heart.

Electroencephalograph (EEG) Records the degree of activation in the cerebral cortex through "brain waves."

Emotional hot system Processing system in the brain that generates automatic approach-avoidance, or fight-or-flight responses; based in the *amygdala*.

Emotional overcloseness In Kohut's view, a state in which the family exposes the child to too much intimacy, stimulation, and intrusiveness.

Emotional stability The opposite of neuroticism, according to Eysenck, who viewed emotional stability-neuroticism as an important trait dimension.

Emotionality Tendency to become physiologically aroused easily and experience frequent and intense negative emotions such as anger, fear, and distress.

Empathic mirroring Learning emotions and behaviors from the examples of others.

Encoding A social cognitive person variable that includes the individual's personal constructs and units for categorizing people, events, and experiences.

Endomorph According to Sheldon, an individual who is obese and correspondingly tends to be relaxed, sociable, and likes to eat.

Entity theorists Those who see abilities and traits as fixed, unchangeable characteristics; they tend to choose goals that will assure them favorable judgment and approval.

Environmental presses According to Murray, contextual or situational pressures that influence personality and its expression.

Environmental-mold traits Those source traits (according to Cattell) that reflect environmental conditions.

Eros One of two sides of the personality, as seen by early psychoanalysts, that represented sexuality and love (see also *Thanatos*).

Error variance The "noise" or the non-essential variance to be discounted from statistical analysis.

Evaluative factor Evaluations such as "good" or "bad."

Excitatory links Activating relationship between two or more schemas in a *network information processing model*.

Executive functions Self-regulatory processes, such as planning, self-control, and willpower.

Existential anxiety An awareness of the nothingness and death that necessarily accompanies being and that must be resolved by enhanced attention to how we choose to lead our lives (in existential theories).

Existentialism A viewpoint initiated by the philosopher Kierkegaard that human beings are completely free and responsible for their own behavior and this responsibility is at the root of the deep dread and anxiety that characterizes human beings.

Expectancies A person variable that includes behavior-outcome and stimulus-outcome expectancies and guides an individual's choices.

Experiment An attempt to manipulate a variable of interest while controlling all other conditions so that their influence can be discounted and the effects of the variable measured.

Experimental group The group in an experiment into which the independent variable is introduced; in order to determine the effects of the independent variable, the results of this group are compared with those in the control group.

Explanatory styles The way in which people interpret and construe the reasons for different events and outcomes.

Explicit motives The individual's more consciously recognized goals.

External control When an individual believes that positive and/or negative events are a result of factors outside of one's control.

Extinction The decrease in the frequency of a response that follows the repetition of the response (or in classical conditioning, the repetition of the conditioned stimulus) in the absence of the unconditioned stimulus.

Extinction schedule Reinforcement for a behavior is withdrawn until gradually the behavior itself stops.

Extraversion (E) (Extraverts) According to Jung, an individual who is conventional, sociable, and outgoing and who reacts to stress by trying to lose himself or herself among people.

Extraversion-introversion According to Eysenck, a basic dimension of personality along which all individuals can be placed at some point.

Factor analysis A mathematical procedure for sorting trait terms or test responses into clusters or factors; used in the development of tests designed to discover basic personality traits; it identifies items that are homogeneous or internally consistent and independent of others.

False memories Memories of events that never actually occurred.

Family therapy A therapeutic approach based on the premise that the roots of problems lie within the family system and therefore must be treated by improving family dynamics and relations.

Field theory Position that construes behavior as determined by the person's psychological life space—by the events in his or her total psychological situation at the moment—rather than by past events or by enduring situation-free dispositions.

Fight or flight reaction Automatic physical and emotional reaction to perceived threat or danger, leading to attack or withdrawal; involves increase in heart rate, metabolic rate, and blood pressure, and a decrease in stomach and intestinal activity.

Fixation A psychodynamic term referring to a process by which a person remains arrested at an early stage of psychosexual development, or moves on but later regresses to that stage.

Free association A technique used in psychoanalytic therapy in which the patient is instructed to report whatever comes to mind, no matter how irrational it may seem.

Functional analysis A system of analysis proposed by Skinner to link the organism's behavior to the precise conditions that control it.

Functional autonomy The idea that adult motives replace the motives of infancy.

Functional magnetic resonance imaging (fMRI) Method of capturing and creating an image of the activity in the brain through measurement of the magnetic fields created by the functioning nerve cells in the brain.

Fundamental attribution error The tendency to focus on dispositions as causal explanations of behavior.

Galvanic skin response (GSR) Changes in electrical activity of the skin due to sweating, as recorded by a galvanometer, and used as an index of emotional state, for example, in a lie detector test.

Gender The social meaning of being a male or a female.

Gender concepts Beliefs about the types of behavior more appropriate for one sex than for the other.

Gender stereotypes Rigid beliefs about what it means to be a man or a woman within a particular culture or society.

Gene A region of DNA that influences a particular characteristic in an organism, and is a unit of heredity.

Generalization Responding in the same way to similar stimuli, for example, when a child who has been bitten by a dog becomes afraid of all dogs.

Generalized conditioned reinforcers Conditioned reinforcers that have been paired with more than one primary reinforcer.

Generalized reinforcers See *generalized conditioned reinforcers*.

Generativity versus self-absorption and stagnation For Erikson, the psychosocial crisis faced by the mature adult where the individual must choose remaining absorbed, productive and vital in work and relationships, versus losing interest in work and other people, disconnecting with the larger world and the human future.

Genital stage The last of Freud's psychosexual stages, in which the individual becomes capable of love and adult sexual satisfaction.

Gestalt theory The completeness or fullness theory of Fritz Perls; focuses on the awareness of one's own experience in dynamic interaction with the environment.

Gestalt therapy An approach developed by F. Perls that aims at expanding the awareness of self and putting the person in touch with his or her own feelings and creative potential; often practiced in groups, use is made of body exercises and the venting of emotions.

Globality Generalizing an event to pertain to many aspects of one's life.

Goal gradients Changes in response strengths as a function of distance from the goal object.

Goal hierarchies Organization of goals in order of their degree of importance to the individual.

Harvard personologists A group of psychologists in the 1940s and 1950s whose study of personality was strongly influenced by the work of Freud and by biosocial, organismic theory stressing the integrated, whole aspect of personality.

Healthy personality According to Maslow, a self-actualized person.

Heritability estimates (index) A measure used in behavior genetic research to try to assess the degree to which a trait or attribute is due to inheritance.

Hierarchy of anxiety (grading the stimuli) A hierarchy of events that range from the most to the least intensely anxiety-provoking.

Higher growth needs Needs for self-actualization fulfillment.

Higher-order conditioning Process that occurs when a conditioned stimulus modifies the response to a neutral stimulus with which it has been associated.

Higher-order motives A hypothesized motive that, unlike thirst or hunger, does not involve specific physiological changes.

Hippocampus A horseshoe-shaped region in the temporal lobe of the brain that regulates emotional responses and complex mental and spatial thought.

Homophobia Dislike and/or discomfort with homosexuality.

Hot cognitions Thoughts that activate strong emotion.

Human agency The individual's ability to proactively influence his or her personal experience.

Human genome The human genetic code consisting of roughly 30,000 to 40,000 individual genes contained in 23 chromosome pairs.

Human-relations training group (T-group)/Sensitivity training group Encounter groups that focus on nonverbal experience and self-discovery.

Humanistic psychology The movement within personality psychology devoted to promoting a "holistic psychology" to study the individual as a whole person, focusing on subjective experience and the self, rather than on sub-processes like learning or perceiving.

Hysteria A neurotic condition consisting of two subcategories: conversion reaction (physical symptoms such as paralysis or loss of sensation without organic cause) and dissociative reaction (disruption of a consistent unitary sense of self that may include amnesia, fugue, and/or multiple personalities).

Hysterical anesthesia Loss of sensation in a part of the body without physiological impairment, reflecting a defensive attempt to avoid painful thoughts and feelings, according to Freud.

Id In Freudian theory, the foundation of the personality and a basic component of the psyche, consisting of unconscious instincts and inherited biological drives; it operates on the pleasure principle.

Ideal self The representation of who you would like to be.

Identification with the aggressor Identification with the father or the "aggressor" during the Oedipal stage of development; motivated by fear of harm and castration by the father.

Identity The sense of self at the level of feelings, social roles and behaviors.

Identity crisis For Erikson, a point in psychological development when the adolescent or young defines his or her identity.

Identity versus role confusion For Erikson, the psychosocial crisis at puberty when the individual struggles to answer "who am I?"—not just verbally, but at the level of feelings, new social roles, and behaviors.

I-E Scale Trait dimension that reflects whether a person perceived locus of control is internal (I) or external (E).

***If* . . . *then* . . . Pattern (Signature)** Distinctive patterns of situation-behavior interactions that characterize an individual (e.g., if situation A, then behavior B).

***If* . . . *then* . . . cultural signatures** Cultural differences, like personality differences, can be expressed in stable relationships between situations and behavior (e.g., Caring if with family, aggressive if with strangers).

Implicit Association Test (IAT) An association task that is used to measure implicit self-esteem; may also be used to evaluate implicit attitudes, beliefs, and values as well.

Implicit methods Indirect and projective methods of personality measurement.

Implicit motives The individual's less conscious, more emotional, and affect-related desires and drives.

Implicit pole The psychological opposite end of a construct, in George's Kelly's theory.

Implicit self-esteem How positively or negatively one regards oneself on indirect measures taken without one's conscious awareness.

Incremental theorists Those who view abilities and traits as open to change; they tend to choose goals that will enhance their competence, though not necessarily guarantee success.

Independent variable Stimulus or condition that the investigator systematically varies in an experiment.

Individualism versus collectivism Two contrasting cultural meaning systems: one focuses on the importance of the individual, the other on the importance of the group or community.

Industry versus inferiority For Erikson, the psychosocial stage when the school-age child needs to feel efficacious, and to develop a sense of being able to master challenges effectively.

Inferiority complex According to Adler, feelings of inferiority in the individual that stem from the experience of helplessness and organ inferiority in infancy; results from a failure to compensate for early weakness through mastery in life tasks.

Inhibition Refers to the extent to which infants or young children are wary of novelty and unfamiliarity, as seen in the shy child.

Inhibitory links De-activating relationship between two or more schemas in a *network information processing model*.

Initiative versus guilt For Erikson, the psychosocial crisis faced by the preschool-age child struggling to gain a sense of goal-directedness and purpose in action-taking, rather than becoming excessively inhibited by punishment fears, and guilt.

Insecure-ambivalent Attitude presented by infants in the Strange Situation whose reunion behavior seemed to be a combination of contact-seeking and anger.

Insecure-avoidant Attitude presented by infants in the Strange Situation who avoided their mother throughout the paradigm, even upon reunion.

Integrity versus despair For Erikson, the psychosocial crisis of adults late in life, conflicted between gaining a satisfying perspective and wisdom or succumbing to despair and feelings of meaninglessness and bitterness about life.

Interactionism Idea that the individual's experiences and actions are the product of dynamic interactions between aspects of personality and situations.

Internal consistency The correlation between different parts of a single measure.

Internal working models In attachment theory, mental representations of the others or self, or of relationships, that guide subsequent experiences and behavior.

Internality Tendency to perceive oneself, and not external circumstances, as responsible for a problem.

Interscorer agreement The degree to which different scorers or judges arrive at the same statements about the same test data.

Interview A verbal method in which a person interacts directly with an interviewer in a one-on-one situation (e.g., to study personality, to survey beliefs).

Intimacy versus isolation For Erikson, the psychosocial crisis faced by young adults struggling between sharing feelings and thoughts with significant others or isolating themselves and focusing on the negative and disappointments.

Intrinsic motivation Motivation (e.g., curiosity, achievement, affiliation, identity, stimulation, and social approval) that does not depend on the reduction of primary drives (such as hunger or sex) and does not have specific physiological correlates.

Introversion (Introverts) Tendency to withdraw into oneself, especially when encountering stressful emotional conflict; according to Jung, the introvert is shy and withdrawn, and prefers to be alone (see also *extravert*).

IQ (Intelligence Quotient) Concept formulated by Binet to summarize an individual's mental level based on test scores; IQ means "mental age" divided by chronological age × 100; the average IQ at any given chronological age is set at 100.

Latency period In Freud's theory of psychosexual stages, the period between the phallic stage and the mature, genital stage, during which the child represses memories of infant sexuality.

Learned drive A motivation that has been transformed from a primary drive by social learning.

Learned helplessness A condition in animals and humans that results from exposure to inescapable painful experiences in which passive endurance persists even when escape becomes possible; it can lead to hopelessness and depression.

Learned optimism Believing that one can induce positive outcomes and is not responsible for negative events.

Level of arousal (LOA) Level of stimulation in the brain.

Levels of analysis Major theoretical approaches to the study of personality that have guided thinking and research.

Libido In Freudian theory, psychic energy that may be attached to different objects (e.g., to the mouth in the oral stage of psychosexual development).

Life/sexual instincts See *Eros*.

Life space Lewin's term for the determinates of an individual's behavior at a certain moment; it includes the person and his or her psychological environment.

"Life tasks" See *current life tasks*.

Macho patterns (machismo) Pride in male physical and sexual prowess.

Mandala One of Jung's archetypes, a circle symbolizing the self's search for wholeness and containing designs often divided into four parts.

Mantra A Sanskrit word used in transcendental meditation.

Marshmallow test A preschool delay of gratification measure used to study delay of gratification in children. The child receives a larger treat (e.g., two marshmallows) if s/he waits until the experimenter returns and a smaller treat (e.g., one marshmallow) if s/he cannot wait.

Mastery-oriented People who believe that their failure is due to lack of effort, not lack of ability.

Meaning in life An individual's sense of purposefulness in his or her life.

Memory task Tasks that examine the kinds of mistakes people make when they are trying to remember, used to gain an understanding of how their mental processes are organized.

Mesomorph An individual who has an athletic build and has a very energetic, assertive, and courageous temperament according to Sheldon.

Methadone A drug that appears promising in the treatment of heroin addiction; blocks the craving for heroin and prevents "highs" if heroin is taken.

Miller Behavioral Style Scale (MBSS) Measure of monitoring-blunting tendencies.

Modeling A technique used in behavior therapy in which the client observes the successful performance of the desirable behaviors by a live or symbolic model; effective in teaching complex, novel responses in short time periods and in overcoming fears (see *observational learning*).

Monitoring A cognitive coping mechanism or style of information processing in which people attend to anxiety-arousing stimuli, often in the hope of controlling them.

Monoamine oxidase (MAO) Enzymes that break down the neurotransmitters after they have passed along the route, maintaining the proper level of neurotransmitters.

Monozygotic twins Identical twins; two organisms that develop from a single fertilized egg cell and share identical genes.

Moral anxiety In Freud's theory, guilt about one's unacceptable feelings, thoughts, or deeds (see also *neurotic anxiety* and *reality anxiety*).

Motivational determinism Freud's belief that everything a person does may be determined by his or her pervasive, but unconscious, motives.

Multiple act criterion A criterion measure consisting of a combination of many acts or behaviors that are expected to be interrelated; combining these components increases the reliability of the measure.

Narrative identity The internal stories that people evolve over time to make sense of their diverse, often conflicting aspects, experiences, and behaviors.

Nature-nurture Phrase delineating the long-standing controversy in psychology over inheritance versus environment as significant determinants of individual differences in personality; nature and nurture are important, and their interaction may be of greatest interest.

Need for achievement (n Ach) Need for achievement (in theory of achievement motivation).

Need for intimacy The motivation to warmly and closely connect, share, and communicate with other people in one's everyday life.

Need for positive regard For Rogers, there is a universal desire for acceptance and love from the important people in one's life.

Need for power Individual's desire to have an impact on other people.

Neo-Freudians Post-Freudian innovators in the field of psychology who expanded on Freud's original work, putting less emphasis on the significance of the id and paying greater attention to the ego and the self.

NEO-PI-R A personality inventory that measures individuals along the Big Five personality trait dimensions.

Network information processing model Model of personality structure that emphasizes the way the person's internal mental representations or schemas are related to each other and interconnected to form a system that functions as an organized network structure.

Neural networks Interconnection of neurons in the brain that are activated during information processing and mental activities.

Neuropharmacology The use of chemicals in treating problems with psychological symptoms and disorders of the nervous system.

Neurotic anxiety In Freud's theory, fear that one's own impulses will go out of control and lead to punishment (see also *moral anxiety* and *reality anxiety*).

Neurotic conflict Clash between id impulses seeking expression and internalized inhibitions.

Neuroticism (N) The opposite of emotional stability, according to Eysenck, who viewed neuroticism-emotional stability as an important trait dimension.

Neurotransmitter systems Physiological pathways that communicate and carry out the functions of signal detection and response via chemical receptors (neurotransmitters).

Neurotransmitters Chemicals that enable the nerve impulses to jump across nerve synapses from one nerve to the next.

Nominal situations The routine activities and places that exist within a given environment.

Nonshared environment All of the aspects of the individual's environment that are not shared with other members of the family (e.g., birth order effects, illness, and peer influences).

Not-thinking According to Dollard and Miller, the learned response to fear, producing the phenomenon of repression in psychodynamic theory.

Object relations theory An approach to psychoanalysis that stresses study of the interactions between individuals, especially in childhood.

Observational learning The process of learning through observation of a live or symbolic model; requires no direct reinforcement.

Oedipus complex According to Freud, the love for the opposite-sex parent during the phallic stage of development, particularly the son's love for the mother and hostility toward the father.

Openness to experience (O) Willingness to try new things, original, independent; opposite of closed-mindedness.

Operant conditioning (instrumental learning) The increase in frequency of an operant response after it has been followed by a favorable outcome (reinforced).

Operants Freely emitted response patterns that operate on the environment; their future strength depends on their consequences.

Operationalization Translation of a construct into something observable and measurable.

Optimal level of arousal (OLA) Arousal level that is most appropriate for performing a given task effectively.

Optimistic orientation A focus on the positive aspects of oneself and in human nature.

Oral stage First of Freud's psychosexual stages, when pleasure is focused on the mouth and on the satisfactions of sucking and eating, as during the first year of life.

Organ inferiority Alfred Adler's term for physical weakness associated with the helplessness of infancy.

Organismic evaluation The self's evaluation of the experiences of the organism (in Rogers' theory).

Organismic experience Experience of the self as a whole organism (in Rogers' theory).

Organized whole Rogers' desired state of being, where the individual functions as an integrated unit.

Ought self The representation of who you believe you should be.

Outcome expectancies Belief that a particular behavior will lead to the anticipated outcome (e.g., that waiting for the promised dessert will actually lead to getting it).

Overcontrolling The tendency to extensively inhibit behavioral impulses.

Overjustification Excessive external reward for a given response; may interfere with the development of intrinsic rewards.

Partial (intermittent) reinforcement Reinforcement in which a response is sometimes reinforced, sometimes not reinforced.

Peak experience According to Maslow, a temporary experience of fulfillment and joy in which the person loses self-centeredness and feels a nonstriving happiness.

Penis envy Envy of the male sex organ; believed by Freud to be universal in women, to be responsible for women's castration complex, and to be central to the psychology of women.

Perceived self-efficacy The belief that one is capable of performing or achieving the relevant task or goal (e.g., "If I jump into that pool, I can swim to the other side").

Perceptual defense Unconscious repressive mechanisms that screen and block threatening visual and auditory inputs.

Performance measures Measures that directly test the individual's ability to perform a task.

Permeability A highly permeable (versus impermeable) construct is one into which a wide range of information can fit (e.g., "good"), in George Kelly's theory.

Permeable boundaries Boundaries between the person and the psychological environment that can be crossed easily.

Person versus situation debate The belief that to the degree that the person was important the situation was not and vice versa.

Person × situation interaction The idea that individual differences in behavior are reflected in the way each person responds to a particular situation and that the way a particular situation will affect behavior depends on the individual.

Person × situation interaction patterns Stable patterns that emerge when the individual's behavior is measured in relation to its situational context.

Personal construct The subjective dimensions through which the individual experiences the world and the self; central unit of George Kelly's theory.

Personal construct theory George Kelly's theoretical approach to personality that tries to see how the person sees or aligns events on his or her own dimensions.

Personal meaning system The individual's system of concepts and feelings that guides and constrains how he or she interprets the self and the world.

Personal narratives The stories people tell themselves to try to make sense of their own lives and experiences.

Personality dispositions Behavioral tendencies or patterns that characterize individuals or types distinctively in reliable ways.

Personality paradox Conflict between intuition of intra-individual consistency and the research results which show a lack of intra-individual consistency.

Personality processing dynamics Stable, distinctive sequences of thoughts, feelings, and behaviors that become activated by particular types of situations in *if . . . then . . .* signatures.

Personality signature Distinctive *if . . . then . . .* situation-behavior profiles that characterize individuals.

Personality structure The internal organization of personality. In the CAPS model, the relatively stable interconnections and organization of expectations, goals, affects, competencies, and behavioral tendencies within the individual's personality system.

Personologists Psychologists who study personality; phrase used by the "Harvard personologists" for their style of personality research.

Personology Intensive psychodynamic study of individual lives as integrated, organized units, conceived by the "Harvard personologists."

Pessimism An explanatory style in which the individual sees negative events as being widespread and largely a result of his or her own doing, while failing to take credit for positive events.

Phallic stage The third of Freud's psychosexual stages (at about age five), when pleasure is focused on the genitals and both males and females experience the "Oedipus complex."

Pharmacotherapy The use of drugs to treat psychological disorders or psychological symptoms.

Phenomenological-Humanistic Level Theory that emphasizes the person's experience as he or she perceives it.

Phenomenology The study of an individual's experience as he or she perceives and categorizes it, with emphasis on the self and interactions with other people and the environment.

Phenothiazines Major tranquilizer drug useful in controlling schizophrenia (also called *antipsychotic drugs*).

Physiological measures Measures of how a person responds physiologically (e.g., change in heart rate, degree of arousal) to different events.

PKU (phenylketonuria) A genetic abnormality in which the gene that produces a critical enzyme is missing; it results in mental retardation if not treated soon after birth.

Placebo An inert substance administered to someone who believes it is an active drug.

Pleasure principle In Freud's theory, the basis for id functioning; irrational, seeks immediate satisfaction of instinctual impulses.

Plethysmograph An instrument that measures changes in blood volume.

Polygraph An apparatus that records the activities of the autonomic nervous system.

Positive psychology A movement in psychology initiated by Seligman to understand human strengths through research and to enhance them through therapeutic and educational interventions.

Positron emission tomography (PET scans) Measures the amount of glucose being used in various parts of the brain, providing an index of activity as the brain performs a particular function.

Possible selves An individual's potential ways of being.

Potency Factor in semantic differential measures represented by scale items like hard-soft, masculine-feminine, strong-weak.

Preconscious Thoughts, experiences, and memories not in a person's immediate attention but that can be called into awareness at any moment.

Predictive validity Correlation between current measure and future behaviors/measures.

Prevention focus Vigilantly attending to potential negative outcomes such as punishment or failure.

Primary biological needs Innate set of needs required for the organism's survival, such as food, water, oxygen, and warmth.

Primary caregiver The main early life care-giver for a child, often the mother.

Primary process thinking Freud's term for the id's direct, reality-ignoring attempts to satisfy needs irrationally.

Primary reinforcers Innate reinforcers that cause automatic responses without the need for conditioning (e.g., food).

Priming The process that increases temporary psychological accessibility of a given construct or cognition.

Principle of contemporaneity According to Lewin, the psychological life space that takes into account only what is happening and experienced at a given point in time.

Principle of interactionism In personality psychology, states that important personality differences may be seen in the ways in which an individual's behavior is effected by and interacts with different situations.

Projection A defense mechanism by which one attributes one's own unacceptable aspects or impulses to someone else.

Projective methods Tests (such as the Rorschach or TAT) that present the individual with materials open to a wide variety of interpretations based on the belief that responses reveal important aspects of the respondent's personality; central in psychodynamic assessment.

Promotion focus Focus on obtaining positive outcomes and gains, such as accomplishments or rewards.

Proprium Allport's term for the region of personality that contains the root of the consistency that characterizes attitudes, goals, and values; not innate, it develops in time.

Prototypes Exemplars or best examples of a construct or schema.

Prototypicality The degree to which the member of a category is representative of that category or exemplifies it.

Psychoanalysis A form of psychotherapy developed by Freud that aims at relieving neurotic conflict and anxiety by airing repressed, unconscious impulses over the course of regular meetings between patient and analyst.

Psychobiography The intensive study of individual lives using narrative methods.

Psychodynamic Behavior Theory Developed by John Dollard and Neal Miller in the late 1940s to integrate some of the fundamental ideas of psychoanalytic theory with the concepts and methods of experimental research on behavior and learning.

Psychodynamic-Motivational Level Approaches, beginning with Freud's work, that probe the motivations, conflicts, and defenses that help explain complex consistencies and inconsistencies in personality.

Psychodynamics In psychoanalytic theory, the processes through which personality is regulated; it is predicated on the concept of repressed, unconscious impulses and the significance of early childhood experience.

Psycholexical approach A research strategy that seeks to classify people into different trait groups by identifying differences among individuals on the basis of ratings with natural language terms (adjectives) that are factor analyzed.

Psychological features The aspects or ingredients of situations that activate the person's characteristic reaction patterns (e.g., being rejected by peers in a social situation).

Psychological oxygen According to Kohut, the psychological deprivation of empathic human responses in important others is analogous to the deprivation of oxygen.

Psychological situation The circumstances and events within a nominal situation that affect behavior.

Psychometric trait approach Approach that emphasizes quantitative measurement of psychological qualities, comparing the responses of large groups of people under standard conditions, often by means of paper-and-pencil tests.

Psychosexual stages According to Freudian theory, development occurs in a series of psychosexual stages; in each stage (oral, anal, phallic, and genital) pleasure is focused on a different part of the body.

Psychosocial crisis According to Erikson's theory, the person's efforts to solve the problems that occur at a given stage of psychosocial development.

Psychosocial stages Erikson's eight stages of development; extending throughout life, each stage centers around a "crisis" or set of problems and the individual's attempts to solve it.

Q-sort (Q-technique) A method of obtaining trait ratings; consists of many cards, on each of which is printed a trait description; the rater groups the cards in a series of piles ranging from those that are least characteristic to those that are most characteristic of the rated person.

Randomization The assignment of research participants to different conditions on the basis of chance; if many participants are used, differences should average out except for the effects produced by the experiment itself.

Rationalization A defense mechanism that occurs when one makes something more acceptable by attributing it to more acceptable causes.

Reaction formation A defense mechanism that occurs when an anxiety-provoking impulse is replaced in consciousness by its opposite.

Reaction time The time it takes an individual to start a given task or response.

Reality anxiety In Freud's theory, the fear of real dangers in the external world (see also *moral anxiety* and *neurotic anxiety*).

Reality principle In Freud's theory, the basis for ego functioning; rational; dictates delay in the discharge of tension until environmental conditions are appropriate.

Reciprocal altruism The recognition that if we help others they are likely to reciprocate in kind.

Reciprocal interaction Interaction between the person and the situation in which both variables influence one another reciprocally.

Reflex An instinctive, unlearned response to a particular stimulus (see also *unconditioned response*).

Regression In psychodynamic theory, reversion to an earlier stage; the return of the libido to its former halting places in development.

Reinforcement (Reinforcer) Any consequence that increases the likelihood that a response will be repeated or strengthened.

Rejection sensitivity A disposition to anxiously expect and easily perceive potential rejection even in ambiguous events.

Relatedness Support and connection with others.

Relational self The self perceived not as a single entity but as an object in relation to other objects, as in Kohut's object relations theory.

Relational therapy A therapeutic process that emphasizes the role of early, current, and analyst-patient relationships in the development and resolution of personality problems.

Relaxation responses Wolpe's preferred conterconditioning method for anxiety; involves elaborate instructions to teach individuals how to consciously relax themselves.

Repression According to psychoanalytic theory, an unconscious defense mechanism through which unacceptable (ego-threatening) material is kept from awareness; the repressed motives, ideas, conflicts, memories, etc. continue to influence behavior.

Repression-sensitization A dimension of differences in defensive patterns of perception, ranging from avoiding the anxiety-arousing stimuli to approaching them more readily and being extra vigilant or supersensitized.

Repressors People who describe themselves as having few problems or difficulties and who do not report themselves as highly sensitive to everyday stress and anxieties.

Resistance Difficulties in achieving progress in psychotherapy due to unconscious defenses as anxiety-producing material emerges during the treatment.

Response Any observable, identifiable activity of an organism.

Role An attempt to see another person through his or her constructs.

Role Construct Repertory Test ("Rep" Test) A technique for measuring personal constructs developed by Kelly.

Rorschach test Projective test consisting of 10 symmetrical inkblots to which the person describes his or her reactions, stating what each blot looks like or might be.

Rumination Dwelling on particular types of cognitions and emotions, usually negative; in a ruminative style of dealing with depression, the person focuses on the fact that he or she is depressed, on the symptoms (like fatigue and disinterest) that are experienced, and on their negative consequences (e.g., "I might lose my job").

Safe haven In attachment theory, the people to whom the young child turns for support and comfort in times of threat or need.

Schemas (schemata) Knowledge structures made-up of collections of attributes or features that have "family resemblance" to each other.

Scholastic Aptitude Test (SAT) A standardized measure of verbal and quantitative skills given routinely to high school seniors before entrance into college.

Secondary dispositions The most specific, defined traits or "attitudes" that influence an individual's behavior.

Secure base Safe haven of dependable comfort in a young child's life from which the world can be explored with trust.

Securely attached A classification of individuals in attachment theory; Characterization of toddlers in Strange Situation who greeted mother positively upon reunion and then returned to play.

Self actualize (self-actualization) The realization of one's human potential.

Self as "agent" The active process of self-construction and purposeful goal pursuit in the course of building a self and a life within the interpersonal world.

Self as "object" The consciousness of the self as a coherent entity.

Self fulfilling prophecy Expectations lead one to behave in such a way that those expectations become reality (e.g., Expectations of success lead to actual success).

Self-actualizing person For Maslow, a person who has the personal qualities listed in Table 9.5.

Self-concept (self) System that serves as a frame of reference for evaluating and monitoring the actual experiences of the organism.

Self-construction A self and identity that gives one's turbulent, confusing life some sense of coherence, direction, and meaningfulness.

Self-determination Actions that are chosen by and have intrinsic value to the person doing them.

Self-disclosure Sharing of stressful, traumatic experiences either in groups or other forms (e.g., diaries).

Self-efficacy Belief that one can do things effectively.

Self-efficacy expectations The person's confidence that he or she can perform a particular behavior, like handling a snake or making a public speech.

Self-enhancing bias Increased likelihood of seeing oneself as causally responsible for actions when they have positive rather than negative outcomes.

Self-enhancing illusions Unrealistically positive view of the self and one's ability to control pure chance situations.

Self-esteem Refers to the individual's personal judgment of his or her own worth.

Self-evaluative standards (self-guides) Standards for assessing oneself.

Selfhood Term used to refer to the awareness of the self as "agent" and "object."

Self-instruction Talking to oneself to control one's behavior; an aspect of some types of control training.

Self-realization A continuous quest to know oneself and to actualize one's potentialities for full awareness and growth as a human being.

Self-regulation The monitoring and evaluation of one's own behavior, modifying one's own behavior and influencing his/her environment.

Self -regulatory competencies The cognitive and attentional mechanisms that help execute goal-directed behavior.

Self-regulatory systems A person variable that includes the individual's rules, plans, and self-reactions for performance and for the organization of complex behavior (see *social cognitive person variables*).

Self-relevant Meaningful to the self.

Self-reports Statements that the individual makes about himself or herself.

Self-schemas Cognitions about the self that arise from past experience and guide the processing of new information.

Self-theory A construction or set of concepts about the self that affect future experience.

Semantic differential Measure that tests individuals on their perceptions of the meanings of diverse words, phrases, and concepts by having them rate each item on a bipolar scale.

Sensation seeking Trait that represents an individual's level of desire to experience new things and take risks.

Sensation seeking scale (SSS) Measure that taps into four different aspects of sensation seeking behavior: thrill and adventure seeking, experience seeking, disinhibition, and boredom susceptibility.

Sense of helplessness Feeling that one's efforts and actions are not effective.

Sensitizers Individuals who are highly sensitive to everyday stress and anxieties.

Sensory anesthesia Loss of sensory ability, such as blindness, deafness, or loss of feeling in a body part.

Sequential priming-pronunciation task A word-pronunciation task, often used to determine the participant's level of sensitivity to personal rejection.

Serotonin A neurotransmitter associated with depression when available in excess amounts in the body.

Sex role identity The degree to which an individual identifies himself or herself as masculine or feminine.

Shadow aspect According to Jung, the unconscious part of the psyche that must be absorbed into the personality to achieve full emotional growth.

Shaping Technique for producing successively better approximations of behavior by reinforcing small variations in behavior in the desired direction and by reinforcing only increasingly close approximations to the desired behavior.

Shared environment (or family environment) Individuals raised in the same family/household.

Sibling rivalry Competition between the siblings of a family that, according to Adler, plays a major role in development.

Signature of personality Stable patterns or profiles that show intraindividual behavior variation as it relates to specific types of situations.

Single-blind method An experimental procedure in which participants do not know whether they are in experimental or control conditions.

Situational test Procedure in which participants are observed performing a task within a lifelike situation; the Harvard personologists used stressful, lifelike tasks under extremely difficult situations to assess OSS candidates and used their performance to make clinical inferences about each person's underlying personality.

Situationism Theory that dispositional consistency is a myth and individual behavior is entirely determined by situational attributes.

Sociability The degree to which the person seeks interpersonal interaction.

Social cognition Research and theory applying cognitive psychology constructs and methodologies to study phenomena of social and personality psychology.

Social Cognitive Level A level of analysis in personality psychology that focuses on the social and cognitive meanings of events or situations for the individual, and the processes through which these meanings lead to social behavior.

Social cognitive person variables Relatively stable social, cognitive, and emotional variables on which individuals differ (e.g., expectations, goals, values, and competencies); sometimes these are called cognitive social person variables.

Social cognitive reconceptualizations of personality Mischel's theory using a variatey of social cognitive person variables to understand individual differences and the nature of consistency and stability in social behavior; focused on analyzing behavior in its situational context, and revealed that people have stable *if* ... *then* ... situation-behavior patterns.

Source traits In R. B. Cattell's theory, the traits that constitute personality structure and determine surface traits and behavior.

Stable intraindividual patterning The idea that the temporal intraindividual variation in behavior is meaningful and stable.

Stable organization of relationships Stable pathways and relationships among the cognitions and affects (the CAUs) available in the personality system in the CAPS model.

Stability The durability of aspects of personality over time.

Stabilizing selection Mechanism that weeds out characteristics at both extremities of a given dimension.

State anxiety A person's momentary or situational anxiety; it varies in intensity over time and across settings.

Statistical significance A statistical computation that reflects how far a given association exceeds that which would be expected by chance.

Stimulus control Behavior that is expressed stably but only under specific, predictable conditions.

Stimulus-outcome relations Stable links between stimuli and other events that allow one to predict the outcomes from the stimuli.

Stimulus-response covariation Stable link between stimulus and response that allow predictions of the response based on the stimulus.

Strange situation An experimental study that puts a young child in an unfamiliar setting to assess individual differences in attachment relations.

Subjective continuity Sense of basic oneness and durability in the self; feeling of consistency and identity.

Subjective values and goals The particular outcomes and goals to which an individual assigns greatest import; a cognitive social person variable.

Sublimation A process through which socially unacceptable impulses are expressed in socially acceptable ways.

Subliminally (subliminal) Occurring outside of a person's consciousness or awareness.

Subordinate goals Goals that are less important on an individual's goal hierarchy (e.g., going to the hardware store) and provide a step in a larger process of goal-pursuit.

Super ordinate goals Goals that are more or most important on an individual's goal hierarchy (e.g., being safe and secure).

Superego In Freud's theory, the conscience, made up of the internalized values of the parents; strives for self-control and perfection; it is both unconscious and conscious.

Super traits Large descriptive categories or factors that result from the clustering of many traits (see also *Big Five Structure*).

Suppression Occurs when one voluntarily and consciously withholds a response or turns attention away from something (see also *repression*).

Surface traits R. B. Cattell's term for clusters of overt or manifest trait elements (responses) that seem to go together; the manifestations of source traits.

Symptom substitution The controversial psychoanalytic belief that new symptoms will automatically replace problematic behaviors that are removed directly (e.g., by behavior therapy) unless their underlying unconscious emotional causes also have been removed.

Systematic desensitization A behavior therapy procedure designed to reduce incapacitating anxiety; an incompatible response (usually relaxation) is paired with progressively more anxiety arousing situations until the individual is able to imagine or be in these situations without becoming anxious.

Systems theory The analysis of units like the family as a system of relationships.

Systems therapy A type of therapy that seeks to understand the individual within the context of the family or system.

Tachistoscope A machine (used in studies of perceptual defense) that projects words onto a screen at different speeds.

Target In an experiment, the participant is assessed on his or her responses to target items or stimuli.

Temperament traits R. B. Cattell's term for traits that determine emotional reactivity.

Temperaments Characteristic individual differences relevant to emotional expression, often visible early in life.

Temporal reliability A high test-retest correlation when the same test is given on multiple occasions to the same group of people.

Tending (response to stress) Responding to stressful situations with nurturance and care-taking behavior (rather than fight or flight reactions).

Test A means of obtaining information about a person through standardized measures of behavior and personal qualities.

Thanatos One of two aspects of the personality considered by early psychoanalysts to represent destruction and aggression; the darker side of human nature (see also *Eros*).

Thematic Apperception Test (TAT) Projective test consisting of a set of ambiguous pictures about which the person being tested is asked to make up an interesting story.

Tokens Items used to barter for rewards, used to assess the effectiveness of different rewards in operant conditioning.

Trait A persistent (enduring) characteristic or dimension of individual differences; defined by Allport as a generalized "neuropsychic system," distinctive to each person, that serves to unify many different stimuli by leading the person to generate consistent responses to them.

Trait anxiety A person's stable, characteristic overall level of anxiety.

Trait approach An approach to personality that categorizes individuals in terms of traits.

Trait structure Unique structure of a trait as it exists in a particular individual.

Trait theorists Psychologists who study personality in terms of the different trait dimensions that characterize each individual.

Trait-Dispositional Level Approach to personality that categorizes individuals in terms of traits or dispositions.

Transactional analysis See *systems theory* and *family therapy*.

Transcendental Meditation (TM) A form of deep meditation in which the meditator sits comfortably with eyes closed and repeats a special Sanskrit word called a "mantra."

Transference In psychoanalysis, the patient's response to the therapist as though the therapist were a parent or some other important figure from childhood; considered and essential aspect of psychoanalytic therapy.

Transformation of motives Defense mechanism in which basic impulses persist but the objects at which they are directed and the manner in which they are expressed are transformed.

Traumatic experiences Experiences that abruptly and severely disrupt a person's life.

Triple typology A classification system that brings together three categories in a meaningful way; in the case of personality, these three categories are types of people, types of behavior, and types of situations.

Trust versus mistrust For Erikson, a psychosocial crisis in which the child may have doubts involving trust (e.g., "Am I loved?", "Am I good?", "Are others good?") The resolution of the crisis can impact the child's future sense of trust, drive, and hope.

Twin method Method of assessing genetic influence by comparing the degree of similarity on trait measures for genetically identical twins versus dizygotic twins.

Uncertainty orientation Personality dimension that is defined at one end by individuals who are comfortable dealing with uncertainty and strive to resolve it, and at the other end by those who are uncomfortable with uncertainty and likely to avoid situations that increase their sense of uncertainty.

Unconditioned response (UCR) The unlearned response one naturally makes to an unconditioned stimulus (e.g., withdrawing the hand from a hot object).

Unconditioned stimuli (UCS) Stimuli to which one automatically, naturally responds without learning to do so (e.g., food, electric shock).

Unconscious In psychoanalytic theory, the part of the personality of which the ego is unaware but that profoundly effects actions and behaviors.

Undercontrolling children Children who do not adequately inhibit their behavioral impulses.

Unique traits In Allport's theory, traits that only exist in one individual and cannot be found in another in exactly the same form.

Units of culture Beliefs, values, goals, and ways of construing the world that are transmitted and shared within a particular community or culture.

Value The subjective importance of an outcome or event for an individual.

Variable An attribute, quality, or characteristic that may be given two or more values and measured or systematically varied.

Vicarious conditioning Conditioning of a response to a stimulus through observation.

Visceral responses Internal bodily responses to external events that occur without our willing them or even thinking about them (e.g., increased heart rate, changes in gland secretion).

Willpower The ability to voluntarily self-control for desired but difficult goals, for example, delay of gratification in anticipation of achieving a more far-reaching but distant goal.

Working self-concept The prominent concepts of the self that are foremost in an individual's thought and memory and that can be easily accessed.

Working through Process that occurs in psychoanalytic therapy when the patient, in the context of the transference relationship, re-examines his or her basic problems until their emotional roots are understood and learns to handle them more appropriately.

REFERENCES 

Abramson, L. Y., Seligman, M. E. P., & Teasdale, J. D. (1978). Learned helplessness in humans: Critique and reformation. *Journal of Abnormal Psychology, 87*, 49–74.

Adams, H. E., Wright, L. W., & Lohr, B. A. (1996). Is homophobia associated with homosexual arousal? *Journal of Abnormal Psychology, 105*, 440–445.

Affleck, G., Urrows, S., Tennen, H., & Higgins, P. (1992). Daily coping with pain from rheumatoid arthritis: Patterns and correlates. *Pain, 51*, 221–229.

Ainsworth, M. D. S. (1989). Attachments beyond infancy. *American Psychologist, 44*, 709–716.

Ainsworth, M. S., Blehar, M. C., Waters, E. C., & Wall, S. (1978). *Patterns of attachment*. Hillsdale, NJ: Erlbaum.

Ajzen, I., & Fishbein, M. (1977). Attitude–behavior relations: A theoretical analysis and review of empirical research. *Psychological Bulletin, 84*, 888–918.

Aldwin, C. (1994). *Stress, coping, and development*. New York: Guilford Press.

Alexander, C. N., Robinson, P., Orme-Johnson, D. W., Schneider, R., & Walton, K. (1994). Effects of transcendental meditation compared to relaxation in promoting health and reducing mortality in the elderly. *Homeostasis, 35*, 4–5.

Alicke, M. D. (1985). Global self-evaluation as determined by the desirability and controllability of trait adjectives. *Journal of Personality and Social Psychology, 49*, 1621–1630.

Allen, E. K., Hart, B. M., Buell, J. S., Harris, F. R., & Wolf, M. M. (1964). Effects of social reinforcement on isolated behavior of a nursery school child. *Child Development, 35*, 511–518.

Allik, J., & McCrae, R. R. (2004). Toward a geography of personality traits: Patterns of profiles across 36 cultures. *Journal of Cross-Cultural Psychology, 35*, 13–28.

Alloy, L. B., & Ahrens, A. H. (1987). Depression and pessimism for the future: Biased use of statistically relevant information in predictions for self versus others. *Journal of Personality and Social Psychology, 52*, 366–378.

Allport, G. W. (1937). *Personality: A psychological interpretation*. New York: Holt, Rinehart and Winston.

Allport, G. W. (1940). Motivation in personality: Reply to Mr. Bertocci. *Psychological Review, 47*, 533–554.

Allport, G. W. (1955). *Becoming*. New Haven, CT: Yale University Press.

Allport, G. W. (1961). *Pattern and growth in personality*. New York: Holt, Rinehart and Winston.

Allport, G. W. (1967). Gordon W. Allport. In E. G. Boring & G. Lindzey (Eds.), *A history of psychology in autobiography* (Vol. 5, pp. 1–25). New York: Appleton-Century-Crofts.

American Psychological Association. (1966). *Standards for educational and psychological tests and manuals*. Washington, DC: Author.

Andersen, S. M., & Chen, S. (2002). The relational self: An interpersonal social-cognitive theory. *Psychological Review, 109*, 619–645.

Andersen, S. M., Chen, S., & Miranda, R. (2002). Significant others and the self. *Self and Identity, 1*, 159–168.

Andersen, S. M., Reznik, I., & Chen, S. (1997). The self in relation to others: Cognitive and motivational underpinnings. In J. G. Snodgrass & R. L. Thompson (Eds.), *The self across psychology: Self-recognition, self-awareness, and the self-concept* (pp. 233–275). New York: New York Academy of Science.

Anderson, J. R., & Bower, G. H. (1973). *Human associative memory*. New York: Wiley.

Anderson, J. R., & Lebiere, C. (1998). *The atomic components of thought*. Mahwah, NJ: Erlbaum.

Angier, N. (1998, February 8). Separated by birth? *New York Times Book Review*, p. 9.

Antonovsky, A. (1979). *Health, stress and coping*. San Francisco: Jossey-Bass.

Archer, J. (1990). The influence of testosterone on human aggression. *British Journal of Psychology, 82*, 1–28.

Archibald, H. C., & Tuddenham, R. D. (1965). Persistent stress reaction after combat. *Archives of General Psychiatry, 12*, 475–481.

Arend, R., Gove, F. L., & Sroufe, L. A. (1979). Continuity of individual adaptation from infancy to kindergarten: A predictive study of ego-resiliency and curiosity in preschoolers. *Child Development, 50*, 950–959.

Argyle, M., & Little, B. R. (1972). Do personality traits apply to social behavior? *Journal of Theory of Social Behavior (Great Britain), 2*, 1–35.

Armor, D. A., & Taylor, S. E. (2002). When predictions fail: The dilemma of unrealistic optimism. In T. Gilovich,

D. Griffin, & D. Kahneman (Eds.), *Heuristics and biases: The psychology of intuitive judgment* (pp. 334–347). New York: Cambridge University Press.

Aronfreed, J. (1966, August). The internalization of social control through punishment: Experimental studies of the role of conditioning and the second signal system in the development of conscience. *Proceedings of the XVIIIth International Congress of Psychology, 35*, 219–230.

Aronfreed, J. (1968). *Conduct and conscience: The socialization of internalized control over behavior*. New York: Academic Press.

Aronfreed, J. (1994). Moral development from the standpoint of a general psychological theory. In B. Puka (Ed.), *Defining perspectives in moral development. Moral development: A compendium* (Vol. 1, pp. 170–85). New York: Garland.

Aronson, E. (1972). *The social animal*. San Francisco: Freeman.

Aronson, E., & Mettee, D. (1968). Dishonest behavior as a function of differential levels of induced self-esteem. *Journal of Personality and Social Psychology, 9*, 121–127.

Asch, S. E. (1946). Forming impressions of personality. *Journal of Abnormal and Social Psychology, 41*, 258–290.

Ashmore, R. D. (1990). Sex, gender, and the individual. In L. A. Pervin (Ed.), *Handbook of personality: Theory and research* (pp. 486–526). New York: Guilford Press.

Aspinwall, L. G., & Staudinger, U. M. (2002). *A psychology of human strengths: Fundamental questions and future directions for a positive psychology*. Washington, DC: American Psychological Association.

Aspinwall, L. G., & Taylor, S. E. (1997). A stitch in time: Self-regulation and proactive coping. *Psychological Bulletin, 121*, 417–436.

Atkinson, J. W. (Ed.). (1958). *Motives in fantasy, action and society*. Princeton, NJ: Van Nostrand.

Ayduk, O., Downey, G., & Kim, M. (2001). Rejection sensitivity and depressive symptoms in women. *Personality and Social Psychology Bulletin, 27*, 868–877.

Ayduk, O., Downey, G., Testa, A., Yen, Y., & Shoda, Y. (1999). Does rejection elicit hostility in rejection sensitive women? *Social Cognition, 17*, 245–271.

Ayduk, O., May, D., Downey, G., & Higgins, T. (2003). Tactical differences in coping with rejection sensitivity: The role of prevention pride. *Personality and Social Psychology Bulletin, 29*, 435–448.

Ayduk, O., Mendoza-Denton, R., Mischel, W., Downey, G., Peake, P. K., & Rodriguez, M. (2000). Regulating the interpersonal self: Strategic self-regulation for coping with rejection sensitivity. *Journal of Personality and Social Psychology, 79*, 776–792.

Ayduk, O., & Mischel, W. (2002). When smart people behave stupidly: Inconsistencies in social and emotional intelligence. In R. J. Sternberg (Ed.), *Why smart people can be so stupid* (pp. 86–105). New Haven, CT: Yale University Press.

Ayduk, O., Mischel, W., & Downey, G. (2002). Attentional mechanisms linking rejection to hostile reactivity: The role of "hot" vs. "cool" focus. *Psychological Science, 13*, 443–448.

Ayllon, T., & Azrin, N. H. (1965). The measurement and reinforcement of behavior of psychotics. *Journal of the Experimental Analysis of Behavior, 8*, 357–383.

Ayllon, T., & Haughton, E. (1964). Modification of symptomatic verbal behaviour of mental patients. *Behaviour Research and Therapy, 2*, 87–97.

Baker, T. B., Piper, M. E., McCarthy, D. E., Majeskie, M. R., & Fiore, M. C. (2003). Addiction motivation reformulated: An affective processing model of negative reinforcement. *Psychological Review, 111*, 33–51.

Ball, D., Hill, L., Freeman, B., Eley, T. C., Strelau, J., Riemann, R. et al. (1997). The serotonin transporter gene and peer-rated neuroticism. *NeuroReport, 8*, 1301–1304.

Baltes, P. B., Staudinger, U. M., & Lindenberger, U. (1999). Life span psychology: Theory and application to intellectual functioning. *Annual Review of Psychology, 50*, 471–507.

Bandura, A. (1965). Vicarious processes: A case of no-trial learning. In L. Berkowitz (Ed.), *Advances in experimental social psychology* (Vol. 2, pp. 1–55). New York: Academic Press.

Bandura, A. (1969). *Principles of behavior modification*. New York: Holt, Rinehart and Winston.

Bandura, A. (1973). *Aggression: A social learning analysis*. Englewood Cliffs, NJ: Prentice-Hall.

Bandura, A. (1977). *Social learning theory*. Englewood Cliffs, NJ: Prentice-Hall.

Bandura, A. (1978). Reflections on self-efficacy. In S. Rachman (Ed.), *Advances in behavior research and therapy* (Vol. 1, pp. 237–269). Elmsford, NJ: Pergamon.

Bandura, A. (1982). Self-efficacy mechanisms in human agency. *American Psychologist, 37*, 122–147.

Bandura, A. (1986). *Social foundations of thought and action: A social cognitive theory*. Englewood Cliffs, NJ: Prentice-Hall.

Bandura, A. (1989). Human agency in social cognitive theory. *American Psychologist, 44*, 1175–1184.

Bandura, A. (1997). *Self-efficacy: The exercise of control*. New York: Freeman.

Bandura, A. (2001). Social cognitive theory: An agentic perspective. *Annual Review, 52*, 1–26.

Bandura, A., & Adams, N. E. (1977). Analysis of self-efficacy theory of behavioral change. *Cognitive Therapy and Research, 1*, 287–310.

Bandura, A., Adams, N. E., & Beyer, J. (1977). Cognitive processes mediating behavioral change. *Journal of Personality and Social Psychology, 35*, 125–139.

Bandura, A., Blanchard, E. B., & Ritter, B. (1969). Relative efficacy of desensitization and modeling approaches for inducing behavioral, affective, and attitudinal changes. *Journal of Personality and Social Psychology, 13*, 173–199.

Bandura, A., & Mischel, W. (1965). Modification of self-imposed delay of reward through exposure to live and symbolic models. *Journal of Personality and Social Psychology, 2*, 698–705.

Bandura, A., Taylor, C. B., Ewart, C. K., Miller, N. M., & Debusk, R. F. (1985). Exercise testing to enhance wives' confidence in their husbands' cardiac capability soon after clinically uncomplicated acute myocardial infarction. *American Journal of Cardiology, 55*, 635–638.

Bandura, A., & Walters, R. H. (1959). *Adolescent aggression*. New York: Ronald Press.

Bargh, J. A. (1996). Automaticity in social psychology. In E. T. Higgins & A. W. Kruglanski (Eds.), *Social psychology: Handbook of basic principles* (pp. 169–183). New York: Guilford Press.

Bargh, J. A. (1997). The automaticity of everyday life. In R. S. Wyer, Jr. (Ed.), *The automaticity of everyday life: Advances in social cognition* (Vol. 10, pp. 1–61). Mahwah, NJ: Erlbaum.

Bargh, J. A. (2001). Caution: Automatic social cognition may not be habit forming. *Polish Psychological Bulletin, 32*, 1–8.

Bargh, J. A., & Barndollar, K. (1996). Automaticity in action: The unconscious as a repository of chronic goals and motives. In P. M. Gollwitzer & J. A. Bargh (Eds.), *The psychology of action: Linking cognition and motivation to behavior* (pp. 457–481). New York: Guilford Press.

Bargh, J. A., Chen, M., & Burrows, L. (1996). Automaticity of social behavior: Direct effects of trait construct and stereotype activation on action. *Journal of Personality and Social Psychology, 71*, 230–244.

Bargh, J. A., & Ferguson, M. J. (2000). Beyond behaviorism: On the automaticity of higher mental processes. *Psychological Bulletin, 126*, 925–945.

Bargh, J. A., Gollwitzer, P. M., Lee-Chai, A., Barndollar, K., & Trätschel, R. (2001). The automated will: Nonconscious activation and pursuit of behavioral goals. *Journal of Personality and Social Psychology, 31*, 101–114.

Bargh, J. A., Raymond, P., Pryor, J. B., & Strack, F. (1995). Attractiveness of the underling: An automatic power → sex association and its consequences for sexual harassment and aggression. *Journal of Personality and Social Psychology, 68*, 768–781.

Bargh, J. A., & Williams, E. L. (2006). The automaticity of social life. *Current Directions in Psychological Science, 15*, 1–4.

Barlow, D. H. (1988). *Anxiety and its disorders: The nature and treatment of anxiety and panic*. New York: Guilford Press.

Barnouw, V. (1973). *Culture and personality*. Homewood, IL: Dorsey Press.

Baron, R. A., & Richardson, D. R. (1994). *Human aggression* (2nd ed.). New York: Plenum Press.

Barrett, L. F., & Barrett, D. J. (2001). Computerized experience-sampling: How technology facilitates the study of conscious experience. *Social Science Computer Review, 19*, 175–185.

Barrick, M. R., & Mount, M. K. (1991). The Big Five personality dimensions and job performance: A meta-analysis. *Personnel Psychology, 44*, 1–26.

Bartussek, D., Diedrich, O., Naumann, E., & Collet, W. (1993). Introversion–extraversion and event-related potential (ERP): A test of J. A. Gray's theory. *Personality and Individual Differences, 14*, 565–574.

Bates, B., & Goodman, A. (1986). The effectiveness of encounter groups: Implications of research for counseling practice. *British Journal of Guidance and Counseling, 14*, 240–251.

Bates, J. E., & Wachs, T. D. (Eds.). (1994). *Temperament: Individual differences at the interface of biology and behavior*. Washington, DC: American Psychological Association.

Baumeister, R. F. (1996). Self-regulation and ego threat: Motivated cognition, self deception, and destructive goal setting. In P. M. Gollwitzer & J. A. Bargh (Eds.), *The psychology of action: Linking cognition and motivation to behavior* (pp. 27–47). New York: Guilford Press.

Baumeister, R. F. (1997). Identity, self-concept, and self-esteem: The self lost and found. In R. Hogan, J. Johnson, & S. Briggs (Eds.), *Handbook of personality psychology* (pp. 681–710). San Diego, CA: Academic Press.

Baumeister, R. F. (1998). The self. In D. T. Glibert, S. T. Fiske, & G. Lindzey (Eds.), *The handbook of social psychology* (Vol. 1, 4th ed., pp. 680–740). New York: Oxford University Press.

Baumeister, R. F. (2002). Ego depletion and self-control failure: An energy model of the self's executive function. *Self and Identity, 1*, 129–136.

Baumeister, R. F., & Cairns, K. H. (1992). Repression and self-presentation: When audiences interfere with self-deceptive strategies. *Journal of Personality and Social Psychology, 62*, 851–862.

Baumeister, R. F., & Heatherton, T. F. (1996). Self-regulation failure: An overview. *Psychological Inquiry, 7*, 1–15.

Baumeister, R. F., & Tice, D. M. (1996). Rethinking and reclaiming the interdisciplinary role of personality psychology: The science of human nature should be the center of the social sciences and humanities. *Journal of Research in Personality, 30*, 363–373.

Beck, A. T., Rush, A. J., Shaw, B. F., & Emery, G. (1979). *Cognitive therapy of depression*. New York: Guilford Press.

Bell, J. E. (1948). *Projective techniques*. New York: Longmans, Green.

Bell, R. Q., & Costello, N. (1964). Three tests for sex differences in tactile sensitivity in the newborn. *Biologia Neonatorum, 7*, 335–347.

Bell, R. Q., & Darling, J. (1965). The prone head reaction in the human newborn: Relationship with sex and tactile sensitivity. *Child Development, 36*, 943–949.

Bell, R. Q., Weller, G., & Waldrop, M. (1971). Newborn and preschooler: Organization of behavior and relations between periods. *Monographs of the Society for Research in Child Development, 36* (Nos. 1 & 2).

Bellak, L., & Abrams, D. M. (1997). *The Thematic Apperception Test, the Children's Apperception Test, and the Senior Apperception Technique in clinical use* (6th ed.). Boston: Allyn & Bacon.

Bem, D. J. (1983). Constructing a theory of the triple typology: Some (second) thoughts on nomothetic and idiographic approaches to personality. *Journal of Personality, 51*, 566–577.

Bem, D. J., & Allen, A. (1974). On predicting some of the people some of the time: The search for cross-situational consistencies in behavior. *Psychological Review, 81*, 506–520.

Bem, D. J., & Funder, D. C. (1978). Predicting more of the people more of the time: Assessing the personality of situations. *Psychological Review, 85*, 485–501.

Ben-Shahar, Y., Robichon, A., Sokolowski, M. B., & Robinson, G. E. (2002). Influence of gene action across different time scales on behavior. *Science, 296*, 741–744.

Benedict, R. (1934). *Patterns of culture*. New York: Mentor.

Benjamin, J., Li, L., Patterson, C., Greenberg, B. D., Murphy, D. L., & Hamer, D. H. (1996). Population and familial association between the D4 dopamine receptor gene and measures of novelty seeking. *Nature Genetics, 12*, 81–84.

Benson, H. (1975). *The relaxation response*. New York: Morrow.

Berger, S. M. (1962). Conditioning through vicarious instigation. *Psychological Review, 69*, 450–466.

Berlyne, D. (1960). *Conflict, arousal, and curiosity*. New York: McGraw-Hill.

Berntzen, D. (1987). Effects of multiple cognitive coping strategies on laboratory pain. *Cognitive Therapy and Research, 11*, 613–623.

Berzonsky, M. D., & Neimeyer, G. J. (1994). Ego identity status and identity processing orientation: The mediating role of commitment. *Journal of Research in Personality, 28*, 425–435.

Betancourt, H., & Lopez, S. R. (1993). The study of culture, ethnicity, and race in American psychology. *American Psychologist, 48*, 629–637.

Bijou, S. W. (1965). Experimental studies of child behavior, normal and deviant. In L. Krasner & L. P. Ullmann (Eds.), *Research in behavior modification* (pp. 56–81). New York: Holt, Rinehart and Winston.

Birbaumer, N., & Ohman, A. (1993). *The structure of emotion: Psychophysiological, cognitive, and clinical aspects*. Seattle, WA: Hogrefe & Huber.

Block, J. (1961). *The Q-sort method in personality assessment and psychiatric research*. Springfield, IL: Charles C. Thomas.

Block, J. (1971). *Lives through time*. Berkeley, CA: Bancroft.

Block, J. (1977). Advancing the psychology of personality: Paradigmatic shift or improving the quality of research. In D. Magnusson & N. S. Endler (Eds.), *Personality at the crossroads: Current issues in interactional psychology* (pp. 37–64). Hillsdale, NJ: Erlbaum.

Block, J. (1995). A contrarian view of the five-factor approach to personality description. *Psychological Bulletin, 117*, 187–215.

Block, J. (2001). Millennial contrarianism: The five-factor approach to personality description 5 years later. *Journal of Research in Personality, 35*, 98–107.

Block, J., & Block, J. H. (1980). The role of ego-control and ego resiliency in the organization of behavior. In W. A. Collins (Ed.), *The Minnesota Symposium on Child Psychology* (Vol. 13, pp. 39–101). Hillsdale, NJ: Erlbaum.

Block, J., & Block, J. H. (2006). Nursery school personality and political orientation. *Journal of Research in Personality, 40*, 734–749.

Block, J., Weiss, D. S., & Thorne, A. (1979). How relevant is a semantic similarity interpretation of personality ratings? *Journal of Personality and Social Psychology, 37*, 1055–1074.

Block, J. H., & Martin, B. (1955). Predicting the behavior of children under frustration. *Journal of Abnormal and Social Psychology, 51*, 281–285.

Blum, G. S. (1953). *Psychoanalytic theories of personality*. New York: McGraw-Hill.

Blum, G. S. (1955). Perceptual defense revisited. *Journal of Abnormal and Social Psychology, 51*, 24–29.

Bock, P. K. (2000). Culture and personality revisited. *American Behavioral Scientist, 44*, 32–40.

Bolger, N., & Romero-Canyas, R. (in press). Integrating personality traits and processes: Framework, method, analysis, results. In Y. Shoda, D. Cervone, & G. Downey (Eds.), *Persons in context: Building a science of the individual*. New York: Guilford Press.

Bolger, N., & Schilling, E. A. (1991). Personality and the problems of everyday life: The role of neuroticism in exposure and reactivity to daily stressors. *Journal of Personality, 59*, 355–386.

Bonanno, G. A. (2001). Grief and emotion: A social–functional perspective. In M. S. Stroebe & R. O. Hansson (Eds.), *Handbook of bereavement research: Consequences, coping, and care* (pp. 493–515). Washington, DC: American Psychological Association.

Bonarius, J. C. J. (1965). Research in the personal construct theory of George A. Kelly: Role construct repertory test and basic theory. In B. A. Maher (Ed.), *Progress in experimental personality research* (pp. 1–46). New York: Academic Press.

Borkenau, P., Riemann, R., Spinath, F. M., & Angleitner, A. (2006). Genetic and environmental influences on person × situation profiles. *Journal of Personality, 74*, 1451–1479.

Bornstein, R. F., Riggs, J. M., Hill, E. L., & Calabrese, C. (1996). Activity, passivity, self-denigration, and self-promotion: Toward an interactionist model of interpersonal dependency. *Journal of Personality, 64*, 637–673.

Borsboom, D., Mellenbergh, G. J., & Van Heerden, J. (2004). The concept of validity. *Psychological Review, 111*, 1061–1071.

Bouchard, T. J., & Loehlin, J. C. (2001). Genes, evolution, and personality. *Behavior Genetics, 31*, 243–273.

Bouchard, T. J., Lykken, D. T., McGue, M., Segal, N. L., & Tellegen, A. (1990). Sources of human psychological differences: The Minnesota study of twins reared apart. *Science, 250*, 223–228.

Boudin, H. M. (1972). Contingency contracting as a therapeutic tool in the deceleration of amphetamine use. *Behavior Therapy, 3*, 604–608.

Bower, G. H. (1981). Mood and memory. *American Psychologist, 36*, 129–148.

Bowers, K. (1973). Situationism in psychology: An analysis and a critique. *Psychological Review, 80*, 307–336.

Bowlby, J. (1969). *Attachment and loss* (Vol. 1). London: Hogarth Press.

Bowlby, J. (1982). Attachment and loss: Retrospect and prospect. *American Journal of Orthopsychiatry, 52*, 664–678.

Braungart, J. M., Fulker, D. W., & Plomin, R. (1992). Genetic influence of the home environment during infancy: A sibling adoption study of the HOME. *Developmental Psychology, 28*, 1048–1055.

Brazier, D. (1993). The necessary condition is love: Going beyond self in the person-centered approach. In D. Brazier (Ed.), *Beyond Carl Rogers* (pp. 72–91) London: Constable.

Brooks, D. (2006, May 7). Marshmallows and public policy. *New York Times*, pp. 4–13.

Brown, G. W. (1998). Genetic and population perspectives on life events and depression. *Social Psychiatry and Psychiatric Epidemiology, 33*, 363–372.

Brown, J. D. (1986). Evaluations of self and others: Self-enhancement biases in social judgment. *Social Cognition, 4*, 353–376.

Brown, J. D., & Dutton, K. A. (1995). The thrill of victory, the complexity of defeat: Self-esteem and people's emotional reactions to success and failure. *Journal of Personality and Social Psychology, 68*, 712–722.

Brown, J. S. (1942). The generalization of approach responses as a function of stimulus intensity and strength of motivation. *Journal of Comparative Psychology, 33*, 209–226.

Brown, J. S. (1948). Gradients of approach and avoidance responses and their relation to level of motivation. *Journal of Comparative and Physiological Psychology, 41*, 450–465.

Brown, K. W., & Moskowitz, D. S. (1998). Dynamic stability of behavior: The rhythms of our interpersonal lives. *Journal of Personality, 66*, 105–134.

Bruner, J. (1992). Another look at New Look 1. *American Psychologist, 47*, 780–783.

Bruner, J. S. (1957). Going beyond the information given. In H. Gruber, G. Terrell, & M. Wertheimer (Eds.), *Contemporary approaches to cognition* (pp. 258–290). Cambridge, MA: Harvard University Press.

Bruner, J. S., & Postman, L. (1947). Emotional selectivity in perception and reaction. *Journal of Personality, 16*, 69–77.

Buss, A. H. (1961). *The psychology of aggression*. New York: Wiley.

Buss, A. H. (1989). Personality as traits. *American Psychologist, 44*, 1378–1388.

Buss, A. H., & Plomin, R. (1984). *Temperament: Early developing personality traits*. Hillsdale, NJ: Erlbaum.

Buss, A. H., Plomin, R., & Willerman, L. (1973). The inheritance of temperaments. *Journal of Personality, 41*, 513–524.

Buss, D. M. (1987). Selection, evocation, and manipulation. *Journal of Personality and Social Psychology, 53*, 1214–1221.

Buss, D. M. (1991). Evolutionary personality psychology. *Annual Review of Psychology, 42*, 459–491.

Buss, D. M. (1996). The evolutionary psychology of human social strategies. In E. T. Higgins & A. W. Kruglanski

(Eds.), *Social psychology: Handbook of basic principles* (pp. 3–38). New York: Guilford Press.

Buss, D. M. (1997). Evolutionary foundations of personality. In R. Hogan, J. A. Johnson, & S. R. Briggs (Eds.), *Handbook of personality psychology* (pp. 317–344). San Diego, CA: Academic Press.

Buss, D. M. (1999). Human nature and individual differences: The evolution of human personality. In L. A. Pervin & O. P. John (Eds.), *Handbook of personality: Theory and research* (2nd ed., pp. 31–56). New York: Guilford Press.

Buss, D. M. (2001). Human nature and culture: An evolutionary psychological perspective. *Journal of Personality, 69*, 955–978.

Buss, D. M., & Craik, K. H. (1983). The act of frequency approach to personality. *Psychological Review, 90*, 105–126.

Buss, D.M., & Schmitt, D.P. (1993). Sexual strategies theory: An evolutionary perspective on human mating. *Psychological Review, 100*, 204–232.

Butler, L. D., & Nolen-Hoeksema, S. (1994). Gender differences in response to depressed mood in college sample. *Sex Roles, 30*, 330–346.

Byrne, D. (1964). Repression–sensitization as a dimension of personality. In B. A. Maher (Ed.), *Progress in experimental personality research* (Vol. 1, pp. 169–220). New York: Academic Press.

Byrne, D. (1966). *An introduction to personality*. Englewood Cliffs, NJ: Prentice-Hall.

Byrne, D. (1969). Attitudes and attraction. In L. Berkowitz (Ed.), *Advances in experimental social psychology* (Vol. 4, pp. 35–90). New York: Academic Press.

Cacioppo, J. T., Berntson, G. G., & Crites, S. L., Jr. (1996). Social neuroscience: Principles of psychophysiological arousal and response. In E. T. Higgins & A. W. Kruglanski (Eds.), *Social psychology: Handbook of basic principles* (pp. 72–101). New York: Guilford Press.

Cacioppo, J. T., & Gardner, W. L. (1999). Emotion. *Annual Review of Psychology, 50*, 191–214.

Cacioppo, J. T., & Petty, R. E. (1982). The need for cognition. *Journal of Personality and Social Psychology, 42*, 116–131.

Caldwell, B. M., & Bradley, R. H. (1978). *Home observation for measurement of the environment*. Little Rock: University of Arkansas Press.

Campbell, J., & Dunnette, M. (1968). Effectiveness of T-group experiences in managerial training and development. *Psychological Bulletin, 70*, 73–104.

Cannon, W. B. (1932). *The wisdom of the body*. New York: Norton.

Cantor, N. (1990). From thought to behavior: "Having" and "doing" in the study of personality and cognition. *American Psychologist, 45*, 735–750.

Cantor, N. (1994). Life task problem-solving: Situational affordances and personal needs. *Personality and Social Psychology Bulletin, 20*, 235–243.

Cantor, N., Kemmelmeier, M., Basten, J., & Prentice, D. A. (2002). Life task pursuit in social groups: Balancing self-exploration and social integration. *Self and Identity, 1*, 177–184.

Cantor, N., & Kihlstrom, J. F. (1987). *Personality and social intelligence*. Englewood Cliffs, NJ: Erlbaum.

Cantor, N., & Mischel, W. (1977). Traits as prototypes: Effects on recognition memory. *Journal of Personality and Social Psychology, 35*, 38–48.

Cantor, N., & Mischel, W. (1979). Prototypes in person perception. In L. Berkowitz (Ed.), *Advances in experimental social psychology* (Vol. 12, pp. 3–52). New York: Academic Press.

Cantor, N., Mischel, W., & Schwartz, J. (1982). A prototype analysis of psychological situations. *Cognitive Psychology, 14*, 45–77.

Cantor, N., Norem, J., Langston, C., Zirkel, S., Fleeson W., & Cook-Flannagan, C. (1991). Life tasks and daily life experience. *Journal of Personality, 59*, 425–451.

Capecchi, M. R. (1994). Targeted gene replacement. *Scientific American, 270*, 52–59.

Carlson, R. (1971). Where is the personality research? *Psychological Bulletin, 75*, 203–219.

Carlson, S. M., & Beck, D. M. (in press). Symbols as tools in the development of executive function. In A. Winsler, C. Fernyhough, & I. Montero (Eds.), *Private speech, executive functioning, and the development of verbal self-regulation*. New York: Cambridge University Press.

Carlson, S. M., Davis, A. C., & Leach, J. G. (2005). Less is more: Executive function and symbolic representation in preschool children. *Psychological Science, 16*, 609–616.

Carter, C. S. (1998). Neuroendocrine perspectives on social attachment and love. *Psychoneuroendocrinology, 23*, 779–818.

Cartwright, D. S. (1978). *Introduction to personality*. Chicago: Rand McNally.

Carver, C. S. (1996). Emergent integration in contemporary personality psychology. *Journal of Research in Personality, 30*, 319–334.

Carver, C. S., Coleman, A. E., & Glass, D. C. (1976). The coronary-prone behavior pattern and the suppression of fatigue on a treadmill test. *Journal of Personality and Social Psychology, 33*, 460–466.

Carver, C. S., Pozo, C., Harris, S. D., Noriega, V., Scheier, M. F., Robinson, D. S., et al. (1993). How coping mediates the effects of optimism on stress: A study of women with early stage breast cancer. *Journal of Personality and Social Psychology, 65*, 375–391.

Carver, C. S., & Scheier, M. F. (1981). *Attention and self-regulation: A control theory approach to human behavior*. New York: Springer-Verlag.

Carver, C. S., & Scheier, M. F. (1990). Principles of self-regulation: Action and emotion. In E. T. Higgins & R. M. Sorrentino (Eds.), *Handbook of motivation and cognition* (Vol. 2, pp. 3–52). New York: Guilford Press.

Carver, C. S., & Scheier, M. F. (1998). *On the self-regulation of behavior*. New York: Cambridge University Press.

Carver, C. S., & White, T. L. (1994). Behavioral inhibition, behavioral activation, and affective responses to impending reward and punishment: The BIS/BAS scales. *Journal of Personality and Social Psychology, 67*, 319–333.

Casey, B. J., Thomas, K. M., Welsh, T. F., Badgaiyan, R., Eccard, C. H., Jennings, J. R., et al. (2000). Dissociation of response conflict, attentional control, and expectancy with functional magnetic resonance imaging (fMRI). *Proceedings of the National Academy of Sciences, 97*, 8728–8733.

Casey, B. J., Tottenham, N., & Fossella, J. (2002). Clinical, imaging, lesion, and genetic approaches toward a model of cognitive control. *Developmental Psychobiology, 40*, 237–254.

Casey, B. J., Trainor, R. J., Orendi, J. L., Schubert, A. B., Nystrom, L. E., Giedd, J. N., et al. (1997). A developmental functional MRI study of prefrontal activation during performance of a go–no-go task. *Journal of Cognitive Neuroscience, 9*, 835–847.

Cashdan, S. (1988). *Object relations theory: Using the relationship*. New York: Norton.

Caspi, A. (1987). Personality in the life course. *Journal of Personality and Social Psychology, 53*, 1203–1213.

Caspi, A. (1998). Personality development across the life course. In W. Damon (Series Ed.) & N. Eisenberg (Vol. Ed.), *Handbook of child psychology: Vol. 3. Social, emotional, and personality development* (3rd ed., pp. 311–388). New York: Wiley.

Caspi, A. (2000). The child is father of the man: Personality continuities from childhood to adulthood. *Journal of Personality and Social Psychology, 78*, 158–172.

Caspi, A., & Bem, D. J. (1990). Personality continuity and change across the life course. In L. A. Pervin (Ed.), *Handbook of personality: Theory and research* (pp. 549–575). New York: Guilford Press.

Caspi, A., McClay, J., Moffitt, T. E., Mill, J., Martin, J., Craig, I. W., et al. (2002). Role of genotype in the cycle of violence in maltreated children. *Science, 297*, 851–854.

Caspi, A., Roberts, B. W., & Shiner, R. L. (2005). Personality development: Stability and change. *Annual Review of Psychology, 56*, 453–484.

Caspi, A., Sugden, K., Moffitt, T. E., Taylor, A., Craig, I. W., Harrington, H., et al. (2003). Influence of life stress on depression: Moderation by a polymorphism in the 5-HTT gene. *Science, 301*, 386–389.

Cattell, R. B. (1950). *A systematic theoretical and factual study*. New York: McGraw-Hill.

Cattell, R. B. (1965). *The scientific analysis of personality*. Baltimore: Penguin Books.

Cervone, D. (1991). The two disciplines of personality psychology [Review of *Handbook of personality: Theory and research*]. *Psychological Science, 2*, 371–376.

Cervone, D. (2004). The architecture of personality. *Psychological Review, 111*, 183–204.

Cervone, D. (2005). Personality architecture: Within-person structures and processes. *Annual Review of Psychology, 56*, 423–452.

Cervone, D., & Mischel, W. (2002). Personality Science. In D. Cervone & W. Mischel (Eds.), *Advances in personality science* (pp. 1–26). New York: Guilford.

Cervone, D., Shadel, W. G., & Jencius, S. (2001). Social-cognitive theory of personality assessment. *Personality and Social Psychology Review, 5*, 33–51.

Cervone, D., & Shoda, Y. (1999). Social cognitive theories and the coherence of personality. In D. Cervone and Y. Shoda (Eds.), *The coherence of personality: Social-cognitive bases of consistency, variability, and organization?* (pp. 3–33). New York: Guilford Press.

Chaiken, S., & Bargh, J. A. (1993). Occurrence versus moderation of the automatic attitude activation effect: Reply to Fazio. *Journal of Personality and Social Psychology, 64*, 759–765.

Chamorro-Premuzic, T., & Furnham, A. (2003). Personality predicts academic performance: Evidence from two longitudinal university samples. *Journal of Research in Personality, 37*, 319–338.

Chan, D. W. (1994). The Chinese Ways of Coping Questionnaire: Assessing coping in secondary school teachers and students in Hong Kong. *Psychological Assessment, 6*, 108–116.

Chan, W., & Mendoza-Denton, R. (2004, April). *Sensitivity to race-based rejection among Asian Americans*. Paper presented at the annual meeting of the Western Psychological Association, Phoenix, AZ.

Chaplin, W. F., John, O. P., & Goldberg, L. R. (1988). Conceptions of states and traits: Dimensional attributes with ideals as prototypes. *Journal of Personality and Social Psychology, 54*, 541–557.

Chartrand, T. L., & Bargh, J. A. (1996). Automatic activation of impression formation and memorization goals: Nonconscious goal priming reproduces effects of explicit task instructions. *Journal of Personality and Social Psychology, 71*, 464–478.

Chaves, J. F., & Barber, T. X. (1974). Acupuncture analgesia: A six-factor theory. *Psychoenergetic Systems, 1*, 11–20.

Chen, S., & Andersen, S.M. (1999). Relationships from the past in the present: Significant-other representations and transference in interpersonal life. In M. P. Zanna (Ed.), *Advances in Experimental Social Psychology* (Vol. 31, pp. 123–190). San Diego, CA: Academic Press.

Chen-Idson, L., & Mischel, W. (2001). The personality of familiar and significant people: The lay perceiver as a social cognitive theorist. *Journal of Personality and Social Psychology, 80*, 585–596.

Cheng, C. (2003). Cognitive and motivational processes underlying coping flexibility: A dual-process model. *Journal of Personality and Social Psychology, 84*, 425–438.

Cheng, C., Chiu, C., Hong, Y., & Cheung, J. S. (2001). Discriminative facility and its role in the quality of interactional experiences. *Journal of Personality, 69*, 765–786.

Cheng, C., Hui, W., & Lam, S. (2000). Perceptual style and behavioral pattern of individuals with functional gastrointestinal disorders. *Health Psychology, 19*, 146–154.

Cherney, S. S., Fulker, D. W., Emde, R. N., Robinson, J., Corley, R. P., Reznick, J. S., et al. (1994). Continuity and change in infant shyness from 14 to 20 months. *Behavior Genetics, 24*, 365–379.

Chiu, C., Dweck, C. S., Tong, J. Y., & Fu, J. H. (1997). Implicit theories and conceptions of morality. *Journal of Personality and Social Psychology, 73*, 923–940.

Chiu, C., Hong, Y., & Dweck, C. S. (1997). Lay dispositionism and implicit theories of personality. *Journal of Personality and Social Psychology, 73*, 19–30.

Chiu, C., Hong, Y., Mischel, W., & Shoda, Y. (1995). Discriminative facility in social competence: Conditional versus dispositional encoding and monitoring-blunting of information. *Social Cognition, 13*, 49–70.

Chodoff, P. (1963). Late effects of concentration camp syndrome. *Archives of General Psychiatry, 8*, 323–333.

Claes, L., Van Mechelen, I., & Vertommen, H. (2004). Assessment of situation–behavior profiles and their guiding cognitive and affective processes: A case study from the domain of aggressive behaviors. *European Journal of Social Assessment, 20*, 216–226.

Clark, L. A., & Watson, D. (1999). Temperament: A new paradigm for trait psychology. In L. A. Pervin & O. P. John (Eds.), *Handbook of personality: Theory and research* (2nd ed., pp. 399–423). New York: Guilford Press.

Cloninger, C. R. (1988). A unified biosocial theory of personality and its role in the development of anxiety states: A reply to commentaries. *Psychiatric Developments, 2*, 83–120.

Cobb, S. (1976). Social support as moderator of life stress. *Psychosomatic Medicine, 38*, 300–314.

Cohen, D. (1998). Culture, social organization, and patterns of violence. *Journal of Personality and Social Psychology, 75*, 408–419.

Cohen, D. (2007). Methods in cultural psychology. In S. Kitayama & D. Cohen (Eds.), *Handbook of cultural psychology*. New York: Guilford Press.

Cohen, D., & Nisbett, R. E. (1994). Self-protection and the culture of honor: Explaining southern violence. *Personality and Social Psychology Bulletin, 20*, 551–567.

Cohen, D., & Nisbett, R. E. (1997). Field experiments examining the culture of honor: The role of institutions in perpetuating norms about violence. *Personality and Social Psychology Bulletin, 23*, 1188–1199.

Cohen, D., Nisbett, R. E., Bowdle, B. F., & Schwarz, N. (1996). Insult, aggression, and the southern culture of honor: An "experimental ethnography." *Journal of Personality and Social Psychology, 70*, 945–960.

Cohen, D., Vandello, J., Puente, S., & Rantilla, A. (1999). "When you call me that, smile!": How norms for politeness, interaction styles, and aggression work together in southern culture. *Social Psychology Quarterly, 62*, 257–275.

Cohen, S., & McKay, G. (1984). Social support, stress, and the buffering hypothesis: A theoretical analysis. In A. Baum, J. E. Singer, & S. E. Taylor (Eds.), *Handbook of psychology and health, Vol. 4. Social psychological aspects of health* (pp. 253–267). Hillsdale, NJ: Erlbaum.

Colby, K. M. (1951). *A primer for psychotherapists*. New York: Ronald Press.

Coles, R. (1970). *Uprooted children*. New York: Harper & Row.

Collaer, M. L., & Hines, M. (1995). Human behavioral sex differences: A role for gonadal hormones during early development? *Psychological Bulletin, 118*, 55–107.

Collins, N. L., & Feeney, B. C. (2000). A safe haven: An attachment theory perspective on support seeking and caregiving in intimate relationships. *Journal of Personality and Social Psychology, 78*, 1053–1073.

Collins, N. L., & Feeney, B. C. (2004). Working models of attachment shape perceptions of social support: Evidence from experimental and observational studies. *Journal of Personality and Social Psychology, 87*, 363–383.

Conner, T., Barrett, L. F., Bliss-Moreau, E., Lebo, K., & Kashub, C. (2003). A practical guide to experience-sampling procedures. *Journal of Happiness Studies, 4*, 53–78.

Contrada, R. J., Cather, C., & O'Leary, A. (1999). Personality and health: Dispositions and processes in disease susceptibility and adaptation to illness. In L. A. Pervin & O. P. John (Eds.), *Handbook of personality: Theory and research* (2nd ed., pp. 576–604). New York: Guilford Press.

Contrada, R. J., Leventhal, H., & O'Leary, A. (1990). Personality and health. In L. A. Pervin (Ed.), *Handbook of personality: Theory and research* (pp. 638–669). New York: Guilford Press.

Cooper, J., & Fazio, R. H. (1984). A new look at dissonance theory. In L. Berkowitz (Ed.), *Advances in experimental social psychology, Vol. 17. Theorizing in social psychology: Special topics* (pp. 229–262). New York: Academic Press.

Cooper, J. R., Bloom, F. E., & Roth, R. H. (1996). *The biochemical basis of neuropharmacology* (7th ed.). New York: Oxford University Press.

Coopersmith, S. (1967). *The antecedents of self-esteem*. San Francisco: Freeman.

Cosmides, L. (1989). The logic of social exchange: Has natural selection shaped how humans reason? Studies with the Wason selection task. *Cognition, 31*, 187–276.

Cosmides, L., & Tooby, J. (1989). Evolutionary psychology and the generation of culture: II. Case study: A computational theory of social exchange. *Ethology and Sociobiology, 10*, 51–97.

Costa, P. T., Jr., & McCrae, R. R. (1988). Personality in adulthood: A six-year longitudinal study of self-reports and spouse ratings on the NEO personality inventory. *Journal of Personality and Social Psychology, 54*, 853–863.

Costa, P. T., Jr., & McCrae, R. R. (1992a). Normal personality assessment in clinical practice: The NEO personality inventory. *Psychological Assessment, 4*, 5–13.

Costa, P. T., Jr., & McCrae, R. R. (1992b). *Revised NEO Personality Inventory (NEO-PI-R) and NEO Five Factor (NEO-FFI): Professional manual*. Odessa, FL: Psychological Assessment Resources.

Costa, P. T., Jr., & McCrae, R. R. (1997). Longitudinal stability of adult personality. In R. Hogan, J. Johnson, & S. Briggs (Eds.), *Handbook of personality psychology* (pp. 269–291). San Diego, CA: Academic Press.

Costa, P. T., Jr., McCrae, R. R., & Dye, D. A. (1991). Facet scales for agreeableness and conscientiousness: A revision of the NEO-personality inventory. *Personality and Individual Differences, 12*, 887–898.

Cote, S., & Moskowitz, D. S. (1998). On the dynamic covariation between interpersonal behavior and affect: Prediction from neuroticism, extraversion, and agreeableness. *Journal of Personality and Social Psychology, 75*, 1032–1046.

Coyne, J. C., & Downey, G. (1991). Social factors and psychopathology: Stress, social support, and coping process. *Annual Review of Psychology, 42*, 401–425.

Crocker, J. (2002). Contingencies of self-worth: Implications for self-regulation and psychological vulnerability. *Self and Identity, 1*, 143–149.

Crocker, J., Major, B., & Steele, C. (1998). Social stigma. In D. T. Gilbert & S. T. Fiske (Eds.), *The handbook of social psychology* (4th ed., pp. 504–553). New York: McGraw-Hill.

Csikszentmihalyi, M. (1990). The domain of creativity. In M. Runco & R. S. Albert (Eds.), *Theories of creativity* (Vol. 115, pp. 190–212). Thousand Oaks, CA: Sage.

Csikszentmihalyi, M. (1993). *The evolving self*. New York: HarperCollins.

Dabbs, J. M., Jr. (1992). Testosterone and occupational achievement. *Social Forces, 70*, 813–824.

Dabbs, J. M., Jr., & Morris, R. (1990). Testosterone, social class, and antisocial behavior in a sample of 4,462 men. *Psychological Science, 1*, 209–211.

D'Andrade, R. G. (1966). Sex differences and cultural institutions. In E. E. Maccoby (Ed.), *The development of sex differences* (pp. 174–204). Stanford, CA: Stanford University Press.

Daniels, A. C. (1994). *Bringing out the best in people: How to apply the astonishing power of reinforcement*. New York: McGraw-Hill.

Daniels, D., Dunn, J. F., Furstenberg, F. F., Jr., & Plomin, R. (1985). Environmental differences within the family and adjustment differences within pairs of adolescent siblings. *Child Development, 56*, 764–774.

David, J. P., Green, P. J., Martin, R., & Suls, J. (1997). Differential roles of neuroticism, extraversion, and event desirability for mood in daily life: An integrative model of top-down and bottom-up influences. *Journal of Personality and Social Psychology, 73*, 149–159.

Davidson, R. J. (1993). The neuropsychology of emotion and affective style. In M. Lewis & J. M. Haviland (Eds.), *Handbook of emotions* (pp. 143–154). New York: Guildford Press.

Davidson, R. J. (1995). Cerebral asymmetry, emotion, and affective style. In R. J. Davidson & K. Hugdahl (Eds.), *Brain asymmetry* (pp. 361–387). Cambridge, MA: MIT Press.

Davidson, R. J., Ekman, P., Saron, C. D., Senulis, J. A., & Friesen, W. V. (1990). Approach–withdrawal and cerebral asymmetry: Emotional expression and brain physiology I. *Journal of Personality and Social Psychology, 58*, 330–341.

Davidson, R. J., & Fox, N. A. (1989). The relation between tonic EEG asymmetry and ten-month-olds' emotional response to separation. *Journal of Abnormal Psychology, 98*, 127–131.

Davidson, R. J., Putnam, K. M., & Larson, C. L. (2000). Dysfunction in the neural circuitry of emotion regulation—A possible prelude to violence. *Science, 289*, 591–594.

Davidson, R. J., & Sutton, S. K. (1995). Affective neuroscience: The emergence of a discipline. *Current Opinion in Neurobiology, 5*, 217–224.

Davis, J. M., Klerman, G., & Schildkraut, J. (1967). Drugs used in the treatment of depression. In L. Efron, J. O. Cole, D. Levine, & J. R. Wittenborn (Eds.), *Psychopharmacology: A review of progress* (pp. 719–747). Washington, DC: U.S. Clearing-House of Mental Health Information.

Davison, G. C., & Neale, J. M. (1990). *Abnormal psychology: An experimental clinical approach* (5th ed.). New York: Wiley.

Davison, G. C., Neale, J. M., & Kring, A. M. (2004). *Abnormal psychology* (9th ed.). Hoboken, NJ: Wiley.

Deaux, K., & Major, B. (1987). Putting gender into context: An interactive model of gender-related behavior. *Psychological Review, 94*, 369–389.

Deci, E. L. (1975). *Intrinsic motivation*. New York: Plenum Press.

Deci, E. L., & Ryan, R. M. (1980). The empirical exploration of intrinsic motivational processes. In L. Berkowitz (Ed.), *Advances in experimental social psychology* (Vol. 13, pp. 39–80). New York: Academic Press.

Deci, E. L., & Ryan, R. M. (1987). The support of autonomy and the control of behavior. *Journal of Personality and Social Psychology, 53*, 1024–1037.

Deci, E. L., & Ryan, R. M. (1995). Human autonomy: The basis for true self-esteem. In M. Kernis (Ed.), *Efficacy, agency, and self-esteem* (pp. 31–49). New York: Plenum Press.

Deci, E. L., & Ryan, R. M. (2000). The support of autonomy and the control of behavior. In E. T. Higgins & A. W. Kruglanski (Eds.), *Motivational science: Social and personality perspectives* (pp. 128–145). New York: Psychology Press.

Dehaene, S., Izard, V., Pica, P., & Spelke, E. (2006). Core knowledge of geometry in an Amazonian indigene group. *Science Magazine, 9*, 381–384.

Depue, R. A., & Collins, P. F. (1999). Neurobiology of the structure of personality: Dopamine, facilitation of incentive motivation, and extraversion. *Behavioral and Brain Sciences, 22*, 491–569.

DeRaad, B., Perugini, M., Hrebickova, M., & Szarota, P. (1998). Lingua franca of personality: Taxonomies and structures based on the psycholexical approach. *Journal of Cross Cultural Psychology, 29*, 212–232.

Derryberry, D. (2002). Attention and voluntary self-control. *Self and Identity, 1*, 105–111.

Derryberry, D., & Reed, M. A. (2002). Anxiety-related attentional biases and their regulation by attention control. *Journal of Abnormal Psychology, 111*, 225–236.

Derryberry, D., & Rothbart, M. K. (1997). Reactive and effortful processes in the organization of temperament. *Development and Psychopathology, 9*, 633–652.

Diamond, M. J., & Shapiro, J. L. (1973). Changes in locus of control as a function of encounter group experiences: A study and replication. *Journal of Abnormal Psychology, 82*, 514–518.

Dickens, W. T., & Flynn, J. R. (2001). Heritability estimates versus large environmental effects: The IQ paradox resolved. *Psychological Review, 108*, 346–369.

Diener, C. I., & Dweck, C. S. (1978). An analysis of learned helplessness: Continuous changes in performance, strategy, and achievement cognitions following failure. *Journal of Personality and Social Psychology, 36*, 451–462.

Diener, E., & Lucas, R. E. (2000a). Explaining differences in societal levels of happiness: Relative standards, need fulfillment, culture and evaluation theory. *Journal of Happiness Studies, 1*, 41–78.

Diener, E. & Lucas, R. E. (2000b). Subjective emotional well-being. In M. Lewis & J. M. Haviland-Jones (Eds.), *Handbook of emotions* (pp. 325–337). New York: Guilford Press.

Dobson, K. S., & Craig, K. D. (1996). *Advances in cognitive-behavioral therapy*. Thousand Oaks, CA: Sage.

Dodge, K. A. (1986). A social information processing model of social competence in children: Cognitive perspectives on children's social behavioral development. *Minnesota Symposium on Child Psychology, 18*, 77–125.

Dodge, K. A. (1993). New wrinkles in the person-versus situation debate. *Psychological Inquiry, 4*, 284–286.

Dodgson, P., & Wood, J. V. (1998). Self-esteem and the cognitive accessibility of strengths and weaknesses after failure. *Journal of Personality and Social Psychology, 75*, 178–197.

Dollard, J., & Miller, N. E. (1950). *Personality and psychotherapy: An analysis in terms of learning, thinking, and culture*. New York: McGraw-Hill.

Downey, G., & Feldman, S. I. (1996). Implications of rejection sensitivity for intimate relationships. *Journal of Personality and Social Psychology, 70*, 1327–1343.

Duckworth, A. L., Steen, T. A., & Seligman, M. E. P. (2005). Positive psychology in clinical practice. *Annual Review of Clinical Psychology, 1*, 629–651.

Dunford, F. W. (2000). The San Diego Navy experiment: An assessment of interventions for men who assault their wives. *Journal of Consulting and Clinical Psychology, 68*, 468–476.

Dunn, J., & Plomin, R. (1990). *Separate lives: Why siblings are so different*. New York: Basic Books.

Dunnette, M. D. (1969). People feeling: Joy, more joy, and the "slough of despond." *Journal of Applied Behavioral Science, 5*, 25–44.

Durham, W. H. (1991). *Coevolution*. Stanford, CA: Stanford University Press.

Durston, S., Thomas, K. M., Yang, Y., Ulug, A. M., Zimmerman, R. D., & Casey, B. J. (2002). A neural basis for the development of inhibitory control. *Developmental Science, 5*, 9–16.

Dweck, C. S. (1975). The role of expectations and attributions in the alleviation of learned helplessness. *Journal of Personality and Social Psychology, 31*, 674–685.

Dweck, C. S. (1990). Self-theories and goals: Their role in motivation, personality, and development. In R. A. Dienstbier (Ed.), *Nebraska Symposium on Motivation* (Vol. 38, pp. 199–235). Lincoln: University of Nebraska Press.

Dweck, C. S., & Leggett, E. L. (1988). A social-cognitive approach to personality and motivation. *Psychological Review, 95*, 256–273.

Dworkin, R. H. (1979). Genetic and environmental influences on person–situation interactions. *Journal of Research in Personality, 13*, 279–293.

D'Zurilla, T. (1965). Recall efficiency and mediating cognitive events in "experimental repression." *Journal of Personality and Social Psychology, 1*, 253–257.

Eagly, A. H. (1987). *Sex differences in social behavior: A social-role interpretation*. Hillsdale, NJ: Erlbaum.

Eagly, A. H. (1995). The science and politics of comparing women and men. *American Psychologist, 50*, 145–158.

Eagly, A. H., & Crowley, M. (1986). Gender and helping behavior: A meta-analytic review of the social psychological literature. *Psychological Bulletin, 100*, 283–308.

Eagly, A. H., & Steffen, V. J. (1986). Gender and aggressive behavior: A meta-analytic review of the social psychological literature. *Psychological Bulletin, 100*, 309–330.

Eaves, L. J., Eysenck, H. J., & Martin, N. G. (1989). *Genes, culture, and personality: An empirical approach*. London: Academic Press.

Ebstein, R. P., Gritsenko, I., Nemanov, L., Frisch, A., Osher, Y., & Belmaker, R. H. (1997). No association between the serotonin transporter gene regulatory region polymorphism and the Tridimensional Personality Questionnaire (TPQ) temperament of harm avoidance. *Molecular Psychiatry, 2*, 224–226.

Ebstein, R. P., Novick, O., Umansky, R., Priel, B., Osher, Y., Blaine, D., et al. (1996). Dopamine D4 receptor (D4DR) exon III polymorphism associated with human personality trait of novelty seeking. *Nature Genetics, 12*, 78–80.

Edelman, G. M. (1992). *Bright air, brilliant fire: On the matter of the mind*. New York: Basic Books.

Ehrlich, P. R. (2000). *Human natures: Genes, cultures, and the human prospect*. Washington, DC: Island Press.

Eigsti, I., Zayas, V., Mischel, W., Shoda, Y., Ayduk, O., Dadlani, M. B., et al. (2006). Predicting cognitive control from preschool to late adolescence and young adulthood. *Psychological Science, 17*, 478–484.

Eisenberg, N., Fabes, R. A., Guthrie, I. K., & Reiser, M. (2002). The role of emotionality and regulation in children's social competence and adjustment. In A. Caspi (Ed.), *Paths to successful development: Personality in the life course* (pp. 46–70). New York: Cambridge University Press.

Eisenberg, N., Spinrad, T. L., & Morris, A. S. (2002). Regulation, resiliency, and quality of social functioning. *Self and Identity, 1*, 121–128.

Eizenman, D. R., Nesselroade, J. R., Featherman, D. L., & Rowe, J. W. (1997). Intraindividual variability in perceived control in an older sample: The MacArthur successful aging studies. *Psychology and Aging, 12*, 489–502.

Ekman, P. (Ed.). (1982). *Emotion in the human face* (2nd ed.). New York: Cambridge University Press.

Ekman, P., Friesen, W. V., & Ellsworth, P. (1972). *Emotion in the human face*. Elmsford, NY: Pergamon Press.

Ellsworth, P. C., & Carlsmith, J. M. (1968). Effects of eye contact and verbal content on affective response to a dyadic interaction. *Journal of Personality and Social Psychology, 10*, 15–20.

Emmons, R. A. (1991). Personal strivings, daily life events, and psychological and physical well-being. *Journal of Personality, 59*, 453–472.

Emmons, R. A. (1997). Motives and goals. In R. Hogan, J. A. Johnson, & S. R. Briggs (Eds.), *Handbook of personality psychology* (pp. 485–512). San Diego, CA: Academic Press.

Endler, N. S., & Hunt, J. M. (1968). S-R inventories of hostility and comparisons of the proportions of variance from persons, responses, and situations for hostility and anxiousness. *Journal of Personality and Social Psychology, 9*, 309–315.

English, T., & Chen, S. (in press). Culture and self-concept stability: Consistency across and within contexts among Asian- and European-Americans. *Journal of Personality and Social Psychology*.

Epstein, S. (1973). The self-concept revisited or a theory of a theory. *American Psychologist, 28*, 405–416.

Epstein, S. (1979). The stability of behavior: I. On predicting most of the people much of the time. *Journal of Personality and Social Psychology, 37*, 1097–1126.

Epstein, S. (1983). Aggregation and beyond: Some basic issues on the prediction of behavior. *Journal of Personality, 51*, 360–392.

Epstein, S. (1990). Cognitive-experimental self-theory. In L. A. Pervin (Ed.), *Handbook of personality: Theory and research* (pp. 165–192). New York: Guilford Press.

Epstein, S. (1994). Trait theory as personality theory: Can a part be as great as the whole? *Psychological Inquiry, 5*, 120–122.

Epstein, S., & Fenz, W. D. (1962). Theory and experiment on the measurement of approach–avoidance conflict. *Journal of Abnormal and Social Psychology, 64*, 97–112.

Erdelyi, M. H. (1985). *Psychoanalysis: Freud's cognitive psychology*. New York: Freeman.

Erdelyi, M. H. (1992). Psychodynamics and the unconscious. *American Psychologist, 47*, 784–787.

Erdelyi, M. H. (1993). Repression: The mechanism and the defense. In D. M. Wegner & J. W. Pennebaker (Eds.), *Handbook of mental control* (pp. 126–148). Englewood Cliffs, NJ: Prentice-Hall.

Erdelyi, M. H., & Goldberg, B. (1979). Let's not sweep repression under the rug: Towards a cognitive psychology of repression. In J. F. Kihlstrom & F. J. Evans (Eds.), *Functional disorders of memory* (pp. 355–402). Hillsdale, NJ: Erlbaum.

Erdley, C. A., & Dweck, C. S. (1993). Children's implicit personality theories as predictors of their social judgments. *Child Development, 64*, 863–878.

Eriksen, C. W. (1952). Individual differences in defensive forgetting. *Journal of Experimental Psychology, 44*, 442–446.

Eriksen, C. W. (1966). Cognitive responses to internally cued anxiety. In C. D. Spielberger (Ed.), *Anxiety and behavior* (pp. 327–360). New York: Academic Press.

Eriksen, C. W., & Kuethe, J. L. (1956). Avoidance conditioning of verbal behavior without awareness: A paradigm of repression. *Journal of Abnormal and Social Psychology, 53*, 203–209.

Erikson, E. H. (1950). *Childhood and society*. New York: Norton.

Erikson, E. H. (1963). *Childhood and society* (2nd ed.). New York: Norton.

Erikson, E. H. (1968). *Identity: Youth and crisis*. New York: Norton.

Eslinger, P. J. (1996). Conceptualizing, describing, and measuring components of executive function: A summary. In G. R. Lyon & N. A. Krasnegor (Eds.), *Attention, memory, and executive function* (pp. 367–395). Baltimore: Brookes.

Exline, R., & Winters, L. C. (1965). Affective relations and mutual glances in dyads. In S. Tomkins & C. Izard (Eds.), *Affect, cognition, and personality* (pp. 319–350). New York: Springer.

Exner, J. E. (1993). *The Rorschach: A comprehensive system, Vol. 1: Basic foundations* (3rd ed.). New York: Wiley.

Eysenck, H. J. (1961). The effects of psychotherapy. In H. J. Eysenck (Ed.), *Handbook of abnormal psychology: An experimental approach* (pp. 697–725). New York: Basic Books.

Eysenck, H. J. (1967). *The biological basis of personality*. Springfield, IL: Charles C. Thomas.

Eysenck, H. J. (1973). Personality and the law of effect. In D. E. Berlyne & K. B. Madsen (Eds.), *Pleasure, reward, preference* (pp. 133–168). New York: Academic Press.

Eysenck, H. J. (1983). Cicero and the state–trait theory of anxiety: Another case of delayed recognition. *American Psychologist, 38*, 114–115.

Eysenck, H. J. (1990). Biological dimensions of personality. In L. A. Pervin (Ed.), *Handbook of personality: Theory and research* (pp. 244–276). New York: Guilford Press.

Eysenck, H. J. (1991). Personality, stress, and disease: An interactionist perspective. *Psychological Inquiry, 2*, 221–232.

Eysenck, H. J., & Eysenck, M. W. (1985). *Personality and individual differences: A natural science approach*. New York: Plenum Press.

Eysenck, H. J., & Eysenck, M. W. (1995). *Mindwatching: Why we behave the way we do*. London: Prion Books.

Eysenck, H. J., & Rachman, S. (1965). *The causes and cures of neurosis: An introduction to modern behavior therapy based on learning theory and the principles of conditioning*. San Diego, CA: Knapp.

Fairweather, G. W. (1967). *Methods in experimental social innovation*. New York: Wiley

Fairweather, G. W., Sanders, D. H., Cressler, D. L., & Maynard, H. (1969). *Community life for the mentally ill: An alternative to institutional care*. Chicago: Aldine.

Feeney, B. C., & Collins, N. L. (2001). Predictors of caregiving in adult intimate relationships: An attachment theoretical perspective. *Journal of Personality and Social Psychology, 80*, 972–994.

Feeney, B. C., & Collins, N. L. (2003). Motivations for caregiving in adult intimate relationships: Influences on caregiving behavior and relationship functioning. *Personality and Social Psychology Bulletin, 29*, 950–968.

Fenz, W. D. (1964). Conflict and stress as related to physiological activation and sensory, perceptual and cognitive functioning. *Psychological Monographs, 78*, No. 8 (Whole No. 585).

Ferster, C. B., & Skinner, B. F. (1957). *Schedules of reinforcement*. New York: Appleton.

Festinger, L. (1957). *A theory of cognitive dissonance*. Stanford, CA: Stanford University Press.

Fischer, W. F. (1970). *Theories of anxiety*. New York: Harper.

Fiske, A. P. (2002). Using individualism and collectivism to compare cultures—A critique of the validity and measurement of the constructs comment on Oyserman et al. (2002). *Psychological Bulletin, 128*, 78–88.

Fiske, D. W. (1994). Two cheers for the Big Five. *Psychological Inquiry, 5*, 123–124.

Fitch, G. (1970). Effects of self-esteem, perceived performance, and choice on causal attribution. *Journal of Personality and Social Psychology, 16*, 311–315.

Flavell, J. H., & Ross, L. (Eds.). (1981). *Social cognitive development: Frontiers and possible futures*. New York: Cambridge University Press.

Fleeson, W. (2001). Toward a structure- and process-integrated view of personality: Traits as density distributions of states. *Journal of Personality and Social Psychology, 80*, 1011–1027.

Fleming, J., & Darley, J. M. (1986). *Perceiving intention in constrained behavior: The role of purposeful and constrained action cues in correspondence bias effects*. Unpublished manuscript, Princeton University, Princeton, NJ.

Flint, J., Corley, R., DeFries, J. C., Fulker, D. W., Gary, J. A., Miller, S., et al. (1995). A simple genetic basis for a complex psychological trait in laboratory mice. *Science, 269*, 1432–1435.

Flynn, F. J. (2005). Having an open mind: The impact of openness to experience on interracial attitudes and impression formation, *Journal of Personality and Social Psychology, 88*, 816–826.

Foa, E. B., & Kozak, M. J. (1986). Emotional processing of fear: Exposure to corrective information. *Psychological Bulletin, 99*, 20–35.

Fodor, I. (1987). Moving beyond cognitive-behavior therapy: Integrating Gestalt therapy to facilitate personal and interpersonal awareness. In N. S. Jacobson (Ed.), *Psychotherapists in clinical practice: Cognitive and behavioral perspectives* (pp. 190–231). New York: Guilford Press.

Forgas, J. P. (1983). Episode cognition and personality: A multidimensional analysis. *Journal of Personality, 51*, 34–48.

Fournier, M. A., Moskowitz, D. S., & Zuroff, D. C. (in press). An integrative framework for the study of behavioral dispositions and behavioral signatures. *Journal of Personality and Social Psychology*.

Fox, N. A., Bell, M. A., & Jones, N. A. (1992). Individual differences in response to stress and cerebral asymmetry. *Developmental Neuropsychology, 8*, 161 184.

Fox, N. A., Henderson, H. A., Rubin, K. H., Calkins, S. D., & Schmidt, L. A. (2001). Continuity and discontinuity of behavioral inhibition and exuberance: Psychophysiological and behavioral influences across the first four years of life. *Child Development, 72*, 1–21.

Fox, N. A., Schmidt, L. A., Calkins, S. D., Rubin, K. H., & Copan, R. J. (1996). The role of frontal activation in the regulation and dysregulation of social behavior during the preschool years. *Development and Psychopathology, 8*, 89–102.

Fraley, R. C., & Shaver, P. R. (1997). Adult attachment and the suppression of unwanted thoughts. *Journal of Personality and Social Psychology, 73*, 1080–1091.

Francis, D. D., Szegda, K., Campbell, G., Martin, W. D., & Insel, T. R. (2003). Epigenetic sources of behavioral differences in mice. *Nature Neuroscience, 6*, 445–226.

Frank, K. G., & Hudson, S. M. (1990). Behavior management of infant sleep disturbance. *Journal of Applied Behavior Analysis, 23*, 91–98.

Fransella, F. (1995). *George Kelly*. London: Sage.

Frawley, P. J., & Smith, J. W. (1990). Chemical aversion therapy in the treatment of cocaine dependence as part of a multimodal treatment program: Treatment outcome. *Journal of Substance Abuse Treatment, 7*, 21–29.

Freud, S. (1924). *A general introduction to psychoanalysis*. New York: Boni and Liveright. (Original work published 1920)

Freud, S. (1933). *New introductory lectures on psychoanalysis* (W. J. H. Sproutt, Trans.). New York: Norton.

Freud, A. (1936). *The ego and the mechanisms of defense*. New York: International Universities Press.

Freud, S. (1940). An outline of psychoanalysis. *International Journal of Psychoanalysis, 21*, 27–84.

Freud, S. (1953). *Fragments of an analysis of a case of hysteria*. Standard edition, Vol. 7. London: Hogarth Press. (Original work published 1905)

Freud, S. (1955a). *The interpretation of dreams* (Vol. 4). London: Hogarth Press. (Original Work published 1899)

Freud, S. (1955b). *On transformations of instinct as exemplified in anal eroticism*. Standard edition, Vol. 18. London: Hogarth Press. (Original work published 1917)

Freud, S. (1957a). *Instincts and their vicissitudes*. Standard edition, Vol. 14. London: Hogarth Press. (Original work published 1915)

Freud, S. (1957b). *Leonardo da Vinci: A study in psychosexuality*. Standard edition, Vol. 2. London: Hogarth Press. (Original work published 1909)

Freud, S. (1958). A note on the unconscious in psychoanalysis. In J. Strachey (Ed. & Trans.), *The standard edition of the complete psychological works of Sigmund Freud* (Vol. 12, pp. 255–266). London: Hogarth Press. (Original work published 1912)

Freud, S. (1959a). *Collected papers, Vols. I–V*. New York: Basic Books.

Freud, S. (1959b). *Formulations regarding the two principles of mental functioning*. Collected papers, Vol. IV. New York: Basic Books. (Original work published 1911)

Freud, S. (1960). *Psychopathology of everyday life* Vol. 6. London: Hogarth Press. (Original work published 1901)

Freud, S. (1963). *The sexual enlightenment of children*. New York: Macmillan.

Friedman, L. (1999). *Identity's architect: A biography of Erik H. Erikson*. New York: Pantheon.

Friedman, M., & Roseman, R. H. (1974). *Type A behavior and your heart*. New York: Knopf.

Friedman, H. S., Tucker, J. S., Schwartz, J. E., Tomlinson-Keasey, C., Martin, L. R., Wingard, D. L., et al. (1995). Psychosocial and behavioral predictors of longevity: The aging and death of the "Termites." *American Psychologist, 50*, 69–78.

Fromm, E. (1941). *Escape from freedom*. New York: Holt, Rinehart and Winston.

Fromm, E. (1947). *Man for himself*. New York: Holt, Rinehart and Winston.

Funder, D. C. (1991). Global traits: A neo-Allportian approach to personality. *Psychological Science, 2*, 31–39.

Funder, D. C. (2001). Personality. *Annual Review of Psychology, 52*, 197–221.

Funder, D. C., & Colvin, C. R. (1997). Congruence of others' and self-judgments of personality. In R. Hogan, J. Johnson, & S. Briggs (Eds.), *Handbook of personality psychology* (pp. 617–647). San Diego, CA: Academic Press.

Gable, S. L., Reis, H. T., & Elliot, A. J. (2000). Behavioral activation and inhibition in everyday life. *Journal of Personality and Social Psychology, 78*, 1135–1149.

Gay, P. (1988). *Freud: A life for our time*. New York: Norton.

Gazzaniga, M. S., & Heatherton, T. F. (2006). *Psychological science: Mind, brain, and behavior* (2nd ed.). New York: Norton.

Geen, R. G. (1984). Preferred stimulation levels in introverts and extraverts: Effects on arousal and performance. *Journal of Personality and Social Psychology, 46*, 1303–1312.

Geen, R. G. (1997). Psychophysiological approaches to personality. In R. Hogan, J. A. Johnson, & S. R. Briggs (Eds.), *Handbook of personality psychology* (pp. 387–416). San Diego, CA: Academic Press.

Giese, H., & Schmidt, S. (1968). *Studenten sexualitat*. Hamburg: Rowohlt.

Gilbert, D. T., & Malone, P. S. (1995). The correspondence bias. *Psychological Bulletin, 117*, 21–38.

Gilligan, C. (1982). *In a different voice: Psychological theory and women's development*. Cambridge, MA: Harvard University Press.

Gilmore, D. D. (1990). *Manhood in the making*. New Haven, CT: Yale University Press.

Gitlin, M. J. (1990). *The psychotherapist's guide to psychopharmacology*. New York: Free Press.

Gladwell, M. (2005). *Blink, the power of thinking without thinking*. New York: Little, Brown.

Glass, D. C. (1977). *Behavior patterns, stress, and coronary disease*. Hillsdale, NJ: Erlbaum.

Glass, D. C., Singer, J. E., & Friedman, L. N. (1969). Psychic costs of adaptation to an environmental stressor. *Journal of Personality and Social Psychology, 12*, 200–210.

Goldberg, L. R. (1973). *The exploitation of the English language for the development of a descriptive personality taxonomy*. Paper presented at the 81st Annual Convention of the American Psychological Association, Montreal, Canada.

Goldberg, L. R. (1990). An alternative "description of personality": The Big-Five factor structure. *Journal of Personality and Social Psychology, 59*, 1216–1229.

Goldberg, L. R. (1992). The development of markers for the Big-Five factor structure. *Psychological Assessment, 4*, 26–42.

Goldberg, L. R., Grenier, J. R., Guion, R. M., Sechrest, L. B., & Wing, H. (1991). *Questionnaires used in the prediction of trustworthiness in pre-employment selection decisions*. Washington, DC: American Psychological Association.

Goldberg, L. R., & Lewis, M. (1969). Play behavior in the year old infant: Early sex differences. *Child Development, 40*, 21–31.

Goldner, V., Penn, P., Shoinberg, M., & Walker, G. (1990). Love and violence: Gender paradoxes in volatile attachments. *Family Process, 29*, 343–364.

Goldsmith, H. H. (1991). A zygosity questionnaire for young twins: A research note. *Behavior Genetics, 21*, 257–269.

Goldsmith, H. H., & Campos, J. J. (1986). Fundamental issues in the study of early temperament: The Denver twin temperament study. In M. E. Lamb, A. L. Brown, & B. Rogoff (Eds.), *Advances in developmental psychology* (pp. 231–283). Hillsdale, NJ: Erlbaum.

Gollwitzer, P. M. (1990). Action phases and mind-sets. In E. T. Higgins & R. M. Sorrentino (Eds.), *Handbook of motivation and cognition: Foundations of social behavior* (Vol. 2., pp. 53–92). New York: Guilford Press.

Gollwitzer, P. M. (1999). Implementation intentions: Strong effects of simple plans. *American Psychologist, 54*, 493–503.

Gollwitzer, P. M., & Bargh, J. A. (Eds.). (1996). *The psychology of action: Linking cognition and motivation to behavior*. New York: Guilford Press.

Gollwitzer, P. M., & Moskowitz, G. B. (1996). Goal effects on action and cognition. In E. T. Higgins & A. W. Kruglanski (Eds.), *Social psychology: Handbook of basic principles* (pp. 361–399). New York: Guilford Press.

Gormly, J., & Edelberg, W. (1974). Validation in personality trait attribution. *American Psychologist, 29*, 189–193.

Gosling, S. D., & John, O. P. (1999). Personality dimensions in non-human animals: A cross-species review. *Current Directions in Psychological Science, 8*, 69–73.

Gosling, S. D., Kwan, V. S. Y., & John, O. P. (2003). A dog's got personality: A cross-species comparative approach to personality judgments in dogs and humans. *Journal of Personality and Social Psychology, 85*, 1161–1169.

Gough, H. G. (1957). *Manual, California psychological inventory*. Palo Alto, CA: Consulting Psychologists Press.

Gove, F. L., Arend, R. A., & Sroufe, L. A. (1979). *Competence in preschool and kindergarten predicted from infancy*. Paper presented at the annual meeting of the Society for Research in Child Development, San Francisco.

Grant, H., & Dweck, C. S. (1999). A goal analysis of personality and personality coherence. In D. Cervone & Y. Shoda (Eds.), *Social-cognitive approaches to personality coherence* (pp. 345–371). New York: Guilford Press.

Gray, J. A. (1991). The neuropsychology of temperament. In J. Strelau & A. Angleitner (Eds.), *Explorations in temperament: International perspective on theory and measurement* (pp. 105–128). New York: Plenum Press.

Greenberg, J. R., & Mitchell, S. (1983). *Object relations in psychoanalytic theory*. Cambridge, MA: Harvard University Press.

Greenberg, J., Solomon, S., Pyszczynski, T., & Rosenblatt, A. (1992). Why do people need self-esteem? Converging evidence that self-esteem serves an anxiety-buffering function. *Journal of Personality and Social Psychology, 63*, 913–922.

Greenwald, A. G. (1980). The totalitarian ego: Fabrication and revision of personal history. *American Psychologist, 7*, 603–618.

Greenwald, A. G. (1992). New look 3: Unconscious cognition reclaimed. *American Psychologist, 47*, 766–779.

Greenwald, A. G., Banaji, M. R., Rudman, L. A., Farnham, S. D., Nosek, B. A., & Mellott, D. S. (2002). A unified theory of implicit attitudes, stereotypes, self-esteem, and self-concept. *Psychological Review, 109*, 3–25.

Greenwald, A. G., & Farnham, S. D. (2000). Using the Implicit Association Test to measure self-esteem and self-concept. *Journal of Personality and Social Psychology, 79*, 1022–1038.

Greenwald, A. G., Oakes, M. A., Hoffman, H. G. (2003). Targets of discrimination: Effects of race on responses to weapons holders. *Journal of Experimental Social Psychology, 39*, 399–405.

Griffitt, W., & Guay, P. (1969). "Object" evaluation and conditioned affect. *Journal of Experimental Research in Personality, 4*, 1–8.

Grigorenko, E. L. (2002). In search of the genetic engram of personality. In D. Cervone & W. Mischel (Eds.), *Advances in personality science* (pp. 29–82). New York: Guilford Press.

Grilly, D. M. (1989). *Drugs and human behavior*. Boston: Allyn & Bacon.

Grolnick, W. S., & Ryan, R. M. (1989). Parent styles associated with children's self-regulation and competence in school. *Journal of Educational Psychology, 81*, 143–154.

Gross, J. J. (1998). Antecedent- and response-focused emotion regulation: Divergent consequences for experience, expression, and physiology. *Journal of Personality and Social Psychology, 74*, 224–237.

Gross, J. J., & John, O. P. (2003). Individual differences in two emotion regulation processes: Implications for affect, relationships, and well-being. *Journal of Personality and Social Psychology, 85*, 348–362.

Grossberg, J. M. (1964). Behavior therapy: A review. *Psychological Bulletin, 62*, 73–88.

Grunbaum, A. (1984). *The foundations of psychoanalysis*. Berkeley: University of California Press.

Guilford, J. P. (1959). *Personality*. New York: McGraw-Hill.

Gunnar, M. R., & Donzella, B. (2002). Social regulation of the cortisol levels in early human development. *Psychoneuroendocrinology, 27*, 199–220.

Gunnar, M. R., Larson, M. C., Hertsgaard, L., Harris, M. L., & Brodersen, L. (1992). The stressfulness of separation among nine-month-old infants: Effects of social context variables and infant temperament. *Child Development, 63*, 290–303.

Guthrie, E. R. (1935). *The psychology of learning*. New York: Harper & Brothers.

Habermas, T., & Bluck, S. (2000). Getting a life: The emergence of the life story in adolescence. *Psychological Bulletin, 126*, 748–769.

Hair, E. C., & Graziano, W. G. (2003). Self-esteem, personality and achievement in high school: A prospective longitudinal study in Texas. *Journal of Personality, 71*, 971–994.

Halverson, C. (1971a). Longitudinal relations between newborn tactile threshold, preschool barrier behaviors, and early school-age imagination and verbal development. Newborn and preschooler: Organization of behavior and relations between period. *SRCD Monograph, 36*.

Halverson, C. (1971b, September). *Relation of preschool verbal communication to later verbal intelligence, social maturity, and distribution of play bouts*. Paper presented at the annual meeting of the American Psychological Association, Washington, D.C.

Hamer, D., & Copeland, P. (1998). *Living with our genes: Why they matter more than you think*. New York: Doubleday.

Hampson, S. E., & Goldberg, L. R. (2006). A first large cohort study of personality trait stability over the 40 years between elementary school and midlife. *Journal of Personality and Social Psychology, 91*, 763–779.

Harackiewicz, J. M., Manderlink, G., & Sansone, C. (1984). Rewarding pinball wizardry: Effects of evaluation and cue on intrinsic motivation. *Journal of Personality and Social Psychology, 47*, 287–300.

Haring, T. G., & Breen, C. J. (1992). A peer-mediated social network intervention to enhance the social integration of persons with moderate and severe disabilities. *Journal of Applied Behavior Analysis, 25*, 319–333.

Harlow, R. E., & Cantor, N. (1996). Still participating after all these years: A study of life task participation in later life. *Journal of Personality and Social Psychology, 71*, 1235–1249.

Harmon-Jones, E., & Allen, J. J. (1997). Behavioral activation sensitivity and resting frontal EEG asymmetry: Covariation of putative indicators related to risk for mood disorders. *Journal of Abnormal Psychology, 106*, 159–163.

Harris, F. R., Johnston, M. K., Kelley, S. C., & Wolf, M. M. (1964). Effects of positive social reinforcement on regressed crawling of a nursery school child. *Journal of Educational Psychology, 55*, 35–41.

Hart, C. L., Haney, M., Foltin, R. W., & Fischman, M. W. (2000). Alternative reinforcers differentially modify cocaine self-administration by humans. *Behavioral Pharmacology, 11*, 87–91.

Hart, C.L., Ward, A.S., Haney, M., Foltin, R.W., & Fischman, M.W. (2001). Methamphetamine self-administration by humans. *Psychopharmacology, 157*, 75–81.

Harter, S. (1983). Developmental perspectives on the self-system. In E. M. Hetherington (Ed.), P. H. Mussen (Series Ed.), *Handbook of child psychology* (Vol. 4, pp. 275–385). New York: Wiley.

Harter, S. (1999). *The construction of the self: A developmental perspective*. New York: Guilford Press.

Hartshorne, H., & May, A. (1928). *Studies in the nature of character: Vol. 1. Studies in deceit*. New York: Macmillan.

Hauser, M. D. (2006). *Moral minds: How nature designed our universal sense of right and wrong*. New York: Ecco.

Hawkins, R. P., Peterson, R. F., Schweid, E., & Bijou, S. W. (1966). Behavior therapy in the home: Amelioration of problem parent–child relations with the parent in a therapeutic role. *Journal of Experimental Child Psychology, 4*, 99–107.

Hazan, C., & Shaver, P. (1987). Romantic love conceptualized as an attachment process. *Journal of Personality and Social Psychology, 52*, 511–524.

Hazan, C., & Shaver, P. R. (1994). Attachment as an organizational framework for research on close relationships. *Psychological Inquiry, 5*, 1–22.

Hebb, D. O. (1955). Drives and the CNS (conceptual nervous system). *Psychological Review, 62*, 243–259.

Heckhausen, H. (1969). Achievement motive research: Current problems and some contributions towards a general theory of motivation. In W. J. Arnold (Ed.), *Nebraska Symposium on Motivation* (pp. 103–174). Lincoln: Nebraska University Press.

Heider, F. (1958). *The psychology of interpersonal relations*. New York: Wiley.

Heine, S. J., Lehman, D. R., Markus, H. R., & Kitayama, S. (1999). Is there a universal need for positive self-regard? *Psychological Review, 106*, 766–794.

Heitzman, A. J., & Alimena, M. J. (1991). Differential reinforcement to reduce disruptive behaviors in a blind boy with a learning disability. *Journal of Visual Impairment and Blindness, 85*, 176–177.

Heller, W., Schmidtke, J. I., Nitschke, J. B., Koven, N. S., & Miller, G. A. (2002). States, traits, and symptoms: Investigating the neural correlates of emotion, personality, and psychopathology. In D. Cervone & W. Mischel (Eds.), *Advances in personality science* (pp. 106–126). New York: Guilford Press.

Henderson, V., & Dweck, C. S. (1990). Adolescence and achievement. In S. Feldman & G. Elliot (Eds.), *At the threshold: Adolescent development* (pp. 308–329). Cambridge, MA: Harvard University Press.

Herman, C. P. (1992). Review of W. H. Sheldon "Varieties of Temperament." *Contemporary Psychology, 37*, 525–528.

Hershberger, S. L., Lichtenstein, P., & Knox, S. S. (1994). Genetic and environmental influences on perceptions or organizational climate. *Journal of Applied Psychology, 79*, 24–33.

Hetherington, E. M., & Clingempeel, W. G. (1992). Coping with marital transitions: A family systems perspective. *Monographs of the Society for Research in Child Development*, Nos. 2–3, Serial No. 277.

Higgins, E. T. (1987). Self-discrepancy: A theory relating self and affect. *Psychological Review, 94*, 319–340.

Higgins, E. T. (1990). Personality, social psychology, and person–situation relations: Standards and knowledge activation as a common language. In L. A. Pervin (Ed.), *Handbook of personality: Theory and research* (pp. 301–338). New York: Guilford Press.

Higgins, E. T. (1996a). Ideals, oughts, and regulatory focus: Affect and motivation from distinct pains and pleasures.

In P. M. Gollwitzer & J. A. Bargh (Eds.), *The psychology of action: Linking cognition and motivation to behavior* (pp. 91–114). New York: Guilford Press.

Higgins, E. T. (1996b). Knowledge activation: Accessibility, applicability, and salience. In E. T. Higgins & A. W. Kruglanski (Eds.), *Social psychology: Handbook of basic principles* (pp. 133–168). New York: Guilford Press.

Higgins, E. T. (1997). Beyond pleasure and pain. *American Psychologist, 52*, 1280–1300.

Higgins, E. T. (1998). Promotion and prevention: Regulatory focus as a motivation principle. In M. P. Zanna (Ed.), *Advances in experimental social psychology* (Vol. 30, pp. 1–46). New York: Academic Press.

Higgins, E. T., King, G. A., & Mavin, G. H. (1982). Individual construct accessibility and subjective impressions and recall. *Journal of Personality and Social Psychology, 43*, 35–47.

Higgins, E. T., & Kruglanski, A. W. (Eds.). (1996). *Social psychology: Handbook of basic principles*. New York: Guilford Press.

Higgins, S. T., Heil, S. H., & Lussier, J.P. (2004). Clinical implications of reinforcement as a determinant of substance use disorders. *Annual Review of Psychology, 55*, 431–461.

Hogan, R. T. (1991). Personality and personality measurement. In M. D. Dunnette & L. M. Hough (Eds.), *Handbook of industrial and organizational psychology* (2nd ed., Vol. 2, pp. 873–919). Palo Alto, CA: Consulting Psychologists Press.

Holahan, C. J., & Moos, R. N. (1990). Life stressors, resistance factors, and improved psychological functioning: An extension of the stress resistance paradigm. *Journal of Personality and Social Psychology, 58*, 909–917.

Hollander, E., Liebowitz, M. R., Gorman, J. M., Cohen, B., Fyer, A., & Klein, D. F. (1989). Cortisol and sodium lactate-induced panic. *Archives of General Psychiatry, 46*, 135–140.

Holmes, D. S. (1974). Investigations of repression: Differential recall of material experimentally or naturally associated with ego threat. *Psychological Bulletin, 81*, 632–653.

Holmes, D. S. (1992). The evidence for repression: An examination of sixty years of research. In J. L. Singer (Ed.), *Repression and dissociation* (pp. 85–102). Chicago: University of Chicago Press.

Holmes, D. S., & Houston, K. B. (1974). Effectiveness of situation redefinition and affective isolation in coping with stress. *Journal of Personality and Social Psychology, 29*, 212–218.

Holmes, D. S., & Schallow, J. R. (1969). Reduced recall after ego threat: Repression or response competition? *Journal of Personality and Social Psychology, 13*, 145–152.

Holmes, J. (1993). *John Bowlby and attachment theory*. New York: Routledge.

Hong, Y., Benet-Martinez, V., Chiu, C., & Morris, M. W. (2003). Boundaries of cultural influence: Construct activation as a mechanism for cultural differences in social perception. *Journal of Cross-Cultural Psychology, 34*, 453–464.

Hong, Y., Chan, G., Chiu, C., Wong, R. Y. M., Hansen, I. G., Lee, S., Tong, Y., & Fu, H. (2003). How are social identities linked to self-conception and intergroup orientation? The moderating effect of implicit theories. *Journal of Personality and Social Psychology, 85*, 1147–1160.

Hong, Y., & Mallorie, L. M. (2004). A dynamic constructivist approach to culture: Lessons learned from personality psychology. *Journal of Research in Personality, 38*, 59–67.

Horowitz, L. M., Rosenberg, S. E., Ureno, G., Kalehzan, B. M., & O'Halloran, P. (1989). Psychodynamic formulation, consensual response method, and interpersonal problems. *Journal of Consulting and Clinical Psychology, 57*, 599–606.

Howes, D. H., & Solomon, R. L. (1951). Visual duration threshold as a function of word-probability. *Journal of Experimental Psychology, 41*, 401–410.

Howland, R. H. (1991). Pharmacotherapy of dysthymia: A review. *Journal of Clinical Psychopharmacology, 11*, 83–92.

Hoyenga, K. B., & Hoyenga, K. T. (1993). *Gender-related differences: Origins and outcomes*. Boston: Allyn & Bacon.

Hoyle, R. H., Kernis, M. H., Leary, M. R., & Baldwin, M. (1999). *Selfhood: Identity, esteem, regulation*. Boulder, CO: Academic Press.

Huber, G. L., Sorrentino, R. M., Davidson, M. A., & Epplier, R. (1992). Uncertainty orientation and cooperative learning: Individual differences within and across cultures. *Learning and Individual Differences, 4*, 1–24.

Humphreys, M. S., & Kashima, Y. (2002). Connectionism and self: Distributed representational systems and their implications for self and identity. In Y. Kashima & M. Foddy (Eds.), *Self and identity: Personal, social, and symbolic* (pp. 27–54). Mahwah, NJ: Erlbaum.

Ickovics, J. (1997, August). *Smithsonian seminar on health and well-being*, sponsored by the Society for the Psychological Study of Social Issues and the American Psychological Society conducted at the Ninth Annual Conference of the American Psychological Society, Washington, DC.

Inkeles, A. (1996). *National character: A psycho-social study*. New Brunswick, NJ: Transaction.

Isen, A. M., Niedenthal, P. M., & Cantor, N. (1992). An influence of positive affect on social categorization. *Motivation and Emotion, 16*, 65–78.

Jaccard, J. J. (1974). Predicting social behavior from personality traits. *Journal of Research in Personality, 7*, 358–367.

Jackson, D. N., & Paunonen, S. V. (1980). Personality structure and assessment. In M. R. Rosenzweig & L. W. Porter (Eds.), *Annual review of psychology* (Vol. 31, pp. 503–551). Palo Alto, CA: Annual Reviews.

Jacobs, W, J., & Nadel, L. (1985). Stress-induced recovery of fears and phobias. *Psychological Review, 92*, 512–531.

Jahoda, M. (1958). *Current concepts of positive mental health*. New York: Basic Books.

James, W. (1890). *The principles of psychology* (Vols. 1 & 2). New York: Holt.

James, W. (1903). *The varieties of religious experience*. New York: Longmans.

Jang, K. L. (1993). *A behavioral genetic analysis of personality, personality disorder, the environment, and the search for sources of nonshared environmental influences*. Unpublished doctoral dissertation, University of Western Ontario, London, Ontario.

Janis, I. L. (1971). *Stress and frustration*. New York: Harcourt.

Jasper, H. (1941). Electroencephalography. In W. Penfield & T. Erickson (Eds.), *Epilepsy and cerebral localization* (pp. 380–454). Springfield, IL: Charles C. Thomas.

Jersild, A. (1931). Memory for the pleasant as compared with the unpleasant. *Journal of Experimental Psychology, 14*, 284–288.

John, O. P. (1990). The Big-Five factor taxonomy: Dimensions of personality in the natural language and questionnaires. In L. A. Pervin (Ed.), *Handbook of personality: Theory and research* (pp. 66–100). New York: Guilford Press.

John, O. P. (2001, February). *What is so big about the Big Five, anyway?* Invited address presented at the 2nd annual meeting of the Society of Personality and Social Psychology, San Antonio, TX.

John, O. P., Caspi, A., Robins, R. W., Moffitt, T. E., & Stouthamer-Loeber, M. (1994). The "Little Five": Exploring the nomological network of the five-factor model of personality in adolescent boys. *Child Development, 65*, 160–178.

John, O. P., Hampson, S. E., & Goldberg, L. R. (1991). The basic level in personality-trait hierarchies: Studies of traits use and accessibility in different contexts. *Journal of Personality and Social Psychology, 60*, 348–361.

Johnson, W., McGue, M., Krueger, R. F., & Bouchard, T. J. Jr.. (2004). Marriage and personality: A genetic analysis. *Journal of Personality and Social Psychology, 86*, 285–294.

Jones, A. (1966). Information deprivation in humans. In B. A. Maher (Ed.), *Progress in experimental personality research* (Vol. 3, pp. 241–307). New York: Academic Press.

Jourard, S. M. (1967). Experimenter-subject dialogue: A paradigm for a humanistic science of psychology. In J. Bugental (Ed.), *Challenges of humanistic psychology* (pp. 109–116). New York: McGraw-Hill.

Jourard, S. M. (1974). *Healthy personality: An approach from the viewpoint of humanistic psychology*. New York: Macmillan.

Joy, V. L. (1963, August). *Repression-sensitization and interpersonal behavior*. Paper presented at the annual meeting of the American Psychological Association, Philadelphia.

Jung, C. G. (1963). *Memories, dreams, reflections*. New York: Pantheon.

Jung, C. G. (1964). *Man and his symbols*. Garden City, NY: Doubleday.

Kagan, J. (1964). The acquisition and significance of sex typing and sex role identity. In M. Hoffman & L. Hoffman (Eds.), *Review of child development research* (Vol. 1, pp. 137–167). New York: Russell Sage.

Kagan, J. (2003). Biology, context, and developmental inquiry. *Annual Review of Psychology, 54*, 1–23.

Kagan, J. (2006). *An argument for mind*. New Haven, CT: Yale University Press.

Kagan, J., Reznick, J. S., & Snidman, N. (1988). Biological bases of childhood shyness. *Science, 240*, 167–171.

Kagan, J., & Snidman, N. (1991). Infant predictors of inhibited and uninhibited profiles. *Psychological Science, 2*, 40–44.

Kahneman, D., & Snell, J. (1990). Predicting utility. In R. M. Hogarth (Ed.), *Handbook of personality: Theory and research* (pp. 66–100). New York: Guilford Press.

Kammrath, L. K., Mendoza-Denton, R., & Mischel, W. (2005). Incorporating *if ... then ...* personality signatures in person perception: Beyond the person–situation dichotomy. *Journal of Personality and Social Psychology, 88*, 605–618.

Kamps, D. M., Leonard, B. R., Vernon, S., Dugan, E. P., Delquadri, C., Gershon, B., et al. (1992). Teaching social skills to students with autism to increase peer interactions in an integrated first-grade classroom. *Journal of Applied Behavior Analysis, 25*, 281–288.

Kaplan, B. (1954). *A study of Rorschach responses in four cultures*. Cambridge, MA: Harvard University.

Kardiner, A. (1945). *Psychological frontiers of society*. New York: Columbia University Press.

Karoly, P. (1980). Operant methods. In F. H. Kanfer & A. P. Goldstein (Eds.), *Helping people change: A textbook of methods* (2nd ed.). Elmsford, NY: Pergamon Press.

Kashima, Y. (2001). Culture and social cognition: Toward a social psychology of cultural dynamics. In D. Matsumoto

(Ed.), *The handbook of culture and psychology* (pp. 325–360). New York: Oxford University Press.

Kashima, Y., Kashima, E., Farsides, T., Kim, U., Strack, F., & Werth, L. et al. (2004). Culture and context-sensitive self: The amount and meaning of context-sensitivity of phenomenal self differ across cultures. *Self and Identity, 3*, 125–141.

Kayser, A., Robinson, D. S., Yingling, K., Howard, D. B., Corcella, J., & Laux, D. (1988). The influence of panic attacks on response to phenelzine and amitriptyline in depressed outpatients. *Journal of Clinical Psychopharmacology, 8*, 246–253.

Kazdin, A. E. (1974). Effects of covert modeling and model reinforcement on assertive behavior. *Journal of Abnormal Psychology, 83*, 240–252.

Kazdin, A. E., & Wilson, G. T. (1978). *Evaluation of behavior therapy: Issues, evidence and research strategies*. Cambridge, MA: Ballinger.

Kelley, H. H. (1973). The processes of casual attribution. *American Psychologist, 28*, 107–128.

Kelley, H. H., Holmes, J. W., Kerr, N. L., Reis, H. T., Rusbult, C. E., & Van Lange, P. A. M. (2003). *An atlas of interpersonal situations*. Cambridge University Press.

Kelley, H. H., & Stahelski, A. J. (1970). The social interaction basis of cooperators' and competitors' beliefs about others. *Journal of Personality and Social Psychology, 16*, 66–91.

Kelly, E. L. (1955). Consistency of the adult personality. *American Psychologist, 10*, 659–681.

Kelly, G. A. (1955). *The psychology of personal constructs* (Vols. 1 & 2). New York: Norton.

Kelly, G. A. (1958). Man's construction of his alternatives. In G. Lindzey (Ed.), *Assessment of human motives* (pp. 33–64). New York: Holt, Rinehart and Winston.

Kelly, G. A. (1962). Quoted in B. A. Maher (Ed.), (1979), *Clinical psychology and personality: The selected papers of George Kelly*. Huntington, NY: Kreiger.

Kelly, G. A. (1966). Quoted in B. A. Maher (Ed.), (1979), *Clinical psychology and personality: The selected papers of George Kelly*. Huntington, NY: Kreiger.

Kendall, P. C., & Panichelli-Mindel, S. M. (1995). Cognitive-behavioral treatments. *Journal of Abnormal Child Psychology, 26*, 107–124.

Kendler, K. S., Karkowski, L. M., & Prescott, C. A. (1999). Causal relationship between stressful life events and the onset of major depression. *American Journal of Psychiatry, 156*, 837–841.

Kenrick, D. T., & Funder, D. C. (1988). Profiting from controversy: Lessons from the person-situation debate. *American Psychologist, 43*, 23–34.

Kenrick, D. T., Sadalla, E. K., Groth, G., & Trost, M. R. (1990). Evolution, traits, and the stages of human courtship: Qualifying the parental investment model. *Journal of Personality, 58*, 97–116.

Kernberg, O. (1976). *Object relations theory and clinical psychoanalysis*. New York: Jason Aronson.

Kernberg, O. (1984). *Severe personality disorders*. New Haven, CT: Yale University Press.

Kessler, R. C. (1997). The effects of stressful life events on depression. *Annual Review of Psychology, 48*, 191–214.

Kihlstrom, J. F. (1999). The psychological unconscious. In L. A. Pervin & O. P. John (Eds.), *Handbook of personality: Theory and research* (2nd ed., pp. 424–442). New York: Guilford Press.

Kihlstrom, J. F. (2003). Implicit methods in social psychology. In C. Sansone, C. C. Morf, & A. Panter (Eds.), *Handbook of methods in social psychology* (pp. 195–212). Thousand Oaks, CA: Sage.

Kihlstrom, J. F., Barnhardt, T. M., & Tataryn, D. J. (1992). The psychological unconscious: Found, lost, and regained. *American Psychologist, 47*, 788–791.

Kim, M. P., & Rosenberg, S. (1980). Comparison of two-structured models of implicit personality theory. *Journal of Personality and Social Psychology, 38*, 375–389.

Kitayama, S. (2002). Culture and basic psychological processes—toward a system view of culture: Comment on Oyserman et al. (2002). *Psychological Bulletin, 128*, 89–96.

Kitayama, S., & Markus, H. R. (1999). Yin and yang of the Japanese self: The cultural psychology of personality coherence. In D. Cervone & Y. Shoda (Eds.), *The coherence of personality: Social-cognitive bases of consistency, variability, and organization* (pp. 242–302). New York: Guilford Press.

Kitayama, S., Markus, H. R., Matsumoto, H., & Norasakkunkit, V. (1997). Individual and collective processes in the construction of the self: Self-enhancement in the United States and self-criticism in Japan. *Journal of Personality and Social Psychology, 72*, 1245–1267.

Klein, D. F., Gittelman, R., Quitkin, F., & Rifkin, A. (1980). *Diagnosis and drug treatment of psychiatric disorders: Adults and children* (2nd ed.). Baltimore: Williams & Wilkins.

Klein, D. F., & Klein, H. M. (1989). The definition and psychopharmacology of spontaneous panic and phobia: A critical review I. In P. J. Tyrer (Ed.), *Psychopharmacology of anxiety* (pp. 135–162). New York: Oxford University Press.

Klohnen, E. C., & Bera, S. (1998). Behavioral and experiential patterns of avoidantly and securely attached women across adulthood: A 31-year longitudinal perspective. *Journal of Personality and Social Psychology, 74*, 211–223.

Knafo, A., & Plomin, R. (2006). Parental discipline and affection and children's prosocial behavior: Genetic and environmental links. *Journal of Personality and Social Psychology, 90*, 147–164.

Kobak, R. R., & Sceery, A. (1988). Attachment in late adolescence: Working models, affect regulation, and representations of self and others. *Child Development, 59*, 135–146.

Koestner, R., & McClelland, D. C. (1990). Perspectives on competence motivation. In L. A. Pervin (Ed.), *Handbook of personality: Theory and research* (pp. 549–575). New York: Guilford Press.

Kohut, H. (1971). *The analysis of the self*. New York: International Universities Press.

Kohut, H. (1977). *The restoration of the self*. New York: International Universities Press.

Kohut, H. (1980). *Advances in self psychology*. New York: International Universities Press.

Kohut, H. (1984). *How does analysis cure?* Chicago: University of Chicago Press.

Kolb, B., & Whishaw, I. Q. (1998). Brain plasticity and behavior. *Annual Review of Psychology, 49*, 43–64.

Komarraju, M., & Karau, S. J. (2005). The relationship between the Big Five personality traits and academic motivation. *Personality and Individual Differences, 39*, 557–567.

Koriat, A., Melkman, R., Averill, J. R., & Lazarus, R. S. (1972). The self-control of emotional reactions to a stressful film. *Journal of Personality, 40*, 601–619.

Kosslyn, S. M, Cacioppo, J. T, Davidson, R. J, Hugdahl, K., Lovallo, W. R, Spiegel, D., et al. (2002). Bridging psychology and biology: The analysis of individuals in groups. *American Psychologist, 57*, 341–351.

Krahe, B. (1990). *Situation cognition and coherence in personality: An individual-centered approach*. Cambridge, UK: Cambridge University Press.

Kramer, P. D. (1993). *Listening to Prozac*. New York: Viking.

Kross, E., Ayduk, O., & Mischel, W. (2005). When asking "*why*" doesn't hurt: Distinguishing rumination from reflective processing of negative emotions. *Psychological Science, 16*, 709–715.

Ksir, C., Hart, C.L., & Ray, O. (2005). *Drugs, society, and human behavior* (11th ed.). New York: McGraw-Hill.

Kuhl, J. (1984). Volitional aspects of achievement motivation and learned helplessness: Toward a comprehensive theory of action control. In B. A. Maher (Ed.), *Progress in experimental personality research* (Vol. 13, pp. 91–171). New York: Academic Press.

Kuhl, J. (1985). From cognition to behavior: Perspectives for future research on action control. In J. Kuhl (Ed.), *Action control from cognition to behavior* (pp. 267–275). New York: Springer-Verlag.

Kuhnen, C., & Knutson, B. (2005). The neural basis of financial risk taking. *Neuron, 47*, 763–770.

Kunda, Z. (1990). The case for motivated reasoning. *Psychological Bulletin, 108*, 480–498.

Kunda, Z. (1999). *Social cognition: Making sense of people*. Cambridge, MA: MIT Press.

Lader, M. (1980). *Introduction to psychopharmacology*. Kalamazoo, MI: Upjohn.

LaHoste, G. J., Swanson, J. M., Wigal, S. S., Glabe, C., Wigal, T., King, N., et al. (1996). Dopamine D4 receptor gene polymorphism is associated with attention deficit hyperactivity disorder. *Molecular Psychiatry, 1*, 128–131.

Laing, R. D. (1965). *The divided self: An existential study in sanity and madness*. New York: Penguin.

Lamiell, J. T. (1997). Individuals and the differences between them. In R. Hogan, J. Johnson, & S. Briggs (Eds.), *Handbook of personality psychology* (pp. 117–141). San Diego, CA: Academic Press.

Landfield, A. W., Stern, M., & Fjeld, S. (1961). Social conceptual processes and change in students undergoing psychotherapy. *Psychological Reports, 8*, 63–68.

Lang, P. J., & Lazovik, A. D. (1963). Experimental desensitization of a phobia. *Journal of Abnormal and Social Psychology, 66*, 519–525.

Langer, E. J. (1975). The illusion of control. *Journal of Personality and Social Psychology, 32*, 311–328.

Langer, E. J. (1977). The psychology of chance. *Journal for the Theory of Social Behavior, 7*, 185–207.

Langer, E. J., Janis, I. L., & Wolfer, J. A. (1975). *Reduction of psychological stress in surgical patients*. Unpublished manuscript, Yale University.

Larsen, R. J., Diener, E., & Emmons, R. A. (1986). Affect intensity and reactions to daily life. *Journal of Personality and Social Psychology, 51*, 803–814.

Larsen, R. J., & Kasimatis, M. (1990). Individual differences in entrainment of mood to the weekly calendar. *Journal of Personality and Social Psychology, 58*, 164–171.

Larsen, R. J., & Kasimatis, M. (1991). Day-to-day physical symptoms: Individual differences in the occurrence, duration, and emotional concomitants of minor daily illnesses. *Journal of Personality, 59*, 387–424.

Lawson, G. W., & Cooperrider, C. A. (1988). *Clinical psychopharmacology: A practical reference for nonmedical psychotherapists*. Rockville, MD: Aspen.

Lazar, S., Bush, G., Gollub, R. L., Fricchione, G. L., Khalsa, G., & Benson, H. (2000). Functional brain mapping of the relaxation response and meditation. *NeuroReport, 11*, 1581–1585.

Lazarus, A. A. (1961). Group therapy of phobic disorders by systematic desensitization. *Journal of Abnormal and Social Psychology, 63*, 504–510.

Lazarus. A. A. (1963). The treatment of chronic frigidity by systematic desensitization. *Journal of Nervous and Mental Diseases, 136*, 272–278.

Lazarus, R. S. (1976). *Patterns of adjustment*. New York: McGraw-Hill.

Lazarus, R. S. (1990). Theory-based stress measurement. *Psychological Inquiry, 1*, 3–13.

Lazarus, R. S. (2006). Emotions and interpersonal relationships: Toward a person-centered conceptualization of emotions and coping. *Journal of Personality, 74*, 9–46.

Lazarus, R. S., Eriksen, C. W., & Fonda, C. P. (1951). Personality dynamics and auditory perceptual recognition. *Journal of Personality, 58*, 113–122.

Lazarus, R. S., & Folkman, S. (1984). *Stress, appraisal, and coping*. New York: Springer.

Lazarus, R. S., & Longo, N. (1953). The consistency of psychological defense against threat. *Journal of Abnormal and Social Psychology, 48*, 495–499.

Leary, M. R. (2002). The self as a source of relational difficulties. *Self and Identity, 1*, 137–142.

Leary, M. R, & Downs, D. L. (1995). Interpersonal functions of the self-esteem motive: The self-esteem system as a sociometer. In M. H. Kernis (Ed.), *Efficacy, agency, and self-esteem* (pp. 123–144). New York: Kluwer Academic/Plenum Press.

Leary, M. R., & Tangney, J. P. (Eds.). (2003). *Handbook of self and identity*. New York: Guilford Press.

Leary, T. (1957). *Interpersonal diagnosis of personality*. New York: Ronald Press.

Leary, T., Litwin, G. H., & Metzner, R. (1963). Reactions to psilocybin administered in a supportive environment. *Journal of Nervous and Mental Diseases, 137*, 561–573.

LeDoux, J. (1996). *The emotional brain*. New York: Simon & Schuster.

LeDoux, J. E. (2001). *Synaptic self*. New York: Viking.

Lemm, K., Shoda, Y., & Mischel, W. (1995). Can teleological behaviorism account for the effects of instructions on self-control without invoking cognition? *Behavioral and Brain Sciences, 18*, 135.

Lepper, M. R., Greene, D., & Nisbett, R. E. (1973). Undermining children's intrinsic interest with extrinsic reward: A test of the "overjustification" hypothesis. *Journal of Personality and Social Psychology, 28*, 129–137.

Lesch, K., Bengel, D., Heils, A., & Sabol, S. Z. (1996). Association of anxiety-related traits with a polymorphism in the serotonin transporter gene regulatory region. *Science, 274*, 1527–1531.

Letzring, T. D., Block, J., & Funder, D. C. (2005). Ego-control and ego-resiliency: Generalization of self-report scales based on personality descriptions from acquaintances, clinicians, and the self. *Journal of Research in Personality, 39*, 395–422.

Levine, R. (1991). *New developments in pharmacology* (Vol. 8, pp. 1–3). New York: Gracie Square Hospitals Publication.

Levy, S. R., Ayduk, O., & Downey, G. (2001). Rejection sensitivity: Implications for interpersonal and inter-group processes. In M. Leary (Ed.), *Interpersonal rejection* (pp. 251–289). New York: Oxford University Press.

Levy, S. R., Stroessner, S. J., & Dweck, C. S. (1998). Stereotype formation and endorsement: The role of implicit theories. *Journal of Personality and Social Psychology, 74*, 1421–1436.

Levy, S. R., West, T., Ramirez, L., & Karafantis, D. M. (2006). The Protestant work ethic: A lay theory with dual intergroup implications. *Group Processes and Intergroup Relations, 9*, 95–115.

Lewicki, P., Hill, T., & Czyzewska, M. (1992). Nonconscious acquisition of information. *American Psychologist, 47*, 796–801.

Lewin, K. (1935). *A dynamic theory of personality*. New York: McGraw-Hill.

Lewin, K. (1936). *Principles of topological psychology*. New York: McGraw-Hill.

Lewin, K. (1951). *Field theory in social science; selected theoretical papers* (D. Cartwright, Ed.). New York: Harper & Row.

Lewinsohn, P. M. (1975). The behavioral study and treatment of depression. In M. Hersen (Ed.), *Progress in behavior modification* (pp. 19–63). New York: Academic Press.

Lewinsohn, P. M., Clarke, G. N., Hops, H., & Andrews, A. (1990). Cognitive-behavioral treatment for depressed adolescents. *Behavior Therapy, 21*, 385–401.

Lewinsohn, P. M., Mischel, W., Chaplin, W., & Barton, R. (1980). Social competence and depression: The role of illusory self-perceptions. *Journal of Abnormal Psychology, 89*, 203–212.

Lewis, M. (1969). Infants' responses to facial stimuli during the first year of life. *Developmental Psychology, 1*, 75–86.

Lewis, M. (1990). Self-knowledge and social development in early life. In L. A. Pervin (Ed.), *Handbook of personality: Theory and research* (pp. 486–526). New York: Guilford Press.

Lewis, M. (1999). On the development of personality. In L. A. Pervin & O. P. John (Eds.), *Handbook of personality: Theory and research* (2nd ed., pp. 327–346). New York: Guilford Press.

Lewis, M. (2002). Models of development. In D. Cervone & W. Mischel (Eds.), *Advances in personality science* (pp. 153–176). New York: Guildford Press.

Lewis, M., & Haviland-Jones, J. M. (Eds.). (2000). *Handbook of emotions* (2nd ed.). New York: Guilford Press.

Lewontin, R. (2000). *The triple helix: Gene, organism, and environment*. Cambridge, MA: Harvard University Press.

Lieberman, M. A., Yalom, I. D., & Miles, M. B. (1973). *Encounter groups: First facts*. New York: Basic Books.

Lieberman, M. D. (2007). Social cognitive neuroscience: A review of core processes. *Annual Review of Psychology, 58*, 259–289.

Liebert, R. M., & Allen, K. M. (1967). *The effects of rule structure and reward magnitude on the acquisition and adoption of self-reward criteria*. Unpublished manuscript, Vanderbilt University, Nashville, TN.

Lief, H. I., & Fox, R. S. (1963). Training for "detached concern" in medical students. In H. I. Lief, V. F. Lief, & N. R. Lief (Eds.), *The psychological basis of medical practice* (pp. 12–35). New York: Harper.

Lietaer, G. (1993). Authenticity, congruence, and transparency. In D. Brazier (Ed.), *Beyond Carl Rogers* (pp. 17–46). London: Constable.

Lindzey, G., & Runyan, W. M. (2007). *A history of psychology in autobiography* (Vol. 9). Washington, DC: American Psychological Association.

Linscheid, T. R., & Meinhold, P. (1990). The controversy over aversives: Basic operant research and the side effects of punishment. In A. C. Repp & N. N. Singh (Eds.), *Perspectives on the use of nonaversive and aversive interventions for persons with developmental disabilities* (pp. 435–450). Sycamore, IL: Sycamore.

Linton, R. (1945). *The cultural background of personality*. New York: Appleton.

Linville, P. W., & Carlston, D. E. (1994). Social cognition of the self. In P. G. Devine, D. C. Hamilton, & T. M. Ostrom (Eds.), *Social cognition: Impact on social psychology* (pp. 143–193). New York: Academic Press.

Loehlin, J. C. (1992). *Genes and environment in personality development*. Newbury Park, CA: Sage.

Loehlin, J. C., McCrae, R. R., Costa, P. T. J., & John, O. P. (1998). Heritabilities of common and measure-specific components of the big five personality factors. *Journal of Research in Personality, 32*, 431–453.

Loehlin, J. C., & Nichols, R. C. (1976). *Heredity, environment, and personality: A study of 850 sets of twins*. Austin: University of Texas Press.

Loftus, E. F. (1993). The reality of repressed memories. *American Psychologist, 48*, 518–537.

Loftus, E. F. (1994). The repressed memory controversy. *American Psychologist, 49*, 443–445.

Loftus, E. F., & Klinger, M. R. (1992). Is the unconscious smart or dumb? *American Psychologist, 47*, 761–765.

Lott, A. J., & Lott, B. E. (1968). A learning theory approach to interpersonal attitudes. In A. G. Greenwald, T. C. Brock, & T. M. Ostrom (Eds.), *Psychological foundations of attitudes* (pp. 67–88). New York: Academic Press.

Lovaas, O. I., Berberich, J. P., Perloff, B. F., & Schaeffer, B. (1966). Acquisition of imitative speech by schizophrenic children. *Science, 151*, 705–707.

Lovaas, O. I., Berberich, J. P., Perloff, B. F., & Schaeffer, B. (1991). Acquisition of imitative speech by schizophrenic children. *Focus on Autistic Behavior, 6*, 1–5.

Luciano, M. Wainwright, M. A., Wright, M. J., & Martin, N. G. (2006). The heritability of conscientiousness facets and their relationship to IQ and academic achievement. *Personality and Individual Differences, 40*, 1189–1199.

Lyons, D. (1997). The feminine in the foundations of organizational psychology. *Journal of Applied Behavioral Science, 33*, 7–26.

Lyons, M. J., Goldberg, J., Eisen, S. A., True, W., Tsuang, M. T., Meyer, J. M., et al. (1993). Do genes influence exposure to trauma: A twin study of combat. *American Journal of Medical Genetics (Neuropsychiatric Genetics), 48*, 22–27.

Lyubomirsky, S., & Nolen-Hoeksema, S. (1993). Self-perpetuating properties of dysphoric rumination. *Journal of Personality and Social Psychology, 65*, 339–349.

Lyubomirsky, S., & Nolen-Hoeksema, S. (1995). Effects of self-focused rumination on negative thinking and interpersonal problem solving. *Journal of Personality and Social Psychology, 69*, 176–190.

Maccoby, E. E., & Jacklin, C. N. (1974). *The psychology of sex differences*. Stanford, CA: Stanford University Press.

MacDonald, K. (1998). Evolution, culture, and the Five-Factor Model. *Journal of Cross-Cultural Psychology, 29*, 119–149.

Madison, P. (1960). *Freud's concept of repression and defense: Its theoretical and observational language*. Minneapolis: University of Minnesota Press.

Magnusson, D. (1990). Personality development from an interactional perspective. In L. A. Pervin (Ed.), *Handbook of personality: Theory and research* (pp. 193–224). New York: Guilford Press.

Magnusson, D. (1999). Holistic interactionism: A perspective for research on personality development. In L. A. Pervin & O. P. John (Eds.), *Handbook of personality: Theory and research* (2nd ed., pp. 219–247). New York: Guilford Press.

Magnusson, D., & Endler, N. S. (1977). Interactional psychology: Present status and future prospects. In D. Magnusson & N. S. Endler (Eds.), *Personality at the crossroads: Current issues in interactional psychology* (pp. 3–31). Hillsdale, NJ: Erlbaum.

Maher, B. A. (1966). *Principles of psychotherapy: An experimental approach*. New York: McGraw-Hill.

Maher, B. A. (1979). *Clinical psychology and personality: The selected papers of George Kelly*. Huntington, NY: Wiley.

Main, M., Kaplan, N., & Cassidy, J. (1985). Security in infancy, childhood, and adulthood: A move to the level of representation. In I. Bretherton & E. Waters (Eds.), *Growing points in attachment theory and research. Monographs of the Society for Research in Child Development, 50* (209), 66–104.

Malmo, R. B. (1959). Activation: A neuropsychological dimension. *Psychological Review, 66*, 367–386.

Malmquist, C. P. (1986). Children who witness parental murder: Post traumatic aspects. *Journal of the American Academy of Child Psychiatry, 25*, 320–325.

Manke, B., McGuire, S., Reiss, D., Hetherington, E. M., & Plomin, R. (1995). Genetic contributions to children's extrafamilial social interactions: Teachers, friends, and peers. *Social Development, 4*, 238–256.

Marcia, J. E. (1966). Development and validation of ego identity status. *Journal of Personality and Social Psychology*, 3, 551–558.

Marcia, J. E. (1980). Identity in adolescence. In J. Adelson (Ed.), *Handbook of adolescent psychology* (pp. 159–187). New York: Wiley.

Marcus, G. (2004). *The birth of the mind*. New York: Basic Books.

Maricle, R. A., Kinzie, J. D., & Lewinsohn, P. (1988). Medication-associated depression: A two and one-half year follow-up of a community sample. *International Journal of Psychiatry in Medicine, 18*, 283–292.

Marks, I. M. (1987). *Fears, phobias, and rituals*. New York: Oxford University Press.

Marks, I. M., & Nesse, R. M. (1994). Fear and fitness: An evolutionary analysis of anxiety disorders. *Ethology and Sociobiology, 15*, 247–261.

Marks, J., Stauffacher, J. C., & Lyle, C. (1963). Predicting outcome in schizophrenia. *Journal of Abnormal and Social Psychology, 66*, 117–127.

Markus, H. (1977). Self-schemata and processing information about the self. *Journal of Personality and Social Psychology, 35*, 63–78.

Markus, H., & Cross, S. (1990). The interpersonal self. In L. A. Pervin (Ed.), *Handbook of personality: Theory and research* (pp. 576–608). New York: Guilford Press.

Markus, H. R., & Kitayama, S. (1991). Culture and the self: Implications for cognition, emotion, and motivation. *Psychological Review, 98*, 224–253.

Markus, H. R., & Kitayama, S. (1998). The cultural psychology of personality. *Journal of Cross-Cultural Psychology, 29*, 63–87.

Markus, H. R., Kitayama, S., & Heiman, R. J. (1996). Culture and basic psychological principles. In. E. T. Higgins & . A. W. Kruglanski (Eds.), *Social psychology: Handbook of basic principles* (pp. 857–913). New York: Guilford Press.

Markus, H., & Nurius, P. (1986). Possible selves. *American Psychologist, 41*, 954–969.

Martin, L. L., & Tesser, A. (1989). Toward a motivational and structural theory of ruminative thought. In J. S. Uleman & J. A. Bargh (Eds.), *Unintended thought* (pp. 306–323). New York: Guilford Press.

Martin, L. L., Tesser, A., & McIntosh, W. D. (1993). Wanting but not having: The effects of unattained goals on thoughts and feelings. In D. M. Wegner & J. Pennebaker (Eds.), *Handbook of mental control* (pp. 552–572). Englewood Cliffs, NJ: Prentice-Hall.

Martin, L. R., Friedman, H. S., Tucker, J. S., Tomlinson-Keasey, C., Criqui, M. H., & Schwartz, J. E. (2002). A life course perspective on childhood cheerfulness and its relation to mortality risk. *Personality and Social Psychology Bulletin, 28*, 1155–1165

Maslow, A. H. (1965). Some basic propositions of a growth and self-actualization psychology. In G. Lyndzey & C. Hall (Eds.), *Theories of personality: Primary sources and research* (pp. 307–316). New York: Wiley.

Maslow, A. H. (1968). *Toward a psychology of being* (2nd ed.). New York: Van Nostrand.

Maslow, A. H. (1971). *The farther reaches of human nature*. New York: Viking.

Matas, W. H., Arend, R. A., & Sroufe, L. A. (1978). Continuity of adaptation in the second year: The relationship between quality of attachment and later competence. *Child Development, 49*, 547–556.

Matthews, K. A. (1984). Assessment of type A, anger, and hostility in epidemiological studies of cardiovascular disease. In A. Ostfeld & E. Eaker (Eds.), *Measuring psychosocial variables in epidemiological studies of cardiovascular disease*. Bethesda, MD: National Institutes of Health.

Matute, H. (1994). Learned helplessness and superstitious behavior as opposite effects of uncontrollable reinforcement in humans. *Learning and Motivation, 25*, 216–232.

May, R. (1961). Existential psychology. In R. May (Ed.), *Existential psychology* (pp. 11–51). New York: Random House.

McAdams, D. P. (1990). Motives. In V. Derlega, B. Winstead, & W. Jones (Eds.), *Contemporary research in personality* (pp. 175–204). Chicago: Nelson Hall.

McAdams, D. P. (1992). The five-factor model in personality: A critical appraisal. *Journal of Personality, 60*, 329–361.

McAdams, D. P. (1995). What do we know when we know a person? *Journal of Personality, 63*, 365–396.

McAdams, D. P. (1999). Personal narratives and the life story. In L. A. Pervin & O. P. John (Eds.), *Handbook of personality: Theory and research* (2nd ed., pp. 478–500). New York: Guilford Press.

McAdams, D. P. (2005a). *The redemptive self: The stories Americans live by*. New York: Oxford University Press.

McAdams, D. P (2005b). Studying lives in time: A narrative approach. In R. Levy, P. Ghisletta, J.-M. LeGoff, D. Spini, & E. Widmer (Eds.), *Advances in life course research: Toward an interdisciplinary perspective on the life course* (Vol. 10, pp. 237–258). London: Elsevier.

McAdams, D. P. (2006). *The person: A new introduction to personality psychology* (4th ed.). Hoboken, NJ: Wiley.

McAdams, D. P., & Constantian, C. A. (1983). Intimacy and affiliation motives in daily living: An experience sampling analysis. *Journal of Personality and Social Psychology, 45*, 851–861.

McAdams, D. P., Jackson, R. J., & Kirshnit, C. (1984). Looking, laughing, and smiling in dyads as a function of intimacy, motivation, and reciprocity. *Journal of Personality, 52*, 261–273.

McAdams, D. P., & Powers, J. (1981). Themes of intimacy in behavior and thought. *Journal of Personality and Social Psychology, 40*, 573–587.

McCardel, J. B., & Murray, E. J. (1974). Nonspecific factors in weekend encounter groups. *Journal of Consulting and Clinical Psychology, 42*, 337–345.

McClanahan, T. M. (1995). Operant learning (R-S) principles applied to nail-biting. *Psychological Report, 77*, 507–514.

McClelland, D. C. (1961). *The achieving society*. New York: Van Nostrand.

McClelland, D. C. (1985). How motives, skills and values determine what people do. *American Psychologist, 40*, 812–825.

McClelland, D. C. (1992). Motivational configurations. In C. P. Smith, J. W. Atkinson, D. C. McClelland, & J. Veroff (Eds.), *Motivation and personality. Handbook of thematic content analysis* (pp. 87–99). New York: Cambridge University Press.

McClelland, D. C., Atkinson, J. W., Clark, R. A., & Lowell, E. L. (1953). *The achievement motive*. New York: Appleton.

McConnell, A. R., & Leibold, J. M. (2001). Relations among the Implicit Association Test, discriminatory behavior, and explicit measures of racial attitudes. *Journal of Experimental Social Psychology, 37*, 435–442.

McCrae, R. R. (2004). Human nature and culture: A trait perspective. *Journal of Research in Personality, 38*, 3–14.

McCrae, R. R., & Allik, J. (2002). *The five-factor model of personality across cultures*. New York: Kluwer Academic/Plenum Press.

McCrae, R. R., & Costa, P. T., Jr. (1985). Updating Norman's "adequacy taxonomy": Intelligence and personality in dimensions in natural language and in questionnaires. *Journal of Personality and Social Psychology, 49*, 710–721.

McCrae, R. R., & Costa, P. T., Jr. (1987). Validation of the Five-Factor model of personality across instruments and observers. *Journal of Personality and Social Psychology, 52*, 81–90.

McCrae, R. R., & Costa, P. T., Jr. (1989). The structure of personality traits: Wiggins' circumplex and the five-factor model. *Journal of Personality and Social Psychology, 56*, 586–595.

McCrae, R. R., & Costa, P. T., Jr. (1990). *Personality in adulthood*. New York: Guilford Press.

McCrae, R. R., & Costa, P. T., Jr. (1996). Toward a new generation of personality theories: Theoretical contexts for the five-factor model. In J. S. Wiggins (Ed.), *The five-factor model of personality: Theoretical perspectives* (pp. 51–87). New York: Guilford Press.

McCrae, R. R, & Costa, P. T., Jr. (1997). Conceptions and correlates of openness and to experience. In R. Hogan, J. Johnson, & S. Briggs (Eds.), *Handbook of personality psychology* (pp. 825–847). San Diego, CA: Academic Press.

McCrae, R. R., & Costa, P. T., Jr. (1999). A five-factor theory of personality. In L. A. Pervin & O. P. John (Eds.), *Handbook of personality: Theory and research* (2nd ed., pp. 139–153). New York: Guilford Press.

McCrae, R. R, Costa, P. T., Jr., Del Pilar, G. H, Rolland, J., & Parker, W. D. (1998). Cross-cultural assessment of the five-factor model: The Revised NEO Personality Inventory. *Journal of Cross-Cultural Psychology, 29*, 171–188.

McEwan, I. (2005). *Saturday*. New York: Anchor.

McFarland, C., & Buehler, R. (1997). Negative affective states and the motivated retrieval of positive life events: The role of affect acknowledgment. *Journal of Personality and Social Psychology, 73*, 200–214.

McGinnies, E. (1949). Emotionality and perceptual defense. *Psychological Review, 56*, 244–251.

McGuire, S., Neiderheiser, J. M., Reiss, D., Hetherington, E. M., & Plomin, R. (1994). Genetic and environmental influences on perceptions of self-worth and competence in adolescence: A study of twins, full siblings, and step siblings. *Child Development, 65*, 785–799.

McHenry, J. J., Hough, L. M., Toquam, J. L., Hanson, M. A., & Ashworth, S. (1991). Project A validity results: The relationship between predictor and criterion domains. *Personnel Psychology, 43*, 335–354.

Meehl, P. E. (1990). Why summaries of research on psychological theories are often uninterpretable. *Psychological Reports, 66*, 195–244.

Meehl, P. E. (1997). Credentialed persons, credentialed knowledge. *Clinical Psychology-Science and Practice, 4*, 91–98.

Meichenbaum, D. (1993). Changing conceptions of cognitive behavior modification: Retrospect and prospect. *Journal of Consulting and Clinical Psychology, 61*, 202–204.

Meichenbaum, D. H. (1995). Cognitive-behavioral therapy in historical perspective. In B. Bongar & L. E. Beutler (Eds.), *Comprehensive textbook of psychotherapy* (pp. 140–158). New York: Oxford University Press.

Meichenbaum, D. H., & Smart, I. (1971). Use of direct expectancy to modify academic performance and attitudes of college students. *Journal of Counseling Psychology, 18*, 531–535.

Meltzer, H. (1930). The present status of experimental studies of the relation of feeling to memory. *Psychological Review, 37*, 124–139.

Mendoza-Denton, R. (1999). Lay contextualism in stereotyping: Situational qualifiers of stereotypes in intuitive theories of dispositions (Doctoral dissertation, Columbia University, 1999). *Dissertation Abstracts International: Section B: The Sciences and Engineering, 60*, 412.

Mendoza-Denton, R., Ayduk, O., Mischel, W., Shoda, Y., & Testa, A. (2001). Person × situation interactionism in self-encoding (I am . . . when . . .): Implications for affect regulation and social information processing. *Journal of Personality and Social Psychology, 80*, 533–544.

Mendoza-Denton, R., Ayduk, O., Shoda, Y. & Mischel, W. (1997). A cognitive–affective processing system analysis of reactions to the O.J. Simpson verdict. *Journal of Social Issues, 53*, 565–583.

Mendoza-Denton, R., Downey, G., Purdie, V. J., Davis, A., & Pietrzak, J. (2002). Sensitivity to status-based rejection: Implications for African-American students' college experience. *Journal of Personality and Social Psychology, 83*, 896–918.

Mendoza-Denton, R., & Mischel, W. (2007). Integrating system approaches to culture and personality: The Cultural Cognitive–Affective Processing System (C-CAPS). In S. Kitayama & D. Cohen (Eds.), *Handbook of cultural psychology* (pp. 175–195). New York: Guilford Press.

Mendoza-Denton, R., Page-Gould, E., & Pietrzak, J. (2005). Mechanisms for coping with status-based rejection expectations. In S. Levin & C. Van Laar (Eds.), *Stigma and group inequality: Social psychological perspectives* (pp. 151–170). Mahwah, NJ: Erlbaum.

Mendoza-Denton, R., Shoda, Y., Ayduk, O., & Mischel, W. (1999). Applying CAPS theory to cultural differences in social behavior. In W. J. Lonner, D. L. Dinnel, D. K. Forgays, & S. A. Hayes (Eds.), *Merging past, present, and future: Selected papers from the 14th International Congress of the International Association for Cross-Cultural Psychology* (pp. 205–217). Lisse, The Netherlands: Swets & Zeitlinger.

Merluzzi, T. V., Glass, C. R., & Genest, M. (Eds.). (1981). *Cognitive assessment*. New York: Guilford Press.

Metcalfe, J., & Jacobs, W. J. (1998). Emotional memory: The effects of stress on "cool" and "hot" memory systems. In D. L. Medin (Ed.), *The psychology of learning and motivation: Advances in research and theory* (Vol. 38, pp. 187–222). San Diego, CA: Academic Press.

Metcalfe, J., & Mischel, W. (1999). A hot/cool-system analysis of delay of gratification: Dynamics of willpower. *Psychological Review, 106*, 3–19.

Milgram, N. (1993). War-related trauma and victimization: Principles of traumatic stress prevention in Israel. In J. P. Wilson & B. Raphael (Eds.), *International handbook of traumatic stress syndromes* (pp. 811–820). New York: Plenum Press.

Milgram, S. (1974). *Obedience to authority*. New York: Harper & Row.

Miller, N. E. (1948). Theory and experiment relating psychoanalytic displacement to stimulus response generalization. *Journal of Abnormal and Social Psychology, 43*, 155–178.

Miller, N. E. (1959). Liberalization of basic S-R concepts: Extensions to conflict behavior, motivation, and social learning. In S. Koch (Ed.), *Psychology: A study of a science* (Vol. 2, pp. 196–292). New York: McGraw-Hill.

Miller, N. E. (1963). Some reflections on the law of effect produce a new alternative to drive reduction. In M. R. Jones (Ed.), *Nebraska Symposium on Motivation* (Vol. 11, pp. 65–112). Lincoln: University of Nebraska Press.

Miller, N. E., & Dollard, J. (1941). *Social learning and imitation*. New Haven: Yale University Press.

Miller, S. M. (1979). Coping with impending stress: Physiological and cognitive correlates of choice. *Psychophysiology, 16*, 572–581.

Miller, S. M. (1981). Predictability and human stress: Towards a clarification of evidence and theory. In L. Berkowitz (Ed.), *Advances in experimental social psychology* (Vol. 14, pp. 203–256). New York: Academic Press.

Miller, S. M. (1987). Monitoring and blunting: Validation of a questionnaire to assess styles of information seeking under threat. *Journal of Personality and Social Psychology, 52*, 345–353.

Miller, S. M. (1992). Individual differences in the coping process: What to know and when to know it. In B. N. Carpenter (Ed.), *Personal coping: Theory, research, application* (pp. 77–91). Westport, CT: Praeger.

Miller, S. M. (1996). Monitoring and blunting of threatening information: Cognitive interference and facilitation in the coping process. In I. G. Sarason, G. R. Pierce, & B. R. Sarason (Eds.), *Cognitive interference: Theories, methods, and findings* (pp. 175–190). Mahwah, NJ: Erlbaum.

Miller, S. M., & Green, M. L. (1985). Coping with threat and frustration: Origins, nature, and development. In M. Lewis & C. Soarni (Eds.), *Socialization of emotions* (Vol. 5, pp. 263–314). New York: Plenum Press.

Miller, S. M., & Mangan, C. E. (1983). The interacting effects of information and coping style in adapting to gynecologic stress: Should the doctor tell all? *Journal of Personality and Social Psychology, 45*, 223–236.

Miller, S. M., Shoda, Y., & Hurley, K. (1996). Applying cognitive-social theory to health-protective behavior: Breast self-examination in cancer screening. *Psychological Bulletin, 119*, 70–94.

Miller, T. Q., Smith, T. W., Turner, C. W., Guijarro, M. L., & Hallett, A. J. (1996). A meta-analytic review of research on hostility and physical health. *Psychological Bulletin, 119*, 322–348.

Minuchin, S., Lee, W., & Simon, G. M. (1996). *Mastering family therapy: Journeys of growth and transformation.* New York: Wiley.

Mischel, H. N., & Mischel, W. (1973). *Readings in personality*. New York: Holt, Rinehart & Winston.

Mischel, H. N., & Mischel, W. (1983). The development of children's knowledge of self-control strategies. *Child Development, 54*, 603–619.

Mischel, T. (1964). Personal constructs, rules, and the logic of clinical activity. *Psychological Review, 71*, 180–192.

Mischel, W. (1965). Predicting the success of Peace Corps volunteers in Nigeria. *Journal of Personality and Social Psychology, 1*, 510.

Mischel, W. (1968). *Personality and assessment*. New York: Wiley.

Mischel, W. (1969). Continuity and change in personality. *American Psychologist, 24*, 1012–1018.

Mischel, W. (1973). Toward a cognitive social learning reconceptualization of personality. *Psychological Review, 80*, 252–283.

Mischel, W. (1974). Processes in delay of gratification. In L. Berkowitz (Ed.), *Advances in experimental social psychology* (Vol. 7, pp. 249–292). New York: Academic Press.

Mischel, W. (1981a). Metacognition and the rules of delay. In J. H. Flavell & L. Ross (Eds.), *Social cognitive development: Frontiers and possible futures* (pp. 240–271). New York: Cambridge University Press.

Mischel, W. (1981b). Personality and cognition: Something borrowed, something new? In N. Cantor & J. Kihlstrom (Eds.), *Personality, cognition, and social interaction* (pp. 3–19). Hillsdale, NJ: Erlbaum.

Mischel, W. (1984). Convergences and challenges in the search for consistency. *American Psychologist, 39*, 351–364.

Mischel, W. (1990). Personality dispositions revisited and revised: A view after three decades. In L. A. Pervin (Ed.), *Handbook of personality: Theory and research* (pp. 111–134). New York: Guilford Press.

Mischel, W. (2004). Toward an integrative science of the person. *Annual Review of Psychology, 55*, 1–22.

Mischel, W. (2007). Walter Mischel. In G. Lindzey & W. M. Runyan (Eds.), *A history of psychology in autobiography* (Vol. IX, pp. 229–267). Washington, DC: American Psychological Association.

Mischel, W., & Ayduk, O. (2002). Self-regulation in a cognitive-affective personality system: Attentional control in the service of the self. *Self and Identity, 1*, 113–120.

Mischel, W., & Ayduk, O. (2004). Willpower in a cognitive-affective processing system: The dynamics of delay of gratification. In R. F. Baumeister & K. D. Vohs (Eds.), *Handbook of self-regulation: Research, theory, and applications* (pp. 99–129). New York: Guilford Press.

Mischel, W., & Baker, N. (1975). Cognitive appraisals and transformations in delay behavior. *Journal of Personality and Social Psychology, 31*, 254–261.

Mischel, W., Cantor, N., & Feldman, S. (1996). Principles of self-regulation: The nature of willpower and self-control. In E. T. Higgins & A. W. Kruglanski (Eds.), *Social psychology: Handbook of basic principles* (pp. 329–360). New York: Guilford Press.

Mischel, W., & Ebbesen, E. B. (1970). Attention in delay of gratification. *Journal of Personality and Social Psychology, 16*, 239–337.

Mischel, W., Ebbesen, E. B., & Zeiss, A. R. (1972). Cognitive and attentional mechanisms in delay of gratification. *Journal of Personality and Social Psychology, 21*, 204–218.

Mischel, W., Ebbesen, E. B., & Zeiss, A. R. (1973). Selective attention to the self: Situational and dispositional determinants. *Journal of Personality and Social Psychology, 27*, 129–142.

Mischel, W., Ebbesen, E. B., & Zeiss, A. R. (1976). Determinants of selective memory about the self. *Journal of Consulting and Clinical Psychology, 44*, 92–103.

Mischel, W., & Moore, B. (1973). Effects of attention to symbolically-presented rewards on self-control. *Journal of Personality and Social Psychology, 28*, 172–179.

Mischel, W., & Morf, C.C. (2003). The self as a psycho-social dynamic processing system: A meta-perspective on a century of the self in psychology. In M. R. Leary & J. P. Tangney (Eds.), *Handbook of self and identity* (pp. 15–43). New York: Guilford Press.

Mischel, W., & Peake, P. K. (1982). In search of consistency: Measure for measure. In M. P. Zanna, E. T. Higgins, & C. P. Herman (Eds.), *Consistency in social behavior: The Ontario symposium* (Vol. 2, pp. 187–207). Hillsdale, NJ: Erlbaum.

Mischel, W. & Shoda, Y. (1994). Personality psychology has two goals: Must it be two fields? *Psychological Inquiry, 5*, 156–159.

Mischel, W., & Shoda, Y. (1995). A cognitive–affective system theory of personality: Reconceptualizing situations, dispositions, dynamics, and invariance in personality structure. *Psychological Review, 102*, 246–268.

Mischel, W., & Shoda, Y. (1998). Reconciling processing dynamics and personality dispositions. *Annual Review of Psychology, 49*, 229–258.

Mischel, W., & Shoda, Y. (1999). Integrating dispositions and processing dynamics within a unified theory of personality: The cognitive affective personality system (CAPS). In L. Pervin & O. John (Eds.), *Handbook of personality: Theory and research* (2nd ed., pp. 197–218). New York: Guilford Press.

Mischel, W., Shoda, Y., & Peake, P. K. (1988). The nature of adolescent competencies predicted by preschool delay of gratification. *Journal of Personality and Social Psychology, 54*, 687–696.

Mischel, W., Shoda, Y., & Rodriguez, M. L. (1989). Delay of gratification in children. *Science, 244*, 933–938.

Mischel, W., & Staub, E. (1965). Effects of expectancy on working and waiting for larger rewards. *Journal of Personality and Social Psychology, 2*, 625–633.

Miyake, A., Friedman, N. P., Emerson, M. J., Witzki, A. H., & Howerter, A. (2000). The unity and diversity of executive functions and their contributions to complex "frontal lobe" tasks: A latent variable analysis. *Cognitive Psychology, 41*, 49–100.

Molina, M. A. N. (1996). Archetypes and spirits: A Jungian analysis of Puerto Rican Espiritismo. *Journal of Analytical Psychology, 41*, 227–244.

Monro, R. (1955). *Schools of psychoanalytic thought*. New York: Holt, Rinehart and Winston.

Morf, C. C. (2006). Personality reflected in a coherent idiosyncratic interplay of intra- and interpersonal self-regulatory processes. *Journal of Personality, 74*, 1527–1556.

Morf, C. C., Ansara, D., & Shia, T. (2001). *The effects of audience characteristics on narcissistic self-presentation*. Manuscript in preparation, University of Toronto.

Morf, C. C., & Rhodewalt, F. (2001a). Expanding the dynamic self-regulatory processing model of narcissism: Research directions for the future. *Psychological Inquiry, 12*, 243–251.

Morf, C. C., & Rhodewalt, F. (2001b). Unraveling the paradoxes of narcissism: A dynamic self-regulatory processing model. *Psychological Inquiry, 12*, 177–196.

Morf, C. C., Weir, C. R., & Davidov, M. (2000). Narcissism and intrinsic motivation: The role of goal congruence. *Journal of Experimental Social Psychology, 36*, 424–438.

Morris, A. S., Silk, J. S., Steinberg, L., Sessa, F. M., Avenevoli, S., & Essex, M. J. (2002). Temperamental vulnerability and negative parenting as interacting of child adjustment. *Journal of Marriage and the Family, 64*, 461–471.

Morse, W. H., & Kelleher, R. T. (1966). Schedules using noxious stimuli I. Multiple fixed-ratio and fixed-interval termination of schedule complexes. *Journal of the Experimental Analysis of Behavior, 9*, 267–290.

Moskowitz, D. S. (1982). Coherence and cross-situational generality in personality: A new analysis of old problems. *Journal of Personality and Social Psychology, 43*, 754–768.

Moskowitz, D. S. (1988). Cross-situational generality in the laboratory: Dominance and friendliness. *Journal of Personality and Social Psychology, 54*, 829–839.

Moskowitz, D. S. (1994). Cross-situational generality and the interpersonal circumplex. *Journal of Personality and Social Psychology, 66*, 921–933.

Mulaik, S. A. (1964). Are personality factors raters' conceptual factors? *Journal of Consulting Psychology, 28*, 506–511.

Murphy, S. T., & Zajonc, R. B. (1993). Affect, cognition, and awareness: Affective priming with optimal and suboptimal stimulus exposures. *Journal of Personality and Social Psychology, 64*, 723–739.

Murray, H. (1967). An autobiography. In E.G. Boring & G. Lindzey (Eds.), *A history of psychology in autobiography* (Vol. 5, pp. 285–310) New York: Appleton-Century-Crofts.

Murray, H. A., Barrett, W. G., & Homburger, E. (1938). *Explorations in personality*. New York: Oxford University Press.

Mussen, P. H., & Naylor, H. K. (1954). The relationship between overt and fantasy aggression. *Journal of Abnormal and Social Psychology, 49*, 235–240.

Nee, D. E., Wager, T. D., & Jonides, J. (in press). A meta-analysis of neuroimaging activations from interference-resolution tasks. *Cognitive, Affective, Behavioral Neuroscience*.

Neisser, U. (1967). *Cognitive psychology*. New York: Appleton.

Nelson, R. J., Demas, G. E., Huang, P. L., Fishman, M. C., Dawson, V. L., Dawson, T. M., et al. (1995). Behavioural abnormalities in male mice lacking neuronal nitric synthase. *Nature, 378*, 383–386.

Nemeroff, C. J., & Karoly, P. (1991). Operant methods. In F. H. Kanfer & A. P. Goldstein (Eds.), *Helping people change: A textbook of methods* (4th ed., Vol. 52). New York: Pergamon Press.

Nesse, R. M. (2001). *Evolution and the capacity for commitment*. New York: Russell Sage.

Newcomb, T. M. (1929). *Consistency of certain extrovert–introvert behavior patterns in 51 problem boys*.

New York: Columbia University, Teachers College, Bureau of Publications.

Niedenthal, P. M. (1990). Implicit perception of affective information. *Journal of Experimental Social Psychology, 25*, 505–527.

Nilson, D. C., Nilson, L. B., Olson, R. S., & McAllister, B. H. (1981). *The planning environment report for the Southern California Earthquake Safety Advisory Board*. Redlands, CA: Social Research Advisory and Policy Research Center.

Nisbett, R. (1990). Evolutionary psychology, biology, and cultural evolution. *Motivation and Emotion, 14*, 255–263.

Nisbett, R. E. (1997, May). *Cultures of honor: Economics, history, and the tradition of violence*. Address given at the Ninth Annual Convention of the American Psychological Society, Washington, DC.

Nisbett, R. E., & Cohen, D. (1996). *Culture of honor: The psychology of violence in the south*. Boulder, CO: Westview Press.

Nisbett, R. E., Peng, K., Choi, I., & Norenzayan, A. (2001). Culture and systems of thought: Holistic vs. analytic cognition. *Psychological Review, 108*, 291–310.

Nisbett, R. E., & Ross, L. D. (1980). *Human inference: Strategies and shortcomings of social judgment*. Englewood Cliffs, NJ: Prentice-Hall.

Noftle, E. E., & Shaver, P. R. (2006). Attachment dimensions and the big five personality traits: Associations and comparative ability to predict relationship quality. *Journal of Research in Personality, 40*, 179–208.

Nolen-Hoeksema, S. (1997, May). *Emotion regulation and depression*. Closing plenary session at the Ninth Annual American Psychological Society Convention, Washington, DC.

Nolen-Hoeksema, S. (2000). The role of rumination in depressive disorders and mixed anxiety/depressive symptoms. *Journal of Abnormal Psychology, 109*, 504–511.

Nolen-Hoeksema, S., Parker, L. E., & Larson, J. (1994). Ruminative coping with depressed mood following loss. *Journal of Personality and Social Psychology, 67*, 92–104.

Norem, J. K., & Cantor, N. (1986). Anticipatory and post-hoc cushioning strategies: Optimism and defensive pessimism in "risky" situations. *Cognitive Therapy and Research, 10*, 347–362.

Norman, W. T. (1961). Development of self-report tests to measure personality factors identified from peer nominations. USAF ASK Technical Note, No. 61–44.

Norman, W. T. (1963). Toward an adequate taxonomy of personality attributes: Replicated factor structure in peer nomination personality ratings. *Journal of Abnormal and Social Psychology, 66*, 574–583.

Ochsner, K. N., & Gross, J. J. (2004). Thinking makes it so: A social cognitive neuroscience approach to emotion regulation. In R. F. Baumeister & K. D. Vohs (Eds.), *The handbook of self-regulation: Research, theory, and applications* (pp. 229–255). New York: Guilford Press.

Ochsner, K. N., & Gross, J. J. (2005). The cognitive control of emotion. *Trends in Cognitive Sciences, 9*, 242–249.

Ochsner, K. N., & Lieberman, M. D. (2001). The emergence of social cognitive neuroscience. *American Psychologist, 56*, 717–734.

O'Connell, D. F., & Alexander, C. N. (1994). Recovery from addictions using transcendental meditation and Maharishi Ayur-Veda. In D. F. O'Connell & C. N. Alexander (Eds.), *Self-recovery: Treating addictions using transcendental meditation and Maharishi Ayur-Veda* (pp. 1–12). New York: Haworth Press.

O'Connor, T. G., Hetherington, E. M., Reiss, D., & Plomin, R. (1995). A twin–sibling study of observed parent–adolescent interactions. *Child Development, 66*, 812–829.

O'Donohue, W., Henderson, D., Hayes, S., Fisher, J., & Hayes, L. (Eds.). (2001). *The history of the behavioral therapies: Founders, personal histories*. Reno, NV: Context Press.

Office of Strategic Services Administration. (1948). *Assessment of men*. New York: Holt, Rinehart and Winston.

Ofshe, R. J. (1992). Inadvertent hypnosis during interrogation: False confession due to dissociative state, misidentified multiple personality and the satanic cult hypothesis. *International Journal of Clinical and Experimental Hypnosis, 40*, 125–156.

Ofshe, R. J., & Watters, E. (1993). Making monsters. *Society, 1*, 4–16.

Oishi, S. (2004). Personality in culture: A neo-Allportian view. *Journal of Research in Personality, 38*, 68–74.

Oishi, S., Diener, E., Napa Scollon, C., & Biswas-Diener, R. (2004). Cross-situational consistency of affective experiences across cultures. *Journal of Personality and Social Psychology, 86*, 460–472.

O'Leary, V. (1997, August). *Smithsonian seminar on health and well-being*, sponsored by Society for the Psychological Study of Social Issues and American Psychological Society conducted at the Ninth Annual Conference of the American Psychological Society, Washington, DC.

Opler, M. K. (1967). Cultural induction of stress. In M. H. Appley & R. Trumbull (Eds.), *Psychological stress* (pp. 209–241). New York: Appleton.

Ornstein, R. E. (1972). *The psychology of consciousness*. San Francisco: Freeman.

Ornstein, R. E., & Naranjo, C. (1971). *On the psychology of meditation*. New York: Viking.

Osgood, C. E., Suci, G. J., & Tannenbaum, P. H. (1957). *The measurement of meaning*. Urbana: University of Illinois Press.

Overall, J. (1964). Note on the scientific status of factors. *Psychological Bulletin, 61*, 270–276.

Pagano, R. R., Rose, R. M., Stivers, R. M., & Warrenburg, S. (1976). Sleep during transcendental meditation. *Science, 191*, 308–309.

Parker, J. D. A., & Endler, N. S. (1996). Coping and defense: A historical overview. In M. Zeidner & N. S. Endler (Eds.), *Handbook of coping: Theory, research, applications* (pp. 3–23). New York: Wiley.

Patterson, C. J., & Mischel, W. (1975). Plans to resist distraction. *Developmental Psychology, 11*, 369–378.

Patterson, G. R. (1976). The aggressive child: Victim and architect of a coercive system. In L. A. Hamerlynck, L. C. Handy, & E. J. Mash (Eds.), *Behavior modification and families: Vol. 1. Theory and research* (pp. 267–316). New York: Brunner/Mazel.

Patterson, G. R. (Ed.). (1990). *Depression and aggression in family interaction*. Hillsdale, NJ: Erlbaum.

Patterson, G. R., & Fisher, P. A. (2002). Recent developments in our understanding of parenting: Bidirectional effects, causal models, and the search for parsimony. In M. H. Bornstein (Ed.), *Handbook of parenting: Vol. 5. Practical issues in parenting* (2nd ed., pp. 59–88). Mahwah, NJ: Erlbaum.

Paul, G. L. (1966). *Insight vs. desensitization in psychotherapy*. Stanford, CA: Stanford University Press.

Paulhus, D. L., Fridhandler, B., & Hayes, S. (1997). Psychological defense: Contemporary theory and research. In R. Hogan, J. A. Johnson, & S. R. Briggs (Eds.), *Handbook of personality psychology* (pp. 543–579). San Diego, CA: Academic Press.

Payne, K. B. (2001). Prejudice and perception: The role of automatic and controlled processes in misperceiving a weapon. *Journal of Personality and Social Psychology, 81*, 181–192.

Peake, P., Hebl, M., & Mischel, W. (2002). Strategic attention deployment in waiting and working situations. *Developmental Psychology, 38*, 313–326.

Pedersen, N. L., Plomin, R., McClearn, G. E., & Friberg, L. (1988). Neuroticism, extraversion, and related traits in adult twins reared apart and reared together. *Journal of Personality and Social Psychology, 55*, 950–957.

Pederson, F. A. (1958). *Consistency data on the role construct repertory test*. Unpublished manuscript, Ohio State University, Columbus.

Pennebaker, J. W. (1993). Social mechanisms of constraint. In D. M. Wegener & J. W. Pennebaker (Eds.), *Handbook of mental control* (pp. 200–219). Englewoood Cliff, NJ: Prentice-Hall.

Pennebaker, J. W. (1997). Writing about emotional experiences as a therapeutic process. *Psychological Science, 8*, 162–166.

Pennebaker, J. W., Colder, M., & Sharp, L. K. (1990). Accelerating the coping process. *Journal of Personality and Social Psychology, 58*, 528–537.

Pennebaker, J. W., & Graybeal, A. (2001). Patterns of natural language use: Disclosure, personality, and social integration. *Current Directions in Psychological Science, 10*, 90–93.

Pennebaker, J. W., Kiecolt-Glaser, J. K., & Glaser, R. (1988). Disclosure of traumas and immune function: Health implications for psychotherapy. *Journal of Consulting and Clinical Psychology, 56*, 239–245.

Perls, F. S. (1969). *Gestalt therapy verbatim*. Lafayette, CA: Real People Press.

Perry, J. C., & Cooper, S. H. (1989). An empirical study of defense mechanisms, I. Clinical interviews and life vignette ratings. *Archives of General Psychiatry, 46*, 444–452.

Pervin, L. A. (1994). A critical analysis of trait theory. *Psychological Inquiry, 5*, 103–113.

Pervin, L. A. (1996). *The science of personality*. New York: Wiley.

Pervin, L. A. (1999). The cross-cultural challenge to personality. In Y. Lee & C. R. McCauley (Eds.), *Personality and person perception across cultures* (pp. 23–41). Mahwah, NJ: Erlbaum.

Peterson, C., & Seligman, M. E. P. (1987). Explanatory style and illness. *Journal of Personality, 55*, 237–265.

Peterson, C., Seligman, M. E. P., & Vaillant, G. E. (1988). Pessimistic explanatory style is a risk factor of physical illness: A thirty-five-year longitudinal study. *Journal of Personality and Social Psychology, 55*, 23–27.

Peterson, D. R. (1968). *The clinical study of social behavior*. New York: Appleton.

Petrie, K. J., Booth, R. J., Pennebaker, J. W., Davison, K. P., & Thomas, M. G. (1995). Disclosure of trauma and immune response to a hepatitis vaccination program. *Journal of Consulting and Clinical Psychology, 63*, 787–792.

Phares, E. J. (1976). *Locus of control in personality*. Morristown, NJ: General Learning Press.

Phillips, K., & Mathews, A. P., Jr. (1995). Quantitative genetic analysis of injury liability in infants and toddlers. *American Journal of Medical Genetics (Neuropsychiatric Genetics), 60*, 64–71.

Pierce, T., Baldwin, M. K., & Lydon, J. E. (1997). A relational schema approach to social support. In G. R. Pierce, B. Lakey, I. G. Sarason, & B. R. Sarason (Eds.), *Sourcebook of Social Support and Personality* (pp. 19–47). New York: Plenum Press.

Pike, A., Reiss, D., Hetherington E. M., & Plomin, R. (1996). Using MZ differences in the search for nonshared environmental effects. *Journal of Child Psychology and Psychiatry, 37*, 695–704.

Pine, D. S., Cohen, P., Johnson, J. G., & Brook, J. S. (2002). Adolescent life events as predictors of adult depression. *Journal of Affective Disorders, 68*, 49–57.

Pinker, S. (1997). How the mind works. New York: Norton.

Plaud, J. J., & Gaither, G. A. (1996). Human behavioral momentum: Implications for applied behavior analysis and therapy. *Journal of Behavior Therapy and Experimental Psychiatry, 27*, 139–148.

Plaks, J. E., Shafer, J. L., & Shoda, Y. (2003). Perceiving individuals and groups as coherent: How do perceivers make sense of variable behavior? *Social Cognition, 21*, 26–60.

Plaud, J. J., & Gaither, G. A. (1996). Behavioral momentum: Implications and development from reinforcement theories. *Behavior Modification, 20*, 183–201.

Plomin, R. (1981). Ethnological behavioral genetics and development. In K. Immelmann, G. W. Barlow, L. Petrinovich, & M. Main (Eds.), *Behavioral development: The Bielefeld interdisciplinary project*. Cambridge, UK: Cambridge University Press.

Plomin, R. (1990). The role of inheritance in behavior. *Science, 248*, 183–188.

Plomin, R. (1994). The Emanuel Miller Memorial Lecture 1993: Genetic research and identification of environmental influences. *Journal of Child Psychology and Psychiatry, 35*, 817–834.

Plomin, R., & Caspi, A. (1999). Behavioral genetics and personality. In L. A. Pervin & O. P. John (Eds.), *Handbook of personality theory and research* (2nd ed., pp. 251–276). New York: Guilford Press.

Plomin, R., Chipuer, H. M., & Loehlin, J. C. (1990). Behavioral genetics and personality. In L. A. Pervin (Ed.), *Handbook of personality: Theory and research* (pp. 225–243). New York: Guilford Press.

Plomin, R., Chipuer, H. M., & Neiderhiser, J. M. (1994). Behavioral genetic evidence for the importance of non-shared environment. In E. M. Hetherington, D. Reiss, & R. Plomin (Eds.), *Separate social worlds of siblings: Impact of nonshared environment on development* (pp. 1–31). Hillsdale, NJ: Erlbaum.

Plomin, R., DeFries, J. C., McClearn, G. E., & Rutter, M. (1997). *Behavioral genetics* (3rd ed.). New York: Freeman.

Plomin, R., Manke, B., & Pike, A. (1996). Siblings, behavioral genetics, and competence. In G. H. Brody (Ed.), *Sibling relationships: Their causes and consequences* (pp. 75–104). Norwood, NJ: Ablex.

Plomin, R., McClearn, G. E., Pedersen, N. L., Nesselroade, J. R., & Bergeman, C. S. (1988). Genetic influence on childhood family environment perceived retrospectively from the last half of the life span. *Developmental Psychology, 24*, 738–745.

Plomin, R., Owen, M. J., & McGuffin, P. (1994). The genetic basis of complex human behaviors. *Science, 264*, 1733–1739.

Plomin, R., & Rende, R. (1991). Human behavioral genetics. *Annual Review of Psychology, 42*, 161–190.

Plomin, R., & Saudino, K. J. (1994). Quantitative genetics and molecular genetics. In J. E. Bates & T. D. Watts (Eds.), *Temperament: Individual differences at the interface of biology and behavior* (pp. 143–171). Washington, DC: American Psychological Association.

Poortinga, Y. H., & Hemert, D. A. (2001). Personality and culture: Demarcating between the common and the unique. *Journal of Personality, 69*, 1033–1060.

Polster, E., & Polster, M. (1993). Frederick Perls: Legacy and invitation. *Gestalt Journal, 16*, 23–25.

Posner, M. I., & Rothbart, M. K. (1991). Attentional mechanisms and conscious experience. In M. Rugg & A. D. Milner (Eds.), *The neuropsychology of consciousness* (pp. 91–112). San Diego, CA: Academic Press.

Posner, M. I., & Rothbart, M. K. (1998). Attention, self-regulation, and consciousness. *Philosophical Transactions of the Royal Society of London B, 353*, 1915–1927.

Potter, W. Z., Rudorfer, M. V., & Manji, H. K. (1991). The pharmacologic treatment of depression. *New England Journal of Medicine, 325*, 633–642.

Powell, G. E. (1973). Negative and positive mental practice in motor skill acquisition. *Perceptual and Motor Skills, 37*, 312–313.

Purdie, V., & Downey, G. (2000). Rejection sensitivity and adolescent girls' vulnerability to relationship-centered difficulties. *Child Maltreatment, 5*, 338–349.

Rachman, S. (1967). Systematic desensitization. *Psychological Bulletin, 67*, 93–103.

Rachman, S. J. (1996). Trends in cognitive and behavioural therapies. In P. M. Salkovskis (Ed.), *Trends in cognitive and behavioural therapies* (pp. 1–23). New York: Wiley.

Rachman, S., & Cuk, M. (1992). Fearful distortions. *Behaviour Research and Therapy, 30*, 583–589.

Rachman, S., & Hodgeson, R. J. (1980). *Obsessions and compulsions*. Englewood Cliffs, NJ: Prentice-Hall.

Rachman, S., & Wilson, G. T. (1980). *The effects of psychological therapy*. Oxford, UK: Pergamon Press.

Ramsey, E., Patterson, G. R., & Walker, H. M. (1990). Generalization of the antisocial trait from home to school settings. *Journal of Applied Developmental Psychology, 11*, 209–223.

Rapaport, D. (1967). *The collected papers of David Rapaport*. New York: Basic Books.

Raush, H. L., Barry, W. A., Hertel, R. K., & Swain, M. A. (1974). *Communication conflict and marriage*. San Francisco: Jossey-Bass.

Raymond, M. S. (1956). Case of fetishism treated by aversion therapy. *British Medical Journal, 2*, 854–857.

Redd, W. H. (1995). Behavioral research in cancer as a model for health psychology. *Health Psychology, 14*, 99–100.

Redd, W. H., Porterfield, A. L., & Anderson, B. L. (1978). *Behavior modification: Behavioral approaches to human problems*. New York: Random House.

Reiss, D., Neiderhiser, J. M., Hetherington, E. M., & Plomin, R. (2000). *The relationship code: Deciphering genetic and social influences on adolescent development*. Cambridge, MA: Harvard University Press.

Rhodewalt F., & Eddings, S. K. (2002). Narcissus reflects: Memory distortion in response to ego-relevant feedback among high- and low-narcissistic men. *Journal of Research in Personality, 36*, 97–116.

Richards, J. M., & Gross, J. J. (2000). Emotion regulation and memory: The cognitive costs of keeping one's cool. *Journal of Personality and Social Psychology, 79*, 410–424.

Riemann, R., Angleitner, A., & Strelau, J. (1997). Genetic and environmental influences on personality: A study of twins reared together using the self- and peer report NEO-FFI scales. *Journal of Personality, 65*, 449–476.

Riger, S. (1992). Epistemological debates, feminist voices: Science, social values, and the study of women. *American Psychologist, 47*, 730–740.

Rimm, D. C., & Masters, J. C. (1974). *Behavior therapy: Techniques and empirical findings*. New York: Academic Press.

Rippetoe, P. A., & Rogers, R. W. (1987). Effects of components of protection-motivation theory on adaptive and maladaptive coping with a health threat. *Journal of Personality and Social Psychology, 52*, 596–604.

Roazen, P. (1974). *Freud and his followers*. New York: Meridian.

Roberts, B. W., Kuncel, N. R., Shiner, R., Caspi, A., & Goldberg, L. R. (in press). The power of personality: The comparative validity of personality traits, socio-economic status, and cognitive ability for predicting important life outcomes. *Perspectives on Psychological Science*.

Robinson, J. L., Kagan, J., Reznick, J. S., & Corley, R. (1992). The heritability of inhibited and uninhibited behavior: A twin study. *Developmental Psychology, 28*, 1030–1037.

Rodriguez, M. L., Mischel, W., & Shoda, Y. (1989). Cognitive person variables in the delay of gratification of older children at-risk. *Journal of Personality and Social Psychology, 57*, 358–367.

Roese, N. J., Pennington, G. L., Coleman, J., Janicki, M., Li, N. P., & Kenrick, D. T. (2006). Sex differences in regret: All for love or some for lust? *Personality and Social Psychology Bulletin, 32*, 770–780.

Rogers, C. R. (1942). *Counseling and psychotherapy: Newer concepts in practice*. Boston: Houghton Mifflin.

Rogers, C. R. (1947). Some observations on the organization of personality. *American Psychologist, 2*, 358–368.

Rogers, C. R. (1951). *Client-centered therapy: Its current practice, implications and theory*. Boston: Houghton Mifflin.

Rogers, C. R. (1955). Persons or science? A philosophical question. *American Psychologist, 10*, 267–278.

Rogers, C. R. (1959). A theory of therapy, personality and interpersonal relationships, as developed in the client-centered framework. In S. Koch (Ed.), *Psychology: A study of a science* (Vol. 3, pp. 184–526). New York: McGraw-Hill.

Rogers, C. R. (1963). The actualizing tendency in relation to "motives" and to consciousness. In M. R. Jones (Ed.), *Nebraska Symposium on Motivation* (pp. 1–24). Lincoln: University of Nebraska Press.

Rogers, C. R. (1967). Autobiography. In E. Boring & G. Lindzey, *A history of psychology in autobiography* (Vol. V, pp. 343–384). New York: Appleton-Century-Crofts.

Rogers, C. R. (1970). *Carl Rogers on encounter groups*. New York: Harper & Row.

Rogers, C. R. (1974). In retrospect: Forty-six years. *American Psychologist, 29*, 115–123.

Rogers, C. R., & Dymond, R. F. (Eds.). (1954). *Psychotherapy and personality change, co-ordinated studies in the client-centered approach*. Chicago: University of Chicago Press.

Rogers, T. B. (1977). Self-reference in memory: Recognition of personality items. *Journal of Research in Personality, 11*, 295–305.

Rogers, T. B., Kuiper, N. A., & Kirker, W. S. (1977). Self-reference and the encoding of personal information. *Journal of Personality and Social Psychology, 35*, 677–688.

Romer, D., & Revelle, W. (1984). Personality traits: Fact or fiction? A critique of the Shweder and D'Andrade systematic distortion hypothesis. *Journal of Personality and Social Psychology, 47*, 1028–1042.

Rorer, L. G. (1990). Personality assessment: A conceptual survey. In L. A. Pervin (Ed.), *Handbook of personality: Theory and research* (pp. 693–720). New York: Guilford Press.

Rosch, E. (1975). Cognitive reference points. *Cognitive Psychology, 1*, 532–547.

Rosch, E., Mervis, C., Gray, W., Johnson, D., & Boyce-Braem, P. (1976). Basic objects in natural categories. *Cognitive Psychology, 8*, 382–439.

Rosenhan, D. L. (1973). On being sane in insane places. *Science, 179*, 250–258.

Rosenthal, R., & Jacobson, L. (1968). *Pygmalion in the classroom: Teacher expectation and pupils' intellectual development*. New York: Holt, Rinehart & Winston.

Rosenthal, R., & Rubin, D. (1978). Interpersonal expectancy effects: The first 345 studies. *Behavioral and Brain Sciences, 3*, 377–415.

Rosenzweig, S., & Mason, G. (1934). An experimental study of memory in relation to the theory of repression. *British Journal of Psychology, 24*, 247–265.

Ross, L. D. (1977). The intuitive psychologist and his shortcomings: Distortions in the attribution process. In L. Berkowitz (Ed.), *Advances in experimental social psychology* (Vol. 10, pp. 173–220). New York: Academic Press.

Ross, L. & Nisbett, R. E. (1991). *The person and the situation: Perspectives of social psychology*. New York: McGraw-Hill.

Rossini, E. D., & Moretti, R. J. (1997). Thematic Apperception Test (TAT) interpretation: Practice recommendations from a survey of clinical psychology doctoral programs accredited by the American Psychological Association. *Professional Psychology Research and Practice, 28*, 393–398.

Roth, S., & Newman, E. (1990). The process of coping with sexual trauma. *Journal of Traumatic Stress, 4*, 279–297.

Rothbart, M. K., Derryberry, D., & Posner, M. I. (1994). A psychobiological approach to the development of temperament. In J. E. Bates & T. D. Wachs (Eds.), *Temperament: Individual differences at the interface of biology and behavior* (pp. 83–116). Washington, D.C.: American Psychological Association.

Rothbart, M. K., Posner, M. I., & Gerardi, G. M. (1997, April). Effortful control and the development of temperament. Symposium presented at the biennial meeting of the Society for Research in Child Development, Washington, DC.

Rotter, J. B. (1954). *Social learning and clinical psychology*. Englewood Cliffs, NJ: Prentice-Hall.

Rotter, J. B. (1966). Generalized expectancies for internal versus external control of reinforcement. *Psychological Monographs, 80*, 1–28.

Rotter, J. B. (1972). Beliefs, social attitudes, and behavior: A social learning analysis. In J. B. Rotter, J. E. Chance, & E. J. Phares (Eds.), *Applications of a social learning theory of personality* (pp. 335–350). New York: Holt, Rinehart and Winston.

Roussi, P., Miller, S. M., & Shoda, Y. (2000). Discriminative facility in the face of threat: Relationship to psychological distress. *Psychology and Health, 15*, 21–33.

Rowan, J. (1992). What is humanistic psychotherapy? *British Journal of Psychotherapy, 9*, 74–83.

Rowe, D. C. (1981). Environmental and genetic influences on dimensions of perceived parenting: A twin study. *Developmental Psychology, 17*, 203–208.

Rowe, D. C. (1983). A biometrical analysis of perceptions of family environment: A study of twin and singleton sibling kinships. *Child Development, 54*, 416–423.

Rowe, D. C. (1997). Genetics, temperament, and personality. In R. Hogan, J. Johnson, & S. Briggs (Eds.), *Handbook of personality psychology* (pp. 367–386). San Diego, CA: Academic Press.

Royce, J. E. (1973). Does person or self imply dualism? *American Psychologist, 28*, 833–866.

Rubin, I. J. (1967). The reduction of prejudice through laboratory training. *Journal of Applied Behavioral Science, 3*, 29–50.

Rubin, K. H., Cheah, C. S. L., & Fox, N. (2001). Emotion regulation, parenting, and display of social reticence in preschoolers. *Early Education, and Development, 12*, 97–115.

Runyan, W. M. (1997). Studying lives: Psychobiography and the conceptual structure of personality psychology. In R. Hogan, J. Johnson, & S. Briggs (Eds.), *Handbook of personality psychology* (pp. 41–69). San Diego, CA: Academic Press.

Runyan, W. M. (2005) Evolving conceptions of psychobiography and the study of lives: Encounters with psychoanalysis, personality psychology and historical science. In W. T. Schultz (Ed.), *Handbook of psychobiography* (pp. 19–41). New York: Oxford University Press.

Rushton, J. P., Fulker, D. W., Neale, M. C., Nias, D. K. B., & Eysenck, H. J. (1986). Altruism and aggression: The heritability of individual differences. *Journal of Personality and Social Psychology, 50*, 1192–1198.

Rusting, C. L., & Nolen-Hoeksema, S. (1998). Regulating responses to anger: Effects on rumination and distraction on angry mood. *Journal of Personality and Social Psychology, 74*, 790–803.

Rutter, M. (2006, May). *Why the different forms of gene–environment interplay matter*. Keynote address, Association for Psychological Science, 18th Annual Convention, New York, NY.

Rutter, M., Dunn, J., Plomin, R., Simonoff, E., Pickles, A., Maughan, B., et al. (1997). Integrating nature and nurture: Implications of person-environment correlations and interactions for developmental psychopathology. *Development and Psychopathology, 9*, 335–364.

Ryan, R. M. (1982). Control and information in the intrapersonal sphere: An extension of cognitive evaluation theory. *Journal of Personality and Social Psychology, 43*, 450–461.

Ryan, R. M., & Deci, E. L. (2001). On happiness and human potentials: A review of research on hedonic and eudaimonic well-being. *Annual Review of Psychology, 52*, 141–166.

Sadalla, E. K., Kenrick, D. T., & Vershure, B. (1987). Dominance and heterosexual attraction. *Journal of Personality and Social Psychology, 52*, 730–738.

Saley, E., & Holdstock, L. (1993). Encounter group experiences of black and white South Africans in exile. In D. Brazier (Ed.), *Beyond Carl Rogers* (pp. 201–216). London: Constable.

Sapolsky, R. M. (1996). Why stress is bad for your brain. *Science, 273*, 749–750.

Sarason, I. G. (1966). *Personality: An objective approach*. New York: Wiley.

Sarason, I. G. (1979). *Life stress, self-preoccupation, and social supports*. Presidential address, Western Psychological Association.

Sartre, J. P. (1956). Existentialism. In W. Kaufman (Ed.), *Existentialism from Dostoyevsky to Sartre* (pp. 222–311). New York: Meridian.

Sartre, J. P. (1965). *Existentialism and humanism* (P. Mairet, Trans.). London: Methuen.

Saucier, G., & Goldberg, L. R. (1996). Evidence for the Big Five in analyses of familiar English personality adjectives. *European Journal of Personality, 10*, 61–77.

Saudino, K. J., & Eaton, W. O. (1991). Infant temperament and genetics: An objective twin study of motor activity level. *Child Development, 62*, 1167–1174.

Saudino, K. J., & Plomin, R. (1996). Personality and behavioral genetics: Where have we been and where are we going? *Journal of Research in Personality, 30*, 335–347.

Saudou, F., Amara, D. A., Dierich, A., LeMur, M., Ramboz, S., Segu, L., et al. (1994). Enhanced aggressive behavior in mice lacking 5-HT1B receptor. *Science, 265*, 1875–1878.

Schachter, D. (1995). *Searching for memory*. New York: Basic Books.

Schank, R., & Abelson, R. P. (1977). *Scripts, plans, goals, and understanding*. Hillsdale, NJ: Erlbaum.

Scheier, M. F., & Carver, C. S. (1987). Dispositional optimism and physical well-being: The influence of generalized outcome expectancies on health. *Journal of Personality, 55*, 169–210.

Scheier, M. F., & Carver, C. S. (1992). Effects of optimism on psychological and physical well-being: Theoretical overview and empirical update. *Cognitive Therapy and Research, 16*, 201–228.

Scheier, M. F., Weintraub, J. K., & Carver, C. S. (1986). Coping with stress: Divergent strategies of optimists and pessimists. *Journal of Personality and Social Psychology, 51*, 1257–1264.

Schmidt, F. L., Ones, D. S., & Hunter, J. E. (1992). Personnel selection. *Annual Review of Psychology, 43*, 627–670.

Schmidt, L. A., & Fox, N. A. (1999). Conceptual, biological, and behavioral distinctions among different categories of shy children. In L. A. Schmidt & J. Schulkin (Eds.), *Extreme fear, shyness, and social phobia: Origins, biological mechanisms, and clinical outcomes* (pp. 47–66). New York: Oxford University Press.

Schmidt, L. A., & Fox, N. A. (2002). Individual differences in childhood shyness: Origins, malleability, and developmental course. In D. Cervone & W. Mischel (Eds.), *Advances in personality science* (pp. 83–105). New York: Guilford Press.

Schneider, D. J. (1973). Implicit personality theory: A review. *Psychological Bulletin, 73*, 294–309.

Schooler, J. W. (1994). Seeking the core: The issues and evidence surrounding recovered accounts of sexual trauma. *Consciousness and Cognition, 3*, 452–469.

Schooler, J. W. (1997). Reflections on a memory discovery. *Child Maltreatment, 2*, 126–133.

Schooler, J. W., Bendiksen, M., & Ambadar, Z. (1997). Taking the middle line: Can we accommodate both fabricated and recovered memories of sexual abuse? In M. Conway (Ed.), *False and recovered memories* (pp. 251–292). Oxford, UK: Oxford University Press.

Schutz, W. C. (1967). *Joy: Expanding human awareness*. New York: Grove.

Schwartz, C. E., Wright, C. I., Shin, L. M., Kagan, J., & Rauch, S. L. (2003). Inhibited and uninhibited infants "grown up": Adult amygdalar response to novelty. *Science, 300*, 1952–1953.

Schwarz, N. (1990). Feelings and information: Informational and motivational functions of affective states. In R. M. Sorrentino & E. T. Higgins (Eds.), *Handbook of motivation and cognition: Foundations of social behavior* (Vol. 2, pp. 527–561). New York: Guilford Press.

Sears, R. R. (1936). Functional abnormalities of memory with special reference to amnesia. *Psychological Bulletin, 33*, 229–274.

Sears, R. R. (1943). *Survey of objectives studies of psychoanalytic concepts* (Bulletin 51). New York: Social Sciences Research Council.

Sears, R. R. (1944). Experimental analysis of psychoanalytic phenomena. In J. McV. Hunt (Ed.), *Personality and the behavior disorders* (pp. 306–332). New York: Ronald Press.

Sedlins, M., & Shoda, Y. (2007, January). *Mental organization and memory: Gender affects confusion errors for celebrity names*. Poster session presented at the annual conference of the Society for Personality and Social Psychology, Memphis, TN.

Segal, N. L. (1999). *Entwined lives: Twins and what they tell us about human behavior*. New York: Plume.

Seligman, M. E. P. (1971). Phobias and preparedness. *Behavior Therapy, 2*, 307–320.

Seligman, M. E. P. (1975). *Helplessness—On depression, development, and death*. San Francisco: Freeman.

Seligman, M. E. P. (1978). Comment and integration. *Journal of Abnormal Psychology, 87*, 165–179.

Seligman, M. E. P. (1990). *Learned optimism*. New York: A. A. Knopf.

Seligman, M. E. P. (2002). *Authentic happiness: Using the new positive psychology to realize your potential for lasting fulfillment*. New York: Free Press.

Seligman, M. E. P., & Hager, J. L. (1972). *Biological boundaries of learning*. New York: Appleton-Century-Crofts.

Seligman, M. E. P., Reivich, K., Jaycox, L., & Gillham, J. (1995). *The optimistic child*. Boston: Houghton Mifflin.

Sellers, R. M., Caldwell, C. H., Schmeelk-Cone, K. H., & Zimmerman, M. A. (2003). Racial identity, racial discrimination, perceived stress, and psychological distress among African American young adults. *Journal of Health and Social Behavior, 44*, 302–317.

Sethi, A., Mischel, W., Aber, L., Shoda, Y., & Rodriguez, M. (2000). The role of strategic attention deployment of self-regulation: Prediction of preschoolers' delay of gratification from mother–toddler interactions. *Developmental Psychology, 36*, 767–777.

Shaver, P. R., & Mikulincer, M. (2005) Attachment theory and research: Resurrection of the psychodynamic approach to personality. *Journal of Research in Personality, 39*, 22–45.

Shelton, J. N. (2000). A reconceptualization of how we study issues of racial prejudice. *Personality and Social Psychology Review, 4*, 374–390.

Shoda, Y. (1990). *Conditional analyses of personality coherence and dispositions*. Unpublished doctoral dissertation, Columbia University, New York.

Shoda, Y. (2007). Computational modeling of personality as a dynamical system. In R. W. Robins, R. C. Fraley, & R. F. Krueger (Eds.), *Handbook of research methods in personality psychology*. New York: Guilford Press.

Shoda, Y., LeeTiernan, S., & Mischel, W. (2002). Personality as a dynamical system: Emergence of stability and consistency from intra- and inter-personal interactions. *Personality and Social Psychology Review, 6*, 316–325.

Shoda, Y., & Mischel, W. (1993). Cognitive social approach to dispositional inferences: What if the perceiver is a cognitive-social theorist? *Personality and Social Psychology Bulletin* [Special issue on Dispositional Inferences], *19*, 574–585.

Shoda, Y., & Mischel, W. (1998). Reconciling processing dynamics and personality dispositions. *Annual Review of Psychology, 49*, 229–258.

Shoda, Y., & Mischel, W. (2000). Reconciling contextualism with the core assumptions of personality psychology. *European Journal of Personality, 14*, 407–428.

Shoda, Y., Mischel, W., & Peake, P. K. (1990). Predicting adolescent cognitive and self-regulatory competencies from preschool delay of gratification: Identifying diagnostic conditions. *Developmental Psychology, 26*, 978–986.

Shoda, Y., Mischel, W., & Wright, J. C. (1989). Intuitive interactionism in person perception: Effects of situation–behavior relations on dispositional judgments. *Journal of Personality and Social Psychology, 56*, 41–53.

Shoda, Y., Mischel, W., & Wright, J. C. (1993a). Links between personality judgments and contextualized behavior patterns: Situation–behavior profiles of personality prototypes. *Social Cognition, 4*, 399–429.

Shoda, Y., Mischel, W., & Wright, J. C. (1993b). The role of situational demands and cognitive competencies in behavior organization and personality coherence. *Journal of Personality and Social Psychology, 56*, 41–53.

Shoda, Y., Mischel, W., & Wright, J. C. (1994). Intra-individual stability in the organization and patterning of behavior: Incorporating psychological situations into the idiographic analysis of personality. *Journal of Personality and Social Psychology, 67*, 674–687.

Showers, C., & Cantor, N. (1984, April). *Defensive pessimism: A "hot" schema and protective strategy*. Paper presented at the annual meeting of the Eastern Psychological Association, Baltimore.

Shweder, R. A. (1975). How relevant is an individual difference theory of personality? *Journal of Personality, 43*, 455–485.

Shweder, R. A. (1990). Cultural psychology—what is it? In J. W. Stigler, R. A. Shweder, & G. Herdt (Eds.), *Cultural psychology: Essays on comparative human development* (pp. 1–43). Cambridge, UK: Cambridge University Press.

Shweder, R. A. (1991). *Thinking through cultures: Expeditions in cultural psychology*. Cambridge, MA: Harvard University Press.

Shweder, R. A., & Much, N. C. (1987). Determinants of meaning: Discourse and moral socialization. In W. M. Kurtines & J. L. Gewirtz (Eds.), *Moral development through social interaction* (pp. 197–244). New York: Wiley.

Silverman, L. H. (1976). Psychoanalytic theory: The reports of my death are greatly exaggerated. *American Psychologist, 31*, 621–637.

Simons, A. D., & Thase, M. E. (1992). Biological markers, treatment outcome, and 1-year follow-up in endogenous depression: Electroencephalographic sleep studies and response to cognitive therapy. *Journal of Consulting and Clinical Psychology, 60*, 392–401.

Singer, C. J. (1941). *A short history of science to the nineteenth century*. Oxford, UK: Clarendon Press.

Singer, J. A., & Salovey, P. (1993). *The remembered self: Emotion and memory in personality*. New York: Free Press.

Singer, J. L. (1988). Sampling ongoing consciousness and emotional experience: Implications for health. In M. J. Horowitz (Ed.). *Psychodynamics and cognition* (pp. 297–346). Chicago: University of Chicago Press.

Skinner, B. F. (1953). *Science and human behavior*. New York: Macmillan.

Skinner, B. F. (1955). Freedom and the control of men. *American Scholar, 25*, 47–65.

Skinner, B.F. (1967). An autobiography. In E. G. Boring & G. Lindzey (Eds.), *A history of psychology in autobiography* (Vol. 5, pp. 387–413). New York: Appleton-Century-Crofts.

Skinner, B. F. (1974). *About behaviorism*. New York: Knopf.

Smith, C. A., & Lazarus, R. S. (1990). Emotion and adaptation. In L. A. Pervin (Ed.), *Handbook of personality: Theory and research* (pp. 609–637). New York: Guilford Press.

Smith, E. E., & Jonides, J. (1999). Storage and executive processes in the frontal lobes. *Science, 283*, 1657–1661.

Smith, E. E., & Medin, L. (1981). *Categories and concepts*. Cambridge, MA: Harvard University Press.

Smith, R. G., Iwata, B. A., Vollmer, R., & Pace, G. M. (1992). On the relationship between self-injurious behavior and self-restraint. *Journal of Applied Behavior Analysis, 25*, 433–445.

Smyth, J. M. (1998). Written emotional expression: Effect sizes, outcome types, and moderating variables. *Journal of Consulting and Clinical Psychology, 66*, 174–184.

Snyder, M., & Cantor, N. (1998). Understanding personality and social behavior: A functionalist strategy. In D. T. Gilbert, S. T. Fiske, & G. Lindzey (Eds.), *The handbook of social psychology* (4th ed., Vol. 1, pp. 635–679). New York: McGraw-Hill.

Snyder, M., & Uranowitz, S. (1978). Reconstructing the past: Some cognitive consequences of person perception. *Journal of Personality and Social Psychology, 36*, 941–950.

Snygg, D., & Combs, A. W. (1949). *Individual behavior*. New York: Harper & Row.

Sorrentino, R. M., & Roney, C. J. (1986). Uncertainty orientation, achievement-related motivation, and task diagnosticity as determinants of task performance. *Social Cognition, 4*, 420–436.

Sorrentino, R. M., & Roney, C. J. R. (2000). *The uncertain mind: Individual differences in facing the unknown*. Philadelphia: Psychology Press/Taylor & Francis.

Spelke, E. S. (2000). Core knowledge. *American Psychologist, 55*, 1233–1243.

Spiegel, D. (1981). Vietnam grief work using hypnosis. *American Journal of Clinical Hypnosis, 24*, 33–40.

Spiegel, D. (1991). Neurophysiological correlates of hypnosis and dissociation. *Journal of Neuropsychiatry, 3*, 440–445.

Spiegel, D., & Cardena, E. (1990). New uses of hypnosis in the treatment of posttraumatic stress disorder. *Journal of Clinical Psychiatry, 51*(10 Suppl.), 39–43.

Spiegel, D., & Cardena, E. (1991). Disintegrated experience: The dissociative disorders revisited. *Journal of Abnormal Psychology, 100*, 366–378.

Spiegel, D., Koopman, C., & Classen, C. (1994). Acute distress disorder and dissociation. *Australian Journal of Clinical and Experimental Hypnosis, 22*, 11–23.

Spiegel, D., Kraemer, H. C., Bloom, J. R., & Gottheil, E. (1989). Effect of psychosocial treatment on survival of patients with metastatic breast cancer. *Lancet, 2*, 888–891.

Spinelli, E. (1989). *The interpreted world: An introduction to phenomenological psychology*. Thousand Oaks, CA: Sage.

Spitzer, R. L., Kroenke, K., & Williams, J. B. W. (1999). Validation and utility of a self-report version of PRIME-MD: The PHQ Primary Care Study. *Journal of the American Medical Association, 282*, 1737–1744.

Srivastava, S., John, O. P., Gosling, S. D., & Potter, J. (2003). Development of personality in early and middle adulthood: Set like plaster or persistent change? *Journal of Personality and Social Psychology, 84*, 1041–1053.

Sroufe, L. A. (1977). *Knowing and enjoying your baby*. Englewood Cliffs, NJ: Prentice-Hall.

Sroufe, L. A., & Fleeson, J. (1986). Attachment and the construction of relationships. In W. Harte & Z. Rubin (Eds.), *Relationships and development* (pp. 51–72). Hillsdale, NJ: Erlbaum.

Staats, C. K., & Staats, A. W. (1957). Meaning established by classical conditioning. *Journal of Experimental Psychology, 54*, 74–80.

Stams, G. J. M., Juffer, F., & van IJzendoorn, M. H. (2002). Maternal sensitivity, infant attachment, and temperament in early childhood predict adjustment in middle childhood: The case of adopted children and their biologically unrelated parents. *Developmental Psychology, 38*, 806–821.

Staub, E., Tursky, B., & Schwartz, G. E. (1971). Self-control and predictability: Their effects on reactions to aversive stimulation. *Journal of Personality and Social Psychology, 18*, 157–162.

Stayton, D. J., & Ainsworth, M. D. S. (1973). Individual differences in infant responses to brief, everyday separations as related to infant and maternal behaviors. *Developmental Psychology, 9*, 226–235.

Steele, C. M. (1997). A threat in the air: How stereotypes shape intellectual identity and performance. *American Psychologist, 52*, 613–629.

Steele, C. M. (1999). Thin ice: "Stereotype threat" and Black college students. *Atlantic Monthly, 284*, 44–54.

Steele, S. (2000, October 30). Engineering mediocrity. *The Daily Report*, the Hoover Institution Office of Public Affairs. Retrieved March 23, 2007, from: http://www.hoover.org/pubaffairs/dailyreport/archive/2867071.html

Stelmack, R. M. (1990). Biological bases of extraversion: Psychophysiological evidence. *Journal of Personality, 58*, 293–311.

Stelmack, R. M., & Michaud-Achorn, A. (1985). Extraversion, attention, and habituation of the auditory evoked response. *Journal of Research in Personality, 19*, 416–428.

Steuer, F. B., Applefield, J. M., & Smith, R. (1971). Televised aggression and the interpersonal aggression of preschool children. *Journal of Experimental Child Psychology, 11*, 442–447.

Stigler, J. W., Shweder, R. A., & Herdt, G. (1990). *Cultural psychology: Essays on comparative human development*. New York: Cambridge University Press.

Stone, A. A., Shiffman, S. S., & DeVries, M. (1999). Rethinking our self-report assessment methodologies. In D. Kahneman, E. Diener, & N. Schwarz (Eds.), *Well-being: The foundations of hedonic psychology* (pp. 26–39). New York: Russell Sage.

Strauman, T. J., Vookles, J., Berenstein, V., Chaiken, S., & Higgins, E. T. (1991). Self-discrepancies and vulnerability to body dissatisfaction and disordered eating. *Journal of Personality and Social Psychology, 61*, 946–956.

Strelau, J., & Zawadzki, B. (2005). The functional significance of temperament empirically tested. In A. Eliasz, S.E. Hampson, & B. de Raad (Eds.), *Advances in personality psychology* (2nd ed., pp. 19–46) New York: Psychology Press.

Stuss, D. T., & Knight, R. T. (Eds.). (2002). *Principles of frontal lobe function*. New York: Oxford University Press.

Sulloway, F. J. (1996). *Born to rebel: Birth order, family dynamics, and creative lives*. London: Little, Brown.

Sutton, S. K. (2002). Incentive and threat reactivity: Relations with anterior cortical activity. In D. Cervone & W. Mischel (Eds.), *Advances in personality science* (pp. 127–150). New York: Guilford Press.

Sutton, S. K., & Davidson, R. J. (1997). Prefrontal brain asymmetry: A biological substrate of the behavioral approach and inhibition systems. *Psychological Science, 8*, 204–210.

Sutton, S. K., & Davidson, R. J. (2000). Resting anterior brain activity predicts the evaluation of affective stimuli. *Neuropsychologia, 38*, 1723–1733.

Swann, W. B., Jr. (1983). Self-verification: Bringing social reality into harmony with the self. In J. Suls & A. G. Greenwald (Eds.), *Social psychology perspectives* (Vol. 2, pp. 33–66). Hillsdale, NJ: Erlbaum.

Talbot, M. (2006, September 4). The Baby Lab. *The New Yorker*, pp. 90–101.

Tart, C. (1970). Increases in hypnotizability resulting from a prolonged program for enhancing personal growth. *Journal of Abnormal Psychology, 75*, 260–266.

Taylor, S. E. (1995). *Health psychology* (3rd ed.). New York: McGraw-Hill.

Taylor, S. E. & Armor, D. A. (1996). Positive illusions and coping with adversity. *Journal of Personality, 64*, 873–898.

Taylor, S. E., & Brown, J. D. (1988). Illusion and well-being: A social psychological perspective on mental health. *Psychological Bulletin, 103*, 193–210.

Taylor, S. E., Klein, L. C., Lewis, B. P., Gruenewald, T. L., Gurung, R. A. R., & Updegraff, J. A. (2000). Biobehavioral responses to stress in females: Tend-and-befriend, not fight-or-flight. *Psychological Review, 107*, 411–429.

Taylor, S. E., Lerner, J. S., Sage, R. M., Lehman, B. J., & Seeman, T. E. (2004). Early environment, emotions, responses to stress, and health. *Journal of Personality* [Special issue on Personality and Health], 72, 1365–1393.

Taylor, S. E., & Schneider, S. (1989). Coping and the simulation of events. *Social Cognition, 7*, 174–194.

Tellegen, A., Lykken, D., Bouchard, T., Wilcox, K., Segal, N., & Rich, S. (1988). Personality similarity in twins reared apart. *Journal of Personality and Social Psychology, 54*, 1031–1039.

Tennen, H., Suls, J., & Affleck, G. (1991). Personality and daily experience: The promise and the challenge. *Journal of Personality, 59*, 313–338.

Tesser, A. (1993). The importance of heritability in psychological research: The case of attitudes. *Psychological Review, 100*, 129–142.

Tesser, A. (2002). Constructing a niche for the self: A biosocial, PDP approach to understanding lives. *Self and Identity, 1*, 185–190.

Tett, R. P., Jackson, D. N., & Rothstein, M. (1991). Personality measures as predictors of job performance: A meta-analytic review. *Personnel Psychology, 44*, 703–742.

Thomas, A., & Chess, S. (1977). *Temperament and development*. New York: Brunner/Mazel.

Thompson-Schill, S. L., Braver, T. S., & Jonides, J. (2005). Editorial: Individual Differences. *Cognitive, Affective and Behavioral Neuroscience, 5*, 115–116.

Thoresen, C., & Mahoney, M. J. (1974). *Self-control*. New York: Holt, Rinehart and Winston.

Toner, I. J. (1981). Role involvement and delay maintenance behavior in preschool children. *Journal of Genetic Psychology, 138*, 245–251.

Triandis, H. C. (1997). Cross-cultural perspectives on personality. In R. Hogan, J. Johnson, & S. Briggs (Eds.), *Handbook of personality* (pp. 440–459). San Diego, CA: Academic Press.

Triandis, H. C., Lambert, W. W., Berry, J. W., Lonner, W., Heron, A., Brislin, R. W., et al. (1980). *Handbook of cross-cultural psychology*. Boston: Allyn & Bacon.

Triandis, H. C., & Suh, E. M. (2002). Cultural influences on personality. *Annual Review of Psychology, 53*, 133–160.

Trilling, L. (1943). *E. M. Forster*. Norfolk, CT: New Directions Books.

Trivers, R. L. (1971). The evolution of reciprocal altruism. *Quarterly Review of Biology, 46*, 35–57.

Truax, C. B., & Mitchell, K. M. (1971). Research on certain therapist interpersonal skills in relation to process and outcome. In A. E. Bergin & S. I. Garfield (Eds.), *Handbook of psychotherapy and behavior change* (pp. 299–344). New York: Wiley.

Tsuang, M. T., Lyons, M. J., Eisen, S. A., True, W. T., Goldberg, J., & Henderson, W. (1992). A twin study of drug exposure and initiation of use. *Behavior Genetics, 22*, 756.

Tudor, T. G., & Holmes, D. S. (1973). Differential recall of successes and failures: Its relationship to defensiveness, achievement motivation, and anxiety. *Journal of Research in Personality, 7*, 208–224.

Tupes, E. C., & Christal, R. E. (1958). Stability of personality trait rating factors obtained under diverse conditions. USAF WADC Technical Note, No. 58–61.

Tupes, E. C., & Christal, R. E. (1961). Recurrent personality factors based on trait ratings. USAF ASD Technical Report, No. 61–67.

Tversky, A. (1977). Features of similarity. *Psychological Review, 84*, 327–352.

Tversky, A., & Kahneman, D. (1974). Judgment under uncertainty: Heuristics and biases. *Science, 185*, 1124–1131.

Tyler, L. E. (1956). *The psychology of human differences*. New York: Appleton.

Urban, M. S., & Witt, L. A. (1990). Self-serving bias in group member attributions of success and failure. *Journal of Social Psychology, 130*, 417–418.

Usher, R. (1996, October 14). A tall story for our time. *Time Magazine—European Edition*, pp. 10–14 (article can be retrieved at http://www.vwl.uni-muenchen.de/ls_komlos/covereu.html).

Vallacher, R. R., Read, S. J., & Nowak, A. (2002). The dynamical perspective in personality and social psychology. *Personality and Social Psychology Review, 6*, 264–273.

Vallacher, R. R., & Wegner, D. M. (1987). Action identification theory: The representation and control of behavior. *Psychological Review, 94*, 3–15.

Vanaerschot, G. (1993). Empathy as releasing several micro-processes in the client. In D. Brazier (Ed.), *Beyond Carl Rogers* (pp. 47–71). London: Constable.

Vandello, J. A., & Cohen, D. (2004). When believing is seeing: Sustaining norms of violence in cultures of honor. In M. Schaller & C. S. Crandall (Eds.), *The psychological foundations of culture* (pp. 281–304). Mahwah, NJ: Erlbaum.

Van Der Ploeg, H. M., Defares, P. B., & Spielberger, C. D. (1982). Zelf–Analyse Vragenlijst (ZAV) [State–trait anger scale (STAS)]. Lisse, The Netherlands: Swets & Zeitlinger.

Vandenberg, S. G. (1971). What do we know today about the inheritance of intelligence and how do we know it? In R. Cancro (Ed.), *Intelligence: Genetic and environmental influences* (pp. 182–218). New York: Grune & Stratton.

Van Mechelen, I., & Kiers, H. A. L. (1999). Individual differences in anxiety responses to stressful situations: A three-mode component analysis model. *European Journal of Personality, 13*, 409–428.

Vansteelandt, K., & Van Mechelen, I. (1998). Individual differences in situation–behavior profiles: A triple typology model. *Journal of Personality and Social Psychology, 75*, 751–765.

Vernon, P. E. (1964). *Personality assessment: A critical survey*. New York: Wiley.

Wager, T. D., Jonides, J., Smith, E. E., & Nichols, T. E. (2005). Toward a taxonomy of attention shifting: Individual differences in fMRI during multiple shift types. *Cognitive, Affective and Behavioral Neuroscience, 5*, 127–143.

Wager, T. D., Sylvester, C. Y., Lacey, S. C., Nee, D. E., Franklin, M., & Jonides, J. (2005). Common and unique components of response inhibition revealed by fMRI. *NeuroImage, 27*, 323–340.

Walker, A. M., & Sorrentino, R. M. (2000). Control motivation and uncertainty: Information processing or avoidance in moderate depressives and nondepressives. *Personality and Social Psychology Bulletin, 26*, 436–451.

Walker, G. (1991). *In the midst of winter: Systematic therapy with families, couples, and individuals with AIDS*. New York: Norton.

Wallace, A. F. C. (1961). *Culture and personality*. New York: Random House.

Waller, N. G., & Shaver, P. R. (1994). The importance of non-genetic influences on romantic love styles: A twin-family study. *Psychological Science, 5*, 268–274.

Walters, R. H., & Parke, R. D. (1967). The influence of punishment and related disciplinary techniques on the social behavior of children: Theory and empirical findings. In B. A. Maher (Ed.), *Progress in experimental personality research* (Vol. 4, pp. 179–228). New York: Academic Press.

Watkins, C. E., Campbell, V. L., Nieberding, R., & Hallmark, R. (1995). Contemporary practice of psychological assessment by clinical psychologists. *Professional Psychology, Research and Practice, 26*, 54–60.

Watson, D. (1988). The vicissitudes of mood measurements: Effects of varying descriptors, time frames, and response formats on measures of positive and negative affect. *Journal of Personality and Social Psychology, 55*, 128–141.

Watson, J. B., & Rayner, R. (1920). Conditioned emotional reaction. *Journal of Experimental Psychology, 3*, 1–14.

Watson, R. I. (1959). Historical review of objective personality testing: The search for objectivity. In B. M. Bass & I. A. Berg (Eds.), *Objective approaches to personality assessment* (pp. 1–23). Princeton, NJ: Van Nostrand.

Weidner, G., & Matthews, K. A. (1978). Reported physical symptoms elicited by unpredictable events and the type A coronary-prone behavior pattern. *Journal of Personality and Social Psychology, 36*, 1213–1220.

Weigel, R. H., & Newman, S. L. (1976). Increasing attitude–behavior correspondence by broadening the scope of the behavioral measure. *Journal of Personality and Social Psychology, 33*, 793–802.

Weinberger, J. (2002). *Unconscious processes*. New York: Guilford Press.

Weiner, B. (1974, February). *An attributional interpretation of expectancy value theory*. Paper presented at the AAAS Meetings, San Francisco.

Weiner, B. (1990). Attribution in personality psychology. In L. A. Pervin (Ed.), *Handbook of personality: Theory and research* (pp. 465–484). New York: Guilford Press.

Weiner, B. (1995). *Judgments of responsibility: A foundation for a theory of social conduct*. New York: Guilford Press.

Weir, M. W. (1965). Children's behavior in a two-choice task as a function of patterned reinforcement following forced-choice trials. *Journal of Experimental Child Psychology, 2*, 85–91.

West, S. G., & Finch, J. F. (1997). Personality measurement: Reliability and validity issues. In R. Hogan, J. Johnson, & S. Briggs (Eds.), *Handbook of personality psychology*. (pp. 143–165). San Diego, CA: Academic Press.

Westen, D. (1990). Psychoanalytic approaches to personality. In L. A. Pervin (Ed.), *Handbook of personality: Theory and research* (pp. 21–65). New York: Guilford Press.

Westen, D., & Gabbard, G. O. (1999). Psychoanalytic approaches to personality. In L. A. Pervin & O. P. John (Eds.), *Handbook of personality: Theory and research* (2nd ed., pp. 57–101). New York: Guilford Press.

Wheeler, G. (1991). *Gestalt reconsidered: A new approach to contact and resistance*. New York: Gardner Press.

Wheeler, R. E., Davidson, R. J., & Tomarken, A. J. (1993). Frontal brain asymmetry and emotional reactivity: A biological substrate of affective style. *Psychophysiology, 30*, 82–89.

White, B. L. (1967). An experimental approach to the effects of experience on early human behavior. In J. P. Hill (Ed.), *Minnesota Symposia on Child Psychology* (Vol. 1, pp. 201–226). Minneapolis: University of Minnesota Press.

White, M., & Epston, D. (1990). *Narrative means to therapeutic ends*. New York: Norton.

White, R. W. (1952). *Lives in progress*. New York: Holt, Rinehart & Winston.

White, R. W. (1959). Motivation reconsidered: The concept of competence. *Psychological Review, 66*, 297–333.

White, R. W. (1964). *The abnormal personality*. New York: Ronald Press.

White, R. W. (1972). *The enterprise of living*. New York: Holt.

Whiting, B. B., & Whiting, J. W. M. (1975). *Children of six cultures: A psycho-cultural analysis*. Cambridge, MA: Harvard University Press.

Whiting, J. W. M., & Child, I. L. (1953). *Child training and personality: A cross-cultural study*. New Haven, CT: Yale University Press.

Wiedenfield, S. A., Bandura, A., Levine, S., O'Leary, A., Brown, S., & Raska, K. (1990). Impact of perceived self-efficacy in coping with stressors on components of the immune system. *Journal of Personality and Social Psychology, 59*, 1082–1094.

Wiedenfeld, S. A., O'Leary, A., Bandura, A., Brown, S., Levine, S., & Raska, K. (1990). Impact of perceived self-efficacy in coping with stressors on components of the immune system. *Journal of Personality and Social Psychology, 59*, 1082–1094.

Wiggins, J. S. (1979). A psychological taxonomy of trait-descriptive terms: The interpersonal domain. *Journal of Personality and Social Psychology, 37*, 395–412.

Wiggins, J. S. (1980). Circumplex models of interpersonal behavior in personality and social psychology. In L. Wheeler (Ed.), *Review of personality and social psychology* (pp. 265–294). Thousand Oaks, CA: Sage.

Wiggins, J. S. (1997). In defense of traits. In R. Hogan, J. Johnson, & S. Briggs (Eds.), *Handbook of personality psychology* (pp. 95–115). San Diego, CA: Academic Press.

Wiggins, J. S., Phillips, N., & Trapnell, P. (1989). Circular reasoning about interpersonal behavior: Evidence concerning some untested assumptions underlying diagnostic classification. *Journal of Personality and Social Psychology, 56*, 296–305.

Wiley, R. C. (1979). *The self concept: Vol. 2. Theory and research on selected topics*. Lincoln: University of Nebraska Press.

Wilson, G. T., & O'Leary, K. D. (1980). *Principles of behavior therapy*. Englewood Cliffs, NJ: Prentice-Hall.

Wilson, M. I., & Daly, M. (1996). Male sexual proprietariness and violence against wives. *Current Directions in Psychological Science, 5*, 2–7.

Wilson, T. D. (2002). *Strangers to ourselves: Discovering the adaptive unconscious*. Cambridge, MA: Harvard University Press.

Winder, C. L., & Wiggins, J. S. (1964). Social reputation and social behavior: A further validation of the peer nomination inventory. *Journal of Abnormal and Social Psychology, 68*, 681–685.

Winter, D. G. (1973). *The power motive*. New York: Free Press.

Winter, D. G. (1993). Power, affiliation, and war: Three tests of a motivational model. *Journal of Personality and Social Psychology, 65*, 532–545.

Wittgenstein, L. (1953). *Philosophical investigations*. New York: Macmillan.

Wolf, R. (1966). The measurement of environments. In A. Anastasi (Ed.), *Testing problems in perspective* (pp. 491–503). Washington, DC: American Council on Education.

Wolff, P. H. (1966). The causes, controls, and organization of behavior in the neonate. *Psychological Issues, 5*, 1–105.

Wolpe, J. (1958). *Psychotherapy by reciprocal inhibition*. Stanford, CA: Stanford University Press.

Wolpe, J. (1963). Behavior therapy in complex neurotic states. *British Journal of Psychiatry, 110*, 28–34.

Wolpe, J. (1997). From psychoanalytic to behavioral methods in anxiety disorders: A continuing evolution. In J. K. Zeig (Ed.), *The evolution of psychotherapy: The third conference* (pp. 107–116). New York: Brunner/Mazel.

Wolpe, J., & Lazarus, A. A. (1966). *Behavior therapy techniques: A guide to the treatment of neuroses*. Elmsford, NY: Pergamon Press.

Wolpe, J., & Rachman, S. (1960). Psychoanalytic evidence: A critique based on Freud's case of Little Hans. *Journal of Nervous and Mental Diseases, 31*, 134–147.

Woodall, K. L., & Matthews, K. A. (1989). Familial environments associated with Type A behaviors and psychophysiological responses to stress in children. *Health Psychology, 8*, 403–426.

Wortman, C. B., & Brehm, J. W. (1975). Responses to uncontrollable outcomes. In L. Berkowitz (Ed.), *Advances in experimental social psychology* (Vol. 8, pp. 278–336). New York: Academic Press.

Wright, J. C., Lindgren, K. P., & Zakriski, A. L. (2001). Syndromal versus contextualized assessment of childhood psychopathology: Differentiating environmental and dispositional determinants of behavior. *Journal of Personality and Social Psychology, 81*, 1176–1189.

Wright, J. C., & Mischel, W. (1982). The influence of affect on cognitive social learning person variables. *Journal of Personality and Social Psychology, 43*, 901–914.

Wright, J. C., & Mischel, W. (1987). A conditional approach to dispositional constructs: The local predictability of social behavior. *Journal of Personality and Social Psychology, 53*, 1159–1177.

Wright, J. C., & Mischel, W. (1988). Conditional hedges and the intuitive psychology of traits. *Journal of Personality and Social Psychology, 55*, 454–469.

Wright, J. H., & Beck, A. T. (1996). Cognitive therapy. In R. E. Hales & S. C. Yudofsky (Eds.), *The American Psychiatric Press synopsis of psychiatry* (pp. 1011–1038). Arlington, VA: American Psychiatric Press.

Wright, L. (1998). *Twins and what they tell us about who we are*. Hoboken, NJ: Wiley.

Young, J. E., Weinberger, A. D., & Beck, A. T. (2001). Cognitive therapy for depression. In D. H. Barlow (Ed.), *Clinical handbook of psychological disorders: A step-by-step treatment manual* (3rd ed., pp. 264–308). New York: Guilford Press.

Youngblade, L. M., & Belsky, J. (1992). Parent-child antecedents of 5-year-olds' close friendships: A longitudinal analysis. *Developmental Psychology, 28*, 700–713.

Zahn-Waxler, C., Robinson, J. L., & Emde, R. N. (1992). The development of empathy in twins. *Developmental Psychology, 28*, 1038–1047.

Zajonc, R. B. (1980). Feeling and thinking: Preferences need no inferences. *American Psychologist, 35*, 151–175.

Zakriski, A. L., Wright, J. C., & Underwood, M. K. (2005). Gender similarities and differences in children's social behavior: Finding personality in contextualized patterns of adaptation. *Journal of Personality and Social Psychology, 88*, 844–855.

Zayas, V., & Shoda, Y. (2005). Do automatic reactions elicited by thoughts of romantic partner, mother, and self relate to adult romantic attachment? *Personality and Social Psychology Bulletin, 31*, 1011–1025.

Zayas, V., & Shoda, Y. (2007). Predicting preferences for dating partners from past experiences of psychological abuse: Identifying the "psychological ingredients" of situations. *Personality and Social Psychology Bulletin, 33*, 123–138.

Zayas, V., Shoda, Y., & Ayduk, O. N. (2002). Personality in context: An interpersonal systems perspective. *Journal of Personality, 70*, 851–900.

Zelazo, P. D., & Müller, U. (2002). Executive function in typical and atypical development. In U. Goswami (Ed.), *Blackwell handbook of childhood cognitive development* (pp. 445–469). Malden, MA: Blackwell.

Zeller, A. (1950). An experimental analogue of repression, I. Historical summary. *Psychological Bulletin, 47*, 39–51.

Zirkel, S. (1992). Developing independence in a life transition: Investing the self in the concerns of the day. *Journal of Personality and Social Psychology, 62*, 506–521.

Zuckerman, M. (1978). Sensation seeking. In H. London & J. E. Exner (Eds.), *Dimensions of personality* (pp. 487–559). New York: Wiley Interscience.

Zuckerman, M. (1979). Attribution of success and failure revisited: Or the motivational bias is alive and well in attribution theory. *Journal of Personality, 47*, 245–287.

Zuckerman, M. (1983). A rejoinder to Notarius. *Journal of Personality and Social Psychology, 45*, 1165–1166.

Zuckerman, M. (1984). Sensation seeking: A comparative approach to a human trait. *Behavioral and Brain Sciences, 7*, 413–471.

Zuckerman, M. (1990). The psychophysiology of sensation seeking. *Journal of Personality, 58*, 313–345.

Zuckerman, M. (1991). *The psychobiology of personality*. Cambridge, NY: Cambridge University Press.

Zuckerman, M. (1993). P-impulsive sensation seeking and its behavioral, psychophysiological, and biochemical correlates. *Neuropsychology, 28*, 30–36.

Zuckerman, M. (1994). *Behavioral expressions and biosocial bases of sensation seeking*. New York: Cambridge University Press.

Zuckerman, M., Persky, H., Link, K. E., & Basu, G. K. (1968). Responses to confinement: An investigation of sensory deprivation, social isolation, restriction of movement and set factors. *Perceptual and Motor Skills, 27*, 319–334.

NAME INDEX

T

U

SUBJECT INDEX